Mastering Elder Law

Carolina Academic Press Mastering Series
RUSSELL L. WEAVER, SERIES EDITOR

Mastering Administrative Law
William R. Andersen

Mastering Bankruptcy
George W. Kuney

Mastering Civil Procedure
David Charles Hricik

Mastering Constitutional Law
John C. Knechtle, Christopher Roederer

Mastering Corporate Tax
Reginald Mombrun, Gail Levin Richmond, Felicia Branch

Mastering Corporations and Other Business Entities
Lee Harris

Mastering Criminal Law
Ellen S. Podgor, Peter J. Henning, Neil P. Cohen

Mastering Criminal Procedure, Volume 1: The Investigative Stage
Peter J. Henning, Andrew Taslitz, Margaret L. Paris, Cynthia E. Jones, Ellen S. Podgor

Mastering Elder Law
Ralph C. Brashier

Mastering Evidence
Ronald W. Eades

Mastering Family Law
Janet Leach Richards

Mastering Intellectual Property
George W. Kuney, Donna C. Looper

Mastering Legal Analysis and Communication
David T. Ritchie

Mastering Legal Analysis and Drafting
George W. Kuney, Donna C. Looper

**Mastering Negotiable Instruments (UCC Articles 3 and 4)
and Other Payment Systems**
Michael D. Floyd

Mastering Products Liability
Ronald W. Eades

Mastering Professional Responsibility
Grace M. Giesel

Mastering Secured Transactions
Richard H. Nowka

Mastering Statutory Interpretation
Linda D. Jellum

Mastering Tort Law
Russell L. Weaver, Edward C. Martin, Andrew R. Klein,
Paul J. Zwier II, Ronald W. Eades, John H. Bauman

Mastering Elder Law

Ralph C. Brashier
CECIL C. HUMPHREYS PROFESSOR OF LAW
THE UNIVERSITY OF MEMPHIS

CAROLINA ACADEMIC PRESS
Durham, North Carolina

Library of Congress Cataloging in Publication Data

Brashier, Ralph C., 1957-
  Mastering elder law / Ralph C. Brashier.
     p. cm.
  ISBN 978-1-59460-448-5 (alk. paper)
  1. Older people--Legal status, laws, etc.--United States. 2. Old age pen-
sions--Law and legislation--United States. 3. Estate planning--United States.
4. Social security--Law and legislation--United States. 5. Older people--
Medical care--Law and legislation--United States. I. Title.
  KF390.A4.B73 2010
  344.7303'26--dc22

                                        2009038010

Carolina Academic Press
700 Kent Street
Durham, NC 27701
Telephone (919) 489-7486
Fax (919) 493-5668
www.cap-press.com

Printed in the United States of America

Contents

Series Editor's Foreword

The Carolina Academic Press Mastering Series is designed to provide you with a tool that will enable you to easily and efficiently "master" the substance and content of law school courses. Throughout the series, the focus is on quality writing that makes legal concepts understandable. As a result, the series is designed to be easy to read and is not unduly cluttered with footnotes or cites to secondary sources.

In order to facilitate student mastery of topics, the Mastering Series includes a number of pedagogical features designed to improve learning and retention. At the beginning of each chapter, you will find a "Roadmap" that tells you about the chapter and provides you with a sense of the material that you will cover. A "Checkpoint" at the end of each chapter encourages you to stop and review the key concepts, reiterating what you have learned. Throughout the book, key terms are explained and emphasized. Finally, a "Master Checklist" at the end of each book reinforces what you have learned and helps you identify any areas that need review or further study.

We hope that you will enjoy studying with, and learning from, the Mastering Series.

Russell L. Weaver
Professor of Law & Distinguished University Scholar
University of Louisville, Louis D. Brandeis School of Law

Preface

I thank my colleagues Donna Harkness, William Kratzke, Janet Richards, Dorothy Wells, and Nicholas White for their insightful comments and suggestions on drafts of various chapters of this book. I am grateful to Richard Townley and Shannon Wiley for their research assistance and to Cheryl Foshee Edwards for her administrative assistance.

I also thank the students in my Elder Law classes at the University of Memphis. Their passion and commitment provide a constant source of inspiration. Their interest and curiosity provide a constant opportunity to learn new things and to see old things afresh. Their stories and the stories of their families provide a constant reminder of the increasing importance of Elder Law and of the need for lawyers to serve America's growing elderly population.

Mastering Elder Law

Chapter 1

Elder Abuse

Roadmap

- Elder abuse includes
  - Physical abuse
  - Sexual abuse
  - Exploitation
  - Emotional abuse
  - Neglect
  - Abandonment
  - Self-neglect
- State Adult Protective Services provisions and other state statutes often address elder abuse and provide for
  - Reporting
  - Investigating
  - Services to the elder
  - Remedies for the abuse

A. Introduction

Elder abuse is a serious, disturbing, and often misunderstood social problem. No one knows the actual incidence of abuse in the United States; however, it is probably far greater than most people realize. It is only since the 1970s that Americans have begun to acknowledge elder abuse as a distinct social problem. Even today, the problem of elder abuse receives far less attention than child abuse. Many seriously incapacitated elders are as dependent and vulnerable as young children, however. Not surprisingly, some of the provisions that states have enacted to redress the problem are patterned after child abuse laws.

A bill introduced in Congress in the first part of the twenty-first century estimated that anywhere between 500,000 and 5,000,000 elders are abused, neglected, or exploited in the United States each year. Elder Justice Act of 2002 (S.G. 2933, introduced Sept. 13, 2002). In the mid-1990s, the National Center of Elder Abuse noted that reported incidents of abuse more than doubled in the years between 1986 and 1994. In 2000, Adult Protective Services agencies across the country received over 470,000 reports of elder/adult abuse or mistreatment.

There are several reasons why precise figures identifying abuse are difficult to obtain and why those that exist are suspect. The problem of elder abuse is addressed primarily by state law, and states define elder abuse in different ways. Conduct that constitutes abuse in one state may not be abuse in a neighboring state, and therefore compilations of state abuse statistics may be misleading. Moreover, most conduct that is clearly elder abuse under applicable state law probably goes unreported. The abused elder with severely diminished capacity may be unable to report the abuse, and an abuser is unlikely to report his own violation of the law. Particularly when the abuse occurs within the home, no other witnesses may be available to report the abuse. Then, too, in many instances family members of the elder may be unaware that the elder is being abused under applicable state law. An adult son who is the caregiver for his elderly mother may not know that slapping her or withholding her food in order to make her "behave" is in fact abuse. If his mother employed such tactics against him when he was a child, he may ignorantly believe that his conduct is proper because, in his view, "Mother is just being obstinate and mean."

Another difficulty in classifying elder abuse is identifying the population subject to being abused as elders. Laws that define the elderly based on chronological age paint with a very broad brush. The functional age of two seventy-year olds may differ substantially. Yet as in so many areas of law, arbitrary classifications based on birth date are generally easier to craft and enforce. As we shall see, under some state and federal laws, elders are protected from abuse or exploitation based on chronological age alone. Recognizing that the problem of abuse and exploitation is more commonly linked to the victim's vulnerability than her age, however, some states have enacted Adult Protective Services statutes that attempt to protect all vulnerable adults from abuse, regardless of age. Such statutes may further contain special provisions that treat vulnerable adults of a defined age as elderly.

Finally, the difficulty of identifying incidents of elder self-neglect contributes to the uncertainty of statistics on elder abuse. Although it is convenient to lump self-neglect with other kinds of elder abuse, self-neglect is arguably different in form and kind from other types of elder abuse. The prevailing view is that a capable individual who knowingly ignores her own needs cannot commit self-neglect; in contrast, an individual who is unable to meet her own needs may commit self-neglect. Capacity exists in a multitude of forms and shades, however, and distinguishing eccentricity from incapacity is often difficult. Further, self-neglect is unlike other forms of abuse in that the perpetrator of the abuse is also the victim. Self-neglect thus involves no bad actor to condemn or punish. One can understand why some observers argue that self-neglect might be more properly considered as a separate problem, rather than included more generally as simply another form of elder abuse.

This chapter examines various kinds of elder abuse and looks at some important statutory measures that states have enacted to redress them. The chapter examines state Adult Protective Services (APS) provisions and other significant laws designed to combat elder abuse. Such provisions vary substantially among the states, however. Thus, while the examination in this chapter provides an overview, the lawyer must always refer to the specific provisions applicable in the jurisdiction in which he or she practices.

Before examining the kinds of elder abuse and state statutory provisions redressing them, we begin with two very difficult questions: why does elder abuse occur and who is likely to be an abuser?

B. Causes of Abuse

A growing body of literature examines the causes of elder abuse. That literature, along with the substantiated reports of elder abuse, also provides information about those individuals most likely to engage in elder abuse. Before proceeding with this discussion, however, a word of caution is appropriate: the causes of elder abuse are many and varied, and experts themselves disagree on the significance of different factors that may contribute to abuse. Although abusers in substantiated cases of abuse often share certain traits or characteristics, many abusers are never prosecuted, charged, or perhaps even suspected. Because abuse often occurs in the privacy of the home, a significant portion of elder abuse almost certainly goes undetected. Abusers come from all walks of life. Some abusers may outwardly appear to be pillars of the community.

Even though no particular set of circumstances will inevitably lead to abuse or allow us to predict with certainty who will engage in abusive behavior, empirical evidence and common sense allow us to identify various warning signs. The lawyer who represents the elderly or individuals with elderly family members should be able to identify common factors that raise red flags concerning potentially abusive situations. Depending upon state law, the lawyer may have a duty to report known or reasonably suspected incidents of abuse—a duty that can trump his duty of confidentiality to the client.

Some commentators believe that the stress of caring for a vulnerable elder often leads to elder abuse by the caregiver. Other commentators believe that caregiver stress is not, in and of itself, a major source of elder abuse. Rather, they stress contributing factors such as the caregiver's financial dependence upon the elder or the caregiver's own drug or alcohol abuse problems as more likely causes. Whether or not caregiver stress alone results in a significant portion of elder abuse, it is clear that such stress can compromise the quality of care provided by the caregiver. When members of the elder's family cannot afford the assistance of hired caregivers, they should attempt to share the caregiving responsibilities. When one family member shoulders the entire responsibility for the elder's care, it is important for the caregiver to find occasional relief from that responsibility. Such relief might come from various sources, including social services programs and church-sponsored temporary elder care that provide a "caregiver's day out." When the caregiver is a paid employee, the family should carefully screen all applicants and perform thorough background checks. Once the caregiver is hired, the family should remain very actively involved in the elder's life, making unannounced visits and perhaps using video monitors as needed.

The condition of the elder often plays a role in determining whether she will be the victim of abuse. A seriously incapacitated elder who cannot report abuse is an easy target for physical abuse, particularly when she has no one other than the caregiver to check on her. The attitude of the elder may contribute to the likelihood for abuse. Some vulnerable elders are kind and generous, while others are mean-spirited and deliberately disrespectful of their caregivers. The physically incapacitated parent who controls the purse strings may feel entitled to complain and whine regardless of the care provided by her caregiver. While no words or actions of the vulnerable elder justify abuse by the caregiver, they undoubtedly play a role in some instances of elder abuse.

The abuser's upbringing may also play a role in some cases of abuse. An individual who was reared in an environment in which physical and mental abuse was regularly used as a means of controlling him may assume that such abuse is a proper means for controlling the behavior of a vulnerable elder. Slapping, hitting, and beating may seem outrageous to most of us, but many children are reared in households where such treatment is common. When they become caregivers for their parents or others, they simply perpetuate the cycle of violence. Even in households where children are reared free from violence, parents often engage in emotional abuse. When children brought up in such an environment become caregivers, they too may engage in emotional abuse, particularly in the form of criticism, name-calling, and threats.

Most observers believe that abuse occurs primarily within the home or community, not in institutional settings. They further note that family members, not paid caregivers, are the most likely abusers. In some instances, a family member who is the principal or sole caregiver of an elderly person may lack the capacity to give proper care. In other instances, the family caregiver is capable, but he nonetheless neglects the elderly family member. Many cases involve adult children who undertake the caregiver role and then allow their parents to exist in deplorable conditions. Some of these children begin the caregiving role adequately, but become less and less dependable over time. On occasion, children abuse their parents as a form of revenge for the real or imagined wrongs their parents have committed against them. Sometimes children, consciously or not, wish to hasten a parent's death so that the children can obtain freedom from the caregiving responsibility or can receive an expected inheritance from the elder. Family members who take financial advantage of an elder often rationalize their behavior. They convince themselves that they have "earned" their inheritance and deserve it now. Alternatively, they convince themselves that the incapacitated elder would have wanted them to have the money or other assets currently if she were fully capable.

Elderly spouses, like their younger counterparts, may engage in abusive behavior towards each other. In many cases, the abuse is a continuation of abusive behavior that began long before the couple grew old. Often such cases are more properly viewed as incidents of continuing domestic violence rather than elder abuse. In other cases, the abusive or violent behavior begins only after the couple is old. Sometimes the onset of abuse beginning in old age stems from the abuser's diminished capacity. In other instances, the abusive spouse is fully capable but has failed to recognize or accept the growing vulnerability of the other spouse. In any event, when abuse occurs within the family, one should consider whether the conduct is covered not only by state elder abuse statutes, but also by domestic violence statutes.

In institutional settings, abusers are often low-paid employees, unhappy with their lives and the demands of their jobs. Their institutional employer may have failed to perform required background checks before hiring them and to train them properly after hiring them.

Studies indicate that men are more likely to engage in abusive behavior generally; nonetheless, women constitute a substantial percentage of elder abusers. Men are also more likely to engage in *physically* abusive behavior. Male or female, caregivers who have substance abuse problems or gambling addictions seem particularly likely to engage in abusive behavior. Concerning potential victims, elderly women are more likely to suffer abuse than are elderly men. Also, the oldest of the old are most likely to be victims of elder abuse.

Although studies of abuse can play an important role in identifying some circumstances and settings ripe for abuse, they also reveal the apparent randomness of some abusive behavior. Abusers may be rich or poor, educated or uneducated, male or female, intelligent or not so intelligent. Some abusers are genuinely unaware that their conduct is abusive. Feeling unimportant in other realms of their lives, some abusers engage in abusive behavior in an unwitting effort to make themselves feel powerful. Other abusers employ abusive tactics to make sure the elder knows "who is in control." Worst of all, some abusers appear to be inherently evil. Such abusers may engage in elder abuse for the "fun" of it.

C. Kinds of Abuse

Broadly defined, elder abuse includes both active abuse and passive abuse. Passive abuse most often consists of the failure of a caregiver to take the reasonable and necessary steps to protect the elder and his welfare. Passive elder abuse is commonly called neglect. In many states, it may also include elder self-neglect.

Much abusive behavior towards the elderly is punishable under older civil or criminal actions such as battery, negligence, and fraud. Nonetheless, society's growing concern for the abused elderly has led to new causes of action aimed specifically at abuse. Because elder abuse as a distinct crime has a relatively short history, definitions of elder abuse continue to evolve. Courts and commentators have sometimes observed that abuse requires a pattern of wrongful behavior. Some statutes still incorporate this view. Under this view, an individual who knowingly and intentionally strikes a vulnerable elder on one occasion might be guilty of a criminal battery, but he would not be guilty of elder physical abuse.

As one court has noted, however, requiring a pattern of behavior permits the perpetrator to have at least one free strike before his conduct can be considered "abusive." When not specifically required by statute, such a result seems inconsistent with the purpose of the legislation to protect the elderly. Thus, some courts and legislatures have more recently concluded that a single incident of seriously harmful behavior involving the improper use of force against an elder should be sufficient to support a charge of physical abuse. State definitions of sexual abuse of a vulnerable adult (which often is a particular form of physical abuse) seldom require a pattern of improper sexual conduct towards the elderly victim. A Florida statute provides that elder neglect "may be based on repeated conduct *or on a single incident or omission* that results in, or could reasonably be expected to result in, serious physical or psychological injury, or a substantial risk of death, to an elderly person...." Fla. Stat. Ann. § 825.102(3)(a) (emphasis added).

Even when abuse undoubtedly occurs, often the elder will be incapable of reporting the abuse. On other occasions, the elder is capable of reporting the abuse, but refrains from doing because she is embarrassed about the abuse, particularly if a family member is the abuser. She may also refrain from reporting the abuse because she fears that the abuser will retaliate by making the abuse even greater. If she is living in the home, she may fear that her report of abuse will cause her to be moved elsewhere, possibly to a place where she will suffer even more. Many elders living in the community appear to believe that, no matter how great the abuse they suffer while in the community, a nursing home is always a worse place in which to live.

The following discussion examines several particular kinds of active abuse as well as neglect and self-neglect. We paint here with a broad brush, noting that specific forms of abuse and their definitions will depend upon applicable state law.

1. Active Abuse

Active abuse of an elder tends be one of three kinds: physical, sexual, or financial. Financial abuse is also frequently termed "exploitation" under state elder abuse statutes.

a. Physical Abuse

Physical abuse involves the improper use of force by anyone against an elder. Striking, hitting, slapping, beating, whipping, kicking, shoving, pushing, and burning of an elder can constitute physical abuse. Other examples of physical abuse can include improperly forcing the elder to eat, to accept unwanted medication, or to be placed under physical restraints. The abuser may improperly place the elder under physical restraints not only to punish the elder, but also to prevent her from reporting other incidents of abuse against her. Physical abuse often manifests itself in bruises, bleeding, internal injuries, and broken bones. It may also cause behavioral changes in the victim.

Many of the reported incidents of physical abuse have arisen in institutional settings. Institutional employees have, among other things, hit, slapped, pushed, shoved, kicked, and stomped on their elderly charges. In one incident, a nursing employee forced the patient to eat her own feces. In another, a nursing home employee slapped the patient while bathing him, leaving a handprint on the patient's face that was visible six to twelve hours later.

b. Sexual Abuse

Although many states define sexual abuse as a specific form of abuse, it is often a particularized form of physical abuse. It occurs when someone engages the elder in sexual contact without the elder's consent. Although sexual abuse may occur through the use of force, it may also occur when the elder is tricked, threatened, or coerced into sexual contact against her will. Sexual contact with an incapacitated elder (one who is unable to give consent) also constitutes sexual abuse.

Some statutes extend sexual abuse to include involuntary exposure of the elder to sexually explicit material or language. The National Center for Elder Abuse defines sexual abuse to include coerced nudity or sexually explicit photographing of an elder.

c. Exploitation

Financial abuse, or exploitation, is probably far more widespread than reported incidents suggest. In its broadest sense, exploitation occurs when someone improperly acquires or uses an elder's funds, benefits, or other assets.

Fiduciaries are among those who frequently exploit an elder's assets. For example, a representative payee of the elder's monthly Social Security benefits may improperly apply those funds for his own use. Similarly, the elder's guardian or conservator may use the elder's funds in a self-interested manner. Although a guardian or conservator generally must account to the supervising court for his expenditures and actions, the accounting often comes too late to protect the elder's estate. An agent under a durable power of attorney can even more easily exploit the elderly principal's estate, since the agent's actions are generally not subject to a court-required accounting. Exploitation may also occur when the elder creates an agency bank account so that her agent can sign checks for her, and the agent subsequently proceeds to write checks for the agent's own benefit. Unfortunately, some of the most startling instances of exploitation involve lawyers taking advantage of a vulnerable adult client. Each year sees a new crop of reported cases in which a lawyer improperly includes himself as a beneficiary in the client's will, obtains and misuses the client's durable power of attorney, or otherwise acts in a self-interested way in breach of his fiduciary obligations to the client.

Dishonest caregivers are also in a convenient position for exploiting the elder's assets. If the elder has access to her own funds, often it is not difficult for the caregiver to steal cash or forge checks. When the caregiver is not a family member, the caregiver's inclusion in the elder's will is often a red flag indicating coercion, duress, undue influence, or deception exerted upon the elder. The elder's contracts with a caregiver that seem unduly favorable to the caregiver are also warning signs of exploitation.

Isolation of the elder by a caregiver, family member, or other person is often a warning sign that exploitation, neglect, or other another form of abuse is occurring. For example, a caregiver who has coerced or tricked an elder into executing a will or making various financial transactions in the caregiver's favor may attempt to prevent third parties from all contact with the elder. In such cases, the abuser may remove the elder to an undisclosed location or, alternatively, carefully monitor all visits, phone calls, or correspondence from third parties.

Local merchants, door-to-door salespeople, fly-by-night home repairmen, and those operating telephone or mail marketing or soliciting schemes often prey on the vulnerable elderly. (Disreputable telemarketers often maintain and circulate among themselves a "mooch" or "sucker" list of elderly individuals who are considered easy targets.) State exploitation statutes may be broad enough to cover such conduct. Alternatively or in addition, state consumer protection statutes may cover such conduct. Federal mail fraud and telemarketing statutes may also come into play. 18 U.S.C. § 1341 (mail fraud); 18 U.S.C. § 2325 (Senior Citizens Against Marketing Scams Act).

In institutional settings, employees may find it easy to steal the belongings or money of a resident with diminished capacity. On occasion, the operator of the institution is involved in such acts.

The ways in which family members, friends, neighbors, caregivers, and strangers can take financial advantage of a vulnerable elder are limited only by the imagination. The elderly population in America on the whole is quite wealthy, and in many instances the exploiter is unlikely to be caught. When an exploiter is caught, often nothing remains of the elder's misappropriated assets to be recovered.

d. Emotional Abuse

Some states criminalize emotional or mental abuse of an elder. There are very few reported cases, although emotional abuse may well be more common than physical abuse. Emotional abuse occurs when someone inflicts mental or psychological anguish upon the elder. It may result from words or conduct of the abuser. For example, emotional abuse can result from words or actions of a caregiver towards the elder that are threatening, intimidating, humiliating, harassing, or insulting. In a well-known case from Delaware, an aide at a nursing home was convicted of emotional abuse after apparently engaging in abusive language towards an eighty-five year old patient in a wheelchair, telling the patient to "kiss my butt," lifting her nurse's uniform, and then placing her rear end on the meal table of the patient's wheelchair for the patient to kiss. Robinson v. Delaware, 600 A.2d 356 (Del. 1991).

Broadly-worded statutes that simply purport to criminalize emotional abuse without further defining the abuse and the setting and circumstances under which it occurs are problematic. Such statutes may be subject to constitutional attack for vagueness if they fail to provide the reasonable person with an understanding of what conduct is forbidden and if they are worded so that they result in arbitrary and discriminatory enforcement by the state. For example, the Delaware statute in *Robinson* withstood a vagueness attack because it only protected a patient or resident within a facility and required that a defendant knowingly perform the acts targeted or directed towards such a patient or resident. The statute also withstood an overbreadth attack because it did not reach a substantial amount of constitutionally protected speech, since the statute applied only to acts occurring within a facility, not to acts in a public setting.

2. Neglect

a. Neglect by a Caregiver

Neglect occurs when a person with a duty of care towards the elder violates those duties. For example, elder neglect may occur when the elder's caregiver fails to ensure that the elder is provided with adequate food and water, hygiene, medicine, and a safe and healthy environment.

As its name suggests, neglect is a form of negligence. One cannot be guilty of elder neglect unless one has a duty of care towards the elder in question. Moreover, one who has a duty of care can only be guilty of neglect concerning those matters covered by the duty.

A duty of care may arise from one of several sources. In the case of hired caregivers, the duty typically arises by express contract from the caregiving agreement. In institutional settings, for example, the contract between the elder (or her proxy) and the nursing home or other institutional residence imposes a duty upon the institution to care for the elderly resident. (The duty may be supplemented by statutory duties as well.) A duty of care may also arise by implied contract, as when an adult child informally becomes her vulnerable parent's sole caregiver in return for bed and board in the parent's household (perhaps along with other benefits).

A duty of care may also be voluntarily assumed, as when a neighbor (without expectation of reimbursement) becomes an elder's sole source of care.

Once the volunteer has assumed the sole caregiving role, third parties will often believe that they need not be concerned for the vulnerable elder. In such settings, the volunteer cannot simply abandon those duties even though she is performing them gratuitously.

A duty of care may also be imposed by statute. In a number of states, adult children have a responsibility to support their indigent parents; however, states seldom enforce such statutes. Not surprisingly, such statutes have not played a major role in elder neglect cases, although they are sometimes cited by courts in such cases. More important are state statutes that impose a duty of care on adult family members or other adult individuals who live in the same household with the elder. For example, Jane agrees to care for her elderly mother in Jane's home in return for the mother's promise to pay the monthly mortgage note on the home. Because Jane has a contractual agreement with her mother, Jane can clearly be guilty of caregiver neglect. If the state also has a statute extending a duty of care to adult members of the household, Jane's husband can also be guilty of neglect if he lives in Jane's house, even though he has no contractual obligation to care for his mother-in-law and has not assumed that duty voluntarily.

A duty of care may also arise from the legal relationship between parties. For example, parents must care for their minor children and guardians must care for their wards. More commonly today, however, such common law duties of care are expressly incorporated into state statute.

Although the problems of abuse and neglect are grave, broadly-worded statutes that purport to impose a duty on every citizen to prevent abuse and neglect are problematic. In People v. Heitzman, 886 P.2d 1229 (Cal. 1994), the California Supreme Court was faced with such a statute. In essence, the statutory language seemed to impose criminal felony liability not only upon the elder's caregiver, but also upon any person who permitted elder abuse when he knew or reasonably should have known of the circumstances likely to produce great bodily harm or death to an elder.

The case involved an egregious incident of elder neglect. The defendant was the elder's daughter, who was not the elder's caregiver but was a frequent visitor in the home where he lived. Despite the statute's wording, the court rejected the argument that the statute imposed a duty upon all citizens to prevent the abuse or neglect of an elder. Such a construction would make the statute void for vagueness, for it (1) would not provide adequate notice to the class of persons under an affirmative duty to prevent abuse and neglect and (2) would be susceptible to arbitrary and discriminatory enforcement. The court also rejected the argument that a duty to prevent abuse or neglect could be imposed upon the defendant based on her duty under California law to support her indigent parent. The court noted that such an argument would do nothing to protect an elderly parent who was not indigent, and presumably the state legislature was concerned with the protection of all elders and not just those who are indigent. To avoid declaring the abuse statute unconstitutional, however, the court imposed a clarifying construction. Under the construction, a third party (who is not a caregiver) can be criminally liable for permitting elder neglect when (1) the third party stands in a special relationship to the individual inflicting the abuse or permitting the neglect and (2) the third party has a duty to supervise and control that individual's conduct. The daughter was not guilty under this clarifying construction.

Among the signs frequently indicating elder neglect are the following: malnutrition, dehydration, bedsores, other festering sores, unattended medical needs, lice and maggots on the body, a fetal or cachetic body position, a mattress soaked or crusted with urine and feces, a lack of adequately controlled temperature in the elder's environment, and terrible odors emanating from the elder or her environment.

b. Abandonment

Abandonment occurs when a person with a duty of care deserts the elder under circumstances that are likely to endanger the elder's health and well-being. It is a particular form of neglect in which the person with the duty of care renounces (usually implicitly rather than expressly) his obligation toward the elder without finding a replacement caregiver. Abandonment can result from a permanent or temporary renunciation of the obligation by the person having the duty of care. For example, an adult child who is the caregiver for her elderly mother might permanently abandon her mother by driving away for parts unknown after leaving her mother at a shopping mall. Alternatively, the daughter might temporarily abandon her mother by going off on vacation for a few days, leaving her vulnerable mother alone at home and unable to attend to herself.

c. Self-Neglect

Many state statutes recognize self-neglect as a form of elder abuse. It occurs when the health or well-being of an elder is endangered by her failure to properly care for herself because of her diminished capacity.

It is important to distinguish the incapacitated elder from the capable elder who can properly care for herself but knowingly and voluntarily chooses not to do so. The capable elder who understands her options and their probable outcomes cannot be guilty of self-neglect, even if her decisions are not those that a reasonable person would make. The state respects her autonomy and privacy and allows her to fail or refuse to act in ways that promote or preserve her health and well-being.

In contrast, the state's interest in protecting its vulnerable citizens may justify state intervention to prevent self-neglect by an elder with diminished capacity. Even here, however, the state should intervene only as necessary. Balancing the state interest with the autonomy of the individual is a delicate and difficult task, however. Moreover, it is often difficult to determine whether objectively bad decisions that endanger the health or well-being of the elder are the result of diminished capacity or are the result of knowing, voluntary decisions. Further compounding the difficulty is the fact that elder self-neglect often occurs when the elderly individual lives alone. When no one else is in the home to witness the elder's actions, a great deal of self-neglect probably goes unrecognized and unreported. Third parties such as grocery store employees or bank tellers who have limited interaction with the elder may not suspect the self-neglect or may simply choose not to become involved. In many states, such third parties have no duty to report suspected cases of self-neglect.

Because of the difficulty of detecting self-neglect, the lack of an "evil" third party engaging in the neglect, and the concern for respecting the elder's autonomy to the maximum extent consistent with her best interest, some commentators suggest that self-neglect may be the most difficult form of abuse to redress.

As with neglect, self-neglect often results in malnutrition, dehydration, unattended medical needs, unsanitary living conditions, and extremely bad odors emanating from the person or his environment.

D. Adult Protective Services

1. Lack of Federal Funding

Federal government funding of elder abuse prevention and education programs is quite small. A 2002 study revealed that the federal government spent $153.5 million on programs directly addressing elder abuse, which was slightly more than two percent spent by the federal government on programs addressing child abuse. Most of the money comes through the Department of Health and Human Services under the Social Services Block Grant program. Block grant funds are used to support Adult Protective Services (APS) agencies in a number of states. The Older Americans Act (OAA) provides for the National Center on Elder Abuse (NCEA) as a program of the United States Administration on Aging. 42 U.S.C. §3001 et seq. Monies under the OAA, however, do not fund state adult protective services.

2. APS Provisions Generally

Today, all states have laws concerning the provision of adult protective services for certain of their vulnerable adult citizens, including the elderly. Often these laws contain aspirational statements listing many various services the state hopes or desires to provide. For example, such a list of services might include "medical care, mental health and mental retardation services, including in-home assessments and evaluations; in-home services including homemaker, home-health, chore, meals; emergency services including shelter; financial assistance; legal services; transportation; counseling; foster care; day care; respite care; and other services as needed to carry out the intent of this part." Tenn. Code Ann. §71-6-101. Because of the costs of such programs and the lack of funding for such services, the statutory language seldom guarantees that the state will provide all such services.

The adults protected under APS statutes vary among the states. Many statutes do not limit the provision of services to the vulnerable elderly. Instead, they make the services available to all vulnerable adults. A state may have enacted special provisions within or separate from the APS statutes for vulnerable adults who are elderly. Some protective services provisions for the elderly are based on age alone, not upon the individual's vulnerability or disability. See http://www.abanet.org/aging/about/pdfs/Age_Threshold_Eligibility_Criteria_for_Adult_Protective_Services_by_State.pdf.

In many states, the APS provisions apply regardless of whether the adult is living in the community. In those states, agencies charged with investigative duties under the APS statutes may investigate reports of violations regardless of where the purported victim resides. In other states, however, APS investigations are initially available only to those who are living in the community, not to those living in a long-term care facility or other institution. In this latter group of states, a resident of a long-term care facility or other institution must initially look to the state Long Term Care Ombudsman Program or to other programs or state laws when the institutionalized resident is abused, neglected, or otherwise denied his rights.

State APS statutes also differ significantly in the range of actions and the kinds of actions considered abusive. The reporting provisions and the investigation provisions also vary substantially among the states. Some APS statutes themselves include criminal penalties for those who abuse, neglect, exploit, or otherwise mistreat the elderly. The APS statutes may also include civil remedies for the victim or his survivors.

3. APS Principles and Practices

The overarching goal of APS provisions is to ensure the safety and well-being of vulnerable adults and elderly persons who have no one to assist them and who are abused or suffering from self-neglect or are at risk of suffering abuse or self-neglect. According to the NCEA, the "guiding value" is that every APS action "must balance the duty to protect the safety of the vulnerable adult with the adult's right to self-determination." A consensus statement from the National Association of Adult Protective Services Administrators lists best practice guidelines concerning APS provisions. Under the guidelines, APS personnel should, among other things, do the following: recognize that the adult's interests are the primary concern in an intervention; avoid projecting their personal values on others; seek informed consent before providing services; involve the adult in formulating the service plan, to the extent possible; attempt to maximize the adult's independence; employ least restrictive services first; use family and informal support systems if those systems serve the best interest of the adult; use substituted judgment consistent with the adult's known values; and do no harm. See http://www.ncea.aoa.gov.

4. The APS Case

State intervention in an elder abuse setting typically begins with the report of abuse or suspected abuse. Once the report is made, the state APS agency or another agency or law enforcement group is charged with investigation. During the investigation, the state must assess the safety and well-being of the alleged victim and must also respect his right of self-determination concerning the proposed provision of protective services. In some instances, the state must conduct a hearing to determine whether it can force protective services upon the purported victim.

When a victim has received protective services or is otherwise determined to have been abused, neglected, or mistreated by a third party, the APS statutes may permit the state to prosecute the perpetrator and may provide the victim with a civil remedy against the perpetrator.

The following discussion examines the steps in a typical APS case and some of the problems commonly encountered in those steps.

a. Reporting

In most instances, the state must rely on citizen-reporters to inform it of the abuse or suspected abuse. Most states mandate that certain categories of persons report elder abuse when they have reasonable grounds to suspect such abuse. Those within the mandate often include health care professionals, such as doctors and nurses, as well as social workers and law enforcement personnel. Other individuals are not required to report abuse, but are generally encouraged to so. Individuals who are not required to report abuse are voluntary reporters. The distinction between mandated and voluntary reporters is potentially important, because state statutes may provide that failure to make a mandated report is a crime. In fact, however, the crime is typically only a misdemeanor, and conviction may only be available when the failure to report was willful or knowing. To date, states have seldom prosecuted a mandated reporter who failed to make the abuse report.

Some commentators have suggested that certain professionals who fail to make a mandated report may be guilty of malpractice. Even if a malpractice action is unavailable against the professional who fails to make a mandated report, he may be subject to license revocation or suspension, or face a charge of unprofessional conduct. The great majority of states do not provide the victim of abuse with an express private cause of action against a person who fails to make a mandated report. In the somewhat analogous area of child abuse, state courts have also generally held that an individual's failure to make a mandated report is not negligence per se.

Some states extend the mandatory reporting obligation to anyone who knows of or has reason to suspect elder abuse. In contrast—and perhaps somewhat surprisingly—a very few states do not require anyone to report elder abuse or suspected elder abuse.

It appears that much known or suspected elder abuse goes unreported. Observers have noted several possible reasons for the failure to report: uncertainty concerning whether a reasonable suspicion of abuse exists; the desire not to become entangled in the private affairs of others; the desire not to be involved in potential legal proceedings; fear that a report and investigation could place the victim in a worse position; concern for protecting the victim's confidentiality, if the victim is a patient or client; and fear of retaliation against the reporter by the victim, the abuser, or others if the reporter's identity is revealed.

APS provisions, however, often provide that the reporter's identity is confidential. Some statutes provide that the reporter's identity may only be revealed as ordered by a court for good cause. Also, APS provisions often provide that a reporter is presumed to act in good faith and is immune from civil or criminal liability for making a report in good faith.

Provisions in some states expressly give an employee a private cause of action (perhaps even permitting punitive damages) against anyone who causes an adverse change in his employment status as a result of his report of elder abuse or his cooperation in an elder abuse investigation or proceeding. Such a provision could be very important, for example, when a nursing home employee reports suspected abuse or provides information or testimony to investigating or prosecuting officials. APS provisions in other states, however, provide no such protections against employer retaliation. Even when a state abuse statute generally prohibits employer retaliation against an employee who reports suspected elder abuse or who cooperates with investigating officials, in some instances the reporting employee may have no private cause of action against an employer who retaliates against him. If the statute does not include an express private cause of action for the aggrieved employee, some courts have refused to imply the existence of such an action.

The content of the report is usually confidential. Observers believe such confidentiality is essential to protect the privacy and best interests of the alleged victim. APS statutes commonly make it unlawful for anyone to use or disclose information in the report except in connection with the subsequent investigation, the provision of services, or other actions necessary to accomplish the purposes of the APS program (such as sharing the information with law enforcement personnel). Some states retain reports in a central registry, a practice that can facilitate investigations. Placing all reports in a central registry also helps to identify repeat victims and abusers.

The report typically may be made to the appropriate state agency (for example, the state department of human services) in writing or orally. The report should contain all relevant information that is known, including the name, address, and age the purported victim; those responsible for her care; the nature and extent of the abuse, neglect, or exploitation (and any history of abuse of the victim); the identity of the perpetrator; and the identity of the complainant, if possible.

APS provisions frequently require coordination among several state agencies. APS provisions often require the agency receiving the report to notify the appropriate law enforcement agency. If the APS provisions also cover institutional abuse, the provisions may require the agency receiving the report to notify appropriate licensing authorities.

When the complainant makes his report to the proper agency, the agency is to contact other agencies as required by law and to initiate an investigation. APS provisions may indicate that the agency then should make a written report of the initial findings and include a recommendation for further action, if appropriate.

APS statutes often are silent on the consequences when the appropriate state agency fails to make the investigation contemplated by the statutes or fails to make the investigation in a timely manner. Suppose A, a vulnerable elder, gives B her durable power of attorney. A is subsequently institutionalized, and B exploits A's estate by misusing the power of attorney for himself. R reports suspected abuse, but the agency does not follow up until six months later, allowing B to further exploit A's estate. If A (or her estate) brings an action to recover the additional funds exploited by B during the period in which the agency failed to investigate, she will probably lose. Under the public duty doctrine, an individual cannot recover from a state agency unless she can show that the agency's duty was not merely to protect the public at large, but also to protect her as an individual.

b. Investigation

To aid in determining whether protective services are needed, APS provisions typically authorize representatives of the investigating agency to enter the private premises where the alleged victim resides. In some cases, the alleged victim or her caregiver refuses to permit the agency representative to enter the premises. In such cases, the agency may have to obtain a search warrant based on a showing of probable cause that abuse is occurring or has occurred.

Health, financial, law enforcement, and other records of both the elder and the alleged perpetrator of abuse are frequently important in the APS investigation. The records often contain relevant information relating to mental capacity, physical problems, substance abuse, unexplained or unusual transfers or withdrawals of funds, and so forth. APS provisions may give the agency representative investigating the case access to such records. If the representative is refused any information covered by the provisions, he may obtain such information by court order or perhaps by a judicial or administrative subpoena. The information obtained from such records is to be treated as confidential except as necessary for use in the investigation or related proceedings.

c. Services

If the investigation reveals that protective services are necessary and the elder agrees to such services, her caregiver may not interfere with such services. If the capable elder does not agree to such services, however, then such services generally may not be provided against her wishes. This principle respects the elder's right of self-determination.

If the elder refuses services but the agency believes that she lacks the capacity to consent to or refuse services, then the agency may seek court authorization to provide the services it believes to be necessary. If the elder is not in imminent danger of suffering irreparable physical or mental harm within a relatively short period, then the agency may seek a hearing to determine her capacity to consent to protective services. The elder must be given several days of advance notice in which to prepare for the hearing. If the judge concludes that the elder needs protective services and lacks capacity to consent, the judge may authorize the provision of protective services.

If the elder refuses services but the agency believes that she lacks the capacity to consent to or refuse services and also that she is in *imminent danger* without the provision of services, the agency may seek a court order authorizing the immediate provision of services. If the court finds that the elder lacks capacity and is in imminent danger, it may order immediate provision of protective services. The order may direct the removal of the elder from her current abode if necessary. In such emergency situations, no hearing is held before the services are authorized. To protect the elder's constitutional rights, however, the state must afford her a hearing shortly after such emergency order is entered.

A determination that the elder lacks the capacity to consent to services is typically not a determination of incapacity for other purposes. Thus the determination is not a substitute for a determination that the elder requires a guardian or conservator or that she should be committed to a mental institution.

Usually the elder who is financially capable of paying for the protective services received must reimburse the state or agency for those services. Otherwise, the state bears the cost of the protective services provided.

d. Remedies

Much elder abuse is prosecuted under traditional criminal laws such as criminal negligence, criminal battery, false imprisonment, and fraud. Some elder abuse is prosecuted under newer crimes now included within the state's criminal code. Some state APS statutes also contain their own distinct criminal provisions against perpetrators of abuse. Depending both upon the state and the severity of the crime, such crimes may be classified as misdemeanors or felonies. For example, simple neglect by a caregiver may be a misdemeanor, while gross neglect may be a felony.

When family members are convicted of elder abuse or neglect, courts sometimes impose seemingly light sentences or merely place the abuser on probation. In other instances, however, courts show no leniency to family abusers. Frequently the state will be unable to prove its case if the elder is unable or unwilling to cooperate. The elder may be especially reluctant to testify against a family member, and often no one but the elder and her abuser witness the abuse or neglect. In egregious cases, however, medical testimony often provides sufficient evidence to support charges of abuse or neglect. For example, when a forensic pathologist convincingly testifies that the autopsy on an alleged neglect victim indicates that she had eaten no food for at least thirty days prior to her death, a jury is likely to be convinced of the caregiver's guilt.

The abused elder herself may sue the perpetrator based on traditional civil actions such as negligence, battery, fraud, and so forth. Some state APS statutes also create a specific civil action for abuse, neglect, and exploitation against the perpetrator. The elder or her representative (such as a guardian or conservator) may bring the action. The statute may specifically state that the action does not abate at the death of the elder. Such a provision is important, for the perpetrator would have great incentive to delay the action if the action simply terminated at the elder's death.

Civil actions under APS statutes may authorize the recovery of compensatory damages as well as costs, attorney fees, and punitive damages in proper circumstances. Compensatory damages include damages for pain and suffering. The Arizona Supreme Court determined that pain and suffering damages survived the death of the elder abuse victim under its APS statutes, despite a general statute elsewhere in the code forbidding the recovery of pain and suffering damages after an injured person's death. The court noted that pain and suffering damages are often the only significant damages suffered by an abused elder, since her medical bills are covered by Medicare or Medicaid and she is unlikely to have suffered a diminution in earning capacity or property damage. In re Denton, 945 P.2d 1283 (Ariz. 1997).

E. Miscellaneous Matters

In this final part of the chapter, we discuss various topics related to elder abuse that are not covered elsewhere. These topics include (1) the ability of an abuser to benefit from the estate of the victim; (2) the availability of elder abuse actions against medical providers; (3) miscellaneous evidentiary and criminal matters; (4) abuse registries; and (5) nursing home litigation.

1. Limiting the Financial Benefits Available to Abusers

a. Caregivers

It is not uncommon for an elderly person to execute a durable power of attorney or a new will in favor of her caregiver. When the caregiver is unrelated to the elder and is a Johnny-come-lately in the elder's life, red flags immediately pop up. Traditionally, those who object to such documents must attack them under common-law theories such as undue influence, lack of capacity, fraud, or duress. A few states have begun to adopt new kinds of statutes, however, that limit certain financial benefits available to caregivers in various circumstances.

California, for example, has adopted a "care custodian" statute that generally invalidates provisions in an instrument executed by a dependent adult in favor of her caregiver. The provisions are not invalid, however, if the care custodian is related by blood or marriage to the transferor or is the transferor's cohabitant or registered domestic partner; if an independent attorney counsels the transferor, reviews and approves the instrument and signs a certificate of independent review concerning such provision; if the instrument is approved by a court after full disclosure; or if the court finds clear and convincing evidence (without considering the testimony of the caregiver) that the caregiver did not procure the transfer by fraud, menace, duress, or undue influence. Cal. Prob. Code §§ 21350–21356. Recent cases interpreting the statute have concluded that the term care custodian was intended to apply to practical nurses or other caregivers hired to provide in-home care. It was not intended to apply to the dependent's new or old friends, even though they may assist the dependent elder in meeting her daily needs.

b. Probate Laws and Estate Benefits

Under the probate laws of most states, an abuser does not lose the right to benefit at the death of a person unless the abuser's action falls under a slayer statute—in other words, unless the abuser feloniously and intentionally caused the death of the person. Because most abuse, even when felonious and intentional, does not result in the death of the victim, the abuser is typically able to receive an intestate share, a devise, life insurance proceeds, survivorship interests, or other assets when the victim dies.

A few states, however, have enacted statutes that now limit an abuser's right to inherit or benefit from the victim. Oregon has extended its slayer statute to prevent abusers as well as slayers from benefitting from their wrongful conduct. The statutes define an abuser as one convicted of a felony for physical abuse or financial abuse. The abuser is only precluded from benefitting, however, if the victim dies within five years after the abuser's conviction. Or. Rev. Stat. §§ 112.455–.525.

In Illinois, "[p]ersons convicted of financial exploitation, abuse, or neglect of an elderly person or a person with a disability shall not receive any property, benefit, or other interest by reason of the death of that elderly person or person with a disability, whether as heir, legatee, beneficiary, survivor ... or in any other capacity." The abuser is treated as having predeceased the victim. (The abuser does not forfeit his pre-existing interest in the property, however.

Thus, if the abuser and the victim were joint tenants with equal interest, the victim's one-half interest would pass as though she survived the abuser and the abuser would retain his one-half interest.) The statute does not apply, however, if the victim knew of the conviction and subsequent to conviction demonstrated her intent to transfer the property, benefit, or interest to the abuser. 755 Ill. Stat. Ann. 5/2-6.2.

In Maryland, a person convicted under a statute relating to financial exploitation of vulnerable adults or adults who are 68 or older is generally disqualified from benefitting from the victim's estate, insurance proceeds, or property, whether by operation of law or pursuant to a legal document executed by the victim before the abuser's conviction and before the abuser has made full restoration to the victim. Md. Crim. Law Code § 8-801.

Under an Arizona statute, if a person who is in a position of trust and confidence to a vulnerable adult improperly uses the vulnerable adult's assets, a court may order that the person forfeit all or a portion of various statutory benefits that the person would otherwise receive. These benefits include an intestate share, an elective share, an omitted spouse's share, an omitted child's share, a homestead allowance, an exempt property allowance, and a family allowance. The court may also revoke dispositions that the vulnerable adult made to the person under a governing instrument and may convert survivorship properties held by the vulnerable adult with the person into tenancies in common. Ariz. Rev. Stat. § 46-456.

A California statute covers a large range of abusive conduct and limits, but does not altogether prohibit, inheritance by an abuser. The statute provides that a person is deemed to have predeceased the decedent-victim if clear and convincing evidence has proved that the person is liable for physical abuse, neglect, or fiduciary abuse of the decedent who was an elder or dependent adult; the person is found to have acted in bad faith; the person has been found to have been reckless, oppressive, fraudulent, or malicious in the commission of any of these acts; and the decedent at the time of the acts and thereafter until his death has been found to have been substantially unable to manage his or her financial resources or to resist fraud or undue influence. If the person has been convicted under the penal code provisions for false imprisonment or crimes against elder or dependent adults, then he is also deemed to have predeceased the decedent. If following the physical abuse, neglect, or fiduciary abuse, the victim was substantially able to manage his or her financial resources and to resist fraud or undue influence, then the section does not apply. In any event, if the person is deemed to have predeceased the victim under the statute, he apparently does not completely lose the ability to benefit from the estate of the victim. Rather, "predeceased" for purposes of the statute means that he loses the right to receive any property, damages, or costs that are awarded to the decedent's estate based on the abuse. Cal. Prob. Code § 259.

Courts have often stated that a principal policy underlying a slayer's statute is to ensure that no one profit from his wrongful acts. At least some probate courts are willing to extend the policy using their inherent equitable powers. In a 1998 South Dakota case, two brothers financially exploited their elderly uncle. Although the brothers were each to receive one-third of their uncle's estate, the state supreme court refused to allow them to receive any part of the punitive damages award they had had to pay to the estate because of the abuse. Estate of O'Keefe, 583 N.W.2d 138 (S.D. 1998).

Developments such as these are noteworthy. With increasing recognition of the problem of elder abuse, more state legislatures and courts will probably restrict the benefits an abuser may receive from the estate of his victim. Because much elder abuse is financially motivated, such measures seem particularly appropriate.

2. Medical Malpractice and Elder Abuse

In some instances, a plaintiff has attempted to bring an abuse or neglect action against a medical or health care provider or facility. For example, such actions might be brought by an elder who suffered extensively from continuing but improper or inadequate medical treatment of an injury, or who was repeatedly denied adequate palliative relief. For the plaintiff, the abuse or neglect action may be more attractive than a medical malpractice action for various reasons. Often the abuse or neglect action will have a longer statute of limitations period, will permit the recovery of damages unavailable under malpractice actions, and will not require the use of expert witnesses.

In some states, abuse and neglect statutes generally exclude actions against health care providers and their employees. In such instances, the plaintiff may have to bring her claim under medical malpractice or professional negligence statutes, or under other provisions governing claims against health care providers.

Some abuse or neglect statutes provide that they do not cover actions within the scope of a medical malpractice or professional negligence statute. At least some courts have concluded that willful, intentional, and reckless conduct by a health care provider is not professional negligence, and thus is not within the scope of the malpractice or professional negligence statute. When the plaintiff's complaint is based on such conduct, his claim is one of elder abuse and is governed by abuse and neglect statutes. Delaney v. Baker, 971 P.2d 986 (Cal. 1999).

3. Evidentiary and Criminal Matters

Sentencing guidelines in some instances will permit sentencing enhance-ment in cases involving elderly victims. For example, enhancement may be permitted when the defendant knew or should have known that the victim was a vulnerable victim, and the offense level may be increased if the offense in-volved a large number of vulnerable victims.

If the crime in question is defined as involving an elderly victim (for ex-ample, "assault on the elderly"), defendants have occasionally asserted that they cannot be held criminally liable when they did not know or have reason to know that the victim was elderly. The better view, accepted by some courts, would seem to reject this argument. The subjective knowledge of the perpe-trator may be difficult or impossible to know, and accepting the argument would often permit perpetrators to escape prosecution under the statute when the victim's apparent or functional age is substantially less than her chronological age. For example, in one case a state high court refused to substantiate a re-port of abuse in the absence of evidence that the perpetrator knew or should have known of the victim's status as an elderly or disabled adult.

At one time, Florida had a special hearsay exception pertaining to out-of-court statements made by an elderly person who was the victim of abuse or violence. California had a somewhat similar hearsay exception. Although the exceptions purported to included restrictions designed to ensure the reliabil-ity of the statements, courts in both states ultimately declared the exceptions to be unconstitutional.

Some elderly criminals have argued that because of their shortened life ex-pectancies, a long sentence that would be constitutional for a younger person is cruel and unusual punishment as applied to them. They have also argued that their continued incarceration after serving a substantial prison term consti-tutes elder abuse. Most observers reject both of these arguments.

4. Abuse Registries

Although there is no national registry of those who have abused a vulner-able or elderly adult, states typically maintain some form of registry or reg-istries. State APS statutes may include provisions about an abuse registry. See http://www.abanet.org/aging/about/pdfs/AbuseRegistriesComparisonChart.pdf. Also, federal law requires states to maintain a registry of all individuals who have completed nurse aide training programs in the state and to include documented findings of neglect, abuse, or misappropriation of resident property involving those individuals listed in the registry. 42 U.S.C. § 1396r(e)(2)(A).

Most commonly, a perpetrator's name may be entered in a state abuse reg-istry based on a criminal conviction or, alternatively, on a finding by a state agency after the alleged abuser was afforded administrative due process. The details con-cerning registries vary substantially from state to state.

In some states, the abuse registry is available for public inspection; in oth-ers it is not. Information in the nurse aide registry required under federal statute must be available for public inspection. In any event, the information in an APS or other state registry is typically available to nursing homes and other licensed facilities that hire employees to work with their elderly residents. Such information is also available to state and professional licensing boards. State statutes often require certain entities—such as residential facilities for the eld-erly—to check the registry before hiring employees.

5. Nursing Home Litigation

Most elder abuse occurs in the community. Nevertheless, institutional abuse seems to hold greater interest for plaintiffs' lawyers, probably because of the per-ceived greater financial rewards that come from suing a nursing home. A nurs-ing home can be held liable for acts resulting from its own negligence and may be vicariously liable for the acts of its employees. For example, in a case where an employee abuses a resident, the nursing home's negligence may be shown in part from the nursing home's failure to engage in proper background checks on the employee; to adequately train the employee; to adequately supervise the employee; to maintain adequate documentation about training and su-pervision; and so forth.

Most active abuse in institutional settings appears to be committed by lower level employees, particularly nurse aides. There is no national registry of in-dividuals who have committed elder abuse. Thus a nurse aide whose name is placed in the registry of one state may move to another state and be able to obtain a nurse aide position there. Because state law often requires the nurs-ing home only to check the registry of the state where it is located, the prior history of abuse in another state will not be detected.

A nursing home is not vicariously liable for all misconduct of an employee. In cases where aides have actively abused residents, courts have looked at var-ious factors in determining whether the employer can be held liable when the employee acted willfully or recklessly. A nursing home that can prove it has engaged in proper background checks, training, supervision, and documen-tation is much less likely to be held vicariously liable for the intentional and reck-less abusive acts of a lower level employee. If the nursing home did not know or have reason to know that the employee would abuse a patient, it may be able to convince a court that the intentional and reckless abusive act was not within the scope of employment and not subject to its control.

Checkpoints

- Concerning elder abuse generally, you should
  - Understand various theories about why abusers engage in abusive conduct
  - Understand that elder abuse is a widespread social problem that has only begun to be recognized in recent decades
  - Be able to recognize warning signs of elder abuse
- Concerning kinds of elder abuse, you should be able to define and distinguish
  - Physical abuse
  - Sexual abuse
  - Exploitation
  - Emotional abuse
  - Neglect
  - Abandonment
  - Self-neglect
- Concerning statutory provisions addressing elder abuse, you should understand
  - The role of Adult Protective Services agencies
  - The way in which reporting statutes work
  - The way in which an abuse investigation is conducted
  - Services available to the abused elder
  - Criminal and civil remedies for the abuse
- Concerning miscellaneous matters relating to elder abuse, you should understand
  - The nature of new statutory developments that limit an abuser's ability to benefit financially from his abuse
  - The potential statutory hurdles against bringing an elder abuse claim against a medical provider
  - Various evidentiary and criminal matters such as the possibility of sentencing enhancement
  - The importance of abuse registries
  - The general nature of nursing home litigation

Chapter 2

Guardianships and Conservatorships

Roadmap

- Guardians and conservators
  - Are appointed by courts in proceedings governed by state law
  - Should be appointed only when appointment serves the best interest of the respondent in the proceeding
  - Are appointed to make personal decisions for, or manage the estate of, individuals who are incapacitated
  - Are fiduciaries who are to act in the best interest of the ward or protected person
- Statutory reforms in recent years require
  - Observance of the due process rights of the respondent in the proceeding
  - The use of the least restrictive alternative
- The Uniform Probate Code provides detailed statutory guidance for guardians and conservators concerning
  - The circumstances under which appointment is proper
  - Procedural matters
  - Duties and powers, including
    - Powers by default
    - Actions that require court approval

A. Overview

1. Generally

When a person lacks or loses the ability to manage her assets or make personal decisions, family members or other interested persons may petition the proper court for a guardianship or conservatorship. A guardian or conservator is a court-appointed fiduciary obligated to make decisions that serve the best interest of the ward, protected person, or disabled person. Although anyone at any age may need the services of a guardian or conservator, a high percentage of guardianship and conservatorship cases involve an elderly respondent suffering from dementia, Alzheimer's, or other diseases resulting in significant mental deterioration. Thus the topic of guardianships and conservatorships is quite important in the study of elder law.

A person's inability to manage her assets or make personal decisions does not necessarily warrant the appointment of a fiduciary for her. If, while capable, a person validly appoints an agent to act on her behalf in the event of her incapacity, then often the agent will be able to make financial and personal decisions for her when she can no longer do so. Durable powers of attorney are perhaps the principal means used today to avoid the costs, delay, and potential embarrassment associated with guardianship or conservatorship proceedings. Lawyers and estate planners increasingly advise their clients of the importance of durable powers of attorney for estate matters and health care, and correspondingly the use of such documents is rising. These and other so-called advance directives, however, are not without dangers of their own. (Advance directives and other planning tools are discussed in Chapters 3 and 4.) For the many individuals who do not have a validly appointed agent or other fiduciary to act for them, significant diminution of mental capacity may lead to a guardianship or conservatorship proceeding.

2. State Authority

Guardianship and conservatorship proceedings are governed almost exclusively by state law. A state's power to intervene in the private lives of its incapacitated citizens for their protection arises principally from its role as *parens patriae*. The parens patriae doctrine, which originated in English common law, allows the state to act on behalf of its citizens who are unable to act for themselves.

Today all states have codified that power in guardianship and conservatorship statutes. These statutes vary significantly among the states, however, in terminology, detail, procedures, and powers delegated to courts. This chapter focuses on general principles and trends in guardianship and conservatorship law. Because of the substantial differences among state law, however, the lawyer must always consult the particular statutes, cases, and court rules applicable in his jurisdiction.

A number of states have adopted the Uniform Veterans Guardianship Act (UVGA) to govern guardianship proceedings involving certain veterans. The UVGA makes the Administrator of Veterans' Affairs a party in interest in a proceeding for the appointment or removal of a guardian of a ward who receives veterans' benefits. Nonetheless, the proceedings themselves are generally governed by state law.

The parens patriae doctrine should result in state beneficence, but not state overreaching. A judicial finding that a person is incapacitated and needs a guardian or conservator can severely curtail the autonomy of that person. Recognizing this, state guardianship and conservatorship laws should carefully balance the state's interest in protecting its incapacitated citizens with the individual's right of autonomy. In the 1980s, newspaper accounts exposed an alarming lack of respect for the latter in state courts. When presented with petitions from family members of a respondent, courts often declared the respondent incapacitated and stripped her of substantially all rights without providing her advance notice and a true opportunity to be heard. Even when the respondent was only partly incapacitated, courts often gave the successful petitioners full powers and virtually complete control to make financial or personal decisions for her.

The newspaper expose´ revealed not only the informality of state guardianship and conservatorship proceedings, but also the lack of procedural and substantive protections afforded a respondent. In 1988, the ABA convened the Wingspread conference, which was the first interdisciplinary national guardianship symposium. The Wingspread conference and the recommendations it produced led to substantial reform of state guardianship and conservatorship laws. States began to include statutory provisions designed to ensure (1) that a respondent receives procedural due process and also (2) that judicial determinations restrict an incapacitated person's autonomy only to the extent necessary to further her best interests.

Some observers question the impact of these changes. It generally appears that a respondent's procedural due process rights are more likely to be respected today than in the past, at least in the early stages of the guardianship or conservatorship process. It does not appear that statutory changes designed to respect and maximize the autonomy of an incapacitated individual have had great success.

3. The UPC and State Terminology

What is the difference between guardianship and conservatorship? The answer depends upon state law. A person who needs a guardian under the laws of State A might require a conservator under the laws of State B.

The modern trend is reflected in Article V of the Uniform Probate Code (revised 1998 version), which incorporates the Uniform Guardianship and Protective Proceedings Act (1997). These provisions, vetted and approved by leading scholars, are far more detailed and protective of a respondent's rights than are the conservatorship and guardianship laws of many states. Article V has been adopted in a few states. Other states have begun to borrow selectively from its provisions, and its influence will probably increase in the coming years. (An earlier version of Article V is still the basis for the guardianship and conservatorship laws of several states. Other states also selectively borrowed from that version. In this chapter, however, references to the UPC or Article V are to the 1998 version.)

Under the UPC, a conservator is a person who is appointed by a court to manage the estate of a protected person. A guardian is a person who has been appointed by a court to make personal decisions for a ward. A respondent is an individual for whom a guardianship, conservatorship, or other protective order is sought.

This bifurcation of substitute decision making into personal matters and estate (or financial) matters is characteristic of guardianship and conservatorship laws throughout the country. Unlike the UPC, however, the laws of some states designate the court-appointed fiduciary a conservator regardless of whether he is appointed to make personal or estate decisions, or both, for the incapacitated person. The laws of other states use the term guardian to refer to the court-appointed fiduciary regardless of whether he is appointed to make personal or estate decisions, or both, for the incapacitated person. The laws of yet other states may use other terms for the court-appointed fiduciary. This chapter will employ the UPC distinction: a guardian makes personal decisions; a conservator makes financial decisions.

Terminology concerning the incapacitated person also varies among the states. When a fiduciary is appointed to make financial decisions, some states employ the UPC approach and refer to the incapacitated person as a protected person. (One might note that section 5-409(d) of the UPC provides that the appointment of a conservator is not a determination of "incapacity." As a practical matter, however, the UPC permits the appointment of a conservator only when the protected person is at least partly incapable of managing her estate. Moreover, the clarifying comment to the statute provides that the appointment of a conservator under the UPC is not a determination of incapacity for guardianship purposes. For the sake of convenience, in this chapter we refer to an incapacitated person as one who requires either a guardian or conservator, or both, acknowledging that the capacity examination for management of the person and management of the estate may differ.)

Some states refer to the person under a conservatorship as a conservatee, and yet others use a term such as disabled person. When a fiduciary is appointed to make personal decisions for the incapacitated person, states often mirror the UPC and refer to the incapacitated person as a ward. Some states use other terms, however.

The UPC provisions seek to maximize individual autonomy. They permit the use of guardianships and conservatorships only as a last resort, when no less restrictive alternative will meet the needs of the respondent. When the respondent needs a guardianship or conservatorship, the UPC grants the guardian or conservator only those powers necessary to meet the respondent's needs. Consistent with its goal of maximizing autonomy, the UPC provides that guardians and conservators should include the ward or protected person, when feasible, in the decision making process.

B. When Should a Guardian or Conservator Be Appointed?

The modern view is that capacity exists along a spectrum. A person may be incapable of making some decisions while capable of making others. Thus, she may require a guardian or conservator with limited powers to assist her in the areas in which she is incapacitated. The modern view is espoused by the UPC and by increasing numbers of state statutes. An older view, still reflected in the statutory language of some states, is that a person is either competent or incompetent. This older view seldom recognizes shades of gray between the extremes. Courts employing this older approach generally award the guardian or conservator full or plenary powers once they have determined the respondent is "incompetent." Even in states whose statutory language seems to incorporate the modern approach, some judges may in fact employ the older view.

When is a person incapacitated? The UPC states than an incapacitated adult is an individual who "is unable to receive and evaluate information or make or communicate decisions to such an extent that the individual lacks the ability to meet essential requirements for physical health, safety, or self-care, even with appropriate technological assistance." UPC § 5-102(5). A determination of incapacity under this definition requires an assessment of the individual's functional abilities. Courts increasingly employ this test of functional ability in determining capacity. Note that an individual does not have to make "responsible" or "good" decisions to be capable. It is her ability to evaluate and communicate decisions to meet her essential needs that is important.

Courts often point out certain factors that do not reflect incapacity. Most important in elder law, courts frequently note that a respondent's old age alone is not a sufficient reason for the imposition of a guardianship or conservatorship. Physical incapacity is not a reason for court appointment of a guardian or conservator if the respondent can evaluate information and communicate decisions to meet her needs. Irresponsible or bad decisions, frequent though they may be, do not warrant the appointment of a management fiduciary if the respondent makes the decisions knowingly, intentionally, and voluntarily. Eccentricity, absent-mindedness, and illiteracy are not themselves reasons for a guardianship or conservatorship. Courts have also indicated that a conservatorship should not be imposed on a respondent merely to ensure that her estate will be protected for her expectant heirs and devisees.

C. The Petition and the Proceeding

1. Petition and Contents

The guardianship or conservatorship proceeding begins with the filing of a petition in the appropriate court. In most states, guardianship and conservatorship proceedings are handled in probate courts or more generalized courts that handle probate matters. If the petitioner is seeking the appointment of a fiduciary to make personal decisions and manage the property of the respondent, typically one petition can consolidate both requests.

In most states, any person interested in the welfare of the person alleged to be incapacitated can file the petition. The UPC and the laws of many states permit an individual to file a voluntary petition seeking the appointment of a guardian or conservator for herself. As the UPC commentary notes, however, such a petition is only effective if she possesses the requisite capacity to file the petition; however, if she possesses that level of capacity, then the more prudent route in most instances would be for her instead to appoint an agent under a duly-executed durable power of attorney. In any event, courts should examine voluntary petitions warily to ensure that the petitioner is not filing the petition under the duress or undue influence of others.

The UPC and many states carefully detail the information that the petitioner must include in the guardianship or conservatorship petition. Under the UPC guardianship provisions, the petitioner must include his name, residence and address, his relationship to the respondent, and his interest in the appointment. To the extent known, the petition should state the respondent's name, age, principal residence, current address, and proposed residence if the petition is granted. The petition should also provide the name and address of the respondent's spouse or other adult with whom she has resided for more than six months; her adult children or, if none, her brothers and sisters, or if none, at least one adult nearest in kinship to her who can be found; the person responsible for her care or custody; and her legal representative. This list of persons identifies those individuals who are most likely to have useful information concerning the respondent. (For example, the respondent's legal representative may know of the existence of a durable power of attorney that would obviate the guardianship action.) The individuals on the list are also to be given notice of proceedings in the matter.

The petition must state the reason why the guardianship is necessary and provide a brief description of the nature and extent of the alleged incapacity. The petition must also identify the proposed guardian and state why he should be selected. The petition must indicate whether it requests a limited or unlimited guardianship. If the request is for a limited guardianship, the petition must indicate the powers to be granted to the limited guardian. If the request is for an unlimited guardianship, the petition must state the reason why a limited guardianship is inappropriate.

Finally, the guardianship petition should provide a general statement of the respondent's property (including any insurance or pension), an estimate of its value, and the source and amount of any other anticipated income or receipts. UPC § 5-304.

The UPC's requirements for a petition requesting the appointment of a conservator are generally similar to the requirements for a guardianship petition, although variation exists in the details. For example, among the individuals specifically mentioned who may petition for the appointment of a conservator is a person who would be adversely affected by lack of effective management of the property and business affairs of the person to be protected by the appointment. A petition for a conservator must also set forth the name and address of any person nominated as conservator by the respondent. If the petition requests a limited conservator, then the petition must specify the property to be placed under the conservator's control. If the petition requests an unlimited conservatorship, the petition must state why a limited conservatorship is inappropriate. UPC § 5-404.

As with almost all aspects of guardianship and conservatorship law, the lawyer must carefully consult the requirements of the particular jurisdiction. Information required to be included in the petition varies substantially among the states. For example, some states may require that a recent medical report on the respondent be attached to a guardianship or conservatorship petition, or that an asset management plan be attached to a conservatorship petition.

2. Jurisdiction and Venue

In most cases, jurisdiction and venue are straightforward. Under the UPC and in most jurisdictions, the applicable court (typically the court hearing probate matters) has jurisdiction over guardianship proceedings for individuals domiciled or present in the state and over conservatorship proceedings for individuals domiciled in or having property located in the state. The court also has jurisdiction over property that subsequently comes into the control of a guardian or conservator under state law. The court that appointed a guardian or conservator may transfer jurisdiction to a court in another county of the state or to another state if doing so will serve the best interest of the ward or protected person.

Venue for a guardianship proceeding is typically in the county in which the respondent resides; in emergency settings, it may also be where the respondent is present. Venue for a protective proceeding is in the county where the respondent resides; however, if the respondent does not reside in the state, it is in the county where the respondent's property is located.

Occasionally, litigation arises concerning jurisdiction. For example, if two adult sons live in different states and their mother lives part of the year with each, each son might decide to file a petition in his state of domicile. The UPC provides that when a petition is filed in one state and then a second petition is filed in another state, the court in the second state must notify the court in the first state. After consultation between the two courts, the second court may then assume or decline jurisdiction in accord with the best interest of the respondent, ward, or protected person. UPC § 5-107. Ordinarily, deference should be granted to the decision of the original court.

A guardian or conservator appointed in one state may petition for appointment in another state if venue in the second state is or will be established. For example, if Ann was properly appointed as guardian of her mother in State A and the two subsequently move to State B because of Ann's job, Ann can petition the proper court in State B to recognize her guardianship without having a full-blown proceeding. Under the UPC, the court in State B can appoint Ann as guardian upon proof of her appointment in State A and her presentation of a certified copy of the portion of the court record from State A as specified by the court in State B. Notice of hearing on the petition and a copy of the petition must be given to the respondent. Also, to discourage forum shopping, ensure the transparency of the process, and protect the interests of others, notice of hearing and a copy of the petition must be given to those people who would be entitled to notice on a regular petition for appointment of a guardian or conservator. The court in State B will appoint Ann unless it concludes such appointment would not be in the best interest of the respondent. UPC § 5-107(c).

3. Procedure and Due Process

Before the latter part of the twentieth century, guardianship and conservatorship laws and proceedings often showed little concern for providing a respondent with advance notice and a true opportunity to be heard. In the statutory reform occurring since the late 1980s, lawmakers in most states have specifically addressed those concerns.

a. Notice and Service

The UPC provides that those required to be notified of a hearing on a guardianship or conservatorship petition must be given that notice at least fourteen days before the hearing. (The fourteen-day notice rule, which has been part of the UPC since its promulgation in 1969, may be altered by a court for good cause.) Such notice must be given in plain language. Proof of notice must be made before or at the hearing and must be filed in the proceeding. The respondent, ward, or protected person is not permitted to waive notice under any circumstances. Others entitled to notice may waive notice by a writing signed by them or their attorney that is filed in the proceeding.

The UPC also permits an interested person who is not otherwise entitled to notice to file a request for notice with the clerk of the court where the proceeding is pending. The request must contain a statement stating the interest of the person and the address of the person to whom such notice is to be given. Among others, interested persons may include creditors, governmental agencies, and perhaps even members of the media or watch-dog agencies.

The guardianship or conservatorship laws of some states purport to grant judges general discretion to waive statutory requirements. Even so, service of process upon the respondent would appear non-waivable because of the respondent's due process rights. The UPC provides that a copy of a petition for guardianship and notice of the hearing on the petition must be served personally on the respondent. Failure to do so is jurisdictional; without personal service and proper notice to the respondent, the court cannot grant the petition. The UPC conservatorship notice requirements are similar; however, if the respondent's whereabouts are unknown or personal service cannot be made, the statute borrows the applicable state's rules for substituted service.

b. GALs and Visitors

The UPC permits a court to appoint a guardian ad litem (GAL) at any stage of the proceeding if it concludes that representation would otherwise be inadequate. The court is to state the duties of the GAL on the record and provide its reasons for appointment. As long as no conflict of interest exists, a GAL may represent several individuals or interests. UPC § 5-115.

In most states, the GAL is appointed to act as a court advisor. Usually he is appointed to confer with the respondent and draw impressions concerning the respondent's probable need for a fiduciary. He may also be expected to explain to the respondent the nature of the proceeding and her procedural rights. He then reports to the court.

State law may prefer that a GAL be a lawyer. In many states, no GAL will be appointed if the respondent has her own lawyer who will represent her at the proceeding. In some cases when the respondent has no lawyer of her own, courts have appointed a GAL as both a court advisor and as lawyer for the respondent. Such appointments are unfortunate and should be considered improper. They create an inherent conflict of interest for the GAL, for he cannot simultaneously serve as a neutral court advisor and an advocate for his client.

The UPC requires the appointment of a "visitor" to assist the court when a guardianship or conservatorship petition is filed concerning an adult respondent. The visitor has specific obligations, many of which coincide with the obligations of GALs under the laws of non-UPC states.

When a guardianship or conservatorship petition is filed, under the UPC the court is to appoint a visitor who has training or experience in the kind of incapacity alleged. The visitor may or may not be a lawyer. In guardianship proceedings, the visitor must interview the respondent in person; explain to the respondent the substance of the petition, the nature of the proceeding, and the general powers and duties of a guardian; inform the respondent of her rights; inform the respondent that proceeding costs and expenses will be paid from her estate; and determine her views regarding the proposed guardian and the guardianship. The visitor must also interview the petitioner and the proposed guardian; visit the respondent's dwelling and proposed dwelling; and obtain information from the respondent's physician and others concerning the respondent's physical or mental condition. Following his investigation, the visitor must file a written report with the court summarizing, among other things: the daily functions that the respondent can manage (independently or with assistance of supportive services or benefits) and cannot manage; the propriety of a guardianship and whether less restrictive alternatives are available; the propriety of a limited guardianship; the qualifications of the proposed guardian and whether the respondent approves of the proposed guardian; and whether a professional evaluation or further evaluation is necessary. (Note that the UPC no longer requires a professional evaluation of the respondent in every case.) If the state does not provide for mandatory counsel, the visitor must make a recommendation to the court concerning whether a lawyer should be appointed for the respondent. UPC § 5-305.

In conservatorship proceedings, the visitor must interview the respondent in person; explain to the respondent the substance of the petition and the nature of the proceeding; inform the respondent of her rights; inform the respondent that proceeding costs and expenses will be paid from her estate; and inform her of the general powers and duties of a conservator and determine her views regarding the proposed conservator and the conservatorship. The visitor must also interview the petitioner and the proposed conservator. The visitor must file a report with the court that discusses, among other things, the following: the propriety of a conservatorship and whether less restrictive alternatives are available; the propriety of a limited conservatorship; the qualifications of the proposed conservator and whether the respondent approves of the proposed conservator; and whether a professional evaluation or further evaluation is necessary. If the state does not provide for mandatory counsel, the visitor must make a recommendation concerning whether a lawyer should be appointed for the respondent. UPC § 5-406.

c. Counsel

Should the state require that a lawyer represent the respondent in a guardianship or conservatorship proceeding? One might instinctively answer yes, but further reflection could lead to a different answer. For example, does a person in a persistent vegetative state need a lawyer to defend against a guardianship or conservatorship petition? She is clearly incapacitated. If she has no duly-appointed agent to act for her and if state law does not bestow on anyone else the power to act for her, she will need a court-appointed fiduciary. Does her estate need to incur the further cost of paying for legal representation, particularly if a GAL or court-appointed visitor will assist the court in assuring that her best interest is served?

In fact, legal scholars disagree on the propriety of mandatory appointment of counsel in guardianship and conservatorship proceedings. Recognizing this, the UPC provides two alternatives from which a state may choose. UPC §§ 5-305, 5-406.

Alternative 1 does not require the appointment of a lawyer in all cases. Instead, it provides that the court shall appoint a lawyer to represent the respondent in the proceeding if (1) requested by the respondent; (2) recommended by the visitor; or (3) the court determines that the respondent needs representation. Alternative 2 provides that unless the respondent is represented by a lawyer, the court shall appoint a lawyer to represent the respondent in the proceeding, regardless of her ability to pay.

d. The Professional Evaluation

State laws often require that the petition be accompanied by a recent medical, psychological, or other appropriate professional evaluation of the respondent. If one is not available at that time, then it must be submitted at or (preferably) before the hearing. If the respondent refuses to submit to such an evaluation, the court may order her to do so. While the recommendation contained in a professional evaluation is not determinative in a guardianship or conservatorship proceeding, it is often highly persuasive. In contested proceedings, however, it is not uncommon to have multiple, conflicting professional recommendations.

The professional evaluation is no longer mandatory under the UPC. Although the court may order such an evaluation, it must do so only when the respondent demands to have a professional evaluation. UPC § 5-306. The UPC provision is a practical one. It recognizes the respondent's right to have a professional evaluation, but saves the respondent's estate from the pointless costs of additional examinations and evaluations when she is unquestionably incapacitated.

The UPC and the laws of several non-UPC states provide that the results of a professional evaluation as well as any written report of a visitor (or GAL) are confidential. These records are available to the court; to the respondent (for any reason); and, for purposes of the proceeding, to the visitor (or GAL) and the lawyers for the petitioner and respondent. For good cause, the court may make such records available to others. UPC §§ 5-307, 5-407. The sealing of such records can be important to protect the privacy of the respondent.

e. Burden and Standard of Proof

Unless an appropriate court has previously determined that the respondent is incapacitated, the respondent in a guardianship or conservatorship proceeding is presumed capable of managing herself and her affairs. Thus the petitioner bears the burden of proving the respondent's incapacity at the hearing. At one time, it was not uncommon for states to require only that the petitioner prove the respondent's incapacity by a preponderance of the evidence. Today, statutes generally adopt a clear and convincing standard of proof. A state may, however, even require a petitioner to prove beyond a reasonable doubt that a proposed ward is incapacitated and in need of a guardian. New Hampshire takes such a stringent approach. N.H. Rev. Stat. § 4640-A:8.

The UPC requires the petitioner to prove incapacity in a guardianship proceeding with clear and convincing evidence. UPC § 5-311. In conservatorship proceedings, however, the UPC takes a bifurcated approach employing different standards of proof. First, the court must determine by clear and convincing evidence that the respondent is unable to manage her property and business affairs because of an impairment in the ability to receive and evaluate information or make decisions (even with the use of technological assistance) or because she is missing, detained, or unable to return to the country. Second, the court must determine by a preponderance of the evidence that she has property that will be wasted or dissipated unless management is provided, or that money is needed for the support and welfare of those who are entitled to her support, and that protection is necessary or desirable to obtain or provide money. UPC § 5-401(2).

f. At the Hearing

States do not always require the respondent to attend the guardianship or conservatorship hearing. Some state laws permit the respondent to waive her right to attend; others provide that she must attend unless excused for good cause. The UPC takes the latter approach. The UPC similarly provides that a proposed guardian or conservator shall attend the hearing unless excused by the court for good cause.

The respondent must be given the opportunity to be heard. The UPC provides that she may present evidence and subpoena witnesses and documents, examine witnesses (including any court-appointed physician, psychologist, or other individual qualified to evaluate the alleged impairment) and the visitor, and otherwise participate in the hearing.

The UPC provides that the hearing may be held in a location convenient to the respondent. Even when such provisions are not a part of a state's statutes, some judges are willing to conduct the hearing where the respondent lives, is hospitalized, or is institutionalized. The court may be able to get a better picture of the respondent's true capacities when she is in familiar and comfortable surroundings.

The court may close the hearing upon the request of the respondent and a showing of good cause. The court may permit others to participate in the proceeding upon their request, if such participation will serve the best interest of the respondent.

A number of states permit the respondent to have a jury trial upon request. More often than not, however, respondents do not want a jury to hear and decide the issue of incapacity. They often consider the prospect embarrassing and do not wish to have the purported evidence of their incapacity paraded before a group of strangers.

g. The Least Restrictive Alternative

One of the most important goals of modern guardianship and conservatorship reform was to stem their overuse. As commentary to the UPC states, "a guardian should be appointed only when necessary, only for as long as necessary, and with only those powers as are necessary." UPC § 5-311. The same is true regarding a conservator.

An examination of state statutes would seemingly indicate that the reform has been substantially successful in satisfying this goal. Many state legislatures have mandated that courts employ the *least restrictive alternative* (LRA) consistent with the respondent's best interest in matters concerning guardianships and conservatorships. Unfortunately, these modern statutory mandates are often ignored by courts. Thus, many courts still routinely grant full powers to guardians and conservators without questioning the propriety of such grants. It is much easier for a court to issue an order granting plenary powers to the guardian or conservator than to look for alternatives to guardianship or conservatorship or to craft an order detailing specific powers removed from the ward or protected person and granted to the fiduciary.

Under strict adherence to the LRA principle, a court should not automatically grant a guardianship or conservatorship even when the evidence clearly and convincingly establishes the incapacity of a respondent who has no duly-appointed agent to act for her. For example, the court generally should not appoint a guardian or conservator if the incapacitated respondent's needs are adequately met by services provided through a state agency (such as social services or human services). Those services are a less restrictive alternative than guardianship or conservatorship. Section 5-412 of the UPC also explicitly permits court-ordered protective arrangements without the appointment of a conservator. Thus, if an individual needs only limited assistance, such as help in supervising a single but important financial transaction, the court might appoint someone to assist her in this one matter without formally designating the assistant as a conservator. (Even when informal alternatives are available, the respondent is still entitled to procedural protections like those afforded in a conservatorship proceeding.)

If there is no less restrictive alternative than guardianship or conservatorship, the LRA mandate still requires a court to distinguish carefully those areas in which the respondent does not need a fiduciary to act for her. This requirement results from the statutory acknowledgment that incapacity exists along a spectrum. To maximize and encourage the respondent's autonomy, independence, and self-reliance, the court should grant the guardian or conservator only those powers necessitated by the respondent's incapacity. In other words, courts should only grant plenary power when the respondent is fully incapacitated. Limited guardianships and conservatorships are preferred over full or plenary guardianships and conservatorships.

Modern statutes often not only require courts to use LRA, but also require courts to state specifically those powers that are being removed from the respondent and granted to the fiduciary. To discourage routine grants of plenary powers, some statutes further require the court to indicate in its order the findings that support its decision. In those states, some appellate courts have indicated that a lower court's generalized statement such as "the court finds the respondent to be incapacitated and thus in need of a guardian or conservator with full powers" is insufficient to satisfy the statutory requirement.

4. The Guardian or Conservator

a. Priority Lists and the Respondent's Best Interest

Once the court properly determines that a guardianship or conservatorship is necessary, it must determine who should be appointed to that fiduciary position. In the typical scenario, the court appoints the person nominated in the guardianship or conservatorship petition. In some instances, the court will hold a separate hearing to determine the appointment. This is particularly likely when several family members are each claiming to be the best person for the position, or when the court decides it needs further information about a proposed fiduciary or about a proposed fiduciary's alleged conflicts of interest.

Courts repeatedly indicate that their responsibility is to appoint the individual who is most likely to further the best interest of the ward or protected person. Nonetheless, many states and the UPC provide a priority list for judicial consideration. The UPC priority list reads generally as follows: (1) a guardian or conservator currently acting for the respondent; (2) a person nominated by the respondent to be her guardian or conservator, if the respondent had sufficient capacity to express a preference; (3) an agent nominated by the respondent under a durable power of attorney to make health care decisions or manage her property; (4) the respondent's spouse; (5) an adult child of the respondent; (6) a parent of the respondent; (7) an adult with whom the respondent has resided for more than six months before the petition is filed. UPC §§ 5-310, 5-413.

The UPC conservatorship provisions further permit persons falling within groups (1), (4), (5), or (6) to designate in writing a substitute to serve in their stead. To be considered as the respondent's nominee under category (2), the nominee does not have to be formally designated in writing; the respondent may even nominate someone orally at the hearing, if the respondent has sufficient capacity at that time.

Category (7) is a modern development that permits recognition of the respondent's domestic partner or companion if the two resided together for six months. Most states do not yet have a provision similar to this. Some courts have refused to appoint a long-term gay or lesbian partner as guardian or conservator of the incapacitated person, even under circumstances in which a spouse would undoubtedly have been appointed. Despite modern statutory developments that purport to follow a best interest standard, the lesson remains clear for gays, lesbians, and others in nontraditional family arrangements: execute a document (preferably a formal legal document) that nominates the preferred person to serve as guardian or conservator. Persons in nontraditional relationships may also want to appoint their significant other as agent under a durable power of attorney.

When two or more persons have equal priority, the UPC provides that the court is to choose the one who is best qualified. Moreover, the UPC provisions clearly indicate that a court may decline to appoint a person having priority if the appointment of such person would not serve the best interest of the respondent. In all states, the bottom line is this: the court should appoint the person who will further the best interest of the ward or protected person.

Under certain conditions, the guardianship provisions permit a spouse of a person to appoint a standby guardian for that person (who is believed to be incapacitated) by will or other signed writing. Similarly, the guardianship provisions permit a parent of an unmarried child to appoint a standby guardian for a child (who is believed to be incapacitated) by will or other signed writing. UPC § 5-302. Standby guardians are discussed more fully later in this chapter.

b. Conflicts and Self-Interest

Courts will not appoint a person as guardian or conservator if he has a conflict of interest that impedes his ability to act in the best interest of the ward or protected person. For example, when the respondent is in a long-term care institution, the UPC prohibits the appointment of an owner, operator, or employee of that facility unless that person is related to the respondent by blood, marriage, or adoption. The prohibition stems from the fear that such a nonfamily member would act in his own interest, engaging in financial exploitation of the ward or protected person.

Judicial concern about financial exploitation is generally greater in conservatorship cases than in guardianship cases because a conservator has control of some or all of the protected person's estate. For example, if Betty needs a conservator and her closest relative is her adult son who is taking advantage of her incapacity to squander her large estate, he should not be appointed her conservator. This is so even if Betty, while unaware of his actions, nominated him as her conservator. If Betty has no other close relatives, friends, or advisors who will serve her best interest, the court should consider appointing a bank or other professional fiduciary.

Although many concerns about fiduciary appointment center on the threat of financial exploitation, problems and conflicts also arise in other settings. Sometimes no one who is willing to serve as a fiduciary seems very deserving or capable. In such circumstances, the court may ultimately conclude that the best interest of the respondent will be served by choosing the least harmful of the various potential fiduciaries. The court may choose a professional guardian or conservator for the respondent whose estate is large enough; however, many respondents do not have ample assets to afford a professional fiduciary.

Many states have established public guardianship programs for incapacitated individuals who have no one to serve as their guardian or conservator. A public guardian is generally a guardian of last resort. The systems vary among the states, but often permit a public agency or a nonprofit group and their employees to serve as guardians for incapacitated individuals with few resources. A public guardian often serves many wards at one time.

c. Letters and Bond

Once the court has chosen the guardian, the court will issue letters of guardianship. Once the court has chosen a conservator and after the conservator has posted any required bond, the court will issue letters of conservatorship. The UPC requires the guardian or conservator to file an acceptance of office before the letters are issued. In so doing, the fiduciary personally submits to the ongoing jurisdiction of the court in all proceedings relating to the guardianship or conservatorship.

Because of the substantial danger of estate depletion that results when a conservator mismanages or steals from the protected person's estate, state law may require the conservator to obtain a bond conditioned on the faithful performance of his duties. The UPC permits the court to require such a bond. Unless otherwise specified, the bond is to equal the value of the property in the conservator's control, plus one year's estimated income, and minus the value of assets that he cannot sell, convey, or remove without court order. UPC § 5-415.

The letters of guardianship or conservatorship are important documents that third parties will often want to see before they transact business with the fiduciary. Limitations on the guardian's or conservator's powers should be indicated on the letters. Under the UPC, third parties are charged with knowledge of restrictions on the letters and may be liable for failing to adhere to those restrictions.

The UPC further provides that an authenticated or certified copy of the letters may serve as proof of the appointment and the fiduciary's authority to act. This provision offers assurances to third parties (who might otherwise be reluctant or unwilling to transact business with the fiduciary) that the fiduciary indeed has the power to act for the ward or protected person.

d. Compensation and Liability

Like the laws of many states, the UPC provides that a guardian or conservator is entitled to reasonable compensation. The UPC permits compensation to be made without court order. If the court later determines that the compensation was excessive, it may order reimbursement to the ward or protected person's estate. In contrast to the UPC approach, in some states the court must first establish the reasonableness of the compensation, which may not be paid without a court order.

In many instances, fiduciaries who are spouses or adult children of the respondent will render their services gratuitously. If the respondent has little or no estate, those willing to serve as fiduciaries may have no choice but to render their services free of charge.

In most states and under the UPC, a respondent who is not indigent must pay for the guardianship or conservatorship proceeding and costs associated with it. These costs can be substantial, particularly in contested proceedings. Fees to be paid include those for the petitioner's lawyer, the respondent's lawyer, the GAL, any court-appointed visitor, and medical/professional evaluations.

Some states provide that if the guardianship or conservatorship petition is unsuccessful, the petitioner must pay the costs of the proceeding. Although such provisions help to prevent the filing of frivolous petitions, they may also dissuade some interested persons from bringing petitions that probably should be filed.

Once the guardian or conservator is appointed, he may require the assistance of others to fulfill his fiduciary duties. For example, in managing a large estate for a protected person, a conservator may hire, among others, investment professionals, lawyers, and accountants. Those whom the guardian or conservator reasonably hires to assist him in fulfilling his duties are typically entitled to compensation from the ward or protected person's estate. A guardian need not use his own funds on the ward.

A guardian is not personally liable to a third person for acts of the ward unless a parent would be liable for the acts of a child under similar circumstances. Moreover, the guardian is not liable for injuries to the ward when the guardian has exercised reasonable care under the circumstances. For example, if the guardian reasonably selects a surgeon to perform a necessary operation on the ward, the guardian is not responsible for injuries resulting from the surgeon's malpractice.

In signing documents and acting on behalf of the incapacitated person or her estate, the guardian or conservator should always indicate his representative capacity and include the name of the individual or estate he serves. For example, Section 5-430 of the UPC provides that, except as otherwise agreed, a conservator is not personally liable on a contract properly entered into for the estate unless he fails to identify the estate and his representative capacity. Although third parties may bring their claims against the estate by proceeding against the conservator in a fiduciary capacity, the conservator is not personally liable unless personally at fault.

5. Temporary Guardianships

a. Emergency Guardianships

When a person is believed to be incapacitated and in imminent danger of substantial harm to her health, safety, or welfare, she may require the immediate appointment of a guardian or conservator. For such situations when no one else has authority or is willing to act in her behalf, states generally have provisions that allow courts to appoint an emergency guardian without adherence to all of the procedural rules governing typical guardianship or conservatorship proceedings. Some states refer to the emergency guardian as a temporary guardian.

A court may appoint an emergency guardian based on its finding from an ex parte affidavit or testimony that the respondent is incapacitated and in imminent danger of substantial harm. No notice is required to be given to the respondent in an emergency scenario. If an emergency guardian is appointed for the respondent without notice, however, due process concerns mandate that she be given a speedy post-appointment hearing to contest the propriety of the appointment. The UPC provides for such a hearing within five days after the appointment. UPC § 5-312.

b. Standby Guardianships

Most elderly parents of a child with developmental disabilities are concerned about what will happen to the child when they die or become unable to care for him. An elderly person whose spouse has Alzheimer's may have similar concerns. In such settings, Sections 5-302 and -303 of the UPC permit the appointment of a standby guardian who can act immediately upon the death or incapacity of the concerned parent or spouse.

By will or other signed writing (including a durable power of attorney or trust instrument), a parent can appoint a standby guardian for an unmarried child who the parent believes is incapacitated. Also by will or other signed writing, one spouse may appoint a standby guardian for the other spouse who the appointing spouse believes is incapacitated. These writings can specify the powers and limitations to be placed on such a guardian. The appointment becomes effective upon the death of the parent or spouse making the appointment, upon adjudication of the appointing person's incapacity, or upon a physician's written determination that that the appointing person is no longer able to care for the incapacitated person.

The guardian becomes eligible to act upon filing a notice of acceptance of appointment along with the appointing instrument. This filing must be made within thirty days after the appointment becomes effective. The guardian must also give written notice to the appointing person (if living), the incapacitated person, a person having the care or custody of the incapacitated person, and the incapacitated person's nearest adult relative. Any of these persons may object in writing to the appointment, and the written objection terminates the appointment.

If the appointing person so desires, she may petition a court to confirm the appointment in advance. A court may give such advance approval if it finds the appointing person will likely become unable to care for the incapacitated person within two years (or other time period as the adopting jurisdiction decides is appropriate). Advance judicial approval means that the appointment cannot be terminated by simple written objection upon the death or incapacity of the appointing person.

If the appointing person does not obtain advance judicial confirmation, the guardian must also file a petition for confirmation of the appointment within thirty days after filing the notice of acceptance of appointment. The UPC indicates that in seeking this confirmation, the regular procedures for appointing a guardian apply.

In many instances, it will be in the best interest of the incapacitated child or spouse for the court to convert the standby guardianship into a regular guardianship. The ability to appoint a standby guardian, especially one who is confirmed in advance by a court, provides the concerned parent or spouse with some peace of mind that an incapacitated loved one will not be neglected immediately following the appointing parent's or appointing spouse's death or own incapacity.

D. Fiduciary Responsibilities and Decision Making

The responsibilities of a guardian or conservator should vary with the capacity of the ward or protected person. In a limited guardianship or conservatorship in which the court grants the fiduciary only very limited authority to act, the fiduciary role may be simple and straightforward. When the guardian or conservator has plenary authority, however, his responsibilities may be difficult and time-consuming. In many instances, the court order will give him little guidance on the proper course of action. The following discussion examines general principles governing the duties and powers of guardians and conservators.

1. Best Interest

The fundamental principle governing all actions by a guardian or conservator is to serve the best interest of the ward or protected person. The guardianship or conservatorship itself is established only when it will serve the respondent's best interest; correspondingly, the guardian or conservator must continue to act to further the ward or protected person's best interest.

The modern view is that the best interest of the ward or protected person is served by granting him the maximum level of autonomy consistent with his abilities. In the absence of a specific statutory directive or court order mandating a particular decision, the guardian or conservator should act only as necessary in light of the limitations of the ward or protected person. Progressive statutes such as Section 5-314 of the UPC further emphasize that, to the extent possible, the guardian or conservator should involve the ward or protected person in the decision making process and encourage him to develop or regain the capacity to act in his own behalf. Thus, as part of the decision making process, a guardian or conservator should carefully consider the reliably-expressed wishes of the ward or protected person.

2. Substituted Judgment

In some instances, the ward or protected person can no longer express his wishes or, alternatively, can no longer express his wishes in a reliable fashion. Is the guardian or conservator then free to make decisions based on the guardian's or the conservator's conclusion as to what will serve the ward or protected person's best interest, without regard to what the ward or protected person probably would have wanted had he retained capacity?

In states where guardianship and conservatorship reform has taken root and grown, the answer increasingly is no. In these states, the guardian or conservator should generally make decisions that are consistent with preferences reliably expressed by the ward or protected person when he was able to do so. If the ward or protected person never specifically expressed a preference on the matter in question, then the decision of the guardian or conservator should generally be consistent with the personal values demonstrated by the ward or protected person to the extent those values are known or can be ascertained. Fiduciary decision making based on the prior expressed wishes or personal values of the ward or protected person involves the use of substituted judgment.

The underlying premise of substituted judgment is that the best interest of the incapacitated person is usually served by decisions consistent with those he made or probably would have made when capable. One should note, however, that statutes in some states define substituted judgment in ways that differ from its traditional meaning. Note also that when a conservator is making a property management investment decision, the use of traditional substituted judgment may result in a decision that conflicts with the conservator's obligation to act as a prudent trustee. In such a situation, the latter obligation will often trump principles of substituted judgment.

3. Statutory Guidance

State guardianship and conservatorship statutes often list a guardian's or conservator's default powers and duties. When the guardianship or conservatorship order does not address a specific question facing the guardian or conservator, these lists of powers and duties may be helpful in guiding the fiduciary. Items on such lists are often general; however, some may be quite specific. For example, the conservatorship statutes of some states contain detailed information on a conservator's permissible investment of a protected person's estate. The UPC provisions concerning the duties and powers of guardians and conservators are emphasized in the following sections.

a. The Duties and Powers of a Guardian

Unless limited by court order, guardians make decisions about the ward's support, care, education, health, and welfare. They must exercise reasonable care, diligence, and prudence, and act at all times in the best interest of the ward. Under LRA principles, guardians assert their authority only as necessitated by the ward's limitations. Guardians encourage the ward to participate in decision making, when feasible. In making decisions, guardians also consider the personal values and expressed wishes of the ward.

Section 5-314 of the UPC provides that a guardian shall (1) become personally acquainted with the ward and maintain contact so that he will know the ward's capacities, limitations, needs, opportunities, and physical and mental health; (2) take reasonable care of the ward's personal effects and, if necessary, bring proceedings to protect the ward's property; (3) spend the ward's money received by him to meet the ward's need for support, care, education, health, and welfare; (4) conserve excess money to meet the ward's future needs (but if a conservator has been appointed for the ward's estate, then the guardian is to pay the excess to the conservator for the ward's future needs); (5) notify the court immediately if the ward's condition changes to allow the ward to exercise rights previously removed; and (6) notify the court if the ward's address changes.

Powers of the guardian are discussed in Section 5-315 of the UPC. The statute provides that, unless otherwise limited by the court, a guardian may (1) apply for and receive money payable to the ward or her custodian for her support (including governmental benefits, insurance proceeds, and benefits under contracts, wills, trusts, conservatorships, or custodianships); (2) take custody of the ward and establish her place of dwelling as consistent with an order from a proper court relating to custody (but may move the ward's dwelling to another state only upon express authorization of the court); (3) commence actions or proceedings against a person for support of the ward or to pay money for the ward's benefit (but only if a conservator with such authority has not been appointed); (4) consent to medical or other care or treatment or service for the ward (subject to the provisions of the ward's valid health-care power of attorney); (5) consent to marriage (or perhaps even divorce, if the state so decides) of the ward; (6) delegate decision making responsibilities affecting the ward's well-being to the ward herself, when reasonable under all of the circumstances; and (7) consent to the adoption of the ward, if specifically authorized by the court.

In making medical decisions for a ward, a guardian must learn whether the ward has an advance health-care directive. If she does, the terms of the directive trump the guardian's wishes, unless a court directs otherwise. Also, the guardian may not revoke the directive without court permission. If the ward's wishes are not clearly expressed in the directive, the guardian must act consistently with the ward's known personal values and other expressed wishes. A number of states impose other requirements that may preclude a guardian from acting unless he obtains an express court order or complies with other statutory provisions. The UPC itself provides that a guardian cannot initiate commitment proceedings to have the ward institutionalized except in accordance with applicable state procedures concerning involuntary civil commitment.

Guardians seldom encounter questions of marriage and divorce for their wards. In some instances, however, marriage or divorce may be in the best interest of the ward. For example, divorce of the ward from an increasingly abusive spouse may be consistent with the values the ward expressed when she was capable and may also protect her from physical or emotional harm. Nevertheless, state courts disagree on the propriety of permitting a guardian to institute a divorce action for the ward. The older view is that dissolution of a marriage is so inherently personal in nature that no one, not even a court-appointed fiduciary, can bring a divorce action for an incapacitated person. The modern trend, however, is to the contrary. It recognizes that a ward may have the capacity to reliably express her wish to be divorced and that, even when she does not have such capacity, in some instances divorce will be consistent with her best interest and her probable wishes had she retained capacity.

Most states now permit an adult to be adopted, although the restrictions vary among the states. In permitting a court to authorize the guardian to consent to adoption of the ward, the UPC recognizes that such adoptions may be in the best interest of the ward. For example, an elderly widow may wish to adopt an incapacitated adult stepchild whom she reared, thereby establishing a legal parent-child connection between them and providing the child with certain protections and benefits. In such circumstances, adult adoption would permit legal recognition of the family tie and also serve the welfare of the child.

To ensure that the best interest of the ward is served and continues to be served, the guardian must make periodic reports to the court. Section 5-317 of the UPC and the laws of most states mandate an initial written report to the court when the guardianship is established and at least an annual written report thereafter. Under the UPC provisions, the report should state or provide (1) the current mental, physical, and social condition of the ward; (2) the living arrangements of the ward throughout the reporting period; (3) the medical, vocational, educational, and other services received by the ward along with an opinion from the guardian concerning the adequacy of the ward's care; (4) a summary of the guardian's visits with the ward, his actions on behalf of the ward, and the degree to which the ward has participated in decision making; (5) if the ward is institutionalized, the guardian's opinion as to whether the current care, treatment, or habilitation plan is in the ward's best interest; (6) plans for the ward's future care; and (7) the guardian's recommendation concerning the need for continued guardianship and changes in the scope of the guardianship. The section further permits the court to appoint a visitor to review such reports, interview the guardian or ward, or make other investigations as the court directs.

As a practical matter, a large number of guardianships and conservatorships are inadequately monitored. The UPC requires the court to establish a system for monitoring guardianships, and many state laws include detailed provisions for reports and accounts by guardians and conservators. Even though a guardian's or conservator's failure to report and account can potentially lead to fines, sanctions, removal, and personal liability, a disturbing number of guardians and conservators either fail to file a timely report or file a report that does not include all of the required information. Often these failures go unpunished. Moreover, when reports are filed, courts (or those appointed by courts to review the reports) may engage in only a cursory review or fail to review them at all. Adequate monitoring of guardianships and conservatorships, including the annual reports filed by the fiduciaries, is essential to ensure that the best interest of the ward or protected person is being served. It appears that the judicial system in many areas of the country has far to go in ensuring an adequate monitoring system for guardianships and conservatorships.

b. The Duties and Powers of a Conservator

The UPC provides in section 5-410 that once a court determines that a conservatorship is needed, that court has all the powers over the estate and business affairs of the protected person that the protected person herself would have if not under a conservatorship. These powers may be exercised for the benefit of the protected person and individuals dependent on the protected person for support. The court may exercise the powers directly or, more commonly, through a conservator. In many states, and under an earlier version of the UPC, judicial power is more limited in at least one important way: the court has all the powers mentioned above *except* the power to make a will for the protected person.

i. Duties

In discussing the general duties of a conservator, Section 5-418 of the UPC begins by stating that the conservator is a fiduciary who shall observe the standards of care applicable to a trustee. Even in states where statutes do not explicitly hold the conservator to trustee standards, courts have often examined such standards to determine whether a conservator has breached his fiduciary duty.

Employing LRA principles, the UPC further provides that conservators may assert their authority only as necessitated by the protected person's limitations. The UPC encourages the conservator to have the protected person participate in decision making, to act in her own behalf, and to develop or regain the ability to manage her estate. (Typical of laws pre-dating the guardianship reform movement, the laws of many states do not specifically impose upon the conservator a duty to encourage the protected person to regain or develop autonomy.)

Within sixty days of appointment, the conservator must file a detailed inventory of the estate. It is to be accompanied by an oath or affirmation that the conservator believes the inventory to be complete and accurate to the best of his knowledge. UPC § 5-419.

Within the same sixty-day period, the conservator is to file a management plan for the estate. The plan should be based on the actual needs of the protected person and should consider her best interest. It should include steps to develop or restore the protected person's ability to manage her estate, an estimate of the duration of the conservatorship, and projections of expenses and resources. UPC § 5-418.

In making investments, distributions, and otherwise exercising his powers, the conservator must consider the protected person's existing estate plan. The conservator has the power to examine the protected person's will and other donative, nominative, and appointment instruments executed by the protected person. UPC § 5-418.

As it does with guardianships, the UPC requires courts to establish a system for monitoring conservatorships that includes the filing and review of reports and plans of the conservator. The UPC requires a conservator to report annually unless otherwise directed by the court. The conservator's report must list estate assets under the conservator's control; list receipts, disbursements, and distributions for the reporting period; list the services provided to the protected person; state recommendations concerning changes in the conservatorship plan; state recommendations concerning the continued need for the conservatorship; and state any recommendations that would change the scope of the conservatorship. UPC § 5-420.

The conservator also must file a report upon resignation or removal, upon termination of the conservatorship, and at other times as directed by the court. (In many states, a conservator's reports are known as accountings or settlements.) After proper notice and hearing, court approval of an intermediate report adjudicates liabilities over matters adequately disclosed in the report. Court approval of a final report adjudicates liabilities over all previously unresolved liabilities concerning the conservatorship.

The UPC permits the court to appoint a visitor to review a report or plan, interview the conservator or the protected person, and make other investigations. The court may require the conservator to submit the estate assets for examination in connection with a report. UPC § 5-420.

ii. General Powers

(a) Title to Property

Once the conservator is appointed, he receives legal title to the property subject to the conservatorship. Thereafter, he is able to act the same as a trustee who is vested with legal title to trust assets. The letters of conservatorship evidence the vesting of this title and may be recorded to give notice to third parties of the conservator's power to act.

Once legal title is vested in the conservator, the protected person generally has no ability to transfer his interest. The UPC includes an exception, however, for certain bona fide purchasers of tangible personal property from the protected person. If the tangible personal property is of the kind in which title is normally transferred by delivery of possession, then the person who in good faith and for security or substantially equivalent value receives such property from the protected person is treated as though the protected person had valid title.

Like a trustee, a conservator must not engage in self-dealing. Section 5-423 of the UPC provides that when a conservator's transaction concerning the estate is affected by a substantial conflict of interest between his personal and fiduciary interests, the transaction is voidable unless expressly authorized by the court after notice to interested persons. This general rule of voidability extends to transactions involving the conservator's spouse, descendants, agent, or lawyer, as well as to a corporation or other entity in which the conservator has a substantial beneficial interest.

(b) Powers by Default

UPC section 5-425 provides a conservator with a long list of default powers. The conservator has not only these powers, but also any other powers granted by applicable state law to a trustee, except as limited by the court in its order of appointment and the letters of conservatorship.

The statute provides that the conservator, acting reasonably and to accomplish the purpose of his appointment, may (1) collect and retain estate assets; (2) receive additions to the estate; (3) continue, or participate in, a business or other enterprise; (4) acquire an undivided interest in an estate asset in which the conservator in any fiduciary capacity holds an undivided interest; (5) invest estate assets as though he were a trustee; (6) deposit estate monies in a financial institution, including one the conservator operates; (7) acquire, dispose of, manage, develop, improve, exchange, partition, change the character of, or abandon estate assets; (8) repair, alter, demolish, or raze buildings or structures; (9) subdivide, develop, or dedicate land for public use, adjust boundaries, and dedicate easements to public use without consideration; (10) enter leases; (11) enter into natural resource or mineral leases and arrangements; (12) grant options; (13) vote securities; (14) pay fees associated with securities; (15) sell or exercise stock subscription or conversion rights; (16) consent to reorganization, consolidation, merger, dissolution, or liquidation of a corporation or other business enterprise; (17) hold a security without disclosure of the conservatorship to permit title to pass by delivery; (18) insure estate assets and insure the conservator against liability concerning a third person; (19) borrow and advance money; (20) pay, contest, and settle claims against the estate, and release claims of the estate to the extent they are uncollectible; (21) pay taxes, assessments, guardian and conservator compensation, and other expenses; (22) allocate income and expenses between income and principal of the estate (as provided by other applicable state law); (23) pay sums to the protected person or individuals in fact dependent upon the protected person, either through direct payment or by payment to a third person or entity on behalf of the protected person or dependent; (24) prosecute or defend claims, actions, or proceedings to protect estate assets and to protect the conservator in performing his fiduciary duties; and (25) execute and deliver instruments to accomplish or facilitate the exercise of powers vested in the conservator. The foregoing list merely provides a summary. The powers are described in more detail in the statute, and several provisions concerning the powers contain additional limiting language.

Section 5-427 provides additional instructions for distributing the estate's income or principal to the protected person or an individual in fact dependent upon the protected person. Although the conservator may generally make such distributions for the support, care, education, health, and welfare of the protected person or dependent without further court order, the conservator must consider (1) the size of the estate, the estimated duration of the conservatorship, and the probability that the protected person may become self-sufficient and able to manage his estate; (2) the accustomed standard of living of the protected person or dependent; and (3) other money or sources used for the support of the protected person. The conservator also must consider recommendations made by a guardian concerning the proper standard of support, care, education, health, and welfare for the protected person or the protected person's dependent. Payments may be made to any person as reimbursement for expenses the conservator might have incurred or in advance for services to be rendered to the protected person (where advance payments are customary or reasonably necessary).

In contrast to Section 5-425 of the UPC, traditional conservatorship laws that still apply in a number of states are much less generous in providing default powers to a conservator. In those states, the conservator must often obtain express court approval, for example, before selling realty or changing the nature of estate investments. In theory, a requirement for prior authorization serves as a prophylactic measure to protect the estate from mismanagement. It acknowledges that corrective measures applied after the mismanagement are often ineffective to protect the protected person and her estate. Nonetheless, one can argue that the traditional approach is inefficient: it imposes burdensome and time-consuming requirements on prudent, honest, and responsible conservators while having little effect on careless, dishonest, and irresponsible conservators who will simply ignore the requirements.

Because the responsibilities of estate administration can be many and complex, it is common for conservators (especially those having plenary powers) to delegate some of their functions to third parties. The UPC does not permit the conservator to delegate the entire administration of the estate, but does permit the conservator to delegate the performance of functions that a prudent trustee of comparable skills might delegate in similar circumstances. UPC § 5-426. The conservator must exercise reasonable care, skill, and caution in (1) selecting an agent; (2) establishing the terms and scope of the delegation; (3) reviewing periodically the agent's performance; and (4) redressing the agent's actions that would constitute a breach of trust if such actions were undertaken by the conservator. If the conservator takes these steps, he is not responsible to the protected person or estate for the actions of the agent. The statute also requires the agent to use reasonable care in his actions and provides that the agent's acceptance of the delegation also places the agent within the jurisdiction of the state courts.

iii. Actions Requiring Court Approval

While the UPC permits the conservator to exercise many powers through its default provisions, it nonetheless requires him to obtain express court authorization for certain actions after giving notice to interested persons. Under Section 5-411, the conservator must generally give notice and obtain judicial approval to make gifts. Notice and judicial approval is not required, however, if the estate is ample to provide for the protected person and those in fact dependent upon him; if the gifts are ones that the protected person might have been expected to make; and if the aggregate amount of gifts in any calendar year does not exceed twenty percent of the income of the estate.

A conservator must give notice and obtain express judicial approval to transfer, release, or disclaim contingent and expectant property interests (including marital property interests and survivorship interests); to release or exercise a power of appointment; to exercise rights to elect options and change beneficiaries under insurance policies and annuities (or to surrender policies and annuities for cash); and to exercise rights to an elective share from the estate of the protected person's deceased spouse and to disclaim or renounce interests by testate or intestate succession or by inter vivos transfer.

The conservator also must give notice and obtain express judicial approve to create a revocable or irrevocable trust of estate property, to revoke or amend a trust revocable by the protected person, or to make, amend, or revoke the will of a protected person. Many states today permit courts to approve a conservator's proposal to create, amend or revoke trusts for estate planning purposes. Only a very few, however, permit a third party to make, amend, or revoke the will of another person. The power of testation has historically been considered too personal to be exercised by a court, conservator, or indeed anyone other than the testator. The UPC provision permitting a conservator to make, amend, or revoke a protected person's will upon court approval thus substantially departs from traditional rules.

In approving any of these proposed actions by the conservator, the court is to consider primarily the decision that the protected person would have made, if that decision is ascertainable. This is an implicit requirement for the use of substituted judgment. The court is also to consider the financial needs of the protected person and those in fact dependent upon her; the interests of creditors; any resulting reduction in tax liabilities; the effect on eligibility for governmental assistance; the protected person's prior pattern of giving or level of support; the protected person's existing estate plan; the protected person's life expectancy and the likelihood that the conservatorship will terminate before her death; and any other relevant factors.

E. Terminating the Guardianship or Conservatorship

1. Generally

Once a guardianship or conservatorship has been established for an elderly person, more often than not it will continue until the elder's death. In some instances, however, the ward or protected person will regain capacity and seek to terminate the guardianship or conservatorship. In most states, a termination petition may be filed by the ward or protected person or any other person interested in his welfare. In many states, the ward or protected person who seeks to terminate the guardianship or conservatorship does not have to file a formal petition. The court will consider his request to terminate even if it is informally communicated to the court.

Although statutes today are generally clear about the standard of proof required to impose a guardianship or conservatorship, they are often less clear about the standard of proof required in a termination proceeding. Some statutes merely indicate that the petitioner must show that the ward or protected person is no longer incapacitated or that the guardianship or conservatorship is no longer in his best interest. Section 5-318 of the UPC provides that when the petitioner presents a prima facie case for termination, the opposing party then has the burden of establishing by clear and convincing evidence that continuation of the guardianship is in the best interest of the ward.

At least some states require annual notice to the ward or protected person of his right to petition for restoration of capacity or modification of the guardianship or conservatorship.

2. Terminating the Fiduciary Appointment

A successful petition for termination of a guardianship or conservatorship is one way to terminate the appointment of a guardian or ward. The appointment of a guardian or conservator will also terminate upon the death of the ward or protected person, upon the resignation or removal of the guardian or conservator, and upon the death of the guardian or conservator. The resignation of a guardian or conservator is not effective until his petition to resign is approved by the court supervising the guardianship or conservatorship.

The ward or protected person or any person interested in his welfare may generally file a petition to remove a guardian or conservator. Section 5-112 of the UPC provides that such a petition may be filed on the ground that removal is in the ward or protected person's best interest or for other good cause. In many cases, good cause is the guardian's or conservator's recently-discovered substantial breach of fiduciary duty.

Once the appointment is terminated, the guardian or conservator must still file any necessary accountings, inventories, or settlements relating to his service.

If a guardian or conservator fails to effectively perform his duties, a court may appoint a temporary substitute guardian or conservator without immediately terminating the permanent appointment. The UPC permits the appointment of a temporary substitute guardian for up to six months.

3. Successor Guardian

The UPC permits the court to appoint a successor guardian to serve in the event of a vacancy in the fiduciary position. For example, the elderly parent of an incapacitated adult child may petition to be the child's guardian and conservator and at the same time seek to have the child's sibling appointed as successor guardian and conservator. The child's sibling can then step into the guardian and conservator role upon the death or incapacity of the parent.

Petitions for resignation or removal of the guardian or conservator may also contain a request for the appointment of a successor guardian.

Checkpoints

- Concerning guardianships and conservatorships generally, you should understand that

  - Proceedings are governed by state law, and terminology varies among the states

  - Under the UPC, guardians are appointed to make personal decisions for a ward, and conservators are appointed to manage the estate of a protected person

- Concerning guardianship and conservatorship proceedings, you should understand

  - The appointment process, under which a guardian or conservator should be appointed only when a respondent is incapacitated and requires guardian or conservator assistance

  - The least restrictive alternative doctrine, which requires that courts impose the least restrictive alternative consistent with the respondent's abilities

  - The due process protections that the law affords to the respondent to the proceeding

  - The role of guardians ad litem and visitors

  - The typical burden and standard of proof

  - The role of a priority list among candidates for appointment as guardian or conservator

  - The nature and value of modern guardianship and conservatorship reform

- Concerning guardians and conservators, you should understand

  - The role of substituted judgment and best interest determinations

  - Fiduciary compensation

  - Duties and powers of the fiduciary, including

    - Powers by default

    - Actions requiring court approval

  - How the fiduciary role is terminated

  - The role of temporary, emergency, and successor guardians and conservators

Chapter 3

Wealth Management and Property Transfers

Roadmap

- The elderly often want to use wealth management tools that will help them avoid the need for a guardian or conservator and that will ensure the orderly passage of their property at death
- Durable powers of attorney
  - Uniform Durable Power of Attorney 1979
  - Uniform Power of Attorney Act 2006
- Nonprobate properties
  - Survivorship properties
  - PODs, TODs, and Totten trusts
  - Revocable trusts
  - Insurance
  - Gifts
- Probate properties
  - Intestate property
  - Testamentary succession (wills)

A. Introduction

As people age, they often grow increasingly concerned about who will manage their assets should they become incapacitated. They also grow concerned about the orderly transfers of their assets at death. Today, when a client consults a lawyer about preparing her estate plan, the lawyer will typically explain to her the potential advantages (and disadvantages) of the durable power of attorney (DPOA). If an individual becomes incapacitated and has no valid DPOA, a court may have to appoint a conservator to manage her estate. In contrast, if an individual becomes incapacitated but has a valid DPOA, the individual's duly-appointed agent can act for her concerning the assets covered by the DPOA. This chapter discusses the durable power of attorney and other advance planning tools that individuals may use in an attempt to avoid a conservatorship should they become incapacitated.

This chapter also discusses various forms of nonprobate and probate transfers that are most likely to be of interest to the elderly person of average means. The discussion includes a primer on survivorship properties, intestate succession, and wills.

B. Durable Powers of Attorney

1. Alternatives to Conservatorship

If an individual fails to make property management arrangements before becoming incapacitated, often the state must appoint a conservator (or guardian, depending upon state terminology) to manage her property. Conservatorship proceedings can be burdensome, time-consuming, and costly. Moreover, the attendant examinations, investigations, and revelations can be embarrassing. No one is happy in being the respondent in a conservatorship proceeding.

Individuals have long used funded, revocable trusts for various property management purposes. Among those purposes may be a desire to ensure that their property is protected and used according to their wishes should they later become incapacitated. Properly crafted, the revocable trust may be an adequate solution for some people. The revocable trust, however, can be a less satisfactory solution than certain other alternatives, and this is particularly so for the elder of modest means. The trust may be expensive to create and fund, and it creates a new property-owning entity potentially subject to its own complex set of rules. If the trust uses a professional or other third-party trustee to manage the assets, the trust may incur significant trustee fees.

Hoping to avoid conservatorship proceedings and yet not wanting (or not willing or able to pay for) a revocable trust, an elder sometimes may simply place her most substantial assets in a standard form of co-ownership. The elder may be unaware of the distinctions between co-ownership relationships, on the one hand, and principal and agent relationships, on the other. If the elder creates a true co-ownership relationship, she has given up significant rights to the property currently. This often is not what she intended to do.

In the last part of the twentieth century, an estate planning tool—one simpler in many ways than the revocable trust or concurrent ownership—became widely available. The durable power of attorney (DPOA) permits an individual having contractual capacity (the "principal") to name an agent (called an "attorney-in-fact" under older statutes and case law) to protect and manage her estate even if or when she is incapacitated. The DPOA will usually eliminate the need for a conservatorship proceeding should the elder become incapacitated. The DPOA allows the principal to name her agent(s), to define the authority of her agent(s), and to delineate the circumstances and time at which that authority begins and ends. A standard DPOA, particularly one that is based on a form provided by state statute, often costs little to draft and execute. Moreover, the DPOA does not provide an agent with a property interest in the assets of the principal.

A durable power of attorney is a special form of advance directive. An advance directive is a legal document that allows an individual to name someone who may act for her or to describe actions (or a range of actions) that someone may take on her behalf, or both. In this chapter we discuss the principal-agent relationship under the durable power of attorney for financial (or estate) matters. In Chapter 4, we take up medical advance directives such as living wills and health-care powers of attorney (also called health-care proxies). Most state statutory law contemplates or requires that a DPOA for financial matters and medical advance directives be executed as separate documents.

Individuals have long-used *nondurable* powers of attorney to appoint agents to act on their behalf. Under common-law agency rules, however, an agent's authority expires as provided in the agency agreement or at the incapacity or death of the principal, whichever first occurs. In contrast, an agent's authority under a *durable* power of attorney does not terminate at the incapacity of the principal.

In the absence of information to the contrary in the DPOA, the agent's authority is immediately effective when the principal executes the DPOA. Both the agent and the competent principal can thus transact the principal's business at that time. Often, however, a principal does not want to name an agent who has the power to act while the principal herself remains capable of protecting and managing her own property. What this principal wants is an agent whose powers spring into effect only when the principal becomes incapacitated. Today, a principal can effectuate such wishes through a *springing* durable power of attorney (SDPOA).

2. Uniform Durable Power of Attorney Act 1979

In enacting durable power of attorney statutes, more than two-thirds of the states have relied in substantial part upon the Uniform Durable Power of Attorney Act 1979 (last amended in 1987). One court has noted that the core purpose of the Act is to establish an alternative to conservatorship. The following discussion outlines the chief provisions of the Act.

a. Creation of a DPOA

Under Section 1 of the Act, a principal may create a durable power of attorney with a writing that contains language such as "This power of attorney shall not be affected by subsequent disability or incapacity of the principal" or other words that show the intent of the principal that the agent's authority is to continue past the principal's disability or incapacity. Section 1 also expressly contemplates the use of an SDPOA. The section notes that a principal can create an SDPOA with such language as "This power of attorney shall become effective upon the disability or incapacity of the principal."

The SDPOA can create problems if not carefully drafted. For example, P executes an SDPOA by merely using the language quoted in the last line of the preceding paragraph. Two years later, P becomes somewhat forgetful and also makes questionable asset management decisions. The SDPOA, however, fails to define "incapacity" or how it is determined. Is P now incapacitated, entitling the agent to act? What if P's family members, doctor, lawyer, and the agent disagree on the question of her capacity? Without guidance from the SDPOA itself, P may wind up before a court for a judicial determination of her incapacity. This is precisely what she hoped to avoid by executing the SDPOA.

In sum, a springing SDPOA should not only include language that clearly shows the principal's intent to authorize the agent to act when the principal becomes incapacitated, but also carefully define how her incapacity is to be determined. For example, the principal might provide that "my incapacity shall be established when three of my five children agree that I can no longer adequately manage my assets in a prudent and responsible manner." Another principal might be concerned that such a provision could easily lead to intra-family conflict among the children; yet another principal might fear that her children could not act in a disinterested manner. These principals might prefer to have their incapacity determined by more neutral parties, such as a treating physician, a lawyer, an accountant, or perhaps some combination of this group. The document can provide for the determination of incapacity in any number of ways. Whatever method the principal chooses, it should be described clearly in the SDPOA.

The Uniform Durable Power of Attorney Act 1979 does not include a form power of attorney among its provisions. It also does not have provisions concerning execution requirements. A substantial minority of states, however, make available a statutory form power of attorney document that can include a durable power. Some of these states use the form document included in section 1 of the Uniform Statutory Form Power of Attorney Act (1988). The form document from the 1988 Act contemplates both execution by the signature of the principal and notarization. The comment to section 1 also suggests that the form include a place for witness signatures. As a practical matter, even if a state DPOA statute does not specifically require witness signatures or notarization, other state laws may require the signature of witnesses or notarization if the principal wants the agent to have the authority to engage in certain transactions, such as those involving transfers of realty.

b. Agent Powers

Section 2 of the 1979 Act provides that all acts of the agent "during any period of disability or incapacity of the principal have the same effect and inure to the benefit of and bind the principal and [her] successors in interest as if the principal were competent and not disabled." The purpose of the section is clear: to authorize an agent to step into the shoes of the incapacitated principal. In practice, however, agents sometimes encounter difficulties when attempting to transact affairs for the incapacitated principal. Unlike letters of conservatorship, DPOAs are relatively new legal documents and are not issued by a court. Without additional corroborative evidence to support the agent's assertion of authority to act, banks, businesses, and other third parties may be reluctant to recognize the agent's designation on a DPOA. The third party may also want confirmation in writing that the principal is now incapacitated and unable to act for herself. When the agent first seeks to transact business with a third party, it may thus be prudent for the agent to bring not only the DPOA, but also affidavits from the principal's physician, lawyer, family members, or other appropriate persons with relevant information, to provide supporting evidence of the agent's current authority to act.

Section 2 also states that the DPOA, once properly executed, remains effective despite the passage of time unless the DPOA states a termination date. In this respect, the DPOA is like a will. Thus P, the principal of an SDPOA without a termination date, does not need to re-execute the document periodically for it to be effective. If P becomes incapacitated fifteen years after executing an SDPOA in which her incapacity is the springing event, her agent may begin to act for P at that time. (Of course, as part of regular updates to her estate plan while she retains capacity, P may want to update the SDPOA sporadically, just as she updates her will from time to time.)

Section 4 provides that death of a principal does not terminate the authority of an agent who exercises the power in good faith without actual knowledge of the principal's death. Thus the section protects those who engage in business transactions with the agent in such circumstances. This section, which applies both to DPOAs and to nondurable powers of attorney, is a departure from common-law principles. At common-law, an agent's power terminated immediately upon the death of the principal.

Section 5 confirms the validity of an agent's acts taken in good faith reliance upon the power of attorney. The section provides that an agent's affidavit that he did not, when exercising the power, have actual knowledge that the power of attorney had been terminated by the principal's death, disability, or incapacity is conclusive proof of the nonrevocation or nontermination of the power at that time for acts made in good faith reliance. The section further provides that if the exercise of the power requires execution and delivery of a document that is recordable (such as a deed or other instrument pertaining to realty), the affidavit when authenticated for record is also recordable.

c. Agent Interaction with Court-Appointed Fiduciaries

Although many individuals execute a DPOA at least in part to avoid a conservatorship, occasional circumstances arise in which the principal will require a court-appointed fiduciary despite the existence of a DPOA. Such might be the case if the DPOA does not give the agent power over all of the principal's assets, and the principal thus needs a conservator or other fiduciary to make decisions concerning the assets excluded from the agent's authority. Alternatively, the court may appoint a conservator when the agent under the DPOA violates his duties to the principal.

Section 3 of the Act provides that if, after the execution of the DPOA, a court appoints a conservator or other fiduciary charged with management of the principal's property, the agent is accountable to the conservator or other fiduciary as well as to the principal. The agent is not accountable to a guardian of the person, however. The statute further gives the conservator or other fiduciary the same power to revoke or amend the DPOA that the principal would have had if not disabled or incapacitated.

The provision further permits the principal to nominate in her DPOA a person to serve as her conservator or guardian if one is necessary. The court is to make any subsequent appointment based on that nomination unless good cause exists not to do so or unless the person is otherwise disqualified. As a practical matter, the principal will often want to nominate the agent as guardian or conservator, particularly if the principal fears that family members may bring conservatorship proceedings to prevent the agent from acting under the DPOA. The nomination of the agent as conservator will serve as a disincentive to family members who might bring a conservatorship action merely to gain control of the estate.

If an agent is violating his fiduciary duties to the principal by engaging in self-dealing or dishonest behavior, a court will typically find that good cause exists not to appoint the agent as conservator. This is so even if the DPOA nominates the agent as conservator and expressly attempts to hold the agent harmless for any wrongful acts whatsoever.

The agent must act in the principal's best interests. Some states that have substantially adopted the Uniform Durable Power of Attorney Act 1979 add a specific provision to emphasize the agent's fiduciary obligations.

3. Uniform Power of Attorney Act 2006

a. Overview

The Uniform Durable Power of Attorney Act 1979 leaves many important questions unaddressed. Consequently, states adopting the 1979 Act have often added their own provisions to address those unanswered questions. In 2006, the Uniform Power of Attorney Act (UPOAA) was promulgated to provide a more detailed model statute for state adoption. The UPOAA includes numerous provisions based on state legislative trends and the conclusions of its drafters about best practices.

The UPOAA provides many more default rules than the 1979 Act. One major problem the UPOAA addresses is the historical reluctance of many third parties to recognize the validity of a power of attorney and to deal with a duly-appointed agent. The UPOAA also seeks to promote flexibility in its power-of-attorney provisions. Because of the substantial risk that a dishonest agent may exploit the principal's assets, the 2006 Act also includes measures to protect the principal from financial abuse. Finally, the 2006 Act is designed to replace both the Uniform Durable Power of Attorney Act 1979 and the Uniform Statutory Form Power of Attorney Act 1988. The new Act will probably be adopted in whole or in part by a number of states in the coming years.

b. Creation, Effect, and Termination

Since the advent of DPOAs, principals have used them as a form of insurance against conservatorships. Under the 1979 Act and most state statutes, a POA is durable only if the principal includes language indicating her intent that it be so. The drafters of the 2006 Act believe, however, that the typical principal wants her power of attorney to be durable. Thus, the UPOAA adopts a new default rule: a power of attorney created under the UPOAA is durable *unless* it expressly provides that it is terminated by the principal's incapacity. UPOAA § 104. (Incidentally, the UPOAA uses the modern term "incapacity" and drops the term "disability." The UPOAA defines incapacity consistent with the definition contained in the conservatorship provisions of the uniform acts. Moreover, because the layperson is often confused over the term "attorney-in-fact," the new Act drops that term and simply uses the term agent.) The UPOAA's provisions do not apply to a power to make health-care decisions, certain other special powers, or powers created on a form prescribed by a government or a governmental subunit for a governmental purpose. UPOAA § 103.

Unlike the 1979 Act, the UPOAA contains execution provisions for a power of attorney. The basic execution requirements are minimal. The UPOAA provides that the power of attorney must be signed by the principal or signed in her conscience presence by someone whom she has directed to sign for her. UPOAA § 105. The Act does not require notarization for the power of attorney to be valid; however, notarization provides an important beneficial presumption. If the power of attorney is notarized or is acknowledged by another individual authorized by law to take acknowledgments, then the principal's signature is presumed to be genuine.

Although the UPOAA does not require notarization, as a practical matter every power of attorney should be notarized when possible. If certain powers are designated to the agent, notarization may be required for the agent to act regarding those powers. If the power of attorney provides the agent with authority over the principal's real property, for example, the power of attorney will need to be recorded in the proper realty records for the agent to engage in realty transactions. To record the power of attorney, however, state law will generally require that the principal's signature be notarized or witnessed.

Like prior law, the UPOAA makes the power of attorney effective when executed unless the power of attorney provides that it will not be effective until a future date or until the occurrence of a future event or contingency. The UPOAA, however, also includes default rules for the principal who fails to provide certain relevant information. If the future event is the principal's incapacity and the document fails to state who is to make the determination of incapacity, the statute provides that a physician or proper mental health professional may make the determination. If the principal has designated someone to determine whether she is incapacitated, that person may also act as her personal representative pursuant to the Health Insurance Portability and Accountability Act (HIPAA) and thereby obtain access to her health information. UPOAA § 109.

The UPOAA recognizes the validity of a power of attorney that is executed in compliance with (1) state law before the enactment of the UPOAA; (2) the laws of another jurisdiction; or (3) the requirements for a military power of attorney. A copy or an electronically transmitted copy of a power of attorney has the same effect as the original unless another statute provides otherwise.

UPOAA § 106. (State real estate recording statutes, for example, may require the presentation of an original power of attorney.)

The principal may indicate the law of the jurisdiction that is to govern the meaning and effect of a power of attorney. Such information regarding controlling law is often important when the principal owns real estate in more than one jurisdiction. If the principal fails to designate the controlling law, by default the controlling law is that of the jurisdiction where the power of attorney was executed. UPOAA § 107.

Under the UPOAA, an agent's authority terminates when (1) the principal revokes the authority; (2) the agent dies, becomes incapacitated, or resigns; (3) the power of attorney itself terminates; or (4) an action is filed for marital dissolution (divorce), annulment, or legal separation between the principal and agent. The principal can override this last rule if she so provides in the power of attorney. UPOAA § 110(b). For example, P names her husband A as her agent and further provides that his authority to act will not terminate in the event of their divorce or legal separation. When P becomes incapacitated, A divorces her to enable her to qualify for public benefits. Because of the specific provision in P's power of attorney, A's authority to act continues past the divorce.

Like the 1979 Act, the UPOAA provides that mere lapse of time does not affect the validity of a power of attorney. The UPOAA also provides that the principal's execution of a subsequent power of attorney does not revoke an existing power of attorney unless the subsequent power of attorney provides that the prior power of attorney is revoked or that all other powers of attorney are revoked. UPOAA § 110(f).

The termination of an agent's authority or a power of attorney is ineffective as to the agent or third parties who act in good faith without actual knowledge of the termination. UPOAA § 110(d). If A as agent enters into a contract with a third party B in good faith, and they are unaware that A's power has terminated because of the principal's death, then the contract is binding on the principal's estate. Incidentally, B can enforce the contract against the principal's estate even if A had been aware that he no longer had authority to act, as long as B acted in good faith without actual knowledge of the termination of A's authority.

c. Encouraging Recognition by Third Parties

In the past, third parties have often refused or been reluctant to recognize an agent's authority under a DPOA. Acknowledging this problem, the UPOAA includes specific provisions promoting acceptance and imposing liability upon third parties who improperly refuse to accept the power of attorney document. The provisions apply only to *acknowledged* powers of attorney, however.

Section 119 of the UPOAA provides that a third party with no actual knowledge of improprieties concerning an acknowledged power of attorney or the agent's acts may rely on the power of attorney. This section promotes third-party acceptance of the DPOA by placing the risk of an agent's improper acts on the principal or her estate. The third party having no actual knowledge of improprieties does not have a duty to investigate. Nonetheless, the statute does permit the third party to request and rely upon (1) an agent's certification (under penalty of perjury) of any fact matter; (2) an English translation of provisions in a power of attorney not in English; and (3) counsel opinion relating to the power of attorney, if the third party provides in writing or other record the reason for the request.

Section 120 imposes liability upon a third party who improperly refuses to accept an acknowledged power of attorney. Adopting states may choose to apply this section to any acknowledged power of attorney or, alternatively, only to an acknowledged *statutory* form power of attorney. Once presented with the acknowledged power of attorney (or acknowledged statutory form power of attorney, if the state chooses the narrower option), the third party has seven business days in which to accept or, if it wishes, to request a certification, a translation, or counsel opinion under Section 119. If the third party seeks the certification, translation, or counsel opinion, then it has five business days in which to accept once the proper certification, translation, or opinion of counsel is presented.

In any event, a third party does not have to accept an acknowledged power of attorney if (1) the third party has no obligation to transact matters with the principal herself; (2) the transaction would be inconsistent with federal law; (3) the third party has actual knowledge that the power of attorney or the agent's authority has been terminated before its exercise; (4) the agent refuses the third party's request for certification, translation, or opinion of counsel; (5) the third party believes in good faith that the power is not valid or the agent lacks authority, regardless of whether a certification, translation, or opinion of counsel has been requested or provided; or (6) the third party makes, or has actual knowledge that someone else has made, a good faith report to appropriate state adult protection services offices that the principal may be subject to abuse by the agent or someone acting for or with the agent.

If none of these bases for refusal to accept the acknowledged power of attorney exists, then the third party who nonetheless refuses to accept the power of attorney not only potentially faces a court order mandating acceptance, but also liability for reasonable attorney fees and costs incurred in the action confirming the power of attorney and mandating acceptance by the third party. Several states that have not adopted the UPOAA have similar provisions designed to promote acceptance of powers of attorney.

d. Agents Generally

Section 108 of the UPOAA permits the principal to nominate, in the power of attorney, a conservator or guardian of her estate or person should she later require a court-appointed fiduciary. If a court subsequently appoints someone other than the agent as conservator of the estate, then the agent is accountable to the conservator as well as to the principal. In a notable change from the 1979 Act, however, the UPOAA does not give the conservator or other court-appointed fiduciary the power to revoke or amend the power of attorney. The power to limit, suspend, or terminate the power of attorney is instead reserved to the court.

Section 111 of the UPOAA addresses some very practical concerns involving co-agents and successor agents. Although most observers believe it is generally inadvisable for the principal to name more than one agent with current authority to act, principals have the power to name two or more co-agents with such concurrent authority to act. The UPOAA provides that in such cases, each agent may exercise his or her authority independently unless the power of attorney provides otherwise. (Some principals do provide otherwise and require, for example, that co-agents may act only upon unanimous consent or, alternatively, only by majority vote in the case of three or more co-agents.)

A well-drafted power of attorney will usually name one or more successor agents to act if an agent resigns, dies, becomes incapacitated, is not qualified to serve, or declines to serve. The UPOAA recognizes the power of the principal to designate one or more successor agents in all of these circumstances. It also permits the principal to grant her agent or other person the authority to designate one or more successor agents.

A successor agent may not act until all predecessor agents are no longer serving. By default, a successor agent has the same authority as that of the original agent. The lawyer should carefully point out this provision to the client, because the provision can be a trap for the unwary. For example, a principal who names her spouse as agent may give him broad powers that expressly include the power to make gifts and change estate planning documents. If the principal then names one of her children as successor agent, by default the child will have the same authority should that child later become the agent. In some instances, the principal may want the child as successor agent to have such broad authority; however, the principal might be reluctant to provide the child with the power to make gifts and change estate planning documents if the principal fears that the child might misuse those powers or that the child's use of the powers might create discord with or among the principal's other children.

Section 111 further provides that, as a default rule, an agent who neither participates in nor conceals a breach of fiduciary duty committed by another agent is not liable for the actions of that other agent. If, however, an agent has actual knowledge of a breach or imminent breach of fiduciary duty by another agent, he must "notify the principal and, if the principal is incapacitated, take any action reasonably appropriate in the circumstances to safeguard the principal's best interest." If he fails to do so, he is liable for reasonably foreseeable damages that otherwise could have been avoided.

An agent is entitled to reimbursement for expenses he reasonably incurred on behalf of the principal. But what of agent compensation for services? Principals often fail to discuss agent compensation in the power of attorney. Sometimes principals assume that a close family member will serve as agent without compensation. Courts also may engage in the presumption that a close family member renders services gratuitously. Historically, agent claims for compensation have led to mixed results when the power of attorney provided no guidance on the matter. Section 112 of the UPOAA addresses this problem with a default rule: in the absence of a provision concerning compensation, an agent is entitled to reasonable compensation under the circumstances. This standard leaves much wriggle room. For example, a request for compensation that might otherwise appear unreasonably large might in fact be reasonable "under the circumstances" if the agent is attempting to maximize his compensation to reduce the principal's estate so that the principal can qualify for governmental assistance. Of course, if the principal knows the terms of compensation that she wants for the agent, she should include those terms in the power of attorney. If compensation is specified in the power of attorney, the default rule does not apply.

The power of attorney document does not create a fiduciary duty on the part of a person named as agent. The agent is generally not a fiduciary until he knows of his appointment and accepts that appointment. Section 113 provides that acceptance occurs when he exercises his authority or performs duties as an agent or when he engages in other assertions or conduct indicating acceptance. As a practical matter, the principal should confer with a person before naming that person as agent. During the discussion, the principal can explain her proposed power of attorney and ascertain whether the other person is willing to serve as her agent. If he is willing to serve, their discussion will give him time to contemplate and prepare for the role. This approach is usually much preferable to that in which the agent first learns of his designation only after the principal has become incapacitated. Neither the 1979 Act nor the UPOAA requires the agent to sign the power of attorney. Nonetheless, it is a good practice to have the agent sign to demonstrate his agreement to serve in that role. The agent's signature on the power of attorney will help to encourage acceptance of the agent's authority by third parties. The agent's signature on the power of attorney also gives third parties a sample of his signature when he later attempts to transact business on the principal's behalf.

Section 118 provides a default rule for agent resignation. If the principal has capacity, the agent may merely give notice to the principal. If the principal has become incapacitated, the agent must also give notice to the principal's conservator and a co-agent or successor agent. If there is no conservator or co-agent or successor agent, then the agent must give notice to the principal's caregiver, someone else who the agent reasonably believes has sufficient interest in the principal's welfare, or a governmental agency with authority to protect the principal's welfare. A well-drafted durable power of attorney, however, will specifically address resignation and not rely on the default rule.

e. Agent Duties

Section 114(a) of the UPOAA imposes certain duties upon agents that a power of attorney cannot alter. The mandatory provisions state that the agent who has accepted appointment shall act (1) in conformity with the principal's reasonable expectations as known and, otherwise, in conformity with the principal's best interest; (2) in good faith; and (3) within the scope of his authority. Under the first of these duties, the agent must normally do what the principal herself would have done if the agent knows what she would have done. As discussed in Chapter 2, this approach is consistent with the modern notion that surrogate decision makers should first employ "substituted judgment" before making a "best interest" decision. This order of dcision making attempts to recognize and preserve the incapacitated individual's right of self-determination.

If the principal knows her wishes to be at odds with those of a reasonable person, then the principal should expressly elaborate upon those wishes within the power of attorney or in some other reasonably reliable document that will be made known to the agent. A written statement concerning such wishes is not required by the UPOAA, but such a statement will assist the agent and deter challenges to his decisions made in accordance with the principal's written statement.

Section 114(b) imposes default duties that a principal may alter in the power of attorney. Among these default duties imposed upon an agent who has accepted appointment are the following: (1) to act loyally for the principal's benefit; (2) to act in a way that does not create a conflict of interest that impairs the agent's ability to act impartially in the principal's best interest; (3) to act with the care, competence, and diligence ordinarily exercised by agents in similar settings; (4) to keep a record of all transactions, receipts, and disbursements made on the principal's behalf; (5) to cooperate with the individual who has the authority to make health-care decisions for the principal; and (6) to attempt to preserve the principal's estate plan to the extent the plan is actually known and is consistent with the principal's best interest. Section 114(c) provides that if the agent acts in good faith, the agent is not liable to a beneficiary of the principal's estate plan should the agent fail to preserve the plan.

At common law, an agent must act solely for the benefit of a principal. In contrast, the UPOAA provides that an agent who acts with "care, competence, and diligence" for the principal's best interest is not liable simply because he also benefits from the act or has a conflicting interest concerning the principal's property or affairs. The UPOAA position reflects a reasonable compromise that allows principals to choose agents such as family members who have inherent conflicts of interest such as those resulting from co-ownership of property or inheritance expectancies.

The agent is not liable for a decline in the value of the principal's property absent a breach of duty to the principal. If the principal chooses the agent because of the agent's special skills or expertise (or in reliance on the agent's claim that he has such special skills or expertise), then a court is to consider those skills or expertise in determining whether the agent acted with care, competence, and diligence. In some instances, a principal chooses an agent who happens to have special skills, but not because of those special skills. For example, a mother might choose her son, who happens to be a lawyer, as her agent. If she does not want to impose upon him the higher standard that might otherwise apply to a lawyer, she should indicate this fact in the power of attorney to avoid later questions about the proper standard of care in the event someone alleges that he breached his fiduciary duty.

In fact, the UPOAA allows a principal to include an exoneration provision that relieves the agent of liability for breach of duty. Although most principals do not wish to include such a provision, at least an occasional principal might choose to include such a provision to dissuade contentious relatives from attacking the agent's acts. An exoneration provision is generally binding; however, the UPOAA provides that such a provision is ineffective to relieve the agent from liability (1) for breaches of duty committed "dishonestly, with an improper motive, or with reckless indifference to the purposes of the power of attorney or the best interest of the principal" or (2) when it was included in the power of attorney as the result of an abuse of a fiduciary or confidential relationship with the principal. UPOAA § 115.

Section 114(f) of the UPOAA provides that the agent does not generally have to disclose disbursements, receipts, or transactions in his role as agent except as ordered by a court or as requested by the principal, another fiduciary acting for the principal (such as a conservator), a government agency with authority to protect the principal's welfare, or the principal's personal representative or successor in interest at death.

f. Agent Liability

Section 117 of the UPOAA provides that an agent who violates the Act is liable for the amount required to restore the principal's property to the value it would have had absent the violation. The agent must also repay to the principal (or her successors) attorney fees and costs paid on the agent's behalf. The comment to the section notes that these amounts are in addition to any civil or criminal penalties the agent may face under other state laws. (Section 123 of the UPOAA provides that remedies provided under the Act "are not exclusive and do not abrogate any right or remedy" under other state laws outside the Act.)

The UPOAA grants standing to a sizable number of people or entities who might wish a court to construe a power of attorney or to review the agent's conduct. Among those granted standing are the following: the principal; the agent; a conservator, guardian, or other fiduciary acting on the principal's behalf; a person who can make health-care decisions for the principal; a spouse, parent, or descendant of the principal; a person who is a presumptive heir of the principal; an individual named to receive a beneficial interest at the principal's death or to receive an interest in a trust created by or for the principal; a government agency authorized to protect the principal's welfare; the principal's caregiver or anyone demonstrating a sufficient interest in the principal's welfare; and anyone asked to accept the power of attorney. UPOAA § 116.

Because of the great risk of financial abuse that accompanies the durable power of attorney, some states have special provisions to protect the principal's estate and her family. In some states, for example, once the principal has become incapacitated, her next of kin may seek a court order requiring that the agent post a bond to insure the estate against his breach of duties.

g. Agent Authority

Powers of attorney may grant the agent broad general authority, specific authority, or a combination of both. Not uncommonly, a power of attorney provides the agent "with the authority to do all acts that I could do." In the absence of legislation to guide them, courts have sometimes struggled with such broadly-worded general provisions. Borrowing from the law of fiduciaries, courts have often concluded that such broad language does not in fact provide the agent with the authority to do anything the principal could have done. The UPOAA agrees with this conclusion and distinguishes agent authority that can be provided by general grant from agent authority that can be provided only by specific grant.

i. Authority That May Be Designated Only by Specific Grant

Section 201 of the UPOAA lists certain things that an agent can do only with a *specific* grant of authority. These things include the following: (1) create, amend, revoke, or terminate an inter vivos trust; (2) make a gift; (3) create or change rights of survivorship; (4) create or change beneficiary designations; (5) delegate authority granted under the power of attorney; (6) waive the principal's right to be a beneficiary of a joint and survivor annuity, including a survivor benefit under a retirement plan; or (7) exercise fiduciary powers that the principal has authority to delegate. The section also requires a specific grant for the agent to be able to disclaim property, including a power of appointment, unless other laws of the jurisdiction permit such disclaimer and the jurisdiction does not wish to change those other laws.

If the power of attorney grants an agent such a specific power but does provide otherwise, then an agent who is not an ancestor, spouse, or descendant of the principal has no authority to create in himself (or in anyone to whom he owes a legal obligation or support) an interest in the principal's property. For example, if a power of attorney contains an express or specific provision granting an agent a power to change beneficiary designations, a spouse as agent could name herself as the beneficiary, but an agent unrelated to the principal could not do so.

Interestingly, although Section 201 of the UPOAA permits the principal to grant the agent specific authority that could substantially affect the principal's estate plan, it does not permit the principal to grant the agent authority to make, amend, or revoke the principal's will. This is consistent with common law, under which no one can make, amend, or revoke another's will. The drafters of the UPOAA apparently believed that the will making power is too personal to delegate. (In contrast, the drafters of the Uniform Probate Code and the Uniform Guardianship and Protective Proceedings Act now grant default will making authority to a conservator who obtains court approval. See Chapter 2.)

If the power of attorney grants the agent the specific authority to make gifts but does not elaborate further, then the default rules of Section 217 apply. In such cases, the agent is only authorized to make gifts of the principal's property in an amount that does not exceed, for each donee, the annual federal gift tax exclusion amount. If the principal's spouse consents to a split gift, then the gift amount for each donee may not exceed twice the annual federal gift tax exclusion limit. (Similarly, an agent may consent for the principal to a split gift by the principal's spouse in an amount not exceeding twice the annual federal gift tax exclusion limit.)

The agent must determine that any such gifts are consistent with the principal's objectives that are actually known by the agent. If the principal's objectives are not known, then the agent must determine that the gifts are consistent with the principal's best interest. Among the relevant factors in making a best interest determination are the value and nature of the principal's property; the principal's probable needs and obligations; minimization of taxes; the principal's eligibility for governmental assistance; and the principal's personal history in making or joining in making gifts.

ii. Authority That May Be Designated by General Grant

The UPOAA permits the principal to use a general grant that will provide her agent with the authority to act on many matters. For example, Section 201(c) provides that if the principal grants her agent the authority "to do all acts that I could do," then the agent has the general authority provided in sections 204 through 216 of the UPOAA. The principal may also incorporate the authority described in sections 204 through 217 by reference. Thus, if a principal uses the descriptive term for a subject within those sections or includes a specific section number within those sections, that section is incorporated into the power of attorney. The principal of course retains the power to modify the authority incorporated by reference. UPOAA § 202.

The authority described in sections 204 through 217 concerns the following matters: real property; tangible personal property; stocks and bonds; commodities and options; banks and other financial institutions; operation of an entity or business; insurance and annuities; estates, trusts, and other beneficial interests; claims and litigation; personal and family maintenance; benefits from governmental programs or civil or military service; retirement plans; taxes; and gifts. The authority granted concerning each of these matters is typically extensive. For example, under Section 204 concerning real property, a partial list of the agent's authority permits the agent to do the following: manage or conserve the real property; lease, receive, acquire or reject an interest in real property; grant or dispose of an interest; mortgage an interest; use, develop, alter, replace, remove, erect, or install structures or other improvements; change the form of title; or even dedicate to public use, with or without consideration, easements or other real property interests of the principal.

Several non-UPOAA states have statutory lists concerning authority the principal may bestow upon her agent by general grant. Before incorporating any statutory authority by general grant, the principal and her lawyer should always carefully review that authority to ensure that it reflects the principal's wishes.

Section 203 of the UPOAA provides rules of construction that apply by default when the principal incorporates one of the subjects in sections 204 through 217 or grants her agent the authority to do anything that the principal could do. Under the rules of construction, the agent is generally authorized to engage in many acts, including the following: demand and obtain monies to which the principal is entitled; enter into, rescind, cancel, terminate, reform, restate, release, or modify contracts; execute, deliver, and record documents; initiate or participate in alternative dispute resolution or intervene in litigation; seek court or governmental assistance on behalf of the principal; hire, pay, and fire an attorney; communicate with government representatives and employees; access communications intended for the principal and communicate on her behalf; and "do any lawful act with respect to the subject and all property related to the subject."

h. Statutory Forms

i. Power of Attorney

The trend is for states to provide a statutory form power of attorney that laypersons and lawyers can use. The increasing use of such statutory forms, which typically the principal can tailor to meet her particular needs, facilitates acceptance by third parties. Because the documents are drafted and executed in a standardized, statutorily-authorized form, third parties gradually become familiar with such documents and are less inclined to balk when an agent presents such a document for acceptance.

Section 301 of the UPOAA provides a statutory form power of attorney based on the earlier substantive provisions found in the Act. The UPOAA form begins with a part entitled "Important Information." Among other things, this introductory part warns the principal that, by default, the power of attorney will become effective immediately and will be effective whether or not the principal is incapacitated. It also informs the principal that the agent will be entitled to reasonable compensation. (The principal can alter these default rules by providing contrary provisions under the "Special Instructions" part of the form.) The form then contains parts entitled "Designation of Agent" and "Designation of Successor Agent(s)." The principal must designate an agent, but is not required to name successor agents.

The following three parts of the form concern the agent's authority to act on the principal's behalf. The first of these parts is entitled "Grant of General Authority." This part lists separately each of the subjects that a principal may incorporate by reference under sections 204 through 216 (concerning real estate, tangible personal property, stocks and bonds, and so forth). The principal may place her initials by any of the subjects over which she wishes to provide her agent with general authority. If she wants to provide her agent with general authority over all of the subjects, she may simply place her initials by the final item in the list, which reads "All Preceding Subjects."

The second of the parts concerning agent authority is entitled "Grant of Specific Authority." It is included as an option for the principal who wants to provide her agent with the authority to do any or all of those acts described in Section 201(a) (such as changing beneficiary designations and making gifts). These are acts that require an express grant by the principal because of the increased risk that they pose for reducing the principal's estate or altering her estate plan. The part contains a cautionary note to the principal concerning these risks. The part then lists separately each of the areas under Section 201(a) over which a principal may specifically authorize the agent to act. The principal may place her initials by any of these areas over which she wishes to provide her agent with authority.

The third part concerning agent authority ("Limitation on Agent's Authority") informs the principal that an agent who is not her ancestor, spouse, or descendant may not use her property to benefit the agent (or to benefit a person to whom the agent owes an obligation of support), unless the principal provides such authority in the "Special Instructions" part of the form.

The Special Instructions part of the form then follows. Completion of this part of the form is optional. Any principal who wants to deviate from the default rules of the UPOAA, however, will want to include the relevant information here. For example, if the principal desires a springing power of attorney, she would so provide in this part. If she wants to give her agent authority to make gifts of unlimited amounts (and thereby avoid the default rules of section 217), she would so indicate in this part of the form.

The next part of the form, "Effective Date," simply restates that the power of attorney is effective immediately unless the principal has indicated otherwise in the Special Instructions part. The following part of the form permits the principal to nominate a conservator in the event one is needed. Another part provides that anyone may rely on the validity of the power of attorney or a copy unless the person knows that it has terminated or is invalid.

The execution part of the form, entitled "Signature and Acknowledgment," provides a signature line for the principal and contains additional lines for her printed name, her address, and her telephone number. Following those lines is a space for the document to be properly acknowledged. As discussed earlier, the UPOAA does not require acknowledgment for the power of attorney to be effective. Proper acknowledgment, however, is designed to promote acceptance by third parties. Sections 119, 120.

The document concludes with a part addressed to the agent. Entitled "Important Information for Agent," it describes his general duties, the termination of his authority, and his potential liability for damages caused by his violation of the UPOAA or by acting outside the authority granted.

The comment to the form indicates that use of the statutory form is optional. A power of attorney that "substantially complies" with the form, however, is deemed to be a statutory form power of attorney under the Act.

ii. Agent's Certification

As previously noted, Section 120 of the UPOAA provides that a third party may request agent certification before accepting a power of attorney document. The Act provides a form certification document for use in those settings in which certification is requested.

Using the form document, the agent certifies under penalty of perjury that the principal granted him authority to act as agent and (1) that the principal is alive and has not revoked the power of attorney or that the power of attorney and the agent's authority have not terminated; (2) that if the power was to become effective upon the occurrence of an event or contingency, then the event or contingency has occurred; and (3) that if he was named as a successor agent, then the prior agent is no longer willing or able to serve. Because the third party may have specific requests not covered by those certifications, the form document also includes a blank space in which the agent may certify other matters as requested by the third party.

The document is to be signed by the agent and properly acknowledged.

iii. Miscellaneous Practical Concerns

For a DPOA to be valid, it must be executed by a principal who understands what she is doing. For example, in In re Thames, 544 S.E.2d 854 (S.C. Ct. App. 2001), the court noted that a principal must have contractual capacity to execute or revoke a valid power of attorney. Moreover, it is the principal's competence at the time of the execution or revocation that is determinative.

In practice, DPOAs are sometimes executed by principals of questionable capacity. Although an elder may have orally expressed her wishes about the management of her property should she become incapacitated, she may also have procrastinated about the execution of a contemplated DPOA. In such situations, it is not uncommon for her family members to seek her signature on a DPOA only after she has experienced substantial mental decline. If harmony prevails within her family following such an execution, no one is likely to challenge the document. For any number of reasons, however, family members or others may eventually take issue with the decisions of an agent. If this happens regarding a DPOA executed by a principal of questionable capacity, the DPOA may well be susceptible to a successful challenge.

The lawyer can attempt to protect the elderly client from this problem by explaining why it is important that a principal be capable of contracting at the execution of a DPOA. If the capable client is wary of "giving up control," the explanation would indicate that she and she alone currently retains complete control over her estate if she uses a springing DPOA; that she can decide how her incapacity is to be determined; that she can place limitations on the agent's power; and that she can revoke the DPOA at any time while she remains capable. The lawyer might further explain that the rules of professional responsibility would prevent him from supervising the execution of a DPOA at a later time under circumstances in which she clearly lacks capacity.

To execute a valid DPOA, the UPOAA merely requires a writing signed by the principal. Nevertheless, a lawyer supervising the execution of a DPOA should err on the side of caution. Even if state law has adopted the UPOAA, a prudent lawyer will typically demand more than the mere signature of the principal. The document should not only be signed by the principal, but also dated and acknowledged or notarized according to state law. If possible, the signature should also be witnessed by at least two disinterested people. (A rare state may even require that the DPOA be executed and attested in compliance with the formalities of the statute of wills. South Carolina is one such state.) Although witnessing is not required under the laws of many states, the use of witnesses is a good practice. If a challenge arises to the adequacy of the execution or to the capacity of the principal at the time of execution, the testimony of the witnesses can greatly assist in thwarting that challenge. In most instances, the DPOA should also be signed by the agent. Most states do not require that the agent sign (or that the agent even be aware of the DPOA at the time of its execution); however, the agent's signature on the document can be very helpful. The agent's signature on the document at the time of execution indicates the agent's awareness of the designation and his willingness to serve. Moreover, third parties may be more inclined to recognize the DPOA and transact business with the agent if his signature is affixed to the DPOA at the time of execution by the principal.

The UPOAA makes a copy of the DPOA as effective as the original. Some third parties, however, have been historically unwilling to transact business with an agent unless the agent provides them with an original DPOA. For this reason, lawyers often have the principal execute multiple originals. Moreover, some institutions such as banks have frequently refused to acknowledge a power of attorney unless it is completed on a form provided by the institution. Third-party demands such as these will probably decrease as use of a statutory form DPOA becomes more commonplace and as third parties increasingly face the threat of litigation, costs, and attorney fees for refusing to recognize a DPOA executed by a principal with whom they would otherwise be obligated to do business. Nonetheless, the lawyer needs to be aware that such problems may linger for yet a while and can cause substantial inconvenience if the agent needs to act quickly.

The Social Security Administration does not recognize a power of attorney for purposes of negotiating Social Security or Supplemental Security Income payments. If the recipient of Social Security or Supplemental Security Income is unable to manage those funds, her agent's power of attorney does not automatically entitle the agent to assume management. Rather, the agent will still have to apply to become the recipient's "representative payee."

If the principal is creating a springing DPOA, she may not wish to provide the agent with the DPOA document (and copies or multiple originals) until the springing event occurs. For example, the principal may leave the documents with her lawyer with the instruction for the lawyer to release the DPOA to the agent when the principal is deemed incapacitated by the process described in the document. If the principal chooses to retain the DPOA, the lawyer should advise her to keep the DPOA in a place of safekeeping that will be accessible to the agent or others in the event of the principal's incapacity. The lawyer should warn the principal against placing the DPOA in her safe deposit box unless someone else also has unfettered access to the box. Under general principles, if the principal places a DPOA in a safe deposit box to which she alone has access, no one may be able to obtain the document quickly should the principal become incapacitated.

In drafting a power of attorney, the lawyer should include specific language concerning the principal's intent as to whether it is durable. The UPOAA makes all powers durable by default, but the default rule in many states is still to the contrary. The lawyer should not rely on a default rule, but rather include specific language on the matter. If the principal's incapacity is the springing event for effectiveness, the DPOA should carefully explain how incapacity is to be determined.

A principal executing a springing DPOA may not want the agent's authority to continue if the principal regains capacity. For such a principal, the lawyer should ensure that the document provides for automatic revocation of the agent's authority when the principal has regained capacity. The document should also detail the conditions under which the principal will be determined to have regained capacity. Similarly, the document should carefully address the terms and conditions regarding an agent's compensation. If the DPOA does not discuss compensation, then in some states by statute the agent will be entitled to reasonable compensation; in others, courts will struggle to determine the principal's intent. In these latter cases, a court may presume that the agent's services were rendered gratuitously, particularly if the agent is a close member of the principal's family.

The lawyer should warn the principal about the potential pitfalls when using joint agents. If the principal nonetheless decides to use joint agents, the DPOA should describe each agent's authority. The DPOA should also include a mechanism for resolving disputes between or among the joint agents on matters over which they both have power.

The lawyer should carefully discuss with the principal her wishes concerning the scope of the agent's authority. In many states and under the UPOAA, statutory provisions will allow the principal to incorporate certain powers by reference or provide interpretative guidance if the principal gives the agent the authority "to do anything that I could do." In the absence of statutory guidance, courts may struggle in interpreting broad general grants. These courts will often search the DPOA for further indications of the principal's intent. For example, in In re Estate of Kurrelmeyer, 895 A.2d 207 (Vt. 2006), the principal's DPOA included a clause authorizing his wife as agent to do all that he could do, including any act and thing "whatsoever necessary." In addition to this broad language, the DPOA specifically gave the agent the authority to execute and deliver trust instruments and to add assets to any trust he had created. Examining the various granting clauses, the court concluded that the wife as agent could create a trust and add assets to it to accomplish estate planning objectives. The court did not find such an action to be an invalid usurpation of the principal's last will and testament, as his children had alleged. The court did note, however, that the wife as agent still had a fiduciary duty, and that the DPOA expressly prohibited her from making gifts to herself.

The authority of an agent to make gifts has been particularly troublesome for courts. Again, statutes in many states may provide guidance. For example, a governing statute may provide that a broad general grant in which the principal authorizes the agent "to do anything I can do" authorizes the agent to make certain gifts (often limited as to amount and to potential donees). In the absence of statutory guidance, most courts have held that an agent cannot make a gift to himself without an express grant of such authority. The temptation for an agent to make gifts to himself appears particularly strong, and many an agent is apparently unaware of (or at least undeterred by) the fiduciary restriction against self-dealing. Sometimes the agent begins to transfer the principal's assets outright to himself almost immediately after his authority to act commences. Alternatively, the agent may provide himself with a right of survivorship to the principal's assets. Courts frequently set such gifts or transfers aside as beyond the scope of the agent's authority. Alternatively, courts may find that the gifts or transfers were the product of fraud, duress, or undue influence.

Disgruntled family members will sometimes attack a principal's DPOA in an effort to gain control over the principal's person or estate. These attacks are usually brought as part of a conservatorship or guardianship proceeding filed by the disgruntled family members. For example, in In re Brubaker, 27 Pa. D. & C. 4th 200 (1994), a son petitioned for a guardian for his father, a 93-year old man alleged to be incapacitated because of his advanced age and "the infirmities that come with such a passage of years." Evidence indicated that the father had expressed a desire not to see his sons, and the court observed that the real purpose of the petition was apparently to resolve this family dispute. The court noted, however, that eleven years earlier the father had executed a valid power of attorney. Moreover, the agent was presently exercising it to accomplish the goals for which the petitioning son sought the guardianship. Thus no guardian was needed for the principal. The court also noted that it would not entertain such spurious guardianship petitions based merely on family disputes, particularly when the respondent had a valid power of attorney specifically designed to obviate the need for such petitions.

It is generally a good practice for the principal to nominate a conservator in the DPOA document. Often the principal will choose to name her agent as the conservator. In the absence of a nominee's wrongdoing or other disqualifying factors, a court will generally appoint the principal's nominee should a conservator later be needed. By nominating the agent as conservator, the principal can often thwart attacks that disgruntled family members might otherwise bring against the agent or the power of attorney.

A principal executing a financial DPOA will often wish to execute a health care proxy at the same time. The statutes of most states contemplate the use of separate documents for the financial DPOA and the health care DPOA. Even if state law permits both kinds of advance directive to be combined in one form, and even if the principal intends to name the same person as financial agent and health care agent, it is generally better practice to use separate documents. The financial DPOA and the health care proxy address substantially different matters.

Finally, the lawyer should carefully discuss with the client the importance of choosing a reliable, knowledgeable, and trustworthy agent. Unlike a guardian or conservator, an agent generally has no duty to file an inventory or make an annual accounting to a supervising court. Although most people consider the avoidance of judicial formalities and costs to be among the most attractive aspects of the DPOA, the informalities of the DPOA pose the substantial risk that an agent's abuse of authority will go undetected. If the lawyer makes the principal aware of this problem, the principal may choose to impose non-judicial inventory or accounting duties on the agent. Again, some states address these and similar matters by statute. For example, a state statute may allow the principal's expectant heirs or other close family members or expectant beneficiaries to petition a court to require a bond of the agent to protect the principal's estate.

C. Nonprobate Properties

Nonprobate properties are, as their name indicates, properties that do not generally pass through probate at the death of the owner. Such properties include the following: assets with right of survivorship, payable-on-death and transfer-on-death accounts, Totten trusts, life insurance proceeds, assets in a revocable trust, realty under a revocable deed, and assets that are the subject of a gift causa mortis.

Although a complete discussion of these properties is beyond the scope of this book, the following material provides an overview of some ways in which nonprobate properties are likely to be of interest to the elderly person. A word of warning is appropriate here: state law determines most of the applicable rules regarding nonprobate properties, and striking disparities exist among the states. For example, revocable deeds are permitted in an increasing minority of states, but remain legally-unrecognized in a majority of states.

1. Generally

Individuals most commonly use nonprobate assets to allow those assets to pass at death directly to others, without the potential cost, delay, and intrusiveness of probate proceedings. At one time, nonprobate properties were sometimes pejoratively viewed as a "poor man's will." Today, however, nonprobate assets are respectfully referred to as will substitutes and are increasingly used in the estate plans of people from all social and economic strata.

Beyond avoidance of probate, the relative merits of nonprobate properties are mixed. Some individuals place their assets in a form of nonprobate ownership hoping to gain favorable tax treatment, to avoid the claims of creditors, or to avoid obligations to family members. Often these individuals are disappointed to learn that the particular form of nonprobate ownership they have chosen provides no advantageous tax treatment or that it even results in disadvantageous tax treatment. Correspondingly, although a particular form of nonprobate ownership may allow the individual to avoid the claims of her creditors in some settings, that same form of ownership may subject the asset to the claims of the individual's co-owners. Increasingly, states have enacted laws that effectively eliminate the owner's ability to use nonprobate assets to avoid his obligations to his family.

Although certain forms of nonprobate ownership will allow a third party to manage assets for the elder who becomes incapacitated, almost none of these forms of nonprobate ownership is as flexible as the durable power of attorney. Significantly, the elder who chooses to use a nonprobate form of ownership so that a surrogate can manage her property typically must convey a property interest to that person or to an entity with whom the surrogate is affiliated. In contrast, the durable power of attorney provides the agent with authority to act, but does not itself convey a property interest to the agent.

2. Survivorship Properties

The joint tenancy and the tenancy by the entirety are the two principal forms of survivorship property recognized in the United States. They have roots extending far back into the common law, and their precise workings today vary significantly from state to state. They are forms of concurrent ownership. If one co-owner becomes incapacitated, the other co-owner or co-owners may continue to manage the property. (The same is true with a tenancy in common, the third principal form of concurrent ownership at common law. The tenancy in common, however, does not contain a right of survivorship. The respective interest of each co-owner in a tenancy in common passes through that co-owner's probate estate.) When one joint tenant dies, the right of survivorship causes her interest to pass by operation of law to the surviving co-tenant or co-tenants. When one tenant by the entirety dies, the surviving tenant by the entirety becomes the sole owner of the property by operation of law.

Historically, most joint tenancies and tenancies by the entirety occurred in connection with the ownership of real estate. Today, however, bank accounts (and other kinds of personalty) are also frequently held in joint tenancies or tenancies by the entirety. The following materials first discuss the survivorship rules that apply to realty and then discuss the special rules that often apply to bank accounts.

a. The Joint Tenancy

To create a joint tenancy, the grantor must clearly express his intent to do so. (If there is ambiguity, a court will typically construe the grant as a tenancy in common, which today is generally the default form of co-ownership unless the grantor's clear intent is to the contrary. In a few states, however, a grant to a husband and wife without further elaboration is presumed to be a tenancy by the entirety and not a tenancy in common.)

The language required to show clear intent to create a joint tenancy varies from state to state. In most states, it appears that "to X and Y as joint tenants" or "to X and Y as joint tenants with right of survivorship" will suffice. In at least some states, however, the latter language will create a joint life estate in X and Y with an indestructible contingent remainder in the survivor.

At common law, joint tenancy rules required that co-owners have unity of possession, interest, time, and title. In other words, at creation all co-owners had a right to use and enjoy the property, had an equal interest in the property, received that interest at the same time, and derived that interest from the same source. Many states today have relaxed those rules.

A person who wants to use a joint tenancy to allow someone to manage her realty (including her home) in the event of her incapacity will usually execute a deed naming herself and another as joint tenants. Elder grantors often select an adult child as a joint tenant. (Note that if common law rules still prevail in the jurisdiction, the elder cannot create a joint tenancy in such a direct manner, because she and her co-owner will not have received their interests at the same time or from the same source. In jurisdictions still applying common law rules, she must use a "straw party." Thus she would have to convey the entire property to a third party who in turn conveys it to her and her child as joint tenants.)

Once the joint tenancy is created, the elder's co-tenant has an ownership interest in the property. As a co-owner, each joint tenant is responsible for paying taxes on income the property produces. Liability for income tax may be a disincentive for placing income-producing property in a joint tenancy if the new co-tenant is in a higher tax bracket than the original owner.

A joint tenant has a presumptive right to use and enjoy the property, to convey his interest in the property, and to force a partition of the property. A partition may result when one co-tenant demands to own his interest outright, without any responsibilities to co-tenants. A partition may be in-kind or by sale. If the property is susceptible to being divided into parts, then it may be partitioned in kind. Often property such as a home cannot be divided in kind. Instead, it is sold and the proceeds are divided among the co-tenants according to their interests.

For example, assume that an elderly widow who is living alone decides to grant a joint tenancy interest in her home to her adult son. At the time the joint interest is created, she believes she can rely on the son to care for her at that home if she becomes incapacitated. If, however, the son subsequently decides that he wants to live in the home, to sell or convey his interest in the home, or to use the home in a way that conflicts with the elder's use, the elder may rue the day she created the joint tenancy. Once she has made a completed gift of an interest in the home to her son, she will not be able unilaterally to withdraw the property from the joint tenancy and reclaim sole ownership. Moreover, since the joint tenancy creates a property interest in her son, his creditors can generally reach his interest in the home, forcing a sale if necessary.

While the elder is sole owner of the home, she can mortgage her interest if she wishes. Once the home is in a joint tenancy, however, few professional lenders will be willing to make a loan on the interest of one joint tenant alone. When one joint tenant is able to and does mortgage her interest alone, states disagree about the effect of the mortgage on the joint tenancy. Most of them today appear to view the mortgage as a lien that does not destroy the joint tenancy. Under this view, if the elder mortgages her interest only and has not repaid the mortgage debt at her death, her son would succeed to ownership of the entire property free of the mortgage. Had she retained the home solely in her name, the home would have passed through probate and been subject to the mortgagee's claim.

If the elder does create a joint tenancy as a tool for avoiding conservatorship, she should take care to obtain the co-tenant's written agreement concerning use, possession, and enjoyment of the property. Most courts will recognize such agreements, including reasonable provisions in which the parties agree to refrain from partitioning the property during their joint lifetimes.

Most laypersons and a surprising number of lawyers are unaware that the right of survivorship accompanying a joint tenancy is not trumped by a will provision. For example, X might decide to place her home in a joint tenancy with her daughter, Y. Later X decides that she wants her son, Z, to have her interest when she dies. Thus X executes a will leaving her interest to Z. The will provision, however, will have no effect, since X's joint tenancy interest passes at death by operation of law to Y. Y becomes the sole owner of the home. To accomplish X's wishes, X must sever her interest from the joint tenancy through a lifetime transfer. To do so, X could deed her interest to a straw party who then deeds the interest back to her. X's interest will then be held as a tenant in common, not as a joint tenant. The interest may then pass through her will to her son. (In some states, X can sever her interest by a direct conveyance from herself as a joint tenant to herself as a tenant in common, without using a straw party.)

Some case law indicates that a lawyer commits malpractice if he knows that his client's property is held in a joint tenancy and yet fails to effectuate a proper severance of her interest to accomplish her testamentary wishes regarding that interest.

b. The Tenancy by the Entirety

For hundreds of years, the tenancy by the entirety could only be held by a married couple. Not all states recognize the tenancy by the entirety, and the variation in treatment among states that recognize it is even greater than that for joint tenancies. If a state recognizes the tenancy by the entirety and also now recognizes gay marriages, civil unions, or domestic partnerships, the tenancy by the entirety is also generally available to couples in those marriages, unions, or partnerships. For the sake of convenience, in this discussion we refer to all such couples as spouses and to their relationship as a marriage.

At common law, neither member of the couple could separately convey any interest in the tenancy by the entirety. Neither could unilaterally demand a partition. In fact, the spouses were considered to be one person. A conveyance to a married couple was deemed to be a tenancy by the entirety if nothing else was stated in the document. The default rule still applies in some states; other states, however, presume that a tenancy in common arises unless the document language clearly shows the grantor's intent to create a tenancy by the entirety.

Today, states also disagree about whether the creditors of one spouse alone can reach that debtor spouse's interest in tenancy by the entirety property. States that recognize a creditor's interest in such cases disagree about the nature of such interest and its effect on the tenancy.

Because the tenancy by the entirety must be held by spouses, and most spouses are typically around the same age, the tenancy by the entirety is often less satisfactory than a joint tenancy as a hedge against conservatorship. The elderly person may be a widow or widower, may never have been married, or may have a spouse who himself is incapacitated. Often the elderly person seeking a property manager through co-ownership wants someone younger, such as a child, to manage the property in the event of her incapacity.

As with the joint tenancy, the survivorship aspect of the tenancy by the entirety cannot be trumped by a will provision. Unlike the joint tenancy, however, the spouse has no unilateral right to sever the tenancy by the entirety under common law rules. Unless her spouse joins in the severance, the surviving spouse will own the property outright under common law rules.

If a married couple divorces, the property they held as tenants by the entirety typically becomes a tenancy in common in the absence of provisions otherwise.

c. Joint Bank Accounts

i. Generally

As a hedge against conservatorship, quite often an elderly person will name someone as a joint tenant on her bank account (or other account involving intangible assets). As a practical matter, this arrangement is generally preferable to a joint tenancy in realty, since a bank account gives the co-tenant immediate access to monies as needed for the care of the elder. Again, however, the new co-tenant acquires a property interest from the elder. If the new co-tenant wishes, typically he may withdraw all of the monies in the account for his own use and the elder will have no recourse against the bank.

In most states, joint accounts are presumed to be owned by the co-tenants in proportion to their net contributions to the account. Assume that Mary, an elder, names her adult son Sam as joint holder of a bank account. She deposited all of the funds in the account and thus all of the funds presumably belong to her. Nonetheless, the son as co-tenant may withdraw funds from the account, even if Mary becomes incapacitated. Thus the son can use the funds to pay his mother's bills and purchase items for her when she can no longer do so herself. Note, however, that he can also withdraw funds for his own use, because the bank has no duty to inquire as to the purpose of the withdrawal. For tax purposes, Mary will be deemed to have made a gift to Sam when he withdraws monies from the account for his own benefit with no obligation to account to his mother. 26 C.F.R. § 25.2511-1. In theory, if he withdraws funds for himself contrary to their agreement, Mary may have a conversion action against him. If she is incapacitated, however, often she will be unaware of what he is doing. In any event, the bank is protected against the son's wrongful conduct. If the son cannot or does not repay her, she and her estate bear the loss.

The treatment of creditors during the joint lives of the co-tenants is also problematic. If Sam incurs debt, his creditors may attempt to reach monies in the joint account. In some states, his creditors can force a partition of the account and reach one-half of the value of the account. In other states, Sam's creditors are initially presumed able to reach the entire balance of the account subject to Mary's right to keep the value of her deposits that she can clearly prove. If Mary has not retained good records, proving her deposits may be difficult. The proof problem may be exacerbated if she has also become incapacitated when the son's creditors attempt to reach the account.

As a will substitute, joint bank accounts are generally less satisfactory than joint tenancies of realty if the elder's goal is to avoid the claims of her creditors at death. In most states, if the elder dies owning real estate in a joint tenancy, the realty passes at her death to the surviving joint tenant and is not subject to the claims of her creditors. In contrast, if the elder dies owning funds in a joint bank account, the funds generally pass at her death to the surviving joint tenant but are subject to the claims of her creditors if her estate is otherwise insufficient to satisfy their claims.

ii. The Agency or "Convenience" Account

The foregoing discussion examined the typical rules associated with a true joint bank account. Very often, however, an elder names another person as a co-tenant of a joint bank account, but in fact does not truly intend to create a joint bank account. Rather, the elder intends to create an account in which the other named party will act as an agent on her behalf in the event of her incapacity. The account is set up only for the convenience of the elder, not to bestow an actual property interest in the account to another person. This agency or so-called "convenience" account contains no right of survivorship. Thus at the death of the elder, the balance of the account passes through her probate estate to her heirs or will beneficiaries.

In a few states, if the elder signs a bank card establishing the account as a "joint" account, then as a matter of law the account is treated as a true joint account. Courts in those states will not accept evidence to show that the elder intended to create an agency or convenience account. The person named as joint tenant succeeds to the balance by right of survivorship upon the death of the elder.

In most states, however, the elder or her estate may overcome the presumption of a joint account that results from the bank card. To overcome that presumption and establish that the account is in fact an agency or convenience account, the elder or her estate must show with clear and convincing evidence that her intent was only to create an agency relationship with the other person, not a true joint tenancy.

A constant stream of litigation concerning alleged convenience accounts produces new opinions each year. A typical scenario is as follows: E, an elder, has two children, a son S and a daughter D. E's will devises her estate equally to the two. Most of E's assets are in a bank account. Because E fears that she may become incapacitated, she names S as a co-tenant of her bank account by checking a box next to "joint account" on the card the bank uses to establish new accounts. (S lives nearby and D lives across the country.) E dies and S claims all remaining funds in the account by right of survivorship. If the account is a true joint account, it is nonprobate property that passes directly to S. If clear and convincing evidence demonstrates that E's intent was merely to make S her agent, however, then in most states the account balance is probate property that passes under E's will equally to S and D.

One reason for the continuing confusion resulting in this area is that bank forms historically provided depositors relatively few options in selecting the kind of account, and an agency account was not among the options. Section 6-204 of the UPC provides a model form that, if widely adopted, could substantially reduce joint account/agency account litigation. The form sets forth a variety of clearly-described options from which the depositor may select, including an account with an agency designation. The depositor who chooses the agency account is to indicate whether the agency designation remains valid following the depositor's disability or incapacity.

3. PODs and Totten Trusts

a. POD and TOD Accounts

Payable-on-death (POD) accounts are perhaps the most obvious form of will substitute. In the typical setting, a depositor establishes an account whose balance is to be paid at her death to one or more named beneficiaries. The depositor retains complete control over the account during her lifetime, and thus can close the account, change beneficiary designations, change the nature of the account, or add to or withdraw from the account. If the account remains in POD form at her death, then the balance passes directly (i.e., outside of probate) to the named beneficiary or beneficiaries.

POD accounts are ubiquitous today, but were once highly disfavored by courts. Historically, courts viewed POD accounts as an infringement upon the protections afforded by statutes of wills, which generally required a substantial number of steps for a valid execution. In contrast, a depositor can establish a POD account quickly, cheaply, without ceremony or witnesses. The things that once made the POD account unpopular with courts are the very things that make it so very popular today.

Recently joining the increasingly popular nonprobate parade is the transfer-on-death (TOD) account, which permits the owner of a security account to register a security in beneficiary form. Such registration has no effect on ownership until the owner dies. At the owner's death, the security passes directly to the named beneficiary or beneficiaries.

Because POD accounts and TOD registrations give the designated beneficiaries no interest in the assets during the lifetime of the owner, neither POD accounts nor TOD registrations have significant value as tools to protect against incapacity. Their principal use is to allow assets to pass quickly and cheaply outside of probate. If the owner's estate is otherwise insufficient to satisfy her debts, most assets held in POD form (such as the typical POD bank account) are subject to the claims of the owner's creditors. This is so because the owner maintained complete control over them until her death. Under state or federal law, particular forms of POD or TOD accounts (such as certain United States Savings Bonds made POD) may be exempt from creditors of the estate despite the owner's control up to death.

POD and TOD designations are part of the contract between the owner and a third party (such as the bank where the account is held). While the owner retains the right to change the designations during her lifetime, that right terminates at her death. Consequently, the modern rule is that the owner's will provisions are ineffective to change a POD or TOD designation. UPC §6-213.

A small but increasing number of states now permits the owner of realty to create a TOD deed. Also called a beneficiary or revocable deed, the deed names a grantee-beneficiary who is to receive the realty directly upon the death of the owner. The owner must record the deed, but she retains complete ownership of the realty during her lifetime and may freely revoke the deed until her death. If she has not revoked the deed before her death, then at her death the grantee-beneficiary typically simply records her death certificate and perhaps files an accompanying affidavit. No probate is required.

b. Totten Trusts

The Totten trust derives its informal name from a famous New York case, In re Totten, 71 N.E. 748 (N.Y. 1904). The Totten trust is also known by several other names, including the tentative trust, the "in trust for" (ITF) account, or the savings account trust. The creation of a Totten trust is simple: the depositor establishes an account "as trustee" or "in trust for" a named beneficiary. The depositor retains complete control over the account during her lifetime. If she does not revoke the account during her lifetime, at her death the balance passes outside probate to the beneficiary.

Although the Totten trust and the POD account serve essentially the same purpose, they have different theoretical bases. By viewing the Totten trust as a tentative form of trust, courts often recognized Totten trusts even when they routinely rejected POD designations. The common law generally permitted the depositor who created a Totten trust to revoke that trust by an express provision in his will.

Today, the Uniform Probate Code treats the Totten trust simply as a form of POD account to which POD principles apply. Thus in states that have adopted the UPC rule, the Totten trust cannot be revoked by a provision in the depositor's will.

4. Revocable Trusts

The trust is a very flexible property tool. It can be established for any purpose that does not violate the law or public policy. The revocable trust (also popularly known as a form of "living" trust) is an effective way for some people to ensure that their property will be managed as they wish in the event of incapacity. At common law, a trust is generally deemed irrevocable unless the settlor—i.e., the person who creates and funds the trust—expressly indicates at creation her intent for the trust to be revocable. The Uniform Trust Code 2000 (UTC), which has been adopted by a growing minority of states, reverses the common law rule and provides that a trust is revocable unless the settlor provides otherwise. The UTC rule seems to be more consistent with the intent of the typical settlor, but lawyers and their clients should be aware that the common law rule still applies in most states.

The settlor who creates the revocable trust retains the power to terminate or amend the trust as long as she remains capable. The settlor can provide as much detail as she wishes in the trust instrument to guide the trustees concerning the management of the assets placed in the trust. She may name herself as trustee or co-trustee (although she cannot be both the sole trustee and the sole beneficiary) to manage the property until the event of her incapacity.

If the settlor's estate is complex or if she has no individual whom she believes can adequately manage it, she will often choose a professional trustee, such as a bank trust department. Third parties are much less inclined to balk at doing business with a well-established, professional trustee than with an agent under a durable power of attorney. Professional trustees are also generally fully aware of their fiduciary duties, something that may not be true with a family member or friend who is a trustee or agent. Among the trustee's duties is an obligation to inform and report to beneficiaries, who will often include named individuals who will take at the settlor's death. This duty allows beneficiaries to keep check on the trustee's actions.

For some elders, however, the cost of establishing and maintaining a revocable trust may overshadow its potential benefits. Probably the greatest advantage of the revocable trust is the settlor's ability to provide detailed tailoring of its provisions. The more the settlor wishes to tailor the trust provisions to meet her individual needs, however, the more she will probably have to pay for the lawyer's drafting fees. Other costs also make the revocable trust an impractical alternative for some individuals. To fund the trust, the settlor will typically need her lawyer to prepare any necessary documents of transfer (such as deeds) so that the trustee can obtain legal title to and thereby manage the trust assets. If the settlor chooses a professional trustee to manage the trust assets, she may incur substantial trustee compensation fees. Even when the settlor chooses an individual trustee who agrees to serve without compensation, she should be aware that the trust is a legal entity that may require the regular expenditure of funds for accountings, tax return preparation, and so forth.

In recent years, the rise of an overzealous, slick, and highly commercial "trust industry" has tainted the reputation of the living trust. Various organizations have solicited customers (particularly elders) through mass mailings that tout the importance and advantages of living trusts and that emphasize the worst aspects of probate. When someone responds to these solicitations, a salesperson from the organization visits and provides a high pressure sales pitch. Often these salespeople answer specific legal questions and advise the customer about the customer's precise legal needs. If the sale is made, the customer's information is forwarded to a central office where paralegals actually prepare the living trust. The trust instrument typically consists of many pages of boilerplate and one or two pages concerning the customer's particular needs. An in-house attorney supposedly reviews each completed trust package. Ultimately, such organizations may charge the customer over $1000 for services. Some courts have concluded that these organizations are assisting or engaging in the unauthorized practice of law, since the salespersons who provide tailored legal advice are almost never lawyers. Such organizations may also be guilty of commingling client funds if they simply deposit customer fees into a general account.

Lawyers, too, sometimes tout the advantages of the living trust without fully considering the client's needs and financial condition. As a means of avoiding conservatorship, the durable power of attorney is generally easier to establish and less expensive. If the client has a trusted friend or family member who agrees to serve as agent, the DPOA may be a more practical solution than the revocable trust.

Lawyers may also inadvertently or intentionally overstate the advantages of the revocable trust. The revocable trust does not itself provide the settlor with any federal estate tax benefits. Also, as with other nonprobate properties that function as will substitutes, assets in a revocable trust are today increasingly subject to the claims of a decedent's creditors at death. Uniform Trust Code § 505. (It is worth noting, however, that creditors typically must first exhaust probate assets before reaching revocable trust assets.) At one time, settlors could use a revocable trust as a way to effectively disinherit a surviving spouse by having the assets pass to third parties outside probate. The modern approach, however, treats the surviving spouse as a creditor and allows the surviving spouse to reach the trust assets as necessary to satisfy the decedent's statutory obligations to her. Chief among these obligations in most separate-property jurisdictions is the survivor's right to an elective (or "forced") share of the deceased spouse's estate.

As a will substitute, the revocable trust typically permits the trust assets to pass directly to the named trust beneficiaries without the potential cost, delay, and intrusiveness of the probate process. (As mentioned above, however, in some instances creditors may be able to bring the assets before the probate court.) If the settlor's goal is to avoid probate entirely, however, she should ensure that all of her assets are in the revocable trust or are otherwise placed in a form of nonprobate ownership. Most notably, if the settlor owns assets that require a document of title and she does not place them in some nonprobate form (such as a revocable trust or co-tenancy with right of survivorship), her estate will typically require probate to provide the needed document of title to her heirs or will beneficiaries.

The elder should be aware that revocable trusts, joint accounts, and durable powers of attorney are not mutually exclusive ways to protect against conservatorship or to avoid probate. Often it will make sense for the elder to use all three or any two of the three along with other estate planning tools.

Finally, it is important to note that certain irrevocable trusts can play an important role in the estate plan of some elders, although not generally for the purpose of avoiding conservatorship. For example, trusts satisfying very specific requirements may help qualify an individual for Medicaid in proper circumstances. This topic is discussed more fully in Chapter 9.

5. Insurance

Life insurance provides money payments directly to a named beneficiary at the death of the insured. If the beneficiary predeceases the insured and the policy does not name an alternate beneficiary, then the proceeds are generally paid to the insured decedent's estate. The insured retains the right to change the beneficiary designation at any time before death. Because the insurance policy represents a contract between the insured and the insurance company, the insured cannot change the beneficiary designation by will.

State statutes often exempt life insurance proceeds from most claims of the decedent's creditors. Increasingly, however, state elective share statutes consider a deceased spouse's life insurance policies in determining the amount of the surviving spouse's elective share. Under the UPC, the value of the proceeds is taken into account in the consideration of the couple's wealth for purposes of determining the ultimate elective share amount to which a surviving spouse is entitled. Some states include only the cash surrender value of the policy in the married decedent's estate for purposes of determining the surviving spouse's elective share amount. Other states do not include the insurance proceeds at all in determining the surviving spouse's elective share amount.

Since life insurance proceeds are paid at the insured's death, the policy does not generally provide significant protection against conservatorship.

6. Gifts

a. Generally

Certain forms of revocable gifts may be considered nonprobate assets that function as testamentary substitutes.

Gifts are generally classified as inter vivos or causa mortis. A completed inter vivos gift in which the donor retains no power to revoke removes the subject of the gift from the donor's estate completely. For example, if an elderly parent makes a completed gift of land to a child, the land no longer belongs to the parent. In contrast, if the parent places land in a revocable trust reserving a life interest for herself and providing a remainder interest to her child, the asset remains in the parent's estate until her death, at which time it passes outside of probate to the child.

All gifts require at least three elements: intent of the donor to make a gift; delivery of the item to the donee; and acceptance by the donee. A donor may make a current gift of a future interest such as a remainder or executory interest. For example, a person who retains a legal life estate in realty and deeds the remainder outright to her child without consideration makes an effective gift currently, even though the child will not enjoy the right to possess the land until the donor's death. At the time such a gift has been effectively made, the donor immediately loses substantial rights regarding the property. In the absence of circumstances that would support claims such as fraud, duress, undue influence, or lack of capacity, the donor has no unilateral ability to "undo" the completed gift.

When dealing with personal property, actual delivery of the item is generally the best form of delivery. Modern courts, however, will often accept substitute delivery by constructive or symbolic means, particularly if actual delivery is impossible or highly impractical under the circumstances. Delivery can also be accomplished through the use of an agent. If the donor has no right to recall the subject of the gift once it is placed in the agent's hands, then delivery has been effectuated at that time.

A completed inter vivos gift over which the donor retains no rights generally means that the donated asset is no longer in the donor's estate. Nonetheless, the transfer or its value may have a continuing impact upon her estate. For example, the transfer may be important for determining whether the donor is financially eligible for certain public benefits; whether the donor's creditors can reach the transferred asset; whether gift tax returns must be filed and whether estate and gift taxes ultimately are owed; and whether the donor's surviving spouse may have the value of the transfer imputed to the donor's estate in determining the survivor's elective share.

b. Causa Mortis

The relatively uncommon gift causa mortis is a gift that is made in contemplation of imminent death. The gift causa mortis functions explicitly as a will substitute. For example, an elderly woman is told that she must have emergency heart surgery. She hands her niece a diamond bracelet and states, "I want you to have this if I die." The woman then dies during the surgery. The niece now owns the bracelet, which does not pass through her aunt's probate estate. Unlike the typical inter vivos gift, the gift causa mortis can be revoked by the donor at any time prior to her death.

Courts are often wary of gifts causa mortis. When someone challenges the validity of an alleged gift causa mortis, courts frequently require that the donee prove the validity of the gift with clear and convincing evidence. Courts have not always agreed upon the nature of the apprehension of death that will support a gift causa mortis. A general concern that one may die soon, however, is typically insufficient to support a gift causa mortis. Most cases recognizing the gift causa mortis involve a threat of imminent death to the donor from serious illness or surgery. In recent years, however, some courts have upheld a gift causa mortis when the donor's underlying illness was a mental illness that caused her to commit suicide.

At common law, a gift causa mortis is automatically revoked if the donor of the gift causa mortis survives the contemplated cause of death. If the donor who recovers does not request the return of the item, however, the circumstances may allow a court to infer that the donor intended to make an inter vivos gift upon recovery.

The law governing basic gifts is largely nonstatutory in most states. That law is often quirky. For example, if A lends (bails) an item to B and then decides to make an inter vivos gift of the item to B, no redelivery from A to B is required. A can simply tell B that the item is his and B becomes the owner. If A lends an item to B and then decides to make a gift causa mortis of the item to B because A learns that she is dying, A must redeliver the item to B under common law rules.

Except in extreme deathbed scenarios when there is no time for an alternative mode of transfer, the gift causa mortis should be avoided. The property owner can usually find a better way of transferring the asset in question.

D. Probate Properties

Any assets owned by the decedent that do not pass as nonprobate assets and in which her interest does not otherwise expire at her death are part of her probate estate. Formally, probate assets are assets that should pass pursuant to state intestate or testate succession laws. Informally, however, surviving family members often distribute the probate assets of a decedent among themselves without regard to the technical niceties of the law of intestate succession or the law of wills. For example, if A dies intestate and her assets include only items of personalty, her heirs might simply agree upon a division of the assets that satisfies them. If any of her probate assets requires a judicial declaration concerning title (e.g., realty), then the heirs will need to have the estate formally probated in the proper court.

In recent years, probate has gained a reputation as something that one should seek to avoid. Obviously, lawyers will charge for their services in connection with probate, and the estate must be held open for a period of time to allow creditors to file their claims. Nonetheless, most estates travel through the probate process without incurring unreasonable cost or delay. Many states have special statutes to simplify and expedite the probate of small estates. Although wills become public documents once they are probated, most people do not seem to find this objectionable. Moreover, even when an individual provides for her most substantial assets to pass outside of probate, she will often need or want a will to dispose of any remaining assets. Thus, drafting wills and supervising their execution remains a common task requested of the lawyer representing elderly clients.

Focusing on the Uniform Probate Code (UPC), the following discussion presents an overview of the general principles of intestate succession and the law of wills. The UPC has helped to streamline the probate process in those states that have adopted it in full. The UPC has also improved the probate process in those states that have borrowed substantially from its provisions. As with many other areas of elder law, however, probate laws still vary substantially across the country. The lawyer should be thoroughly familiar with the probate laws that will apply to her clients.

1. Intestate Succession

When an individual dies owning probate assets and yet having no effective will, how should her assets be distributed? As mentioned above, in some cases her family can amicably agree privately among themselves, without the need for judicial involvement. If the family cannot agree, or if clear title to a property is required, then the estate will be probated. In such cases, the distribution of the estate will be governed by the laws of intestate succession. An intestate succession statute is a legislative guess of how the typical decedent would want her estate distributed.

a. General Patterns of Distribution

With few exceptions, intestate succession statutes contain arbitrary, fixed, objective patterns of distribution. They do not permit a court to inquire into the personal preferences of the particular decedent. The persons who succeed to the decedent's estate under the intestate succession law are known as her heirs. Today, one intestate succession statute usually covers both realty and personalty owned by the decedent. Historically, states often had separate statutory schemes for realty and personalty, and those individuals who received the decedent's personalty were known as her next-of-kin.

The decedent's surviving spouse typically receives the first cut of the decedent's estate. (In a small but growing minority of states, the decedent's legally-recognized nonmarital partner receives this benefit.) Once the spouse is provided for, the decedent's issue or descendants receive their cut. In a large number of estates, distribution will end at that point. In some states, the decedent's parents may share part of the estate with the surviving spouse if the decedent leaves no descendants.

If the decedent has no spouse or issue, then the decedent's parents or their issue generally succeed to the property. For the elderly decedent without spouse or issue and whose parents have predeceased her, this means that her brothers and sisters and the issue of predeceased brothers and sisters will succeed to her estate. A substantial majority of states makes no distinctions between the decedent's whole- and half-blood relatives. Thus, if Jane dies intestate survived by her whole-blood sister Kay and her half-blood brother Larry, the two survivors will split her estate equally. A handful of states provide that whole-blood relatives take twice as much as half-blood relatives. One state, Mississippi, provides that whole-blood relatives take to the complete exclusion of half-blood relatives of the same degree.

If the decedent has no surviving spouse, issue, parents, or issue of parents, then the decedent's grandparents and their issue generally take. For the elderly decedent in this category, this often means her first cousins and the issue of predeceased first cousins will succeed to her estate (because her grandparents and her uncles and aunts will have predeceased her).

The modern trend, as exemplified by the UPC, does not permit distribution beyond these categories. If no survivor exists within these categories, then the estate escheats to the state. Under such rules, if the decedent's closest surviving relative is her grandparent's sibling, the decedent's estate would escheat because the grandparent's sibling does not fall within the prescribed categories.

b. Methods of Distribution
i. The Surviving Spouse

The modern approach to intestate distribution provides the surviving spouse with a base monetary amount (e.g., the first $150,000 of the estate) and a fixed part of any excess (e.g., one-half of the remaining part of the estate). The UPC uses this "base amount plus a fixed part of the excess" approach. Under the UPC, the base amount varies with family structure, but the recommended amount is never less than the first $150,000 of the decedent's estate. The fixed part of the excess also varies with family structure. When the decedent and her surviving spouse have surviving issue from their relationship and neither has surviving issue outside that relationship (i.e., when they are in a traditional nuclear family relationship), the surviving spouse receives everything under the UPC. UPC § 2-102.

An older approach, still used in a number of states, simply provides the surviving spouse with a fixed-fractional part of the estate. For example, the statute may generally provide that the surviving spouse receives one-third of the intestate estate while the remaining two-thirds passes to the decedent's issue. For small estates, such statutes can provide substantially less protection for the surviving spouse than those statutes that guarantee the surviving spouse a base fee. For example, if Mark dies intestate with an estate of $75,000 and is survived his wife Nancy and their children Ron and Sam, the UPC would give Nancy the entire amount. A fixed-fractional statute providing the surviving spouse with only one-third of the decedent's estate would give Nancy only $25,000, with the remaining $50,000 to pass to the children. Fixed-fractional statutes not only tend to ignore the survivor's probable needs, but also appear to ignore the typical wishes of the decedent. The few and limited studies undertaken tend to indicate that the typical decedent wants first and foremost to protect the surviving spouse.

ii. Representation

When survivors take not in their own stead, but as issue of a predeceased individual who otherwise would have taken, the survivors are said to take by "representation." For example, assume that the applicable provision of the intestate succession statute provides that the estate is to be distributed "to the brothers and sisters of the decedent and to the issue of predeceased brothers and sisters by representation." A slightly complex but not atypical scenario will demonstrate the concept. Alice dies intestate. Her sister Betty has predeceased her, but Betty's daughter Brenda survives her. Alice's brother Carl has predeceased her, but his sons Dan and Earl survive. Carl's daughter Fran predeceased Carl, but Fran's daughters Gail and Heather survive. Finally, Alice's sister Irene predeceased her. Irene's daughter Jan also predeceased Alice, but Jan's son Ken survives.

In this example, all of the named survivors are Alice's heirs. Alice has no living sibling, so all of the surviving individuals named will be taking by representation, because they are issue of a predeceased sibling of Alice. Representation, however, involves different methods of allocation that depend upon the law of the jurisdiction.

The oldest form of representation is "strict" or "pure" per stirpes. Under this form of representation, Alice's estate is initially divided into equal parts among the individuals in the category who take in their own right (Alice's siblings, had any of them been living) and among those predeceased individuals who would have taken in their own right but have left issue capable of taking their part (Betty, Carl, and Irene). The estate in our example is therefore divided into thirds. Betty's one-third will pass to her issue, Carl's one-third will pass to his issue, and Irene's one-third will pass to her issue. Once the distribution begins, a per stirpes approach means that heirs will take from the share their predeceased parent would have received. Betty's one-third will pass to Brenda. Carl's one-third will be divided into thirds. Thus, Carl's sons Dan and Earl will take one-ninth each. The remaining one-ninth that Fran would have taken passes to her issue, Gail and Heather (one-eighteenth each). Irene's one-third would have passed to Jan, but Jan also predeceased Alice. That one-third thus passes to Jan's issue, Ken.

A more modern distributional scheme adopted by many states is sometimes called "modern" per stirpes. Under this scheme, the first division of the estate is made at the nearest generational level where there is a living relative who is eligible to take. Because none of Alice's siblings survived her, the niece/nephew level is the nearest generational level to Alice in which a living relative is eligible to take. Thus, the estate is first divided into fifths, one each for Brenda, Dan, Earl, Fran, and Jan. (These are the five nieces and nephews who are either living or, alternatively, who are predeceased but have living issue eligible to take.) Brenda, Dan, and Earl are living and each takes one-fifth of Alice's estate. After this initial cut, per stirpes principles apply. Fran's one-fifth passes to her daughters Gail and Heather (one-tenth each). Jan's one-fifth passes to her son Ken.

The UPC defines representation in yet another fashion. Sometimes called "per capita at each generational level," the approach presumes that a decedent would want survivors at the same generational level to take the same amount from her estate. Thus, all nieces and nephews should receive the same fractional distribution. All grand-nieces and grand-nephews should receive the same fractional distribution. As under the modern per stirpes approach, the first division of the estate is made at the nearest generational level where there is a living relative eligible to take. Thus, the estate is first divided into fifths, one each for Brenda, Dan, Earl, Fran, and Jan. (Fran and Jan must be counted even though they are predeceased, because they left surviving issue eligible to take.) Brenda, Dan, and Earl each receive one-fifth of Alice's estate. The remaining two-fifths of Alice's estate will now pass equally to her grand-nieces (Gail and Heather) and her grand-nephew (Ken). Each of them thus receives two-fifteenths of Alice's estate. UPC § 2-106.

c. Nontraditional Families

Today, American families come in all shapes and sizes. In contrast, most intestacy statutes employ a "one size fits all" approach to inheritance. Such intestate succession statutes may ignore members of a decedent's family if that family form is unusual or even slightly nontraditional. For example, although stepparent-stepchild relationships exist throughout American society, the great majority of intestacy statutes effectively exclude stepparents and stepchildren as potential heirs of each other. Ann may have reared her stepson Joe from the time he was an infant and may refer to him as "my son," but he is very unlikely to be an heir at her death. (California has a statute that permits stepchild inheritance in rare circumstances. A few other states and the UPC allow a stepchild to take as a last resort if the decedent has no other surviving family members as defined by the intestacy statute. Provisions favoring stepchildren rarely apply, however.)

Similarly, gay, lesbian, and unmarried straight couples in long-term committed relationships are not potential heirs of each other in a large majority of states. In jurisdictions that permit such couples to register and gain statewide legal recognition, these couples generally must carefully avail themselves of that registration process to become potential heirs of each other.

The layperson may assume that the default rules of inheritance law will recognize the relationships that she most treasured. As we have seen, however, the default rules are arbitrary classifications that are not trumped by the probable wishes of a particular decedent. The need for a will thus becomes especially important for individuals in nontraditional families.

In some instances, intestate succession statutes have begun to include certain people outside the nontraditional family. These provisions are discussed in the following paragraphs.

i. Adopted Children

Adoption creates a new legal parent-child relationship. Most states today treat the adopted child as a member of the adoptive parent's family for inheritance purposes. For example, if Ann dies intestate survived by Joe, her former stepson whom she legally adopted, then Joe will be her heir because he is her legally-recognized child.

In the great majority of states, a child adopted into a completely new family is no longer a potential heir of the biological parents who gave the child up for adoption. For example, if Mary and Bill's biological child Kim was adopted into a new family, and Mary and Bill subsequently had two children whom they reared, only the two later children would be Mary and Bill's legal children and heirs when Mary and Bill die. (A handful of states, however, do include Kim as a potential heir of Mary and Bill.)

New family adoption occurs when the child is adopted by two "new" parents. The new family adoption is in contrast with the blended family adoption. Blended family adoptions are very frequent today. In the most common form of blended family adoption, the spouse of one of the child's legal parents adopts the child. (In other words, the child's stepmother or stepfather adopts the child.) States have taken different approaches to the inheritance treatment of children in the stepparent adoption setting. For example, assume that Alice and Bill are a married couple with one child, Carol. Alice and Bill obtain a divorce, and Alice receives primary custody of Carol. Alice then marries Dick. Dick wants to adopt Carol, and Bill agrees that he may do so. Following the adoption, Carol is the legally-recognized child of Alice and Dick. She is not the legal child of Bill. Under one approach to stepparent adoption, following the adoption Alice will be a potential heir from and through Alice and Dick, but not a potential heir from and through Bill. (This approach is consistent with the new family adoption approach discussed above.) The UPC, however, uses a different approach. The UPC provides that Carol is a potential heir not only from and through Alice and Dick (her legal parents), but also from and through Bill (who severed his legal relationship with Carol to allow another man to become her legal father). Thus, if Bill subsequently had two more children and then died intestate with no spouse, the UPC would divide his estate among his two legally-recognized children and Carol. UPC § 2-119(b). Finally, a third approach to stepparent adoption, used in some states, permits Carol to inherit from and through Bill only if the adoption occurred after Bill's death.

On rare occasion, a couple takes a child into their home and erroneously believes that they have legally adopted the child. For example, the couple may have failed unwittingly to sign the necessary papers or to obtain the necessary signatures from others. If the purported adoption is not legally recognized, then the child cannot take as a legal child of the couple under intestate succession statutes. In a number of states, however, equity may give the child partial relief under principles of equitable adoption or virtual adoption. If the couple took the child in when he was young and led the child to mistakenly believe and rely upon the belief that he was legally adopted, then the child may take a child's intestate share at the death of either "equitable" parent. The doctrine only applies if the equitable parent dies intestate, and its does not establish a legal relationship between the couple and the child for other purposes. In most courts, the child thus has no further inheritance rights regarding other members of the "equitable family" such as the couple's legally-recognized children. Moreover, the doctrine only applies to benefit the equitably-adopted child. If the equitably-adopted child dies before the equitably-adoptive parents, the equitably-adoptive parents have no claim on the child's intestate estate.

ii. Nonmarital Children

Today, a substantial and growing minority of American children are born to unmarried mothers. Until the last third of the twentieth century, nonmarital children were routinely excluded as heirs of their fathers. In response to decisions from the United States Supreme Court, today all states permit nonmarital children to inherit from and through their fathers in some circumstances.

If, during the lifetime of the father, the child (or her proxy) establishes his paternity legally, then in any state the child is a potential heir from and through that legal father. In many states, the child may also become an heir from and through a father if she establishes his paternity with clear and convincing evidence after his death during the probate process. Thus if eighty-five year-old John dies intestate survived by the two children of his long-term marriage and also by a sixty-year old nonmarital child whom he never met, in some states the nonmarital child will be able to claim one-third of John's intestate estate if she proves paternity. (Note that in some states that otherwise permit a nonmarital child to prove paternity posthumously, statutes of repose may prevent an older nonmarital child from asserting such a claim. Such a statute might provide, for example, that a child cannot establish paternity for inheritance purposes once three years have passed following the child's attainment of the age of majority.)

Similarly, if Jean, a grandmother, dies intestate survived by her predeceased son's three marital children and also by that son's nonmarital child who had legally proved his paternity, Jean's estate will be divided into fourths. This is so even if Jean did not know about the nonmarital child.

Intestate succession laws have not kept pace with the rapid evolution in family structures. Thus it becomes even more important for individuals to have a will. The will can account for the testator's specific wishes. For example, if John wants to leave his entire estate to his two marital children and to exclude any nonmarital children he may have fathered, he can so provide in his will. (To make his intent clear, John will probably want to include a clause specifically disinheriting any nonmarital child or other person asserting a claim as his issue. This will help to avoid the nonmarital child's claim that she was "pretermitted," or inadvertently omitted.)

iii. Children of Assisted Reproductive Technology

Thousands of American children have been conceived through assisted reproductive technology (ART). This technology includes artificial insemination and embryo implantation. Couples unable to conceive through intercourse and single persons without partners have increasingly used the technology to become parents. Many states have not addressed the inheritance rights of such children. It generally appears that inheritance rights flow from determinations of legal parentage, but legal parentage of children of ART is often unclear in many settings in many states. Again, the prudent course for inheritance purposes is to accomplish the client's wishes by specific will provisions, thereby avoiding the uncertainties in the default rules of intestate succession.

d. Advancements

Sometimes a parent will give a child a substantial gift that is intended to count as an advance against the child's inheritance. For example, a father might give his son $50,000 towards the purchase of a home with the understanding that the lifetime gift will count against the son's inheritance. Years later the father dies intestate with an estate of $150,000, survived by his son and daughter. If the law of advancements applies, the daughter will receive $100,000 and the son $50,000 at their father's death. Because the son's lifetime gift is taken into account, each of the two children ultimately receives $100,000 from the father, a distribution consistent with their intestate shares had no gift been made. The advancement concept applies only when the decedent dies intestate as to all or part of his assets.

The common law presumed that a substantial lifetime gift to a child was to be counted against the child's inheritance. The UPC provisions, however, treat a lifetime gift as an advancement only if the donor indicated his intent that the gift be an advancement in a contemporaneous writing or if the donee acknowledged the gift as an advancement in a writing. Thus, in the above scenario, a state applying the common law would treat the gift as an advancement, but a UPC state would do so only if the understanding was evidenced by a writing satisfying the statutory requirements. The UPC does not limit the advancement concept to children of the donor; rather, it extends the advancement concept to heirs generally.

Under the UPC, if the donee predeceases the donor, the advancement does not count in distributing the donor's estate unless the writing provides otherwise.

e. Family Protection Provisions (Excluding the Elective Share)

Many states provide the decedent's surviving spouse and certain children with a right to a set amount of exempt personal property and an allowance from the decedent's estate. The exempt property award and the allowance typically come "off the top": in other words, they pass free of the claims of the decedent's general creditors and have priority over devises made in the will and over intestate distributions. The laws governing the awards and their size vary significantly among the states. The UPC provides for a maximum of $15,000 of exempt property to the surviving spouse; if no surviving spouse exists, the award is to the decedent's children. Such property typically consists of household furnishings, cars, personal effects, and so forth. UPC § 2-403.

The UPC permits the personal representative of the estate to provide an allowance of up to $2,250 per month for one year to the surviving spouse and the decedent's minor children whom the decedent was obligated to support and also those children who were in fact being supported by the decedent. UPC §§ 2-404, 405. Note that while the exempt property award and the allowance may help to tide the family over during the period of probate administration, as financial protection for the surviving family they are not terribly generous.

Many states also provide homestead protection for the surviving spouse and certain of the decedent's children. In some states, the home and a generous amount of contiguous land may be included in the award, free of the claims of the decedent's general creditors. In contrast, some states do not set aside realty, but instead provide for a homestead allowance free of the claims of the decedent's general creditors. As its name implies, the homestead allowance is a monetary award. The UPC incorporates the allowance approach and suggests a homestead allowance of $22,500 for the surviving spouse; if no surviving spouse exists, the allowance is divided among the decedent's minor and dependent children. UPC § 2-402.

2. Testamentary Succession (Wills)

A will allows an individual—the testator—to direct the distribution of her estate according to her wishes. Testamentary freedom is said to be a hallmark of American inheritance law. Even so, significant limitations on testamentary freedom exist.

a. Execution

American courts traditionally demanded strict adherence to the execution requirements of the applicable statute of wills. If the execution deviated from those requirements, courts often refused to probate the document even though it clearly represented the desires of the decedent. Courts in some states now recognize a will despite execution errors, as long as the execution is in substantial compliance with the statute of wills.

The UPC even includes a harmless error rule that allows a court to probate a document not executed in compliance with the statute of wills as long as the will proponent demonstrates with clear and convincing evidence that the decedent intended the document to be her will. UPC § 2-503. Even in states where the court has such a dispensing power to ignore flaws in execution, the good lawyer will carefully supervise the execution to ensure that all of the statutory requirements are met.

i. Attested Wills

Most wills are formal wills attested by witnesses. These are the only kinds of wills permitted in about one-half of the states. The remaining states recognize a formal, attested will, but also permit a testator to prepare an informal, handwritten ("holographic") will that does not require witness signatures. The UPC recognizes both forms of wills. UPC § 2-502.

The statutory requirements for attested wills vary among the states. Generally, the will must be signed by the testator or by someone acting on his behalf, in his presence, and at his request. (The ability to use a proxy signature can be extremely important for the physically incapacitated testator.) The formal will also requires the signatures of witnesses. Most states require the signature of two individuals requested by the testator to serve as witnesses to the will execution. A couple of states require three witnesses. Placement of the signatures may be important in some jurisdictions.

Witnesses should not be beneficiaries of the will, for a number of states void or limit devises to interested witnesses. (Statutes limiting bequests to interested witnesses are often a trap for the testator who prepares her own will.) In most states that limit devises to an interested witness, however, the signature of an interested witness is ignored if it is not necessary for the will to be properly executed. In other words, if the state only requires two witnesses, and the interested witness and two disinterested witnesses sign the will, the limitation does not apply. The UPC does not limit devises to interested witnesses. UPC § 2-505.

Under the statutes of many states, the witnesses must sign in the presence of the testator. Some states also require the witnesses to sign in the presence of each other. Even if the state does not impose such requirements, the prudent practice is to ensure that all of the signatures are obtained when the testator and witnesses are gathered together and that each sees the other sign the will.

Most well-drafted wills provide for witnesses to sign following an "attestation clause." The attestation clause states, in essence, that the testator is of sound and disposing mind and acting free from undue influence and duress. This language is intended to help prove the testator's capacity and intent. The attestation clause also tracks the execution requirements of the statute to help prove that the execution was proper. Thus the clause will state, for example, that the testator acknowledged the document as his will; that the testator signed the document before the witnesses; that the testator requested the witnesses to sign the document; and that the witnesses then signed the document in the testator's presence and in the presence of each other. In sum, a properly drafted and signed attestation clause will provide a presumption that the testator possessed capacity, that the testator intended the document to be her will, and that the will was properly executed.

Many lawyers now routinely attach an affidavit to the will at the time of its execution so that the will can be self-proved during the probate process. The affidavit contains a signed statement by the testator of his capacity and intent and a signed statement by the witnesses that includes the same information contained in an attestation clause. (If the affidavit is not included at the time of will execution, it may be executed and attached to the will at a later time.) When the testator dies, the sworn, acknowledged statements of the testator and witnesses generally allow the will to be probated without the need to call the witnesses before the probate court. Thus, the self-proving affidavit expedites the probate process. The UPC self-proved will provision is found in Section 2-504.

ii. Holographic Wills

As mentioned earlier, about half the states permit an individual to prepare and sign a handwritten will. Often such holographic wills are written by individuals who do not trust lawyers or want to pay for their services. Unfortunately, this mistrust and frugality often results in a confusing document that ultimately must be construed in a will contest. Laypersons often use legal terms imprecisely in their holographic wills. Moreover, when an individual once writes a holographic will, she is very likely to write others. If she produces several such holographic wills that are undated and that have inconsistent provisions, more confusion arises. Although modern courts will generally strive to accomplish the testator's intent, ascertaining intent from a poorly written holographic will or a series of inconsistent, undated holographic wills can be extremely difficult.

Not all holographic wills present interpretation problems. Some are written carefully and precisely and function as effectively as formal, attested wills. A lawyer may even recommend that a client execute a holographic will in some testator's intent, ascertaining intent from a poorly written holographic will or a series of inconsistent, undated holographic wills can be extremely difficult.

Not all holographic wills present interpretation problems. Some are written carefully and precisely and function as effectively as formal, attested wills. A lawyer may even recommend that a client execute a holographic will in some instances, such as when the client is dying and there is no time to prepare and execute a formal attested will. The holographic will can also be useful to the testator who has a formal, attested will to govern the distribution of the principal items of value in her estate, but who frequently changes her mind about the distribution of many small items of tangible personalty. If such a testator limits her holographic will to those small items of tangible personal property, often she will do no harm to the overall estate plan carefully prepared by her lawyer in accordance with her wishes. The practical difficulty, however, is constraining the testator/client once she begins to draft holographic wills. (The UPC and a number of states provide a better alternative than the holographic will for bequeathing tangible personalty outside the principal will document. This alternative, which allows the testator to list such items and their intended recipient in a signed writing made at any time, is discussed later in this chapter.)

The requirements for a valid holographic will vary. Some states require the entire document to be in the handwriting of the testator; others require the material parts or portions to be in the testator's handwriting. The UPC, again reflecting more liberal developments, requires only that the material portions be in the testator's handwriting. UPC § 2-502(b). Some states require the testator's signature at the end of the document, while others permit the signature anywhere within the document.

In states taking a stringent approach to holographic wills, courts may refuse to probate a document that is not entirely in the testator's handwriting. For example, courts in such states may refuse to accept as a holographic will a form will with pre-printed passages supplemented by the handwritten wishes of the testator. This is so even if the decedent's intent and wishes are clear. Courts in such states would also probably refuse to allow the testator to incorporate by reference provisions from other documents that are not in the testator's handwriting. In contrast, a court employing the UPC approach would generally recognize such documents as valid holographic wills so long as the material portions were in the testator's handwriting. Even if the material portions were found not to be in the testator's handwriting, a court employing the UPC approach could still permit probate of the holographic and nonholographic materials under the harmless error rule, as long as clear and convincing evidence demonstrated that the decedent intended the entire document to be his will.

b. Revocation

An individual's testamentary desires may change over time. Such changes are particularly likely to occur when the natural objects of her bounty change, as often happens following marriages, divorces, births, and deaths. Thus the individual may want or need to update her will from time to time. Her new will may completely or partly revoke the older will, depending upon the circumstances and the laws of the jurisdiction.

i. Generally

A will can be revoked by a revoking document or by a physical act of revocation. Most states also provide for automatic revocation (i.e., revocation by operation of law) in some instances.

(a) Revocation by Writing

The typical document of revocation is a subsequently-executed will with a clause that expressly revokes all previous wills of the testator. A subsequently-executed will without such a clause will nonetheless revoke any or all parts of an earlier will that are inconsistent with the provision of the later will. Under the UPC, a subsequent will that does not contain an express revocation clause is presumed to replace rather than supplement an earlier will if the subsequent will contains a complete disposition of the estate. UPC § 2-507(c). If the subsequent will does not contain a complete disposition of the estate, the subsequent will is presumed to supplement the earlier will. In the latter case, the only provisions revoked in the earlier will are those that are inconsistent with the subsequent will. UPC § 2-507(d).

Today, most states also recognize a document that merely revokes all prior wills without providing for an alternative distribution of the estate; however, the document must be executed in compliance with the statute of wills to be effective.

(b) Revocation by Physical Act

The testator may revoke a will by her physical act performed on the will with the intent to revoke. The physical act of revocation may also be performed by a third party in the presence of the testator and at her request. Physical acts of revocation include burning, tearing, canceling, obliterating, or destroying the will or any of its parts. Courts have noted that revocation by physical act is often inherently ambiguous. If the testator was a chain smoker who had singed many items with cigarette ashes, do burn marks on her will indicate her intent to revoke? When physical act revocation is alleged, courts are likely to admit extrinsic evidence liberally in an effort to ascertain the testator's intent.

Most states permit partial revocation by physical act. For example, a testator may partly revoke her will by marking through a specific provision but otherwise leaving the document intact. Other states do not permit partial revocation of a will by physical act. In such states, the will must stand or fall in its entirety when physical act revocation is alleged.

Wills often contain one or more codicils, which are provisions that supplement the underlying will. The codicil itself is a testamentary document and must be executed in compliance with the statute of wills. Traditionally, revocation of a codicil has no effect on the validity of the underlying will. In contrast, revocation of the underlying will typically also serves to revoke the codicil.

Codicils can create confusion about the testator's wishes, especially when a will contains several codicils. (Problems grow even worse if some of the codicils are undated or are not numbered.) Today, word processing programs can easily generate a new will document that includes the client's amended wishes. In light of this modern development, careful lawyers now often avoid the use of codicils. When the client wants to amend her will, the lawyer simply amends the language of the original document in the word processing file, prints the entire new document containing the amendments, then supervises the execution of that document. In this manner, no codicil is necessary and the questions that codicil sometimes cause are avoided.

(c) Revocation by Operation of Law

Revocation of a will or some of its provisions may occur by operation of law. State statutes often provide that divorce of the testator revokes all will provisions for the testator's ex-spouse. The UPC provides not only for automatic revocation of provisions for the ex-spouse, but also for revocation of all provisions for the relatives of the ex-spouse. UPC § 2-804. (Note, however, that provisions for the testator's issue with the ex-spouse are not revoked.) The same rules apply in the event of the annulment of the testator's marriage.

Slayer statutes can also cause a revocation by operation of law. In most states, a slayer statute prevents a killer from benefitting financially from the person whom he feloniously and intentionally killed. In such instances, the killer cannot take under the will of his victim. The UPC slayer statute is found in Section 2-803. The UPC generally provides that persons precluded from taking by operation of law are treated as though they had disclaimed their interests. UPC § 2-803(e). The precise effect and requirements of slayer statutes vary among the states.

State statutes may include other instances of revocation by operation of law. For example, some states revoke a testator's will if, after will execution, the testator marries and has children. In a few states, a spouse who has abandoned the testator may not take under the testator's will. A noteworthy development in the field of elder law is the increased adoption of statutes that preclude abusers of elderly or vulnerable adults from benefitting from the estates of their victims. (For more discussion of this topic, see Chapter 1.)

ii. Revival

A testator may revive a will that she has revoked. Assume that Tess, a testator, executes Will 1, which contains a complete disposition of her estate. Later, Tess executes Will 2, which also contains a complete disposition of her estate. Yet later, Tess tears up Will 2 with the intent to revoke it. What happens to Will 1?

As with most will doctrines, the rules of revival depend upon state law. In one group of states, Will 1 automatically springs back to life, or is revived, when Tess tears up Will 2. (Courts in some of these states may not reach this conclusion if Will 2 contained a clause expressly revoking Will 1.) In a second group of states, courts do not automatically revive Will 1, but instead search for Tess's intent concerning revival. Her intent will determine whether Will 1 is revived. In a third group of states, Tess cannot revive Will 1 by physical act revocation of Will 2; instead, she must re-execute Will 1 or she must execute a new will that brings the provisions of Will 1 back to life.

In the scenario described above, the UPC presumes that Will 1 remains revoked, but nonetheless allows revival if evidence indicates that the testator wished to revive Will 1. UPC § 2-509(a).

Now suppose that Tess did not tear up Will 2, but instead executed Will 3, which revoked Will 2 and did not contain a complete disposition of the estate. The UPC provides in this circumstance that Will 1 is not revived except to the extent it appears from the terms of Will 3 that the testator intended Will 1 to take effect. Thus, part of Tess's estate will pass through intestate succession if Will 3 does not indicate that Will 1 is to be revived. UPC § 2-509(c).

iii. Dependent Relative Revocation

Under the doctrine of dependent relative revocation (DRR), a court will ignore the testator's revocation of a testamentary document if the revocation was based on the testator's mistake of law or fact and if the testator would not have made the revocation in the absence of his mistake. For example, Tom executes Will 1, leaving all of his estate to his long-term gay partner. (The state is one that does not permit gay couples to marry or enter into a civil union or register as domestic partners.) Tom later executes Will 2, leaving a small bequest to the couple's housekeeper and the remainder of his estate to his partner. When the housekeeper subsequently predeceases Tom, Tom destroys Will 2 by physical act, mistakenly believing that by doing so he is reviving Will 1. Tom, however, lives in a state where he can revive Will 1 only by re-execution or another testamentary document. Tom then dies having taken no further action regarding his estate.

Without the doctrine of DRR, Tom would die intestate and his entire estate would pass to others than his long-term partner, who was clearly the principal object of Tom's bounty. DRR, however, will allow the court to ignore Tom's revocation of Will 2, since the revocation was based on Tom's mistaken belief that he was reviving Will 1. In this manner, Will 2 is given effect and the bulk of Tom's estate will still pass to his partner.

DRR applies only when it helps to promote the testator's intent. Courts are usually generous in allowing the use of extrinsic evidence to prove the testator's probable wishes.

Courts in some states apply the doctrine liberally, others more stringently. Some courts apply the doctrine only when the revocation in question is by physical act.

c. Construction

Many doctrines and default rules exist to assist a court when construing a will. Some of the more important ones are discussed in the following paragraphs.

i. Integration

A will is integrated when all of its pages in their final form were present before the testator at the time of execution and she intended those pages to be part of her will. Later substitutions of pages or provisions cannot be probated unless they, too, are executed in compliance with the statute of wills.

ii. Incorporation by Reference

Most states and the UPC permit a testator to incorporate an extrinsic writing or parts of an extrinsic writing into the will. UPC § 2-510. For example, a testator may provide that a certain sum of money is "to pass according to the provisions of the living trust my late husband established for our relatives." At the testator's death, the probate court may refer to the provisions of the trust instrument, even though it is not a document executed by the testator in compliance with the statute of wills.

A document can only be incorporated by reference if it exists at the time the testator executes her will. The doctrine applies only if the testator intended to incorporate the extrinsic document, and the doctrine requires that the testator adequately identify the document she seeks to incorporate. Some courts require a very precise description of the document sought to be incorporated, but most courts require only a sufficient description.

Historically, most courts refused to allow a holographic will to incorporate extrinsic writings not in the handwriting of the testator. In states that take a liberal approach to holographic wills and emphasize the testator's intent, courts may allow holographic wills to incorporate non-holographic writings.

iii. Republication

When a testator executes a codicil to a will, often a presumption arises that she is in essence re-executing the entire will. In so doing, she is said to republish or ratify the original will provisions (except to the extent that they are altered by the codicil). Modern courts uphold the presumption if it furthers the intent of the testator; if not, the presumption is rebutted. Nonetheless, a lawyer representing the testator should be aware of the potential problem and take care to ascertain and indicate the testator's intent concerning republication if she executes a codicil.

For example, assume that the testator's original will devises "my current fractional interest in Blackacre to my son." At the time of will execution, the testator owns one-third of Blackacre. Two years after will execution, she purchases an additional one-third interest in Blackacre. Three years after will execution, she executes a codicil that names a new executor for her estate but says nothing about Blackacre or her desire whether to republish the underlying will. If republication applies, her son will receive the two-thirds interest. If not, he will receive only the one-third interest she originally owned. The court will attempt to ascertain her intent in making this determination.

iv. Events of Independent Significance

Events occurring after the execution of the will may affect the distribution of assets provided for under the will. This is not a problem as long as a reason exists for the event that is separate and apart from the effect of the event upon will distribution. For example, the testator may devise "my household furnishings to John." Subsequent to will execution, the testator may change her household furnishings frequently and substantially. Such a change (event) is presumably undertaken for the testator's benefit to satisfy the testator's comfort and aesthetic taste, and presents no problem at her death. John may take the furnishings. The UPC recognizes the doctrine in Section 2-512.

v. Lists of Tangible Personal Property

The UPC and some states permit the testator's will to refer to a written statement or list that will dispose of items of tangible personal property not otherwise specifically disposed of by the will. That written statement or list must be signed by the testator and must describe the tangible personalty with reasonable certainty. The writing may not dispose of money. The list can be prepared at any time. UPC § 2-513. This provision is important, for it allows a court to refer to the list even though it was prepared after the will was executed (and thus could not be incorporated by reference) and because it allows a court to refer to the list even though the only purpose of the list is to dispose of property under the will (and thus could not be considered an act of independent significance).

vi. Additions to Trusts

The UPC and most states have a statutory provision that permits the testator to devise property to the trustee of a trust even if that trust is altered after will execution or is to be established after will execution. UPC § 2-511. In the absence of such authority, probate courts had to rely on doctrines such as incorporation by reference or events of independent significance to uphold such devises when possible. Incorporation by reference could only work, however, when the trust was in existence at will execution. Moreover, changes in the trust subsequent to will execution could only be recognized by the probate court if they qualified as events of independent significance. The newer statutes permitting will additions to trusts avoid the need to rely on those doctrines.

vii. Antilapse

When a devisee predeceases the testator and the devise contains no alternative provision, the devise may lapse or it may be saved through an antilapse doctrine for the devisee's issue. If the devise lapses, it usually falls into the residue of the testator's estate; if the will has no residuary clause, then the subject of the devise will pass through intestate succession.

The UPC and most states assume that testators are not concerned about protecting devises from lapse when the devisee is someone outside her close family circle. Thus an antilapse statute will often protect devises to the testator's grandparents and their descendants. The UPC also extends antilapse protection to devises to stepchildren. It does not extend antilapse protection to devises to spouses, however. UPC § 2-603. In contrast to the limited antilapse statutes such as that of the UPC are broad antilapse statutes used in some states to protect any devisee who leaves issue.

Antilapse rules are default rules that apply only when the testator did not provide contrary provisions in her will. For example, the testator might include a devise "to my daughter Meg, but if she does not survive me by ten days, then to my son Ned." If Meg does not survive the testator by ten days, the alternate devisee Ned will receive the property. Antilapse protection does not apply for the benefit of Meg's issue because the testator has provided explicit instructions concerning the property.

In many states and under the UPC, a person is treated as having predeceased the decedent if he does not survive the decedent by 120 hours. UPC § 2-702. Under the older approach to survivorship, a person needs to survive the decedent only by a moment to be a survivor. This older, "last gasp" approach to survivorship is still employed in a number of states. The older approach can create substantial proof problems.

viii. Class Gifts

As its name implies, a class gift in a will is a devise to a group of people (e.g., "my nieces"). Antilapse questions can arise in the class gift context. In most states, if the class gift is to "my nieces" and one niece predeceases the testator but leaves issue, the issue of the predeceased niece succeed to her interest because nieces are among the relatives who are protected by the state antilapse statute. If the predeceased niece leaves no issue, however, typically the devise is divided among the remaining members of the class (i.e., the other nieces).

An increasingly practical problem involving class gifts is the interpretation of terms such as "issue," "descendants," "grandchildren," and the like. Such class gift language has become more problematic because of changing family structures and DNA evidence that can prove biological connections between people who have not lived together as family.

The UPC generally provides as a default rule that children of assisted reproduction, gestational children, nonmarital children, and adopted children are included in class gifts in accordance with the rules of intestate succession regarding parent-child relationships. UPC § 2-705. If the transferor is not the adoptive parent, however, an adopted child is not considered within the class gift to the adoptive parent's children unless (1) the adoption occurred before the adoptee was eighteen; (2) the adoptive parent was the adoptee's foster parent or stepparent; or (3) the adoptive parent functioned as a parent of the adoptee before the adoptee turned eighteen. Similarly, if the transferor is not the genetic parent, a child of a genetic parent is not considered that genetic parent's child "unless the genetic parent, a relative of the genetic parent, or the spouse or surviving spouse of the genetic parent or of a relative of the genetic parent functioned as a parent of the child" before the child's eighteenth birthday.

For example, assume that the testator leaves a substantial devise to "my grandchildren." Aware of the provision, the testator's gay son adopts his thirty-year-old partner. When the testator dies, her son's adoptee will not take part in the class gift because the adoption did not occur before the adoptee was eighteen, the adoptive parent was not the adoptee's foster parent or stepparent, and the adoptive parent did not function as the adoptee's parent before the adoptee turned eighteen. In contrast, if the adoptive parent includes a class gift to "my children" in his will, the adoptee would be included.

Even in states that have no statutory provisions similar to those of the UPC, probate courts have sometimes noted that they retain the inherent equitable power to refuse to recognize an adoption that was undertaken primarily to manipulate inheritance rights under a third party's will.

ix. Abatement and Exoneration

When the testator's assets are insufficient to satisfy her creditors and to fulfill the will devises, then the devises must abate as necessary to satisfy the creditors. Before abating devises, the testator's property unprovided for by will (i.e., passing through intestacy) will be used to satisfy her creditors. Once the property not disposed of by will is used up, the devises generally abate in the following order: (1) residuary devises; (2) general devises; and (3) specific devises. Residuary devises are characterized by will phrases that leave "the residue" or "the balance" or "everything else" to named beneficiaries. General devises are most commonly legacies (sums of money), such as "$10,000 to Jane." Specific devises are those that designate specific assets to a beneficiary, such as "my Steinway piano to Mary." A fourth category of devise, the demonstrative devise, is a hybrid. It is typically a legacy that is intended to come from a specific source, but that may be paid from general assets of the estate if necessary. For example, "$10,000 to Nick from the sale of my antique glass collection" would be a demonstrative legacy if the testator intended for Nick to have $10,000 even if her antique glass collection sold for less than that amount. A demonstrative legacy is treated as specific to the extent of the value of the intended source and as general to the extent that the source is insufficient to satisfy the legacy.

If only part of a classification of devises is required to satisfy debts, then abatement among the devisees within that classification is determined pro rata. If the testator's general devises are "$10,000 to Jan" and "$40,000 to Ken," and if $5000 from the general devises must be used to satisfy the testator's creditors, $1000 will come from Jan's legacy and $4,000 from Ken's.

Under the modern approach to abatement, states do not distinguish realty and personality. Some states, however, still engage in the older presumption that favors realty over personalty. In these states, personalty typically abates before realty.

Abatement rules are default rules that may be changed by explicit provisions in the testator's will. If the principal object of the testator's bounty is her residuary beneficiary, for example, the testator might want to indicate clearly in the will that general and specific devises are to abate before the residuary devise. The UPC provision also permits a court to ignore the statutory abatement order if the application of that order would defeat the testator's express or implied purpose. UPC § 3-902.

Although the typical default order of abatement for devises is residuary, general, and specific, a number of states use a different default order in certain settings. For example, in some states abatement may be pro rata when the abatement is the result of an elective share awarded to the testator's surviving spouse. The testator can avoid the default rules of abatement, however, by providing an explicit order of abatement in her will.

At common law, if a testator devised specific realty subject to a mortgage, the devisee was entitled to receive the realty and to have the mortgage debt satisfied from the testator's residuary estate. This principle, known as exoneration, still applies in a number of states. In contrast, the modern approach adopted by the UPC and many states treats realty the same as all other assets. The devisee of realty subject to a mortgage receives the property subject to that debt. UPC § 2-607. Principles of exoneration and nonexoneration are default rules that a testator can alter by explicit language in her will. The UPC statute, however, indicates that a general directive from the testator such as "all of my debts are to be paid" is not enough to overcome the presumption of nonexoneration.

x. Ademption

Ademption by extinction is a principle under which a specific devise fails because the subject matter of the devise is no longer in the testator's estate at her death. Thus, if the testator devises "my 1961 Thunderbird" to John and then disposes of the Thunderbird before her death, the devise is adeemed by extinction. John receives nothing. Under the majority approach, courts examine only whether the subject matter of the specific devise is in the testator's estate at death; if it is not, the devise is adeemed. This approach (called the "identity" theory of ademption) does not investigate the testator's intent. Thus, if the testator in the earlier example had traded the 1961 Thunderbird for a 1963 Thunderbird with the intent that John receive the replacement vehicle, John would be out of luck.

A number of states have begun to reject the identity theory or at least to make significant inroads upon its arbitrary application. For example, the UPC gives a specific devisee the right to any balance of the purchase price owed to the testator at his death from the testator's sale of the property that was the subject of the devise; to any condemnation award remaining to be paid to the testator for the taking of the property; to any proceeds remaining to be paid to the testator for injury to the property; and to any real property or tangible personal property owned by the testator at death that the testator acquired as a replacement for the specifically devised property. (Thus, John would be able to take the replacement car in the example in the preceding paragraph.) In other circumstances, the UPC expressly permits the court to consider the testator's intent in determining whether ademption has occurred. UPC § 2-606.

Many states and the UPC also now have explicit provisions concerning ademption and the effect of a conservator's or agent's transfers on the will of the incapacitated ward or principal. Such provisions are often especially important for the elderly client and her intended will beneficiaries. The provisions typically state that the specific devisee is entitled to a general pecuniary devise equal to the net sales price received by the conservator or agent on account of the transfer. Similarly, the specific devisee is entitled to a general pecuniary devise equal to the amount of any condemnation award, insurance proceeds, or other recovery the conservator or agent obtains for the specifically devised property. These provisions often terminate such protection for the specific devisee, however, if a court determines that the incapacity of the principal or ward has ended and the principal or former ward then survives that determination for a defined period of time. UPC § 2-606.

Ademption by satisfaction occurs when the testator makes a devise and then makes a gift of the property during her lifetime to satisfy the devise. This form of ademption, which applies only to devises, is the counterpart of the advancement, which applies only to intestate property. States following the UPC approach invoke the ademption by satisfaction doctrine only when the will provides that the gift is to be deducted; when the testator declared in a contemporaneous writing that the gift is in satisfaction of the devise or is to be counted against the value of the devise; or when the devisee indicates in writing that the gift is in satisfaction of the devise or is to be counted against the value of the devise. UPC § 2-609. For example, if the testator bequeaths $10,000 to Ben and subsequently gives Ben $5,000 with a writing indicating that the gift is to count against the bequest, a partial ademption by satisfaction occurs. At the testator's death, Ben will receive the remaining $5,000 of his bequest.

d. Disinherited Family Members

American testators are generally free to leave their assets as they wish. In all states but Louisiana, Americans may even disinherit their minor and dependent children in the absence of a court order providing otherwise. In fact, only one family member — the testator's surviving spouse — receives significant and widespread protection from disinheritance in the United States. In separate-property states, statutes typically grant the surviving spouse a forced or elective share to protect her against disinheritance or to recognize her contributions to the marital partnership. (Exceptions exist, however. For example, Georgia permits a testator to disinherit the surviving spouse. Even in Georgia, the surviving spouse is entitled to other family protection provisions.) Community property principles protect spouses from disinheritance in community-property states.

The testator's disinheritance of family members will have no effect on certain benefits that flow from the testator and that are mandated by federal law. For example, a testator's will cannot affect his widow's eligibility and right to Social Security auxiliary benefits based on his work record.

The following discussion briefly examines the principal forms of probate protections for disinherited spouses and also examines forms of protection against the testator's inadvertent failure to provide for close family members.

i. Spousal Protection in Separate-Property States

Most states are separate-property or "common law" states. Ownership of assets by two married individuals depends upon title. For example, if the wife earns $100,000 during the marriage and places the money in a bank account in her name only, the money belongs to her. Assume that W is the sole breadwinner in the family and all of the family's significant assets are titled in her name. She executes a will leaving her entire estate to her paramour and nothing to her husband. In the absence of statutory protection against such disinheritance, the wife could in fact effectively disinherit her husband. Almost all separate-property states, however, have enacted statutes to protect substantially against this result. (As discussed previously, most states also give the surviving spouse the benefit of a family allowance, a personal property exemption, and a homestead award. Often, however, those forms of family protections are insignificant, particularly when the homestead award itself is a mere allowance.)

The principal form of statutory protection against disinheritance in separate-property states is the elective-share provision. The earliest form of elective-share provision, still used by some states, guarantees the surviving spouse a fixed portion, such as one-third, of the decedent's net probate estate. This amount is calculated without regard to the survivor's wealth and without regard to the length of the marriage. A state using this approach may have a statute that allows the surviving spouse to include in the decedent's net probate estate the value of assets the decedent transferred outside of probate with the intent to defeat the survivor's elective share. Alternatively, a state may have a statute that includes in the decedent's net probate estate the value of illusory transfers (i.e., transfers over which the decedent retained significant control). The UPC is designed to automatically consider certain assets transferred by the deceased spouse or over which he retained certain rights.

The UPC also takes a substantially different approach to the elective share. It treats marriage as a partnership endeavor. Each year during the early part of the marriage, each spouse is accruing a greater interest in the marital partnership. After fifteen years, the marriage is an equal partnership in which property owned by either spouse is considered to be marital property for elective-share purposes. When one spouse dies after that time, the statute ensures that the surviving spouse retains at least one-half of the couple's total wealth. In determining the surviving spouse's elective share, the statute thus considers the length of the marriage and the total assets (probate and nonprobate) of each spouse. UPC §§ 2-202 to -209. (Recent amendments to the UPC elective-share provisions offer states a deferred marital-property alternative. That alternative examines only property acquired during the marriage other than by gift or inheritance. UPC § 2-203 alternative subsection (b).)

The difference between the traditional elective share and the UPC elective share can be substantial. For example, assume that Betty dies survived by her husband of twenty years. Betty's will disinherits Al and devises everything to her children from a prior marriage. Betty has $90,000 of net probate assets and $90,000 of nonprobate assets. Her husband, Al, has $750,000 of probate assets (those assets that would have passed through probate had he died first) and $1,000,000 of nonprobate assets. In a state with a traditional elective-share of one-third, Al would receive $30,000 of Betty's estate (one-third of her net probate assets) even though he is far, far wealthier than Betty. Under the standard UPC elective-share calculation, Al will receive nothing. He owns more than half of the couple's marital property at Betty's death, and thus the statutory formula provides him with no protection against disinheritance.

Unlike traditional elective-share provisions, the UPC also provides a supplemental elective share for the needy surviving spouse. The UPC suggests that no surviving spouse should be left with less than $75,000 (taking into account the survivor's own wealth) if the combined marital wealth totals at least that amount. For example, now assume that Betty dies with $90,000 of probate assets that she wills exclusively to her children from a prior marriage. Al, her husband of twenty years, has no assets at her death. The principal elective-share provision of the UPC would guarantee Al one-half of the couple's marital wealth, or $45,000. The supplemental elective share, however, would ensure that he receive an additional $30,000 so that he is not left with under $75,000. In a state with a traditional elective share of one-third, Al would simply receive $30,000 and no more.

No matter how clearly stated, the deceased spouse's will provisions disinheriting the surviving spouse cannot trump the elective share. By premarital contract, however, spouses can agree to waive their surviving spouse protection, including that of the elective share. Many states also permit such a waiver in a postnuptial agreement. These contractual agreements are particularly important for many elders who wish to marry and yet preserve all or the bulk of their assets for children and grandchildren from their prior relationships.

ii. Spousal Protection in Community-Property States

An important minority of jurisdictions in the United States employs community-property principles. In these states, most property acquired by the efforts of a married couple is owned by the couple as a community. The spouses are treated as equal partners from the beginning of the marriage. Title to community-property assets is not determinative of ownership. Thus, if the husband earns $100,000 during the marriage and places it in a bank account solely in his name, the property is nonetheless community property. Each spouse has a one-half interest in the community property, and the will of one spouse cannot defeat the community-property interest of the other spouse. Consequently, no elective-share protection is generally needed.

Not all property owned by the spouses is community property, however. Each spouse retains separate ownership of the assets he or she held prior to the marriage. Each spouse also retains separate ownership of the assets he or she acquired during the marriage with such pre-marital assets. Moreover, assets one spouse receives by gift, devise, or inheritance during the marriage are the separate assets of the recipient. Unwittingly or not, spouses often comingle separately-owned assets with community property. When questions arise concerning ownership, tracing the provenance of the assets can be difficult, and a presumption in favor of community property often applies.

When a married couple moves from a separate-property state to a community property state, the separately-owned assets they previously acquired do not change their character. Those assets remain separate property. Because married couples today may live in several states over the course of their marriage, the discrepancies between the separate-property and community-property systems can present problems. Assume that Betty and Al, a married couple, move from a separate-property state to a community-property state upon Al's retirement. Substantially all of the couple's assets are titled in Al's name and remain so after the move. Al disinherits Betty and dies. Under traditional community-property principles, Betty would be unprotected, since the couple has no community property. Several community-property states, however, have now adopted a quasi-community-property statute or other protective statute designed to provide for the surviving spouse when the couple had assets earned in a separate-property state. Such a statute, for example, may allow the court to recharacterize property earned during the marriage as "quasi-community property" and to award the survivor a one-half interest in such property.

Problems may also arise when a married couple moves from a community-property state to a separate-property state. Assume that Al and Betty retire from a community-property state to a separate-property state that has a fixed elective share of one-third. Assume further that all of their $900,000 of assets comes from Al's earnings in the community-property state. The assets are all titled in Al's name. Al dies and his will completely disinherits Betty.

In fact, Betty needs no protection against disinheritance because she owns one-half of the $900,000. All of the $900,000 is community property because it was earned by Al during the marriage in a community-property state. Although title was in Al's name, title is not determinative of community-property ownership. Moreover, the community property retains its character even when the couple moves to a separate-property state. Thus, one would expect Betty to receive $450,000 and the remainder to pass through Al's will. This is indeed what happens in some separate-property states. A number of separate-property states have enacted the Uniform Disposition of Community Property Rights at Death Act, which is designed to ensure this result. In other separate-property states, however, Betty may attempt to claim her one-third elective share from Al's $450,000 interest. If she is successful, she will in fact wind up with substantially more than half of the marital assets.

iii. Marital Contracts

Spouses can forgo their rights to an elective share, homestead, exempt property, and family allowance by written contract, agreement, or waiver. Such waivers are commonly seen in premarital agreements. In particular, elders often want to preserve some or all of their probate assets for their children and grandchildren from prior relationships. Less common than prenuptial agreements are postnuptial agreements. In the absence of specific legislation authorizing the postnuptial agreement, some courts have struggled over the adequacy of consideration underpinning a postnuptial agreement. Some of these courts may impose more stringent requirements upon the parties seeking to create a postnuptial agreement.

The UPC recognizes both premarital and postmarital agreements and makes no distinctions between them in its provisions. UPC § 2-213. The UPC provision provides that a waiver of "all rights" to a present or prospective spouse's property or estate is a waiver of "all rights of elective share, homestead allowance, exempt property, and family allowance by each spouse in the property of the other and a renunciation by each of all benefits that would otherwise pass to him [or her] from the other by intestate succession or by virtue of any will executed before the waiver."

Importantly, several federal courts have held that a marital agreement valid under state law cannot affect the surviving spouse's right to benefits governed by ERISA unless the marital agreement also explicitly satisfies ERISA's requirements. ERISA, the federal law governing many employee benefit plans, recognizes spousal waivers only when (1) the spouse consents in writing; (2) the waiver also designates a beneficiary or form of benefits that cannot be changed without spousal consent (or the spouse expressly permits designation by the participant (the employee-spouse) without further consent); and (3) the spouse's consent acknowledges the effect of such election and is witnessed by a plan representative or a notary public. (ERISA is discussed in more detail in Chapter 6.)

iv. Premarital Wills

Some states and the UPC provide special statutory protection for the surviving spouse of a testator who executed his will before the marriage. These statutes are often called pretermitted or omitted spouse statutes. In fact, under many of these statutes, the spouse may be considered pretermitted or omitted even though she is a devisee, as long as the testator did not provide for her in contemplation of her as his surviving spouse. For example, the testator may have included a small devise for the surviving spouse in his premarital will as a token of their friendship, long before he contemplated marrying her.

Under the UPC premarital will provision, the testator's estate is divided into three parts. One part is that devised to a child of the testator born before the testator married the surviving spouse and who is not a child of the surviving spouse. A second part is that devised to a descendant of such a child or that passes by antilapse to such a child or a descendant of such a child. The third part consists of whatever remains after consideration of the first two parts.

The surviving spouse is entitled to an intestate share of the remainder amount, unless (1) evidence indicates the will was made in contemplation of the testator's marriage to the surviving spouse; (2) the will indicates that its provisions are to be effective even in the event of a subsequent marriage; or (3) the testator provided for the spouse by transfer outside the will and the testator's intent that the transfer be in lieu of a testamentary provision is demonstrated by his statements or can be reasonably inferred from the size of the transfer or other evidence. UPC § 2-301.

For example, assume that Ted devised his entire estate to his son Sam in a premarital will. Ted then married Wanda, who was not Sam's mother. Wanda would receive nothing under the statute. Because the entire estate is devised to Ted's child, there is no remaining amount to provide an intestate share to Wanda. Wanda, however, would be entitled to her elective share against Ted's estate. In contrast, if Ted had devised half of his estate to Sam and half to his friend Bill, then under the premarital will statute Wanda could take an intestate share from the one-half of Ted's estate that was devised to Bill. Alternatively, she could receive her elective share distribution if that would provide her with more of Ted's estate. She could not take under both the premarital will provision and the elective share provision, however.

v. Pretermitted Child Statutes

Most states have statutory provisions for pretermitted or omitted children of the testator. Under the UPC and a majority of states, such statutes apply only when the will does not provide for the testator's children born or adopted *after* the testator executed the will. Some state statutes, however, also protect children born or adopted before the testator executed the will, as long as the will does not provide for them.

The UPC provides for one of two potential distributions to omitted children. First, if the testator had no living child at the time of will execution, then the omitted child receives an amount equal to his intestate share, unless the will devises substantially all of the testator's estate to the child's other parent who survives and is able to take under the will. Second, if the testator has one or more living children at will execution and the will devises property to one or more of those living children, then the omitted child takes a child's portion of the property devised to the children. UPC § 2-302. For example, assume that Mary had two children, Norm and Ora, at the time of will execution. The will devised $60,000 to

Norm, nothing to Ora, and the remainder to charity. After will execution, Mary's child Peter was born. Mary then died without amending her will. If Peter is an omitted child, he will take a one-third of the $60,000. Norm receives the remaining $40,000.

A child is not pretermitted if (1) the will indicates that the omission was intentional or (2) the testator provides for the later-born or later-adopted child by transfer outside the will and the testator's intent that the transfer be in lieu of a testamentary provision is demonstrated by the testator's statements or can be reasonably inferred from the size of the transfer of other evidence. UPC § 2-302.

To avoid the imposition of such a statutory default rule, the drafter of the will should ascertain the testator's intent and clearly state that intent in the will.

e. Will Contests

By far the two most common grounds for contesting the validity of a will are lack of testamentary capacity and undue influence. Other grounds, such as fraud and duress, are much less frequently asserted.

i. Capacity

The capacity required to execute a will is quite low. Along the spectrum of capacity required to execute a legal document, the capacity required for executing a will is generally thought to be the least demanding. Thus a person who lacks legal capacity to enter into a contract may possess testamentary capacity. Even a person whose entire estate is being managed by a court-appointed conservator may possess testamentary capacity. When testamentary capacity is in question, courts examine whether, at the time of will execution, the testator knew generally what she owned, knew the objects of her bounty, and made an orderly plan of disposition that she understood.

The older the testator is at the time of will execution, the more likely it seems that disgruntled family members will challenge the testator's capacity. Several precautionary steps by the testator and her lawyer will help the will survive a challenge. If the will contains an attestation clause signed by disinterested witnesses who indicate their belief that the testator was possessed of "a sound and disposing mind" at will execution, a presumption of the testator's capacity will likely arise. The presumption is even stronger if the witnesses swear to that belief in an affidavit attached to the will. Thus the preference for a formal, attested will over a holographic will becomes even stronger if a will contest seems likely. The lawyer supervising the execution ceremony may want to ensure that the witnesses talk with the testator before the execution so that they can later testify as to the basis for their belief that she possessed capacity at the time of execution.

Some lawyers routinely give the client a standardized, written test for testamentary capacity before will execution. Other lawyers administer such a test when a threat of contest seems likely. Yet other lawyers not only find such tests unhelpful, but also believe that such tests administered selectively may raise a red flag of concern about the testator's capacity.

Testators sometimes use a penalty clause to ward off a will contest, regardless of the alleged grounds. Penalty clauses are discussed at the end of this chapter.

ii. Undue Influence

The will should embody the distributive plan chosen by a testator who is acting freely and voluntarily. A contest alleging undue influence asserts that the will in question is not a free and voluntary expression of the testator's intent, but rather represents the wishes of a third party who has exerted undue influence over the testator.

Everyone is influenced by those with whom she comes in contact, and most individuals are particularly influenced by family members. Only when the influence becomes undue, so as to destroy the testator's free agency, is the will tainted. In ascertaining whether undue influence exists, courts often look for (1) a confidential relationship between the testator and the person alleged to have committed the undue influence and (2) suspicious circumstances. In some instances, a presumption of undue influence arises automatically because of the relationship between the testator and another person in a position considered to be dominant. Among such relationships are doctor-patient, pastor-congregant, and lawyer-client. (The last of these relationships also raises questions of ethical impropriety if the lawyer drafts a will in which he is a beneficiary.) If a testator thus leaves her entire estate to her doctor instead of her family, a presumption of undue influence automatically arises. To rebut the presumption, the dominant party will have to show, typically with clear and convincing evidence, that the testator was not susceptible to undue influence or that the testator received independent, meaningful counsel before executing the will.

A person who unduly influences the testator may persuade the testator to devise assets to a third party (usually someone closely affiliated with the person exerting the undue influence). In doing so, the person exerting the undue that Gina is a bedridden elder who had always planned to leave her estate to her nieces and nephews. Fran, who is Gina's caretaker, unduly influences Gina to devise her assets to Fran's children. Even though Fran's children may be completely innocent parties, a court should refuse to probate the will based on Fran's undue influence. (With the growing concern for deterring and preventing elder abuse, state statutory law may now directly address the problem of the paid caregiver as will beneficiary. See Chapter 1.)

iii. Penalty Clauses

A testator may include a penalty clause (also called an anti-contest or in terrorem clause) in the will to reduce the probability of a will contest. For example, assume that Tina executes her will to leave the bulk of her $500,000 estate to her long-time unmarried partner. Tina is concerned that her daughter, Debbie, who is also Tina's presumptive heir, will contest the will. To help prevent a contest, Tina may include Debbie as a will beneficiary but attach a penalty clause to the provision for Debbie. Tina might thus include a $100,000 legacy for Debbie, but further provide that if Debbie contests the will, the $100,000 is to be added to the bequest to Tina's partner. In that scenario, Debbie may have to make a difficult choice. If Debbie successfully contests the will and Tina thereby dies intestate, Debbie will receive the entire estate. If, however, Debbie unsuccessfully contests the will, then Debbie receives nothing and Tina's partner takes everything.

Modern courts do not invariably uphold penalty clauses following an unsuccessful contest. Instead, they consider whether probable cause existed for instituting the contest. This is the approach of the UPC. UPC § 2-517. In the preceding example, if Debbie unsuccessfully contested Tina's will but the court concluded that Debbie had probable cause for instituting the contest, the court would ignore the penalty clause and Debbie would still receive the $100,000 bequest.

Checkpoints

- Concerning wealth management and property transfers, you should understand that
  - Many elders wish to avoid having a guardianship or conservatorship imposed
  - Many elders use various agency and property tools, including durable powers of attorney as well as more traditional nonprobate and probate devices
- Concerning the durable power of attorney, you should understand
  - A durable power of attorney is a document executed by a principal that will allow her agent to act for her even though she is incapacitated

Checkpoints *continued*

- The distinction between a durable power of attorney immediately effective and a durable power of attorney with a springing power
- The potential advantages and disadvantages of using a durable power of attorney
- The principal distinctions between the Uniform Durable Power of Attorney 1979 and the Uniform Power of Attorney Act 2006
- The general nature of agent powers and duties
- Concerning nonprobate properties, you should understand
  - Nonprobate properties, which are properties that pass to beneficiaries outside probate
  - General principles of survivorship properties, including
    - Joint tenancies and tenancies by the entirety
    - Joint bank accounts and their difference from convenience accounts
  - General principles regarding other nonprobate assets, including
    - POD and TOD accounts
    - Totten trusts
    - Revocable trusts
    - Insurance
    - Gifts inter vivos and causa mortis
- Concerning probate properties, you should understand
  - Probate properties, which are properties that pass through the probate process at the owner's death
  - General principles of intestate succession, including
    - Methods of representation
    - The treatment of individuals in nontraditional families
  - General principles regarding family protection provisions
  - General principles regarding wills, including
    - Rules of execution
    - Methods of revocation
    - Revival and dependent relative revocation
    - Common rules of construction regarding
      - Integration, incorporation by reference, and republication
      - Events of independent significance, lists of tangible personal property, and additions to trusts
      - Antilapse, abatement, and ademption
    - The treatment of disinherited relatives, including
      - Spouses
        - In separate-property states
        - In community-property states
      - Issue
    - Bases for will contests and the treatment of penalty clauses

Chapter 4

Health-Care Decision Making

Roadmap

- Health-care decisions for the elderly often involve questions concerning
  - Informed consent
  - The refusal of life-prolonging treatment
    - By a competent patient
    - By an incompetent patient
  - Advance directives
    - Living wills
    - Durable powers of attorney for health care
  - Assistance in dying
    - Physician assisted suicide
    - Euthanasia

A. Introduction

Although one may experience health problems at any age, health-care decision making is a particularly important concern to the elderly population. Like other patients, elders are concerned about their present and future state of health. Very often, they are also concerned about death and the steps they can take to ensure that, to the extent possible, they control the manner of their death.

This chapter begins by examining the right of a patient to make an informed decision concerning her health care. It then explores how and why courts have generally concluded that a competent patient's right to refuse treatment encompasses a right to refuse life-prolonging or life-saving treatment (i.e., a so-called "right to die"). The chapter also discusses the manner in which states (and the United States Supreme Court) have treated an incompetent patient's rights in cases seeking to terminate or refuse life support.

Medicine increasingly has the tubes and tools to prolong the biological functioning of an individual's body, even if the individual is permanently unconscious. Society continues to struggle with the propriety of life-prolonging or life-sustaining treatment for incompetent patients. Individual preferences vary substantially, even within families. In the last quarter of the twentieth century, states began to enact legislation that allows a competent individual to indicate in advance the course of her treatment by her oral or written instructions or through a duly-appointed agent. Such advance directives can govern the course of her treatment if, when the time for the proposed treatment arises, she is incapable of making that decision. For many elders, such advance directives have become an integral part of their estate plan (using that term in the broadest sense). Thus, this chapter also discusses living wills, health-care powers of attorney, and the integrated statutory approach of the Uniform Health-Care Decisions Act.

The final part of the chapter examines whether a terminally-ill individual has the right to physician assistance in hastening her death. Specifically, it examines how courts have viewed the state's authority to criminalize conduct that assists a suicide. The chapter also examines Oregon's Death with Dignity Act, which was the first state statutory scheme to permit physician assistance in hastening the death of terminally ill patients. Euthanasia, in which a physician not merely assists in hastening the patient's death, but in fact actively causes the patient's death, is briefly examined at the end the chapter.

B. The Right to Be Informed

The typical patient wants to make her own medical treatment decisions. She can make a knowledgeable decision about the best court of treatment for her, however, only if she receives adequate information about her options. Thus the law generally demands that a medical provider obtain an informed consent from the patient before performing surgery or pursuing a course of treatment. This section provides an overview of the origins and meaning of the law of informed consent.

1. Informed Consent

In the landmark case of Schloendorff v. Society of New York Hospital, 105 N.E. 92 (N.Y. Ct. App. 1914), Justice Cardozo wrote, "Every human being of adult years and sound mind has a right to determine what shall be done with his own body." Thus, a doctor who performs surgery on a competent patient without her consent commits a battery under common-law principles. For example, a doctor who erroneously amputates the foot of a patient who had consented to and was scheduled for heart surgery would have no defense to the patient's battery action. Battery is an intentional tort. Because the essence of the claim is the improper touching of the patient, the plaintiff typically does not have to provide expert medical testimony and may even recover an award of punitive damages in proper cases.

Although a doctor may occasionally engage in such wrongful behavior today, typically the doctor and the patient have discussed the procedure performed and the doctor has obtained the patient's consent to that procedure. Later, however, the patient asserts that the doctor failed to provide her with adequate information for her to make an *informed* consent. It is this action — one based on a patient's allegation that she did not receive adequate information to make an informed consent — with which we are primarily concerned in our discussion of medical consent. In most (but not all) states, such actions are governed by state statutes and are treated as a form of negligence claim.

For many years following *Schloendorff*, courts routinely found that a physician could lawfully perform the medical procedure in question as long as he gave the patient advance notice of the procedure and the patient did not object. The level of required physician disclosure was thus minimal. The prevailing paradigm was that of the expert doctor who was in the best position to know and choose the course of the patient's medical treatment. In the mid-twentieth century, however, courts began to require that physicians disclose more to the patient. In Salgo v. Leland Stanford Jr. University, 317 P.2d 170 (Cal. Ct. App. 1957), the court stated that "a physician violates his duty to the patient and subjects himself to liability if he withholds any facts which are necessary to form the basis of an intelligent consent by the patient to the proposed treatment." Today, the paradigm for informed consent is based on patient autonomy. The American Medical Association's Code of Medical Ethics supports this paradigm, rejecting the older, paternalistic view of the all-knowing doctor who satisfies his disclosure obligation without providing the patient adequate information to make an intelligent consent decision.

2. Disclosure

a. What Must Be Disclosed

Modern courts do not always completely agree on what information a physician must disclose to ensure that a patient's consent is informed. Nonetheless, courts often agree on several areas of disclosure. The informed consent process first requires the doctor to inform the patient of the diagnosis. The doctor should also describe the proposed procedure or course of treatment to the patient. In describing the proposed procedure or course of treatment, the doctor should discuss the material risks inherent in that procedure or course of treatment and the probable results of the procedure or course of treatment. Increasingly, courts are also requiring the doctor to disclose comparative data on success rates.

The physician should also inform the patient of medically reasonable alternatives to the procedure or course of treatment that he is recommending. In discussing medically reasonable alternatives, the physician should describe the material risks associated with those alternatives and the probable results of those alternatives.

As just mentioned, the physician generally should disclose the probable results of the proposed procedure or course of treatment and the various medically reasonable alternatives. This prognosis generally should include not only short-term consequences of the procedure or treatment, but also its long-term effects. In proper cases, it could include information on life expectancy. For example, a physician who recommends a course of treatment in response to a patient's life-threatening cancer might be expected to inform the patient of statistical life expectancy data related to the proposed treatment. (Some doctors note that such data have little value as applied to a particular patient, however, and others simply assert the "therapeutic" privilege and refuse to reveal such information.) The physician should also typically include the patient's prognosis without any treatment. The informed consent law of some states requires such disclosure.

The physician must disclose conflicts of interest to the patient. For example, if the physician will benefit from the procedure he is recommending, he should make the benefit known to the patient. The benefit could take any of several forms. It could be financial, as when he receives a portion of the proceeds from a device he proposes to insert into the patient. It could be reputational, as when he is writing a scholarly paper on the procedure he is recommending. Along with his conflicts of interest, the physician should disclose other material factors about himself or his status that a reasonable patient would want to know. Although doctors are seldom forthcoming about personal information such as their substance abuse problems or HIV status, a reasonable patient undergoing major invasive surgery might find such information to be material. Usually failure to disclose such matters is not alleged in informed consent cases, for hospitals often establish procedures to prevent surgery by physicians whose health or abuse problems put patients at risk. Historically, doctors have not been required as part of the informed consent process to detail their experience and qualifications.

In addition to the preceding information, the doctor must always disclose any information required to be disclosed under the informed consent statutes or case law of the jurisdiction.

Finally, to the best of his ability, the doctor must answer truthfully and fully the specific questions posed by the patient. Such questions generally pertain to matters that are material to the patient, and the doctor must neither ignore those questions nor provide evasive answers to conceal information that he might rather not disclose. In Shadrick v. Coker, 963 S.W.2d 726 (Tenn. 1998) the court allowed a plaintiff's action to proceed despite the passing of a statute of repose, because the plaintiff's evidence created a genuine issue of material fact concerning whether the doctor had truthfully and fully answered the plaintiff's questions about the experimental nature of a device implanted in the plaintiff during the plaintiff's initial surgery.

b. Standard of Disclosure

As discussed in the preceding section, to obtain an informed decision from the patient, the physician must generally describe the diagnosis, the proposed treatment (and material risks associated therewith), medically reasonable alternatives (and their material risks), and the prognosis. But is the disclosure standard based on what a reasonable physician similarly situated would consider proper to describe? Or is it instead based on what a reasonable patient would consider material? States disagree. The reasonable physician standard is the older standard, and it still applies in some states. A substantial number of states have adopted a reasonable patient standard, however, and others will probably do so in coming years.

Under the older approach, a plaintiff in an informed consent case must show (1) what a reasonable physician similarly situated would disclose and (2) how the defendant-physician failed to satisfy that disclosure standard. The plaintiff will almost invariably be required to establish this disclosure standard and the defendant's deviation from the standard through the use of one or more expert witnesses. Proponents of this older approach argue that it promotes good medical practice and efficiency. They argue that it is realistic, not paternalistic, to acknowledge that the doctor is in the best position to know what information should be disclosed.

The landmark case for the newer, reasonable patient approach is Canterbury v. Spence, 464 F.2d 772 (D.C. Cir. 1972). Under this approach, the trier-of-fact determines whether the physician's failure to disclose was material from the stance of a reasonable patient in the plaintiff's position. Depending upon state law and the circumstances, the plaintiff may still need an expert to assist in proving her case. Proponents of this newer approach emphasize patient autonomy and self-determination: the patient, not her doctor, has the right to decide what is important in determining what should be done to her body.

c. Physician Defenses

When a patient alleges that her doctor failed to obtain her informed consent to the procedure or course of treatment in question, the doctor may have one or more defenses. Some of these defenses are discussed in the following paragraphs.

Courts have long recognized that the physician may not be required to obtain the patient's informed consent in a genuine emergency scenario. A doctor usually may rely on the emergency doctrine when (1) the patient is unconscious or is otherwise incapable of consenting, and the harm from failing to treat is imminent and outweighs the harm that might result from the treatment; (2) the patient has no advance directive concerning treatment in the scenario at hand or the doctor is unaware of such advance directive; and (3) the doctor has no time to secure the consent of someone authorized to make medical decisions for the patient.

Doctors sometimes withhold material information from a patient from concern that disclosure would cause the patient to become so emotionally distraught as to foreclose a rational decision by the patient. Doctors also sometimes withhold material information from concern that disclosure will exacerbate the patient's illness, complicate or hinder treatment, or lead to psychological damage or severe depression. Doctors assert that their failure to disclose in these circumstances is a therapeutic privilege. Relatively few recent cases exist in which doctors have successfully asserted the therapeutic privilege as a defense when a plaintiff alleges the doctor's failure to obtain an informed consent. Legal commentators generally criticize the so-called privilege as an easily-asserted defense that, if widely acknowledged, could swallow the general duty to disclose. While the defense does exist, even courts have noted that it must be carefully circumscribed. For example, courts have suggested that the doctor who believes disclosure to the patient is clearly inappropriate should at least attempt to make disclosure to and obtain consent from an agent with authority to make medical decisions for the patient. If the patient has no duly-authorized agent, then the doctor should make disclosure to and obtain consent from a close relative of the patient.

If a patient gave an oral informed consent but subsequently asserts that the procedure was performed without consent because her consent was not in writing, in most jurisdictions the physician will prevail. Unless state law requires an informed consent to be evidenced by a writing, the general view is that a patient may consent orally. Although doctors and hospitals routinely require consent to be evidenced by a form signed by the patient, the writing seldom provides the full range of information necessary for an informed consent. Instead, the consent form states that the consent process has been undertaken and that all of the criteria for obtaining an informed consent have been satisfied. If that process has been undertaken and all of the criteria for obtaining an informed consent have been satisfied through oral discussion, in most states the oral consent is perfectly valid.

Occasionally, a patient wants to waive her right to make an informed consent. For example, a cancer patient may tell the doctor, "I do not want to think about this at all. Do whatever you think is best. I trust you." The doctor knows, however, that there are several possible courses of treatment for the patient's cancer, each with its own risks and benefits. While waiver can be a valid defense to a plaintiff's allegation of lack of informed consent, proving the validity of a waiver can be problematic. As a general principle, one cannot waive her right to make an informed consent unless she enters the waiver knowingly. The knowledge requirement seemingly imposes some duty of disclosure on the physician. The extent of disclosure is subject to debate, however. Moreover, if the state recognizes the validity of an oral consent, one may argue that the state must also recognize the validity of a patient's oral waiver of the right to make an informed consent. These are difficult concerns that a doctor understandably should try to avoid. Today, commentators often suggest that, when a patient wishes to waive her right to make an informed consent, the doctor obtain her written permission to make disclosure to and obtain consent from her duly-authorized agent. In so doing, the doctor can avoid the waiver problem completely.

3. Causation

The plaintiff who brings an informed consent case must first prove that the physician failed to disclose the information required to be disclosed under applicable state law. Such proof alone, however, does not entitle her to prevail on her claim. Rather, the plaintiff must also prove that the inadequate disclosure resulted in injury to her. In most jurisdictions, the plaintiff may recover only if she shows that a reasonably prudent patient in her position would have chosen a different course of treatment or care had she been appropriately informed by the physician. A minority of jurisdictions employ a particular patient standard, under which the plaintiff can prove causation if she proves that she would not have consented had the physician provided adequate disclosure.

C. The Right to Refuse
Life-Prolonging Treatment

The law of informed consent acknowledges the competent patient's right to make her own decisions concerning medical treatment. She may choose procedure X over procedure Y or she may refuse any procedure whatsoever. Does her right to refuse treatment include a right to refuse life-prolonging treatment? If it does, does an incompetent patient have a similar right to refuse life-prolonging treatment? In the last part of the twentieth century, courts began to struggle with these questions, which are examined in the following subsections.

1. Competent Patients

a. Bases for the Right to Refuse Treatment

State courts have generally concluded that a competent patient has a right to refuse life-prolonging treatment. In the early case of In re Quackenbush, 383 A.2d 785 (N.J. County Ct. Prob. Div. 1978), a seventy-two year old man had advanced gangrene in both legs. Doctors testified that unless the man's legs were amputated, he would probably die within three weeks. The judge concluded that the man was competent and could refuse the amputation despite state objection.

Moreover, state courts generally do not distinguish the refusal to begin life-prolonging treatment from the refusal to continue life-prolonging treatment already in place. Thus, a competent patient who wishes to discontinue artificial life support such as a ventilator generally has a right to terminate that artificial life support. State courts typically view such a decision as part of the patient's right to direct the course of her medical treatment. They reject the argument that such a decision is tantamount to suicide; instead, they conclude that death results from the patient's underlying illness or injury. (In fact, if the patient's injuries leading to the use of life support were the result of a criminal act, the perpetrator can be prosecuted for homicide when the patient dies upon the removal of the life support at her request. Courts have rejected the criminal defendant's argument that the patient's decision to remove life support is an independent intervening cause of her death.)

Courts have disagreed about the source for the competent patient's right to refuse life-prolonging treatment. State courts in early cases often found that the right springs from the state common law, especially the law of informed consent. Other courts found that the right originated in privacy provisions of a state constitution. Some state courts suggested that the right has its origins in the privacy provisions of the federal Constitution. The United States Supreme Court, however, rejected that position in Cruzan v. Director, Missouri Department of Health, 497 U.S. 261 (1990). Instead, Chief Justice Rehnquist, writing for the Court, assumed that that a competent person has a liberty interest that permits her to refuse lifesaving hydration and nutrition under the due process clause of the fourteenth amendment of the Constitution.

In the vast majority of states, the competent individual today also has an express statutory right through living will or durable power of attorney statutes to indicate her wishes regarding the use of life-prolonging treatment. States disagree concerning the execution requirements and the precision with which she must express her desires for such documents to be legally cognizable. Nevertheless, if the applicable state law is carefully followed, the document can serve as a guide in determining proper treatment decisions if she later becomes incompetent.

b. State Interests

Although most judicial decisions (and virtually all decisions involving elderly patients) have upheld the competent patient's decision to refuse life-prolonging treatment, courts have continued to recognize that state interests may be implicated when a citizen or someone acting for her makes such a decision.

The principal state interests discussed in state court cases are the following: (1) preserving life; (2) protecting the interests of innocent third parties; (3) preventing suicide; and (4) maintaining the ethical integrity of the medical profession. (States typically assert these interests most strenuously when the patient in question is incompetent and unable to speak for herself.) In the 1990s, the United States Supreme Court also noted that the state has an interest in protecting vulnerable groups and in preventing voluntary and involuntary euthanasia.

While the state has an interest in the preservation of human life, most state courts have concluded that this interest must be balanced or reconciled with the individual's interest in refusing medical treatment, especially in scenarios involving incurable illness. Courts have occasionally allowed the state interest in protecting innocent third parties to trump a competent patient's right to refuse treatment. For example, early decisions sometimes required a parent to undergo a simple but life-saving procedure to protect her minor children from being orphaned. Most modern decisions disagree and protect the competent patient's right to refuse treatment even in such cases. Courts have sometimes noted that the state could require an individual to undergo a vaccination if necessary for public safety at large. In general, however, modern courts seldom find that the interests of third parties trump the competent patient's right to refuse life-sustaining treatment.

State courts also generally refuse to equate a decision to refuse life-prolonging medical treatment with a decision to commit suicide. Unlike the person committing suicide, the patient refusing medical treatment may have no desire to die. Moreover, the person committing suicide brings about her own death; the patient refusing life-prolonging medical treatment dies from natural causes (i.e., the underlying disease or medical problem).

The state interest in maintaining the ethical integrity of the medical profession today clearly weighs in favor of affirming the patient's right to refuse life-prolonging treatments or procedures. Although medical schools once taught that lives were to be "saved" (prolonged) whenever possible, modern medical training increasingly emphasizes the patient's right of self-determination and acknowledges the various harms that may result from prolonging a patient's life against her wishes. Doctors now often recognize that the terminally ill patient is more in need of palliative relief than life-extending treatment.

In sum, the interests of the state will rarely be substantial enough to outweigh the decision of a competent elder to refuse life-prolonging treatments or procedures.

c. Life-Prolonging Treatment Following Patient Refusal

Although a competent patient has a right to refuse life-prolonging treatment, commentators have observed that health-care providers sometimes administer such treatment despite the patient's clear refusal. In Anderson v. St. Francis-St. George Hospital, Inc., 671 N.E.2d 225 (Ohio 1996), the patient had watched the suffering of his wife after she was resuscitated. He informed his doctor that he did not want extraordinary life-saving measures to be used on him. Thus, a "no code" order was placed in his chart. Nonetheless, a nurse used a defibrillator to revive him when he developed a potentially fatal irregular heart rhythm. Two days later he had a stroke. He lived for almost two years, but was unable to walk, suffered from incontinence, had trouble speaking, needed assistance in bathing and dressing, and incurred significant medical expenses. When his estate sued his health-care providers for damages, the court found that the essence of the claim was "wrongful living." The Ohio Supreme Court concluded that there is no cause of action for such a claim, observing that it would be impossible to place a price tag on the benefit of life or to award damages on the relative merits of being versus nonbeing. Moreover, the court observed that the estate could not recover on a negligence theory, because the defibrillation was not the "but for" cause of the decedent's stroke. Rather, the defibrillation had merely extended the decedent's life, and his other health problems had caused his stroke. The court acknowledged that the estate might recover for battery, but commented that the damages would be nominal because the battery was physically harmless.

The Anderson court recognized that its holding might initially seem to allow health-care providers to freely ignore a patient's clearly-expressed desire to refuse life-prolonging treatment. The court warned, however, that medical professionals would be subject to appropriate licensing sanctions and also to liability for significant damages for battery in proper cases.

State legislatures and drafters of model acts have recognized the "wrongful extension of life" problem. In partial response, advance directives statutes now often include provisions imposing civil penalties upon health-care providers or institutions that intentionally violate a patient's instructions or advance directive. The Uniform Health-Care Decisions Act suggests that a health-care provider or institution that intentionally violates provisions of the Act (which recognizes various forms of advance directives) be liable for damages of $500 or actual damages resulting from the violation, whichever is greater, plus reasonable attorney fees. UHCDA § 10. The efficacy of such statutory provisions is questionable. Proving that the violation was intentional can be difficult, particularly when the patient was in an emergency situation. Assuming the plaintiff can establish that the violation was intentional, proving actual damages in excess of $500 may be almost impossible if a court takes the views discussed in the *Anderson* case.

In a recent Florida case, the estate representative of a deceased nursing home resident successfully alleged that a nursing home had breached its contract with the resident by taking measures to keep her alive that conflicted with the resident's living will/advance directive. The representative successfully argued that the resident's living will/advance directive was incorporated into the nursing home contract. The defendant, however, obtained summary judgment on the representative's claims under the state advance health care directive statutes and the federal patient self-determination act because the court found that no private cause of action exists under those statutes. Moreover, the representative was unsuccessful in her action for violation of the state nursing home resident's rights statutes, because the infringement she alleged did not itself cause the patient's death and the state recognized no action for wrongful prolongation of life. Scheible v. Joseph L. Morse Geriatric Center, Inc., 988 So. 2d 1130 (Fl. Dist. Ct. App. 2008).

d. Competency

In early cases, health-care providers sometimes asserted that a patient's decision to refuse life-prolonging treatment was itself an indication of the patient's incompetence. If the health-care providers could show that the patient was incompetent and had provided no instructions or advance directive while competent, the providers could then argue the need for a surrogate decision maker who might overrule the patient's refusal. State courts have increasingly acknowledged, however, that competent patients may make treatment decisions that are unusual or perhaps even manifestly incomprehensible to the reasonable person. For example, an elderly person informs a doctor that he will not undergo a simple, relatively non-invasive life-prolonging treatment. Complicating matters, the elder is experiencing fluctuations in mental lucidity. If the elder makes his refusal during lucid moments, or if the refusal is consistent with his attitudes towards life-prolonging treatment before he began experiencing mental fluctuations, courts will generally mandate that the health-care providers respect his decision.

Commentators have suggested a variety of tests for determining a patient's competency to refuse treatment. Most observers generally conclude that a competency test should require that the patient have a basic understanding of the relevant information provided to him and a basic ability to assess that information. The law increasingly demands respect for the unusual beliefs or unconventional values of individuals who possess that basic understanding and ability.

2. Incompetent Patients

a. Bases for the Right to Refuse Treatment

If a competent adult generally has a right to refuse treatment under state law or through a liberty interest protected under the Fourteenth Amendment of the federal Constitution, does an *incompetent* adult have a similar right? State courts have answered "yes," but even so their answers have varied in substantial ways. As Chief Justice Rehnquist noted in Cruzan v. Director, Missouri Department of Health, 497 U.S. 261 (1990), simply answering yes leaves many questions to be answered. If the incompetent person has a right to refuse life-prolonging treatment, someone else must make the decision for her if she left no advance directive or instructions. Who should that third-party decision maker be? How does the state ensure the integrity of a medical decision made by a surrogate?

b. Role of the Judiciary

In the early case of In re Quinlan, 355 A.2d 647 (N.J. 1976), Karen Ann Quinlan suffered severe brain damage that left her in a persistent vegetative state (PVS). A body in a PVS continues to function internally. It maintains temperature, heartbeat, digestive activity, and certain reflexive activity of muscles and nerves. The individual in the PVS, however, does not exhibit self-awareness or true consciousness. The individual is considered to be in a terminal condition, but is not considered terminally ill.

Because Nancy was not brain dead, she was alive under controlling legal and medical standards. The state had no established procedure controlling the scenario. Thus, Karen's father as guardian sought judicial permission to remove her respirator. Ultimately, the state supreme court held that her father as guardian could exercise his daughter's right to privacy by authorizing removal of her respirator upon the concurrence of various parties. The court provided for mandatory involvement of her family, attending doctors, and the hospital ethics committee. The court further noted that upon concurrence of these groups, Karen's life support could be withdrawn without any resulting civil or criminal liability on the part of any participant. (Contrary to medical expectation, Karen did not immediately die when her respirator was eventually removed.)

The following year, the Massachusetts Supreme Court disagreed with the applicable procedures established by the New Jersey Supreme Court. In Superintendent of Belchertown State School v. Saikewicz, 370 N.E.2d 417 (Mass. 1977), Joseph was a sixty-seven year old with an I.Q. of ten. He suffered from leukemia. Without treatment, he would die a relatively painless death within a matter of weeks or months. Joseph had no close relatives who wished to become involved in his treatment. The superintendent of the school where Joseph was institutionalized petitioned for a guardian for Joseph so that the guardian could make a decision concerning treatment. Evidence indicated that proposed chemotherapy would cause pain and discomfort that Joseph would not understand; however, the treatment might provide a thirty-to-forty percent chance of remission and extend his life from two to thirteen months. Balancing various factors, the court agreed with the conclusion of the guardian ad litem that Joseph should not have treatment. The Massachusetts court explicitly rejected the New Jersey approach that would entrust the decision of continuing artificial life support to the patient's guardian, family, attending doctors, and hospital ethics committee. Instead, the court concluded that the ultimate decision-making responsibility in such instances was for duly-established courts of proper jurisdiction.

Modern statutes such as the Uniform Health-Care Decisions Act typically view judicial resolution of such matters as a last resort, even when the proposed treatment is life-prolonging. Such statutes often provide a hierarchical approach to decision making for the incompetent patient. The patient's wishes are given utmost respect. The patient, when competent, may have expressed those wishes in an advance directive or instruction. If not, her agent, surrogate, or guardian may still be aware of her preferences. Under this modern approach, judicial resolution is most likely needed only in unusual settings such as those in which a family member contests the validity of an alleged advance directive, or a class of surrogates entitled to make medical decisions for the patient (such as the patient's adult children) is evenly divided about the propriety of the suggested treatment.

c. The Patient's Wishes

Today, the wishes or presumed wishes of the patient are generally of paramount concern in determining whether life-prolonging procedures or treatment are to be used or removed. This is so even when the patient is now incompetent.

When an incompetent patient was previously competent and at that time reliably expressed her wishes concerning life-prolonging treatment about the circumstances in which she now finds herself, those wishes typically must be followed. (States differ in the ways in which they gauge reliability, however.) Patients often express these wishes formally and directly, through written advance directives such as living wills or health-care powers of attorney. In such cases, little question arises as to the proper course of action.

If the incompetent patient has not previously expressed her wishes about the course of treatment in a manner legally-recognized by the state, a third party must make the treatment decision for the patient. The third party may be her duly-appointed agent, a court-appointed guardian, a surrogate (such as a family member) upon whom the decision falls by operation of state law, or even a state court itself.

When a third party must make the treatment decision for the incompetent patient, state law typically requires the third party to make the decision under the substituted judgment doctrine when possible. This doctrine, in its traditional application, requires the decision maker to act in accordance with the known wishes of the person on whose behalf the decision is made. For example, a principal may have discussed her wishes concerning life-prolonging treatment with her agent and yet have failed to explicitly include those wishes in a living will or a health-care power of attorney. If the agent were later called upon to make a decision for the principal concerning the use of life-prolonging treatment, the agent would be bound by substituted judgment principles to make the decision that the principal indicated she would have made. This is so even if the agent himself would have chosen a different course of action.

In some instances, the decision maker will not have enough information to make a decision based on substituted judgment. For example, the principal may never have indicated formally or informally her wishes concerning a particular treatment. In such an instance, her health-care agent has no basis for making a substituted judgment decision, and yet he has legal authority to act. When the decision maker has insufficient information from which to make a decision based on substituted judgment, then he must make the decision in accordance with the principal's best interest. Although best interest decisions are inherently more objective than substituted judgment decisions, modern statutes do require the decision maker to consider the principal's personal values (to the extent known) when making a best interest decision.

Courts are not always consistent or precise in their definitions and use of the terms "substituted judgment" and "best interest." Thus in *Saikewicz*, the court stated that it was making a substituted judgment decision for the sixty-seven year old patient with an I.Q. of ten. In fact, because the patient had never been able to reliably express his wishes concerning any medical treatment, the court had no basis for making a true substituted judgment decision concerning the proposed chemotherapy for the patient's leukemia. Unwittingly, the court in essence made a decision based on the patient's best interest.

d. Evidentiary Standards and the Role of Courts and Legislatures

When a family member, guardian, or other third party asserts the right of a permanently unconscious or PVS patient to refuse or cease life-prolonging treatments or procedures, how does the state ensure the integrity of the decision? May the state require clear and convincing proof that the decision comports with the patient's wishes?

In Cruzan v. Director, Missouri Department of Health, 497 U.S. 261 (1990), Nancy Cruzan had a car accident that left her comatose for about three weeks. Later she progressed to an unconscious state in which she would orally ingest some nutrition. Ultimately, gastrostomy feeding and hydration tubes were implanted in Nancy to aid in her recovery. She did not progress further, however. Her father eventually requested that the hospital terminate the artificial nutrition and hydration procedures. Unsure of their responsibilities, hospital employees refused to honor the request without court approval. Nancy's parents successfully sought judicial authorization from a state trial court. The court observed that Nancy had once made informal observations to a housemate friend that she would not wish to continue her life unless she could live "at least halfway normally." The Missouri Supreme Court reversed the trial court decision, finding that Nancy's prior remarks were not clear and convincing, inherently reliable expressions of her intent.

The United States Supreme Court affirmed the decision of the state supreme court. The Court noted that state courts may be guided in making such decisions by state constitutions, statutes, and common law, but that the question before the Court was whether the Constitution precluded Missouri from choosing the rule of decision it made. Writing for the Court, Chief Justice Rehnquist assumed that a person has a liberty interest under the Due Process Clause of the Fourteenth Amendment to refuse unwanted medical treatment. (In fact, a majority of justices—including four dissenting justices—indicated their clear belief that such a constitutional right exists.)

The Court further noted, however, that the state does have an interest in the preservation and protection of human life. The Court noted that a state may have legitimate concerns that incompetent patients will not have loved ones to act as surrogates; that family members, even when available, may not always act to protect the patient; that litigation regarding treatment may not be adversarial and thus may fail to adequately protect the patient; and that the state simply may assert an unqualified interest in preserving human life to be weighed against the patient's constitutionally protected interests. In light of these concerns, the Court concluded that a state may constitutionally impose a clear and convincing standard of proof in cases like *Cruzan*. Chief Justice Rehnquist noted that Missouri's approach mandating Nancy's continued treatment in the absence of clear of convincing evidence preserved the status quo, even if the decision were erroneous in a particular setting; in contrast, "an erroneous decision to withdraw life-sustaining treatment ... is not susceptible of correction."

Following the Supreme Court decision in *Cruzan*, new information surfaced concerning Nancy's wishes. A person with whom Nancy had worked recalled that when she and Nancy were feeding brain-damaged children, Nancy had consistently indicated that she would never want anyone to feed her if she were unable to eat on her own. A state court subsequently concluded this information was clear and convincing evidence that Nancy would not have wanted life-sustaining treatment while in a PVS. The artificial nutrition and hydration were terminated, and Nancy died a few days later.

Although some oral statements may be sufficient to satisfy a clear and convincing standard of proof concerning the withdrawal of life-prolonging treatment, most courts agree that generalized statements such as "I would never want to be a vegetable" are insufficient. Note that in those states that impose a stringent standard of proof upon the third party decision maker, some concern exists that the third party decision maker or the patient's family and loved ones will manufacture evidence to meet the clear and convincing standard of proof. There is also concern that a family will initially refuse to consent to treatment for the incompetent patient, for it appears in such states that it is more difficult to terminate existing life-prolonging treatment than to refuse it initially.

Although *Cruzan* has received much attention through the years, the great majority of states that have addressed the matter have refused to impose such a high standard of proof upon those asserting an incompetent patient's right to refuse life-prolonging treatment. (There are notable exceptions, however.) Most state court opinions or modern state advance directive statutes instead focus on the responsibility of the third party decision maker to make the decision based on principles of substituted judgment or in accordance with the patient's best interest. In these states, litigation is typically unnecessary unless someone asserts that the decision maker is acting in bad faith; on erroneous medical opinion; or without authority. Litigation may also arise if there is disagreement among a group of individuals (such as an elder's adult children) with equal decision making authority. State statutes taking this modern approach are based on the view that death and dying is a private matter, that the incompetent patient's family and loved ones typically will act in good faith, and that judges have no particular expertise in such matters and should only be involved when absolutely necessary.

One should also note the now-prevailing view that legislators also have no particular expertise that would allow them to make such decisions for a particular individual. In Bush v. Schiavo, 885 So. 2d 321 (Fla. 2004), however, the Florida legislature enacted such a law. In 1998, Theresa Schiavo was a PVS patient whose husband as guardian sought removal of her artificial life support some eight years after the heart attack leading to her condition. Theresa's parents objected. They had doctors who testified that she could recover. Theresa had no advance directive. Following much litigation, lower state courts granted the husband's request. In October 2003, the feeding tube was removed. Within a week, however, the state legislature passed a statute (known as "Terri's Law") giving the governor the power to issue a one-time stay to prevent withholding of artificial nutrition and hydration from Theresa. The governor issued the stay and litigation began again. The Florida Supreme Court ruled that the statute was unconstitutional as a violation of the separation of powers doctrine. The United States Supreme Court refused to hear the case. The United States House of Representatives tried to subpoena Theresa, her husband, and others. The United States Supreme Court then rejected an emergency appeal from the House of Representatives. In response, Congress passed an unusual piece of legislation that transferred jurisdiction of the case to a United States District Court. The district court, however, ruled in the husband's favor and the Court of Appeals for the Eleventh Circuit affirmed. Theresa ultimately died in 2005, about two weeks after the feeding tube was removed.

Many Americans—even those who believe that artificial nutrition and hydration should never be withdrawn—were appalled by the legislative acts that made the private world of a seriously incapacitated individual into a public spectacle. Criticized by many commentators for using Theresa's plight more for political purposes than from compassion, legislators currently appear unlikely to engage in such individualized legislation in future "right to die" cases.

e. Artificial Nutrition and Hydration as Medical Treatment

In a concurring opinion in *Cruzan*, Justice Sandra Day O'Connor wrote that the liberty guaranteed by the Due Process Clause of the Fourteenth Amendment to refuse medical treatment includes the right to reject artificial delivery of food and water. Four other justices agreed. Today, most legal and medical commentators accept the view that artificial provision of nutrition and hydration is a form of medical treatment that the patient may reject. The view is particularly important for those incompetent patients such as Nancy Cruzan, whose biological functioning can be prolonged for years with such artificial delivery of nutrition and hydration. A minority of observers believe that "food and water" are never medical treatment, no matter how they are provided. In their view, artificial delivery of nutrition and hydration cannot be refused under informed consent or other medical theories because no medical treatment is involved.

State legislatures often include special provisions in advance directive laws that emphasize the individual's right to refuse artificial nutrition and hydration. In many state advance directive forms, the person executing the advance directive is asked to clearly indicate her wishes concerning artificial nutrition and hydration. For example, many living will statutory forms provide that artificial nutrition and hydration will be provided unless the person checks a particular box indicating that she does not wish to have such treatment. The optional form provided under the Uniform Health-Care Decisions Act explains to the person completing it that, unless the person limits the authority of her agent, the agent will have the right to determine whether artificial nutrition and hydration will be provided.

When an incompetent patient is unconscious and has no reasonable medical expectation of recovery or is in a PVS, most states do not require clear and convincing evidence of the incompetent patient's wishes before permitting an agent, guardian, or surrogate decision maker to withhold or withdraw life-prolonging medical treatment, including the provision of artificial nutrition and hydration. Instead, state statutes or court opinions usually require the application of the substituted judgment doctrine or the best interest test, without specifically discussing a proof standard. When the incompetent patient is neither permanently unconscious, in a PVS, nor terminally ill, however, virtually all courts have agreed that a surrogate, guardian, or conservator seeking withdrawal of artificial nutrition and hydration must meet a high standard of proof.

In Conservatorship of Wendland, 110 Cal. Rptr. 2d 412 (2001), Robert was comatose for several months following a 1993 vehicular accident. He had no advance directive. His wife visited him daily and authorized treatment, including artificial provision of nutrition and hydration. Eventually he regained consciousness, but was severely disabled, mentally and physically. He could not talk, but he did demonstrate clear though inconsistent interaction with his environment. He could not walk, feed himself, eat, drink, or control his bowel and bladder functions. Years passed by. Physicians believed he was minimally conscious and unlikely to experience further cognitive recovery. On three occasions, his feeding tube became dislodged and his wife authorized surgery for reinsertion. When the tube became dislodged a fourth time, she declined to authorize the surgery. Robert's treating physician, other physicians, and the hospital ombudsman all apparently supported her decision. The twenty-member hospital ethics committee unanimously approved her decision.

Robert's mother and sister objected and obtained a temporary restraining order. Robert's wife then successfully sought to be appointed as his conservator. Her subsequent attempt to have the artificial nutrition and hydration withdrawn led to further litigation. Ultimately, the California Supreme Court held that in those exceptional cases in which a conservator proposes to end the life of a *conscious* but incompetent conservatee, the conservator must prove, by clear and convincing evidence, (1) that the decision is in accordance with the conservatee's wishes or (2) that if the conservatee's wishes cannot be proven, the decision is in the conservatee's best interest. The court affirmed the lower court's decision that the wife had failed to present such clear and convincing evidence. (Robert died of pneumonia in the month before the California Supreme Court issued its opinion.)

The California court did emphasize important distinctions between a conservator and a duly-appointed agent for health-care decisions. The court noted that a conservator is not an agent of the conservatee, is not freely designated by the conservatee, and cannot be presumed to have a special knowledge of the conservatee's health-care wishes. Thus, the court concluded that the imposition of the high standard of proof upon a conservator in the *Wendland* setting is appropriate. The same argument would apply to any decision maker not duly appointed by the incompetent-but-conscious person.

The Uniform Health-Care Decisions Act does not distinguish the conscious-but-incapacitated individual from other incapacitated individuals. The Act also does not impose a particular standard of proof upon a guardian or surrogate making a health-care decision for an incapacitated person. Rather, it simply relies upon substituted judgment and the fallback best interest test.

D. Advance Directives

A medical advance directive permits an individual to inform health-care providers and others concerning her wishes for medical treatment (including the use of life-prolonging measures, such as artificial nutrition and hydration) in the event the individual becomes incapacitated. The two most commonly-discussed forms of advance directives are durable powers of attorney for health care and so-called "living wills." In fact, older forms of advance care directives also exist. For example, an individual's oral instructions to her health-care provider are also a form of advance directive. These include instructions such as DNR ("do not resuscitate") and similar notations placed on a patient's medical chart pursuant to her oral request.

In the last quarter of the twentieth century, state legislatures across the country began to enact living will statutes that allow the patient to indicate her desired course of her treatment in the event she becomes terminally ill or is in a terminal condition. States also began to enact health-care power of attorney statutes (often called "health-care proxy statutes") that allow a competent principal to appoint a health-care agent to make medical decisions for her.

Carefully-planned advance directives can help the patient and her loved ones avoid legal, medical, religious, political, and ethical quagmires that may otherwise arise if she becomes incapacitated and in need of medical treatment. Acknowledging this fact and spurred to action in the aftermath of *Cruzan*, Congress enacted The Patient Self-Determination Act of 1991. 42 U.S.C. §§ 1395cc(f), 1396a(w). The Act requires health-care facilities participating in Medicare or Medicaid programs (1) to inform the competent adult patient about her right to make medical decisions, including her right to formulate advance directives under state law; and (2) to record in the patient's medical records whether she has an advance directive. Commentators have observed, however, that such information is often thrust upon the patient without providing her an adequate explanation of the information or a significant opportunity to act upon it. Moreover, it is the patient's responsibility to place her advance directive in the hands of the medical provider.

The following discussion examines legal issues concerning living will statutes and health-care power of attorney statutes. It also examines the Uniform Health-Care Decisions Act (UHCDA), a model act whose provisions allow the individual to complete a living will and to appoint a health-care agent in one document. The UHCDA also establishes a helpful list of default decision makers when the individual has not provided for an agent and has left no living will or other instructions. The discussion begins by examining common-law procedures when the incompetent individual has no advance directive.

1. In the Absence of an Advance Directive

When an incapacitated individual has no advance directive and state law does not create a default decision maker for her, often the process of medical decision making for her will depend upon the circumstances. In many cases, the process will be accomplished informally. In others, however, the patient's family or the medical provider will resort to judicial proceedings.

In the informal setting, medical providers will often follow the wishes of the patient's closest relatives if those relatives clearly agree upon a course of treatment (or non-treatment) and their decision does not require treatment that is medically inappropriate. When family members cannot agree or the health-care provider is concerned about potential liability should the health-care provider follow their request, court proceedings are likely to result. In such instances, the proceedings often begin with the appointment of a guardian to make medical decisions for the patient. In simple cases, the court may provide the guardian with the authority to make the particular decision in question; however, if the decision the guardian proposes to make is novel, controversial, or stringently opposed by some family members of the patient, the court may require the guardian to present evidence (often based on substituted judgment or best interest principles) supporting her proposed decision. In the latter case, proceedings may drag on for months or even years.

Acknowledging the potential problems of medical decision making for the incapacitated individual with no advance directive and no judicially-appointed guardian, a number of states have enacted statutory default provisions that allow her close relatives or others especially interested in her care (such as a domestic partner) to make medical decisions for her. The statutes usually establish a hierarchical approach to default appointment. The patient's spouse is typically first in line as the default decision maker, followed by the patient's adult children. The list of potential default decision makers varies among the states. Section 5 of the UHCDA recognizes a "surrogate" who may make medical decisions for an incapacitated patient when the patient has provided no medical instructions and has no agent or guardian to make decisions for her. The UHCDA provides the surrogate with broad powers. In contrast, some state statutes limit the range of medical decisions the default decision maker can make. For example, in some states the statute may not permit the default decision maker to refuse life-sustaining treatment for the patient; alternatively, it may permit the decision maker to authorize the removal of artificial nutrition and hydration only if the decision maker obtains physician certification that the artificial nutrition and hydration are merely prolonging the dying process and that the patient is unlikely to regain capacity.

As previously discussed, statutes providing for a surrogate or default decision maker often expressly indicate that all medical decisions should be made on the basis of substituted judgment or, if necessary as a fallback, in the best interest of the patient.

2. Living Wills

Living will statutes typically permit the capable individual (the "declarant") to indicate in a signed writing her treatment wishes if she later becomes incapacitated, is terminally ill or in a medically terminal condition and near death. Most declarants execute a living will to refuse extraordinary measures in such circumstances and to die a "natural death with dignity." Thus, living will statutes in some states are called "Natural Death" or "Death with Dignity" provisions. (Note, however, that "Death with Dignity" statutes in Oregon and Washington are not living will provisions, but rather are physician-assisted suicide laws.)

a. Execution and Revocation

State statutes usually require that the living will be witnessed or notarized. The statutes also often contain provisions that preclude interested parties from serving as witnesses to the living will or that require at least one witness to be disinterested. Depending upon state law, interested parties may include expectant will beneficiaries or heirs, those with claims against the declarant's estate, the declarant's attending physician, employees of the attending physician, and employees of any health-care facility in which the declarant is a patient at the time of execution.

Today, the vast majority of states do not require recordation of a living will. Like a testamentary will, the living will validly executed by a competent declarant remains effective until the declarant revokes it. The declarant typically may revoke her living will expressly or impliedly by writing. Thus, a signed notation on the living will by the declarant that "I hereby revoke this document" should suffice as an express revocation. An implied revocation of an earlier living will would occur if the declarant executed a new living will whose terms were inconsistent with those of the earlier living will. The declarant may also revoke the living will by an oral statement made to her health-care provider, who is to place a notation in her records concerning the revocation. Even if the method of revocation chosen by the declarant is not expressly recognized in the state living will statutes, the revocation itself is likely to be valid if it demonstrates a clear expression of the declarant's intent no longer to be bound by the living will. Thus various forms of informal extrinsic evidence should support revocation if they are sufficiently reliable as an indication of a competent declarant's revocatory intent. In fact, a few states are so concerned about erroneously enforcing a living will that they permit a declarant to revoke the living will regardless of her mental state or competency.

Many living will statutes also address the validity of a living will executed by a declarant under the laws of another jurisdiction. Today, states often recognize a living will executed by a declarant as long as the living will was executed (1) in accordance with the laws of the state being asked to recognize the living will or (2) in accordance with the laws of the state where the declarant resided at the time of execution. Even if the living will document proves invalid under applicable state law, in some circumstances it may still present clear and convincing evidence of the declarant's intentions. Such might be the case, for example, where the competent declarant reliably expressed her wishes in the writing, but a court concludes that the writing is not a living will under state law because of a de minimis flaw in execution.

b. Language and Interpretation

Statutes often indicate that a living will is enforceable when the patient suffers from a terminal illness or a terminal condition that will result in her death within a reasonably short time frame regardless of the use of life-sustaining medical treatment. Technically, a person may be in a terminal condition, such as a PVS, without being terminally ill. (The PVS patient has no chance of recovering higher cortical and cognitive function, but she may suffer no underlying illness.) State statutes, however, may define the terms terminal illness or terminal condition narrowly or broadly or may use only one of the terms. For example, a state living will statute may use the term "terminal condition" broadly to include any disease, illness, injury or condition from which there is no reasonable medical expectation of recovery. A state may define "persistent vegetative state" separately from "terminal condition."

How imminent must death be before the living will can take effect? Most state statutes do not provide a specific time frame, and the "reasonably short time" contemplated by most state statutes leaves much room for argument. Even acknowledging this wriggle room, such statutes may effectively preclude giving current effect to the living will of an incompetent person in the early stages of a terminal illness or condition who could live several years or more. The interpretation problems increase when one also considers the frequent statutory requirement that the death must be expected to occur within a reasonably short time *regardless* of the use of medical treatment. A literal interpretation of such a requirement would often mean that the living will of a PVS patient could not be given effect, because a PVS patient may live for years with the use of artificial nutrition and hydration, which today are considered to be medical treatment by the medical profession and most judicial decisions.

c. The Value and Limitations of the Living Will

State living will statutes provide an individual with the opportunity to express her desires in advance concerning future medical treatment if she later is incapacitated, in a terminal condition or suffers from a terminal illness, has no reasonable medical hope of recovery, and is likely to die within a relatively short period of time. A properly-executed living will for the patient who finds herself under these conditions provides clear and convincing evidence of her wishes. (For example, the Missouri Supreme Court in *Cruzan* indicated that artificial nutrition and hydration would not have been forced upon Nancy Cruzan had she executed a living will indicating her wishes not to have such treatment.)

The statutory requirements for a living will to become effective are many, however. Moreover, living will statutes often do not offer options for incapacitated persons who are terminally ill or in a terminal condition but who are not expected to die soon (such as some patients with Alzheimer's) or who have reasonable medical hope of recovery (such as some patients who object to treatment for personal reasons). What if, prior to becoming incompetent, such a patient indicated in her living will her clear desire to refuse life-prolonging treatment in all circumstances? A question may arise as to the current efficacy of the living will, since she is not in circumstances contemplated under the living will statute. It is increasingly clear, however, that any such question must be resolved in favor of upholding the patient's clearly expressed wishes. It is true that a court might conclude that such provisions are not a valid part of the patient's living will, since the provisions relate to circumstances not contemplated by the legislature when drafting the statute; however, other state laws—and very likely the federal Constitution—ultimately mandate recognition of the patient's clearly- and reliably-expressed desires concerning medical treatment, wherever they may be found.

Because most living will statutes are designed to apply only in very narrow circumstances, many commentators suggest that the individual execute a more flexible advance planning device, the health-care power of attorney. The individual may use the health-care power of attorney as a supplement to her living will; alternatively, because of the potentially comprehensive powers and instructions she can include within a power of attorney, she may simply rely on the power of attorney alone. As we shall see later in the chapter, some states permit the individual to complete a living will and a health-care power of attorney in one document.

3. Health-Care Powers of Attorney

In a concurring opinion in *Cruzan*, Justice Sandra Day O'Connor indicated that states may be constitutionally required to give effect to the treatment decisions of an incapacitated patient's duly-appointed proxy. Today, most commentators appear to assume that if the individual has a constitutional right to direct the course of her medical treatment, then states are indeed constitutionally bound to follow the medical treatment decisions of her duly-appointed agent under a durable power of attorney for health care (DPOAHC).

By the time of the *Cruzan* opinion in 1990, statutes in a number of states permitted a competent individual to appoint an agent to make medical decisions for her during her incapacity. Since that time, many other states have enacted DPOAHC provisions that explicitly permit the principal to appoint an agent for purposes of medical decision making. Even if the federal Constitution does not require the state to follow the decisions of the duly-appointed agent, a state's own DPOAHC statutes may do so, expressly or impliedly.

a. Execution and Revocation

Like state living will laws, state DPOAHC statutes vary in their requirements for execution. Typically DPOAHC statutes require a writing signed by the principal and two witnesses. The statutes may also require notarization; alternatively, the statutes may permit notarization to serve in lieu of the witness requirement. Like living will statutes, DPOAHC statutes may require that one or both witnesses be disinterested. Interested witnesses may include expectant heirs or will beneficiaries as well as health-care providers and their employees.

Some states provide model forms for the DPOAHC; however, any such form must allow the principal to express her wishes in detail, since the goal of the DPOAHC is to provide the individual with a flexible tool in which she can express her wishes to her agent as she believes necessary. Perhaps reflecting concern about the potential for undue influence or coercion exerted upon the principal, some state statutes preclude certain individuals (for example, the operator of a health-care institution or his employees) from being named as agent. Other statutes permit certain individuals (such as the principal's guardian) to be named agent only if the principal takes certain precautions, such as obtaining the advice of legal counsel.

A principal may prepare her own DPOAHC; increasingly, however, DPOAHCs are considered to be basic estate planning documents and are drafted by the principal's lawyer. Some states require that when the DPOAHC is drafted or prepared by someone other than the principal, the DPOAHC must incorporate a statutory warning statement to the principal that explains the importance and effect of the document.

DPOAHC statutes are typically separate and apart from durable power of attorney statutes for estate management. Some state statutes explicitly provide that the appointment of an agent for estate management gives the agent no power to act as the principal's health-care agent (or vice-versa). Even if the statutes are silent on this point, the execution requirements for the two documents may differ. In such states, the individual who seeks to combine the two forms of agency in one document must take special care to ensure statutory compliance with both sets of statutes. Most commentators suggest that if the individual wants both a DPOAHC and a durable power of attorney for estate matters, the prudent course is to execute two separate documents.

States seek to ensure that a principal who desires to revoke her DPOAHC can do so easily. Most states allow the principal to revoke the DPOAHC in writing or orally. Statutes often provide that the principal may revoke by notifying the agent; alternatively, she may revoke by notifying her health-care provider, who is to include a notation of the revocation in her medical records. It seems likely, however, that a state will recognize any clear and reliable indication from a capable principal of her desire to revoke the DPOAHC, even if the method she chooses is not specifically recognized in the statute.

When a principal revokes a DPOAHC, she may wish to obtain the document and all copies and to destroy them or clearly mark them as revoked. It is the principal's responsibility to make the agent or the health-care provider aware that she has revoked the DPOAHC. An agent who acts in good faith under the DPOAHC without knowledge that it has been revoked is generally immune from criminal prosecution and civil liability.

When one spouse designates the other as her agent under a DPOAHC and the couple subsequently divorces, state DPOAHC statutes often revoke the ex-spouse's agency power by operation of law. Such revocation reflects the legislative assumption that most individuals would not want to have an ex-spouse as a medical decision maker. Because the ultimate goal should be to effectuate the intent of the individual, however, the automatic revocation provision usually will not apply if the principal provides in the DPOAHC document that the agency designation is to remain effective even in the event of the couple's divorce.

A principal who spends substantial time living in different jurisdictions should ensure that her DPOAHC is valid in each of those jurisdictions. Fortunately, states now often recognize not only a DPOAHC executed in accordance with their own laws, but also a DPOAHC executed in compliance with the laws of the state where the principal was residing at the time of execution.

b. Medical Providers and Insurance Companies

If the health-care provider complies with the wishes of the agent based on the provider's good faith belief that the agent is duly appointed and is not acting inconsistently with the desires of the principal, the provider is not subject to criminal prosecution, civil liability, or professional disciplinary action.

Some DPOAHC statutes provide that a health-care provider is not subject to criminal prosecution, civil liability, or professional disciplinary action for failing to comply with the agent's request to withdraw health-care necessary to keep a principal alive. One presumes that state legislatures do not intend for such provisions to give any health-care provider carte blanche to substitute its decision for that of the agent in determining the propriety of life-sustaining treatment for the principal. If that were the state legislative intent, the statute might very well be unconstitutional. Instead, such provisions presumably apply to permit health-care providers to refuse to honor such a request due to matters of conscience. Such might be the case, for example, when the principal is a patient in a church-affiliated hospital and the hospital is bound by religious tenets to continue life-sustaining treatment in all circumstances. In such a case, state statutes often provide that the health-care provider is to arrange for the prompt and orderly transfer of the patient to the care of another health-care provider. Whether the transfer can in fact occur promptly depends upon the setting. In some instances, no other health-care provider may be willing to take the patient. Nonetheless, by statutorily requiring transfer of the patient to another health-care provider who will accede to the wishes of her agent, the state in theory protects the patient's right to have her wishes honored.

Many state DPOAHC statutes explicitly state that health-care providers, medical service plans, health maintenance organizations, insurers, and similar entities may not condition admission to a health-care institution (or the provision of treatment or insurance) on the requirement that the patient execute a DPOAHC. They also provide that the principal's execution of a DPOAHC does not affect the principal's existing life insurance policy or the sale, procurement, or issuance of any life insurance policy. A decision to withhold or withdraw medical treatment from a principal does not impair or invalidate her life insurance policy.

c. Rights and Obligations of an Agent

By default, the agent under a DPOAHC typically has the same rights that the principal would have concerning information about the principal's health care, including the right to receive and review medical records and to consent to the disclosure of medical records. Although the principal often wants her agent to have full access and control to such information, she may not always desire this. If the principal is giving the agent limited powers to act in special circumstances, she may want the agent to have only the information that relates to those circumstances. She can limit the agent's rights to information about her health care if she so provides in the DPOAHC.

The agent is bound to honor the known wishes of the principal. (A court may terminate or modify an agent's powers if it finds the agent has acted in bad faith.) In the absence of DPOAHC provisions to the contrary, the agent typically has priority over any other person to act for the principal. In making medical decisions, the agent thus has priority over the principal's closest relatives (including the principal's spouse) and over the principal's court-appointed guardian. Depending upon state law, a DPOAHC that bestows blanket powers upon the agent may entitle the agent not only to make medical treatment decisions, but also to make organ donations, authorize an autopsy, and even direct the disposition of the principal's remains.

In the unusual scenario in which a principal executes a living will subsequent to the execution of the DPOAHC, the living will does not typically revoke the agent's powers unless the living will indicates the declarant's intent to revoke the DPOAHC. Rather, the two documents operate together, and the agent is bound by any provisions in the living will.

4. The Uniform Health-Care Decisions Act

As previously emphasized, living will and health-care power of attorney statutes vary significantly among the states. These differences can present problems in our highly mobile society, for they mean that a person's advance directives may satisfy the laws of one state but not those of a neighboring state. State statutes that provide family members or others with default authority to make decisions for an incapacitated adult patient also differ substantially. Even within a state, legislatures have often created various health-care decision making statutes at different times, resulting in inconsistencies and confusion and, in some instances, gaps in coverage.

The Uniform Health-Care Decisions Act (UHCDA) is a comprehensive model statutory scheme designed to eliminate such inconsistencies, confusion, and gaps in coverage. The UHCDA has been adopted in several states. Far preferable to the piecemeal approach still existing in many states, the Act is likely to gain increasing importance in coming years. In fact, some states that are not currently considered UHCDA jurisdictions have begun to borrow from its provisions. (Borrowing only bits and pieces from a uniform act can create other problems if state legislatures are not careful, however.)

Promulgated in 1993, the prefatory note to the UHCDA provides an overview of the Act. The prefatory note indicates that the Act is centered on six concepts, paraphrased below:

1. *To acknowledge that the competent individual has the right to direct the course of her health care in all circumstances, even if her decision to refuse or discontinue care results in death.* She may name an agent with limited authority or with the authority to make all health-care decisions she could make. She may provide instructions or define an agent's authority as broadly or as narrowly as she desires.

2. *To provide a single, comprehensive statutory scheme to replace existing legislation.* The Act authorizes health-care decisions (a) by the individual's agent when the individual does not wish to or cannot make decisions for herself; (b) by designated surrogates (such as close family members or friends) when no agent or guardian has been appointed or is reasonably available; and (c) as a last resort, by courts.

3. *To simplify and facilitate the making of advance directives for health care.* The individual's instructions may be written or oral; a power of attorney need only to be signed, not witnessed or acknowledged; and the statute provides an optional advance directive form.

4. *To ensure, to the extent possible, that health-care decisions concerning the individual are governed by her wishes on the issues to be resolved.* An agent or surrogate must act in accordance with the individual's instructions and in accordance with her other wishes to the extent those wishes are known. When she did not provide instructions and her wishes are unknown, the agent or surrogate must act in her best interest, taking into account her personal values that are known. A guardian also must act in accordance with her instructions and cannot revoke her advance directive without express court approval.

5. *To promote compliance by health-care providers and institutions.* Providers and institutions must comply with a patient's instructions. They must comply with a reasonable interpretation of that instruction or other health-care decision made by a person authorized to make decisions for the patient. They may refuse to comply, however, for reasons of conscience or when the instruction or decision would require medically ineffective care or care contrary to applicable health-care standards.

6. *To provide a procedure for the resolution of disputes that minimizes litigation.* For cases of last resort, the Act authorizes courts to be the decision maker and specifies who may bring a petition.

Uniform Health-Care Decisions Act prefatory notes (paraphrased).

a. Definitions

Section 1 of the UHCDA contains definitions applicable throughout the Act. The Act defines capacity as "an individual's ability to understand the significant benefits, risks, and alternatives to proposed health care and to make and communicate a health-care decision." It defines an advance health-care directive as a *power of attorney for health care* or an *individual instruction*. An individual instruction is "an individual's direction concerning a health-care decision for the individual." The term broadly encompasses various forms of direction, including living wills, other writings in which the individual expresses her health-care wishes, and oral directions from the individual to be recorded in her health-care record. The individual instruction may pertain to a specific health-care matter or decision or may be general.

A "health-care decision" is one made by the individual or her agent, guardian, or surrogate. The comment to the section indicates that the term "is to be given the broadest possible construction." The definition explicitly includes a decision to provide, withdraw, or withhold artificial nutrition and hydration and all *other forms* of health care. Thus, the Act acknowledges artificial nutrition and hydration as medical treatment.

Unless an exception applies, health-care institutions (i.e., hospitals, nursing homes, residential-care facilities, home health agencies, and hospices) and health-care providers (i.e., doctors and others licensed or authorized to provide health care) must comply with a health-care decision made by a person with authority to do so. The "primary physician" is a physician named by the individual, her agent, guardian, or surrogate to have primary responsibility for the individual's health care. The primary physician is also the individual's "supervising health-care provider"; however, if the individual has no primary physician or the primary physician is not reasonably available, then the supervising health-care provider is the health-care provider who undertakes primary responsibility for the individual's health care.

b. Execution, Interpretation, and Revocation

Section 2 of the UHCDA provides that a power of attorney must be in writing and signed by the principal. The Act does not permit the oral designation of an agent. Consistent with its desire to minimize impediments to the making of advance health-care directives, the Act does not require that the written power of attorney be witnessed or acknowledged. (To encourage the practice, however, the optional form provided by the UHCDA includes spaces for the signatures of two witnesses.) The principal may authorize her agent to make any health-care decision she could have made while possessing capacity. An owner, operator, or employee of a residential long-term health-care institution where the principal is receiving care cannot be the principal's agent unless related to the principal by blood, marriage, or adoption.

The document may also include individual instructions. Thus, the Act permits the power of attorney, instructions characteristic of a living will, and other instructions to be combined in a single document.

Unless the power of attorney specifies otherwise, it becomes effective only upon a determination that the principal lacks capacity and ceases to have effect upon a determination that the principal has regained capacity. The principal's primary physician makes those determinations as well as a determination that another condition exists that affects an individual instruction or the authority of an agent, unless the written advance health-care directive specifies otherwise.

An agent is to make health-care decisions in compliance with the principal's individual instructions and other wishes of the principal known to the agent. The Act does not use the term "substituted judgment." In the absence of instructions or known wishes, the agent must make health-care decisions in accordance with the agent's determination of the principal's best interest; however, the Act provides that the agent shall consider the principal's personal values, to the extent known, when making a best interest determination.

The Act provides that an advance health-care directive is valid if it complies with the Act, regardless of when or where executed or communicated. Because the Act imposes minimal requirements for the execution of a valid advance health-care directive, almost any advance directive valid under the laws of a non-UHCDA jurisdiction will be valid in a jurisdiction that has adopted the UHCDA.

Section 3 of the UHCDA provides that an individual may revoke her advance health-care directive, in part or whole, in any manner that communicates her intent to revoke. One exception to this rule exists: an individual may revoke her designation of an agent only by a signed writing or by personally informing her supervising health-care provider. The health-care provider, agent, guardian, or surrogate who is informed of a revocation is to promptly communicate the fact of revocation to the supervising health-care provider and any health-care institution at which the individual is receiving care.

When an individual has multiple advance health-care directives with conflicting provisions, a later health-care directive is deemed to revoke an earlier one to the extent of the conflict. A decree of divorce, dissolution of marriage, legal separation, or annulment revokes a prior designation of the spouse as an agent unless the decree or a power of attorney for health care provides otherwise.

c. Optional Form

The UHCDA provides an optional form, consisting of four parts, that an individual may use to create an advance health-care directive. UHCDA § 4. The individual who uses the form is free to modify all or any part of the form. The form contains a prefatory explanation that describes in clear and succinct language the different parts of the form, the purpose of those parts, the individual's rights, and the default rules that apply to the advance health-care directive. For example, the explanation informs the individual that unless she limits the authority of her agent, her agent may make all health-care decisions, including a decision to provide, withhold, or withdraw artificial nutrition and hydration. The explanation notes that, after completing the form, the individual is to sign and date the form at the form's end. The explanation also recommends that the individual (1) request that two other persons sign as witnesses; (2) give a copy of the signed and completed form to her physician, any other health-care providers she has, any health-care institution at which she is receiving care, and her health-care agent(s) named in the form; and (3) talk to the person she has named as agent to ensure that the agent understands her wishes and is willing to take on the responsibility of making health-care decisions for her.

Part one of the form permits the individual to establish a power of attorney. The comment to the form indicates that the drafters intentionally began the form with the power of attorney to "reflect the reality that the appointment of an agent is a more comprehensive approach to the making of health-care decisions than is the giving of an individual instruction, which cannot possibly anticipate all future circumstances which might arise." The power of attorney form begins with a space for the designation of an agent. Another space follows for the optional designation of a first alternate agent to serve if the principal revokes the agent's authority or if the agent is not willing, able, or reasonably available to make a health-care decision for her. The form also includes a space for the optional designation of a second alternate agent to serve if the principal revokes the authority of her agent or first alternate agent or if they are unwilling, unable, or not reasonably available to serve.

The form states that the agent is authorized to make all of the principal's health-care decisions (including decisions to provide, withhold, or withdraw artificial nutrition and hydration) except as limited by the principal. A space then follows in which the principal may add such limitations. If the space is insufficient, the principal may include her limitations on additional sheets of paper. The form contains a box for the individual to check if she wants to make the agent's power immediately effective; otherwise, the power will become effective when her primary physician determinates that she is unable to make her own health-care decisions. The form contains a paragraph explaining the agent's obligation to act in accordance with the power of attorney, with any instructions the principal gives in the second part of the form, and with the principal's other wishes to the extent they are known to the agent. The explanation of the agent's obligation further indicates that when the principal's wishes are unknown to the agent, the agent is to make a decision in the principal's best interest, taking into account the principal's personal wishes to the extent they are known by the agent. Part one concludes with a default provision nominating the agent as guardian of the principal's person if one needs to be judicially appointed. If the agent is unwilling, unable, or not reasonably available to act as guardian, the default nomination falls upon the alternate agents in the order designated.

Like most power of attorney forms, the UHCDA form does not require the formal acceptance by an agent. The comment indicates that the drafters did not wish to add another execution formality to the advance health-care directive that might reduce further the number of individuals who would complete such a directive. Nonetheless, the comment strongly encourages practitioners to include a formal acceptance provision, for two reasons: (1) because a designated agent has no duty to act until he accepts, formal acceptance reduces the risk that an agent will refuse to act if the need later arises, and (2) formal acceptance increases the likelihood that the principal will discuss her views and personal values with the agent.

Part two of the UHCDA optional form allows the individual to indicate her instructions for health care. This part of the form includes the living will component and allows the individual to make any other instructions she wishes. The individual need not fill out this part of the form if she is content to allow her agent to make end-of-life decisions. If she wishes to complete part two, however, the form allows the individual to mark a box indicating her end-of-life wishes (1) to prolong life "as long as possible within the limits of generally accepted health-care standards" or (2) not to prolong life if (i) she has an incurable and irreversible condition that will result in her death in a relatively short time, (ii) she becomes unconscious and, to a reasonable degree of medical certainty, will not regain consciousness, or (iii) the probable risks and burdens of treatment would outweigh the expected benefits. Part two of the form also provides that, by default, artificial hydration and nutrition must be provided, withheld, or withdrawn in accordance with the wishes she has indicated concerning her end-of-life decisions; however, she may check a box that will require artificial hydration and nutrition to be provided in all circumstances. Unless she provides to the contrary, by default the form directs that she receive treatment for alleviation of pain or discomfort at all times, even if the treatment hastens her death. Finally, part two allows the individual to add other instructions or to alter the options provided by the form.

Part three allows the individual to donate her organs, tissues, or body parts upon her death. If she chooses to donate, she may limit the donation to specific organs, tissues, or body parts. Alternatively, she may donate any organs, tissues, or body parts that are needed. Unless the donor indicates otherwise, the gift can be used for transplant, therapy, research, or education purposes. If the individual does not want her donation used for some of those purposes, however, she may strike those to which she objects.

Part four of the form allows the individual to designate a primary physician and an alternate to serve as primary physician if the first doctor named is not willing, able, or reasonably available to act as primary physician.

Following part four, the form indicates that a copy of the form has the same effect as the original. At the end of the document, the individual is to sign and print her name, provide her address, and date the form. The form also contains spaces for two witnesses to sign and print their names, provide their addresses, and date the form. As previously noted, the form does not require the signatures of witnesses; however, the drafters of the Act strongly encourage the use of witness signatures.

d. Surrogates

The UHCDA recognizes the authority of a surrogate to make health-care decisions for an incapacitated individual when the individual has no agent or guardian or when her agent or guardian is not reasonably available. UHCDA § 5.

The individual may designate her surrogate by personally informing the supervising health-care provider. For those circumstances in which the individual makes no such designation or her designee is not reasonably available, the Act establishes a default list of those who may serve as surrogate. The list, in order of priority of eligibility to serve as surrogate, is as follows: the spouse (unless legally separated); an adult child; a parent; or an adult brother or sister. (The list of relatives includes those of the half-blood and by adoption.) If no one in the preceding list is reasonably available, then the surrogate may be an adult "who has exhibited special care and concern for the patient, who is familiar with the patient's personal values, and who is reasonably available." Note that the Act does not treat domestic partners or longtime companions as spouses. Although partners or companions might qualify in the final default category, they could only act if no family members higher in the priority list were willing to act or were reasonably available. Thus, a person in an unmarried, committed relationship who wants her partner to have the right to make medical decisions for her should be sure to execute the power of attorney naming the partner as agent. (If the relationship ends, however, the individual should also be sure to revoke the power of attorney if she no longer wants her ex-partner to act for her, because there is no revocation by operation of law in that circumstance.) Alternatively, an individual's oral designation of her partner as surrogate should also give the partner the authority to make decisions for the individual; however, an oral designation is perhaps more susceptible to attack than is a power of attorney.

The individual retains the right to disqualify anyone from serving as her surrogate. The individual may indicate her desire to disqualify a person either through a signed writing or by personally informing her supervising health-care provider. For example, a widowed patient without an agent or guardian might inform her supervising health-care provider that "under no circumstances is my daughter Gladys to make any medical decisions for me." If the patient has three other adult children, those other children could act as surrogate; Gladys could not.

A person who assumes the authority of a surrogate is to communicate his role to those family members in the priority list who can be readily contacted. (Any member of a class authorized to serve as surrogate may assume authority to act, even though there are other members of the class.) Like an agent, a surrogate is to make health-care decisions that comply with the patient's individual instructions and other wishes that are known. Otherwise, the surrogate is to make such decisions based on the surrogate's determination of the individual's best interest, considering the patient's personal values to the extent known.

The broad authority of the surrogate reduces the probability that health-care decisions for an individual will have to be made by a court when the individual has no agent or guardian. In fact, the UHCDA specifically states that a surrogate's health-care decision is effective without judicial approval. Nonetheless, the UHCDA recognizes that judicial resolution may be necessary in some instances, such as when multiple members of a class assume the authority to act as surrogate and are deadlocked concerning the proper course of treatment. For example, assume that an incapacitated, widowed patient's four adult children all decide to act. They disagree about the proper course of treatment. The UHCDA provides that if there is a majority view among the children, then the health-care provider shall comply with that view. If, however, the class is evenly divided, then the class and all individuals having lower priority are disqualified from making the decision. In such cases, the parties may have to seek a judicial determination to resolve the dilemma.

A surrogate may not be an owner, operator, or employee of a residential long-term health-care institution at which the patient is receiving care. An exception applies if the owner, operator, or employee is related to the patient by blood, marriage, or adoption.

To ensure the propriety of the surrogate's assumption of authority, the supervising health-care provider may require an individual claiming the right to act as surrogate to provide a written declaration under penalty of perjury that includes facts and circumstances reasonably sufficient to establish the claimed authority. The commentary notes that the health-care provider does not have a duty to investigate the qualifications of such person, however.

e. Guardians

The UHCDA contains three statements in its provision concerning decisions by a guardian. First, a guardian must comply with the ward's individual instructions and cannot revoke the ward's advance health-care directives in the absence of express authority from the appointing court. Second, unless a court order provides to the contrary, an agent's health-care decision takes precedence over a guardian's decision. Finally, as with health-care decisions by agents and surrogates, health-care decisions by guardians are effective without judicial approval. UHCDA § 6.

f. Health-Care Information and Health-Care Providers

Unless a patient's advance health-care directive provides otherwise, a person authorized to make health-care decisions for a patient has "the same rights as the patient to request, receive, examine, copy, and consent to the disclosure of medical or any other health-care information." UHCDA § 8.

Section 7 of the UCHDA imposes various obligations on health-care providers. Before implementing any health-care decision made for a patient, the supervising health-care provider, if possible, must promptly communicate to the patient the decision and the identity of the person making the decision.

When a supervising health-care provider becomes aware of the existence of a patient's advance health-care directive, a revocation of such directive, or a designation or disqualification of a surrogate, then the provider is to record that information in the patient's health-care record. If the advance health-care directive, its revocation, or the designation or disqualification of a surrogate is in writing, the provider is to request a copy. If a copy is provided, then the provider is to arrange for it to be maintained in the patient's health-care record.

A primary physician who makes or learns of a determination that a patient lacks or has regained capacity is to promptly record that information in the patient's health-care record and to communicate that determination to the patient (if possible) and to any person authorized at that time to make health-care decisions for the patient. The same rule applies if a primary physician makes or learns of another condition that affects an individual instruction or that affects the authority of an agent, guardian, or surrogate.

As a general rule, a health-care provider or health-care institution must comply with an individual instruction of the patient and with a reasonable interpretation of that instruction by a person with authority to make health-care decisions for the patient. Also, when a health-care decision is made by a person with authority to act for the patient, the provider or institution must comply with that person's decision to the same extent as if the decision had been made by the patient while having capacity. The Act contains two exceptions to these rules, however. First, the provider may decline to comply for reasons of conscience. Similarly, an institution may decline to comply if the instruction or decision is contrary to a policy of the institution that is expressly based on reasons of conscience and if the policy was timely communicated to the patient or the person then authorized to make health-care decisions for the patient. Second, a provider or institution may decline to comply if the instruction or decision would require medically ineffective health care or health care contrary to generally accepted health-care standards applicable to the health-care provider or institution.

The provider or institution that declines to comply must promptly inform the patient (if possible) and her authorized decision-maker; must provide continuing care until a transfer can be made; and, unless the patient or her authorized decision-maker refuses assistance, must make all reasonable efforts to assist in a transfer of the patient to another provider or institution willing to comply with the instruction or decision.

Tracking provisions of federal law, the UHCDA also states that a health-care provider or institution may not require or prohibit the execution or revocation of an advance health-care directive as a condition for providing health care.

g. Immunities

Section 9 of UHCDA protects health-care providers and institutions from liability for their actions made in good faith. If the provider or institution acts in good faith and in accordance with generally accepted health-care standards applicable to the provider or institution, it is not subject to civil or criminal liability or to discipline for unprofessional conduct for (1) complying with the health-care decision of a person having apparent authority (including a decision to withhold or withdraw care); (2) declining to comply with a health-care decision of a person because it believed that person lacked authority; or (3) complying with an advance health-care directive and assuming that the directive was valid when made and had not been revoked or terminated.

The same section also grants immunity from civil or criminal liability, and from discipline for unprofessional conduct, to agents and surrogates who make their health-care decisions in good faith.

h. Statutory Damages

A health-care provider or institution that intentionally violates the UHCDA is subject to liability to the aggrieved individual for $500 or actual damages resulting from the violation, whichever is greater, plus reasonable attorney fees. The $500 amount is bracketed in the Act, and the drafters suggest that a state legislature adopting the Act will need to determine for itself the proper amount necessary to effect statutory compliance by providers and institutions. UHCDA § 10.

A person who intentionally "falsifies, forges, conceals, defaces, or obliterates" an individual's health-care directive or revocation of that directive without the individual's consent is subject to liability to the individual for damages of $2,500 or actual damages, whichever is greater, plus reasonable attorney fees. The same applies to a person who "coerces or fraudulently induces" the individual to give, revoke, or not make an advance health-care directive.

The statutory comment notes that the damages provided under the section are in addition to other available remedies.

i. Miscellaneous Provisions

While the UHCDA is designed to reduce judicial involvement in the realm of private, personal health-care decisions, the Act also acknowledges that judicial relief will sometimes be necessary. The Act provides a list of those individuals and others who may petition for injunctive or other equitable relief. This list includes the patient, the patient's agent, guardian, or surrogate, as well as a health-care provider or institution involved with the patient's care. It also includes an individual who is in the priority list to serve as surrogate (i.e., various family members and also adults who have exhibited special care and concern for the patient). UHCDA § 14. The section authorizes equitable relief only. The comment to the section notes that those seeking money damages can pursue such damages through other avenues.

The Act engages in a rebuttable presumption that an individual has capacity to make a health-care decision, to give or revoke an advance health-care directive, and to designate or disqualify a surrogate. UHCDA § 11. The individual having capacity always has a paramount right to make her own health-care decisions.

Because an individual may be receiving treatment or care from several providers or even at several institutions, the Act provides that a copy of a written advance health-care directive, revocation of such a directive, or designation or disqual-ification of a surrogate has the same effect as the original. UHCDA § 12.

The Act also contains a section of general rules concerning its effect. UHCDA § 13. The fact that an individual has not made an advance health-care direc-tive, or that she has revoked an advance health-care directive, does not create any presumption concerning her intention regarding health care. Death that results from the withholding or withdrawal of health care under the Act does not constitute a suicide or homicide. It also does not legally impair or invali-date an insurance policy or an annuity providing a death benefit, regardless of any terms of the policy or the annuity to the contrary. The Act notes that it "does not authorize or require a health-care provider to provide health care contrary to generally accepted health-care standards applicable to the health-care provider or institution."

The Act also carefully notes that it "does not authorize mercy killing, as-sisted suicide, euthanasia, or the provision, withholding, or withdrawal of health care, to the extent prohibited by other statutes" of the enacting state. It is to these topics we turn in the final parts of this chapter.

E. Assistance in Dying

1. Generally

The state has an interest in preventing suicide. State statutes may allow law enforcement officials to arrest a person without a warrant if that person is at-tempting to commit suicide. State statutes may even permit a person to use non-deadly force as necessary against another person to prevent that other person from committing suicide. Most states have statutes criminalizing the act of assisting suicide. What is the relationship between the state interest in preventing suicide and medical decisions that hasten death?

Most medical ethicists and the medical profession no longer view life prolon-gation as appropriate in all cases. A terminally ill, competent patient may gener-ally exercise her right to refuse or withdraw life-prolonging treatment. Health-care providers may comply with the patient's wishes to withdraw or refuse life-prolonging treatment; further, they may provide palliative relief as she dies from the under-lying illness. Modern courts agree that such a patient is not committing suicide and that such providers are not assisting a suicide. Thus, health-care providers can facilitate the dying process by removing or withholding treatment upon the request of the patient, even though her request will clearly hasten her death. In effect, a terminally ill, competent patient whose life is dependent upon a ventilator or other life-prolonging device, medication, or medical procedure, may choose to die more quickly by refusing or terminating such treatment.

For a terminally ill, competent patient whose life is not dependent upon a ventilator or other life-prolonging device, medication, or medical procedure, the choice to die is not so easily effectuated. At the end of the twentieth century, some providers indicated that they would be willing to actively assist such patients end their lives with prescribed lethal medication if not for state laws banning assisted suicide. Some of these providers and their patients brought constitutional challenges to state assisted-suicide bans. The United States Supreme Court addressed such challenges in companion cases in 1997.

2. Assisted Suicide and the Constitution

In Washington v. Glucksberg, 521 U.S. 702 (1997), the plaintiff-doctors asserted that a mentally competent, terminally ill adult has a fourteenth-amendment due process liberty interest that extends to her personal choice to commit physician assisted suicide. The United States Supreme Court rejected the argument. The Court found that Washington's then-existing assisted suicide ban did not violate the fourteenth amendment either on its face or as applied to competent, terminally ill adults who wish to hasten their deaths by obtaining lethal medication prescribed by their doctors.

Examining the nation's history, legal traditions, and practices, the Court noted that assisted-suicide bans exist in almost every state (and indeed in almost every western democracy). Such bans are longstanding expressions of state commitment to the protection and preservation of human life. The Court observed that the constitutionally-protected right of a competent person to refuse lifesaving hydration and nutrition (which the Court had assumed in *Cruzan*) is entirely consistent with the nation's history and constitutional traditions concerning informed consent, battery, and refusal of unwanted medical treatment. In contrast, an individual's decision to commit suicide with the assistance of another has never enjoyed such legal protection. Because the asserted right was not a fundamental liberty interest, the only remaining question was whether Washington's assisted-suicide ban was rationally related to a legitimate government interest. The Court found that it unquestionably was.

Examining state interests, the Court noted that a state has an unqualified interest in the preservation of human life and need not adopt a sliding-scale approach that depends upon the medical condition and the wishes of the person whose life is at stake. The Court also noted the state's interest in preventing suicide and in studying, identifying, and treating its causes. The Court also observed the American Medical Association's conclusion that "[p]hysician-assisted suicide is fundamentally incompatible with the physician's role as healer" and noted that the state has an interest protecting the integrity and ethics of the medical profession. The Court then discussed the state's interest in protecting vulnerable groups— including the poor, the elderly, and disabled persons—from abuse, neglect, and mistakes. The Court observed that if physician-assisted suicide were permitted, many individuals might choose it to spare their families the substantial costs associated with end-of-life health care. The Court indicated that the state interest in protecting vulnerable groups goes beyond protecting them from coercion; in fact, "it extends to protecting disabled and terminally ill people from prejudice, negative and inaccurate stereotypes, and 'societal indifference.'" The Court found that assisted-suicide bans help promote a state policy that values the lives of the vulnerable no less than the lives of the young and healthy. Finally, the Court observed that a state might legitimately fear that permitting assisted suicide would lead to voluntary or even involuntary euthanasia.

In Vacco v. Quill, 521 U.S. 793 (1997), plaintiffs alleged that New York's assisted-suicide ban violated the equal protection clause of the fourteenth amendment. Pointing out that New York permits a competent person to refuse life-sustaining treatment and arguing that a terminally ill competent person's desire for physician-assisted suicide is "essentially the same thing," the plaintiffs asserted that New York's ban on assisted suicide thus violates the equal protection clause. The Court rejected the argument, finding that the distinction between assisted suicide and withdrawing life-sustaining treatment is logical, important, and certain rational. The distinction is widely recognized and endorsed in the medical profession and in our legal traditions.

The Court also examined the question of physician intent in various scenarios. The Court observed that a physician who honors a patient's request to withdraw or refuse life-sustaining medical treatment may only intend to respect the patient's wishes. Even when a doctor provides aggressive palliative care that may hasten a patient's death (something the physician is expressly permitted to do under many assisted-suicide statutes), the doctor's intent may only be to ease the patient's pain. In contrast, a doctor who assists a suicide must "necessarily and indubitably" intend that the patient "be made dead." The Court noted that it had previously recognized, at least implicitly, a distinction between "letting a patient die" and "making a patient die."

3. State Law: Oregon's "Death with Dignity" Act

The Supreme Court decisions in Glucksberg and Vacco uphold the validity of state assisted-suicide laws; however, the decisions do not mandate that states enact or maintain such provisions. In fact, the Glucksberg opinion noted that states have been engaged in a thoughtful, serious examination of physician-assisted suicide. The opinion also noted that Oregon voters had enacted through ballot initiative a "Death with Dignity Act" in 1994. That Act legalizes physician-assisted suicide for competent, terminally ill adults. Ore. Stat. Ann. §§ 127.800–.997. In late 2008, Washington voters themselves rejected the assisted-suicide ban that the United States Supreme Court had found constitutional in *Glucksberg.* The Washington statutes legalizing physician-assisted suicide went into effect in March of 2009 and are based on the provisions of the Oregon Act. Wash. Rev. Code §§ 70.245.010–.220. (In an opinion not yet released for permanent publication at the time this book goes to press, the Montana Supreme Court has ruled that a terminally ill patient's consent to physician assistance in dying provides the assisting physician with a state statutory defense against a charge of homicide as long as no consent exceptions apply. Baxter v. State, 2009 WL 5155363 (Mont. 2009).)

The Oregon Act has withstood several direct and indirect attacks on the state and federal level. In 2001, for example, then-United States Attorney General John Ashcroft issued an Interpretive Rule indicating that the use of controlled substances to assist suicide is not a legitimate medical practice and that dispensing or prescribing them for that purpose is unlawful under the Controlled Substances Act. If carried out, the rule would have led to the revocation of the drug licenses of Oregon doctors who assist suicide with drug prescriptions. In 2006, the United States Supreme Court concluded that the Controlled Substances Act does not permit the United States Attorney General to prohibit doctors from prescribing regulated drugs for use in physician-assisted suicide. Gonzales v. Oregon, 546 U.S. 243 (2006).

The Oregon Act is described below.

a. The Written Request

To initiate a written request for medication to end her life "in a humane and dignified manner," the Act requires that the person making the request be a capable adult resident of Oregon who has been determined by her attending physician and a consulting physician to be suffering from a terminal disease and who has voluntarily expressed her wish to die. She is capable if a court or her attending physician, consulting physician, psychiatrist or psychologist opines that she has the ability to make and communicate health decisions to health-care providers.

Factors demonstrating Oregon residency include, but are not limited, to the following: possession of an Oregon driver's license; registration to vote in Oregon; evidence that the person owns or leases property in Oregon; and filing of an Oregon tax return for the most recent tax year.

A "terminal disease" is an incurable and irreversible disease that has been medically confirmed and will, within reasonable medical judgment, produce death within six months. "Medically confirmed" indicates that the medical opinion of the attending physician has been confirmed by a consulting physician who has examined the patient and her relevant medical records. A "qualified patient" is one who has satisfied the statutory requirements to obtain a prescription for medication to end her life in a humane and dignified manner.

The written request must be signed and dated by the patient and witnessed by two individuals who, in her presence, attest that to the best of their knowledge and belief the patient is capable, acting voluntarily, and is not being coerced to sign the request. At least one of the witnesses must be someone who is not (1) a relative of the patient; (2) entitled to part of the qualified patient's estate by will or operation of law at her death; or (3) an owner, operator, or employee of a health-care facility where the qualified patient is receiving medical treatment or is a resident. The patient's attending physician at the time the request is signed cannot be a witness. If the patient is in a long-term care facility at the time of the written request, one of the witnesses must be an individual designated by the facility and having qualifications specified by the Oregon Department of Human Services.

b. The Attending and Consulting Physicians

The statute requires the attending physician to make the initial determination of whether the patient has a terminal disease, is capable, and has made her request voluntarily. The attending physician must also request the patient to demonstrate Oregon residency. Very importantly, the Act requires the attending physician to ensure that the patient is making an informed decision by informing the patient of the medical diagnosis; the prognosis; the potential risks associated with taking the medication to be prescribed; the probable result of taking the medication to be prescribed; and the feasible alternatives, including comfort care, hospice care, and pain control. The attending physician must refer the patient to a consulting physician for medical confirmation of the diagnosis and a determination that the patient is capable and acting voluntarily. The attending physician or consulting physician is to refer the patient for counseling if either is of the opinion that the patient may be suffering from a psychiatric or psychological disorder or depression causing impaired judgment. In that event, no medication to end a patient's life is to be prescribed until the counselor determines that the patient is not suffering from a psychiatric or psychological disorder or depression causing impaired judgment.

The attending physician also is to recommend that the patient notify her next of kin of her decision. The attending physician is to counsel her about the importance of having another person present when she takes the medication and of not taking the medication in a public place. (The Act provides that a governmental entity that incurs costs resulting from a patient terminating her life in a public place shall have a claim against her estate to recover costs and reasonable attorney fees.) The attending physician must also inform the patient of her opportunity to rescind the request at any time in any manner. The Act imposes a fifteen-day waiting period between the patient's initial oral request and the writing of a prescription for the medication, and the attending physician must offer the patient an opportunity to rescind at the end of that fifteen-day waiting period.

Immediately prior to writing the prescription, the attending physician is to verify that the patient is making an informed decision and complete all the documentation required for the patient's medical record by the statute. The information to be included is designed to ensure a voluntary, informed decision by a capable adult patient who is suffering from a terminal disease.

The attending physician is to ensure that all appropriate statutory steps have been taken before writing the prescription. The attending physician may dispense the medications directly and may also dispense ancillary medications designed to reduce discomfort, if the physician is registered as a dispensing physician with the Board of Medical Examiners, has a current Drug Enforcement Administration certificate, and complies with any applicable administrative rule. Alternatively, the attending physician, acting with the patient's consent, may contact a pharmacist and inform the pharmacist of the prescription and deliver the written prescription personally or by mail to the pharmacist. The pharmacist may then dispense the medication either to the patient, the attending physician, or an expressly identified agent of the patient.

The attending physician may also sign the patient's death certificate.

c. The Timing of Requests and the Fifteen-Day Waiting Period

To receive a prescription for life-ending medication, a qualified patient must make an oral request, a written request, and then must reiterate the oral request to her attending physician no less than fifteen days after making the initial oral request. At the time of the second oral request, the attending physician must offer the patient an opportunity to rescind the request. No prescription can be written until the attending physician has offered the qualified patient an opportunity to rescind the request. The patient may rescind her request at any time, in any manner, without regard to her mental state.

No less than fifteen days shall elapse between the patient's initial oral request and the writing of the prescription. In addition, no less than forty-eight hours shall elapse between the patient's written request and the writing of a prescription.

In sum, once the patient begins the process with her initial oral request, at least fifteen days must pass before she can receive the prescription. If her written request comes after the thirteenth day following the initial oral request, or if her second oral request comes more than fifteen days after her initial oral request, then the waiting period will be longer.

d. Reporting Requirements; Effect of Death under the Act

The Oregon Department of Human Services is to annually review a sample of records required to be maintained under the Act. Also, any health-care provider dispensing medication under the act must file a copy of the dispensing record directly with the department. Except as otherwise required by law, however, the information collected is not a public record and is not available for public inspection. Even so, the Act requires the department to generate and make available to the public an annual statistical report of information it has collected.

Under the Act, no provision in a contract, will, or other agreement, whether written or oral, is valid to the extent it affects whether a person may make or rescind a request for life-ending medication. Moreover, no obligation under a currently-existing contract can be conditioned on or affected by the making or rescinding of a request by the person for life-ending medication.

The sale, procurement, or issuance of any life, health, or accident insurance or annuity policy (or the rate charged for any policy) cannot be conditioned on or affected by the making or rescinding of a request by a person for life-ending medication. A patient's decision to ingest such medication has no effect upon a life, health, or accident insurance or annuity policy.

The Act carefully notes that nothing within its provisions is to be construed to authorize a physician or any other person to end a patient's life by lethal injection, mercy killing or active euthanasia. Actions lawfully taken under the statute are not for any purpose to be considered suicide, assisted suicide, mercy killing, or homicide.

e. Immunities, Liabilities, and Penalties

If a person participates in good faith compliance with the provisions of the Act, that person is not subject to civil or criminal liability or professional disciplinary action. (This immunity extends to those who are present when a qualified patient takes the prescribed medication to end her life.) A professional organization or association or health-care provider may not subject a person to censure, discipline, suspension, loss of license, loss of privileges, loss of membership, or other penalty for participating (or refusing to participate) in good faith compliance with the Act. A patient's request for life-ending medication or the provision of such medication by the attending physician in good faith compliance with the Act does not constitute neglect or provide the sole basis for the appointment of a guardian or conservator.

The state does not require health-care providers to honor a patient's request for life-ending medication. If a provider is unable or unwilling to carry out the patient's request for life-ending medication and the patient transfers to a new health-care provider, the prior health-care provider must transfer, upon request, a copy of the patient's relevant medical records.

One health-care provider may prohibit another provider from participating in a Death-With-Dignity request on the premises of the prohibiting provider if the prohibiting provider has notified the other provider of its policy against Death-With-Dignity requests. The statute also permits the prohibiting provider to impose certain sanctions upon the other provider for violating the policy of the prohibiting provider.

The Act contains a section imposing liability upon those who interfere with the Act. A person who without the patient's authorization willfully alters or forges a request for medication or conceals or destroys the patient's rescission of that request with the intent or effect of causing the patient's death is guilty of a Class A felony. A person who coerces or exerts undue influence on a patient to request medication for the purpose of ending the patient's life, or to destroy a rescission of such a request, is guilty of a Class A felony.

Nothing in the Act limits further liability for civil damages resulting from other negligent conduct or intentional misconduct by any person. Moreover, the statutory penalties under the Act do not preclude criminal penalties applicable under other law concerning conduct that is inconsistent with the Death-With-Dignity Act.

The Act provides a form by which a patient can request medication under the Act. The statute provides that a patient's request for medication under the Act is to be substantially in that form.

F. Euthanasia

In most physician-assisted suicide cases examined by American courts, the physician provides or would be willing to provide the means for the terminally ill, competent patient to hasten her death. Usually the means for hastening death is prescription medication, although in some instances physicians such as Jack Kevorkian have provided the patient with various contraptions or machines that allow her to release lethal chemicals into her body based on her physical movements.

With euthanasia, the physician does more than provide the means for the patient to hasten her death; the physician himself hastens the patient's death directly through lethal injection. No American jurisdiction permits euthanasia. In 1998, Jack Kevorkian went beyond providing his suicide machine to a patient; instead, he administered a lethal injection to Thomas Youk, a fifty-two year-old man suffering from amyotrophic lateral sclerosis (ALS, also known as "Lou Gehrig's disease"). Youk indicated in writing that he sought euthanasia entirely voluntarily to end his "intolerable and hopelessly incurable suffering." Kevorkian filmed the lethal injection and Thomas Youk's resulting death. The film was later shown as part of an interview with Kevorkian on television's "60 Minutes." Kevorkian explained to the interviewer that, with regard to the dying process, euthanasia provides "better control" than assisted suicide. Kevorkian was subsequently convicted of second-degree murder for his action. People v. Kevorkian, 639 N.W.2d 291 (Mich. Ct. App. 2002).

The result is unsurprising. In upholding Washington's assisted-suicide ban, the United States Supreme Court noted in *Glucksberg* in 1997 that a state may fear that permitting assisted suicide would eventually lead to voluntary and even involuntary euthanasia. The Court observed the state's legitimate concern about containing and policing assisted suicide. The Court noted the dangers of the slippery slope: once a terminally ill, competent patient has a right to a physician's assistance in prescribing lethal drugs, this right may expand to include a physician's assistance in administering lethal drugs. Eventually, family members too might participate, either directly or indirectly as agents or duly appointed surrogate decision makers.

Finally, the *Glucksberg* Court painted a disturbing picture of the legalized practice of euthanasia in the Netherlands. Although the term euthanasia typically refers to "the deliberate termination of another's life at her request," the Dutch government's own study indicated that in 1990 there were more than 1000 cases of euthanasia without an explicit request. In addition, there were almost 5000 cases in which doctors administered lethal morphine overdoses without the patients' explicit consent. The Court stated the following:

> This study suggests that, despite the existence of various reporting procedures, euthanasia in the Netherlands has not been limited to competent, terminally ill adults who are enduring physical suffering, and that regulation of the practice may not have prevented abuses in cases involving vulnerable persons, including severely disabled neonates and elderly persons suffering from dementia.

In sum, because there is no right to physician assisted suicide under the Constitution, there is also no constitutional right to euthanasia in the United States. No state has sought to legalize the practice of euthanasia.

Checkpoints

- Concerning health-care decision making generally, you should understand principles of informed consent, the right to refuse life-prolonging treatment, advance directives, and assistance in dying
- Concerning informed consent, you should understand
    - What the physician must disclose
    - The standards of disclosure
    - Physician defenses
    - The requirement of causation
- Concerning the right to refuse life-prolonging treatment, you should understand
    - The bases for a right to refuse treatment
    - The state interests that are implicated when one refuses life-prolonging treatment
    - The results when a provider ignores the patient's decision to refuse treatment
    - The problems that may arise when a third-party seeks to refuse or withdraw life-prolonging treatment from an incompetent patient, including
        - Who should be the third-party decision maker
        - Constitutionally-permissible standards of proof that a state may impose upon the party seeking to refuse or withdraw such treatment for the patient
        - The distinctions between substituted judgment and best interest decisions
- Concerning advance directives, you should understand
    - Living wills
        - Their applicability and limitations
        - General requirements under most state laws
    - Powers of attorney for health care
        - Their applicability
        - General requirements under most state laws

Checkpoints *continued*

- The Uniform Health-care Decisions Act

  - Its applicability and principal concepts

  - Its inclusion not only of provisions for living will instructions and the designation of an agent, but also provisions for a surrogate decision maker when there is no agent or guardian

- Concerning assistance in dying, you should understand

  - State assisted suicide bans

  - The United States Supreme Court rulings that uphold state assisted suicide bans against attack from those seeking physician assisted suicide

  - The general way in which "Death with Dignity" statutes apply in Oregon and Washington to permit physician assisted suicide in very limited circumstances

  - That no constitutional right to euthanasia exists in the United States, and that no state has attempted to legalize euthanasia

Chapter 5

Age Discrimination in Employment

Roadmap

- The federal Age Discrimination in Employment Act (ADEA) protects covered individuals forty and older
- ADEA applies to
  - Hiring and firing decisions
  - Terms and conditions of employment
  - Employer advertisements
- ADEA sets forth various employer defenses
- ADEA lawsuits include those based on claims of
  - Disparate treatment
  - Disparate impact
  - Retaliation
- ADEA remedies include
  - Injunctive relief
  - Back pay
  - Reinstatement or front pay
  - Costs and attorney fees
  - Liquidated damages

A. Overview

The Constitution does not protect employees from age discrimination by private employers. Even a state may engage in age discrimination under the Constitution as long as the age classification in question is rationally related to a legitimate state interest. By the mid-1960s, however, Congress became concerned that a practice of age discrimination based on inaccurate stereotypes was depriving the country of the services of many competent and dedicated older workers. To redress this problem, Congress enacted the Age Discrimination in Employment Act ("ADEA") in 1967.

The ADEA states that its purpose is "to promote employment of older persons based on their ability rather than age; to prohibit arbitrary age discrimination in employment; [and] to help employers and workers find ways of meeting problems arising from the impact of age on employment." 29 U.S.C. §621.

In general, the ADEA is designed to prevent and redress age discrimination against employees and job applicants who are at least forty years old. In its first two decades, the ADEA included an upper age cap at which ADEA protected ended. Since 1987, however, the ADEA's protection applies without any upper age cap. The Supreme Court has held that employers may favor an older employee over a younger one without violating the ADEA, even when both employees are within the protected age group. The ADEA does not prevent or redress age discrimination against employees under age forty.

This chapter discusses the application and limitations of the ADEA. From the outset, however, we should note that many states have their own statutes prohibiting age discrimination in employment. Such state statutes are often called "state ADEAs" or "little ADEAs." Although this chapter occasionally mentions state ADEAs, the details of such state statutes are beyond the scope of the chapter. Nonetheless, be aware that these state ADEAs play an important role in redressing age discrimination in employment; moreover, they may provide protection beyond that provided in the federal ADEA.

B. Law and Regulations

The ADEA statutes are found at 29 U.S.C. §§ 621–634. References to "the Secretary" within ADEA refer to the Secretary of Labor of the United States. The ADEA statutes empower the Equal Employment Opportunity Commission (EEOC) (1) to issue rules and regulations that it considers necessary or appropriate for carrying out the ADEA and (2) to establish reasonable exemptions to and from ADEA provisions that it finds necessary and proper in the public interest. The principal regulations for the ADEA begin at 29 C.F.R. 1625.1.

The statutes and the regulations are available at the EEOC website, www.eeoc.gov. The website also contains many other helpful documents concerning ADEA laws and claims, including the EEOC Compliance Manual and enforcement guidelines. These latter documents lack the force of law, but constitute informed judgment that courts often consider.

C. The ADEA's General Prohibitions

The ADEA makes it unlawful for an *employer* (1) to fail or refuse to hire or to discharge any individual or otherwise discriminate against any individual with respect to compensation, terms, conditions, or privileges of employment, because of such individual's age; (2) to limit, segregate, or classify employees in any way that would deprive or tend to deprive any individual of employment opportunities or otherwise adversely affect his status as an employee, because of such individual's age; or (3) to reduce the wage rate of any employee in order to comply otherwise with the ADEA. 29 U.S.C. 623(a).

The ADEA makes it unlawful for an *employment agency* "to fail or refuse to refer for employment, or otherwise to discriminate against, any individual" because of his age. An employment agency also cannot "classify or refer for employment any individual on the basis of such individual's age." 29 U.S.C. §623(b).

The ADEA also provides that *labor unions* cannot exclude or expel individuals from membership or otherwise discriminate against individuals because of their age. It is unlawful for a labor union "to limit, segregate, or classify its membership, or to classify or fail or refuse to refer for employment any individual, in any way which would deprive or tend to deprive any individual of employment opportunities, or would limit such employment opportunities or otherwise adversely affect his status as an employee or as an applicant for employment, because of his age." Labor unions also may not "cause or attempt to cause an employer to discriminate against an individual" in violation of these rules. 29 U.S.C. §623(c).

The ADEA prohibits discrimination by an employer against any employee or applicant for employment who has opposed any practice generally forbidden by the ADEA, or who has made a charge, testified, assisted, or participated in any manner in an ADEA investigation, proceeding, or in ADEA litigation. The statute effectively prohibits employer retaliation against employees or job applicants who oppose the employer's ADEA violations or who participate in an ADEA claim against the employer. The prohibition against retaliation also extends to employment agencies and labor unions. 29 U.S.C. §623(d).

Under the ADEA, employers cannot print or publish, or cause to be printed or published, any employment notice or advertisement that indicates "any preference, limitation, specification, or discrimination, based on age." 29 U.S.C. §623(e). Similar restrictions extend to employment agencies and labor unions. Because of these restrictions, help wanted notices or advertisements that express a preference for younger applicants, for example by using terms and phrases such as "age 25 to 35," "young," "college student," "boy," or "girl," may violate the ADEA unless an exception applies. Conversely, employers may post help wanted notices or advertisements that express a preference for older individuals, using terms and phrases such as "retirees," or "supplement your pension." The regulations indicate that help wanted notices or advertisements that ask applicants to disclose or state their age do not, in themselves, violate the ADEA. The regulations further indicate, however, that such notices or advertisements will be scrutinized closely to ensure that such requests were made for a lawful purpose; moreover, such notices or advertisements must contain a statement clearly indicating to the applicant that the ADEA prohibits age discrimination against individuals at least forty years of age.

The ADEA contains detailed rules concerning the treatment of employee pension benefit plans. In general, an employer, employment agency, or labor organization cannot establish or maintain a defined benefit plan that requires or permits the cessation of an employee's benefit accrual, or the reduction of the rate of an employee's benefit accrual, because of his age. An employer, employment agency, or labor organization cannot establish or maintain a defined contribution plan that requires or permits the cessation of allocation to an employee's account, or the reduction of the rate at which amounts are allocated to an employee's account, because of age. 29 U.S.C. §623(i).

An employer, employment agency, or labor organization may, however, observe an employee pension benefit plan provision that imposes (without regard to age) a limitation on the amount of benefits that the plan provides, or a limitation on the number of years of service or years of participation that are taken into account for purposes of determining benefit accrual under the plan. Also, the ADEA pension plan provisions are not violated solely because an employee pension benefit plan provides for the attainment of a minimum age as a condition of eligibility for normal or early retirement benefits.

D. Covered Employment

1. Private Employment

The ADEA's definitions effectively exempt most small private employers from its general coverage provisions. The ADEA defines "employer" as "a person engaged in an industry affecting commerce who has twenty or more employees for each working day in each of twenty or more calendar weeks in the current or preceding calendar year." 29 U.S.C. §630(b).

References in the regulations to an employer refer in fact to employers, employment agencies, and labor unions. By regulation, an employment agency is a covered employer regardless of the number of employees the agency may have.

The statutory definition of employee states, somewhat circuitously, that an employee is "an individual employed by any employer." The definitions of employer and employee have resulted in significant litigation concerning who is an ADEA-covered employee and who is an ADEA-covered employer.

a. Determining Employee Status

The ADEA itself provides virtually no guidance in determining who is an employee. The United States Supreme Court, however, has agreed with EEOC guidelines and emphasized that a common-law test should be used in determining employee status under federal antidiscrimination acts.

An individual who is paid for his work may be an independent contractor, and not an employee, if he retains control over his work in a manner dissimilar from that of an employee. Such is often the case when the individual has control or discretion over his schedule, provides his own tools or instruments, does not receive employee benefits or employee tax treatment by the employer, and so forth. For example, if John works for an employer (or for several different employers) as an independent contractor, he is not an ADEA-protected employee. If the employer regularly pays nineteen employees and John, then none of the employees is ADEA protected because the employer does not have twenty employees.

Can a shareholder, director, vice-president, or partner be an ADEA-protected employee? The answer is yes. It is the right of control, and not an individual's title, that determines whether he is an employee. The EEOC guidelines, cited with approval by the Supreme Court, provide various questions to assist in determining employee status. Among them are the following: Can the organization hire or fire the individual or set the rules and regulations of his work? Does the organization supervise the individual's work? Does the individual report to someone higher in the organization? Is the individual unable to influence the organization? Did the parties not intend that the individual be an employee, as expressed in written agreements or contracts? Is the individual excluded from sharing in the profits, losses, and liabilities of the organization?

In determining whether an individual is an employee, generally no one factor is determinative. Courts and the EEOC guidelines indicate that all the incidents of the relationship should be considered. Note, for example, that an entry-level or mid-level partner in a large organization may have little control over his job responsibilities and may have no management responsibilities at the organization; in fact, he may be subject to virtually all of the decisions of a small group of senior, managing partners. In such a case, he may be an employee for ADEA purposes even though his title indicates that he is a "partner."

b. "Twenty or More Employees"

To be subject to the ADEA, the employer must have twenty or more employees for each working day in each of twenty or more calendar weeks in the current or preceding calendar year. The EEOC Compliance Manual counts employees by examining the employer's payroll records for a given week. Any employees who are on the regular payroll (even if they are only part-time or temporary employees) for that entire week are counted. The Supreme Court has approved this approach in a case involving Title VII. (Title VII uses the same definition of "employer" as the ADEA, but imposes only a fifteen-employee per week threshold.)

If facts support piercing the corporate veil, an ADEA plaintiff may combine the number of employees from a parent corporation and its subsidiary to satisfy the twenty-employee threshold. For example, if Subco fires Kathy because she is sixty-five, but Subco has only ten employees, Kathy may still have a valid ADEA claim if she demonstrates that Subco is an integrated enterprise with Parentco, which has fifteen employees.

The twenty weeks must be within one calendar year, but they do not have to be consecutive. For example, if Acme employs twenty employees for sixteen weeks early in the current year and then twenty employees for four more weeks towards the end of the year, Acme is an ADEA-covered employer. This is so even if the alleged discrimination occurs between those two periods, when Acme did not have twenty or more employees. Moreover, because Acme has twenty employees for each of twenty weeks in the current year, it will also be an ADEA-covered employer in the next year, regardless of how many employees it has during that year.

It now appears that the twenty-employee threshold is not an absolute requirement for a court to have subject matter jurisdiction over an ADEA claim. In a 2006 Supreme Court case under Title VII, the employer-defendant first asserted—after the close of the trial on the merits—that it did not have the requisite number of employees. The employer further asserted that its failure to meet the employee-numerosity threshold deprived the court of subject matter jurisdiction. The Supreme Court disagreed, finding that the employee-numerosity threshold related instead to the merits of the claim and had been conceded by the employer when it failed to timely object. In light of the similarities between the definitions of employer under the ADEA and Title VII, the decision presumably extends to ADEA actions.

Even if an ADEA defendant can timely and successfully assert that it does not satisfy the twenty-employee requirement, the ADEA plaintiff is not necessarily without further recourse. State ADEAs or their counterparts may apply to employers with fewer than twenty employees. (Incidentally, some state ADEAs have no lower age threshold at which protection begins; instead, they prohibit age discrimination against employees of any age.)

c. Nonprofit, Charitable, and Religious Organizations

To be subject to ADEA, the employer also must be engaged in "an industry affecting commerce." The term is construed very broadly to cover all activities affecting commerce to the extent permitted by the Constitution. The term includes non-profit and charitable activities.

The ADEA does not expressly exempt religious organizations from its employer mandates. When faced with claims of age discrimination against a religious organization, courts have generally focused on the nature of the employment in question. For example, the decision of a church to fire a janitor is likely to be substantially different from its decision to fire a pastor, even when both of the discharged individuals are within the protected age group. In an ADEA action, the employment decision concerning the janitor is unlikely to involve judicial entanglement in first amendment religious concerns. There is little reason for the case not to proceed. The discharge of the pastor, however, may very well give cause for a court to refuse to hear the alleged ADEA action. If the pastor's action would require the court to become entangled in church doctrine and religious tenets, the court might find that the claim is so pervasively religious that any judicial review would pose a significant risk of first amendment infringement.

d. Operations in Foreign Countries

If an American employer controls a company whose place of incorporation is a foreign country, prohibited acts by that company are typically attributed to the American employer. Whether an employer controls a company is determined by (1) the interrelationship of operations, (2) common management, (3) centralized control of labor relations, and (4) common ownership or financial control of the employer and the corporation. For example, assume that Ann is forty-five years old and works overseas as an employee of a company incorporated overseas but controlled by an American employer. Ann will typically be treated as an ADEA-covered employee as long as the American employer itself is covered by ADEA. (Note also that if Ann works overseas as an employee of an American company that is an ADEA-covered employer, she is also typically protected by the ADEA.)

Section 623(f)(1) provides that it is not unlawful for an employer to take actions otherwise prohibited under the ADEA when such practices involve an employee in a workplace in a foreign country and compliance with the ADEA would cause such employer or a corporation controlled by such employer to violate the laws of the country in which the workplace is located.

EEOC policy and judicial opinions have also concluded that the ADEA applies to an overseas company operating in the United States if the company has twenty employees. Courts have not agreed whether the twenty-employee threshold must be satisfied solely by counting employees within the United States or instead can be satisfied by examining the total number of company employees wherever located.

2. State and Federal Employment

The ADEA statute defines employer to include a state and its political subdivisions, agencies, and instrumentalities. (The statute further provides that the term "employee" does not include any person elected to public office in any state or political subdivision of any state; any person chosen by such officer to be on such officer's personal staff; or an appointee on the policymaking level or an immediate adviser with respect to the exercise of the constitutional or legal power of the office.)

Despite the statutory language, the applicability of ADEA to the state as an employer was severely curtailed by a Supreme Court decision in 2000. In Kimel v. Florida Board of Regents, 528 U.S. 62 (2000), the Supreme Court concluded that the ADEA does not validly abrogate the states' sovereign immunity under the eleventh amendment. The Court concluded that, in enacting the relevant ADEA provisions, Congress (1) had failed to demonstrate any significant pattern of unconstitutional discrimination by states when it included them as employers under the ADEA and (2) had no reason to believe that such prophylactic legislation was necessary.

Following *Kimel*, a private citizen may not bring an ADEA action for damages against a nonconsenting state. The *Kimel* Court, however, stated that its opinion did "not signal the end of the line for employees who find themselves subject to age discrimination at the hand of their state employers." The Court suggested that individuals would still be protected against such discrimination by state ADEAS, which exist in almost every state.

Importantly, the *Kimel* decision does not bind the EEOC (the federal agency charged with enforcing the ADEA). Thus, while a private individual himself may not be able to obtain the relief he would otherwise seek from the state, the EEOC may still be able to do so. Notably, the EEOC's enforcement mandate permits it to bring suit on behalf of an individual against whom a state employer has engaged in ADEA discrimination.

Section 633a of ADEA extends protection against age discrimination to federal government employment.

E. Employer Defenses and Exceptions

The ADEA provides several affirmative defenses for employers under section 623(f). These include the bona fide occupational qualification defense, the "reasonable factor other than age" defense, the bona fide seniority system defense, the bona fide employee benefit plan defense, and the good cause defense. The statutes also permit age discrimination in specified conditions relating to the employment of law enforcement officers, firefighters, and bona fide executives or high policymakers.

1. Bona Fide Occupational Qualification

The ADEA does not prohibit an employer from taking actions otherwise generally prohibited where age is a bona fide occupational qualification (BFOQ) reasonably necessary to the normal operation of the particular business. This defense is intended to be quite narrow, however. If an employer is sued under the ADEA and asserts the BFOQ defense, the employer has the burden of proving that the age limit is reasonably necessary to the essence of the business, and either that (1) all or substantially all individuals excluded from the job involved are in fact disqualified or (2) that some of the individuals so excluded possess a disqualifying trait that cannot be ascertained except by reference to age.

In employee challenges to employer mandatory retirement age policies, employers have often successfully asserted the BFOQ defense when the employment is intimately connected to public safety. If the employer's goal is public safety, however, the ADEA requires that the employer prove that the challenged practice does indeed effectuate that goal and that there is no acceptable alternative that would better advance that goal or equally advance it with less discriminatory impact.

2. Reasonable Factor Other Than Age

An employer may take actions otherwise generally prohibited under the ADEA when the action is based on a "reasonable factor other than age" (RFOA). The employer has the burden of showing that the RFOA exists factually.

Whether an RFOA exists is determined on the basis of all the particular facts and circumstances surrounding each individual situation. For example, the

ADEA does not protect an older worker from job loss that results from an employer's legitimate reduction in force (RIF) or reorganization. If the employer actually uses age as a limiting criterion, however, then of course the RFOA defense is unavailable.

If the employer asserts that an employment practice (including a test required by the employer) is an RFOA and evidence indicates that the practice has an adverse impact on individuals within the protected age group, the practice can only be justified as a business necessity. For example, a test that required the job applicant to identify top pop and rock bands and singers of the past several months would probably eliminate from contention most older applicants. Use of the test would be an ADEA violation unless the tests were a business necessity, which it is unlikely to be unless the essence of the business requires a knowledge of current trends in pop and rock music.

3. Bona Fide Seniority Systems

The ADEA permits an employer to observe the terms of a bona fide seniority system that is not a subterfuge to evade the purposes of the ADEA. A bona fide seniority system must be based on length of service as the primary criterion for the equitable allocation of available employment opportunities and prerogatives among younger and older workers; however, the system may be qualified by such factors as merit, capacity, or ability.

The statute explicitly indicates that no bona fide seniority system shall require or permit the involuntary retirement of a covered employee because of his age.

4. Bona Fide Employee Benefit Plans

An employer may observe the terms of a bona fide employee benefit plan where, for each benefit or benefit package, the actual amount of payment made or cost incurred on behalf of an older worker is no less than that made or incurred on behalf of a younger worker. The employer may also observe the terms of a bona fide employee benefit plan that is a voluntary early retirement incentive plan.

No employee benefit plan or voluntary early retirement incentive plan excuses the employer's failure to hire an individual because of age, however. Also, no such plan can require or permit the involuntary retirement of any protected individual because of his age. The employer has the burden of proving that its actions were lawful in any ADEA civil enforcement proceeding.

5. Good Cause

The ADEA expressly states that it is not unlawful for an employer to discharge or otherwise discipline an individual for good cause. Although the ADEA lists good cause and RFOA defenses separately at 29 U.S.C. §623(f), courts have often treated the two similarly. Dozens of cases lump them together without distinguishing them. In fact, it appears that almost any cause is "good" for ADEA purposes as long as age plays no role in the employment decision.

6. Law Enforcement Officers and Firefighters

If certain conditions are met, the ADEA permits a state, its subdivisions, agencies and instrumentalities, or an interstate agency to fail or refuse to hire, or to discharge, an individual as a law enforcement officer or firefighter because of her age. Such actions are permissible only if made pursuant to a bona fide hiring or retirement plan that is not a subterfuge to evade the purposes of the ADEA. If the practice in question is a mandatory retirement age policy that was enacted after September 30, 1996, the policy cannot require mandatory retirement before the employee reaches age 55. 29 U.S.C. §623(j).

7. Bona Fide Executives or High Policymakers

ADEA does not prohibit compulsory retirement of any employee who is 65 years old and who, for two years immediately preceding retirement, is employed in a bona fide executive or high policymaking position. This exception only applies, however, when the employee is entitled to an immediate non-forfeitable annual retirement benefit from a pension, profit-sharing, savings, or deferred compensation plan (or a combination of such plans) of the employer that equals at least $44,000. 29 U.S.C. §631(c).

F. The ADEA Lawsuit

It seems likely that most age discrimination occurs in the hiring process rather than in the firing process. Nevertheless, far more ADEA lawsuits are brought by discharged employees than by job applicants who are not hired. Two factors help to account for this: first, being fired is generally more emotionally painful than not being hired; and second, an employee who is fired generally has better access to information about the employer to support her

ADEA claim. Charges concerning benefits and conditions of employment, while important, are also much less common than charges resulting from the discharge of an employee.

An employee who voluntary quits generally has no claim for wrongful discharge under the ADEA. If, however, because of her age the employee has been subjected to working conditions so intolerable that a reasonable person would feel compelled to resign, her decision is not truly voluntary. Thus, she may have an ADEA claim under a "constructive" discharge theory.

ADEA cases generally fall into one of two categories: disparate treatment or disparate impact. The great majority of cases are disparate treatment cases, in which the aggrieved employee alleges deliberate, unlawful age discrimination against her. Her allegations may be based on circumstantial evidence or, less often, upon direct evidence of age discrimination against her. In contrast, the aggrieved employee in a disparate impact case asserts that an employer's facially-neutral policy in fact has harsher effects on the ADEA-protected class than on other employees. A third category of ADEA cases involves employee claims of employer retaliation because of the employee's opposition to ADEA violations or participation in an ADEA investigation, proceeding, or litigation.

1. Disparate Treatment

When the plaintiff alleges deliberate age discrimination by the employer against her, her ADEA claim is a disparate treatment claim. If she has only circumstantial evidence of the discrimination, courts will apply the burden-shifting test from *MacDonnell Douglas* (a Title VII Supreme Court opinion) to her claim. In contrast, if she had direct evidence of such discrimination, courts historically applied the "mixed motives" test from *Price-Waterhouse* (another Title VII case from the Supreme Court). As discussed below, in 2009 the Supreme Court ruled that the *Price-Waterhouse* framework does not apply to ADEA claims.

a. Circumstantial Evidence

Most ADEA-covered employers understand the ADEA prohibitions. They are unlikely to provide an employee with direct evidence of their age discrimination against her. When the ADEA plaintiff has only circumstantial or indirect evidence of such discrimination, courts apply the three-part *McDonnell Douglas* burden-shifting test to determine whether she has established her prima facie of discrimination and whether she is entitled to have her case heard before a jury. Many employment law defense attorneys believe juries to be very sympathetic to ADEA plaintiffs, and thus stringently work to avoid having an ADEA case heard by a jury.

The *McDonnell Douglas* test allocates the burden of production and the order of presentation of proof in circumstantial evidence cases. The plaintiff begins by establishing her prima facie case of discrimination. When she does so, a presumption or inference of age discrimination arises, and the burden shifts to the employer to present a legitimate, nondiscriminatory reason for the employment decision. If the employer does so, then the presumption or inference of discrimination under *McDonnell Douglas* disappears. The plaintiff's evidence must then show that the employer's asserted nondiscriminatory reason is pretextual—i.e., that the reason asserted by the employer is in fact intended to cover actual discrimination based on age. If the plaintiff's prima facie case and other evidence create a fact issue as to whether the employer intentionally discriminated against the plaintiff because of her age, then the plaintiff is entitled to have her case heard by a jury. Ultimately, the plaintiff must prove age discrimination by a preponderance of the evidence.

To establish her prima facie case in the wrongful discharge scenario, the plaintiff typically must demonstrate the following: (1) she was a member of the protected ADEA class at the time she was fired by her employer; (2) she was otherwise qualified for the job; (3) she was discharged by her employer; and (4) her employer filled her position with someone younger. The plaintiff may establish her prima facie case even if the replacement employee is within the ADEA-protected class (i.e., the employee is forty or older), as long as the replacement employee is "substantially younger" than the plaintiff.

The mere fact that an employer's asserted legitimate, nondiscriminatory reason (LNR) for the employment decision is pretextual does not necessarily mean the plaintiff who has established her prima facie case may proceed to a jury trial. For example, if the plaintiff's evidence merely shows that the employer's LNR was pretext intended to cover up some other, *non-age* reason for the employment decision, she has demonstrated pretext but still failed to create a fact issue concerning age discrimination.

The Supreme Court has held that the *McDonnell Douglas* rules do not constitute a pleading requirement. The plaintiff's complaint thus does not have to contain factual allegations supporting each element of her *McDonnell Douglas* prima facie case.

b. Direct Evidence

If the plaintiff had direct evidence of age discrimination, for many years federal courts generally employed the framework of *Price-Waterhouse*. Once the plaintiff established that age was a motivating factor in a direct evidence or mixed motive case, then the burden of persuasion shifted to the employer. The employer had to prove, as an affirmative defense, that it would have made the same decision without regard to age considerations. The employer had to prove this by a preponderance of the evidence.

In 2009, the Supreme Court ruled in a 5–4 decision that the *Price-Waterhouse* test does not apply to ADEA actions. The burden of persuasion does not shift to the employer to demonstrate that it would have taken the same action regardless of the plaintiff's age, and this is so even if the plaintiff has produced evidence that age was one motivating factor in the employer's decision. Instead, the plaintiff's burden of persuasion in a mixed motives case is the same as in any other disparate treatment case. The plaintiff must prove by a preponderance of the evidence — whether that evidence is direct or circumstantial — that age was the "but for" cause of the challenged employer decision. Gross v. FBL Financial Services, Inc., 129 S. Ct. 2343 (2009).

2. Disparate Impact

Unlike disparate treatment claims, which examine the employer's intent or motivation, disparate impact claims involve challenges to employment practices that are facially neutral in their treatment of employees, but that in fact have a more adverse impact on the protected group. Plaintiffs in a disparate impact case often use detailed statistical evidence to prove that impact. In Smith v. City of Jackson, 544 U.S. 228 (2005), a divided Supreme Court held that disparate impact claims are permitted under the ADEA. Lower federal courts had disagreed on the availability of such a claim prior to *Smith*.

The plaintiffs alleging disparate impact must isolate and identify the specific employment practice that is responsible for any observed statistical disparities. The plaintiffs cannot merely allege an impact or point to a generalized policy that leads to the impact. Even if the plaintiffs clear this hurdle, the employer will prevail if it shows that its neutral policy is based on a reasonable factor other than age (RFOA). In Meacham v. Knolls Atomic Power Laboratory, 128 S. Ct. 2395 (2008), the Supreme Court observed that RFOA is an affirmative defense and held that the employer thus has the burden of production and the burden of persuasion concerning the RFOA.

3. Retaliation

Section 623(d) makes it unlawful for an employer to discriminate against any of his employees or applicants for employment because such individual has opposed any practice that violates ADEA or because such individual has made a charge, testified, assisted, or participated in any manner in an investigation, proceeding, or litigation under ADEA. In 2008, the Supreme Court concluded that the federal-sector provision, Section 633a, also prohibits retaliation against a federal employee even though no express retaliation language is included in that section. Gomez-Perez v. Potter, 128 S. Ct. 1931 (2008).

In a retaliation case, a plaintiff establishes her prima facie case under the ADEA by showing (1) that she engaged in ADEA-protected activity; (2) that an adverse employment action was taken against her; and (3) that there was a causal connection between her participation in the protected activity and the adverse employment decision.

An employee is protected from retaliation as long as she had a reasonable and good faith belief that she was opposing an unlawful discriminatory practice and the manner of her opposition was reasonable. She is protected from retaliation for participating in the investigation, proceeding, or litigation regardless of the validity or reasonableness of the original allegation of discrimination. EEOC interprets the retaliation provision to protect any employee, regardless of age, who opposes a practice violating the ADEA or who makes a charge, testifies, assists, or participates in an investigation, proceeding, or litigation under ADEA. Thus a thirty-year old employee who testifies on behalf of an older co-worker in an ADEA action is protected against retaliation.

Although the Supreme Court has not addressed the issue, several courts of appeals have refused to recognize ADEA retaliation claims from employees who appear to have been retaliated against solely because of their association with another employee. For example, assume that a married couple works for an ADEA-covered employer. The wife brings an ADEA claim against the employer, but her husband does not participate in any manner in her claim. Nonetheless, shortly thereafter the company discharges her husband. Courts that read Section 623(d) literally would hold that the husband has no standing to bring an ADEA retaliation claim because he neither opposed a practice violating ADEA nor made a charge, testified, assisted, or participated in an investigation, proceeding, or litigation under the ADEA.

At least some of these courts have acknowledged but nevertheless disagreed with EEOC Compliance Manual provisions. The EEOC Compliance Manual indicates that equal employment statutes prohibit discrimination against someone closely related to or associated with an individual who has engaged in a protected activity.

G. Procedural Issues

1. Sixty-Day Waiting Period after Charge Is Filed

A charge is a statement filed with the EEOC by or on behalf of an aggrieved person that alleges that the named prospective defendant has engaged in or is about to engage in actions in violation of the ADEA. To be a charge, the information should be sufficient to be reasonably construed as a request for EEOC to take remedial action to protect the employee's rights or to settle a dispute between the employee and her employer. Federal Express Corp. v. Holowecki, 128 S. Ct. 1147 (2008). A complaint, by contrast, is information (that is not a charge) received from any source that alleges that a named prospective defendant has engaged in or is about to engage in actions in violation of the ADEA.

ADEA generally prohibits nonfederal employees from binging a civil action until sixty days after a charge has been filed with the EEOC. During that time period, EEOC is to promptly attempt to eliminate any alleged unlawful practice by informal methods of conciliation, conference, and persuasion. If these methods fail and EEOC notifies the charging party of the failure before the sixty-day period has run, she may commence an action to enforce her rights without waiting for the sixty days to lapse.

In a state that has its own law prohibiting age discrimination in employment and that has established or authorized a state authority to grant or seek relief from such discriminatory practice, the claimant may not bring suit under the ADEA before the expiration of sixty days after proceedings have been commenced under the state law, unless such proceedings have been terminated before the end of the sixty days. States with such laws are said to be deferral states, because ADEA defers to the state laws and proceedings; states without such laws are nondeferral states.

Most states today are deferral states. When the unlawful practice occurs in a deferral state, the claimant may file her charge simultaneously with the state authority and the EEOC so that the 60-day period applicable to each runs simultaneously.

Federal employees are not subject to a 60-day waiting rule. Instead, they may proceed to federal court after giving EEOC thirty days' notice of an intent to file an ADEA action.

2. Timeliness of the Charge

If the unlawful practice occurs in a nondeferral state, the charge must be filed with the EEOC within 180 days after the alleged unlawful practice occurred.

In a deferral state, the charge must be filed with the EEOC within 300 days after the unlawful practice occurred or within 30 days after receipt by the individual of notice of termination of proceedings under state law, whichever is earlier.

Deferral states may have a worksharing agreement with the EEOC under which a claimant who has filed an ADEA charge with a state authority is deemed to have filed a charge with EEOC and vice-versa. Even in the absence of such a worksharing agreement, EEOC regulations require it to refer a charge to the corresponding state authority.

If the claimant fails to meet the applicable deadline, her ADEA claim is time-barred. Courts, however, may excuse the claimant's failure to meet the applicable filing deadlines if the circumstances warrant equitable modification or estoppel.

3. Civil Actions and Judicial Relief

If a nonfederal employee-claimant files a timely charge with the EEOC and the EEOC does not commence an enforcement action within sixty days, the claimant may commence her own ADEA action. The claimant must file her suit no later than ninety days after receiving notice from the EEOC that her charge has been dismissed or that the EEOC's proceedings have otherwise been terminated by the EEOC. Unlike Title VII, however, the ADEA does not require the claimant to wait for a "right to sue" notice or letter (formally known as a Notice of Dismissal or Termination). In other words, if the sixty-day period waiting period has passed without EEOC commencing an action, the claimant may file her ADEA suit even though she has not yet received a "right to sue" letter from the EEOC. If EEOC commences an action within the sixty-day period, however, the claimant may not bring her own ADEA action.

The ADEA gives the EEOC independent enforcement authority. Thus, EEOC may investigate suspected ADEA violations and bring enforcement actions against employers even though no claimant has filed a charge. The EEOC may bring suit against an employer in federal district court even when a claimant has already properly instituted her own ADEA action against the employer in federal district court and even when EEOC earlier issued a right to sue letter. If EEOC decides to bring such an action shortly after the claimant has brought her action, the court may allow EEOC to intervene. If EEOC decides to bring such an action after the claimant has completed her ADEA litigation in federal court, EEOC cannot obtain damages on behalf of the claimant; however, EEOC may obtain injunctive or other proper relief against the violating employer.

4. Waivers

As part of a severance or termination package, an employer may want an employee to waive any claims she has against the employer.

The ADEA permits an individual to waive her ADEA rights or claims if her waiver is knowing and voluntary. The ADEA states that a waiver is not knowing and voluntary unless, at a minimum (1) the waiver is part of an agreement between the individual and the employer that is written in a way that is calculated to be understood by the individual or by the average individual eligible to participate; (2) the waiver specifically refers to rights or claims arising under the ADEA; (3) the individual does not waive rights or claims that arise after the date the waiver is executed; (4) the individual waives rights or claims only in exchange for consideration in addition to anything of value to which the individual already is entitled; (5) the individual is advised in writing to consult with an attorney prior to executing the agreement; (6) the individual is given a period of at least twenty-one days within which to consider the agreement (forty-five days if the waiver is requested in connection with an exit incentive or other employment termination program offered to a group or class of employees); (7) the agreement provides that for at least seven days following the execution of the agreement, the individual may revoke the agreement, and the agreement shall not become effective or enforceable until the revocation period has expired; and (8) if a waiver is requested in connection with an exit incentive or other employment termination program offered to a group or class of employees, the employer informs the individual in writing in a manner calculated to be understood by the average individual eligible to participate, as to (a) any class, unit or group of individuals covered by such program, any eligibility factors for such program, and any time limits applicable to such program; and (b) the job titles and ages of all individuals eligible or selected for the program, and the ages of all individuals in the same job classification or organizational unit who are not eligible or selected for the program. 29 U.S.C. § 626(f).

In Oubre v. Entergy Operations, Inc., 522 U.S. 422 (1998), the Supreme Court refused to enforce a written waiver under which a former employee purported to release all claims against her former employer in return for severance pay. The Court noted that the agreement did not give her twenty-one days to consider her options; did not give her seven days after she signed in which to change her mind; and did not make specific reference to ADEA claims. Because the agreement did not conform to the statutory requirements, it was not enforceable as a knowing and voluntary waiver.

A waiver made in settlement of an individual's EEOC charge or her judicial action alleging age discrimination is not considered knowing and voluntary unless at a minimum it satisfies requirements (1) through (5) of the preceding paragraph and the individual is given a reasonable period of time within which to consider the settlement agreement.

In disputes over whether a required element of a knowing and voluntary waiver has been satisfied, the party asserting the validity of the waiver has the burden of proving in a court of competent jurisdiction that the waiver was a knowing and voluntary one.

The ADEA specifically provides that no waiver may affect the EEOC's rights and responsibilities to enforce the ADEA. Moreover, no waiver may be used to justify interfering with the protected right of an employee to file an ADEA charge or participate in an investigation or proceeding conducted by the EEOC.

In 14 Penn Plaza LLC v. Pyett, 129 S. Ct. 1456 (2009), the Supreme Court held that a collective-bargaining agreement that clearly and unmistakably requires union members to arbitrate ADEA claims is enforceable as a matter of federal law.

5. Notices and Recordkeeping

Every employer covered by the ADEA must post and keep posted upon its premises a notice pertaining to the applicability of the ADEA as prescribed by the EEOC. The notice must be posted in prominent and accessible places where it can be readily observed by employees, applicants for employment, and union members.

The ADEA also requires that employers retain records relating to its employment practices. Employers must make and keep for three years employee payroll and other records that contain the employee's name, address, date of birth, occupation, rate of pay, and compensation earned each week. For one year from the date of the personnel action in question, every employer must retain records related to (1) job applications, resumes, and other forms of employment inquiry submitted to the employer in response to the employer's advertisement or other notice concerning job openings (including records pertaining to the failure or refusal to hire an individual); (2) promotion, demotion, transfer, selection for training, layoff, recall, or discharge of any employee; (3) job orders submitted by the employer to an employment agency or labor organization for recruitment of personnel for job openings; (4) test papers completed by applicants or candidates for any position that disclose the results of any employer-administered aptitude or other employment test considered by the employer in connection with any personnel action; (5) the results of any physical examination where such examination is considered by the employer in connection with any personnel action; and (6) any advertisements or notices to the public or to employees relating to job openings, promotions, training programs, or opportunities for overtime work.

Every employer must keep on file any employee benefit plan as well as copies of any seniority system and merit system for the full period the plan or system is in effect and for at least one year after its termination. 29 C.F.R. 1627.3.

H. Remedies

The ADEA's enforcement provisions are designed to encourage voluntary compliance by the employer through the informal methods of conciliation, conference, and persuasion. Before instituting an action, EEOC must attempt to eliminate the discriminatory practice and effect voluntary compliance through such methods. ADEA's judicial remedies are discussed under Section 626(b), which incorporates several provisions of the Fair Labor Standards Act. Potential remedies include injunctive relief, back pay, reinstatement or front pay, costs, attorney fees, and liquidated damages.

The ADEA permits courts to issue preliminary and permanent injunctions against an employer. Permanent injunctions may be appropriate when an employer has a history of discriminatory practices or policies based on age, and also when the ADEA claim involves a large number of plaintiffs or potential plaintiffs.

A plaintiff who has lost earnings or benefits because of an ADEA violation is entitled to back pay. Back pay includes not only salary, but also pension contributions and insurance premiums that the employer would have paid. The back pay award should equal the difference between the salary and benefits the employee would have received and the salary and benefits he has received from other sources following the wrongful action by the employer. Wages earned in a new position or pension and severance benefits received from the company are typical offsets used in determining the total back pay award. More often than not, courts do not include Social Security benefits and unemployment benefits as offsets. In a discharge case, the calculation period generally runs from the date of the wrongful discharge to the date that the employee accepts or declines a bona fide offer of reinstatement. The discharged employee has a duty to mitigate his damages.

When an employee is wrongfully discharged under the ADEA, courts generally state that the preferred remedy is reinstatement rather than front pay (an award for future lost earnings). Nevertheless, if the relationship between the employer and employee is hopelessly tainted or fraught with tension, the court may refuse to order reinstatement. In those instances, the plaintiff will receive an award of front pay. If after discharging an employee in violation of the ADEA the employer learns of other information that would have provided good cause for his termination (such as theft from the company), reinstatement will not be ordered and front pay, if any, will be substantially reduced. Back pay, however, would still be appropriate from the time of the ADEA violation until the date the additional information was discovered.

Section 626(b) provides that liquidated damages shall be payable only in cases of willful violation of the ADEA. Willful violations may be found when the employer intentionally violates the ADEA or has shown reckless disregard concerning whether the employer's conduct is prohibited by the ADEA. Liquidated damages typically equal twice the amount of the plaintiff's actual damages (excluding front pay). Liquidated damages are not available against the federal government. Courts have generally concluded that no punitive damages are available under ADEA. Courts appear to agree that ADEA affords no compensatory award for pain and suffering.

The Supreme Court has held that the entire ADEA award to the successful plaintiff is taxable. C.I.R. v. Schleier, 515 U.S. 323 (1995).

Checkpoints

- Concerning the federal Age Discrimination in Employment Act (ADEA), you should understand
  - The ADEA protects covered individuals forty and over from age discrimination by covered employers
  - The ADEA covers hiring and firing decisions; conditions, terms, and privileges of employment; and retaliation claims
- Concerning covered employment, you should understand the definitions of employer and employee, including
  - How to determine employer status
    - Must have twenty employees in twenty weeks in current or preceding calendar year
    - Nonprofit and charitable organizations are not excluded as employers
    - Religious organizations may be included in some circumstances
    - Under the eleventh amendment, nonconsenting states are immune to ADEA suits by private citizens seeking damages
  - How to determine employee status
    - Test is derived from common law, not statute
    - An individual's title is not necessarily determinative of his employee status

Checkpoints *continued*

- Concerning employer defenses, you should understand generally the
    - Bona fide occupational qualification defense
    - Reasonable factor other than age defense
    - Bona fide seniority system defense
    - Bona fide employee benefit plan defense
    - Good cause defense
    - Law enforcement officer and firefighter exception
    - Bona fide executive or high policymaker exception
- Concerning forms of ADEA lawsuits, you should understand
    - The disparate treatment claim
    - The disparate impact claim
    - The retaliation claim
- Concerning procedural issues under ADEA, you should understand
    - The rules for timely filing of a charge
    - The rules for filing private suit in federal district court
    - The role of the EEOC
    - The difference between deferral and nondeferral states and the effect on procedure
    - The rules concerning waiver of ADEA rights
    - The employer's obligation to provide notices and maintain records
- Concerning remedies, you should understand the availability of injunctive relief, back pay, reinstatement or front pay, costs, attorney fees, and liquidated damages

Chapter 6

Social Security, Retirement, and Pension Programs

Roadmap

- Social Security is designed as a safety net for retired and disabled workers and their survivors and dependents
  - Social Security is financed by payroll taxes
  - The amount and receipt of Social Security retirement benefits by the worker depends upon
    - Establishing eligibility through the worker's earnings record and birth date
    - Determining the worker's primary insurance amount
    - Applying penalties such as those for early receipt
    - Applying rewards for delayed receipt
  - Auxiliary benefits based upon a worker's earnings record are often available to the worker's spouse, ex-spouse, surviving spouse, surviving ex-spouse, and dependent or disabled children
  - Social Security also provides disability benefits for disabled workers and their families
  - Social Security appeals are available at four administrative levels prior to judicial review in federal court
- Other important public retirement or pension programs, or both, exist for railroad workers, government employees, members of the armed services, and veterans
- Private-sector pension plans cover millions of American workers
  - Plans are defined benefit plans or defined contribution plans
  - ERISA provides favorable tax treatment to qualified plans and their participants
  - Spousal protections are included in plan provisions
  - Distribution, taxation, and rollover rules play an important role in pension planning

---

A. Social Security

1. Generally

The Social Security program provides benefits for retired and disabled workers who have contributed to the program through employment taxes. The program also provides benefits for various individuals who are related to or dependent upon the worker. Title II of the Social Security Act sets forth the old-age, survivors, and disability insurance (OASDI) program. Like most statutory distributive schemes with widespread applicability, the retirement benefits program is characterized largely by objective categories and rules. A person who fits within the scheme will obtain retirement benefits. In most respects, however, the scheme leaves little room for administrative or judicial discretion.

The program is considered a form of social insurance. In fact, the program contains both insurance and welfare components. A worker's payments into the program are analogous to payments made on an insurance policy. The more one pays into the program, the higher one's monthly retirement benefit. Retired workers with lower earnings, however, receive a proportionately larger return on their payments, and thus the program contains a wealth redistribution component characteristic of welfare.

Despite the wealth redistribution component of the program, the drafters of the program did not envision it as a welfare program for poor workers. The drafters also did not intend the program to be a complete replacement of pre-retirement income. Instead, the goal was to help provide a safety net for all retired or disabled workers and their survivors. Commentators have noted that Social Security is designed to be one leg of a "three-legged stool" of retirement income. The other two legs are the worker's savings and other sources of retirement-related income such as pension benefits. From the inception of the program in the mid-1930s, Congress and the Roosevelt administration indicated that Social Security is to supplement, not to supplant, other resources upon which workers had relied before the enactment of the program.

Nevertheless, Social Security benefits today provide more than half of all income for most elderly recipients. For many, the reliance on Social Security is almost total. A Fact Sheet issued by the Social Security Administration (SSA) in February of 2009 stated, "Among elderly Social Security beneficiaries, 20% of married couples and about 41% of unmarried persons rely on Social Security for 90% or more of their income." The same Fact Sheet indicated that almost a third of the workforce has no savings set aside for retirement, and over half has no private pension coverage.

Americans fail to save for many various reasons. Unlike paying a mortgage or car note, failure to save usually results in no immediate adverse repercussions to the individual. Many workers are so concerned about their present needs and wants that they fail to consider their retirement needs, which seem distant. Society itself promotes consumerism, making it difficult for many individuals to deny themselves and their families the promised happiness that comes with the purchase of slickly advertised goods. Of course, some individuals simply do not earn enough to save. Supporting their families and educating their children takes all of their income. Moreover, some individuals who have diligently saved may see their nest egg reduced substantially or even wiped out as the result of catastrophic illnesses or job loss in middle age. Nest eggs may also diminish or disappear when markets turn sour or investments unexpectedly go bad.

Although the great majority of Americans clearly lack adequate savings for their retirement years, certain groups generally fare better than others. Older individuals who are college graduates are likely to have almost three times the income of individuals who did not complete high school. Older males are likely to have significantly higher income than older females. In addition to this income discrepancy, women are also likely to live longer past retirement, and thus women are more likely to exhaust the income they have accumulated. Race and age also are important factors in predicting who is most likely to rely heavily upon Social Security. Older nonwhites have median incomes around one-third less than that of older whites. Further, as an individual moves into her seventies and eighties, her income is likely to decline.

At the beginning of 2009, the estimated average monthly Social Security benefit for retired workers was $1,112. Although Social Security is often called a federal entitlement program, Congress has the power to amend or repeal the Social Security Act, including the level of benefits, at any time.

2. History and Highlights

During the Great Depression that began in late 1929 and lasted well into the 1930s, thousands of banks collapsed, unemployment soared, and companies across the country were unable to pay the pensions they had promised their retired employees. With savings and pension benefits wiped out and no opportunity for employment, perhaps up to fifty percent of the elderly American population was unable to support itself adequately. Families, friends, charities, and newly-enacted state pension programs could not assist everyone.

As part of the New Deal in response to the economic devastation wreaked by the depression, President Franklin D. Roosevelt signed the Social Security Act in 1935. Although Congress has tweaked the program on several occasions since its enactment, the basic principles underlying the original program have remained substantially consistent.

From the beginning, the program has been financed by payroll taxes contributed by workers and their employers. The tax rate is constant regardless of the worker's earnings, although a worker whose earnings exceed a certain threshold pays no tax to the Social Security program on the excess amount. (The worker does continue to pay a tax on the excess to fund Medicare hospital insurance, however.) The tax is mandatory and now applies to almost all workers.

In determining retirement benefits, the worker's contributions are ultimately "indexed" to account for the changing value of those contributions over time. Early in the program's history, Congress made eligibility for benefits dependent upon the receipt of credits, called "quarters of coverage," earned during the course of employment. Congress also extended the potential list of recipients to include the worker's dependents and certain survivors. Since the 1970s, benefits are automatically increased each year by cost-of-living adjustments (COLAs). In October of 2009, howeveer, SSA announced that there would be no COLA for 2010 in light of the economic downturn.

Workers may receive full retirement benefits when they reach full retirement age (FRA, also called normal retirement age or NRA). For individuals retiring before 2003, FRA was 65. Today, FRA is tied to year of birth. Concerns about the program's future solvency resulted in amendments in the 1980s that ultimately increased FRA to age 67 for individuals born in 1960 or thereafter. Some observers believe that Congress will have to increase FRA further if the program is to remain solvent and benefits constant. In the 1980s, Congress also made a substantial part of Social Security benefits subject to federal income tax for higher income recipients.

The program permits covered workers to receive Social Security retirement benefits before reaching FRA, but in such cases applies a permanent reduction in benefits paid. Workers who receive early Social Security retirement benefits but who also have earnings above a certain threshold face a "retirement earnings" penalty that will further reduce their benefits.

All of these aspects of the Social Security program are discussed in more detail later in this chapter.

3. Laws and Administrative Materials

a. Statutes and Regulations

Title II of the Social Security Act provides the OASDI (old age, survivors, and disability insurance) statutes. The statutes begin at 42 U.S.C. § 401. The

Social Security Administration (SSA) website provides the statutes online at http://www.ssa.gov/OP_Home/ssact/title02/0200.htm. Since 1995, SSA has been an independent agency. It is headed by a Commissioner who is appointed for a six-year term. The SSA is charged with establishing reasonable regulations, rules, and procedures concerning the Act. The federal regulations interpreting the principal concerns regarding Social Security benefits begin at 20 C.F.R. 404. The SSA website provides the regulations online at http://www.ssa.gov/OP_Home/cfr20/404/404-0000.htm. A lawyer should always read the regulations in conjunction with the statute before advising a client.

b. Rulings

The SSA also publishes Social Security Rulings, which include important judicial decisions, the Commissioner's decisions, Office of General Counsel opinions, SSA policy statements, and SSA interpretations of the statutes and regulations. Social Security Rulings become effective when published in the Federal Register. Rulings are binding on all components of the SSA. Unlike regulations, Social Security Rulings are not promulgated pursuant to the requirements of the Administrative Procedures Act. Thus, Social Security Rulings do not have the force of statutes or regulations. Nonetheless, SSA's interpretation of a Social Security statute or regulation is generally entitled to deference unless the interpretation is plainly unreasonable or inconsistent with the clear meaning of the statute or regulation.

One important kind of ruling is an SSA Acquiescence Ruling, which explains SSA's application of decisions from United States Courts of Appeals when those decisions are inconsistent with SSA's national policy or interpretation concerning the law. If a Court of Appeals holding conflicts with SSA's interpretation of the Social Security Act or regulations, SSA will apply the holding at all levels of the administrative review process within the applicable circuit unless the government seeks further judicial review of that holding or otherwise relitigates the issue presented in the decision. When the adverse holding occurs and the government does not seek further judicial review or is unsuccessful on further review, SSA issues a Social Security Acquiescence ruling. The ruling describes the administrative case, discusses the court decision, identifies the issues involved, and explains how SSA will apply the holding. Acquiescence Rulings are generally effective upon publication in the Federal Register and apply to all determinations and decisions made on or after that date unless the Acquiescence Ruling is rescinded.

Even after publication of an Acquiescence Ruling, SSA may relitigate the issue if an "activating event" occurs and either (1) the General Counsel of the SSA, after consulting with the Department of Justice, concurs that relitigation would be appropriate or (2) SSA publishes a notice in the Federal Register that it intends to relitigate. Activating events include the following: (1) an action in both the House and Senate indicating that a circuit court decision on which the ruling was based was decided inconsistently with congressional intent; (2) a statement in a majority opinion of the same circuit indicating that the court might no longer follow its previous decision if a particular issue were presented again; (3) subsequent circuit court precedent in other circuits supporting SSA's interpretation on the issue in question; or (4) a subsequent Supreme Court decision presenting a reasonable legal basis for questioning a circuit court holding upon which the ruling is based.

The SSA will rescind an Acquiescence Ruling if (1) the Supreme Court overrules or limits a circuit court holding that was the basis of the ruling; (2) a circuit court overrules or limits itself on an issue that was the basis of the ruling; (3) a federal law is enacted that removes the basis for the holding in a decision of a circuit court that was the subject of the ruling; or (4) SSA subsequently clarifies, modifies, or revokes the regulation or ruling that was the subject of the circuit court holding or, in certain circumstances, SSA subsequently issues a new regulation making the ruling no longer necessary. 20 C.F.R. 404.985.

The SSA provides both Social Security Rulings and Acquiescence Rulings on its website. The table of contents for Social Security Rulings concerning old age and survivor's insurance is found at http://www.ssa.gov/OP_Home/rulings/oasi-toc.html. The table of contents for Social Security Rulings relating to disability is found at http://www.ssa.gov/OP_Home/rulings/di-toc.html. Acquiescence rulings are found at http://www.ssa.gov/OP_Home/rulings/ar-toc.html.

c. Manuals and Handbooks

SSA's Program Operations Manual System (POMS) is a massive set of guidelines for the use of agency employees in processing claims. Its coverage extends beyond Social Security to Supplemental Security Income (SSI) and Medicare. It explains how agency employees are to evaluate claims and interpret the law. POMS is available for inspection and copying at SSA district offices. It is also available in CD-ROM format from the Government Printing Office. The public version is also available at https://secure.ssa.gov/apps10/poms.nsf/partlist!OpenView.

SSA's Hearings, Appeals, Litigation and Law Manual (HALLEX) provides procedural instructions addressed to appellate decision makers such as Administrative Law Judges and the Appeals Council. It is also a valuable resource to lawyers representing clients in the appeals process. It is available at http://www.socialsecurity.gov/OP_Home/hallex/hallex.html.

SSA also publishes a Social Security Handbook online, which is designed to provide an overview of the statute, regulations, and rulings in terms that are easy to understand. SSA warns that the laws themselves are very complex and that in the event of any conflicts between the Handbook explanations and the laws, regulations, or rulings, the latter control. The Handbook is provided at http://www.socialsecurity.gov/OP_Home/handbook/handbook-toc.html.

4. Financing the Program

a. FICA/SECA Taxes

To finance the Social Security program, the Federal Insurance Contributions Act (FICA) imposes a payroll tax on worker wages and on self-employment income. (The self-employment tax component is referred to as SECA.)

The payroll tax consists of two components: OASDI (old age, survivors', and disability insurance) and HI (hospital insurance). The OASDI component funds Social Security, while the HI component helps to fund Medicare. The OASDI tax applies to wages and income from all covered employment, but does not apply to nonwork sources of income such as pensions, dividends, IRA distributions, interest, or inheritance. The tax does not apply to rents received unless one is in the trade or business of renting real estate, in which case the rents are self-employment income.

For employees, the OASDI tax rate is 6.20 percent of wages up to a maximum amount that changes annually (e.g., $102,000 in 2008 and $106,800 in 2009). Wages exceeding that amount are not subject to further OASDI tax. Observers most frequently note that, because of the annual maximum earnings subject to the OASDI tax, the payroll tax is regressive. In other words, a worker's contributions-to-earnings ratio grows smaller the more she earns in excess of the annual maximum. The HI tax rate is 1.45 percent of an employee's wages and since 1994 has not been subject to a cap. Instead, it applies to all of an employee's wages. The employee's employer must contribute an equal amount under FICA. For example, if an employee earned $100,000 in wages in 2009, her FICA tax would be $7,650 (that is, $6,200 for OASI and $1,450 for HI). Her employer would also pay $7,650 in FICA taxes. (Because the employer bears one-half of the total FICA taxes, commentators suggest that this employee is actually worth $107,650 to the employer.)

For the self-employed, the tax rates are doubled—i.e., 12.40 percent for OASDI up to the yearly maximum amount, and 2.90 percent for HI without a cap. Thus, the total SECA tax is 15.3 percent up to $106,800 in 2009, and the HI portion of the tax continues to apply to all earnings. The self-employed person receives the benefit of two deductions, however. First, in determining the SECA tax she owes, she may reduce her self-employment earnings by 7.65 percent. (Just as the employer's share of the FICA tax—i.e., 7.65 percent—is not considered wages to the employee, one-half of the SECA tax is not considered part of the self-employed person's net earnings.) Second, in determining the income tax she owes, she can deduct from gross income one-half of what she plays in SECA tax on her IRS 1040 form. 26 U.S.C. §§ 164(f), 1402(a)(12).

Although the wages subject to the OASDI tax change each year, the tax percentages themselves have not changed since 1990.

b. The Trust Fund

The Social Security Act provides for a so-called "trust fund" as a separate account in the United States Treasury. FICA taxes are deposited into the trust fund. Withdrawals are made to fund monthly benefits and to cover administrative expenses of the program. By statute, funds not withdrawn for benefits and expenses must be invested in interest-bearing securities of the United States or guaranteed by the United States. Thus, the trust fund is set up so that SSA does not need to make periodic requests for funding from Congress.

The Act also creates a Board of Trustees to hold the funds, report to Congress at least annually, and make recommendations and improvements concerning policies and procedures. The Board of Trustees consists of the Secretary of the Treasury (who is also the managing trustee), the Secretary of Labor, the Secretary of Health and Human Services, the Commissioner of Social Security, and two members of the public who are appointed by the President subject to Senate confirmation and who are not to be members of the same political party. The detailed annual report of the Board is available at the SSA website and provides predictions about the probable future of the program.

c. Who Pays for Whom?

SSA does not deposit the FICA taxes paid by a current worker into a separate account established for the future use of that worker. Instead, the system has been referred to as "pay-as-you-go." The payroll taxes of all current workers are deposited into the trust fund, which is used to pay the current recipients of Social Security benefits. The system thus involves an intergenerational transfer of income from the young to the old.

As long as the revenue generated by the payroll taxes exceeds benefits paid, the reserve increases and the immediate future of the program appears safe. The program will soon face unprecedented numbers of claims, however, as baby boomers reach retirement age. The 2009 Trustees Report predicted that by 2016 program expenditures will exceed revenues and that by 2037 the reserve will be exhausted.

5. Eligibility for Benefits

Benefits under the OASDI program may extend to persons in the following categories: (1) retired workers, (2) disabled workers, (3) dependents of retired or disabled workers, (4) spouses and ex-spouses of a retired worker, and (5) survivors of a deceased worker. To reduce the potential drain on the program when multiple individuals are entitled to benefits upon the earnings record of one worker, the program imposes a cap on the monthly amount allowed to the worker's family. For example, if a widow of a deceased worker and the couple's two dependent children are receiving benefits and their total benefits individually would otherwise exceed the family maximum, each will receive a proportionately reduced monthly sum so that the total amount of the payments does not exceed the family maximum.

The specific formula for determining the maximum family benefit for families of retired or deceased workers involves the use of four different percentages applied to three "bend points" and is provided on the SSA website at http://www.socialsecurity.gov/OACT/COLA/familymax.html. A different formula applies for families of disabled workers and is available at http://www.socialsecurity.gov/OACT/ COLA/dibfamilymax.html.

6. The Earnings Record

Anyone engaged in covered employment must pay FICA taxes and thus must obtain a Social Security number from SSA. The SSA maintains an earnings record for each worker whose wages from employment or self-employment are covered by the Social Security program. The earnings record provides a total picture of the worker's contributions to the Social Security program throughout her period of covered employment.

The information for the record is supplied by employers and by the self-employed. The earnings record is an extremely important document, because calculation of Social Security benefits is based on the information contained in the worker's earnings record.

Each year SSA mails a statement of earnings to all people who are at least twenty-five years old, who are not receiving benefits on their own earnings record, and for whom the SSA has a current address. The mailing occurs about three months before the worker's birthday. A worker or her proxy may also request an earnings record statement to verify the accuracy of the information held by SSA. Social Security Handbook § 1419.

The worker should inspect her earnings record regularly. A worker must request a correction of misreported wages or income within three years, three months, and fifteen days from the end of the calendar year in which the incorrectly listed wages were earned or in which the incorrectly listed self-employment income was earned. Upon expiration of the time period for requesting a correction, the amount of wages or self-employment income listed in the worker's earnings record is generally conclusive in an administrative or judicial proceeding.

The statute and regulations do contain exceptions in which SSA may change the earnings record following the expiration of the general period for requesting corrections; however, these are of limited availability. For example, an exception may apply to permit the correction of obvious clerical errors by SSA or to correct entries based on fraud.

7. Covered Employment

An individual establishes direct eligibility for Social Security benefits by working in covered employment and obtaining credits over a specified time period. (Other individuals may establish derivative or auxiliary eligibility based on their relationship with the worker.) The vast majority of American workers are engaged in covered employment. A 2009 Fact Sheet from SSA indicated that about ninety-four percent of all workers (162 million people) were employed in jobs covered by Social Security. If one works in covered employment, participation is mandatory; no one can opt out.

The principal groups of workers in noncovered employment today are workers under the Railroad Retirement program (a multi-tiered benefit program enacted in 1934, somewhat intertwined with Social Security); federal government employees hired prior to 1984 (who are covered under the Civil Service Retirement System unless they subsequently chose to switch to coverage under the Federal Employees Retirement System); and state and local government agency employees if the agency has not elected coverage. A church or qualified church-controlled organization may elect for religious reasons to have its employees treated as noncovered, in which case the employees' wages are treated as self-employment income. Special rules apply to certain kinds of employment such as agricultural labor or domestic service.

8. Quarters of Coverage

To obtain insured status under the program, a worker must earn a requisite number of credits, called quarters of coverage (QCs). Workers who do not obtain sufficient credits to be insured are not eligible for benefits on their own earnings records.

A worker earns a QC or credit based on wages or self-employment income subject to the FICA tax. In 2009, earnings of $1,090 were required to obtain a credit. The Social Security Act requires the Commissioner to annually adjust the amount of earnings required to obtain a QC and to publish that amount in the Federal Register no later than November 1 preceding the calendar year in which the amount becomes effective. A worker may obtain up to four credits in a calendar year. Thus, if Alice earned $4,360 in 2009, she would receive four credits. Note that even if she earned $436,000 in 2009, she would still receive only four credits for that year.

By regulation, an individual may not earn a credit for a calendar quarter that begins after her death. For example, if for the year 2009 Alice earned $4,360 but died shortly before October 1 (the beginning of the fourth calendar quarter), she could only receive three credits for 2009.

To be fully insured, workers born in 1929 or thereafter need forty credits. Fully insured status potentially entitles the worker and those claiming through her the full panoply of Social Security benefits, as discussed more fully later in this chapter.

To be currently insured, a worker needs six credits during the full thirteen-quarter period ending with the calendar quarter in which she died, most recently became entitled to disability benefits, or became entitled to retirement benefits. Currently insured status results in more limited benefits than fully insured status, but includes benefits for a dependent, unmarried child of a deceased worker as well as benefits for a surviving spouse (or a divorced spouse of the deceased worker) who is caring for a child entitled to benefits (if the child is sixteen or under or disabled). Currently insured status also entitles survivors to a one-time lump sum death payment.

A person may also have disability insured or special insured status. These are discussed later in the chapter.

9. Retirement Benefits

a. Full Retirement Age (FRA)

A worker is eligible for full retirement benefits if she is fully insured and first applies for benefits upon reaching full retirement age (FRA). In early 2009, SSA introduced a "Retire Online" program that allows individuals to complete their applications online. Applicants no longer have to visit the local Social Security office or wait for an appointment with a Social Security representative.

Full retirement age is dependent upon the worker's year of birth, as indicated in the following table:

Full Retirement Age	
Year of Birth	FRA
1937 or earlier	65
1938	65 and 2 months
1939	65 and 4 months
1940	65 and 6 months
1941	65 and 8 months
1942	65 and 10 months
1943–1954	66
1955	66 and 2 months
1956	66 and 4 months
1957	66 and 6 months
1958	66 and 8 months
1959	66 and 10 months
1960 and later	67

b. Delayed Receipt of Benefits

If a worker defers receipt of Social Security retirement benefits past FRA, she will receive a permanently enhanced benefit amount when the benefits begin. Once the worker turns seventy, however, there is no further increase in benefits for deferred receipt.

For example, if Bob was born in 1950, is fully insured, and waits to receive benefits until he reaches age 70 (four years past his FRA of 66), his monthly retirement benefit check will be thirty-two percent more (four years of deferred receipt at eight percent per year) than what he would have received had he begun benefits at his FRA of sixty-six. Once Bob reaches age seventy, he

Benefit Increase for Delayed Retirement Beyond FRA		
Year of Birth	Yearly Rate of Increase	Monthly Rate of Increase
1933–34	5.5%	11/24 of 1%
1935–36	6.0%	1/2 of 1/%
1937–38	6.5%	13/24 of 1%
1939–40	7.0%	7/12 of 1%
1941–42	7.5%	5/8 of 1%
1943 or later	8.0%	2/3 of 1%

should apply for benefits because further deferral will result in no additional increase in his monthly check.

c. Early Receipt of Benefits

In contrast to deferral of benefits past FRA, a worker who is fully insured may choose to begin receiving retirement benefits as early as age sixty-two. Historically, most workers have chosen early receipt. The worker who does so, however, faces a penalty that permanently reduces her benefit amount. The penalty is a percentage reduction applied to each month of early retirement, as follows: (1) for up to thirty-six months of early receipt, 5/9 of one percent for each month; (2) for any additional months of early receipt beyond the first thirty-six, 5/12 of one percent for each of those additional months.

For example, if Callie was born in 1960, her FRA is 67. If she begins re tirement benefits at age 64 (three years early), her benefits will be permanently reduced by twenty percent (i.e., 5/9 of 1% per month times 36 months). If she chooses to begin retirement benefits at age 62 (five years early), her benefits will be permanently reduced by thirty percent (i.e., the twenty percent penalty for the thirty-six months as calculated above *plus* an additional penalty of 5/12 of 1% per month times 24 months for the additional months of early retirement.)

Moreover, if Callie chooses early receipt and continues to work, her Social Security benefits are further reduced under the "retirement earnings test" if her earnings exceed a certain threshold. The retirement earnings test is discussed in the following section.

A person who took early receipt of benefits may subsequently stop early receipt by requesting to withdraw her application (SSA-Form 521). If she does so, she must pay back all benefits received. 20 C.F.R. § 404.640. She may later refile and begin to receive benefits at a higher rate based on her current age. The withdrawal/payback/renewal process makes financial sense for some individuals, particularly if they continued to work and have substantial earnings after early receipt; however, the process is not often used.

d. Retirement Earnings Test

A retirement earnings penalty may apply to an insured worker under FRA who has chosen early receipt of Social Security retirement benefits and who continues to earn wages or self-employment income. The earnings test applies to wages received from an employer and to net earnings from self-employment. It does not apply to the insured's pensions, annuities, capital gains, investment earnings, interest, or government benefits.

In years preceding the year in which the insured reaches FRA, SSA deducts $1 in benefits for every $2 the insured earns above an annual threshold amount. The threshold amount is adjusted each year. In 2009, the threshold was $14,160. Assume that Ann, who is sixty-two, begins receiving early retirement benefits in 2009. She will initially face a permanent reduction of benefits because of her choice to take early receipt, as previously discussed. Ann continues to work, and she earns $19,160. Because her earnings exceed the threshold by $5,000, she will also lose $2500 of the Social Security benefits she would otherwise receive.

In the year in which the worker reaches her FRA, however, SSA only deducts $1 in benefits for every $3 she earns above an annual threshold amount. This threshold amount is different from the threshold amount applicable to earnings in years before the worker reaches FRA. In 2009, the threshold amount for the year in which the worker reaches her FRA was $37,680. Moreover, SSA counts only the earnings the worker received in the months preceding that in which she reached FRA. For example, assume that Bob began receiving early retirement benefits in 2007. In October of 2009, Bob reached FRA. In applying the retirement earnings test, only Bob's earning between January 1 and September 30 are considered. If in those months he has excess earnings of $600, then he will lose $200 of Social Security benefits.

In any event, no retirement earnings penalty applies once the insured reaches FRA. From that time forward, the insured's Social Security benefits are unaffected by her earnings.

Excess earnings of the retired worker are also charged against the total monthly family benefit, thus potentially reducing the monthly benefit to other family members claiming on the worker's earnings record. For example, assume that the retired worker has a $3000 penalty imposed because of the retirement earnings test. If his monthly benefit is $500 and his wife and child each have a monthly auxiliary benefit of $250, no benefits will be payable to the family from January through March. (The total monthly benefit of $1000 times three months equals the $3000 penalty.) Moreover, if an auxiliary beneficiary has excess earnings under the retirement earnings test, her award may be further reduced. In the preceding example, if the wife has an excess earnings penalty of $500, she not only will receive no benefits from January through March (because of her husband's excess earnings), but also will receive no benefits for April and May (because of her excess earnings).

The Social Security program has included a retirement earnings test since its inception, although the test has been amended significantly many times. The merits of the retirement earnings test remain debatable. The test is difficult for SSA to administer, is confusing to beneficiaries, and discourages some willing and able workers from continuing in gainful employment. Eliminating the test, however, would further increase the projected long-range deficit of the Social Security program. Moreover, eliminating the test might encourage many more insured workers to receive permanently-reduced early benefits, to the ultimate disadvantage of their survivors.

10. Derivative (or Auxiliary or Secondary) Benefits

a. Family Members or Ex-Family Members of a Living Worker

i. Spouse

The spouse of a worker is entitled to benefits if she meets the following conditions: (1) the worker has filed for or is receiving retirement or disability benefits; (2) the spouse files for her spousal benefits; (3) she is not entitled to a retirement or disability benefit based on a primary insurance amount that equals or exceeds one-half of the worker's primary insurance amount; (4) she is at least age sixty-two, or she has in her care a child under sixteen or disabled who is entitled to benefits on the worker's earnings record; and (5) she has been married to the worker for one year; or she is the parent of the worker's child (whether the child is living or dead); or she was entitled to certain Social Security benefits based on the record of a fully insured worker in the month before the month she married her current spouse; or she was entitled to certain benefits under the Railroad Retirement Act in the month before the month she married the worker.

A person is a spouse under the Act if the couple was validly married under state law or if state law would treat the claimant as a surviving spouse for the distribution of the worker's personal property for intestate succession purposes. The definition of spouse includes a common-law spouse if she is recognized by state law. A person may also be a spouse if she in good faith entered into a ceremonial marriage with the worker unaware that the marriage would turn out to be invalid, as long as she was living with the worker when he applied for benefits and she meets certain other requirements.

The spouse's benefit is generally equal to one-half of the worker's primary insurance amount. For example, suppose Hal and Wanda are a married couple, both of whom have reached FRA and wish to receive retirement benefits. Hal's earnings record entitles him to a $1000 monthly benefit. Wanda's spousal benefit will be $500. Assume, however, that Wanda's own earnings record entitles her to a $400 monthly retirement benefit. Because Wanda's spousal benefit on Hal's earnings record (one-half of $1000) is larger, SSA automatically pays Wanda the $500 amount.

Since 2000, Hal himself does not have to be receiving benefits for Wanda to receive the spousal auxiliary benefit; it is sufficient if Hal has filed for benefits. For example, if Hal files for benefits and then suspends his actual receipt of benefits, Wanda can receive the spousal benefit. Hal might choose to suspend his receipt currently so that he will receive larger monthly payments when he does begin actual receipt.

If Hal and Wanda are entitled to similar retirement benefits on their own work records and Wanda wants to retire but Hal does not, Hal might currently apply for a spousal benefit on Wanda's work record. When Hal reaches age seventy, he could apply for larger benefits based on his own work record and forego the receipt of further spousal benefit payments.

The spouse's benefit may be less than one-half if (1) total benefits to the family based on the worker's earnings record would otherwise exceed the family maximum; (2) the spouse qualifies for another benefit (such as retirement or disability) that is smaller than her spouse's benefit (in which case only the difference between the spousal benefit rate and the other benefit amount she receives is paid as a spousal benefit); or (3) the spouse receives benefits before FRA.

If the spouse takes early benefits, her penalty is 25/36 of one percent for each month of early receipt prior to FRA, up to thirty-six months. If she takes early receipt more than thirty-six months before FRA, an additional monthly penalty of 5/12 of one percent is imposed by SSA. For example, if Wanda was born in 1960, her FRA is 67. If she chooses to begin spousal retirement benefits at age 64 (three years early), her benefits will be permanently reduced by 5/12 of 1% per month times 36 months. If she chooses to begin retirement benefits at age 62 (five years early), her benefits will be permanently reduced by the preceding amount *plus* an additional penalty of 5/12 of 1% per month times 24 months for the additional months of early retirement.

Note that the spouse's award is based on the worker's primary insurance amount (PIA) (discussed later). This means that while the spouse may be penalized for her own decision to take early receipt of her spousal benefit, she is not penalized for the worker spouse's decision to take early receipt.

ii. Divorced Spouse

The divorced spouse (i.e., the worker's ex-spouse) is entitled to auxiliary benefits if she meets the following conditions: (1) the insured (the worker) is entitled to retirement or disability benefits; (2) the ex-spouse is the insured's divorced spouse from a marriage that was valid or deemed valid under state law; (3) the ex-spouse was married to the insured for at least ten years immediately before the divorce became final; and (4) the ex-spouse is unmarried.

If the insured worker has not yet filed for or received benefits, but is at least sixty-two and is fully insured, the ex-spouse can still receive ex-spouse benefits as long as the divorce has been final for two years. If the worker has reached FRA, however, the two-year waiting period does not apply. The ex-spouse is not entitled to ex-spouse benefits before age sixty-two even if she has a child in her care.

The divorced spouse's benefit is generally one-half of the worker's primary insurance amount. It may be less than one-half, however, if the divorced spouse qualifies for another benefit that is smaller than her ex-spouse's benefit (in which case the ex-spouse's benefit will pay the difference between the ex-spouse benefit rate and the other benefit she receives); or if the ex-spouse receives benefits before FRA. The penalty rates applicable to the spouse who takes early receipt are also used for the divorced spouse who takes early receipt.

If the applicant qualifies for ex-spouse spouse benefits because of two or more marriages that lasted ten years each, SSA will automatically determine which marriage provides the maximum ex-spouse benefits.

The divorced spouse's benefit is not subject to the family maximum cap. It has no effect on the amount received by the worker or any of his family members, and those benefits have no effect on the amount received by the divorced spouse.

iii. Children

A child of a living worker is entitled to benefits if the child meets the following conditions: (1) the child is (or was) dependent upon the worker/parent; (2) the child is unmarried; (3) the child is under 18, or is 18–19 and a full-time elementary or secondary school student, or is age 18 or older under a disability that began before the child was 22; and (4) the worker/parent is entitled to disability insurance benefits or retirement benefits.

The child's monthly benefit rate is one-half of the insured worker/parent's primary insurance amount if the parent is entitled to disability or retirement benefits. It may be less than one-half, however, if the family maximum applies and the benefit rate must be reduced. It may also be less than one-half if the child is disabled and entitled to disability or retirement benefits on his own earnings record. In the latter instance, the child's benefit rate will be the amount by which one-half of the worker's primary insurance amount exceeds the child's disability benefits.

b. Family Members of a Deceased Worker

i. Surviving Spouse

The surviving spouse of a worker can typically receive benefits on the deceased spouse's earnings record if she satisfies the following conditions: (1) the surviving spouse is at least age sixty (or age fifty if she meets disability-related requirements); (2) the deceased spouse died fully insured; (3) the surviving spouse is not entitled to a retirement benefit that is equal to or larger than that she would receive on the deceased spouse's earnings record; (4) she is not currently in a marriage that occurred before she turned sixty (or age fifty is she is disabled); and (5) she was married to the worker at least nine months before his death (unless his death was accidental) or is the parent of his child. A person is a widow or widower under the Act if the couple was validly married under state law or if the state law treats the claimant as a surviving spouse for the distribution of the worker's intestate personal property. A person can be a widow or widower if she in good faith entered into a ceremonial marriage with the worker unaware that the marriage would turn out to be invalid, as long as she was living with the worker at his death and meets certain other requirements. By virtue of the federal Defense of Marriage Act, however, a same-sex marriage otherwise recognized by state law is not a recognized marriage for Social Security purposes, since it is not a union between a man and a woman.

The surviving spouse who has reached FRA is generally entitled to one hundred percent of the retirement benefits received by the deceased spouse. Receipt may begin as early as age sixty (or, if the surviving spouse has a disability, as early as age fifty). SSA imposes a penalty upon the surviving spouse who begins receipt of surviving spousal benefits before her FRA, however. The penalty is calculated by dividing 28.5 percent by the possible number of months of early retirement (which will vary, depending upon the spouse's FRA), and multiplying the result by the actual number of months the individual takes early receipt. In other words, the maximum penalty is 28.5 percent.

Interestingly, FRA is calculated differently when a spouse is claiming surviving spousal benefits rather than retirement benefits: in essence, SSA treats a surviving spouse as if she were born two years earlier. Thus, if she were born in 1957, the 1955 FRA (66 years and 2 months, as shown on the chart provided earlier in the chapter) would apply for purposes of determining the surviving spouse's benefit.

It is perhaps worth noting that a surviving spouse (or any other person) who is convicted of the felonious and intentional killing of a worker cannot become entitled to benefits on that worker's Social Security earnings record.

ii. Surviving Divorced Spouse

An ex-spouse of a deceased worker may generally qualify for widow's or widower's benefits on the worker's earnings records if she satisfies the following conditions: (1) she is at least age sixty (or age fifty if she meets disability-related requirements); (2) the worker died fully insured; (3) she is not entitled to a retirement benefit that is equal to or larger than that she would receive on the worker's earnings record; (4) she is not currently in a marriage that occurred before she turned sixty (or age fifty if she is disabled); and (5) she was married (or deemed to be validly married) to the worker for at least ten years before the divorce became final. 20 C.F.R. §404.336.

iii. Surviving Children and Their Mothers or Fathers

A surviving child is entitled to benefits on the worker/parent's earnings record if she satisfies the following conditions: (1) the worker/parent died either fully or currently insured; (2) the child is the child of the worker/parent; (3) the child is either under 18, or is 18–19 and a full-time elementary or secondary school student, or is 18 or over but under a qualifying disability that began before age 22; (4) the child was dependent upon the worker/parent; and (5) the child is not married. The term "child" includes the worker's child who would have the potential right to inherit intestate personal property from the worker's estate. It may include a stepchild, a grandchild, or a step-grandchild in certain circumstances. In several cases recently litigated across the country, mothers have argued that their children conceived and born after the death of their husbands (but with the sperm of their husbands) are entitled to surviving children's benefits. In states that recognize such children as the lawful child of the deceased husband, the children have indeed received such Social Security benefits.

Each surviving child entitled to benefits receives seventy-five percent of the worker/parent's primary insurance amount, subject to a pro rata reduction if necessary to stay within the family maximum amount of benefits permitted.

A single parent or divorced single parent who is not entitled to benefits as a surviving spouse or divorced surviving spouse may be entitled to a mother's or father's benefit. To receive the benefit, he or she must care for the worker's child who is entitled to a child's insurance benefits, and the child must be under age sixteen or disabled. The benefit is seventy-five percent of the deceased worker's primary insurance amount. Marriage generally ends the mother's or father's entitlement, although re-entitlement may occur if the marriage ends.

iv. Parents of the Deceased Worker

A parent of a deceased worker is entitled to benefits if she satisfies various conditions, including the following: (1) the worker was fully insured at death; (2) the parent is at least sixty-two; (3) the parent is not entitled to a benefit equal to or larger than the amount of the unadjusted parent's insurance benefit after any increase to the minimum benefit; (4) the worker was providing at least one-half of the parent's support at the worker's death or, if the worker was disabled until death, when the worker became disabled; (5) the parent has not married following the worker's death; and (6) the parent is the biological parent of the worker; adopted the worker before the worker turned sixteen; or became the worker's stepparent before the worker turned sixteen.

If only one parent is entitled to the benefit, the rate is eighty-two and one-half percent of the worker's primary insurance amount. If both parents are entitled to the benefit, the rate is seventy-five percent for each parent. There is no penalty for receiving the benefits prior to FRA. As for most other family members, however, a parent's benefits are subject to the family maximum cap.

v. Lump Sum Death Payment

When a worker dies fully or currently insured, some of his family members are generally entitled to a one-time lump sum payment of $255. It is typically paid to the surviving spouse who is living in the household with the worker at his death. If there is no surviving spouse living with the worker at his death, then the award is paid to a surviving spouse who is otherwise eligible for benefits as a surviving spouse, mother, or father for the month the worker dies. In very rare circumstances, the worker may die survived by two surviving spouses (a legal spouse and a deemed spouse), neither of whom was living with the worker at his death. In such cases, the $255 is divided between the spouses.

If no spouse is eligible to receive the payment, the worker's child or children who are eligible for benefits on the worker's earnings records may receive the award.

11. Disabled Workers and Their Families

The Social Security program includes various kinds of disability protection. Among them are the following: (1) monthly cash benefits for a disabled worker;

(2) monthly cash benefits for needy, blind, or disabled individuals; (3) the establishment of a period of disability for a disabled worker (which protects against the loss of or reduction in the disability amount or retirement insurance benefits); (4) monthly cash benefits for a disabled spouse or disabled surviving divorced spouse; (5) monthly cash benefits for a disabled child; and (6) vocational rehabilitation services, employment services, or other support services.

a. Disabled Worker Benefits

An individual is eligible for a disabled worker's benefits if she satisfies the following conditions: (1) she is under a disability; (2) she files a proper and timely application; (3) she has disability insured status; (4) she has completed a five-month waiting period, unless exempt; and (5) she has not reached FRA. The worker has disability insured status if (1) she has at least twenty credits during a forty-calendar quarter period (often called the 20/40 rule); (2) the forty-calendar quarter period ends with the quarter that she is determined to be disabled; and (3) she is fully insured in that calendar quarter. The waiting period is not required if an individual was previously entitled to a period of disability and becomes disabled again within five years following the month in which her previous disability ended; or if she applies only for Supplemental Security Income (SSI) benefits; or if she is entitled to childhood disability benefits.

Members of the disabled worker's family may receive derivative (or auxiliary) benefits on the worker's earnings record.

i. Disability Defined

A worker is disabled if she is unable to engage in substantial gainful activity (SGA) because of physical or mental impairment. She must not only be unable to perform her prior work, but also any other kind of work taking into account her age, education, and experience. She must establish her impairment with objective medical evidence. The evidence should indicate that the impairment will lead to death or last for at least twelve consecutive months. Finally, the worker must also meet the non-medical criteria required to be insured. Less strict rules apply to blind persons at least fifty-five years old.

Disability determinations are independently made on all facts in the applicant's case. Generally the weight SSA gives to the applicant's treating physicians and providers depends upon various factors.

Impairments resulting from the commission of a felony are not covered by disability benefits. Similarly, impairments in which drug or alcohol abuse is a contributing factor are not covered by disability benefits. If SSA determines that the adult applicant's condition is not an impairment as described in its

"Listing of Impairments," or is not medically equally to such an impairment, SSA may still determine that the applicant is disabled based on her residual functional capacity for work. In such cases, SSA looks at how the condition affects the applicant's ability to do work-related activities and also examines her vocational background, including age, education and work experience.

The impairment must be the main reason the applicant cannot work. She is not disabled if she is able to do any of her past relevant work or any other kind of work that exists in significant numbers in the national economy. The following factors are not considered when SSA makes its disability determination: (1) inability of the applicant to get work; (2) lack of work in the local area; (3) hiring practices of employers; (4) technological changes in the industry in which the applicant worked; (5) cyclical economic conditions; (6) no job openings; (7) not actually being hired to do work the applicant could otherwise do; or (8) not wanting to do a particular kind of work.

ii. "Period of Disability" Defined

A period of disability is a continuous period in which the person is disabled. The period is not counted when determining the worker's insured status or the monthly benefit payable to the worker and her family. The beginning date of a period of disability is also important for determining the dependency of a child and a parent.

The worker establishes a period of disability if she satisfies the following conditions: (1) she files an application while she is disabled (or no later than twelve months after the month in which her period of disability ended); (2) she has disability insured status; (3) she was disabled before a final decision was made on her application; and (4) she was disabled for a period of at least five months in a row before reaching FRA or she is exempt from the five-month waiting period requirement.

For Title II, the period of disability begins on the date the worker's disability began if she meets the requirements for disability insured status; otherwise, the period begins on the first day of the calendar quarter after her disability began and she attains disability insured status. The period generally ends with the last day of the month in which the earliest of the following events occurs: the second month after the month her disability ends; the month before the month she reaches FRA; or the month she dies.

iii. Disability Benefit Amount and Duration

The disabled worker's benefit amount is generally the same as her primary insurance amount. In some instances, it may be less if she receives workers' compensation or a public disability benefit based on her work that is paid under a federal, state, or local public law or plan. It may also be less if she is entitled to disabled worker's benefits after a reduced spouse's or retirement insurance benefit.

The last month in which the worker is entitled to disabled worker's benefits is generally whichever of the following first occurs: the second month after her disability ends (with certain exceptions); the month before the month she dies; or the month before the month she reaches FRA. When a worker reaches FRA, her benefits are automatically converted to retirement benefits.

b. Spouses' Benefits Based on Disability

A disabled surviving spouse or surviving divorced spouse age 50–59 can receive disabled surviving spouse's benefits if she satisfies several conditions. She must be disabled. She must have become disabled no later than seven years after the latest of the following months: (1) the month the disabled worker died; (2) the last month she was previously entitled to mother's insurance benefits (or father's insurance benefits if the claimant is male) based on disability on the disabled worker's earnings record; or (3) the month her entitlement to widow's insurance benefits ended because her disability ended. Finally, the surviving spouse typically must have been disabled throughout a waiting period of five full calendar months in a row and must meet the other ("nondisability") general requirements for a surviving spouse or a surviving divorced spouse.

c. Children's Benefits Based on Disability

A disabled child under the age of eighteen may be eligible for Supplemental Security Income under Title XVI, or may be entitled to Title II benefits if the parent is a disabled worker or deceased and was insured. If an adult child became disabled before reaching age twenty-two, she may be entitled to Childhood Disability Benefits under Title II.

12. Determining Cash Benefit Amounts: PIA and AIME

a. Generally

The actual monthly cash benefit one receives from Social Security is almost always based on the worker's Primary Insurance Amount (PIA). The only monthly cash benefit not based on PIA is a special monthly payment to uninsured persons who turned 72 before 1972 who do not qualify for a regular Social Security benefit under the fully insured provisions.

The worker's PIA is derived from the worker's taxable earnings averaged over certain years in which she was in the workforce. The manner in which SSA averages the earnings generally depends upon whether the worker was first eligible for benefits or died before 1979 or, instead, was first eligible or died in 1979 or later. For those in the former category, PIA is based on the workers Average Monthly Earnings (AME). The amounts used are the actual earnings reported by the worker's employers or by the self-employed worker. (This method also applies in limited circumstances to certain workers who first became eligible after 1978.)

For the great majority of workers—those who first became eligible or died in 1979 or later—PIA is based on Average Indexed Monthly Earnings (AIME) over a thirty-five year period. SSA indexes the worker's earnings from 1951 through the second year before the year of the worker's first eligibility or death, whichever comes first. The process of indexing is designed to adjust the earnings over time to account for inflation. The worker's actual reported earnings are used, unindexed, in computing AIME for years that begin with the year before the worker's first year of eligibility.

For example, if Kay turned 65 in 2002, then she would have been first eligible for retirement benefits in 1999, when she was 62. The key year for indexing—two years before she died or first became eligible—is 1997. The average wages for all workers in 1997 is compared to the average wages of all workers for each year after 1950. This will produce an indexing factor that is applied to each year of Kay's wages that are to be indexed. Kay's earnings after 1997 are not indexed, but rather are included as reported. (There is a special indexing formula that may apply for computing widow(er)'s benefits if the worker died before reaching age sixty-two in 1979. There is also a special minimum PIA that may apply to workers who worked in covered employment for at least eleven years at low earnings.)

Not all of Kay's years of earnings will be included in determining Kay's AIME. For the typical worker seeking retirement benefits today, SSA first examines the worker's "elapsed years" (also called "base years"), which are years beginning with the year after the worker turns 21 and ending with the year before her first eligibility (age 62). Thus, the typical worker like Kay will have forty elapsed years. SSA then determines "computation years" by subtracting five from the number of elapsed years. Kay, and typical workers like her, will thus have thirty-five computation years that SSA considers in calculating her AIME. SSA includes the thirty-five years in which the worker had her highest earnings (taking into account any indexing). If Kay continues to have earnings in years past first eligibility, SSA may recalculate to take into account these earnings if they would increase her AIME and PIA. Note also that even if Kay is not in the work force for thirty-five years, the earnings she has will still be averaged over a thirty-five year period. For this reason, a spouse who was a stay-at-home parent will often be better off taking auxiliary benefits on the earnings record of the primary worker spouse rather than taking on her own earnings record.

Once SSA has determined the worker's AIME, it determines the worker's PIA by applying a mathematical formula that breaks AIME into three parts separated by two so-called "bend points." The bend points are monetary amounts that change each year. In 2009, the bend points were $744 and $4483. In calculating PIA, SSA includes ninety percent of the AIME below the first bend point, thirty-two percent of the amount between the bend points, and fifteen percent of the amount above the second bend point. If a retiring worker's AIME calculated in 2009 were no more than $744, then she would have a PIA that is ninety percent of that amount. She would receive a monthly benefit check for that amount, assuming no reductions apply as a result of early receipt or other factors.

Although workers with higher AIMEs have higher PIAs and thus receive larger monthly benefit checks, the application of lower percentages of inclusion in PIA to those parts of AIME above the low bend points means that workers with higher earnings receive a lower percentage return on their investment in the program.

Once the worker applies, PIA is determined and resulting adjustments are made (for example, the penalty for receipt of benefits before the worker reaches FRA). The worker's retirement benefits then typically continue for the remainder of her life. Note that SSA makes no adjustments for life expectancies. If Kay and Jack were born at the same time, had identical earnings in covered employment, and retired at FRA, their PIAs would also be identical. If Jack dies at seventy and Kay dies at ninety, however, she will receive far greater actual benefits from the program. The program's failure to account for life expectancy implicitly favors women over men, and Hispanics, Asians, and whites over blacks.

b. Preventing Windfalls

Some higher earning individuals who are entitled to Social Security benefits are also entitled to pensions from noncovered employment. Because such individuals may not have significant earnings subject to the FICA tax, their AIME may be low (even though they are higher earning individuals). Application of the general rules would include 90% of their AIME below the first bend point; however, this significant return was intended to protect lower income workers. To prevent higher-earning individuals from receiving this disproportionately favorable return, a windfall elimination provision (WEP) applies to certain workers.

The WEP applies to workers who became eligible for Social Security retirement or disability benefits after 1985 and who are also entitled to a pension for which they first became eligible after 1985 based on earnings from employment not covered under Social Security. For such workers who first became eligible for Social Security benefits in 1990 or later, SSA includes 40% (and not 90%) of the AIME up to the first bend point. (The percentages of AIME includable between the bend points and past the second bend point remain the same as under the general formula.) For example, suppose that John became entitled to Social Security retirement benefits in 1995 (after eleven years in covered employment) and a pension (from thirty years of noncovered employment) in that same year. After calculating his AIME, the applicable percentages of inclusion around the bend points would not be 90-32-15, but rather would be 40-32-15.

At least some individuals entitled to a pension from noncovered employment may also have earned Social Security coverage over a substantial period of time. To avoid unduly penalizing these individuals, the WEP increases the initial percentage of inclusion by five percent for each year of Social Security coverage from years twenty through thirty. (To receive credit for years of Social Security coverage, the individual must earn an amount that is adjusted annually.) For example, if John became entitled to Social Security retirement benefits and a pension from noncovered employment in 2000, and he had twenty-one years of Social Security coverage, the applicable percentages of inclusion around the bend points would be 45-32-15. A worker who has thirty or more years of Social Security coverage receives the full inclusion of 90 percent below the first bend point; in other words, the general rules of PIA calculation will apply to him.

One final limitation should be noted: to protect the lower income individual who is subject to the WEP, the WEP as applied to the first bend point may never reduce the Social Security benefit by more than one-half of the noncovered pension benefit. For example, assume that Karen has no more than twenty years of Social Security coverage and is entitled to a pension from noncovered employment. The applicable WEP percentage up to the first bend point is 40 percent. In 2009, the first bend point was $744. The amount of inclusion in her PIA up to the first bend point would initially appear to be $297.60 (i.e., 40% of $744). If Karen's monthly pension amount, however, is $500, then the $744 amount can be reduced by no more than $250 (one-half of her monthly pension). Thus, the amount of inclusion will be $494 (that is, $744–$250) rather than $297.60. 20 C.F.R. § 404.213.

c. Government Pension Offset

When an individual receives a pension from her earnings as a noncovered governmental employment and also draws a Social Security derivative or auxiliary benefit as a spouse, ex-spouse, or surviving spouse, her Social Security benefit is reduced by a government pension offset (GPO). The GPO reduces the spouse's auxiliary benefit by two-thirds of her government pension. 20 C.F.R. § 404.408a. The regulation notes limited exceptions in which the offset does not apply.

Assume that Karen is generally eligible for a $500 monthly spousal benefit; however, her civil service pension (based on her own earnings in noncovered governmental employment) is $600 monthly. Because of the GPO, the $500 is reduced by $400 (two-thirds of Karen's pension). Karen will only receive a spousal benefit of $100. If Karen's pension were $750 or more, the GPO would eliminate her right to any Social Security spousal benefit.

The GPO represents an attempt by Congress to treat government employees who do not pay Social Security taxes somewhat like employees working in the private sector who do pay such taxes.

If Karen had some years of Social Security coverage in addition to her years of noncovered governmental employment, she might seek Social Security benefits on her own earnings records. In such a case, however, her benefits might very well be reduced by the windfall elimination provision discussed previously.

13. Representative Payees

If a Social Security beneficiary is unable to manage or direct the management of her benefits, SSA will select an individual or an organization to serve as the beneficiary's representative payee. For adult beneficiaries, SSA requires convincing evidence of the beneficiary's inability to manage her payments before appointing a representative payee. This evidence may include a court's determination that the beneficiary is unable to handle her financial affairs (e.g., a specific court order in a guardianship proceeding) or a recent signed statement from a physician, psychologist, or qualified medical practitioner in a position to provide an informed opinion. In addition to legal or medical evidence, SSA may base its decision on lay evidence, including its own observations of the beneficiary during a face-to-face interview or statements from relatives, close friends, neighbors, or landlords who are in a position to provide an informed opinion.

In selecting the representative payee, SSA considers various factors, including the proposed payee's relationship and concern for the beneficiary, his ability to act in the beneficiary's best interest, and whether he has custody of the beneficiary. For beneficiaries under eighteen, a parent having custody of the beneficiary is preferred. For adult beneficiaries, SSA's usual order of preference is as follows: a legal guardian, spouse, or other relatives having custody of the beneficiary or showing strong concern for her; a friend having custody or showing strong concern; a public or nonprofit agency or institution, federal institution, or statutory guardian or voluntary conservator; a private institution having custody of the beneficiary; others capable and willing to serve without reimbursement, such as volunteers from community groups or organizations; or a friend without custody but who shows strong concern for the beneficiary's personal welfare. A different order of preference exists for adult beneficiaries with substance abuse problems.

SSA provides the beneficiary with advance notice of its decision to make payments to a representative payee. The beneficiary may object, in which case SSA will review the evidence and issue a determination. The beneficiary may appeal SSA's decision. After payments to a representative payee begin, the beneficiary may request a reevaluation of capability. If a beneficiary shows that she can mange or direct management of her benefits, SSA will begin or resume direct payments to the beneficiary.

The representative payee is to determine the beneficiary's current and future needs and use the funds for the beneficiary's best interest. The beneficiary's current needs come first, and are never to be sacrificed to pay other expenses, to conserve or invest funds, or to accumulate funds for the future. The representative payee is to apply the payments only for the beneficiary's use and welfare. If the beneficiary's current and reasonably foreseeable future needs are being met, however, the representative payee may apply part of the benefits for the support of the beneficiary's spouse, child, or parent who is the beneficiary's legal dependent. Funds not disbursed for the beneficiary's current needs are properly disbursed if they are saved or invested for the beneficiary. The payee should invest accumulations of more than $500 or place them in interest-bearing accounts. Preferred investments include various insured bank accounts and U.S. Savings Bonds. The accounts must be separate accounts showing that the payee holds the property in trust for the beneficiary. The payee may not mingle his own money with that of the beneficiary.

The representative payee must keep written records of all payments received from SSA and receipts to show how the monies were spent or saved. He has a duty to report to SSA any event affecting the beneficiary's payment amount or right to benefits; to provide an accounting when requested by SSA (at least annually); to notify SSA when he cannot serve or is no longer suitable to serve; and to return conserved funds to SSA when he no longer serves as representative payee.

When a beneficiary is in an institution or nursing home that is not receiving Medicaid payments on her behalf, the representative payee's obligation to provide first for the beneficiary's current needs usually includes payments for institutional/nursing home care, for items that will aid in her recovery or release, and for items to meet her personal needs and improve her condition.

If a representative payee misuses the beneficiary's payments, SSA will make restitution to the beneficiary if it was negligent in following procedures to investigate or monitor the representative payee's actions, or if the payee is an organization or person serving fifteen or more beneficiaries. SSA may impose civil monetary penalties of up to $5000 for each instance of misuse by the representative payee. The representative payee may also be subject to an assessment of up to twice the amount of the misused payments. SSA may refer the case for criminal prosecution. The convicted payee may be fined up to $25,000 and imprisoned up to five years.

14. Protection of Payments ("Anti-Assignment")

Under Section 207 of the Social Security Act (42 U.S.C. § 407), a beneficiary's right to future payment is generally not transferable or assignable, and none of the moneys paid or payable or rights existing under the Act are subject to execution, levy, attachment, garnishment, or other legal process, or to the operation of any bankruptcy or insolvency law. Several exceptions exist, however. The principal exceptions in which a beneficiary's Social Security payments may be garnished are for child support and alimony. Moreover, the IRS may levy for taxes owed. SSA itself may also seek a refund of overpayments.

SSA notes that its responsibility for protecting the beneficiary's rights under Section 207 typically ceases when the beneficiary is paid. If the beneficiary maintains the Social Security benefits in a discrete bank account consisting only of the Social Security benefits (so that the benefits are clearly identifiable as Social Security benefits), however, then the benefits continue to have their Section 207 protection.

15. Underpayments and Overpayments

SSA has detailed rules and policies for handling underpayments and overpayments of benefits. Due to the program's complex rules and formulas and the need for periodic adjustments and recalculations to account for changing circumstances of beneficiaries, underpayments and overpayments are not uncommon.

When SSA detects an underpayment, it usually pays the amount owed automatically. No written request is required unless SSA lacks complete information. If the amount is owed to a person now deceased, SSA normally makes payments in the following order: to the surviving spouse if living in the same house with the underpaid person at his death or if entitled to a monthly benefit on the underpaid person's earnings record in the month of his death; children entitled to benefits on the underpaid person's earnings record; parents of the underpaid person entitled to benefits on his earnings record; a surviving spouse not falling into the first category; children not falling into the second category; parents not falling into the third category; and the legal representative of the underpaid person's estate.

When SSA detects an overpayment, it sends a notice to the overpaid individual, his representative payee, or his legal representative. The notice indicates the amount overpaid, how and when the overpayment occurred, the recipient's right to request reconsideration of the overpayment determination, and the action required by the recipient of the overpayment. Generally, SSA will request a full, immediate refund, unless the overpayment can be withheld from the next month's benefit check or another proposed adjustment is available. If the overpaid beneficiary has died, his estate is liable for repayment.

If a beneficiary fails to satisfy overpayment by immediate refund or through withholding or adjustment of future benefits payable, SSA may pursue other relief. SSA may enter into a compromise settlement with the beneficiary, particularly if there is a legitimate dispute over the facts. Alternatively, SSA may grant a waiver if the overpaid beneficiary is without fault, recovery or adjustment would defeat the purpose of the program (for example, because the beneficiary needs substantially all of her income to meet ordinary and necessary living expenses), or recovery would be against equity and good conscience.

If SSA decides that litigation is appropriate, the case is referred to the Department of Justice. SSA also has other debt collection tools, including laws that permit withholding of federal income tax refunds and administrative wage garnishment. SSA may also engage in an administrative offset that permits withholding or reduction of federal payments other than tax refunds.

16. Administrative and Judicial Review

The individual who is dissatisfied with SSA's initial determination concerning her entitlement or continuing entitlement to benefits may pursue her claim through an appeals process, which includes a multi-step administrative component that may ultimately lead to an action in federal district court. The review process typically is as follows: initial determination; reconsideration; hearing before an administrative law judge (ALJ); Appeals Council review; and civil action in federal district court.

An expedited appeals process is available at the reconsideration level or higher if the determination has not become final and the claimant's only issue challenges the constitutionality of a provision of the Social Security Act preventing the payment of benefits or a favorable determination in a non-claim earnings discrepancy case. In such instances, the case may proceed directly to federal district court. The claimant must generally request an expedited appeals process within sixty days after the date she receives notice of the reconsidered determination; at any time after filing a timely request for a hearing but before she receives notice of the ALJ's decision; within sixty days after the date she receives a notice of the ALJ's decision; or at any time after filing a timely request for Appeals Council review but before she receives notice of the Appeals Council's action.

a. Initial Determination

Initial determinations cover a wide variety of topics, including entitlement or continuing entitlement to benefits; reentitlement to benefits; the amount of benefits; the recomputation of benefits; revisions of earnings records; termination of benefits; establishment or termination of a period of disability; need for a representative payee and who should be representative payee if one is needed; overpayments and underpayments of benefits; and so on. SSA mails the claimant or her representative notice of the initial determination, stating reasons for the determination, the effect of the determination, and information about the right to review. The initial determination becomes final unless the claimant or her representative makes a written request for a reconsideration. The request must be made within sixty days after the date of receiving the notice of the initial determination. The request can also be made by any other person who shows in writing that his rights may be adversely affected by the initial determination. The sixty-day deadline may be extended if the claimant can demonstrate good cause (as defined in the regulations) for missing that deadline.

b. Reconsideration

A reconsideration is an independent case review of all evidence in the record. This evidence includes the evidence submitted for the initial determination along with any further evidence and information the claimant or her representative submits for the reconsideration. The reconsideration, which is made in the same office that made the initial determination, is not limited to the issues that the claimant raises. Under SSA policy, the person making the reconsideration decision must have had no part in making the initial determination. Unless Supplemental Security Income payments are in question, the reconsideration does not include a formal conference that allows the claimant to participate or subpoena and cross-examine adverse witnesses.

Once SSA has made the reconsideration determination, it mails the claimant a notice detailing the basis for the determination. The determination becomes final unless the claimant or another person shows that the claimants' rights may be adversely affected by the reconsidered determination and makes a written request for a hearing before an administrative law judge (ALJ) within sixty days after the date of receiving the notice of the reconsidered determination; or the claimant or another person uses the expedited appeals process; or SSA revises the reconsidered determination. The time period for filing a hearing request may be extended for good cause.

c. Hearing

A claimant may request a hearing before an ALJ if she disagrees with the reconsidered determination; if she shows her rights may be adversely affected by the decision; or if the local SSA office has made a reconsidered determination or another kind of determination that by SSA regulation provides the right to such a hearing. The claimant is mailed or served with notice of the hearing at least twenty days before the hearing is to occur. The notice contains a statement of the specific issues to be decided, an explanation of procedures, and other information. A claimant objecting to the issues to be decided must notify the ALJ in writing, stating the reasons for her objections. The ALJ then makes a decision on the objections either in writing or at the hearing.

The hearing usually provides the only opportunity in the administrative review process for the claimant to appear personally before the decision-maker. At the hearing, the claimant may appear in person or by video teleconference; may testify under oath or affirmation; may submit new evidence; may examine the evidence used in the reconsidered determination; and may present and question witnesses. The ALJ has the power to issue subpoenas. The claimant may waive her right to an oral hearing, in which case the ALJ typically makes his decision based on the evidence from the reconsideration determination and from any new evidence submitted by the claimant or any other party.

The ALJ may dismiss the hearing request if the claimant requests dismissal; if the claimant fails to appear at the hearing without waiving her right to appear or establishing good cause for her absence; if the claimant does not file the request within the time limit and does not establish good cause for missing the deadline; if the claimant has no right to a hearing; if a previous decision or determination that has become final was made for the claimant involving the same facts and issues; if the claimant dies and no substitute pursues her request; or if the SSA office has made a fully favorable revised reconsideration determination.

The hearing may proceed along one of several paths. For example, the ALJ may hold the hearing and issue his decision; hold a limited hearing to determine whether the evidence warrants reviewing a prior determination or decision; or send the case back to the local SSA office for a revised determination. The ALJ may also hold a pre-hearing or post-hearing conference on his own or at the request of a party to the hearing. Parties receive notice of a conference at least seven days before it occurs. A record of the conference is made, and agreements and actions of the parties at the conference are binding unless one of the parties objects.

The ALJ usually issues a written decision or dismisses the case after the hearing; however, on occasion he may send the case with a recommended decision to the Appeals Council for its decision.

A decision of the ALJ generally becomes final unless the claimant or another party makes a written request for Appeals Council review within sixty days after receiving notice of the ALJ's decision; or the Appeals Council within sixty days after the ALJ's decision or dismissal decides on its own motion to review the action; or the claimant requests the expedited review process within sixty days after receiving notice of the ALJ's decision.

d. Appeals Council Review

A claimant at the hearing may make a written request for Appeals Council review if she disagrees with the hearing decision or with dismissal of the hearing request. The request should be made within sixty days after the date the party receives notice of the ALJ's action. (Again, the claimant may receive an extension if she proves good cause.) The Appeals Council may dismiss the request. Alternatively, the Appeals Council may grant the request and issue a decision or remand the case to an ALJ. Within sixty days following the ALJ's decision or dismissal, the Appeals Council may decide on its own motion to review the action (including an action that is favorable to a claimant).

The Appeals Council will typically review a case when it appears that the ALJ may have abused his discretion; when the ALJ has made an error of law; when the ALJ has made findings or conclusions or taken action that is not supported by substantial evidence; when the case involves a broad policy or procedural issue that may affect the general public interest; or when there is new and material evidence relating to the period on or before the date of the ALJ's decision that makes the ALJ's findings, conclusions, or action contrary to the weight of the evidence currently in the record. 20 C.F.R. §416.1470.

If the Appeals Council decides to review the case, it may limit the issues it will consider. The Appeals Council considers all evidence in the record before the ALJ and new and material evidence submitted that relates to the period on or before the date of the ALJ's hearing decision. If the Appeals Council decides that additional evidence is needed, it may remand the case to an ALJ to receive evidence and issue a new decision unless the Appeals Council decides that it can obtain the evidence more quickly. The claimant may request an oral argument before the Appeals Council. The Appeals Council grants such a request if it decides that the case raises an important question of law or policy or that oral argument would help it reach a proper decision.

The Appeals Council provides the highest level of SSA administrative decisional review, and thus provides the SSA's final decision.

e. Judicial Review

A claimant unhappy with the result of an Appeals Council decision may file an action in federal district court where the claimant resides or has her principal place of business. The claimant must file the action within sixty days after the date she received the notice of the decision from the Appeals Council. As at other stages of the review process, the time period may be extended if the claimant shows good cause. (The Appeals Council decides whether to grant a claimant an extension for filing in federal district court.) The claimant may also file for an expedited appeal at any time before she receives notice of the Appeals Council's decision.

The court may affirm, modify, or reverse the lower decision. If the claimant appeals, the decision is subject to further judicial review in a federal Court of Appeals. Ultimately, the case may be heard by the United States Supreme Court.

In some instances, the federal district court may remand the case to the Appeals Council. The Appeals Council may then make a decision or itself remand the case to an ALJ. The Appeals Council or ALJ may consider any issues relating to the claim, regardless of whether they were raised in the administrative proceedings leading to the final decision in the case. The regulations specifically authorize the Appeals Council to make a new, independent decision based on the entire record that will be the final decision of the Commissioner after remand or, alternatively, to remand the case to an ALJ for further proceedings.

Under SSA policy, the claimant has no right to review in federal district court when the Appeals Council has dismissed a request for review or when the Appeals Council has denied a request for review of an ALJ's dismissal decision. 20 C.F.R. § 416.1472.

17. Representation of a Claimant

At every point from the initial determination forward, the claimant may choose to be represented by an attorney or other qualified individual. The claimant must notify SSA in writing of her choice to be represented, preferably using SSA's "appointment of representative" form. If the claimant chooses to be represented by someone other than an attorney, the representative must also submit a written acceptance of the appointment to SSA or sign the appointment of representative form.

Once appointed, the representative is entitled to any information about the claim that the claimant herself could access. The representative receives SSA notices and copies of actions, determinations, decisions, and requests for information or evidence. Such information received by the representative has the same force and effect as if received by the claimant. The representative may submit evidence, present facts and law, appear at proceedings (with or without the claimant), and make requests and give notice about proceedings. He cannot testify for the claimant and may not sign applications on the claimant's behalf for benefits or rights.

SSA must authorize fees to be paid to the representative for his services dealing with SSA on behalf of the claimant. SSA uses one of two methods to authorize the representative's fee: the fee agreement or the fee petition. Under the fee agreement process, the claimant and the representative file with SSA a written agreement, signed by each, before the date of a favorable determination by SSA. SSA typically approves the agreement at the time of the favorable determination or decision if the claim results in past-due benefits and if the fee specified in the agreement does not exceed the lesser of a prescribed dollar amount or twenty-five percent of the past-due benefits. 42 U.S.C. § 406. (Effective June 22, 2009, the set amount is $6000. From 2002 until that time, the set amount had been $5300. 75 Fed. Reg. 6080 (Feb. 4, 2009).) If SSA approves the fee agreement, it notifies the claimant and the representative of the past-due benefit amount; the amount payable to the claimant; the amount that the representative may charge and collect; and an explanation that the claimant, the representative, the decision maker, or the claimant's auxiliary beneficiaries have fifteen days after receiving notice to request review of the fee amount. If SSA disapproves of the fee agreement, the claimant or representative has fifteen days after receiving notice of the disapproval to request review.

If SSA's determination of decision is unfavorable or if SSA otherwise denies the fee agreement, the representative who wishes to charge and collect a fee must use the second method of payment: the fee petition. The representative files a fee petition (on an SSA form) after completing his services regarding the claim. He also sends a copy to the claimant. The petition requests a fee and gives detailed information about services rendered and the amount of time the representative spent on the case. In setting the fee, SSA also considers the complexity of the case. Once SSA sets the fee, it notifies the representative and the claimant and provides information about how it set the fee. The claimant, her auxiliary beneficiaries, or the representative may request review of the fee amount within thirty days after receipt of notice.

SSA makes direct payments to a representative from the claimant's past-due benefits. When making such direct payments to the representative, SSA deducts the lower of 6.3 percent of the representative's fee or a prescribed amount ($79 in 2009) to cover administrative costs. The representative cannot demand reimbursement of this amount from the claimant. If the claimant and representative had no fee agreement or SSA disapproved the fee agreement, the representative must file a fee petition within sixty days of notice of a favorable determination to receive direct payment.

The representative must inform SSA if the claimant has deposited monies into a trust or escrow account to ensure payment of the fee, or if the representative has received payments toward the fee from other sources. These amounts are deducted from the fee award before SSA makes the direct payment.

If the case proceeds to court and the claimant obtains a favorable ruling, the court may allow a reasonable attorney fee for services rendered that may include twenty-five percent of the claimant's past due benefits. Under the Equal Access to Justice Act (EAJA), the attorney may also request reimbursement of his expenses incurred in representing a claimant before a governmental agency. The court may authorize such a fee if the claimant prevails and if the court finds that the position of the government was not substantially justified. If the court authorizes both an SSA attorney fee and a fee under EAJA, the attorney must refund the smaller amount to the claimant.

18. Taxation of Benefits

Since the mid-1980s, a portion of a recipient's Social Security benefits are treated as income potentially subject to taxation under federal laws. 26 U.S.C. § 86. IRS applies a formula that first combines all of the beneficiary's income including tax-exempt or tax-excluded amounts (for example, tax-exempt interest), plus one-half of Social Security benefits. If this sum does not exceed a base amount, then no Social Security benefits are subject to taxation. In contrast, if this sum exceeds a base amount (the first threshold) but does not exceed a second threshold amount, the tax formulas generally provide that up to 50% of the Social Security benefits are taxable. The base amount or first threshold is $25,000 for single individuals and $32,000 for married couples filing jointly.

If the formula yields a sum that exceeds the second (and higher) threshold, up to eighty-five percent of benefits can be taxable. For individuals, the second threshold amount is $34,000; for married couples filing jointly, it is $44,000. (Up to 85% of benefits can also be taxable if the taxpayer is married filing separately and lived with the spouse at any time during the year.)

Both the first and second threshold amounts are provided for in the tax statutes and do not change annually. The tax statute is designed to protect lower income persons from paying federal income tax on their Social Security benefits. In fact, SSA points out that most Social Security recipients fall below the first threshold and thus pay no federal income tax on their benefits.

Although state governments are permitted to tax Social Security benefits, most states do not do so. Moreover, the trend is against such taxation. Thus, several states are currently in the process of phasing out state taxation of Social Security benefits. States that continue to tax Social Security benefits have adopted various approaches.

19. Reforming the Program

Social Security benefits cannot be sustained indefinitely at their current level if financing of the program remains unchanged. Predictions in 2008 indicated that before 2020 the fund would collect less than the amount of benefits it must pay; by 2040, the fund would be exhausted. The 2009 Annual Report from the Social Security Board of Trustees revised those estimates to indicate that the fund would experience cash flow deficits beginning in 2016 and that the reserves would be exhausted by 2037. Eventually, Congress will have to address the problem.

Although everyone agrees that the system must be changed or substantially tweaked, the proposals for reform vary significantly. Congress could retain the basic structure of the existing program by increasing the payroll tax rate, by increasing or eliminating the cap on wages subject to payroll tax, or by increasing normal retirement age and the earliest eligibility age. A simple increase in the tax rate would have a disproportionate adverse impact upon workers with lower wages. Increasing retirement age could have a disproportionate adverse impact upon workers in jobs that require strength and endurance.

Under the current system, workers do not own or control any part of their contribution. One controversial idea is to convert a part of the traditional Social Security contribution into an individual account that the worker invests in private funds. Most supporters of this approach suggest that workers would be entitled to two levels of benefits: first, a somewhat traditional, but substantially lower Social Security payment based on her contributions to the fund and, second, the contributions (plus earnings and minus losses) in her private account. In light of the market downturn that began in 2008 and that took even many investment professionals by surprise, privatization proposals seem much less likely now to garner general congressional support.

A different suggestion for reform uses price indexing as the basis for determining Social Security benefits. Currently most or all of the worker's yearly wages are indexed, the sum of the worker's highest thirty-five years is divided by 420 (which is 35 years times 12 months for each year), and a progressive benefit formula is applied to two bend points (the PIA factors) to determine the worker's primary insurance amount (PIA). The workers' benefit checks are then price-indexed annually based on the Consumer Price Index. The price indexing proposal differs from current law by including price indexing earlier in the calculation of benefits. For example, because prices are expected to grow less rapidly than wages, multiplying the PIA factors by the price growth/wage growth fraction would substantially reduce benefit payments over time. This kind of blanket price indexing would adversely affect all recipients—including those who can least afford it. Alternatively, a progressive price indexing scheme might apply price indexing to all the wages of those with the highest earnings, to some of the wages of those within a midrange of earnings, and to none of the wages of those with the lowest earnings. Over time, a progressive price indexing proposal considerably flattens the level of benefits among all workers. For a more detailed discussion of this proposal and others discussed in this subsection, see Kathryn L. Moore, *Social Security Reform: Fundamental Restructuring or Incremental Change?*, 11 Lewis & Clark L. Rev. 341 (2007).

A third proposal is simply for Congress to finance the program through general revenue allocations. Opponents fear that annual budget debates could weaken public support for the program; they also worry that weakening the link between worker contributions and worker benefits could allow the system to spiral out of control. Under an alternative proposal, Congress would allocate some or all of the federal estate revenue (as opposed to general revenue) to the Social Security program.

B. Other Public Retirement and Pension Programs

1. Railroad Worker Benefits

Like the Social Security Act, the federal Railroad Retirement Act (RRA) is a product of the Great Depression. Enacted in 1934, 1935, and 1937, the RRA in many ways parallels the Social Security Act. The RRA, however, provides a system of social insurance for a specific population: vested railroad workers and their families. Not surprisingly, the number of covered employees has declined substantially with the decline of the railroad. At the end of the 1930s, the Act covered 1.2 million workers; by the mid-1990s, the Act covered only slightly more than a quarter of a million workers.

Using its own age and service requirement formulas, the railroad program provides monthly benefits to retired or disabled workers, their spouses, certain ex-spouses, certain dependents, and certain survivors of deceased workers.

The program also pays a lump sum benefit upon the death of the worker, which can vary based on the deceased worker's years of service.

To be a vested (or "career") railroad worker, the worker (1) must have 120 months (ten years) of service in the railroad industry or (2) must have, effective January 1, 2002, at least 60 months of service in the railroad industry, all of which accrued after December 31, 1995. Once a worker is vested, his service and compensation records generally cannot be used for benefit purposes under Social Security. If a worker is nonvested at the time of retirement or at the onset of disability, however, the Railroad Retirement Board generally transfers the worker's records to the Social Security Administration.

A two-tier formula determines annuity amounts. The first tier considers the worker's railroad credits and any Social Security credits. This amount is comparable to a Social Security benefit. The second tier considers only the worker's railroad credits. This amount is more like a pension benefit that is paid in other industries above and beyond the worker's receipt of Social Security.

Although separate from Social Security benefits, Railroad Retirement benefits are coordinated with many various aspects of the Social Security program. (There are notable distinctions, however.) The tier one part of a railroad annuity is typically increased by a cost of living adjustment at the same time and by the same amount that Social Security benefits are increased. The tier two part of the annuity, however, is typically increased annually by 32.5% of the increase in the consumer price index.

A worker's benefits are subject to reduction in several circumstances. For example, benefits may be reduced for workers who retire early (as defined under the system) and also for workers who are first eligible for both tier one benefits and certain government pensions or other payments after 1985.

Railroad retirement tier one payroll taxes for employers and employees are the same as Social Security payroll taxes. Railroad employers and employees, however, also pay a tier two tax to finance tier two benefits, with the employer being taxed at a significantly higher rate than the employee.

The two tiers of a railroad retirement annuity—the Social Security equivalent benefit and the non-Social Security equivalent benefit—are treated differently for federal income tax purposes. Although the worker receives only one monthly benefit, he generally receives two tax statements from the Railroad Retirement Board. The Social Security-equivalent benefit is taxed like a true Social Security benefit. The other part of the annuity is generally taxed like a private pension. The federal statute precludes state and local governments from taxing the tier two benefits and other benefits that exceed Social Security benefits.

The Railroad Retirement Act begins at 45 U.S.C. § 231. The principal regulations can be found beginning at 20 C.F.R. 201.1; regulations discussing the interrelationship between the Social Security program and the Railroad Retirement program begin at 20 C.F.R. 404.1401. Finally, the Railroad Board itself publishes pamphlets and other helpful information concerning the program. These materials are available at www.rrb.gov.

2. Government Employment

a. Federal

The Civil Service Retirement System (CSRS) is a defined benefit, contributory retirement system that covers most employees of the federal government hired before 1984. CSRS became effective in 1920, and was the only major retirement program for federal employees prior to 1984. Federal employees covered by CSRS were excluded from Social Security coverage.

The CSRS program is funded by general revenue, the employer, and employee payroll taxes. CSRS benefits include those for retirement, disability, and survivors. The CSRS annuity is based on a formula that considers the employee's length of service and the employee's highest average basic pay earned during any three consecutive years of service (the employee's "high-3" average). The basic annuity may be reduced because of spousal (or ex-spousal) benefits to be paid after the employee's death, because of the employee's early retirement, or because of the employee's service for which he did not make retirement contributions. The benefits include a COLA. While CSRS employees typically pay no OASI (Social Security) payroll tax, they do pay the HI (Medicare) tax.

Social Security laws were changed in the 1980s, when Congress created the Federal Employees Retirement System (FERS). The change required most new federal employees to participate in the Social Security program by paying OASI taxes. FERS covers most employees hired after 1983 and also covers employees formerly covered by CSRS who elected to transfer to the FERS program. The FERS program officially began on January 1, 1987.

In comparison to CSRS, FERS is more like benefit programs in the private sector. FERS employment offers three forms of benefits: Social Security; a basic benefit plan (BBP); and an optional thrift savings plan (TSP). The employee pays full Social Security taxes, makes a contribution to the BBP, and has the option of making tax-deferred contributions to the TSP. The TSP offers the kind of savings and tax benefits that private companies often offer their employees under 401(k) plans. The employee controls how much of his pay to put into his TSP account.

The BBP of FERS is a defined benefit plan, under which the employer promises a level of benefits tied to a formula. The BBP annuity amount depends on length of service and the employee's "high-3" average pay. For the employee to be vested—i.e., to be eligible to receive retirement benefits from the plan if he leaves federal service before retiring—he must have at least five years of creditable civilian service. The FERS program also includes survivor and disability benefits. COLAs tied to the consumer price index apply to most benefits.

The legislation that created FERS also created the CSRS "offset" plan. CSRS offset employees are employees who are covered by CSRS and also by Social Security. Such employees receive their CSRS annuity, but it is reduced when they become eligible for Social Security benefits (typically at age 62). The reduction amount is the amount of the Social Security benefit attributable to service after 1983 that was covered by both CSRS and Social Security. 5 C.F.R. 831.0005. CSRS survivor and disability benefits are similarly reduced if Social Security survivor or disability benefits are payable.

Court orders relating to divorce or separation can divide a CSRS or FERS annuity; divide a refund of employee retirement contributions; provide a survivor annuity payable upon the death of an employee or retiree; permit a former spouse to maintain coverage under the Federal Employees Health Benefits (FEHB) program; or require an employee or retiree to assign his Federal Employees Group Life Insurance (FEGLI) coverage to a former spouse or children. Lawyers drafting such orders should note that CSRS and FERS are exempted from the ERISA rules that apply to qualified pension plans in the private sector. Lawyers often believe that an order that satisfies ERISA's QDRO rules will be equally effective for CSRS or FERS plans; however, they are frequently wrong. For example, under ERISA the ex-spouse's share of the benefit may begin when the employee reaches minimum retirement age, regardless of whether the employee has retired. This early benefit is not available under CSRS or FERS, however. The Office of Personnel Management (OPM), which administers CSRS and FERS, provides a handbook, available online, for attorneys who are drafting court-orders concerning retirement, health benefits, and life insurance under CSRS, FERS, FEHB, and FEGLI.

In addition to CSRS and FERS, other retirement programs exist for specific groups of federal employees (e.g., the Foreign Service Retirement System); however, the great majority of federal employees are covered by CSRS or FERS. The statutes pertaining to CSRS begin at 5 U.S.C. §8331. The statutes pertaining to FERS begins at 5 U.S.C. §8401. The United States Office of Personnel Management offers online information about CSRS and FERS at www.opm.gov.

b. State and Local

In 2009, the United States Bureau of Labor Statistics (BLS) observed that state and local retirement plans of some sort were available to ninety-two percent of state and local government employees. Most state and local retirement plans traditionally promise to provide the employee a certain level of retirement benefits tied to a formula. This approach contrasts with private sector retirement plans, which increasingly do not provide a defined benefit. Unlike most private sector pension plans, state and local benefit plans typically include a COLA. State and local defined benefit plans usually depend more on employee contributions than do private sector defined benefit plans.

In 2008, BLS indicated that about three times as many state and local employees had access to defined benefit plans as they did to defined contribution plans. An increasing trend, however, is for state and local governments to offer employees an employee-contribution-only plan along with a defined benefit plan.

Although many state and local pension plans were inadequately funded into the 1970s, this problem was substantially reduced in subsequent years. By the early twenty-first century, most plans appeared to be substantially funded and at least reasonably sound. In part, this improvement may have resulted from state laws adopting more stringent accounting standards. More recently, however, state and local plans have been seriously affected by the financial crisis that began in 2008.

State and local plans vary substantially. Not surprisingly, plans for public employees whose jobs are physically demanding tend to have earlier retirement ages and more extensive disability coverage. Such is true for police and firefighters, for example.

Most employees of state and local governments are also covered by the Social Security program. Social Security did not originally include such employees; however, changes in Social Security laws allowed (or required, in some instances) state and local governments to provide Social Security coverage to employees. Today, more than seventy percent of state and local employees participate in the Social Security program. Most of those employees not covered by Social Security are police, firefighters, and teachers. Uncovered employees tend to be concentrated in a few states, including California, Colorado, Illinois, Louisiana, Massachusetts, Ohio, and Texas.

c. Military

Military service performed on or after January 1, 1957 is usually creditable for Social Security benefits. Thus many military retirees and their families receive monthly Social Security benefits under rules that apply to the Social Security program generally.

In addition, the military retirement system provides a funded, noncontributory defined benefit plan that includes retirement, disability, and survivor annuity programs. Upon honorably serving in the military for twenty years, an individual is qualified for retirement pay. Unlike most pension plans, the military pension begins when the qualified individual retires, regardless of his age. An individual who entered the armed services as a teenager and retired twenty years later could thus begin receiving his military pension in his thirties.

The benefit formula for an individual depends upon when the individual first became a member of the armed services. One formula applies to retirees who first became members of the armed services before September 8, 1980; another formula applies to retirees who first became members on or after September 8, 1980 but before August 1, 1986; and a third formula applies to retirees who first became members on or after August 1, 1986. An annual COLA automatically adjusts benefits. Military retirement pay in most cases is fully taxable. Military retirement pay generally cannot be garnished; however, among the notable exceptions are provisions permitting garnishment for alimony and child support. 5 C.F.R. 581.101 et seq. The Uniformed Services Former Spouse's Protection Act provides that state courts may treat military retirement pay as property in divorce cases. 10 U.S.C. § 1408.

The military retirement system applies to members of the Army, Navy, Marine Corps, and Air Force, and is administered by the Department of Defense. Most of the retirement provisions also apply to certain other individuals, including members of the Coast Guard (administered by the Department of Transportation), officers of the Public Health Service (administered by the Department of Health and Human Services), and officers of the National Oceanic and Atmospheric Administration (administered by the Department of Commerce). 5 C.F.R. 831.301.

An individual eligible for a military disability retirement system benefit may also be eligible for Veterans Affairs (VA) disability benefits concerning a service-connected disability. (The two programs use different standards for determining disability.) A VA benefit may replace or partly replace military retirement benefits (on a dollar-to-dollar basis), but cannot be added to the military retirement benefit. Because VA benefits are exempt from federal income taxation, an individual eligible for both kinds of benefits may wish to forego the military benefits in favor of the VA benefit. Moreover, the individual who establishes a service-connected disability entitling him to VA benefits receives numerous other benefits concerning treatment and admittance at VA facilities.

C. Veterans' Benefits

The Department of Veterans' Affairs (VA) oversees a range of benefits for veterans, service members, and their families. Among the most important benefits are disability compensation; a veteran pension; provisions for dependents and survivors; and health care. Other benefit programs cover education; vocational rehabilitation and employment; home loans; life insurance; and burial.

An individual who is discharged from active military service under other than dishonorable conditions is potentially eligible for VA benefits. Active service is full-time service (other than active duty for training) as a member of the Army, Navy, Air Force, Marine Corps, Coast Guard, or as a commissioned officer of the Public Health Service or National Oceanic and Atmospheric Administration.

Under the disability compensation program, the VA will make monthly payments to an individual who is at least ten percent disabled as a result of a disability that resulted from active duty in the armed forces. Disabilities that resulted from an injury or disease existing before service, but that were aggravated by that service, are covered. Moreover, disabilities that resulted from active duty, but that appeared substantially later, are covered. The amount of compensation generally depends upon the percentage of disability. A veteran with a disability rating of at least thirty percent is eligible for additional allowances for dependents. Dependents may include spouses, minor children, children under twenty-three attending school, children permanently incapable of self-support because of a disability that arose before age eighteen, and dependent parents. The amount of this additional payment depends upon the disability rating of the veteran and the number of dependents. As discussed in the preceding section, military retirement pay can affect the VA disability compensation amount.

The VA pension program provides payments to low-income veterans who are permanently and totally disabled or who are sixty-five and older. To be eligible for such payments, a veteran also must satisfy a minimum active period of service requirement—a period that varies, but is never less than ninety days, at least one day of which was during a period of war. The VA recognizes the following war periods: the Mexican Border Period; World War I; World War II; the Korean War; the Vietnam War; and the Gulf War. The Gulf War period runs from August 2, 1990 to a date yet to be set by law or Presidential proclamation.

The VA survivors program provides a death pension to certain low-income spouses and unmarried children of deceased veterans who satisfied the minimum active period of service requirement, at least one day of which was during a period of war. To be eligible, the spouse must not have remarried, and children must be under eighteen, or under age twenty-three if attending school, or have become permanently incapable of self-support because of a disability that arose before age eighteen. An award for dependency and indemnity compensation (DIC) is payable to survivors when the veteran's death resulted from a service-related disability; a disease or injury incurred or aggravated while on active duty; or an injury incurred or aggravated while on inactive duty training. The DIC award is also payable in certain cases when the veteran was totally disabled from a service-connected disability or condition at the time of death, even though the disability or condition did not cause his death.

In addition to the death pension and DIC payments for survivors, VA benefits include educational assistance to qualifying dependents of certain veterans who died of a service-connected disability or who suffer a specified level of disability or who are currently missing in action. A surviving spouse loses eligibility for educational assistance benefits if she remarries before age fifty-seven or is cohabiting with another person who has been held out publicly as her spouse. Children usually must be between eighteen and twenty-six to receive educational benefits.

To honor the deceased veteran, the VA offers various burial benefits. These benefits can include a monument or marker for eligible veterans; a presidential memorial certificate; a burial flag; burial in a VA national cemetery; and in some instances, reimbursement of some burial expenses.

Initial claims for VA benefits are typically made at a local VA office. There is at least one VA office in each state. A claimant who receives an adverse decision may appeal. Appeals most commonly arise because the local office determines that the claimant has no disability, determines the disability is not service connected, or determines that the disability is less severe than the claimant believes it to be. The claimant has one year from the date of the notification of the adverse decision to file an appeal. The claimant should first file a written Notice of Disagreement (NOD) with the office or center that made the decision. (The claimant may then request a file review at the local office. The review may include a personal hearing.) After receiving the NOD, VA will then furnish a "Statement of the Case" (SOC) to the claimant. The SOC explains in detail the evidence, laws, and regulations the VA office used in deciding the claim.

If the claimant wishes to pursue the appeal, the last step in the VA appeal process is to file a Form 9 to establish his right to a "Substantive Appeal." The Form 9 states the benefit sought, the mistakes in the SOC, and may request a personal hearing. The Form 9 must be received by the local VA office within sixty days of the date that the office mailed the SOC or within one year of the date that the office mailed the original decision denying the claim, whichever is later.

The Board of Veterans' Appeals (BVA) rules on the appeal. If he has so requested on the Form 9, the claimant (and his representative, if any) may have a personal hearing with a member of the BVA in Washington, D.C., at a VA regional office, or by videoconference. The hearing is conducted informally, and a transcript is made and sent to BVA with the claimant's file. The Board member later reviews all of the information and makes a decision and sends the claimant a copy. Occasionally the claim is remanded for further information.

During the appeals process, the claimant may be assisted or represented by a veterans' service organization (VSO), an agent, or an attorney if he so chooses. VSOs include The American Legion and Disabled American Veterans, and they often have offices at local VA centers.

The claimant may appeal a final decision of the Board of Veterans' Appeals to the United States Court of Appeals for Veterans Claims. (This court is an independent court that is not part of the Department of Veterans Affairs.) Alternatively, the claimant may try to reopen the claim at the local VA office or may file a motion asking the Board for a reconsideration because of a clear and unmistakable error.

D. Private Sector Pension and Retirement Plans

1. Overview of Employee Benefit Plans

An employee benefit plan is an entity created or maintained primarily or exclusively by an employer to do what its name suggests: to provide benefits to employees. The most important form of plan to help the retired worker meet the cost of living is the pension benefit plan; however, some employers also provide welfare benefit plans, which may afford medical and other non-pension benefits.

Pension plans began to appear formally by the end of the nineteenth century, as America became more industrialized and employers felt increased need for long-term, skilled employees. By promising a pension, companies could better attract and retain those workers. During the Great Depression, however, plans often failed and employee expectations were dashed. The government's concern for the retirement security of its elderly population, which eventually led to the creation of Social Security, also gave rise to strengthened tax and labor laws that spurred the growth of private pension plans. By mid-century, employers increasingly realized the tax advantages of plan formation. Today, it is the tax advantages afforded to employers by qualified employee benefit plans that are primarily responsible for their formation and continued existence. Tens of millions of American workers are covered by private pension plans.

Federal law does not require private employers to offer a benefit plan. Nonetheless, many thousands of employer-sponsored plans exist across the country. They are particularly likely to be found in the manufacturing industry, among large companies, and in employment where workers are unionized. More than 48 million private-sector workers are covered by employer-sponsored pension plans. These private sector plans are generally subject to the requirements of the Employee Retirement Income Security Act (ERISA), discussed below. For general information on pension plans, visit the Department of Labor website at www.dol.gov/ebsa.

2. Kinds of Plans

A pension plan is generally classified as either a defined benefit plan or a defined contribution plan.

a. Defined Benefit Plan

A defined benefit plan is one in which the employer promises to provide the employee a certain level of retirement benefits that is tied to a formula. The formula is usually one of three kinds: a fixed-benefit formula (also called a flat-benefit formula), a career-average formula, or a final-average formula. A fixed-benefit formula promises the employee a certain amount, such as a specific dollar amount or a specific amount based on a percentage of the employee's final pay. Under a career-average formula, a participant's yearly earnings are averaged over the period in which she participates in the plan, and her benefit is a percentage of her average earnings multiplied by the number of her years of service. A final-average formula is similar to the career-average formula, except that it typically averages earnings only from specified years near the end of the employee's career (when her earnings are presumed to be at their highest level), and then calculates her benefit as a percentage of her average final earnings times the number of her years of service.

A defined benefit plan may also consider the employee's projected Social Security benefits, in which case it is considered an integrated plan. An integrated plan's coordination of benefits means that the plan is less costly to the employer, because the employee's plan benefit is reduced by her projected Social Security benefits.

Employees begin to accrue benefits under a defined benefit plan as soon as they become participants. They do not become vested until they have worked for the period of time required by the plan, however. Only when they are vested are participants guaranteed to receive all or a portion of their benefits at retirement age.

Retirement benefits often take the form of an annuity for the life of the retired worker or, alternatively, for the combined lives of the pensioner and her surviving spouse. As mentioned in the section on government employee retirement plans, defined benefit plans that are public (e.g., sponsored by federal, state, or local government) often include a cost-of-living adjustment; private-sector plans usually do not.

A defined benefit plan promises a certain benefit to its participants, regardless of the value of plan's investments. From the stance of the employer, a defined benefit plan is therefore a somewhat risky endeavor. The employer bears the risk that the plan is underfunded or that plan investments will fail. Moreover, most defined benefit plans also require complex actuarial projections to better ensure that funding is adequate to provide the promised level of benefits. Thus, the defined benefit plan is more difficult to administer than a defined contribution plan. In sum, it is not surprising that fewer and fewer single employers now provide defined benefit plans. The number of single-employer plans (plans governing non-union workers) dropped from over 129,000 in 1985 to less than 30,000 in 2004. Those plans remaining tend to be quite large.

b. Defined Contribution Plan

Because of the cost and complexity of defined benefit plan administration and the stricter funding requirements, employers today are increasingly choosing defined contribution plans for their employees. In a defined contribution plan (also called an individual account plan), the employee has a separate account maintained in his name. The defined contribution plan contains no employer promise to provide a certain level of retirement benefits. At retirement, an employee may receive the vested balance in his account. Depending upon the plan, contributions may come from the employer, the employee, or both (often under a matching arrangement).

A defined contribution plan may take any of several forms. It may be a money purchase plan, in which the employer's contributions are mandatory and typically represent a percentage of the employee's salary; a profit sharing plan, in which the employer contributes an amount based on a formula (that is usually, but not necessarily, tied to profits); a target benefit plan, in which the employer contributes an amount projected (but not guaranteed) to provide a certain level of benefits; a stock bonus plan (including the employee stock ownership plan, or ESOP, that invests principally in the employer's own stock); or one of several other kinds of plans.

A cash-or-deferred-arrangement plan (a CODA or 401(k) plan) is an increasingly common and important form of profit-sharing or stock-bonus plan. It permits the employee to choose whether the employer will make contributions to his tax-deferred retirement account or, instead, will pay that same amount to him as compensation. Some employers provide contributions to match those made by the employee to the account. The plan may provide the employee with significant discretion on how the funds in his retirement account are invested. (The equivalent of the 401(k) for educational institutions and nonprofits is the 403(b) account.)

Because the defined contribution plan does not include an employee guarantee of a certain level of benefits, the employee bears the risk that his account will not grow adequately to meet his needs in old age. The employee who makes bad investment choices may find himself with little or no retirement benefits.

3. ERISA

Because of the lack of comprehensive and uniform federal laws regulating pension plans in the private sector, well into the second half of the twentieth century defined benefit plans continued to be underfunded and to fail. In 1963, thousands of workers were affected when an established car manufacturer, Studebaker, collapsed and its pension plans were terminated. This and several other notable incidents eventually led Congress to enact the Employee Retirement Income Security Act (ERISA) in 1974. ERISA preempts state law and imposes stringent rules on covered plans. Government plans are exempt from ERISA. Church plans are also exempt from ERISA if no election for coverage has been made. In sum, ERISA governs most employer and union sponsored retirement plans in private industry.

Title I of ERISA is designed to protect plan participants and their beneficiaries in employee benefit plans. Title I is codified in federal labor laws. Title I includes laws concerning participation, vesting, funding, reporting and disclosure, enforcement and administration, and fiduciary responsibility. Title II contains the tax provisions of ERISA and is codified in federal tax laws. Title III lays out the jurisdictional roles of the Treasury Department and the Labor Department under ERISA.

Title IV of ERISA created the Pension Benefit Guaranty Corporation (PBGC), a federal corporation, to insure that a minimum level of benefits will be paid under covered single employer plans or multiemployer plans in the event of a shortfall resulting from plan termination. (Multiemployer plans are plans to which more than one employer contributes as a result of a collective bargaining agreement. They are sometimes called union plans.) The corporation is funded primarily by premiums paid by companies sponsoring pension plans, by returns on investments, by assets recovered from terminated plans, and by recoveries from terminated sponsors. Importantly, the insurance program extends only to private-sector defined benefit plans, not to public-sector plans (federal, state, and local government) or church plans. Moreover, there is no similar federal guarantee of benefits for participants in defined contribution plans.

a. Qualified and Nonqualified Plans

The heart of Title II is plan qualification. A pension plan is qualified for favorable tax treatment if it satisfies specific, rigorous requirements of the internal revenue code. When an employer makes a contribution to a qualified plan, the amount of the contribution is immediately deductible in determining the employer's taxes, even though the contribution amount will not be distributed to (or included in the income of) the employee at that time. The tax advantages for the employee are also substantial. The earnings that result from the contributions to the pension fund can accumulate tax-free until they are distributed to the employee; thus, the fund can grow more rapidly. Moreover, the employee is not taxed on the contributions to and earnings by the fund until they are distributed to her, at which time she is likely to be in a lower marginal federal income tax bracket.

These tax advantages do not exist for the nonqualified plan. With a nonqualified plan, the employer receives a deduction for its contribution in the year that the employee must include the contribution in her gross income. The employee is usually taxed on the contribution when the employer makes a contribution, even if the employee has no right to a distribution until many years later. Earnings on the fund do not accumulate tax-free.

Although qualified plans are more important in providing retirement security for the typical elderly American, in some instances it suits the employer's purpose to have a nonqualified plan. Nonqualified plans can be cheaper to create, fund, and administer. Moreover, because of anti-discrimination rules that apply to qualified plans, an employer may choose a nonqualified plan to discriminate among employees it wishes to include or exclude. Nonqualified plans are generally covered by trust law rather than the internal revenue code.

b. Plan Participation

To receive benefits under a plan, an employee must participate in the plan. The terms of a retirement plan must be set forth in a formal plan document and a Summary Plan Description (SPD). At a minimum, the employee should examine the SPD, a copy of which she should receive within ninety days of becoming a plan participant. The SPD is designed to provide an overview of the plan. The employee can obtain more detailed information from the formal plan document or the plan administrator.

ERISA requires that participants receive an individual benefit statement at least once a year. Participants should review their statement carefully and report any errors to the plan administrator. Participants in a defined contribution plan typically receive individual benefit statements; those participants should also examine such statements closely.

ERISA's basic rule of eligibility requires that an employee must become eligible to participate in the pension plan at age twenty-one or after completing one year of service, whichever is later. Two special rules may alter the basic rule, however. If a plan provides that a participant's accrued benefits are one hundred percent vested after two years of service, the plan can require two years of service. For tax-exempt plans at educational institutions that provide for one hundred percent vesting after one year of service, the employee must become eligible to participate at age twenty-six or after completing one year of service, whichever is later.

ERISA also prohibits age discrimination against older workers in its plan participation rules. A plan that excludes employees on the basis of age is not a qualified plan.

c. Vesting of Benefits

When an employee becomes eligible and begins to participate in a pension plan, she begins to accrue benefits. Yet upon severance from employment, she may lose those benefits if they have not yet vested. Among ERISA's most important rules are its provisions for the vesting of benefits. When an employee has a nonforfeitable right to plan benefits, her benefits are said to be vested. For employer contributions to vest for the employee's benefit, an employee typically has to work for a specified time period. This period of time is defined in a vesting schedule.

ERISA's tax provisions provide that a defined contribution plan must satisfy one of two vesting schedules. Under a so-called cliff vesting schedule, the plan must provide the employee with a nonforfeitable right to one hundred percent of the employee's accrued benefit derived from employer contributions after three years of service. Alternatively, the plan may satisfy a graded vesting schedule, under which the plan must provide the employee with a nonforfeitable right to twenty percent of her accrued benefit from employer contributions after two years of service; forty percent after three years; sixty percent after four years; eighty percent after five years; and one hundred percent after six years of service. These are minimum requirements; the plan may provide more generous vesting rules.

ERISA's tax provisions also provide that a defined benefit plan must satisfy one of two vesting schedules. Under the cliff vesting schedule, the plan must provide that an employee who has completed at least five years of service has a nonforfeitable right to one hundred percent of her accrued benefit derived from employer contributions. Alternatively, using a graded vesting approach, the plan must provide the employee with a nonforfeitable right to twenty percent of her accrued benefit from employer contributions after three years of service;

forty percent after four years; sixty percent after five years; eighty percent after six years; and one hundred percent after seven years of service. Again, these are minimum requirements; the plan may provide more generous vesting rules.

Importantly, accrued benefits from employer contributions are also deemed to vest when the employee reaches normal retirement age, even if the vesting schedule is not yet otherwise satisfied. Moreover, if the plan itself terminates, an employee's accrued benefits vest even if the vesting schedule is not yet otherwise satisfied.

Note that a contribution made by an employee to her pension plan is always considered vested; however, restrictions may limit the time at which the employee can take the benefit amounts out of the plan.

d. Retirement Benefits

ERISA is also concerned with the timing of benefit payments to the plan participant. Defined benefit plans contain a normal retirement age provision that defines the time at which the employee is irrevocably entitled to receive full retirement benefits. Despite its name, normal retirement age may vary among employees, because it may also be tied to years of service with the employer. Under ERISA, unless the plan provides for an earlier normal retirement age, then normal retirement age is the later of the time at which the participant attains sixty-five or the fifth anniversary of the time the participant began participating in the plan. 26 U.S.C. § 411(a)(8).

All defined bnefit plans and some defined contribution plans require that a participant's benefit be distributed in the form of an annuity that provides monthly payments for the remainder of his life, unless the plan provides an optional form of payment and the participant (and his spouse, if he is married) consent to receive the optional form of payment. When received, these monthly payments represent taxable income to the participant. As an alternative to an annuity, the plan may allow the participant to choose a lump sum payment, which amount is determined by a formula in the plan. A lump sum distribution from a defined contribution plan is typically the balance in the employee's separate account. Lump sum distributions from a qualified plan are taxable in the year received unless rolled over into another qualified plan or into an individual retirement account (IRA).

A defined benefit plan may permit a participant to receive reduced benefits upon early retirement if he meets certain service and age requirements. Under ERISA, however, such a plan must also permit former participants who satisfied the service requirement, but who separated from service prior to reaching the age requirement, to receive such early retirement benefits when they satisfy the age requirements. 26 U.S.C. §401(a)(14). (If a participant in a defined benefit plan leaves his employer before reaching retirement age, usually he must leave the benefits with the plan until he becomes otherwise eligible to receive them.)

The Age Discrimination in Employment Act precludes covered employers from terminating or discriminating against employees forty or over because of their age. Qualified plans must state how they calculate benefits for employees who remain beyond the plan's normal retirement age. Federal law requires the plan to recognize the earnings and service of those employees for pension contribution and benefit purposes.

e. Spousal Rights

The annuity from a defined benefit plan or a money purchase or target benefit plan generally must include survivor benefits for the participant's surviving spouse. (ERISA does not require that a plan provide a survivor annuity unless the participant had been married for a one-year period ending on the earlier of the participant's annuity starting date or the date of the participant's death.) These benefits include the qualified joint and survivor annuity (QJSA) and the qualified preretirement survivor annuity (QPSA). 26 U.S.C. §401(a)(11).

The QJSA provides payments over the combined lifetimes of the participant and his spouse. The QJSA must be no less than the actuarial equivalent of an annuity for the life of the participant only. The amount to the surviving spouse must be at least fifty percent of the benefit amount paid to the participant. 26 U.S.C. §417(c). For example, suppose that Harry's monthly pension payment under a qualified joint and 100% survivor annuity is $1000 per month. At Harry's death, Wanda would continue to receive $1000 per month for life. If the QJSA were a qualified joint and 50% survivor annuity, however, Wanda would only receive $500 per month following Harry's death.

If the participant dies before the annuity starting date, the surviving spouse is protected by the QPSA. Under the QPSA, the surviving spouse's payment will not be less than the actuarial equivalent of the amount that would be payable as a survivor annuity to her under the QJSA. 26 U.S.C. 417(c). For estate tax purposes, the value of the surviving spouse's interest in a QJSA or QPSA is includable in the participant's gross estate, but qualifies for the marital deduction.

A couple may waive the right to the QJSA and QPSA, in which case the participant's monthly annuity check will be larger. To waive these spousal protections, however, the participant must execute a written waiver and the spouse must execute a written consent to the annuity payment without a survivor's benefit. The spouse's signature must be witnessed by a notary or plan representative. Most, but not all, courts reviewing antenuptial agreements have concluded that those agreements fail to meet ERISA requirements for a waiver. One obvious reason is that the consent obtained in an antenuptial agreement is from a person who is not yet a spouse. Even a post-marital agreement may fail to meet ERISA requirements if not carefully drafted and properly witnessed.

For plan years beginning after December 31, 2007, plans required to offer a QJSA must offer a qualified optional survivor annuity (QOSA) as an alternative if the QJSA is waived. The QOSA is the actuarial equivalent of a single annuity for the life of the participant. The annuity is for the life of the participant, with a survivor annuity for the life of the surviving spouse equal to a specified percentage of the amount of the annuity that is payable during the joint lives of the couple. If the QJSA provides a survivor annuity for the life of the surviving spouse that is less than 75 percent of the amount of the annuity that is payable during the joint lives of the participant and the spouse, then the QOSA must provide the survivor annuity percentage of 75 percent. If the QJSA provides a survivor annuity for the life of the surviving spouse that is greater than or equal to 75 percent of the amount of the annuity that is payable during the joint lives of the participant and the spouse, then the QOSA must provide a survivor annuity percentage of 50 percent. 26 U.S.C. §417(g); IRS Notice 2008-30, 2008-12 I.R.B. 638.

Defined contribution plans that are not required to offer a QJSA nonetheless include default provisions to protect the participant's surviving spouse. If the participant dies before receiving his benefits, in most cases the benefits pass directly to the surviving spouse. If the couple wishes a different result, the participant must name a different beneficiary and his spouse must consent by executing a waiver in front of a notary or plan representative.

f. QDROs

To better ensure that a participant's pension benefits will be available to him when he retires, ERISA generally prohibits assignment or alienation of the participant's interest in a pension plan. Exceptions to the anti-assignment rule exist, and the most commonly-encountered exception exists to fulfill the participant's family support or marital property obligations.

Under ERISA, a qualified domestic relations order (QDRO) may establish an alternate payee who is entitled to receive all or part of a participant's payable benefits under a pension plan. A QDRO is a judgment, decree, or order made under state domestic relations law providing for child support; for alimony; or for marital property rights that benefit a spouse, ex-spouse, or other dependent of the participant. The QDRO must contain specific information naming the participant, the alternate payee, the plan affected by the order, the manner in which the benefit is to be calculated and paid to the alternate payee, and the applicable number of payments or time frame for those payments. The QDRO may be part of a divorce decree or court-approved property settlement or it may be a separate order. It may be made in the absence of divorce proceedings, for example, to establish child support or obligations concerning marital property rights.

In drafting a QDRO for court approval, the lawyer will need to read the plan's summary plan description and may need to read other plan documents and talk with the plan administrator. A QDRO will often adopt either a separate payment approach or a shared interest approach. Under a shared interest approach, the alternate payee receives part of each payment made to the participant. This approach is often used when the participant is already receiving payments from the plan. The shared interest approach typically divides the retirement benefit (and not just the payment itself) as part of the couple's marital property.

A QDRO may provide that a former spouse is to be treated as the participant's surviving spouse concerning any or all of his pension benefits. For example, if a QDRO provides that the ex-spouse is to be treated as the participant's surviving spouse in a defined benefit plan, she will be the beneficiary of the QJSA or QPSA. A later spouse of the participant will receive no annuity from the benefits covered by the award. (If additional benefits accrue after the date of the QDRO, the later spouse would be entitled to the QJSA/QPSA from the additional benefits.)

ERISA does not permit the alternate payee under a QDRO to receive a benefit prior to the time the participant reaches his earliest retirement age unless the plan permits earlier payments. For QDRO purposes, earliest retirement age is defined as the earlier of (1) the date on which the participant is entitled to a distribution under the plan or (2) the later of either the date at which the participant turns fifty or the earliest date on which the participant could receive benefits under the plan if the participant separated from service.

In Kennedy v. Plan Administrator for DuPont Savings and Investment Plan, 129 S. Ct. 865 (2009), the Supreme Court examined an ex-spouse's waiver to plan benefits that was a part of the couple's divorce decree. The waiver was not in the form of a QDRO. Moreover, the ex-spouse had not disclaimed her interest in accordance with the plan's specific methods. The Court ruled that the plan administrator had a duty under ERISA to comply with the plan documents, which still listed the ex-spouse at the time of the decedent's death. Thus the ex-spouse could receive the benefits.

g. Distributions and Taxation

Distributions from a defined benefit plan typically take the form of an annuity. As mentioned, ERISA requires that the plan offer a QJSA and QPSA for a married participant. The married couple may waive these survivor annuity provisions in a properly executed writing, in which case the participant may choose a single life annuity. Because such a payment will be made over the life of only one annuitant, the monthly payment will be larger. If the participant's spouse will have her own pension or other significant retirement benefits or income, or if she is unlikely to survive the participant, a waiver of the QJSA and QPSA may make financial sense.

Distributions from a defined contribution plan often are made in a lump sum. A lump sum payment may also be available in lieu of an annuity under a defined benefit plan.

i. Generally

As with most retirement entities or accounts receiving favorable tax treatment, periodic pension payments (such as monthly annuity checks) are generally includible in gross income when received. The same general rule applies to lump sum payments. If the participant made "after-tax" contributions — i.e., he contributed amounts from income on which he had already paid tax — to the plan, however, then the recovery of those amounts (his "investment in the contract," "capital," or "basis") is not taxable. Earnings on those contributions and the remaining part of his pension payments not attributable to his after-tax contributions remain taxable.

To determine what part of the participant's monthly payment is taxable in such cases, the tax code provides a simplified exclusion ratio for qualified plans that divides the "investment in the contract" by the anticipated number of payments based on his age. 26 U.S.C. § 72(d). If the annuity is in joint and survivor form, the anticipated number of payments is based on the combined ages of the annuitants.

For example, assume that Harry begins receiving monthly annuity payments of $1000 from a qualified plan upon his retirement at age 65. His wife Wanda is age 62, and the annuity is a QJSA. Further assume that Harry's investment in the contract is $31,000. In this example, the couple's combined age is 127. The tax code provides that when the combined age of the annuitants is between 121 and 130, the anticipated number of payments is 310. The nontaxable part of Harry's monthly payment is determined by dividing Harry's investment in the contract ($31,000) by the anticipated number of payments (310). In other words, $100 of the monthly pension payment is tax-free (i.e., not includible in gross income) until his full investment of $31,000 has been recovered. Once Harry's investment in the contract has been recovered, any remaining pension payments will be fully includible in gross income. If the investment has not been fully recovered at

Harry's death, then $100 of the monthly payment to Wanda will be tax-free until the investment is fully recovered. The $100 tax-free portion remains constant even if the monthly payment increases, for example, because of a COLA.

If the annuity payments cease before the investment in the contract is fully re-covered, a deduction for the unrecovered amount may be allowed to the annui-tant in his last taxable year. 26 U.S.C. §72(b)(3). Alternatively, the annuity contract may provide for a refund of the unrecovered amount when the annuitant dies. Under the rules that apply to qualified plans, the refund feature does not require an adjustment to the investment in the contract. 26 U.S.C. §72(d)(1)(B).

The tax code does not apply the simplified exclusion ratio for determining the non-taxable part of the monthly payment if the primary annuitant is 75 on the annuity starting date unless there are fewer than five years of guaranteed payments under the annuity. 26 U.S.C. §72(d)(1)(E). Instead, the code uses life expectancies that apply generally to annuities (and not those that relate specifically to qualified plans).

If an annuity provides for a fixed number of payments, the investment in the contract is divided by that specific number of payments to determine the non-taxable portion of the contribution.

Individuals ineligible to participate in a qualified pension plan may want to establish an individual retirement arrangement (IRA) to build a retirement nest egg while deferring tax on the investment's earnings. With a traditional IRA, contributions are deductible, earnings grow tax-free, and distributions are tax-able upon withdrawal. The amount of deductible annual contributions is lim-ited, but increases for persons fifty or over under so called catch-up rules. Withdrawals before age fifty-nine and one-half are generally subject to a ten per-cent early withdrawal penalty; however, withdrawals must begin by age seventy and one-half.

There are various kinds of IRAs. For example, a Simplified Employee Pen-sion (SEP-IRA) is essentially a traditional IRA that is established by an em-ployer for a firm's employees. The employer receives the deduction, the earnings accumulate tax-free, and distributions are taxed to the employee upon receipt. As its name suggests, a SEP-IRA is a simple alternative for the employer who wants to provide some form of retirement nest egg for its employees.

The so-called Roth IRA is notably different from a traditional IRA and sub-ject to special rules. No deduction is allowed to an individual for his contribution to a Roth IRA. Withdrawals (including earnings) are not taxable or subject to an early withdrawal penalty as long as they are qualified distributions. 26 U.S.C. §408A(d). (These rules also apply to "Roth contributions" to a qualified Roth contribution program of an applicable retirement plan. U.S.C. §402A.) Indi-viduals and couples with income above an annual threshold may not contribute to a Roth IRA. Unlike a traditional IRA, there is no mandatory withdrawal from a Roth IRA at age seventy and one-half.

ii. Early Distributions

Congress provides favorable tax treatment to various retirement entities or accounts to encourage Americans to save for their old age. To discourage individuals from receiving early distributions from those entities or accounts, tax laws impose a ten percent tax penalty on many early distributions. 26 U.S.C. §72(t). The penalty is imposed on the portion of the distribution includible in gross income; thus, it does not apply to that part of the distribution attributable to the taxpayer's after-tax contributions. Note that the penalty is in addition to the regular income tax that must be paid on the part of the distribution includible in gross income. For example, if Eve receives an early distribution of $25,000 subject to income taxation, she will owe not only her regular income tax upon the distribution, but also an additional $2500 if the penalty applies.

The tax code does not impose the penalty on all early distributions, however. For example, the code does not apply the penalty to distributions from a qualified pension, profit sharing or stock bonus plan, a qualified annuity plan, or a section 403(b) tax sheltered annuity contract when the distributions (1) were made when the taxpayer has reached fifty-nine and one-half; (2) were made to a beneficiary on or after the death or the employee; (3) were attributable to the taxpayer's disability that makes him unable to engage in any substantial gainful activity by reason of any medically determinable physical or mental impairment that can be expected to result in death or to be of long-continued and indefinite duration; (4) are part of a series of substantially equal periodic payments made at least annually for the taxpayer's life (or life expectancy) or the joint lives (or joint life expectancies) of the taxpayer and his designated beneficiary; (5) are dividends paid concerning stock of a corporation under section 404(k); (6) are made on account of a section 6331 tax levy on the qualified retirement plan; (7) are made (and not otherwise excluded from the penalty under other exceptions) to the extent that the employee is entitled to a deduction for medical expenses paid during the year exceeding 7.5% of adjusted gross income, without regard to whether the employee actually claims those deductions; (8) were made to an alternative payee under a QDRO; or (9) were made to an employee after separation from service, which separation occurred during or after the calendar year in which he reached fifty-five. 26 U.S.C. §72(t).

All but the final two of these exceptions also apply to early distributions from individual retirement arrangements (which include individual retirement accounts and individual retirement annuities). For early distributions from individual retirement plans, however, the statute also excludes from the penalty (1) distributions for qualified higher education expenses for the taxpayer, his spouse, or a child or grandchild of the taxpayer or his spouse (reduced by non-taxable amounts from other sources such as scholarships), and (2) distributions (up to a $10,000 lifetime limitation) for qualified first-time homebuyers including the taxpayer, his spouse, any child, grandchild, or ancestor of the taxpayer or his spouse. 26 U.S.C. §72(t)(7), (8).

The code contains no special exceptions from the penalty for early distributions from CODAs. The code generally provides that a participant in a CODA may not receive distributions earlier than (1) disability, death, or severance from employment; (2) the termination of the plan without establishment or maintenance of another defined contribution plan (other than an employee stock ownership plan); (3) in the case of a profit-sharing or stock bonus plan, the attainment of age fifty-nine and one-half; or (4) in the case of contributions to a profit-sharing or stock bonus plan to which section 402(e)(3) applies, upon hardship of the employee. 26 U.S.C. §401(k)(2)(b)(i).

More generally, certain distributions that might otherwise be subject to the 10 percent early distribution excise tax may avoid that tax with the use of certain rollover arrangements, discussed later.

iii. Deferred Distributions

Just as the tax code generally imposes a penalty tax on early distributions, it also imposes a penalty tax on delayed distributions from qualified plans. Qualified plans include plans described under Internal Revenue Code section 401(a); annuity plans described in section 403(a); annuity contracts described in section 403(b); individual retirement accounts described in section 408(a); and individual retirement annuities described in section 408(b). 26 U.S.C. §4974(c). To avoid the penalty, individuals generally must begin receipt of distributions from account balances by April 1 of the year following the later of (1) the year in which the individual reaches age seventy and one-half, or (2) the year in which he retires. If the employee is a "five percent owner" with respect to the plan year ending in the calendar year in which the employee reaches age seventy and one-half, however, the required beginning date is April 1 of the calendar year following the calendar year in which the employee attains age seventy and one-half (i.e., his actual retirement date is irrelevant). This is also true for traditional individual retirement accounts under section 408(a)(6) or individual retirement annuities under section 408(b)(3). 26 U.S.C. 401(a)(9)(C)(ii).

The amount of the minimum required distribution is generally determined by formulas that are designed to distribute the entire interest over the taxpayer's life or life expectancy, or over the joint lives or joint life expectancies of the taxpayer and a designated beneficiary.

A plan is not disqualified if it fails to make the minimum required distribution to a participant. Rather, the code imposes upon the participant a fifty percent excise tax on the difference between the minimum required distribution and the amount actually distributed to the participant. The IRS may waive the penalty if the taxpayer establishes that the shortfall in the amount distributed was due to reasonable error and that reasonable steps are being taken to remedy the shortfall. 26 U.S.C. § 4974(d).

(In response to the economic downturn that began in 2008, Congress enacted the Worker, Retiree and Employer Recovery Act of 2008. Section 201 of the Act suspended the required minimum distribution rules under 26 U.S.C. 401(a)(9) for the year 2009. The law applies to defined contributions plans, including IRA, 401(k), 403(b), and certain 457(b) accounts. Congress hoped that the provision might allow IRA owners and retirement plan beneficiaries to recoup some of the losses they had suffered in the economic downturn.)

iv. Lump Sum Payment

A pension plan may allow a participant to choose a lump sum distribution in lieu of periodic payments. The retired employee may consider the lump sum more attractive for various reasons. He may believe that he can invest the sum more wisely; he may have special needs that a periodic payment will not meet; he may simply want to wash his hands of any continuing connection to the former employer; and so on.

The lump sum will generally be includible in the individual's gross income in the year it is received. Again, however, he will not be taxed on any part of the lump sum that represents a return on his investment in the contract—i.e., his after-tax contributions. (One might note that the code permits those taxpayers who attained the age of fifty before January 1, 1986 and who receive a lump sum from a pension plan to use a so-called "forward averaging" formula if they meet certain criteria. Although the tax will be imposed upon receipt of the lump sum, the formula for calculating the tax allows those taxpayers to treat the lump sum payment as though it were received over a ten-year period and provides other tax advantages as well.)

To avoid a potentially substantial income tax on the lump sum, the recipient will often "roll over" the funds into another qualified pension plan or other entity as permitted by the tax code. For example, the code permits him to roll the funds over to his IRA within sixty days of receipt of the funds as long as he meets certain other requirements. In many instances, he will be able to transfer the sum directly to another qualified plan.

No less than thirty days before a distribution is made, the plan administrator must provide the participant with a written explanation (which may include certain notice provided electronically) of rules concerning rollovers and direct transfers. The code requires a qualified plan to withhold twenty percent of an eligible rollover distribution that is not transferred directly to an eligible retirement plan. 26 U.S.C. §3405(c); 26 C.F.R. 31.3405(c)-1. The withholding is to help ensure the payment of any tax liability on the lump sum distribution in the event the entire amount is not properly rolled over within sixty days.

If the funds are directly rolled over within sixty days, and do not come into the hands of the employee, there is no withholding. Thus it is prudent for the participant to ensure that the funds are directly transferred to the eligible retirement plan. If the taxpayer receives the lump sum himself (less the twenty percent withholding amount) and wants to roll over the entire amount (one hundred percent) to postpone including that entire amount in income, then he will have to come up with twenty percent from some other source to add it to the eighty percent he actually received. For example, suppose T's lump sum distribution from his employer's qualified plan is $20,000, and the sum will be paid to T. The plan must withhold $4,000 (twenty percent of the lump sum), however, so that T will actually receive only $16,000 in hand. If T simply rolls over the $16,000, then he must include the remaining $4,000 as a taxable distribution for the year. (Moreover, if T is under fifty-nine and one-half, he may incur the ten percent early distribution tax on the taxable distribution.)

Withholding from an eligible rollover distribution is not required if (1) the distribution and all prior eligible rollover distributions received from the plan during the tax year total less than $200 or (2) the distribution consists solely of employer securities, plus cash of not more than $200 in lieu of fractional shares.

Where the withholding rule otherwise would apply, the IRS may waive it in some instances such as the taxpayer's disability or hospitalization or for postal error. IRS automatically waives the sixty-day period in limited circumstances involving no fault of the taxpayer and error on the part of the receiving financial institution.

Rollovers are not always in the best interest of the participant. This may be true, for example, if there is significant net unrealized appreciation on employer stock in the participant's account at the time it becomes eligible for rollover distribution. If the stock is properly rolled over, the taxpayer has no amount included in gross income at that time. Distributions from the rollover account will be taxed as ordinary income, however. In contrast, if the taxpayer does not rollover the stock, it is true that the value of the unappreciated stock will be included in his gross income in the year of distribution; however, if he subsequently sells the stock, the unrealized appreciation will be taxed only at the capital gains rate. If the unrealized appreciation is significant, foregoing rollover may be the wise choice.

The tax code permits many kinds of tax-free rollovers between various forms of retirement accounts or plans. Under 26 U.S.C. § 402(c)(4), an "eligible rollover distribution" is any distribution of all or any part of the balance of the taxpayer's credit in a qualified retirement plan with only a few exceptions. The term does not include (1) a series of substantially equal distributions paid at least annually over the taxpayer's lifetime or expectancy, the joint lives or life expectancies of the taxpayer and his beneficiary, or a period of at least ten years; (2) a required minimum distribution; (3) a hardship distribution; (4) certain corrective distributions and loans; (5) dividends paid on employer securities; and (6) the cost of life insurance coverage. 26 U.S.C. § 402(c)(4); 26 C.F.R. 1.402(c)-(2)

The rollover rules that apply to an employee also generally apply to his surviving spouse who receives a distribution from a qualified retirement plan. The same is true for distributions from a qualified retirement plan to an employee's ex-spouse (or spouse) pursuant to a QDRO. Historically, the rules were not as generous for nonspouses. The Worker, Retiree, and Employer Recovery Act of 2008 (WRERA) contained technical corrections to the Pension Protection Act of 2006, however, that make clear that a nonspouse beneficiary of a deceased employee can rollover a distribution from a qualified retirement plan in a direct trustee-to-trustee transfer to an IRA set up to receive that distribution. The WRERA mandate is effective for plan years beginning after December 31, 2009.

Self-employed individuals are generally treated as employees for rollover purposes. A self-employed individual may establish a qualified plan. His contributions to the plan are deductible and earnings on the contributions accumulate tax-free until distribution. If he receives an eligible rollover distribution, he can roll that distribution (including a lump sum distribution) over into a traditional IRA.

For a general chart concerning various forms of rollovers and their permissibility, see http://www.irs.gov/pub/irs-tege/rollover_chart.pdf.

Regarding the treatment of pension benefits for estate tax purposes, the value of benefits to be paid after the participant's death—including joint and survivor annuities and lump-sum distributions—are includible in his estate.

One should also note that states vary significantly in their treatment of retirement pension income for taxation purposes. Some states exempt almost all pension income from state taxation; several others impose substantial taxes on such income. Some states exempt military and government pensions, but not private pensions, from state taxation. Some states provide partial exclusions regardless of the pension source. For further discussion and a chart comparing state income taxation of retirement income in 2007, see http://www.ncsl.org/programs/fiscal/pitaxret07.htm.

h. Benefit Claims

The Summary Plan Description should contain information outlining the plan's claims procedures. The most common claims relate to benefit qualification and benefit amount. Under federal law, the plan has ninety days from the time the participant files the claim to reach a decision. The plan may take up to 180 days if it notifies the participant that it needs an extension.

If the plan denies the claim, it must provide written notice detailing the specific reasons for the denial and the method for filing an appeal. The participant then has sixty days to request a review. The plan has sixty days to review the appeal (with a possible extension of an additional sixty days if it notifies the participant of the need for the longer period). Again, the plan must then send written notice to the participant concerning the grant or denial of the appeal. A denial requires the plan to explain the reason, provide information about any additional appeal levels, and provide a statement about the participant's right to seek judicial review of the plan's decision.

Checkpoints

- Concerning Social Security, you should understand
  - The FICA tax and the financing of the program
  - The importance of the earnings record
  - How one establishes insured status
  - How retirement benefits are determined, including
    - The way in which primary insurance amount (PIA) is calculated
    - The effect of receiving early retirement benefits and the application of the retirement earnings test
    - The effect of deferred receipt past full retirement age
    - The windfall elimination provision and the government pension offset
  - Who is entitled to auxiliary benefits and how those benefits are calculated
  - The general nature of the Social Security disability program
  - The role of the representative payee
  - The anti-assignment provision of the Social Security Act
  - The administrative and judicial review process

Checkpoints *continued*

- Concerning public retirement or pension programs, you should understand generally
  - The railroad retirement system
  - The federal CSRS and FERS systems
  - The typical aspects of state and local plans
  - The military retirement system
  - Veterans' benefits
- Concerning private-sector pension plans, you should understand
  - The distinctions between defined benefit plans and defined contribution plans
  - The role of ERISA
  - The general treatment of spouses and ex-spouses of plan participants
  - The general rules concerning distributions, taxation, and rollovers

Chapter 7

Supplemental Security Income

Roadmap

- Supplemental Security Income (SSI) provides a minimum level of income to people with limited income and resources who are blind, disabled, or sixty-five or over

- The applicant's countable income determines whether she satisfies the SSI income test

  - Countable income consists of earned income and unearned income

  - Various important exclusions from earned income and unearned income apply in determining countable income

- The applicant's countable resources determine whether she satisfies the SSI resources test

  - Various important exclusions (including the value of the home) apply in determining countable resources

- In various settings, income and resources of another person may be deemed available to the applicant

- The appeals process under SSI is generally similar to that under Social Security

---

A. Introduction

The Supplemental Security Income (SSI) program, which began in 1974, is a federal welfare program administered by the Social Security Administration (SSA). The statutes are located in Title XVI of the Social Security Act beginning at 42 U.S.C. § 1381. The principal regulations for the SSI program are found at 20 C.F.R. part 416. Around 7.3 million people received SSI benefits in 2008.

The program is intended to provide a minimum level of income to people with limited income and resources who are blind or disabled or who are sixty-five or over. Unlike Social Security, SSI is not based on an employment tax. Rather, SSI is funded by the general revenue in the United States Treasury. SSI benefits typically are paid on the first day of each month for which the applicant is entitled to payment. The program operates for the benefit of residents throughout the United States and the Northern Mariana Islands. It may also benefit a child who is a United States citizen living outside the country with a parent in the United States armed forces.

Most states provide a voluntarily supplement to the SSI payment with monies from state funds. States that supplement the SSI payment may enter into an agreement under which SSA administers the state supplemental payment program. If SSA administers the state supplemental program, then the beneficiary only receives one monthly check representing both the federal SSI payment and the state supplemental payment. SSA charges a state to administer a state supplemental payment program. Thus, most states manage their own supplement. In those states, people must apply for the state supplement through the appropriate state agency. A few states are "dual-administration" states in which both SSA and the states administer some state supplements.

Because eligibility for SSI requires the applicant to keep SSA apprised of his complete financial picture, the SSI information also provides a convenient way to determine the applicant's eligibility for Medicaid, the federal/state welfare program for health care. States may contract with SSA to have SSA make Medicaid eligibility decisions for SSI applicants. Most states have entered into such a contract. In those states, application for SSI also constitutes an application for Medicaid.

When an individual applies for SSI, the SSA notifies him of the state food stamp program and makes an application available to him. If everyone in the home signs up for SSI or receives SSI, the SSA will help complete the food stamp application. In other instances, the application is usually made through a local department of social services (or its equivalent). Food stamps, which are issued by the states pursuant to the Food Stamp Act of 1977, are intended to assist SSI beneficiaries in purchasing food and other necessary household items. A state may replace food stamps, however, with a cash payment to people who receive SSI. California, for example, has done this.

If an individual is unable to manage or direct the management of his SSI payments, SSA may select a representative payee to do so.

B. Eligibility Requirements

To receive SSI benefits, one must file an application. The only exception to this rule is for people eligible for assistance under a federal/state matching grant program prior to January of 1974. These people were "grandfathered" into the SSI program and are sometimes referred to as converted recipients.

1. Who May Be a Beneficiary

SSI benefits are available to persons in three categories: those who are sixty-five or older; those who are blind; and those who are disabled. There are no age limitations on the latter two categories. An applicant is blind if his vision with the use of a corrective lens is 20/200 or less in the better eye, or if he has tunnel vision of 20 degrees or less. In determining the disability of an applicant, the SSI program uses the same standards employed under the Social Security program. Thus, a disabled adult is someone unable to engage in substantial gainful activity due to a medically determinable physical or mental impairment that can be expected to result in death, or that has lasted or can be expected to last for a continuous period of not less than twelve months.

An individual may fall into more than one eligibility category. For example, he may be at least sixty five and he may also be blind or disabled or both blind and disabled. Although the benefit rates themselves are consistent across the categories, higher income/resource exclusions for the blind or disabled person may effectively result in a higher benefit for the blind or disabled person. If the person who is at least sixty-five wishes to claim the higher exclusion amounts associated with blindness or disability, he must have an established onset of blindness or disability before the month in which he turned sixty-five.

To receive SSI, the individual must also be a citizen or meet certain other criteria. Most aliens cannot receive SSI unless (1) they are qualified aliens under Department of Homeland Security standards and satisfy further conditions that permit receipt of SSI or (2) they are lawfully admitted for permanent residence (LAPR) and have forty qualifying quarters of creditable work or meet other specified standards. The SSI rules also permit receipt of SSI by (1) noncitizen Indians who are members of a federally recognized Indian tribe; (2) Canadian Indians who are in the United States under Section 289 of the Immigration and Nationality Act (INA); and (3) certain aliens meeting the requirements of the Trafficking Victims Protection Act of 2000 who were victims of a severe form of trafficking in persons.

SSI is unavailable to an individual in any month in which he has an unsatisfied warrant for a felony (or, where unclassified as a felony, a crime punishable by death or imprisonment for more than one year), or in which he has violated a condition of probation or parole under federal or state law.

2. Location of the Beneficiary

Residence at a public institution has a notable effect on eligibility for SSI. As a general rule, residents of a public institution for a full calendar month are ineligible for SSI unless one of several exceptions applies. The exceptions include residence at the following public institutions: a publicly-operated community residence serving no more than sixteen residents; an institution where residence is primarily for educational or vocational training; and a public emergency shelter for the homeless (in which case payment is limited to no more than six months in any nine-month period).

When an individual is a resident of a public or private medical treatment institution throughout a month and Medicaid pays over fifty percent of the cost of care for the month, the SSI payment is generally limited to $30 (less any countable income). Some exceptions, however, allow full payment of SSI to an institutionalized individual. When the individual was eligible for SSI under a special work incentive provision in the month before the first full month he lives in a medical or psychiatric institution, he may receive full payments for two or three months (depending upon the circumstances). Importantly, full SSI benefits may also be paid for the first three full months of institutionalization if the person meets the following conditions: the institution is a medical treatment facility; Medicaid pays more than fifty percent of the cost of care; *and* a physician certifies that the stay in a medical facility is not likely to last more than three months and that the individual needs to maintain and provide for expenses at the home to which he may return.

For example, suppose John enters a public institution and is a resident throughout the month. The institution is a medical treatment facility, and Medicaid pays more than fifty percent of the cost of his care. John is otherwise eligible for SSI. Here, under the general rule, John is eligible for a monthly SSI payment of $30. Note, however, that if John's physician certifies that John's stay will probably not extend beyond three months and that John needs his SSI to provide for the home to which he may return, then John can get his full SSI benefit during the first three full months of his stay.

An individual who is outside the United States for a full calendar month is generally ineligible for SSI benefits for that month. He is deemed to be back in the United States after he has spent thirty consecutive days in the United States, at which point his SSI eligibility may resume. The "calendar month" rule does not apply to a blind or disabled child who is a United States citizen living outside the United State with a parent who is in the United States armed forces. It also does not apply to a student who is temporarily abroad for the purpose of conducting studies not available in the United States, where the student is sponsored by an American educational institution and the studies are designed to enhance the student's ability to obtain gainful employment.

If one is receiving SSI and subsequently goes to prison or jail, he is ineligible for SSI for any full calendar month in which he is in prison or jail.

3. Marriage of the Beneficiary

An individual may obtain SSI whether or not he is married. SSI rules require information about an applicant's marital status, however. If the applicant is married, the SSI rules also require certain details concerning the marriage. Eligible SSI recipients will fall within one of three categories: (1) the eligible individual (an applicant who meets all of the eligibility requirements); (2) the eligible couple (an eligible individual and his eligible spouse); and (3) the ineligible couple (an eligible individual whose spouse does not meet all of the criteria for SSI eligibility).

SSI rules treat a couple as married if (1) they are married under applicable state law and are living in the same household; (2) they are holding themselves out as married in the community where they live; or (3) one member of the couple is entitled to Social Security benefits as the spouse of the other. In most but not all cases, the SSI rules examine the existence of a marriage on the first day of the month. For example, if Hank is legally separated from his wife, Winifred, and is living with Helen and holding Helen out to the community as his wife, Helen will be his spouse for most SSI purposes if he is living with her at the beginning of the month. (This is so even if Hank and Helen break up later in the month and one moves out.) As the example shows, a person's so-called "holding-out" spouse takes precedence over a legally married spouse from whom the person is separated. Of course, marriage may also end by death, divorce, or annulment.

If a married couple is in an institution, SSA does not treat them as married. Instead, they are treated as two potential eligible individuals in determining eligibility and payment amounts. This is so even if the couple shares a room at the institution.

The monthly SSI federal benefit rate (FBR)—which is the maximum monthly amount one can receive—differs for eligible individuals and eligible couples. An eligible couple's FBR is 1.5 times that of an eligible individual. In determining an eligible couple's actual benefit, the SSI program considers the combined countable income of the couple and their combined resources.

4. Continuing Assessment of Eligibility

Because SSI is a program of last resort and the income and resources of recipients change over time, SSA will periodically reexamine the eligibility of SSI recipients to ensure that they are eligible and being paid the proper amounts. SSA conducts reevaluations by mail, telephone, and personal interview. The frequency of reevaluation depends upon the likelihood that the recipient's circumstances will change in a way that affects his eligibility or payment amount.

To assist SSA in ensuring the propriety of continued payment of SSI, the recipient is required to report events or changes in circumstances that affect his eligibility or payment amount. These mandatory reports must account for, among other things, changes in the amount of earned and unearned income; change of residence; marriage, divorce, or separation; absence from the United States; improvement in the condition that caused a disability; death of certain individuals; changes in income or resources for the recipient or for others whose income and resources are attributed to the individual; eligibility for other benefits; change in school attendance; change in household composition; change in citizenship or alien status; other change in status, such as becoming a fugitive felon or violating a condition of probation or parole; and admission to or discharge from a medical facility, public or private institution.

The principal causes of overpayments and underpayments of SSI benefits are recipients' failure to report and recipients' errors in reporting. Failure to report may result in the following monetary penalties: $25 for the first failure to report; $50 for a second failure; and $100 each for all subsequent failures to report. The recipient generally has ten days after the month in which the change occurred to report the change to SSA. SSA may also impose sanctions upon a person who knowingly makes false statements or misrepresentations pertaining to his benefits. The initial sanction is a loss of payments for six months. Subsequent sanctions increase the time periods for which the right to payment is lost.

C. Asset Limitations: Income and Resources

The SSI program is intended to be a program of last resort for persons of limited means. The program takes into consideration the applicant's need based on his income stream and his accumulated resources. When an individual applies for SSI, SSA will inform him of his potential eligibility for benefits other than SSI. The applicant then has thirty days to "take all appropriate steps" to pursue those benefits. Such other sources of benefits may include Social Security and private pension benefits.

So that SSA can fully consider the applicant's initial and continuing needs, the applicant must give SSA permission to contact any financial institution at any time and to request any records pertaining to the applicant. Similarly, people who are responsible for the applicant's support must allow SSA to contact any financial institution at any time and to request any financial records about them.

To receive SSI benefits, an individual or couple must satisfy both an income test and a resources test. As explained in the following paragraphs, the individual or couple cannot have monthly countable income exceeding the federal benefit rate (FBR) and also cannot have countable resources — real or personal property (including cash) — exceeding a certain amount at the beginning of each month. For individuals, that amount is $2000; for a couple, the amount is $3,000.

The FBR is increased annually. In 2009, it is $674 for an eligible individual and $1,011 for an eligible couple.

1. Income

a. Generally

SSI rules consider income to be anything received in a calendar month that is used or can be used to meet one's need for food or shelter. Income may be in cash or in-kind. In-kind income is food or shelter or something that may be used to obtained food or shelter. Among the things that are *not* income for SSI purposes are the following: (1) medical care and services given free of charge or paid for directly to the provider by someone else; (2) any social service or related cash or in-kind item provided by a government social service program; (3) receipts from the sale, exchange, or replacement of a resource; (4) income tax refunds; (5) payments by credit life or credit disability insurance; (6) the proceeds of a loan, including both the money one borrows or the money one receives as repayment of a loan (but interest received for repayment of a loan is income); (7) money paid by someone else directly to a supplier on one's behalf (but note that the goods or services received as a result of the third-party payment may themselves be income); (8) replacement of income already received (for example, replacement of a lost or stolen check); (9) home energy and protection assistance; and (10) items other than food and shelter that would be an excluded non-liquid resource if one retained them. 20 C.F.R. 416.1103.

b. Countable Income

Once SSA determines an applicant's income, it applies all appropriate exclusions to determine the applicant's *countable* income. Calculated on a monthly basis, countable income is subtracted from the monthly federal benefit rate (FBR) to determine the amount of the SSI payment the individual or couple will receive. In 2009, if John is otherwise eligible for SSI and has countable income of $300 in a given month, his SSI check for that month will be $374 (i.e., the $674 individual FBR for 2009 less John's countable income of $300). If John's countable income equals or exceeds the FBR, he is ineligible for a benefit check in that month.

When an individual first establishes eligibility for SSI, his SSI benefit amount in the first month of payment will depend upon his countable income in that month. (The first month of payment is the month following that in which the individual first establishes eligibility.) For example, if John first applies for and establishes eligibility in August, his first payment will occur on September 1. John's countable income for September is considered in determining the amount of his SSI benefit check in that month. In the second month of initial eligibility for payment, John's SSI benefit is based on his countable income in the "first month prior to the current month." In other words, the amount of John's benefit check for October will also depend upon his countable income in September. In all subsequent, continuous months of receipt, SSI benefits are based on countable income in the "second month prior to the current month." Thus John's November check will also depend upon his September countable income, but his December check will depend upon his October countable income, his January check will depend upon his November countable income, and so forth. In sum, once a person has established eligibility and begun to receive benefits, from the third month of payment forward SSA computes the SSI benefit amount based on the individual's countable income from two months before the current month. This estimate process is call retrospective monthly accounting. If John becomes ineligible because of excess resources or income and then reestablishes eligibility after at least one month of ineligibility, the cycle begins again and similar rules apply concerning the treatment of countable income. 20 C.F.R. § 416.420. Proration, however, may occur in the first month an individual re-attains eligibility after a period of ineligibility.

SSA periodically reviews and revises its estimates of countable income whenever there is a report of change or a redetermination. Income is normally considered to be received in the month of actual or constructive receipt. A notable exception is the treatment of self-employment earnings, which are determined on an annual basis and allocated equally over the twelve months of the tax year.

i. Earned Income

In calculating countable income, SSI rules distinguish earned income from unearned income. *Earned income* includes wages; net earnings from self-employment estimated for the current year and spread over twelve months; payments for participating in a sheltered workshop or work activities center program; sickness or disability payments received within the first six months of stopping work; and royalties for publications and honoria for services.

Importantly, SSI rules contain a number of provisions that exclude certain earned income from the countable income total. For the typical recipient, two of these exclusions are very common: first, the initial $65 of earned income each month is excluded from consideration; second, from the remaining earned income (i.e., the amount after the $65 exclusion), one-half is excluded from consideration. Other potential exclusions are mentioned in the following paragraph.

A more complete list of exclusions (in the order applied by SSA) includes the following: those exclusions authorized by federal laws other than Title XVI; the full amount of any federal earned income tax credit payments; the first $30 per calendar quarter of earned income if that income is received infrequently or irregularly; a set monthly amount for a working student regularly attending school; any part of a $20 monthly general income exclusion (described in the next section) that is not used against unearned income; the first $65 of earned income each month (described in the preceding paragraph); the impairment-related work expenses of a disabled (not blind) individual who is under 65 or received SSI based on a disability for the month before turning age 65; one-half of the month's remaining earned income (described in the preceding paragraph); any expenses reasonably attributable to the earning of income for a blind (not disabled) person who is under 65 or received SSI because of blindness for the month before turning age 65; and any earned income used to fulfill an approved Plan to Achieve Self-Support (PASS) in the case of a blind or disabled individual who is under 65 or received SSI based on blindness or disability for the month before turning age 65.

ii. Unearned Income

Unearned income is—as one might expect—any income that is not earned. Examples include food or shelter given to an individual or received by an individual because someone else paid for it; private pensions and annuities; periodic public benefits payments such as Social Security, civil service annuities, VA pension and compensation payments, and workers' compensation; life insurance proceeds and other death benefits to the extent that the total amount is more than the expenses of the deceased person's last illness and burial paid by the individual; gifts and inheritances; support and alimony payments; prizes and awards; dividends and interest; rents and any royalties that are not earned income; various payments that are not considered wages for Social Security purposes, including in-kind payments to agricultural and certain domestic workers, tips under $20 a month, jury fees, and money paid to individual who are residents but not employees of institutions; and military pay and allowances, except basic pay. 20 C.F.R. 416.1121.

SSI rules also exclude many items of unearned income from countable income. For the typical recipient, perhaps the most frequently used exclusion is the general $20 exclusion that applies first against an individual's total unearned income (other than income based on need, such as payments in which the recipient's income is a factor). Any part of this $20 exclusion that is not used against unearned income applies to earned income, as mentioned in the preceding section.

Among other exclusions from unearned income are the following: the value of most benefits provided under a number of federal programs (such as the Food Stamp Act, the Older Americans Act, the National Housing Act, and the National School Lunch and Child Nutrition Act); a public agency's refund of taxes on real property or food; assistance based on need and funded wholly by a state and/or one of its political subdivisions; any part of a grant, scholarship, fellowship, or gift used for paying tuition, fees or other necessary educational expenses (but not amounts set aside or actually used for food or shelter); food raised by an individual or his spouse if consumed by the household; assistance under the Disaster Relief and Emergency Assistance Act or under federal statute because of a catastrophe declared by the President to be a major disaster; the first $60 per calendar quarter of unearned income received infrequently or irregularly; payments to an individual for providing foster care to a child placed in the individual's home by a qualified agency; interest earned on excluded burial funds and appreciation in the value of an excluded burial arrangement left to accumulate and become part of the separately identifiable burial fund; certain home energy and other needs-based support and maintenance assistance; and one-third of support payments made by an absent parent to or for an eligible child. 20 C.F.R. 416.1124.

To see how countable income is calculated and applied against the FBR in a simple example, assume that Jan is eligible for SSI. In 2009, she receives monthly wages of $115 and a Social Security check for $300. Her countable income will be calculated as follows:

Earned income:
> $115 (wages)
>   − 65 (exclusion of first $65)
>   50
>   − 25 (exclusion of one-half of the month's remaining earned income)
> $25 total countable earned income

Unearned income:
> $300 (Social Security benefits)
>   − 20 (exclusion of first $20)
> $280 total countable unearned income

Total countable income:
> $25 countable earned income
>   + 280 countable unearned income
> $305

Jan's monthly SSI benefit:
> $674 federal benefit rate (2009)
> − 305 countable income
> $369

As the example shows, an individual's countable income counts against the maximum monthly SSI benefit (the FBR) dollar for dollar.

2. Valuing In-Kind Support and Maintenance

Income not in the form of cash or negotiable instruments is in-kind income. In-kind income that is unearned and directly satisfies the individual or couple's need for food or shelter is termed "in-kind support and maintenance." SSA uses one of two special rules in determining its value. All other in-kind income is simply valued at current market value.

For in-kind support and maintenance, SSA will apply either the "one-third reduction rule" (VTR, for "value of the reduction") or the "presumed maximum value rule" (PMV). The one-third reduction rule applies when the person (1) lives in another's household throughout a calendar month (excepting permissible temporary absences) and (2) receives both food and shelter from within the household. The person is not living in another's household if he or the spouse with whom he is living has an ownership interest in the home or is liable for payment of any part of the rent for the household. The person is also not living in another's household if he has been placed there under a protective care program; if he pays at least a pro rata share of average household operating expenses; if all household members receive public income-maintenance payments; or if the household does not provide any food. In contrast, a person does live in another individual's household if that other individual (1) provides the support and maintenance, (2) lives there, (3) is not a minor child, and (4) is not an ineligible individual whose income can be deemed to the person.

Under the one-third reduction rule, SSA considers the value of the in-kind support and maintenance to be one-third of the applicable FBR. The value of the one-third reduction applies fully or not at all. When it does apply, no other in-kind support and maintenance is considered. Moreover, the $20 general income exclusion (discussed in the preceding sections) does not apply to income counted under the one-third reduction rule. As mentioned earlier, in 2009 the full FBR for an individual is $674 and for an eligible couple is $1,011. Thus, if the one-third reduction rule applies, the value of the in-kind support and maintenance is $224.66 for an individual and $337.00 for an eligible couple.

SSA applies the presumed maximum value rule to other scenarios involving in-kind support and maintenance. For example, the PMV rule applies if a recipient lives throughout a month in someone's household but does not receive both food and shelter from that person. It also applies if a recipient lives in his own household, but someone outside that household pays for the rent, utilities, or food. It also applies to recipients living in a non-medical institution. Under the PMV rule, SSA presumes that the value of support and maintenance does not exceed one-third of the applicable FBR plus $20. (Thus for 2009, the value considered under the PMV rule is $244.66 for an individual and $357.00 for an eligible couple.) Unlike the one-third reduction rule, however, the PMV rule is rebuttable. If a party shows that the actual value of the food or shelter received is less than the presumed maximum value, SSA will then use the actual value in computing countable income.

3. Resources

To receive an SSI check in a given month, the individual or couple must satisfy not only an income test, but also a resource test. If the individual or couple has excess resources, then no SSI benefits will follow. The existence of resources does not affect the monthly payment amount, however, so long as the eligible individual or couple does not exceed the resource limit. Thus, unlike countable income, countable resources do not reduce the monthly SSI benefit dollar for dollar.

a. Nature and Ownership of Resources

Resources include cash and other assets that one can convert to cash to obtain support and maintenance. If the applicant has the right, authority, or power to sell the property, it is a resource. The SSI program distinguishes between liquid and non-liquid resources. Liquid resources are cash and other resources convertible to cash within twenty working days (such as savings and checking accounts, stocks, bonds, mutual funds, promissory notes, certain trusts, and certain kinds of life insurance). Resources that one cannot convert into cash within twenty working days — including real and personal property — are non-liquid. The distinction becomes important when ascertaining whether the applicant qualifies for conditional SSI payments and whether a resource can be excluded as non-business property essential to self-support.

A special rule applies when resources are owned by multiple persons including the applicant. If the applicant needs the consent of the co-owner(s) to liquidate his share, then that share is not a resource for the applicant if the co-owner(s) refuse to consent.

b. Countable Resources

Just as the SSI rules consider only an applicant's countable income, they also consider only the applicant's countable resources. Since 1989, the applicable countable resource limits have been $2000 for an individual without a spouse and $3000 for an individual with an eligible spouse or a living-with ineligible spouse. Countable resources are determined on a monthly basis and are valued as of the first moment of the month.

In valuing resources, cash is always counted at its face value. Most resources (liquid and non-liquid) are counted at their equity value—i.e., the price at which the resource can be expected to sell on the open market, considering the specific geographic area and accounting for any encumbrances existing on the resource.

c. Resource Exclusions

Title XVI of the Social Security Act mandates a number of exclusions from countable resources. An individual's home that is owned by him or his spouse and that serves as the principal place of residence is excluded from countable resources. Such a home is excluded regardless of value, and includes adjacent land and related buildings on it. Similarly, household goods and personal effects are excluded regardless of value. One vehicle is excluded, regardless of value, if the applicant or a member of his household uses it for transportation.

Property of a trade or business is excluded without limit. The rules also exclude non-liquid non-business income producing property that has an equity value of no more than $6,000 and that produces a net annual return of least six percent of its excluded equity value. (If the equity value exceeds $6000, the excess is countable.) Similarly excluded is non-liquid non-business property that has an equity value of no more than $6,000 and that is used to produce goods or services essential to the applicant's daily activities. (Again, the value of the property in excess of $6,000 is countable.) 20 C.F.R. 416.1222. Liquid non-business property is not excludable.

Life insurance with a cash surrender value that is owned by the applicant or his spouse is excluded from countable resources if the total face value of all policies owned on any one person is not more than $1,500. Insurance with no cash surrender value is not a resource.

Burial spaces for the applicant, his spouse, and members of his immediate family are not considered countable resources. This exclusion extends to vaults, crypts, caskets, mausoleums, urns, and headstones and grave markers. Moreover, money set aside for a burial fund of up to $1500 each for the applicant and his spouse are excluded, as long as the funds are specifically designated for burial and not combined with non-burial assets.

Real property that the applicant owns but cannot sell is excluded under certain conditions. For example, the real property exclusion applies if the applicant owns the property jointly with another owner and (1) it is the principal residence for the other owner and (2) the sale would cause undue hardship to the other owner due to loss of housing. The real property exclusion also applies if the applicant's reasonable efforts to sell his real property have been unsuccessful. Recognizing that it may take several months to convert non-liquid resources to cash for support and maintenance, the SSA may provide conditional SSI payments for nine months while evaluating this exclusion. After nine months, the property is excluded as long as it has not been sold but the applicant continues his efforts to sell.

Among the many other exclusions are provisions concerning disaster assistance, benefits and payments excluded by federal statutes other than Title XVI of the Social Security Act; certain Title XVI or Title II retroactive payments; certain housing assistance; and grants, scholarships, fellowships or gifts provided for tuition, fees, or other necessary educational expenses for nine months after the month of receipt.

An individual with excess countable resources may "spend down" those resources to become eligible for SSI in subsequent months. He may not create eligibility, however, simply by giving away or selling a resource for less than fair market value (FMV). If the individual (or his spouse) transfers an asset for less than FMV, the individual may become ineligible for SSI for up to 36 months. The time frame for ineligibility will depend upon the value of the uncompensated transfer as compared to the applicable SSI benefit rate. Moreover, SSA will report the transfer to the state Medicaid agency, resulting in a potential period of ineligibility for some Medicaid covered services as well.

If an individual uses assets to create a trust on or after January 1, 2000, the income and principal may count as resources. If the trust is revocable, the entire trust is generally an available resource. If the trust is irrevocable but payment may be made to the individual who created it, then the part of the trust from which payment can be made is treated as an available resource. Exceptions that may not treat trust assets as resources apply to certain so-called (d)(4) trusts (e.g., pooled trusts and special needs trusts) and to cases where inclusion would result in undue hardship.

4. Deeming

Not surprisingly, when an eligible individual lives in the same household with his ineligible spouse, the income and resources of the ineligible spouse are considered to be available to the eligible individual. Thus, the income of the ineligible spouse is combined with the income of the eligible individual and compared to the FBR for a couple. In general, when a third party has or shares financial responsibility for the applicant, SSI considers that party's resources and income in determining the applicant's eligibility. This process is known as "deeming." In spouse-to-spouse deeming, an individual can never receive a higher payment than he would have received had no deeming occurred.

Deeming of income and resources occurs in four settings: (1) from an ineligible spouse to an eligible individual living in the same household (as mentioned above); (2) from a parent to a child under age 18; (3) from a sponsor to an alien; and (4) from an essential person to an eligible qualified individual. SSI excludes many items from the deeming of income, however. Moreover, any resources excluded for an eligible individual are similarly excluded for an ineligible spouse or ineligible parent for deeming purposes. In addition, pension funds owned by an ineligible spouse, or by an ineligible parent or spouse of a parent, are excluded from resources for deeming purposes.

D. The Appeals Process

The initial determination is the first decision made on an SSI matter. It typically concerns a question of eligibility or the amount of payment, but may concern any number of other matters. The individual who objects to the initial determination may appeal that decision. Appeals may also be requested by the individual's eligible spouse, a parent, or the representative payee, and the SSA may reexamine an initial determination on its own motion.

Because the SSI program is administered by the SSA, the SSI appeals process is similar to that of the Social Security program. The administrative appeals process begins with a reconsideration. Individuals who disagree with the reconsideration determination may request a hearing before an administrative law judge (ALJ). If dissatisfied with the decision or dismissal by the ALJ, the appellant may request review by the Appeals Council. Throughout the appeals process, the appellant should carefully note the time limits for requesting review. (The time limits may be extended for good cause.) If the case proceeds through the administrative appeals process and the Appeals Council ultimately denies the appellant's request for review or issues a revised decision with which the appellant disagrees, the appellant may proceed to federal district court.

Checkpoints

- Concerning Supplemental Security Income (SSI) generally, you should understand that it is a program for persons of limited means who are blind, disabled, or sixty-five or over
- Concerning SSI eligibility rules, you should understand
  - The examination and treatment of income and resources
  - The effects of institutionalization
  - The effect of marriage
  - The deeming process
- Concerning income, you should understand that
  - In-kind income is income not in the form of cash or a negotiable instrument
  - The recipient's countable income must be less than the SSI federal benefit rate
  - Countable income consists of earned income and unearned income
    - Earned income includes wages, net earnings from self-employment, royalties, honoria, and certain other payments to the applicant
    - Unearned income is any income that is not earned, including Social Security and various other benefit payments, dividends and interest, pensions and annuities
  - Special valuation rules apply to in-kind support and maintenance
    - Important exclusions from earned income and unearned income exist in calculating countable income
- Concerning resources, you should understand that
  - The recipient's countable resources must not exceed the monthly countable resources limit under SSI
  - Countable resources are typically considered on their face value
    - Various important resources are excluded from the determination of countable resources
    - Among the exclusions from countable resources are the home, household goods and personal effects, and one vehicle

Chapter 8

Medicare

Roadmap

- Medicare is government-sponsored health insurance generally available to individuals 65 and over

- Depending on the service, supply, or care in question, Medicare may require the beneficiary to pay deductibles, premiums, copayments, or coinsurance

- Medicare has four main parts, A through D

    - Parts A and B are Original Medicare

        - Part A includes hospital insurance, skilled nursing facility coverage, home health services, and hospice care

        - Part B is supplementary medical insurance for certain doctor services, outpatient services, and other health and medical services

    - Part C covers Medicare Advantage plans that are a newer alternative to Original Medicare

    - Part D is Medicare Prescription Drug Coverage

- Medigap policies are private insurance policies that beneficiaries often purchase to supplement their Medicare coverage

---

A. Introduction and Overview

1. A Limited, Federal Health Insurance Program

Although the United States does not provide universal health care coverage to its citizens, it does make Medicare available to its elderly population. (As this book goes to press, Congress is engaged in serious debate about health care reform, but the prospects for universal health care are mixed.) Medicare is government-sponsored health insurance for people sixty-five or older. Medicare is also available to individuals of any age with end-stage renal disease, which is kidney impairment that appears irreversible and permanent and requires a regular course of dialysis or kidney transplantation to maintain life. Finally,

Medicare is also available to individuals under sixty-five who have certain disabilities. This chapter concentrates on the Medicare program and its application to the elderly population.

Medicare was enacted in 1965 as Title XVIII of the Social Security Act. It was first implemented on July 1, 1966. In 1977, the Health Care Financing Administration (HCFA) was established to administer the Medicare (and Medicaid) program. In 2001, HCFA was renamed the Centers for Medicare and Medicaid Services (CMS).

2. The "Parts" of Medicare

The Medicare program consists of four parts, labeled A through D based on their location within Title XVIII of the United States Code. Individuals eligible for Medicare can choose among the different parts to obtain their health care and prescription drug coverage. The Original Medicare plan consists of Parts A and B. Although Medicare now provides newer alternatives in Part C, the great majority of individuals still choose coverage under Parts A and B. In 2006, Part D became effective and added prescription drug coverage to the Medicare program.

Part A is the "hospital insurance" program under the Original Medicare plan. It not only helps to cover inpatient hospital care, but also skilled nursing facility (SNF) care, certain home health services, and hospice care. Part B is the "medical insurance" program under the Original Medicare plan. It helps to cover medically-necessary services, including doctors' services and outpatient care. Part B also includes coverage for some (but far from all) preventive care.

As an alternative to traditional coverage under Parts A and B, Medicare now provides a Part C program that includes "Medicare Advantage" (MA) plans like those provided by a health maintenance organization (HMO) or preferred provider organization (PPO). These plans are privately managed, but they must be approved by Medicare. They must cover the services covered by Original Medicare. Often these plans offer more extensive coverage than Original Medicare. Usually these plans include Medicare drug coverage. Each MA plan, however, will impose different out-of-pocket costs on its enrollees. The Medicare program also offers other alternative plans—including Medicare Cost plans, demonstrations/pilot programs, and Programs of All-Inclusive Care for the Elderly (PACE). These plans provide coverage under Parts A and B, and some also include drug coverage.

Part D helps to cover the cost of prescription drugs. It is separately available to individuals who choose coverage under the Original Medicare plan and to those who choose a Part C plan that does not include drug coverage.

3. Related Health Care Concerns, Programs, and Insurance

As with most forms of insurance, Medicare does not provide a totally free ride for the covered individual. Throughout this chapter, note carefully the rules concerning deductibles, coinsurance, and copayments associated with the various parts of the Medicare program. A deductible is the amount that the enrollee must pay before the insurance plan will begin to pay for his health care or prescriptions. Coinsurance is an amount the enrollee must pay (usually expressed as a percentage, such as 20 percent for a doctor's visit) as his share of the cost for the Medicare-provided service after he has paid any applicable deductible. A copayment is an amount (usually set in terms of dollars, such as $10 or $20 for a prescription) that the enrollee must pay as his share of the cost for a medical service or supply.

Also note that individuals who fail to meet applicable deadlines or comply with program rules often incur payment penalties, find themselves at least temporarily unable to change plans, or even find themselves without any Medicare coverage for some period of time.

As you read this chapter, keep in mind the existence of another government health care financing program, Medicaid. We will examine Medicaid in detail in the following chapter. For now, however, note that Medicaid is a welfare program intended primarily to address the health care needs of persons of any age who have low income and resources. Some individuals covered by Medicare also qualify for Medicaid coverage. Very importantly, the Medicaid program can help to cover the cost of long-term institutionalization. Such long-term health care costs, which are a serious concern to elderly Americans, are not generally covered by Medicare.

Even the most comprehensive Medicare package leaves notable gaps in health care coverage. To help insure against the substantial costs of health care that an individual might face if his health care need is not covered by Medicare, private insurance companies offer different "Medigap" policies to fill some of those gaps. Medigap policies are not a part of the Medicare program; rather, they are insurance policies that an individual may opt to purchase. Because Medigap policies play an important role in elder health care, however, they are discussed at the end of this chapter. For now, note that Medigap policies also are not designed to cover the cost of years of long-term institutionalization.

B. Laws and Administrative Materials

The Medicare statutes are primarily located at Title XVIII of the Social Security Act. The statutes begin at 42 U.S.C. § 1395. The principal Medicare regulations begin at 42 C.F.R. 405. The Medicare program is administered by the Centers for Medicare and Medicaid Services (CMS). CMS provides a number of online manuals, accessible at http://cms.hhs.gov/Manuals/. Many other Medicare official publications are available online at www.medicare.gov and at www.cms.hhs.gov.

The Medicare statutes require the Secretary of Health and Human Services to mail annually a clear, simple explanation of Medicare benefits and limitations on benefits and payments to each individual entitled to Part A or Part B benefits. This explanation is also mailed to an individual when he enrolls under Part A or Part B. The Secretary also provides a toll-free number at 1-800-MEDICARE to assist individuals seeking information about the Medicare programs. 42 U.S.C. § 1395b-2.

C. The Original Medicare Plans (Parts A and B)

1. Part A

Part A is so-named because its provisions are compiled in Part A of title XVIII of the Social Security Act. Part A covers inpatient hospital care, skilled nursing facility care, home health services, and hospice care.

a. Financing

Medicare Part A is financed through the hospital insurance (HI) part of the FICA tax. (FICA is discussed more fully in Chapter 6.) The tax is a 2.9 percent payroll tax that is divided evenly between a wage earner and his employer. Self-employed individuals pay the entire 2.9 percent themselves. Unlike the retirement and disability parts of the FICA tax, the HI part of the tax is not subject to a wage cap. Whether the covered individual earns $50,000 or $500,000 in a given year, the HI tax applies to the entire amount. The HI tax is deposited in the Federal Hospital Insurance Trust Fund.

Unlike Social Security retirement benefits, which vary according to the tax contributions of the employee, Part A hospital insurance benefits do not vary among covered individuals. All individuals with Part A coverage are entitled to the same benefits, regardless of the actual amount of HI tax paid.

b. Eligibility and Enrollment

i. Premium-Free Hospital Insurance

Part A coverage is available free of charge to an individual who is sixty-five and who qualifies for Social Security or Railroad Retirement benefits. In 2007, CMS estimated that ninety-nine percent of Medicare beneficiaries with Part A coverage have no premium to pay because they have at least forty quarters of Medicare-covered employment.

An individual who has applied for Social Security or Railroad Retirement benefits before the age of sixty-five generally does not need to file an application for Part A coverage. Such an individual is automatically enrolled in Parts A and B. He is issued a Medicare card that indicates his coverage. Coverage begins on the first day of the month in which the individual turns sixty-five.

In contrast, an individual who is eligible but who has not applied for Social Security or Railroad Retirement benefits by the age of sixty-five must apply if he wishes his free Medicare Part A coverage to begin before he receives Social Security retirement benefits. To ensure that Part A coverage begins in the month when the applicant turns sixty-five, he should apply for Medicare three months before his sixty-fifth birthday.

Borrowing from the rules of Social Security (discussed in Chapter 6), the Medicare program makes available premium-free Part A coverage to the spouse, surviving spouse, or ex-spouse of an individual who qualifies or qualified for premium-free Part A coverage. The spouse, surviving spouse, or ex-spouse claiming derivatively must be at least sixty-five years old, however. Like Social Security benefits, premium-free hospital insurance benefits are not available to an ex-spouse who was not married to the worker for at least ten years. Of course, many spouses, surviving spouses, or ex-spouses will be entitled to Part A coverage based on their own work records or, in the case of multiple marriages, on the work record of a different spouse.

Part A also provides premium-free coverage to Medicare-qualified government employees who are at least sixty-five and whose employment was subject only to the hospital insurance portion of the FICA tax. Like others not receiving Social Security benefits at age sixty-five, they need to apply for Part A coverage. The program also covers individuals under sixty-five who have been entitled to Social Security disability benefits for twenty-four calendar months as well as persons with end-stage renal disease. 42 U.S.C. § 426.

ii. Premium Hospital Insurance

Individuals who are not eligible as a Social Security or Railroad Retirement beneficiary or on the basis of government employment may voluntarily enroll for Part A coverage. These individuals, however, must pay a monthly premium. Their Part A coverage is called "premium" hospital insurance and the individuals who voluntarily enroll are known as hospital insurance enrollees. To enroll, the individual must be sixty-five, not eligible for Part A coverage without premium payments, and a United States resident who is either (1) a citizen or (2) a lawful alien admitted for permanent residence who has continuously resided in the United States for five years immediately preceding the first month in which she meets all other requirements for entitlement to hospital insurance. Importantly, the individual who voluntarily enrolls in Part A must also enroll in Part B. 42 C.F.R. 406.20(b).

(a) Enrollment Periods

An individual may enroll for premium hospital insurance only during certain periods: (1) her initial enrollment period; (2) the general enrollment period; (3) a special enrollment period; or (4) a transfer enrollment period (for health maintenance organization (HMO) or competitive medical plan (CMP) enrollees).

The initial enrollment period extends for seven months, from the third month before the month the individual first meets the eligibility requirements through the third month after that first month of eligibility. If Mary will turn sixty-five in August and she is otherwise eligible to voluntarily enroll in Part A, her initial enrollment period will run from May through November of that year. The month of her actual enrollment is important, however. If an individual enrolls during the three months before the first month of eligibility, her entitlement begins with the first month of eligibility. Thus if Mary enrolls at any time from May through July, her coverage will begin in August. If an individual enrolls in the first month of eligibility, entitlement begins with the following month. If the individual enrolls during the month after the first month of eligibility, entitlement begins with the second month after the month of enrollment. Finally, if the individual enrolls in either of the last two months of the enrollment period, entitlement begins with the third month after the month of enrollment.

A general enrollment period runs from January 1 through March 31 of each calendar year. If Mary does not enroll during her initial enrollment period, she may subsequently enroll during the general enrollment period in any year. If an individual enrolls during a general enrollment period, her entitlement begins on July 1. (Moreover, as discussed below, enrollment during a general enrollment period can result in a premium penalty in some situations.)

A special enrollment period (SEP) is provided by statute to permit individuals who have been covered by group health plans through their or their spouse's employment to enroll in Part A without waiting for the general enrollment period. The SEP includes any month during any part of which an individual over age sixty-five is in a group health plan by reason of the current employment status of the individual or her spouse. The SEP ends on the last day of the eighth consecutive month during which the individual is at no time enrolled in a group health plan by reason of current employment status. If the individual enrolls during a month in which she is covered under the group health plan based on current employment status, or if she enrolls during the first full month when no longer covered, then Part A coverage begins on the first day of the month of enrollment or, at her option, on the first day of any of the three following months. If she enrolls in Part A during any later month of the SEP, then Part A coverage begins on the first day of the month following the month of enrollment.

A transfer enrollment period permits an individual to transfer from an HMO or CMP to Part A coverage. A transfer enrollment period begins with any month or any part of a month in which an individual is enrolled in an HMO or CMP and ends with the last day of the eighth consecutive month in which the individual is no longer enrolled in the HMO or CMP. If the individual enrolls in Part A while still enrolled in an HMO or CMP, or during the first month that she is no longer enrolled in the HMO or CMP, Part A coverage begins on the first day of the month of Part A enrollment, or, at her option, on the first day of any of the following three months. If she enrolls in Part A during any of the last seven months of the transfer enrollment period, coverage begins on the first day of the month after the month of enrollment.

(b) Premiums and Penalties

Persons with forty or more quarters of coverage are eligible for Social Security retirement benefits, and thus they and their spouses pay no premiums for Part A coverage.

The basic monthly premium for voluntary enrollees is promulgated each September for the following calendar year. The monthly premium amount reflects an estimate of one-twelfth of the benefits and administrative costs, on a per capita basis, that will be payable from the Federal Hospital Insurance Trust Fund to enrolled individuals for the year in question. 42 U.S.C.A. § 1395i-2(d)(1). In 2009, the monthly premium was $443 for voluntary enrollees with less than thirty quarters of Medicare-covered employment. The premium is substantially reduced for employees with thirty to thirty-nine quarters of coverage. In 2009, their monthly premium was $244.

Voluntary enrollees for premium hospital insurance who enroll after the close of their initial enrollment period have their premium payments increased by ten percent if they have a full twelve months or more of late enrollment. The period over which the enrollee will have to pay the ten percent premium penalty is determined by doubling the number of full twelve-month periods of late enrollment. 42 C.F.R. 406.32. The months to be counted for ascertaining whether the premium increase applies include the months from the end of the initial enrollment period through the end of the general enrollment period, the special enrollment period, or the transfer enrollment period in which the individual enrolls, but excluding (1) months during which the individual was enrolled in an employer group health plan based on the current employment of the individual or her spouse and (2) months that the individual was enrolled in an HMO or CMP.

For example, assume that Nancy's initial enrollment period ended in July 2006, but she did not enroll until January 2007 during the general enrollment period. The months to be counted in this late enrollment are August through March (the months following the end of her initial enrollment period through the end of the general enrollment period). Because this period (eight months) is less than twelve months, however, Nancy incurs no premium penalty. If instead Nancy had first enrolled in January of 2008, then her period of late enrollment would be twenty months (i.e., August of 2006 through March of 2008). Her premium would be increased by ten percent, and she would have to pay this increased premium for two years (i.e., two times one full twelve-month period of late enrollment). After that time, she would pay only the regular premium amount applicable to her. If Nancy had been covered by an employer group health plan until July of 2008 and she enrolled in August of 2008 (the first month of her special enrollment period), then she would have no months countable towards an increased premium.

If the late enrollment for premium hospital insurance is the result of government error, misrepresentation, or inaction, CMS may take whatever action it deems necessary to provide appropriate relief. This includes designation of a special initial or general enrollment period; designation of an entitlement period; adjustment of premiums; a combination of the preceding; or other remedial action.

c. Coverage

Part A hospital insurance helps to cover the costs of the following: (1) inpatient hospital care, including that provided at critical access hospitals and inpatient rehabilitation facilities; (2) inpatient stays at a skilled nursing facility, but not including custodial or long-term care; (3) certain home health services; and (4) hospice care services. Doctor fees and outpatient charges are not covered by Part A, but instead are covered in part by Part B.

Each of the four categories of Part A coverage has its own rules and requirements.

i. Inpatient Hospital Care

Part A hospital stay coverage includes inpatient care at acute care hospitals, critical access hospitals, inpatient care as part of a clinical research study, and inpatient mental health care at a psychiatric hospital. (Critical access hospitals are certain rural hospitals that make available twenty-four hour emergency care services and that are some distance from other hospitals or that are certified by the state as being necessary providers of health care services to residents in the area.)

Part A hospital insurance helps to cover the cost of a semi-private room, meals, general nursing, drugs that are part of the inpatient treatment, and other hospital services and supplies. Part A hospital care coverage does not include a private room unless medically necessary. It also does not include private-duty nursing or a room television or telephone. Coverage for mental health care at a psychiatric hospital is limited to 190 days over the individual's lifetime.

In determining coverage for hospital stays, Medicare employs a concept known as a "spell of illness." The concept is also important in determining coverage for stays at skilled nursing facilities and for home health care purposes. In essence, a spell of illness is simply a benefit period. A spell of illness begins with the first day on which an individual is furnished inpatient hospital services, inpatient critical access hospital services, or extended care services. A spell of illness ends when sixty consecutive days have passed during which time the individual is neither an inpatient of a hospital or critical access hospital nor a skilled nursing facility. 42 U.S.C. § 1395x(a). The day of discharge from the institution counts as one of the sixty days. An individual may have multiple spells of illness within a year.

Medicare Part A provides substantial coverage for the first ninety days of a hospital stay during each spell of illness. In addition, Part A provides the individual with a lifetime reserve of sixty days of coverage that he may use as he wishes for inpatient care.

During the first sixty days of a hospital stay during a spell of illness, the individual pays a Medicare Part A deductible; almost all other costs are paid by Medicare. (Medicare Part A does not pay for the first three pints of blood required by the individual during a calendar year. 42 U.S.C. § 1395e(a)(2).) During days sixty-one through ninety, the individual must pay a daily coinsurance amount. After day ninety, Medicare Part A coverage ends unless the individual dips into his lifetime reserve days. The use of a lifetime reserve day also requires a daily coinsurance payment from the individual. In 2009, the deductible was $1,068; the daily copayment amount for days sixty-one through ninety was $267; the daily copayment amount for a lifetime reserve day was $534. These amounts increase each year. By statute, however, the coinsurance for days sixty-one through ninety is always one-fourth of the deductible amount, and the coinsurance for lifetime reserve days is always one-half of the deductible amount. 42 U.S.C. § 1395e(a)(1).

For example, John enters the hospital under Medicare Part A. He has not used any of his lifetime reserve days when he is admitted. In this setting, John must pay a deductible of $1068 in 2009. If his hospital stay does not exceed sixty days, he will have no further amounts to pay under Part A. If he stays beyond sixty days, however, he must make a daily payment of $267 from day sixty-one through day ninety. If he stays beyond ninety days, Part A provides no benefits unless he chooses to use his lifetime reserve days. In 2009, he must pay $534 for each lifetime reserve day that he uses. If John chooses to use his lifetime reserve days but his hospital stay lasts beyond one hundred and fifty days, Medicare Part A benefits will cease on day one hundred and fifty-one.

If John has a spell of illness, is released for at least sixty consecutive days, and then returns to the hospital, a new spell of illness begins. This is a new spell of illness even if his readmission is the result of the same medical problem that caused his earlier admission. When he is re-admitted to the hospital, he must pay the deductible. If he remains past day sixty, the coinsurance rules require him to make a daily payment. If he stays past day ninety, Part A benefits end unless he still has lifetime reserve days, chooses to use them, and makes the required daily payment.

In contrast, if John is released after a thirty-day hospital stay but reenters the hospital one month later, he will still be within the same spell of illness, because sixty consecutive days have not passed since his earlier hospital stay. When he re-enters the hospital, he will pickup with day thirty-one of his spell of illness. If his second hospital stay lasts beyond thirty days, he must begin to pay the daily payment. If his second hospital stay lasts beyond sixty days, Part A benefits end unless he still has lifetime reserve days, chooses to use them, and makes the required daily payment.

ii. Skilled Nursing Facility Care

A skilled nursing facility (SNF) is an institution (or a distinct part of an institution) that is primarily engaged in providing (1) skilled nursing care and related services for residents who require medical or nursing care or (2) rehabilitation services for injured, disabled, or sick persons. Most SNFs are commonly referred to as nursing homes, but not all SNFs are "Medicare-approved."

To be approved under the Medicare program, an SNF must have a transfer agreement with one or more hospitals under which transfer of patients is made between the hospital and the facility whenever such transfer is medically appropriate as determined by the attending physician. The transfer agreement must also provide for the exchange of medical information concerning patients. The Medicare-approved SNF is also subject to important requirements and restrictions relating to the provision of services, residents' rights, and administration (including the training of employees). The SNF is further subject to any state laws that provide more stringent rules and quality controls. Finally, the SNF must "participate" in Medicare, which means that it is subject to Medicare's price controls on the provision of care and services. By participating in Medicare, the SNF is reimbursed for the care and services it provides during the patient's post-hospital extended care stay at the rate established by Medicare.

Part A SNF coverage applies only to those patients requiring skilled nursing care on a daily basis (by or under the supervision of skilled personnel) or other skilled rehabilitation services, which as a practical matter can only be provided in an SNF on an inpatient basis. 42 U.S.C. § 1395f(a)(2)(B). The regulations provide a helpful list of certain kinds of treatment that are considered to involve skilled nursing or skilled rehabilitative services. Skilled nursing care includes such things as intravenous or intramuscular injections and intravenous feeding; nasopharyngeal and tracheostomy aspiration; treatment of extensive decubitus ulcers or other widespread skin condition; and the application of dressings involving prescription medications and aseptic techniques. The administration of routine oral medications, eye drops, and ointments is not SNF care, nor is the change of dressings for noninfected postoperative or chronic conditions. 42 C.F.R. 409.33. Custodial care and personal care services are not skilled nursing care.

Medicare requires that the SNF care be reasonable and necessary treatment for the patient, and a physician must certify that the patient requires SNF care on a daily basis. If the treatment is rehabilitative services, the "daily basis" requirement is satisfied if the services are needed and provided at least five times a week. A patient is not barred from SNF care by a diagnosis that full recovery or medical improvement is not possible; rather, a patient may require SNF care if such care can maintain the patient's current capacity or prevent further deterioration. A patient's terminal diagnosis does not prevent receipt of SNF care.

For SNF coverage to begin, the individual must have been hospitalized at least three consecutive days before his discharge and transfer to the SNF. Although transfer to the SNF will often be immediate, Medicare will cover the SNF stay as long as he is admitted (1) within thirty days after hospital discharge or (2) within the time that is medically appropriate. 42 U.S.C. § 1395x(i). The condition that requires SNF treatment generally must be connected to the condition that required his inpatient hospital care. Medicare Part A will also cover SNF stays for conditions that arise after the transfer to the SNF while the individual was in the facility for treatment of the condition for which he had received inpatient hospital services.

Part A SNF coverage includes semi-private room, meals, skilled nursing and rehabilitative services, and various other services and supplies. Part A coverage extends to a private room if the patient requires isolation, if the facility has only private rooms, or if the semi-private rooms and ward accommodations are fully occupied. (The same is true for hospital insurance coverage.)

When a patient is transferred from a hospital to an SNF pursuant to the order of the attending physician, Medicare Part A covers the cost of the first twenty days of the patient's SNF stay in its entirety. In days twenty-one through one hundred, however, the patient must make a daily coinsurance payment. The amount the patient must pay is one-eighth of the hospital deductible payment for a spell of illness. (In 2009, the daily payment for SNF care in days 21–100 was $133.50, which is one-eighth of the $1,068 hospital deductible amount.) Part A provides no benefits beyond day one hundred of his SNF stay.

If an individual has a post-hospital SNF stay, is released, and sixty consecutive days pass in which he is not a patient at a hospital or a resident of an SNF, a new spell of illness will begin if he is subsequently readmitted to a hospital and then transferred to an SNF. His first twenty days of his second stay at the SNF will again be covered entirely by Medicare Part A, but he will have a daily payment for the following eighty days of his stay.

An individual who is discharged from an SNF but within thirty days is admitted again to that facility or to another SNF is deemed not to have been discharged.

iii. Home Health Services

Medicare Part A pays for home health care, which includes items and services furnished (1) to an individual who needs skilled care and is under the care of a physician; (2) by a Medicare-participating home health care agency, or by others under arrangements with the agency; (3) pursuant to a plan certified and reviewed at least every two months by a physician; and (4) on a visiting basis in the individual's home (with some exceptions for outpatient services). Home health care services are intended for individuals who are largely confined to their homes or an institution that is neither a hospital nor a skilled nursing facility; however, the individual need not be bedridden to qualify. An individual may be considered homebound even though she is able to leave her home occasionally.

A home health agency is a public agency or private organization (or a sub-unit of an agency or organization) that is primarily engaged in providing skilled nursing services and other therapeutic services. Its policies are established by a group of professional personnel, including one or more physicians and one or more registered professional nurses. Those policies govern its services and provide for supervision of the services by a physician or a registered nurse. The agency maintains clinical records on all patients, and it must be licensed or approved by any applicable state or local law concerning such agencies. Agencies must have an acceptable overall plan and budget under Medicare, must provide appropriate surety bonds, and must satisfy the conditions of participation in the Medicare program. Among other things, these conditions are designed to protect patient rights; ensure proper training and education of agency personnel; and mandate review and assessment of policies and procedures.

Home health items and services include part-time or intermittent nursing care provided by or under the supervision of a registered professional nurse; part-time or intermittent services of a home health aide who has completed a Medicare-approved training program; physical or occupational therapy or speech-language pathology services; medical social services under the direction of a physician; and medical supplies (excluding most drugs and biologicals (serums, vaccines, etc.)) and durable medical equipment. The items and services also include those provided on an outpatient basis under arrangements made by the home health agency that involve equipment that could not be made readily available to the individual at her home. In the outpatient setting, Medicare does not pay for the cost of transportation to and from the individual's home. Payment for home health services also does not include items or services that would not be included if furnished to an inpatient of a hospital under Part A. 42 U.S.C. § 1395x(m).

The term "part-time or intermittent services" means skilled nursing and home health aide services furnished any number of days per week, as long as they are furnished less than eight hours each day and less than twenty-eight hours each week. In special cases subject to review, the services may be furnished less than eight hours each day but up to thirty-five hours each week. Intermittent care is defined as skilled nursing care provided or needed less than seven days each week or less than eight hours of each day for periods of twenty-one days or less. 42 U.S.C. § 1395x(m).

Home health care services do not require the payment of a deductible. They also do not require the payment of a coinsurance amount, except in the case of durable medical equipment (DME). A partial list of DME includes iron lungs, oxygen tents, hospital beds, and wheelchairs (which may include a power-operated vehicle that may be appropriately used as a wheelchair, but only where the use of such a vehicle is determined to be necessary on the basis of the individual's condition) used in the patient's home. The term may also include the seat-lift mechanism in a seat-lift chair, although it does not include the chair. The coinsurance liability of the beneficiary for DME furnished as a home health service is twenty percent of the customary (insofar as reasonable) charge for the services. 42 C.F.R. 409.50. In other words, Medicare will pay for eighty percent of the Medicare-approved amount for the DME.

For persons enrolled in Part A, coverage includes post-institutional home health services furnished during a home health spell of illness for up to one hundred visits during such spell of illness. 42 U.S.C. § 1395d(a)(3). Generally, a home health care "visit" occurs each time an agency employee or other person providing the service enters the beneficiary's home and provides a covered service. If two persons are required to provide the service, two visits may be covered. If two persons are present but only one is needed to provide the individual's care, only one visit may be covered. 42 C.F.R. 409.48.

Post-institutional home health services are those furnished to an individual after his discharge from a hospital or critical access hospital in which he was an inpatient for not less than three consecutive days before such discharge if the services were initiated within fourteen days after the date of such discharge. It also includes services provided after an individual's discharge from a skilled nursing facility where he was provided post-hospital extended care services if the home health services are initiated within fourteen days after the date of such discharge.

A "home health spell of illness" is a period of consecutive days beginning with the first day on which the individual is furnished post-institutional home health services occurring in a month for which he is entitled to benefits under Part A, and ending with the close of the first period of sixty consecutive days thereafter on each of which he is neither an inpatient of a hospital, a critical access hospital, a skilled nursing facility under 42 U.S.C. § 1395i-3(a)(1) or § 1395x(y)(1), nor provided with home health services. 42 U.S.C. § 1395x(tt).

Unlike the home health provisions under Medicare Part A, the home health provisions under Part B do not limit the number of visits. (Part B home health rules also do not require an institutional stay.) Home health care visits that are not covered by Part A can be covered by Part B. Thus despite the stringent Part A rules, in overall effect there is no limit on the number of visits per year by home health care agency personnel.

If intermittent or part-time skilled services provided by a home health agency are necessitated, other home health aide services may also be included in the physician's order when appropriate. Such services may include assistance with bathing, dressing, grooming, shaving, changing bed linens of an incontinent individual, and so forth. Such services are intended to maintain the individual's health or facilitate in the treatment or his injury or illness.

iv. Hospice Care

Hospice care is an alternative that a terminally ill individual covered under Medicare Part A may choose. Unlike the other Part A programs, hospice care aims to provide palliative care and comfort to the dying individual and his family; it does not seek to treat and cure the individual's illness. Hospice care does include, however, a wide range of items, care, and services unavailable under the other Part A programs. To be Medicare-covered, the hospice services must be reasonable and necessary for the palliation or management of the terminal illness or related conditions.

The term "hospice care" broadly refers to items and services provided to the terminally ill individual by a hospice program (or by others under arrangements made by a hospice program) under a written plan established and periodically reviewed by the individual's attending physician and also by the hospice program's interdisciplinary group and medical director or physician member.

The items and services provided by hospice care include the following: (1) nursing care provided by or under the supervision of a registered nurse; (2) physical or occupational therapy, or speech-language pathology services; (3) medical social services under a physician's direction; (4) services of a properly trained home health aide as well as homemaker services; (5) medical supplies (including drugs and biologicals) and the use of medical appliances; (6) physicians' services; (7) short-term inpatient care (including both respite care and procedures necessary for pain control and chronic symptom management) in an inpatient facility; (8) counseling concerning care of the terminally ill individual and adjustment to his death; and (9) any other item or service that is specified in the plan and for which payment may be otherwise made under the Medicare program. Nursing care, home health aide services, and homemaker services can be available on a twenty-four hour, continuous basis, but only during periods of crisis and only as necessary to maintain the terminally ill individual at home.

Respite care is available in the hospice program. Respite care is short-term inpatient care provided to the terminally ill individual only as necessary to give relief to the individual's family members or other persons caring for him. Respite care is available only on an intermittent, nonroutine, and occasional basis and may not be provided consecutively over longer than five days.

In addition to medical, therapeutic, and counseling services available under hospice care, home health aides may provide a variety of personal care services for the individual. These services may include household services to maintain a safe and sanitary environment in the areas of the home used by the patient. For example, the aide may change bed linens or engage in light cleaning and laundering essential to the comfort and cleanliness of the individual. Such services are to be provided under the supervision of a registered nurse.

A hospice program is a public agency or private organization (or a subunit) that primarily engages in providing the items and services described in the preceding paragraphs, that makes services available (as needed) on a twenty-four hour basis, and that provides bereavement counseling for the immediate family of terminally ill individuals. The program provides care and services in the individual's home, on an outpatient basis, or on a short-term inpatient basis. Services such as nursing, physician care, and counseling generally must be provided substantially by the hospice program, although the program can make arrangements for the provision of most other services. The hospice agency or organization must be licensed pursuant to any applicable state or local law.

The program must have an interdisciplinary group of personnel including one registered professional nurse and one social worker employed by the program. It must also include one physician either employed by the program or under contract with the program. The interdisciplinary group must also include one pastoral or other counselor. The group establishes the policies governing the provision of care and services. In addition to these statutory requirements, the regulations contain numerous other conditions of participation for hospice agencies and organizations. 42 C.F.R. 418.50–418.100.

The hospice organization must maintain central clinical records on all patients. It may not discontinue the hospice care because of a patient's inability to pay for such care. It may use volunteers in accordance with governmental standards, but must maintain records on the use of such volunteers and the cost savings and expansion of care and services achieved through the use of volunteers.

For a physician to certify an individual as terminally ill and eligible for hospice care, the physician must conclude that the individual's life expectancy is six months or less. The individual does not have to accept hospice care; such care is provided only if he (or a person authorized under state law to act for him if he is incapacitated) affirmatively elects it. For the terminally ill individual who elects hospice care in lieu of other benefits, the statute provides for two hospice care periods of ninety days each and for an unlimited number of subsequent periods of sixty days each. The periods often run consecutively, but they do not have to do so. For example, a person who has been certified for and elected hospice coverage for a ninety-day period may decide to terminate hospice coverage. He will still have one ninety-day period and an unlimited number of sixty-day periods available to him. The hospice must obtain a written certification of his terminal illness for each of the hospice periods, even if they are running consecutively.

To elect hospice care, the individual (or his representative) files an election statement with a particular hospice. The election statement identifies the hospice that will provide the care; acknowledges that the individual has been given a full understanding of the palliative rather than curative nature of hospice care; indicates the effective date of election (which cannot be earlier than the date of the election statement); contains the signature of the individual (or his representative); and also acknowledges that certain Medicare services are waived by the election. Unless exceptional and unusual circumstances exist, the individual who has elected to receive the care of a particular hospice provider is deemed to have waived all rights to payment (1) for hospice care provided by a different hospice program during the period and (2) for services furnished during the period that are related to the treatment of the individual's terminal condition (or related condition) or that are the equivalent of (or duplicative of) hospice care. This waiver of payment rights, however, does not apply to physicians' services furnished by the individual's attending physician who is not a hospice employee or to services provided by the hospice program (or by others under arrangements made by the program).

An individual can revoke his election for hospice care during a ninety-day or sixty-day hospice period. If he does so, the revocation is a waiver of his right to have payment made for any hospice care benefits for the remaining time in the hospice period. Moreover, the individual is deemed to have been provided with such benefits during the entire period. Thus, if he revokes his election in the midst of his first ninety-day hospice period, he loses the days remaining in that ninety-day period; however, he resumes other Medicare coverage of the benefits he had earlier waived in making the hospice election initially. In contrast, an individual may change from one hospice program to another once during a ninety- or sixty-day period, and such a change is not treated as a revocation of his election for hospice care. Thus, if he changes hospice programs in the midst of his first ninety-day period, the period continues under the new provider.

The individual who elects hospice care has no deductible to pay for hospice services. The hospice may assess a limited coinsurance charge against him for (1) drugs and biologicals and (2) respite care. The individual is liable for a coinsurance payment for each palliative drug and biological prescription furnished by the hospice while he is not an inpatient. The amount of coinsurance for each prescription approximates five percent of the cost of the drug or biological to the hospice, but may not exceed five dollars. The coinsurance payment for each day of respite care is equal to five percent of the payment made by CMS for each respite care day, but the coinsurance liability for respite care during a hospice coinsurance period may not exceed the inpatient hospital deductible applicable in the year in which the coinsurance period began.

An individual on hospice who receives services that are not considered hospice care is liable for Medicare deductibles and coinsurance payments and also for the difference between the reasonable and actual charge on unassigned claims for those other services that are not considered hospice care. Such services include services furnished before or after a hospice election period; services of the individual's attending physician, if the attending physician is not an employee or working under an arrangement with the hospice; and Medicare services received for the treatment of an illness or injury not related to the individual's terminal condition.

2. Part B

Part B provides supplementary medical insurance (SMI) that is available (1) to most individuals age sixty-five or over and (2) to disabled individuals who are under age sixty-five and entitled to hospital insurance. Part B insurance helps to cover medically necessary items and services not covered under Part A. Most importantly, Part B covers certain doctors' services; outpatient services; services furnished by rural health clinics, ambulatory surgical centers, comprehensive outpatient rehabilitation facilities; and other medical and health services. It also covers ambulance services, laboratory and diagnostic services, and medical equipment and supplies. Further, Part B covers home health care not covered by Part A. For example, if home health services are ordered for an individual who was not admitted to a hospital or SNF, Part A coverage is unavailable, but the services can be covered under Part B. Similarly, because Part A limits home health services to one hundred visits per spell of illness, additional visits can be covered under Part B.

Although Part B covers certain expenses in full, in most instances the beneficiary is responsible for a coinsurance amount for the service in question. (Often the coinsurance is twenty percent of the Medicare-approved reasonable charge for the service.) Additionally, the beneficiary must pay a monthly premium for Part B insurance and must satisfy an annual deductible. These aspects of the Part B program are discussed in more detail in the following paragraphs.

a. Financing

Unlike Part A, which is financed by the hospital insurance portion of the FICA tax, Part B is financed by insurance premiums from the beneficiaries and by contributions from federal funds. As required by statute, the premium is designed to cover approximately one-fourth of the average cost of Part B services incurred by beneficiaries aged 65 and over.

b. Eligibility and Enrollment

An individual who is entitled to hospital insurance benefits under Part A is eligible to enroll in Part B. Also eligible is an individual who has attained the age of sixty-five, is a resident of the United States, and is either (1) a citizen or (2) an alien lawfully admitted for permanent residence who has resided in the United States continuously during the five years immediately preceding the month in which he applies for enrollment in Part B. 42 U.S.C. § 1395o. Individuals are not eligible to enroll if they have been convicted of certain crimes against the United States.

i. Initial Enrollment Period; Automatic Enrollment

The initial enrollment period generally begins on the first day of the third month before the month in which the individual first satisfies the eligibility requirements and ends seven months later. For an individual who is sixty-five and eligible for enrollment solely because he is entitled to Part A, the individual is considered as first meeting the eligibility requirements for SMI on the first day he becomes entitled to hospital insurance or would have been entitled if he filed an application for that program.

An individual is automatically enrolled in Part B if he resides in the United States (excepting Puerto Rico), becomes entitled to regular Part A insurance (i.e., non-premium hospital insurance), and does not decline SMI enrollment. In other words, if he wants Part A coverage only, he must affirmatively decline Part B coverage in this setting. SSA will send him a notice of his automatic enrollment and specify a period (which runs for at least two months after the month the notice is mailed) in which he may submit a signed statement indicating that he wishes to decline enrollment in Part B. An individual is automatically enrolled in the third month of the initial enrollment period if he is entitled to Social Security benefits on the first day of the initial enrollment period or establishes entitlement to Part A by filing an application and meeting all other requirements during the first three months of the initial enrollment period. If an individual establishes entitlement to Part A on the basis of an application filed in the last four months of the Part B initial enrollment period, he is automatically enrolled in the month in which the application is filed. 42 C.F.R. 407.17–407.18.

ii. General and Special Enrollment Periods

As with Part A, Part B provides a general enrollment period beginning on January 1 and ending on March 31 of each year. If an individual establishes entitlement to Part A on the basis of an application filed after the Part B initial enrollment period but not during a general enrollment period, he is automatically enrolled for Part B on the first day of the next general enrollment period. If an individual establishes entitlement to Part A hospital insurance on the basis of an application filed during a Part B SMI general enrollment period, he is automatically enrolled on the first day of that period.

Also like Part A, Part B provides a special enrollment period (SEP) pertaining to individuals covered under a group health plan. To use an SEP, individuals must meet the following conditions: (1) they must be eligible to enroll for Part B on the basis of age or disability, but not end-stage renal disease; (2) when first eligible for Part B coverage (the fourth month of their initial enrollment period), they were covered under a group health plan or large group health plan on the basis of current employment status or, if not so covered, they enrolled in Part B during their initial enrollment period; and (3) for all months thereafter, they maintained coverage under either Part B or a group or large group health plan. 42 C.F.R. 407.20. For an individual sixty-five or over who is or was covered by a group health plan, coverage must be by reason of the current employment status of the individual or the individual's spouse.

iii. Request for Individual Enrollment

An individual who meets the eligibility requirements and desires Part B coverage must make a request for enrollment if he is not entitled to Part A; has previously declined enrollment in Part B; has had a previous period of Part B coverage that terminated; resides in Puerto Rico or outside the United States; or is enrolling or reenrolling during an SEP. The request must be signed by the individual or his representative and be filed with SSA or CMS during the initial enrollment period, a general enrollment period, or a special enrollment period.

iv. When Entitlement Begins

If an individual enrolls during the first three months of the initial enrollment period, entitlement begins with the first month of eligibility. If an individual enrolls during the fourth month of the initial enrollment period, entitlement begins with the following month. If an individual enrolls during the fifth month of the initial enrollment period, entitlement begins with the second month after the month of enrollment. If an individual enrolls in either of the last two months of the initial enrollment period, entitlement begins with the third month after the month of enrollment. For example, if John first becomes eligible for Part B in April, his initial enrollment period is January through July of that year. If he enrolls in January, February, or March, his entitlement begins on April 1. If he enrolls in April, his entitlement begins May 1. If he enrolls in May, his entitlement begins July 1. If he enrolls in June, his entitlement begins September 1. If he enrolls in July (the last month of his initial enrollment period), his entitlement begins October 1.

If an individual enrolls or reenrolls during the general enrollment period, entitlement begins on July 1 of that calendar year. For an individual who enrolls or reenrolls during an SEP, the entitlement rules are the same as for Part A enrollment during an SEP. If the individual enrolls during a month in which he is covered under the group health plan based on current employment status, or if he enrolls during the first full month when no longer covered, then Part B coverage begins on the first day of the month of enrollment or, at his option, on the first day of any of the three following months. If he enrolls in Part B during any later month of the SEP, then Part B coverage begins on the first day of the month following the month of enrollment.

v. Government Error

If an individual's enrollment or nonenrollment in SMI is unintentional, inadvertent, or erroneous because of the error, misrepresentation, or inaction of a federal employee or any person authorized by the federal government to act in its behalf, then SSA or CMS may take whatever action it determines necessary to provide appropriate relief. This action may include designation of a special initial or general enrollment period; designation of an entitlement period based on that enrollment period; adjustment of premiums; any combination of the preceding, or any other remedial action that may be necessary to correct or eliminate the effects of the error, misrepresentation, or inaction.

vi. Premiums and Penalties

Medicare Part B requires the beneficiary to pay a monthly premium. Until 2007, all beneficiaries were charged a uniform monthly premium that was adjusted annually. Under a provision of the Medicare Modernization Act of 2003 (which began to be implemented in 2007), Congress decided that higher income beneficiaries should pay more. Beneficiaries are charged according to

modified adjusted gross income in one of five brackets. The adjusted gross income thresholds are themselves adjusted annually.

Part B Premiums per Beneficiary (2009)		
Individual Tax Return and Modified Adjusted Gross Income …	Joint Tax Return and Modified Adjusted Gross Income …	Total Monthly Premium Amount
Less than or equal to $85,000	Less than or equal to $170,000	$96.40
Greater than $85,000 and less than or equal to $107,000	Greater than $170,000 and less than or equal to $214,000	$134.90
Greater than $107,000 and less than or equal to $160,000	Greater than $214,000 and less than or equal to $320,000	$192.70
Greater than $160,000 and less than or equal to $213,000	Greater than $320,000 and less than or equal to $426,000	$250.50
Greater than $213,000	Greater than $426,000	$308.30

Modified adjusted gross income is statutorily defined as adjusted gross income under the federal tax code, increased by the amount of interest received
or accrued during the taxable year that is exempt from income taxation. In
determining the monthly Part B premiums for a given year, the individual's
modified adjusted gross income is based on the individual's last taxable year beginning in the second calendar year preceding the year involved. For example,
a person's premium for 2009 would typically be based on the information on
the tax return he filed in 2008 for tax year 2007.

In fact, few elderly Part B beneficiaries exceed the base threshold. A 2008 fact
sheet issued by CMS predicted that nearly ninety-five percent of beneficiaries
will pay only the base or standard Medicare Part B monthly premium.

For an individual who enrolls after his initial enrollment period and not
pursuant to a special enrollment period, the Part B monthly premium is increased
by ten percent for each full twelve months in which he could have been but
was not enrolled. In counting these twelve-month periods for the person who
first enrolls, the statute generally considers the months elapsed between the
close of his initial enrollment period and the close of the enrollment period
in which he enrolled (excluding months of coverage in a group health care or
large group health care plan by virtue of current employment). 42 U.S.C.

§ 1395r(b). If the increased premium is not a multiple of ten cents, then the increased premium amount is rounded to the nearest multiple of ten cents.

Part B premiums are generally paid in one of three ways: (1) for most people, by automatic deduction from Railroad Retirement benefits, Social Security benefits, or civil service annuities; (2) by direct payment for others without such benefits who must pay their own premiums (preferably paid on a quarterly basis) or whose premiums are paid through a group organization (typically paid on a monthly basis); or (3) by the state through a so-called "state buy-in" agreement benefitting certain individuals with limited income and resources. Unpaid premium amounts constitute an enforceable obligation against the enrollee and his estate. Moreover, the enrollee may be terminated for nonpayment of premiums if he fails to satisfy his debt within the Part B grace period.

c. Deductible

In addition to the monthly premium, Part B includes an annual deductible. In 2009, the annual deductible was $135. The enrollee must meet the annual deductible even if he receives Part B coverage for only a part of the year. Expenses that the enrollee incurs for Part B care generally count toward meeting the annual deductible, with some exceptions. Expenses incurred for the following services are not subject to the annual deductible and do not count toward meeting that deductible: home health services; pneumococcal vaccines and their administration; federally qualified health center services; and certain screening mammography services, screening pelvic examinations, colorectal cancer screening tests, and certain ultrasound screenings for abdominal aortic aneurysms. 42 C.F.R. 410.160.

For example, if John's earliest Medicare Part B reasonable charge in 2009 is a physician's fee of $235, the first $135 will be paid by John and will satisfy his deductible for the year. Payment of the remaining $100 fee will be governed by Part B's coinsurance rules. (Coinsurance rules are discussed in the next section.) John will have no further Part B deductible to pay in 2009.

In addition to the enrollee's responsibility for the annual monetary deductible, the enrollee is also responsible for the cost of the first three units of blood used during the year. This blood deductible is satisfied, however, if the enrollee has met his blood deductible under Part A.

d. Coverage and Coinsurance

Part B includes coverage for a wide array of outpatient medical services and supplies. A few of the many items of coverage include physicians' services; outpatient hospital services and supplies incident to a physician's services; certain drugs and biologicals that the beneficiary cannot give himself; diagnostic tests;

medical supplies, appliances, and devices; emergency medical services; and home health services not covered by Part A. 42 C.F.R. 401.1 et seq.

Once the enrollee has met his yearly deductible, in most instances Medicare Part B will pay a provider or supplier of Part B services 80 percent of the Medicare-approved amount. The enrollee is responsible for paying the remaining 20 percent. This general rule is subject to numerous exceptions, however.

i. Physicians' Services and Charges

Perhaps the most important coverage provided by Part B is that for physicians' services. Part B covers medically necessary services the beneficiary receives from his doctor in the doctor's office, in a hospital, in an SNF, in the beneficiary's home, or anywhere else. It does not cover routine examinations other than a one-time "Welcome to Medicare" exam.

(a) Coinsurance and Limitations on Charges

Physicians' services, like most services covered under Part B, generally require a payment from the Medicare-covered patient. Part B is structured in a manner that not only limits the amount paid by the beneficiary, but also the amount that can be charged by the physician. The Medicare Part B program establishes a "Medicare-approved amount" for each of the various services rendered by a provider or a supplier under the program.

In most states, doctors are permitted to decide whether they will "participate" in the Medicare-reimbursement program. If they choose to participate (or if they are required to participate, as in a few states), then they are only entitled to recover the Medicare-approved amount for the particular service rendered. Doctors who agree to be bound by the Medicare-approved amount are said to "accept assignment" or "take assignment." If a doctor takes assignment, then Medicare will reimburse the doctor for 80 percent of the Medicare-approved amount, and the beneficiary is responsible for the remaining 20 percent. 42 U.S.C. § 1395l(a).

In sum, the Medicare-approved amount is the amount under the Original Medicare plan that a doctor or supplier who accepts assignment can be paid. It includes what Medicare pays and any deductible, coinsurance, or copayment that the beneficiary must pay. The Medicare-approved amount may be (and often is) less than the actual amount a doctor or supplier normally charges.

For example, if John has met his annual deductible and later his participating doctor performs a Part B service for which the Medicare-approved amount is $1000, then Medicare Part B will pay the doctor $800 and John is responsible for paying the remaining $200. Note that because the doctor accepts assignment, $1000 is all the doctor is allowed to recover, even if he would customarily charge $1500 for such a service and even if most doctors would charge $1500 for such a service. When a physician bills on assignment, the bill is submitted directly to the Medicare program and the physician is paid the Medicare-reimbursement amount directly from Medicare Part B.

For the doctor who chooses not to participate in Medicare or not to take assignment, Part B will still only pay 80 percent of the Medicare-approved amount. For a nonparticipating physician (and other nonparticipating suppliers and persons), however, the Medicare-approved amount is statutorily reduced by five percent. 42 U.S.C. § 1395w-4(a)(3). This reduction is intended to provide an incentive for physicians and suppliers to participate. The incentive is somewhat tempered however, in that the nonparticipating physician can charge the Part B beneficiary not only 20 percent of the Medicare approved charge, but also up to an additional 15 percent of the Medicare-approved amount. 42 U.S.C. § 1395w-4(g)(2)(C), (D). When a physician does not participate, he bills the entire charge to the patient. The patient must pay the bill, and the patient has the burden of seeking reimbursement from Medicare. This system is sometimes referred to as balance billing.

For example, if John has met his annual deductible and later his nonparticipating doctor performs a Part B service for which the standard Medicare-approved amount from the fee schedules is $1000, then the Medicare-approved amount for the nonparticipating doctor is $950 (reflecting the five percent reduction). The doctor, however, may bill John for up to 115 percent of the $950 amount. John must pay the entire bill, but he may seek partial reimbursement from Medicare (which will pay 80 percent of the $950 approved amount).

Similar reimbursement rules and limitations apply for many (but not all) other providers and suppliers who participate in Medicare Part B. Some of these rules and limitations are described further in the discussion of other Part B services that follows.

(b) Examples of Covered Services

The range of physician services covered by Part B is quite broad. It includes doctor services for transplants. It also includes a second opinion concerning the need for surgery, and even a third opinion if the first and second opinions differ. In some rural areas, Part B will cover telemedicine under certain conditions in a provider's office, a hospital, or a federally-qualified health center. Telemedicine is the provision of medical or other health services through a communications system (computer, telephone, etc.) by a practitioner in a location different from that of the patient. In each of these cases, the patient pays 20 percent of the Medicare-approved amount for the doctor's service.

Podiatrists' services are covered for medically-necessary treatment of injuries or diseases of the foot. (Routine foot care is excluded.) The beneficiary pays 20 percent of the Medicare-approved amount for medically-necessary treatment. Medicare Part B also covers qualified chiropractic services when manipulation of the spine is medically necessary to correct a subluxation. Moreover, Part B will cover certain services provided by clinical social workers, physician assistants, and nurse practitioners. The beneficiary pays 20 percent of the Medicare-approved amount.

ii. Preventive Services

Medicare Part B does not cover most routine medical examinations. Because disease prevention is generally much less expensive than disease treatment and cure, however, Medicare Part B covers a variety of preventive services. Although little-heralded, these may be among the most important of the Part B services.

All Medicare beneficiaries are entitled to cardiovascular screening once every five years. They pay nothing if their doctor or provider accepts assignment. All women with Medicare age 40 and older can get a screening mammogram once a year. They pay 20 percent of the Medicare-approved amount, with no Part B deductible. All women with Medicare are covered for a Pap test and pelvic exam at least once every twenty-four months. The beneficiary pays nothing for the Pap lab test. For Pap test collection and pelvic and breast exams, the beneficiary pays 20 percent of the Medicare-approved amount with no Part B deductible.

For men over age 50 (coverage begins one day after the fiftieth birthday), Medicare will cover annual prostate cancer screening. The beneficiary has no coinsurance or Part B deductible for a Prostate Specific Antigen (PSA) test. He must pay 20 percent of the Medicare-approved amount if he has a Digital Rectal Examination (after the yearly Part B deductible).

Colorectal cancer screening is also covered by Part B for all Medicare beneficiaries fifty and older. Medicare now waives the Part B deductible for the colorectal cancer screening benefit. The frequency of coverage depends upon the kind of test and whether the beneficiary is at high risk. For example, a screening colonoscopy is covered once every six years for most beneficiaries, but once every twenty-four months for those at high risk. Moreover, the "age 50 and older" requirement does not apply to a screening colonoscopy. As a general rule, the beneficiary must pay 20 percent of the Medicare-approved amount. If a flexible sigmoidoscopy or colonoscopy is done in a hospital outpatient department or an ambulatory surgical center, however, the beneficiary must pay 25 percent of the Medicare-approved amount. Medicare imposes no charge on the beneficiary for a fecal occult blood test.

Medicare Part B's preventive services also include flu shots (once per flu season at no charge if the provider takes assignment); pneumococcal shots (usually only needed once in a lifetime; there is no charge if provider takes assignment); and hepatitis B shots (for those at medium to high risk; the beneficiary pays 20 percent of the approved amount after the yearly deductible). It also includes bone mass measurements at least once every two years for those whose doctors say are at risk for osteoporosis. The beneficiary pays 20 percent of the approved amount after the yearly deductible.

The preventive services also include diabetes screening up to twice annually for those who are at risk for diabetes. The beneficiary pays nothing if the provider accepts assignment. The services also include diabetes glucose monitors, test strips, and lancets for those with diabetes. Beneficiaries pay 20 percent of the Medicare-approved amount after the yearly Part B deductible. If a doctor so requests, Part B will also cover diabetes self-management training for certain beneficiaries who are at risk for complications from diabetes. These beneficiaries must pay 20 percent of the approved amount after the annual deductible.

When referred by a doctor, beneficiaries with diabetes or renal disease (but who are not on dialysis) may also receive medical nutrition therapy to help manage the diabetes or kidney disease. This includes three hours of one-on-one counseling services in the first year and two hours each year after that. A doctor's referral is required each calendar year for subsequent hours. (Additional hours also may be available with a doctor's referral.) The beneficiary pays 20 percent of the Medicare-approved amount after the yearly Part B deductible is met.

Part B also covers an annual glaucoma test for beneficiaries whose doctor says they are at high risk for glaucoma. The beneficiary pays 20 percent of the Medicare-approved amount after the yearly Part B deductible is met.

Medicare beneficiaries who are diagnosed with a smoking-related disease or whose medications are compromised by the use of tobacco can get coverage for counseling to quit smoking. Medicare will cover up to eight personal visits annually. The visits must be ordered by the beneficiary's doctor and provided by a qualified doctor or other Medicare-recognized practitioner. The beneficiary pays 20 percent of the Medicare-approved amount after the Part B deductible is met. CMS notes that smoking-related diseases—which include heart disease, cerebrovascular disease (stroke), multiple cancers, lung disease, weak bones, blood clots, and cataracts—account for the bulk of Medicare spending today.

Finally, Medicare Part B provides a one-time "Welcome to Medicare" comprehensive preventive physical examination for new beneficiaries. Beneficiaries who want to take advantage of this service must schedule it within their first twelve months of Part B coverage. The beneficiary pays 20 percent of the Medicare-approved amount, and the Part B deductible does not apply. Part B will also pay for a one-time ultrasound screening for abdominal aortic aneurysm for beneficiaries who are determined to be at risk and who are referred for the screening as a result of the Welcome to Medicare examination. The beneficiary pays 20 percent of the Medicare-approved amount for such screening. The deductible does not apply.

iii. Miscellaneous Services

Part B covers medically-necessary diagnostic lab services ordered by the beneficiary's treating physician as part of treatment of a medical problem. Such tests include CT scans, MRIs, EKGs, and X-rays. Part B also covers clinical diagnostic laboratory services provided by certified laboratories enrolled in Medicare. Diagnostic tests and lab services are intended to help the doctor diagnose or rule out a suspected illness or condition. In general, the beneficiary pays 20 percent of the Medicare-approved amount for covered diagnostic tests and X-rays performed in a physician's office or independent testing facility. The beneficiary must pay a copayment for diagnostic tests and X-rays in the hospital outpatient settting, but pays nothing for Medicare-covered lab services.

Medicare Part B covers emergency room services. A medical emergency exists when the beneficiary believes that he has an injury or illness that requires immediate medical attention to prevent a disability or death. The beneficiary pays a copayment for each emergency room visit unless he is admitted to the hospital for the same condition within three days of his emergency room visit. In addition to paying a specified copayment for each hospital service, the beneficiary must pay a coinsurance of 20 percent of the Medicare-approved amount for each emergency room doctor who treats the beneficiary.

Medicare Part B covers emergency ground transportation (ambulance services) when the beneficiary needs to be transported to a hospital or skilled nursing facility for medically-necessary services, but only when transportation in any other vehicle could endanger the beneficiary's health. Medicare will even pay for transportation by air if the beneficiary requires immediate and rapid ambulance transportation that ground transportation cannot provide. In some instances, Medicare may provide for non-emergency transportation as ordered by a doctor. Medicare only covers services to the nearest appropriate medical facility able to give the care the beneficiary needs. The beneficiary pays 20 percent of the Medicare-approved amount for ambulance services. All ambulance suppliers must accept assignment. Medicare does not cover transportation for routine health care.

Part B services also include coverage for chemotherapy for outpatients or for patients in a doctor's office or freestanding clinic. (Part A covers chemotherapy for cancer patients who are hospitalized.) Part B also covers radiation therapy for outpatients or patients in freestanding clinics. For outpatient radiation therapy, the beneficiary pays a set copayment. For radiation therapy at a freestanding facility, the beneficiary pays 20 percent of the Medicare-approved amount.

Part B also helps to pay for medically-necessary outpatient physical and occupational therapy and speech-language pathology services if the services are set up pursuant to a plan of treatment by the beneficiary's doctor or therapist and the doctor periodically reviews the plan to see how long therapy is needed. Medicare does not pay for services given by a speech-language pathologist in private practice, although it will pay for services of a Medicare-approved physical or occupational therapist in private practice that are given in the therapist's office or in the patient's home.

iv. Equipment and Supplies

Part B covers durable medical equipment (DME) ordered by a beneficiary's physician for use in the beneficiary's home. To be covered, it must be prescribed by the beneficiary's physician. To qualify as DME, the equipment must be durable (long lasting), used for a medical reason, not generally useful to someone who is not sick or injured, and used in the beneficiary's home. Among the items that are potentially covered are air-fluidized beds, blood sugar monitors, canes (but not those for the blind), commode chairs, crutches, dialysis machines, home oxygen equipment and supplies, hospital beds, infusion pumps, nebulizers, patient lifts, suction pumps, traction equipment, walkers, and wheelchairs. If the doctor or supplier is not enrolled in Medicare, Medicare will not pay the claim submitted by the doctor or supplier.

Typically, the beneficiary pays 20 percent of the Medicare-approved amount for DME. Medicare pays for different kinds of DME in different ways, however. If the supplier is a participating supplier, it must accept assignment. If the DME supplier does not accept assignment, Medicare does not limit what it can charge and the beneficiary may have to pay the entire bill (both his share and Medicare's share) at the time he receives the DME. In some areas, the Medicare beneficiary must use certain Medicare-contracted suppliers to obtain certain DME.

When ordered by a physician, Medicare Part B covers artificial limbs and eyes, and arm, leg, back, and neck braces. The patient pays 20 percent of the Medicare-approved amount. Orthopedic shoes are not covered unless they are a necessary part of the leg brace. Part B does not cover dental plates or other dental devices.

Part B covers power-operated vehicles (scooters), walkers, and wheelchairs as DME if prescribed by the beneficiary's physician. The beneficiary must have a face-to-face examination and a written prescription from a doctor or other treating provider before Medicare will cover a power wheelchair.

Part B also covers ostomy supplies for people who have had a colostomy, ileostomy, or urinary ostomy. Part B covers the amount of supplies that the physician indicates are needed by the patient based on the patient's condition. The patient pays 20 percent of the Medicare-approved amount. Part B generally does not cover common medical supplies like bandages and gauze.

v. Limited Coverage of Prescription Drugs

Part B provides limited outpatient coverage for prescription drugs. (More comprehensive drug coverage is available if a beneficiary joins a Medicare Part D drug plan, discussed later.) Usually Part B coverage is for drugs that are not self-administered.

For example, Part B will cover drugs infused through an item of DME such as an infusion pump or nebulizer, if reasonable and necessary. Part B will also cover antigens prepared by a doctor and administered by a properly-instructed person (this may include the patient in this instance) under doctor supervision. Most injectable drugs given by a licensed medical practitioner are covered if the drug is considered reasonable and necessary for treatment. Among common drugs that may be included are injectable osteoporosis drugs for certain women; erythropoietin by injection for individuals with end-stage renal disease or if needed to treat anemia related to certain other conditions; blood clotting factors by injection for hemophiliacs; immunosuppressive drugs for transplant patients if the transplant was covered by Medicare in a Medicare-certified facility; oral cancer drugs that are available in injectable form; and certain oral anti-nausea drugs used as part of an anti-cancer chemotherapeutic regimen under specified conditions. Generally the beneficiary pays 20 percent of the Medicare-approved amount for covered prescription drugs. Again, however, Part B coverage for prescription drugs is limited.

vi. Home Health Services

A person who qualifies as homebound under Part A is also considered homebound for Part B coverage. Part B will cover the cost of specified home health services when Part A coverage ceases or does not exist. The beneficiary has no coinsurance amount to pay.

vii. Mental Health Services

Part B covers mental health services on an outpatient basis that are provided by a doctor, clinical psychologist, clinical social worker, nurse practitioner, clinical nurse specialist, or physician assistant in an office setting, clinic, or hospital outpatient department. Medicare coverage for outpatient mental health treatment (such as psychotherapy) has historically been far stingier than its coverage for most other outpatient services. In 2009, for example, reimbursement for psychotherapy was limited to 50% of the Medicare-approved amount. Beginning in 2010, however, the coverage will gradually begin to increase. In 2010 and 2011, the patient's share of the cost will generally be limited to 45% of the Medicare-approved amount. In 2012, that percentage decreases to 40%, and in 2013 that percentage decreases to 35%. In 2014 and years thereafter, the patient's share of the cost will be limited to 20% of the Medicare-approved amount.

3. Exclusions and Priority of Payment

a. Items and Services

Section 1395y of the Medicare statutes provides a long list of exclusions from Part A and Part B coverage. Although some of these exclusions have been mentioned in the preceding discussion, it is perhaps worth listing several of them here to demonstrate how substantial the exclusions are.

First, Medicare generally provides no payments for expenses incurred for items or services that are not *reasonable and necessary* for the diagnosis or treatment of illness or injury or to improve the functioning of a malformed body member. In the context of certain medical and health services, the expenses must be reasonable and necessary for the prevention of illness. Medicare now includes a one-time "Welcome to Medicare" examination and includes certain preventive screening procedures. Under the "reasonable and necessary" mantra, however, Medicare imposes limitations on the frequency of various medical screening procedures.

Medicare does not cover routine physical checkups, routine eye exams, routine hearing exams, routine prescriptions for eyeglasses or contact lenses, hearing aids, or exams for fitting hearing aids. Medicare provides only very limited coverage of immunizations. Medicare excludes routine dental work. It excludes most orthopedic shoes and other devices for the feet as well as routine foot care and treatment of flat foot conditions. Medicare does not cover cosmetic surgery except as required for the prompt repair of accidental injury or for improvement of the functioning of a malformed body member.

The reasonable and necessary requirement often leads Medicare to make determinations of "no coverage" for treatments that are deemed experimental. Of course, experimental treatments may evolve into standard medical practices that eventually become Medicare-covered for future patients.

Medicare generally provides no payment when the beneficiary has no legal obligation to pay for items or services furnished to him and which no other person (by reason of his membership in a prepayment plan or otherwise) has a legal obligation to provide or pay for.

Medicare generally does not cover health care while the beneficiary is traveling outside the United States. (Puerto Rico, the U.S. Virgin Islands, Guam, American Samoa, and the Northern Mariana Islands are considered the United States for most (but not all) Medicare purposes.) One very limited exception arises when the individual receives inpatient hospital services outside the United States if (1) the individual is a United States resident and (2) the hospital was closer to, or substantially more accessible from, the residence of the beneficiary than the nearest hospital within the United States that was adequately equipped to deal with, and was available for the treatment of his illness or injury. This might apply to a resident near the Canadian border, for example. Under another very limited exception, Medicare will cover emergency inpatient hospital services outside the United States if (1) the individual was physically present in the United States (or was in Canada while traveling by direct route between Alaska and another state) when the emergency occurred and (2) the hospital was closer to, or substantially more accessible from, his location than was the nearest adequately-equipped and available hospital in the United States. If the inpatient hospital stay is covered under the exception, then so are doctor and ambulance services.

Medicare does not pay for personal comfort items or services (except in the case of hospice care as reasonable and necessary for the palliation or management of terminal illness). Although Congress did not define "personal comfort," the regulations indicate personal comfort services include the use of a telephone and television. The regulations have withstood attack.

Very importantly, Medicare does not cover custodial care (except as permitted under the hospice program as reasonable and necessary for the palliation or management of terminal illness). Medicare also does not cover expenses that constitute "charges imposed by immediate relatives of such individual or members of his household." The latter rule is intended to prevent Medicare reimbursement for items and services that would typically be provided or performed gratuitously by family members of the patient and by those living in his house (including domestic employees). Immediate family is defined broadly to include not only spouses, parents, children, and siblings, but also stepparents, stepchildren, stepsiblings, parents-in-law, children-in law, siblings-in-law, grandparents, grandchildren, and the spouses of grandparents and grandchildren. Moreover, the rule applies to charges for physicians' services furnished by an immediate relative of the beneficiary or by a member of the beneficiary's household, even if the claim is submitted by someone else or by an entity such as a partnership or a professional corporation. 42 C.F.R. 411.12.

b. Medicare as Secondary Payer

Section 1395y discusses the priority of payment when, in addition to Medicare coverage, the beneficiary is covered by an employer group health care plan or the payments in question can reasonably be expected to be made under a worker's compensation plan, under an automobile or liability insurance policy (including a self-insured plan), or under no-fault insurance. In most of these settings, Medicare functions as the secondary plan. The other source of payment is the primary plan, from which payment must first be made before Medicare's obligation to pay kicks in. Where coverage under the primary plan is less than the entire charge, Medicare may pay for the remainder (without regard to deductibles and coinsurance) or some part thereof, based on a limiting formula. Expenses for Medicare-covered services that are paid for by primary payers are credited toward the Medicare Part A and Part B deductibles.

A group health plan generally may not discriminate against current employees age sixty-five or older because they have Medicare; rather, the plan must provide these people the same benefits as those afforded to employees under sixty-five. Small employers are excepted from this rule, however. (A small employer is one who does not have twenty or more employees for each working day in each of twenty or more calendar weeks in the current calendar year or the preceding calendar year.)

Medicare may make payment on the beneficiary's behalf when primary plans do not pay promptly; however, such payments are conditioned on later reimbursement of the program from the primary plan. CMS may sue the primary plan if necessary to recover the payment. If it is necessary for CMS to take legal action, CMS may recover twice the amount that Medicare paid. In CMS actions for recovery of conditional payments, the beneficiary must cooperate or else the government may recover from him.

4. Appeals and Rights

a. Limitation on Liability; Notice

A long-standing provision of Medicare limits the payment liability of beneficiaries for non-covered services or items when they did not know, or could not reasonably have been expected to know, that the services or items would not be covered. 42 U.S.C. § 1395pp.

This limitation on liability extends to non-covered custodial care and services not reasonable and necessary furnished by a provider or by a practitioner or supplier that accepted assignment of benefits. If both the beneficiary and the provider did not know and could not reasonably have been expected to know of the non-coverage, Medicare will pay. Medicare will also provide a notice to the beneficiary and the provider that in similar conditions arising thereafter Medicare will not pay. If an innocent beneficiary pays, but the provider, practitioner, or supplier knew or should have known that the item or service is noncovered, Medicare will indemnify the beneficiary and may recover from the provider, practitioner, or supplier. The regulations provide criteria for determining whether a beneficiary, provider, practitioner, or supplier knew that services were excluded from coverage.

The limitation on liability principle also applies to home health services in settings where the individual was not confined to his home or did not need skilled nursing care on an intermittent basis. The limitation also applies to hospice care when the individual is determined not to be terminally ill.

The limitation on liability principle generally does not protect the beneficiary from liability for non-covered services or items provided by a nonparticipating provider under Part B (other than those provided by a physician). Under the regulations, if a nonparticipating physician provides services that are found to be not reasonable and necessary, then the limitation on liability principle applies and the physician must provide a refund to the beneficiary/patient unless an exception applies. 42 C.F.R. 411.408.

In many instances, the beneficiary will not be able to assert the limitation on liability principle because he will have received advance notice of potential noncoverage. If a doctor, provider, or supplier thinks Medicare may not cover an item or service, it is to provide the beneficiary a written Advance Beneficiary Notice (ABN). The notice explains what items and services Medicare may not cover, why Medicare may not cover those items, and what the items will probably cost. In this manner, the beneficiary can make an informed choice about whether to obtain the item or service. 42 U.S.C. § 1395cc(a)(1)(M)(iv). The beneficiary will have to sign and date the ABN. There are various kinds of ABNs: the general advance beneficiary notice of noncoverage (ABN; CMS R-131), used by doctors, durable medical equipment suppliers, and certain health care providers; the skilled nursing facility advance beneficiary notice (SNFABN); the home health advance beneficiary notice (HHABN); and the hospital-issued notice of non-coverage (HINN).

b. The Appeals Process

i. Premature Discharge and Expedited Appeals

As part of the hospital admissions process, the beneficiary should receive a notice entitled "An Important Message from Medicare About Your Rights" (IM). The IM explains the beneficiary's right to medically necessary services; to be involved in decisions about services and payment; to obtain post-hospital services; and to appeal a discharge decision. The IM also explains the beneficiary's financial responsibility for remaining in the hospital after his discharge date. The beneficiary must sign the IM.

If the beneficiary believes he is being discharged too soon, he may request a Quality Improvement Organization (QIO) to review the decision. A QIO is a group of practicing doctors and other health care experts paid by the federal government to check and improve the care given to people with Medicare. If the beneficiary requests the review no later than the date of discharge, he may remain in the hospital without additional financial responsibility (other than applicable coinsurance or deductibles) while awaiting the decision of the QIO. If the QIO decides against the beneficiary, the beneficiary's additional financial liability will begin if he stays past noon of the day after the QIO gives him its decision.

Similar requests may be made when a beneficiary thinks other Medicare-covered services are ending too soon. The beneficiary should receive and be asked to sign a Notice of Medicare Provider Non-Coverage at least two days before covered services end. Home health agencies, skilled nursing facilities, comprehensive outpatient rehabilitation facilities, and hospices with beneficiaries enrolled in Original Medicare must notify the beneficiaries of the right to an expedited review process when the provider anticipates that Medicare coverage of their services will end. The beneficiary who believes the services are ending prematurely should request the QIO to make an independent review. The request should be made no later than noon of the day before the Medicare-covered services are to end. The QIO redetermination should be made within seventy-two hours.

A second level of appeal results in a reconsideration by a Qualified Independent Contractor (QIC) that again is to be made within seventy-two hours. In appeals levels three through five, the claimant may proceed to a hearing before an administrative law judge, to a Medicare Appeals Council review, and ultimately to federal court. These final three steps are governed by the same rules that apply in the standard appeals process, described below.

ii. Standard Appeals Process

Once Medicare makes a decision on a claim, the beneficiary has a right to a fair, efficient, and timely decision on appeals regarding a health care payment decision or on initial determinations on items or services received. The appeals process is provided for at 42 U.S.C. § 1395ff and further defined in the regulations. There are four levels of administrative appeals for standard and expedited claims under Parts A and B, followed by the right to proceed to federal district court in certain circumstances.

In the standard process, the initial determination is made by a fiscal intermediary (FI), carrier, or Medicare Administrative Contractor (MAC). The FI, carrier, or MAC is a private company that contracts with Medicare. FIs (sometimes just called "intermediaries") usually contract with Medicare to pay Part A and some Part B bills (for example, bills from hospitals). Carriers contract with Medicare to pay physicians and most other Medicare Part B bills. MACs contract with Medicare to pay certain Part A and Part B bills.

When an initial determination is made, the beneficiary should receive a Medicare Summary Notice (MSN) that indicates whether the claim is approved or denied. If the claim is denied, the MSN will include the reason for denial along with information on how to file an appeal.

(a) Redetermination

The beneficiary typically has 120 days from receipt of the MSN in which to file an appeal. The beneficiary can use the MSN itself to make the request by circling items with which the beneficiary disagrees, explaining why, and signing. Alternatively, the beneficiary can make a request by letter or use a redetermination request form provided on the CMS website. The appeal is filed with the company that handled the Medicare claim.

This first level of appeal is called a redetermination. There is no monetary minimum threshold for filing a request for a redetermination. The company will generally send a written decision within sixty days of receiving the beneficiary's request.

(b) Reconsideration

If a beneficiary is dissatisfied with the redetermination decision, he may request a reconsideration. The reconsideration request can be made by letter or by a reconsideration form available from the CMS website. The request is filed with a Qualified Independent Contractor (QIC) that did not take part in the redetermination. The request should be filed within 180 days of the beneficiary's receipt of the redetermination. As with the redetermination request, there is no minimum dollar threshold required to file for a reconsideration.

The QIC will send the beneficiary its written reconsideration within 60 days of receiving the beneficiary's request. If the QIC cannot meet this deadline, it will send a letter that indicates the beneficiary's option to go directly to the next level of appeal.

(c) ALJ Hearing

The third level of appeal provides a hearing before an administrative law judge (ALJ). The beneficiary's request for such a hearing generally must be filed within 60 days of his receipt of the reconsideration decision. Before the beneficiary is entitled to an ALJ hearing, the amount in controversy (AIC) must meet a minimum dollar threshold. The amount is adjusted annually. In 2009, the threshold amount was $120. The reconsideration letter prepared by the QIC will estimate whether the claim satisfies the threshold, but the ultimate determination is for the ALJ. The reconsideration will provide instructions for requesting an ALJ hearing. The ALJ will respond within 90 days of receiving the beneficiary's request for a hearing.

If the ALJ cannot or does not issue a timely decision, the beneficiary may file a written request with the ALJ to proceed to the next level of appeal. 42 C.F.R. 405.1104. If the ALJ issues a timely decision to which the beneficiary objects, the beneficiary may also proceed to the next level of appeal.

(d) MAC Review

The fourth level of appeal is a Medicare Appeals Council (MAC) review. Generally, a beneficiary must submit a MAC review request within sixty days of receiving the ALJ's decision. There is no minimum monetary threshold required for MAC review. The ALJ decision will include instructions for filing a MAC review request.

If the MAC provides review, it sends its written decision within 90 days of receiving the request. Alternatively, if MAC cannot issue a timely decision, the beneficiary may request to proceed to federal court review.

A party may request to appear before the MAC to present oral argument. The MAC grants a request for oral argument if it decides that the case raises an important question of law, policy, or fact that cannot be readily decided based on written submissions alone. Alternatively, the MAC may decide on its own that oral argument is necessary to decide the issues in the case. 42 C.F.R. 405.1124.

(e) Federal Court Review

Federal court review is available in some instances when the beneficiary disagrees with the MAC's decision. The AIC must again meet a monetary threshold, adjusted annually. The AIC threshold for federal court review is substantially greater than the AIC required for an ALJ hearing. In 2009, the amount was $1,220. The request for federal court review must be filed in the appropriate United States District Court within 60 days of the MAC's decision.

D. Part C (Medicare Advantage Plans)

1. Generally

A Medicare Advantage plan (an MA plan) is an optional type of Medicare health plan offered by a private company that contracts with Medicare to provide the beneficiary with all his Medicare Part A and Part B benefits. An MA plan may also be called a Medicare Part C plan. Under the Medicare Part C program, Medicare pays a monthly amount to these private MA plans for the enrollee's care. MA plans include health maintenance organizations, preferred provider organizations, private fee-for-service plans, special needs plans, and Medicare medical savings account plans.

By statute, an individual is generally eligible to enroll in an MA plan if he is entitled to benefits under Part A and is enrolled in Part B. 42 U.S.C. § 1395w-21(a)(3). To enroll, the individual must live in the geographic service area of the plan. (An MA plan may permit him to continue to enroll if he subsequently moves outside the plan's service area, so long as the plan continues to provide him reasonable access to the full range of basic benefits.) An individual may enroll initially if, at the time he first becomes entitled to Part A benefits and enrolled under Part B, at least one plan exists in the area in which he resides. This enrollment period generally runs from three months before the individual turns sixty-five to three months after the month he turns sixty-five. There is also an annual, coordinated election period that runs from November 15 through December 31 for the following plan year. Moreover, an open enrollment and disenrollment period exists during the first three months of each year. During this period, however, the individual cannot add or change to a plan with prescription drug coverage unless he already has Medicare prescription drug coverage. 42 U.S.C. § 1395w-21(e).

An increasing minority of Americans are choosing MA plans over the Original Medicare plan. Enrollment in MA plans varies substantially across the country, but in several states recent enrollment has approached or exceeded thirty percent of the Medicare population. In contrast, in some states enrollment is less than five percent. Among MA plans, by far the most often utilized are HMOs.

A beneficiary enrolled in an MA plan receives Medicare services through the plan, not under Original Medicare Parts A and B. The plan provides all of the enrollee's Part A and Part B benefits and must cover at least all of the medically-necessary services that the Original Medicare plan provides. MA plans, however, can charge different copayments and deductibles for these services. Enrollees in MA plans cannot buy a Medigap policy to cover copayments and deductibles.

A potential advantage of an MA plan is that it may offer extra benefits, such as coverage for routine vision, hearing, dental, and wellness programs not covered by the Original Medicare plan. Most MA plans also provide Medicare prescription drug coverage. Generally, MA plans charge one combined premium for Part A and Part B benefits, Medicare prescription drug coverage (if offered), and extra benefits (if offered). The enrollee's actual out-of-pocket costs under an MA plan will depend on various factors, including the following: whether the plan charges a monthly premium in addition to the Part B premium; whether the plan pays all or only part of the monthly Part B premium; whether the plan has a yearly deductible or additional deductibles; the costs, if any, for each visit or service; the costs of going outside the plan; and the cost of the extra benefits.

Many individuals believe that the potential advantage of extra benefits under an MA plan is outweighed by the limitations of provider networks generally associated with MA plans. The use of provider networks often means that the MA plan enrollee must see doctors who belong to the plan and must use certain hospitals to get covered services. Often the plan will require the enrollee to obtain a referral before seeing a specialist or to obtain prior authorization for certain procedures. If the enrollee uses a provider not in the network, he often pays a higher cost or even the entire cost of the covered service. In some instances, joining an MA plan will cause the enrollee to lose employer or union health care coverage.

It is extremely important for an individual to examine carefully the benefits and limitations before enrolling in an MA plan.

2. Protections for Enrollees (Including Appeals)

Section 1395w-22 imposes requirements for MA plan disclosures, grievance mechanisms, and coverage determinations, reconsiderations, and appeals. The plan must, at the time of enrollment and at least annually thereafter, provide the enrollee with a detailed description of the plan provisions concerning service area, benefits, access, out-of-area coverage, supplemental benefits, and prior authorization rules.

Each year, MA plans send enrollees an Evidence of Coverage. This document details plan benefits, costs to enrollees, and appeals procedures, among other things. Plans may change each year, and an enrollee should receive an Annual Notice of Change each fall. The Annual Notice of Change explains changes in benefits, costs, or service area that will become effective in the following January. If the plan covers prescription drugs, the Annual Notice of Change also details changes to the formulary (the list of covered drugs). If an MA plan leaves the Medicare program, it must inform the enrollee about his options. Typically, the individual is returned to the Original Medicare plan if he does not choose to join another MA plan.

Each MA plan must have a procedure for making determinations about coverage. Determinations that deny coverage must be in writing and include a statement "in understandable language" of the reasons for the denial and a description of the reconsideration and appeals process. The plan must also have procedures for assuring an expedited determination in certain situations. The plan must provide for reconsideration when requested by an enrollee or physician. Independent, outside entities are to review and resolve in a timely manner reconsiderations that affirm certain denials of coverage, in whole or in part.

If the enrollee is still dissatisfied and the amount in controversy exceeds a fairly low threshold ($120 in 2009; adjusted annually), he is entitled to a hearing before an administrative law judge under the Office of Medicare Hearings and Appeals. Further appeal may be made to the Medicare Appeals Council, which may decline review. Ultimately, if the amount in controversy exceeds a more substantial threshold ($1200 in 2009; adjusted annually), the disgruntled enrollee may proceed to federal district court.

Section 1395w-22(j) is designed to further protect enrollees. It provides that a plan may not prohibit or restrict a covered health care professional from advising a patient about the patient's health status or medical care or treatment, regardless of whether benefits for such care or treatment are provided under the plan. The statute also places limitations on physician incentive plans. The statute provides that a plan cannot make a specific payment directly or indirectly to a physician or physician group as an inducement to reduce or limit medically necessary services provided with respect to a specific individual enrolled in the plan.

3. Kinds of MA Plans

There are several categories of MA plans. Substantial differences may exist among the plans within a category, however. The following paragraphs provide a general overview of the major categories or kinds of MA plans.

A Medicare health maintenance organization (HMO) plan is an MA plan that often provides benefits in addition to the mandatory coverage of Part A and Part B benefits. HMOs are available in many parts of the country. With most HMOs, the enrollee can only use the services of doctors, specialists, and hospitals on the plan's list, except in cases of emergency. The enrollee will generally need to choose a primary care physician, because typically the enrollee must obtain a referral from a primary care physician to see a specialist. Enrollee costs may thus be lower than in the Original Medicare plan. A point-of-service (POS) option is an HMO option that allows enrollees to use doctors and hospitals outside the plan for an additional cost. Most plans now offer prescription drug coverage.

A Medicare preferred provider organization (PPO) plan is a plan in which the enrollee pays less if he uses the doctors, hospitals, and providers that belong to the network. The enrollee does not have to choose a primary care physician. In most cases the enrollee does not have to obtain the referral of a primary care physician to visit a specialist. The enrollee may use doctors, hospitals, and providers outside the organization, but usually at an additional cost. Many PPOs now offer prescription drug coverage.

A Medicare private fee-for-service (PFFS) plan allows the enrollee to visit any Medicare-approved physician or hospital accepting the plan's payment. Not all providers will accept the plan's payment or agree to treat the enrollee, however. The insurance plan, rather than the Medicare program, decides how much it will pay and what the enrollee will pay for the services he obtains. Some PFFS plans now offer prescription drug coverage. As with most plans, the enrollee may obtain extra benefits for a higher premium.

A medical savings account (MSA) plan has two parts: a high-deductible health plan and a bank account. Medicare provides the plan with an amount each year for an enrollee's health care, and the plan deposits a part of this money into the enrollee's account. The enrollee uses the money in his account to pay his health care costs. When account money is used for Part A and Part B services, it applies toward the plan's deductible. After the deductible is reached, the plan covers the enrollee's Medicare-covered services. Any money left in the account at year's end is added to the enrollee's next deposit. MSAs do not offer prescription drug coverage. Although the enrollee may choose his doctor or hospital, some plans have network doctors or hospitals that provide services for a lower cost. The enrollee is not required to have a referral from a primary care physician to see a specialist.

A special needs plan (SNP) is an MA plan that provides more focused health care for specific groups of people, such as those who have both Medicare and Medicaid, who reside in certain institutions (like a nursing home), or who have specific chronic or disabling medical conditions (like diabetes, congestive heart failure, mental illness, or HIV/AIDS). The plan may use a care co-ordinator who helps the enrollee develop a personal care plan and coordinate his care. For example, in an SNP for people with both Medicare and Medicaid, the plan may use a care coordinator to help the enrollee obtain assistance from the community and coordinate his health care. Typically, the enrollee must obtain care and services from doctors or hospitals in the plan's network, except in emergencies. SNPs usually have specialists for the diseases or conditions that affect their members. The referral of a primary care physician is usually required to visit a specialist. All SNPs must provide prescription drug coverage.

4. Other Medicare Plans

Some Medicare plans are not MA plans but are still part of the Medicare program. These include Medicare Cost plans, Medicare Demonstrations/Pilot programs, and Programs of All-Inclusive Care for the Elderly (PACE). These plans provide coverage under Part A and Part B and may provide Part D prescription drug coverage. Such plans are often similar to MA plans, but each of them has special rules and exceptions.

Medicare Cost plans are available in certain parts of the country. An individual may enroll even if he only has Part B coverage, and he may enroll at any time the Medicare Cost plan is accepting new members. If the enrollee visits a non-network provider, the services are covered under Original Medicare. He would have to pay the Part B premium and any applicable coinsurance or deductibles under Part A and Part B. The enrollee can leave the plan at any time and return to Original Medicare.

Medicare demonstrations test improvement in Medicare coverage, payment, and quality of care. They usually focus on a specific group of people or are offered only in specific areas, or both. For example, Medicare has a current pilot program for people with Medicare and one or more chronic illnesses.

PACE provides medical, social, and long-term services and prescription drug coverage for frail, elderly people who get health care in the community. It is a joint Medicare and Medicaid program available in some states that have chosen it as an optional Medicaid benefit.

E. Part D

1. Generally

Under Part D, Medicare now offers prescription drug coverage for anyone with Medicare. First effective in January of 2006, Part D is generally considered the most substantial change to the Medicare program since its enactment in 1965.

For most Medicare beneficiaries, a Medicare Part D (prescription drug) plan is a stand-alone drug plan that adds prescription drug coverage to the Original Medicare plan (Parts A and B), some Medicare Cost plans, some Medicare private-fee-for-service plans, and Medicare medical savings account plans. Such Part D plans (sometimes called PDPs) are offered by insurance companies and other private companies approved by Medicare.

Although this discussion will focus on stand-along drug plans, Medicare Advantage plans (Part C) may also offer prescription drug coverage that follows the same rules as Medicare Prescription Drug plans. Enrollees in most MA plans that provide drug coverage must obtain that drug coverage through their MA plan; if they enroll in a separate Medicare Prescription Drug plan, they are disenrolled from the MA plan and returned to the Original Medicare plan. An MA plan including prescription drug coverage is sometimes called an MA-PD plan.

To get coverage under a Part D stand-alone plan, the Medicare beneficiary must join. Each plan can vary in costs and in drugs covered. The plan issues its members a PDP card to use when filling prescriptions. Depending upon the plan, the member may have a copayment or a deductible to meet when filling the prescription.

2. Drug Coverage Rules

All PDPs must generally cover at least two drugs in each category of drugs. Plans can choose which specific drugs are covered in each category, however. In six classes of drugs—anti-psychotics, anti-depressants, anti-convulsants, immunosuppressants, cancer, and HIV/AIDS—PDPs are required to cover almost all of the drugs. Plans are not required, but may choose, to cover certain drugs such as barbiturates and drugs for erectile dysfunction or weight loss. PDPs are generally not allowed to cover over-the-counter drugs.

Many PDPs place drugs into various tiers. The member's copayment then depends in part upon the tier in which the needed drug lies. A four-tiered categorization might appear as follows:

Tier	Copayment	Coverage
1	Lowest copayment	Most generic prescription drugs
2	Medium copayment	Preferred, brand-name prescription drugs
3	Higher copayment	Non-preferred, brand-name prescription drugs
Specialty Tier	Highest copayment	Unique, very high-cost drugs

A preferred brand-name prescription drug is a drug that the plan has determined is less costly, but as effective, as a non-preferred brand-name prescription drug. Drugs covered by a plan may change during the year. If a formulary change affects a drug that a member takes, the plan must notify him at least sixty days in advance. The member may then have to change the drug he takes or pay more for it. In some instances, a plan will allow the member to continue the drug until the end of the year. Alternatively, the member may request an exception or may appeal the plan's decision.

3. Points to Consider

Subject to the limitations of the Part D program, each PDP may impose its own set of rules or limitations. Because each PDP has its own formulary, a prospective member should review a plan carefully to determine whether it includes prescription drugs he currently takes or is likely to need during the year.

A plan may require prior authorization, in which case the member or his physician (or both) must contact the plan before the plan will cover the prescriptions. A plan may impose quantity limits upon drugs. A plan may require step therapy, which requires the member to try one or more similar, lower cost drugs before the plan will cover the drug originally requested.

The plan may cover only a generic brand of the drug the individual is currently taking, or a different brand-name drug for the same illness or condition. As previously mentioned, drug coverage may also change during the year. Some plans permit prescriptions by mail; others utilize only certain pharmacies. Premiums, deductibles, and copayments or coinsurance for each drug vary with each plan.

4. Grievances and Appeals

a. Grievances

A grievance is a complaint or dispute other than a coverage determination (see below) in which a plan member expresses dissatisfaction with any aspect of the operations, activities, or behavior of a Part D plan sponsor, regardless of whether remedial action is requested. A simple grievance might involve a complaint about customer service or the lack of clarity in the plan sponsor's notices or written materials. A complaint about the plan sponsor's decision not to expedite a request for a coverage determination or redetermination can also constitute a grievance.

Grievances may be filed orally or in writing by an enrollee or his appointed representative. They are to be filed no later than 60 days after the event or incident that brought about the grievance. The plan sponsor generally must notify the enrollee of its decision as expeditiously as the enrollee's health requires, but no later than 30 days after it receives the grievance, unless extended by the plan for up to 14 calendar days. If, however, the grievance involves a refusal to grant an enrollee's request for an expedited coverage determination or an expedited redetermination, and the enrollee has not yet purchased or received the drug that is in dispute, then the plan must respond to the grievance within 24 hours.

b. Appeals

i. Coverage Determinations and Exceptions That May Lead to an Appeal

Coverage determinations (in contrast to grievances) are appealable decisions made by a Part D plan sponsor regarding (1) receipt of, or payment for, a prescription drug that an enrollee believes may be covered; (2) a tiering or formulary exception request; (3) the amount the plan sponsor requires the enrollee to pay for a Part D prescription drug; (4) a limit on quantity or dose of a requested drug; (5) a requirement that the enrollee first try another drug; or (6) the enrollee's satisfaction of a prior authorization or other utilization management requirement.

An enrollee, his physician, or his appointed representative may request a standard coverage determination by filing a request in writing with the plan sponsor. The request may be made by use of a Model Coverage Determination Request Form available from the CMS website, a coverage determination request form developed by the plan sponsor or other entity, or any other written document. Physicians may also submit a request on the Model Coverage Determination Request Form for Physicians. Using this form, the physician may request not only a coverage determination or exception, but also submit a statement supporting an exception request or attempt to satisfy a utilization management requirement.

An exception request is one in which the enrollee, his prescribing physician, or his appointed representative seeks to deviate from the plan. For example, the enrollee may request a tiering exception or a formulary exception. A tiering exception seeks to obtain a non-preferred drug at the cost terms applicable to drugs in the preferred tier. A formulary exception seeks to obtain a Part D drug not included on the plan sponsor's formulary. The enrollee's prescribing physician must submit a statement supporting a request for an exception. A plan will grant an exception request when it determines that the drug is medically necessary for the enrollee.

For coverage determination requests that do not involve an exception, the plan sponsor must notify the enrollee of its determination within 72 hours of receipt of the standard request. If the coverage determination involves an exception, however, the relevant time period does not begin until the enrollee's prescribing physician submits his supporting statement to the plan sponsor. For an expedited request for a coverage determination, the time period is 24 hours. A plan will honor an expedited request, which can be made in writing or orally, when it determines, or the enrollee's physician so advises the plan, that the enrollee's life or health may be seriously jeopardized by waiting for a standard decision.

If the coverage determination is unfavorable to the enrollee, the decision will contain the information needed for the enrollee to file a request for a redetermination with the plan sponsor. The redetermination will be the first level of appeal.

ii. Standard Appeals Process

(a) Redetermination

The enrollee or his appointed representative may appeal an adverse determination by a plan sponsor by requesting a redetermination. (In special circumstances, the enrollee, his appointed representative, or his prescribing physician may request an expedited redetermination. The expedited appeals process is discussed separately below.)

A request for a redetermination must be filed with the plan sponsor within 60 calendar days from the date of the notice of the coverage determination. Unless the plan sponsor accepts oral requests, the request should be in writing.

Once the plan sponsor receives a standard request, it must make its decision and notify the enrollee of its decision no later than 7 calendar days after receiving the request.

(b) Reconsideration

If the redetermination is adverse to the plan enrollee, he or his appointed representative may request a reconsideration by the Independent Review Entity (IRE), which is also commonly called the Part D Qualified Independent Contractor (QIC). The enrollee must file the reconsideration request, in writing, within 60 days from the date of the notice of the plan sponsor's redetermination decision. The request can be made through the Request for Reconsideration of Medicare Prescription Drug Denial form, available on the CMS website.

When the IRE receives a standard request, it must make its decision and notify the enrollee of its decision no later than 7 calendar days after receiving the request. If the reconsideration is adverse to the enrollee, then the reconsideration will include information needed by the enrollee to request a hearing with an ALJ.

(c) ALJ Hearing

The enrollee or his appointed representative may appeal an IRE's adverse reconsideration decision by requesting a hearing with an ALJ. To request such a hearing, the amount in controversy must meet a certain threshold. (In 2009 the threshold was $120.) The request, which must be in writing, must be filed within 60 calendar days from the date of the notice of the IRE's reconsideration decision. If the ALJ makes a decision unfavorable to the enrollee, the decision will include information needed by the enrollee to request a review with the Medicare Appeals Council (MAC).

(d) MAC Review

The enrollee or his appointed representative may appeal an ALJ's adverse decision by requesting review by the Medicare Appeals Council (MAC). The request, which must be in writing, must be filed within 60 calendars from the date of the notice of the ALJ's decision. If the MAC's decision is unfavorable or the MAC denies the enrollee's request to review an ALJ's decision, the decision will include information needed by the enrollee to file a request for review by a federal district court.

(e) Federal Court Review

The enrollee or his appointed representative may appeal an unfavorable decision by the MAC (including a refusal to review the ALJ's decision) by seeking review in a federal district court. To obtain such review, the amount in controversy must reach a monetary threshold. (In 2009, the threshold was $1,220.) The enrollee must request the review in the proper federal district court within 60 calendar days from the date of the notice of the MAC's decision.

iii. Expedited Appeals

If a coverage determination is adverse to the enrollee and the enrollee, his physician, or his appointed representative believes that his life or health will be endangered by the standard appeals time frame, the enrollee, his physician, or the enrollee's appointed representative may request an expedited redetermination. Expedited requests may be made in writing or orally. When the plan sponsor receives the expedited request, it has up to 72 hours to make its decision and notify the enrollee.

If the redetermination is adverse to the enrollee, he or his appointed representative may request an expedited reconsideration. The IRE has 72 hours from receipt of the request to make its decision and notify the enrollee.

If the reconsideration is adverse to the enrollee, he or his appointed representative may proceed through the remaining stages of appellate review (an ALJ hearing, MAC review, and federal court) under the same rules that apply in the standard appeals process described above.

5. Enrollment and Payment

a. Generally

One can first enroll in a PDP when he initially becomes eligible for Medicare. This enrollment period begins three months before the individual's sixty-fifth birthday and ends three months after the month in which he turns sixty-five. There is also an enrollment period that runs from November 15 through December 31 of each year. Individuals may enroll at any time if they qualify for extra help. Such individuals would include those who have Medicare and Medicaid, belong to a medical savings program, or get Supplemental Security Income (SSI) benefits.

Depending upon the plan, enrollment may be made by application on paper, online, or even by telephone. PDPs are not allowed to solicit new members by phone. A member of one plan may switch to another plan during any of the enrollment periods described in the preceding paragraph.

b. Premium Penalty

An individual who does not enroll in a PDP when he is first eligible for Medicare must pay a premium penalty for late enrollment. 42 U.S.C. § 1395w-

113. The penalty is one percent of the national base beneficiary premium for each uncovered month (or, if greater, an amount that is actuarially sound for each uncovered month). The penalty is determined at the time the individual joins the plan. The penalty is permanent. Thus, if the individual first enrolls two years after he is eligible for Medicare, he will typically pay a premium that is permanently increased by 24 percent of the national base beneficiary premium for as long as he retains PDP coverage. If the national base beneficiary monthly premium is $50 at the time he joins, he will pay an additional $12 each month for his PDP plan.

The penalty applies to a Medicare-eligible individual who goes without creditable prescription drug coverage for sixty-three continuous days or more. Creditable coverage is that which provides coverage of the costs of prescription drugs having an actuarial value that equals or exceeds the standard prescription drug coverage under Part D. By statute, creditable coverage may include coverage under a PDP or MA-PD; under a Medicaid plan; under a group health benefits plan (including the federal employees health benefits program (FEHBP)); under a state pharmaceutical assistance program described in the Part D statutes; under coverage for veterans, and survivors and dependents of veterans; under military coverage (including TRICARE); and under such other coverage as determined appropriate.

For example, if John has prescription drug coverage through a former or current employer, the employer must provide him with a notice that compares his coverage with that of Medicare's basic prescription drug coverage. The notice may be in a letter, in the plan, or in a benefits handbook. This notice will help John determine whether later enrollment in a PDP will result in a premium penalty. If the group health care plan is creditable, he may postpone joining a PDP. (Medicare warns individuals to keep such notices, because the individuals may need to show the notices as proof of creditable prescription drug coverage if they join a Medicare PDP late.) This is an important decision not only because of the monthly premium associated with the PDP, but also because in some instances joining the PDP may cause him (or his spouse or other dependents) to lose all of the employer coverage.

Assuming John's employer coverage is creditable but comes to an end, he must join a PDP and obtain coverage within sixty-three days to avoid the PDP premium penalty. Most individuals who have TRICARE, VA, or FEHBP prescription drug coverage (all of which are considered creditable) retain it for as long as they qualify. If such coverage ends, these individuals also may avoid the PDP premium penalty by obtaining Medicare PDP coverage within sixty-three days.

Before 2006, some Medigap policies included prescription drug coverage. CMS warns that an individual with such a policy who postpones PDP enrollment may have to pay the late enrollment penalty if the Medigap drug coverage is not equivalent to that of the Medicare Part D program.

c. Payments

PDP payments that a member must make include the monthly premium, a yearly deductible (not charged by all plans), and copayments or coinsurance (paid after any deductible is met).

The member may be able to pay his PDP premium in various ways, depending upon the plan. The premium may be deducted from his checking or savings account, charged to a credit or debit card, billed directly by the plan, or deducted from his Social Security payment. A Medicare beneficiary who belongs to an MA-PD plan does not have a separate monthly premium to pay for prescription drug coverage.

Most PDPs contain various levels of coverage and include a coverage "gap" or so-called "donut hole." (The statutory paradigm is found in Section 1395s-102(b).) Under the typical PDP, the member is responsible first for meeting an annual deductible. (Some PDPs contain no deductible. In return, however, they typically charge a higher monthly premium.) Once the member pays the deductible, the member pays a copayment and the plan pays the remaining charge for the drug until the total payments by the plan and the member (including her deductible) reach a certain amount. Thereafter, the member is solely responsible for paying the costs for covered drugs until the member has spent a defined amount out-of-pocket. (This period in which the member pays all costs is the donut hole.) Finally, once the member has paid the out-of-pocket amount, the coverage gap or donut hole ends, and the member will pay a small copayment or coinsurance amount for each drug until the end of the year. Coverage once the donut hole is closed is often referred to as catastrophic coverage.

Benefit packages offered by a PDP must be at least as valuable as the standard benefit formula. CMS provides the following example of a typical PDP payment structure based on the 2009 standard benefit formula: The member's PDP deductible is $295, and thereafter the member pays a 25 percent copayment and the plan pays the remaining cost of prescriptions until together the plan and the member have paid (including the deductible) $2700. Once total payments reach $2700, the plan requires the member to pay all of her drug costs until she has spent a total of $4350 (including her deductible, her copayments, and her donut hole payments). When the member has spent out-of-pocket $4350, the donut hole is closed and the member will pay only a small copayment or coinsurance amount (amounting to no more than a few dollars) for each drug until year's end.

The coverage gap comes as a surprise to many people examining PDPs. Note that even while he is in the coverage gap, the member must continue to pay his PDP monthly premium. Some PDPs offer at least partial coverage during the gap; however, the member will typically pay higher premiums for such a plan.

F. Medicare/Medicaid "Dual Eligibles"

Medicare can involve substantial premium, deductible, copayment, and coinsurance payments. Some people who qualify for Medicare have such limited income and resources that it is extremely difficult or impossible for them to pay those premium, deductible, copayment, and coinsurance amounts. Some of these people may obtain assistance in paying their out-of-pocket Medicare medical expenses from their state Medicaid program.

Different benefits exist for these individuals who are Medicare beneficiaries and are also eligible for some kind of Medicaid benefit. Such persons are known as "dual eligibles," and their benefits are often known as medical savings programs. Some of these dual eligibles are entitled to full Medicaid benefits and are known as full benefit dual eligibles (FBDE); others are entitled to limited Medicaid benefits.

To supplement their Medicare coverage, FBDEs receive services and supplies available under their state Medicaid program. This means that when services are covered by both Medicare and Medicaid, then Medicare is generally the first payer and Medicaid will only pay the remaining amount (up to the state limit). Medicaid, however, will also cover services not covered by Medicare, such as SNF care beyond the 100-day Medicare limit or items such as eyeglasses and hearing aids.

In addition to FBDEs are several categories of Medicare beneficiaries who receive limited Medicaid benefits to pay out-of-pocket Medicare expenses. These include Qualified Medicare Beneficiaries, Specified Low-Income Beneficiaries, Qualifying Individuals, and Qualified Disabled and Working Individuals.

Qualified Medicare Beneficiaries (QMBs) are those with resources not exceeding twice the standard allowed under the Supplemental Security Income (SSI) program and income not exceeding 100 percent of the federal poverty level (FPL). QMBs are eligible for Medicaid payment of Medicare premiums, deductibles, co-insurance and co-pays. If the QMB does not otherwise qualify for any additional Medicaid benefits, he is a "QMB Only." In contrast, a "QMB Plus" is someone who satisfies QMB standards and also meets the financial criteria for full Medicaid coverage, often by qualifying as "medically needy" as discussed in the chapter on Medicaid.

Specified Low-income Medicare Beneficiaries (SLMB) are those with resources not exceeding twice the standard allowed under the SSI program and
income that exceeds the QMB maximum level but is less than 120 percent of
the FPL. They are eligible for payment of Part B premiums by Medicaid. If the
SLMB does not qualify for any additional Medicaid benefits, he is an "SLMB
Only." In contrast, an "SLMB Plus" is one who meets SLMB standards and also
meets the financial criteria for full Medicaid coverage, often by qualifying as
"medically needy."

Qualifying Individuals (QI) are those not otherwise qualified for full Medicaid benefits who have resources not exceeding twice the standard allowed
under the SSI program and income that exceeds the SLMB maximum level but
is less than 135 percent of the FPL. QIs are eligible for Medicaid payment of
Part B premiums. Such payments are completely federally funded and the total
expenditures are limited by statute, however.

Qualified Disabled and Working Individuals (QDWI) are certain individuals
who were receiving Medicare due to disability, who lost entitlement because
they returned to work, but who may buy Medicare Part A. These individuals, not
otherwise eligible for Medicaid, must have income below 200 percent of the FPL
and resources at or below twice the standard allowed under the SSI program. These
individuals may qualify for Medicaid payment of Part A premiums only.

G. Medicare's Future

The Summary of the 2009 Annual Reports from the Social Security and
Medicare Boards of Trustees paints a bleak picture of the financial condition
and future of the Medicare program. The Summary noted that a Medicare
funding warning had been triggered for the third consecutive year, indicating
that non-dedicated sources of revenues would soon account for over forty-five
percent of Medicare's outlays. The following excerpt from the Summary highlights the financial problems:

> As we reported last year, Medicare's financial difficulties come
> sooner — and are much more severe — than those confronting Social
> Security. While both programs face demographic challenges, rapidly
> growing health care costs also affect Medicare.... [W]hile Medicare's
> annual costs were 3.2 percent of Gross Domestic Product (GDP) in
> 2008, ... they are projected to ... reach 11.4 percent of GDP in 2083.
> The projected 75-year actuarial deficit in the Hospital Insurance (HI)
> Trust Fund is now 3.88 percent of taxable payroll, up from 3.54 per-

cent projected in last year's report. The fund again fails our test of short-range financial adequacy.... The fund also continues to fail our long range test of close actuarial balance by a wide margin. The projected date of HI Trust Fund exhaustion is 2017, two years earlier than in last year's report, when dedicated revenues would be sufficient to pay 81 percent of HI costs. Projected HI dedicated revenues fall short of outlays by rapidly increasing margins in all future years. The Medicare Report shows that the HI Trust Fund could be brought into actuarial balance over the next 75 years by changes equivalent to an immediate 134 percent increase in the payroll tax (from a rate of 2.9 percent to 6.78 percent), or an immediate 53 percent reduction in program outlays, or some combination of the two. Larger changes would be required to make the program solvent beyond the 75-year horizon.

The projected exhaustion of the HI Trust Fund within the next eight years is an urgent concern. Congressional action will be necessary to ensure uninterrupted provision of HI services to beneficiaries. Correcting the financial imbalance for the HI Trust Fund—even in the short range alone—will require substantial changes to program income and/or expenditures.

Part B of the Supplementary Medical Insurance (SMI) Trust Fund, which pays doctors' bills and other outpatient expenses, and Part D, which pays for access to prescription drug coverage, are both projected to remain adequately financed into the indefinite future because current law automatically provides financing each year to meet next year's expected costs. However, expected steep cost increases will result in rapidly growing general revenue financing needs—projected to rise from 1.3 percent of GDP in 2008 to about 4.7 percent in 2083—as well as substantial increases over time in beneficiary premium charges.

It is expected that about one quarter of Part B enrollees will be subject to unusually large premium increases in the next two years. This occurs because it is projected that the other three-quarters of Part B enrollees will not be subject to premium increases in those years due to low projected Social Security benefit COLAs and a "hold-harmless" provision of current law that limits premium increases to the increase in Social Security benefits.

"A Summary of the 2009 Annual Reports: Status of the Social Security and Medicare Programs," available at http://www.ssa.gov/OACT/TRSUM/index.html.

H. Medigap Policies

1. Generally

The formal name for Medigap insurance is Medicare Supplement Insurance. Medigap policies do not constitute part of the federal Medicare program. Rather, Medigap policies are health insurance policies sold by private insurance companies to individuals who choose to purchase them. Medigap policies are designed primarily to fill in some of the gaps for which the individual is otherwise financially responsible (such as premiums, deductibles, copayments, and coinsurance amounts) in the Original Medicare program. Some Medigap policies cover items or services that are not covered at all by Original Medicare.

To obtain a Medigap policy, an individual generally must have Part A and Part B coverage. Medigap policies are designed only to work with Original Medicare. Although Medigap policies purchased before January 1, 2006 may include provisions for prescription drugs, new Medigap policies are prohibited from including such provisions. Thus, today's enrollee in Original Medicare who wants prescription drug coverage must enroll in a Part D prescription drug plan (PDP). Enrollees under pre-2006 Medigap policies without prescription drug coverage may also join a PDP. An enrollee who has an older policy with drug coverage may retain the drug coverage under that policy or may join a PDP. If the Original Medicare enrollee has an older policy with drug coverage and he chooses to join a PDP, he must notify the Medigap insurance company. The insurance company will remove the prescription drug coverage provision from the policy. An individual may not have prescription drug coverage under both a Medigap policy and a PDP.

Congress has attempted to simplify the Medigap purchasing process and protect consumers from overreaching by insurance companies. Under federal law, insurance companies are permitted only to sell standardized Medigap policies. Standardized Medigap policies are currently designated by letters A through L (with exceptions in Massachusetts, Minnesota, and Wisconsin). Some states offer a Medigap policy known as Medicare SELECT. All Medigap policies with the same designation offer the same basic benefits. Thus, a Medigap D policy sold by Company A is generally the same as a Medigap D policy sold by Company B. The only difference is likely to be the price charged by the two insurance companies. Each policy must be clearly identified on its front as "Medicare Supplement Insurance."

Medigap policies are sold to individuals. If a husband and wife both have Original Medicare and want a Medigap policy, they must each buy their own policy. Medigap policies sold after 1992 are generally guaranteed renewable. The insurer cannot drop an insured unless he stops paying his premiums, was untruthful on his Medigap application, or the insurer becomes bankrupt or insolvent.

This discussion of Medigap is principally concerned with minimum federal requirements. States may impose additional requirements upon insurers that provide consumers with additional Medigap rights.

2. Coverage under the Standardized Plans

The following chart (taken from the CMS website in 2009) demonstrates the kinds of coverage provided by standardized Medigap policies.

Medigap Benefits	Medigap Plans A through L											
	A	B	C	D	E	F	G	H	I	J	K	L
Medicare Part A Coinsurance and Medigap Coverage for Hospital Benefits	√	√	√	√	√	√	√	√	√	√	√	√
Medicare Part B Coinsurance or Copayment	√	√	√	√	√	√	√	√	√	√	50%	75%
Blood (first 3 pints)	√	√	√	√	√	√	√	√	√	√	50%	75%
Hospice Care Coinsurance or Copayment											50%	75%
Skilled Nursing Facility Care Coinsurance			√	√	√	√	√	√	√	√	50%	75%
Medicare Part A Deductible		√	√	√	√	√	√	√	√	√	50%	75%
Medicare Part B Deductible			√		√					√		
Medicare Part B Excess Charges						√	80%		√	√		
Foreign Travel Emergency (up to plan limits)			√	√	√	√	√	√	√	√		
At-Home Recovery (up to plan limits)				√			√		√	√		
Preventive Care Coinsurance (included in the Part B coinsurance)	√	√	√	√	√	√	√	√	√	√	√	√
Preventive Care Not Covered by Medicare (up to $120)					√					√		

The chart shows the kinds of benefits that are offered by all Medigap A plans, B plans, and so forth. All Medigap Plans A through J (as well as the Medicare SELECT plan, described later) provide the following basic benefits: Part A inpatient hospital care coinsurance plus coverage for 365 days after Medicare coverage ends; Part B coinsurance or copayments for hospital outpatient services; and the first three pints of blood each year. Plans cover coinsurance only when the insured has paid the deductible, unless the policy plan itself covers the deductible. Although several plans cover foreign travel emergencies, they also include a separate deductible for such emergencies (not noted on the chart).

Plans J and F also offer a high-deductible option. For example, in 2009, the individual under such a plan with the high-deductible had to pay $2,000 in Medigap-covered costs before the Medigap policy paid anything. Moreover, as the chart indicates, Plans K and L provide only partial coverage for several categories of items or services. The chart does not indicate, however, one additional important aspect of such plans: once the individual meets an out-of-pocket yearly limit and his Part B deductible, the plan then pays 100 percent of covered services for the rest of the calendar year. The out-of-pocket limit in 2009 was $4,620 for Plan K and $2,310 for Plan L.

Not every plan will necessarily be offered by an insurance company selling Medigap policies. If an insurance company sells any Medigap policy, however, it must sell a Medigap Plan A policy.

One additional kind of Medigap policy is a Medicare SELECT policy that is sold in some states. In essence, a Medigap SELECT policy is simply one of the Medigap A through L policies that requires the insured to use specific hospitals and, in some instances, specific doctors to obtain full insurance benefits in non-emergency situations. These policies are generally cheaper than Medigap policies without such limitations.

Like the Medicare program, Medigap policies are not designed to provide private-duty nursing, dental care, vision care and eyeglasses, or long-term care.

The reader interested in the standardized Medigap policies offered in Massachusetts, Minnesota, and Wisconsin will find a separate discussion of those policies at the CMS Medigap website.

A change to the Medigap program will begin on June 1, 2010. On that date, new Medigap Plans M and N will be offered, while Plans E, H, I, and J will no longer be sold. Plans M and N are designed to have lower premiums than other Medigap policies. In return, Plan M policy holders will pay half of their Part A deductible and all of their Part B deductible; Plan N policy holders will be responsible for limited co-payment amounts for doctor visits and emergency room visits after the Part B deductible is met.

Moreover, all new policies sold on or after June 1, 2010, will include the cost sharing amount for Part A hospice and respite care. Policies D and G are also altered, and the preventive services and at-home recovery provisions are eliminated.

3. Right to Purchase

For most individuals, the best time to purchase a Medigap policy is during the Medigap open enrollment period. The open enrollment period is a six-month period that begins on the first day of the month in which an individual is both age sixty-five or older and enrolled in Medicare Part B. (The individual may submit his application before his open enrollment period begins, and probably should do so if he has health care coverage that will end when he turns sixty-five.) If, for example, an individual continues to work past age sixty-five and delays enrollment in Part B because he has creditable coverage under his employer's group health coverage, his open enrollment period will not begin at age sixty-five, but will instead begin when he enrolls in Part B.

Medical underwriting principles do not apply during the open enrollment period, which means that the insurance company cannot refuse to sell an individual any of the Medigap policies it offers or charge an additional amount because of the individual's health problems. Moreover, the company cannot delay the coverage starting date. If the newly insured has a pre-existing condition, however, the company may be able to refuse to cover his out-of-pocket costs for health problems for up to six months in certain instances. The company must reduce or eliminate the pre-existing condition waiting period, however, if the individual purchases the policy during the open enrollment period, previously had creditable coverage for at least six months, and was not without such coverage for more than 63 consecutive days.

If an individual applies for a Medigap policy outside the open enrollment period, an insurance company generally may refuse his application unless he has a guaranteed issue right (as described below). In the absence of such a right, the company may use medical underwriting principles in deciding whether to insure the individual and, if it does insure him, what to charge him for the policy.

An individual may have a guaranteed issue right to purchase a Medigap policy outside of his open enrollment period. Guaranteed issue rights (sometimes called "Medigap protections") require insurers offering Medigap policies to sell the individual a Medigap policy even if he has pre-existing conditions, without additional charges because of his health problems. A guaranteed issue right usually occurs when an individual has other health care coverage that changes, or when he has a trial right to a Medicare Advantage plan and can still purchase a Medigap policy in case he changes his mind about the MA plan. (Federal law generally prohibits insurers from selling Medigap policies in certain instances, such as when the individual already has Medicaid or a Medicare Advantage plan.) Even when the individual has a right to purchase a Medigap policy under a guaranteed issue right, that right to purchase may be limited to certain Medigap policy plans.

Guaranteed right situations arise in the following settings: (1) an individual is enrolled in a Medicare Advantage plan and that plan leaves the Medicare program, stops giving care in that area, or the individual moves out of the plan's service area; (2) an individual is in the Original Medicare plan and has employer group health plan or union coverage that pays after Medicare pays and that is now ending; (3) an individual is in the Original Medicare plan, has a Medicare SELECT policy, and is moving out of the Medicare SELECT plan's service area; (4) an individual joined a Medicare Advantage plan or PACE when first eligible for Medicare Part A at age 65 and decided within the first year of joining that he wanted to switch to the Original Medicare plan; (5) an individual dropped a Medigap policy to join a Medicare Advantage plan (or to switch to a Medicare SELECT policy) for the first time, and decides he wants to switch back after being in the plan for less than a year; (6) an individual's Medigap insurance company goes bankrupt and an individual loses his coverage, or the individual otherwise loses his coverage through no fault of his own; or (7) an individual leaves a Medicare Advantage plan or drops his Medigap policy because of company violations or misrepresentations. In most of these cases, the individual must apply for Medigap coverage no later than 63 days after the prior coverage ends.

4. Prices

Although Medigap policies are standardized, each insurance company offering Medigap policies sets its own premiums and determines how it will establish the price. Medigap policies can be priced or rated in one of three ways: (1) community rated ("no-age rated"); (2) issue-age rated; or (3) attained-age rated.

Under community rating, the same monthly premium applies to anyone who has that policy, regardless of his age. Premiums may increase over time because of inflation or other factors, but not because of the age of the insured.

Under issue-age rating, the age of the individual when he purchases the policy determines the premium. The younger the purchaser, the lower the premium will be. Premiums may increase over time because of inflation or other factors, but not because of the increasing age of the insured.

Under attained-age rating, the insured's current age determines the amount of the premium. Thus, premiums are lowest for the younger buyer, but they will increase as he ages. These kinds of policies are often the least expensive initially, but may easily become the most expensive over time. Moreover, premiums also increase because of inflation or other factors.

Before purchasing a Medigap policy, CMS suggests that the individual engage in a multi-step inquiry: (1) decide which benefits are desired and then choose the Medigap plan that best accommodates those desires; (2) learn which insurance companies sell Medigap policies in the state of residence; (3) call the insurance companies selling those policies, ask detailed questions, and compare costs; and (4) purchase the policy. The pricing structure of a standardized Medigap plan can vary significantly among insurance companies. Before making a final decision, the prospective purchaser should consider the financial strength of the various insurance companies offering the Medigap plan that he has chosen. He should also inquire whether the insurance companies offer various discounts (for example, for nonsmokers). For a helpful list of questions that the individual should ask insurance companies before purchasing a Medigap policy, see CMS's most recent annual booklet on choosing a Medigap policy, available online at the CMS website at http://www.cms.hhs.gov/medigap/.

5. Consumer Protection Provisions

Medigap laws are designed to prevent or curb sharp practices by insurance companies. The laws forbid insurers from selling an individual a Medigap policy to an individual known to have an existing Medigap policy, unless the individual indicates in writing that he plans to cancel his existing policy. With limited exceptions, insurers may not sell a Medigap policy to a person known to have Medicaid or to be in a Medicare Advantage Plan. Insurers may not indicate that a Medigap policy is a part of the Medicare program and may not suggest that a Medigap policy has been recommended by the federal government. Insurance company employees selling Medigap policies may not claim to be Medicare representatives.

Checkpoints

- Concerning Medicare Part A, you should understand
  - How Part A is financed
  - The differences in coverage for hospital insurance, SNF care, home health services, and hospice
  - The payment structure (deductibles, copayments, and coinsurance) for the different kinds of coverage under Part A
- Concerning Medicare Part B, you should understand
  - How Part B is financed
  - The general kinds of coverage offered
  - The payment structure (deductibles, premiums, copayments, and coinsurance)
- Concerning the Medicare Advantage program (Part C), you should understand
  - How it differs from Original Medicare (Parts A and B)
  - The various advantages and disadvantages of the program
- Concerning Medicare Part D, you should understand
  - How prescription drug plans work in general
  - The payment structure (deductibles, premiums, copayments, coinsurance, and the "donut hole")
- Concerning all parts of Medicare, you should understand generally the tiers of the appeals process
- Concerning all parts of Medicare, you should understand generally the rules of enrollment and the penalties that accompany untimely enrollment
- Concerning Medigap insurance policies, you should understand
  - Policies are not part of the Medicare program, but instead are obtained privately and are completely optional
  - Policies are intended to supplement coverage under Original Medicare
  - Congress has attempted to simplify the selection process and protect consumers by standardizing policies

Chapter 9

Medicaid

Roadmap

- Medicaid is a welfare program run jointly by federal and state government
  - Each participating state must have a state medical assistance plan
  - Each state plan must be federally approved
- Medicaid states are said to be SSI states or 209(b) states
  - All states provide coverage to the categorically needy
  - SSI states may provide coverage to the medically needy; 209(b) states must do so
- Eligibility is based on income and resources
- Medicaid (unlike Medicare) covers the cost of long-term health care
  - Medicaid provides special rules to protect the community spouse of an institutionalized spouse
  - Medicaid provides special rules to protect the program when an applicant transfers assets in an attempt to create eligibility
- Medicaid includes provisions for liens, adjustments, and recovery against a recipient's estate

---

A. Overview

Medicaid is a joint federal/state welfare program enacted by Congress in 1965. Under the program, the federal government makes annual appropriations to states to help furnish medical assistance and rehabilitation and other services to families with dependent children and to aged, blind, or disabled individuals whose income and resources are insufficient to pay for such necessary assistance or services. In 2006, Medicaid paid for an estimated $320 billion in services.

As of early 2008, Medicaid beneficiaries included nearly 14 million elderly and disabled people and over 44 million people in low-income families. The Medicaid program was enacted with particular concern for poor children, and much of the program is designed for their benefit; however, this chapter emphasizes the aspects of the program that significantly affect the elderly. For the elderly poor, Medicaid covers the cost of many items not covered by the Medicare program. (Medicare is discussed in Chapter 8.) One of the most important of these items is the cost of long-term care. In recent years, Medicaid has paid for nearly half of all nursing home care in the United States. Such payments accounted for more than 35 percent of state Medicaid budgets.

State or local agencies implement the day-to-day operations of Medicaid while operating within the parameters set by federal law. The program is jointly funded by federal and state tax revenues. The state contribution is significant, often ranging between 25 to 50 percent of the total costs of the program. States are not required to participate in the Medicaid program, but all states have chosen to do so. (Puerto Rico, Guam, the United States Virgin Islands, American Samoa, and the Northern Marianna Islands also participate in Medicaid, but under different rules that are not discussed in this chapter.)

B. Statutes, Regulations, and Administration

1. Federal

The federal Medicaid statutes, which were enacted as an amendment to the Social Security Act, begin at 42 U.S.C. § 1396 (Title XIX of the SSA). Throughout the statutes, the Medicaid program is often referred to as "medical assistance." The regulations interpreting and explaining the statutes begin at 42 C.F.R. 430.

The Centers for Medicare and Medicaid Services (CMS) within the Department of Health and Human Services (HHS) is the agency that oversees the program. CMS also maintains the State Medicaid Manual (SMM), which makes available informational and procedural material that state Medicaid agencies need to administer the Medicaid program. Through the manual CMS can issue mandatory, advisory, and optional Medicaid policies and procedures to the state agencies. CMS program transmittals communicate new or changed policies or procedures to be incorporated into a specific CMS program manual. Once difficult to obtain, many of these materials can now be readily accessed online at http://www.cms.hhs.gov/home/regsguidance.asp.

2. State

The federal statute requires each participating state to have its own detailed plan for medical assistance. 42 U.S.C. § 1396a. Each official state medical assistance plan (MAP) is a substantial document that discusses how that state operates its Medicaid program and demonstrates compliance with federal law. The state plan must address many various topics, including administration, eligibility, coverage, and provider reimbursement. The plan may include a large range of materials in different formats. For example, the plan may include not only federal forms in which the state simply places check marks by the options it has chosen, but also policy narratives and various explanatory and interpretative documents. For the state to receive Medicaid appropriations, the plan must be submitted to and approved by the CMS.

Many of these voluminous state plans are now available online. Although most states refer to their programs as state Medicaid programs, some states call their Medicaid programs by other names. For example, California has Medi-Cal, Maine has MaineCare, Massachusetts has MassHealth, and Tennessee has TennCare. To view the website of your state Medicaid agency and its online publications, see http://www.nasmd.org/links/state_medicaid_links.asp.

C. Benefits

1. Generally

The federal Medicaid statutes set forth a long list of benefits that must or may be covered by a state plan. The list of mandated benefits depends upon whether a person is "categorically needy" or "medically needy." (These two classifications are described more fully later. In general, the medically needy are those persons whose financial status exceeds the requirements to be categorically needy but yet is insufficient to pay for their medical care.) For elderly individuals who are considered categorically needy, among the benefits the state must provide are the following: inpatient hospital services (other than services in an institution for mental diseases); outpatient hospital services; rural health clinic services consistent with state law; laboratory and X-ray services; nursing facility services (other than services in an institution for mental diseases); physicians' services; and certain medical and surgical services furnished by a dentist. 42 U.S.C. §§ 1396a(a)(10)(A), 1396d(a); 42 C.F.R. 440.210. Of particular importance to the elderly is the required coverage of nursing facility services.

Among the other services that a state may provide to its elderly poor are the following: medical or remedial care furnished by a licensed practitioner; home health care services; private duty nursing services; clinic services furnished by or under the direction of a physician; dental services; physical therapy and related services; prescribed drugs, dentures, prosthetic devices, and prescription eyeglasses; other diagnostic, screening, preventive, and rehabilitative services; inpatient hospital services and nursing facility services for individuals 65 or over in an institution for mental diseases; hospice care; case management services; respiratory care services; home and community care in certain circumstances for functionally disabled elderly individuals; community supported living arrangements services under certain circumstances; personal care services in certain circumstances; primary care case management services; services under PACE ("Program of All-Inclusive Care for the Elderly") to certain individuals; and any other medical or remedial care recognized by the state and specified by the Secretary of Health and Human Services (HHS). 42 U.S.C. § 1396d(a). (If a state plan entitles an individual to nursing facility services, it must also provide for home health services. 42 U.S.C. § 1396a(10)(D). The categorically needy are thus entitled to home health benefits because the state plan must provide them with skilled nursing facility services; in contrast, the medically needy are entitled to home health services only if the state chooses to provide them with skilled nursing facility services. 42 C.F.R. 440.220.)

The foregoing lists of benefits are significantly broader in scope than those provided under Medicare. Moreover, states may obtain Medicaid waivers from CMS to gain additional flexibility in operating their programs. To obtain a waiver, the state must provide assurances that its proposal is cost-effective, efficient, and not inconsistent with the purposes of Medicaid. "Waiver states" may expand existing benefits or add new benefits as approved in their waivers. For example, a home and community-based services (HCBS) waiver allows the state to provide benefits and services to individuals at home or in the community rather than in an institutional setting. 42 C.F.R. 441 (subpart h). The benefits may include both traditional medical services as well as nonmedical services. Thus, benefits might include case management services; homemaker services; home health aide services; personal care services; adult day health services; respite care services; and other medical and social services as requested by the state and approved by CMS that will contribute to the health and well-being of individuals and their ability to reside in the community. 42 C.F.R. 440.181.

Medical providers and suppliers decide whether to participate in Medicaid. If they participate, then the state agency reimburses them for the services or items supplied to the Medicaid patient. The federal Medicaid statutes generally do not require the patient to pay premiums, deductibles, coinsurance, or copayments. States are permitted, however, to impose certain nominal charges for care and services. Even if the Medicaid patient is responsible for such cost-sharing charges, however, the Medicaid statute prohibits a provider from denying care or services to a Medicaid patient who is unable to pay such amounts.

42 U.S.C. § 1396o.

2. Availability

The Medicaid statutes and regulations contain several directives concerning the amount, duration, and scope of benefits under the program. 42 U.S.C. § 1396a(10); 42 C.F.R. 440.230. The state plan must provide that the "amount, duration, or scope" of medical assistance made available to any categorically needy person will not be less than the medical assistance made available to any other categorically needy person. Also, it cannot be less in amount, duration, or scope than the medical assistance made available to persons who are not categorically needy (i.e., those who are medically needy).

Each state plan must specify the amount, duration, and scope of each service for the categorically needy and for each covered group of medically needy. Each service must be sufficient in amount, duration, and scope to reasonably achieve its purpose. The state may not arbitrarily deny or reduce the amount, duration, or scope of a required service to an otherwise eligible recipient solely because of the recipient's diagnosis, kind of illness, or condition. The state may, however, place appropriate limits on a service based on criteria such as medical necessity or on utilization control procedures.

3. Quality Assurance

To be approved, the state plan must contain detailed assurances concerning state oversight of the program that ensure its integrity and protect Medicaid recipients. A partial listing of the mandated assurances is provided below. Others are mentioned in various parts of this chapter.

The state plan must provide that the state health or other medical agency will establish and maintain health standards for institutions in which recipients of Medicaid may receive services. It must establish or designate a state authority responsible for establishing and maintaining standards, other than those relating to health, for such institutions. The plan must include descriptions of the kinds and numbers of professional medical personnel and supporting staff to be used in administering the plan. It must describe the standards that the state authority will use to establish and maintain standards for institutions at which recipients of Medicaid may receive care. It must also describe other standards and methods that the state will use to assure that medical or remedial care and services provided to recipients of Medicaid are of high quality.

The state plan must require agreements with every person or institution providing services. Under these agreements, the person or institution must keep such records as are necessary to fully disclose the extent of the services provided and to furnish the state or the federal government with information regarding payments claimed as the state or federal government may request. The plan must require any nursing facility receiving payments to satisfy all of the detailed requirements found in 42 U.S.C. § 1396r(b)–(d). These requirements include those relating to the provision of services (including quality assurance, training of personnel, physician supervision, and maintenance of records), residents' rights, and administration (including licensing requirements and sanitary and infection control). The plan must also include a state program that meets the requirements for the licensing of administrators of nursing homes under 42 U.S.C. § 1396g. (Nursing home requirements are discussed more fully in Chapter 11.)

The state plan must provide methods and procedures regarding the utilization of and payment for care and services under the plan as necessary to safeguard against unnecessary utilization of such care and services. These methods and procedures are also to assure that payments are consistent with efficiency, economy, and quality of care, and that they are sufficient to enlist enough providers so that care and services are available under the plan at least to the extent that such care and services are available to the general population in the geographic area.

The state plan must contain various provisions for the reporting of information by health services facilities, organizations, and entities receiving payments under the plan. The plan must also require the state to demonstrate that it operates a Medicaid fraud and abuse control unit (unless the state demonstrates that operation of such a unit would not be cost-effective because of minimal fraud in connection with the provision of covered services and that beneficiaries will be protected from abuse and neglect in connection with the provision of medical assistance without the existence of such a unit). The Medicaid fraud unit investigates and prosecutes violations of all state laws regarding any and all aspects of fraud in connection with any aspect of the provision of medical assistance and the activities of providers of such assistance under the state plan. With the approval of the Inspector General of the relevant federal agency, the unit may also prosecute violations of any aspect of the provision of such services under any federal health care program if the suspected fraud or violation is primarily related to the state plan. 42 U.S.C. § 1396b.

4. Fiscal Integrity: Third-Party Liability

If a Medicaid beneficiary incurs a medical expense for which a third party is liable for payment, sound fiscal policy suggests that the state not pay that expense. The Medicaid statute and regulations adopt and elaborate upon that policy. 42 U.S.C. § 1396k; 42 C.F.R. 135 et seq.

To assist the state in learning of such third party's existence and probable liability, all state plans must require that an individual is eligible for Medicaid only if he assigns to the state any rights to support and to payment for medical care from any third party. The individual must also agree to cooperate with the state in identifying and providing information to the state to assist it in pursuing a third party who may be liable to pay for care and services under the state plan (unless the individual has good cause for refusing to cooperate, a factor which takes into consideration the best interests of the individuals involved).

Medicaid statutes require the state agency to take all reasonable measures to determine the legal liability of such third parties. 42 U.S.C. § 1396(a)(25); 42 C.F.R. 433.138–.139(b) & (c).

D. Eligibility and Coverage

1. Generally

Medicaid recipients must be United States citizens or permanent resident aliens. Section 1396b(v) precludes Medicaid payments to an alien who is not lawfully admitted for permanent residence or otherwise permanently residing in the United States. Even then, Medicaid is only available to such a permanent resident alien if the care is necessary for the treatment of an emergency medical condition, the alien otherwise meets the eligibility requirements under the state plan, and the care is not related to an organ transplant procedure.

Under 1396a(b), a state plan may not otherwise impose a residence requirement that excludes from eligibility an individual residing in the state, regardless of whether the individual's residence is maintained permanently or at a fixed address. The plan also may not impose an age requirement of more than 65 years.

Although the federal statute sets forth the general limitations on eligibility for medical assistance, typically the state Medicaid agency is responsible for making individual decisions concerning eligibility. Federal provisions preclude an agency from imposing an age requirement of more than 65 years when the program provisions are for the "aged." Federal provisions also contain rules for determining the age of an applicant. 42 C.F.R. 435.520(a)(1) & (b); 435.522(a) & (c).

Because Medicaid is a program for the financially needy, the program imposes an income and a resources test. The discussion of detailed requirements for financial eligibility is covered later in this chapter.

2. Coverage

a. Mandatory Coverage: The Categorically Needy

Section 1396a(10)(a)(i) requires that the state plan make certain kinds of medical assistance available to certain categories of people. People who fall within these groups are generally referred to as "categorically needy." Most importantly for elders, a majority of states provides Medicaid coverage to aged, blind, and disabled persons who are eligible for Supplemental Security Income. (Other states provide coverage under the 209(b) option discussed below.) Medicaid must also be available to certain needy families receiving benefits under the TANF ("Temporary Assistance to Needy Families") program.

i. SSI States and 209(b) States

The Supplemental Security Income (SSI) laws were passed seven years after the adoption of the Medicaid program. (SSI is discussed in Chapter 7.) States have two options concerning the provision of Medicaid to persons eligible for SSI.

The first option simply ties Medicaid coverage to receipt of SSI benefits. This option is used by most states, which are known for Medicaid purposes as "SSI states." SSI income and resources rules apply to such Medicaid programs. Thus in these states, all recipients of SSI are eligible for Medicaid. In most of these states, no separate application for Medicaid is required.

A second option allows states to impose more stringent Medicaid eligibility rules than those under the SSI program. States choosing this option are known for Medicaid purposes as "209(b) states," because the option was provided in section 209(b) of the public law of which it was a part. (The option is now codified at 42 U.S.C. § 1396a9(f).) The 209(b) states include Connecticut, Hawaii, Illinois, Indiana, Minnesota, Missouri, Nebraska, New Hampshire, North Dakota, Ohio, Oklahoma, and Virginia.

Fearing that some states would choose to depart from the Medicaid program if required to provide Medicaid benefits to all recipients of SSI, Congress adopted the 209(b) option to permit states to develop their own rules for Medicaid eligibility. Eligibility requirements in 209(b) states, however, cannot be more restrictive than those in effect on January 1, 1972. Moreover, SSI payments (and any state supplements) themselves are not considered part of the individual's income in establishing eligibility for Medicaid in 209(b) states.

Because 209(b) states may impose Medicaid income and resources eligibility requirements that are more stringent than those in SSI states, the Medicaid laws require 209(b) states to provide for "medically needy" individuals. A medically needy individual is someone who would have excess income under state rules but for the consideration of incurred medical (and remedial) expenses. Such a person in effect becomes categorically needy if he is otherwise eligible for Medicaid and the payment of incurred medical costs from his total income brings him within the state's financial eligibility requirements. The individual must "spend down" or pay the amount of incurred medical expense that will make him financially eligible for Medicaid under state law. 42 C.F.R. 435.121(e).

Incurred medical expenses that are subject to payment by a third party (other than a public program of the state or its political subdivision) are not considered in the spend-down process. States choosing the 209(b) option must allow this spend-down process with regard to excess income. They may, but are not required to, extend the spend-down process to excess resources.

Unlike 209(b) states, SSI states are not required to cover the medically needy, but they may choose to do so. Because most states are SSI states, the medically needy classification and the spend-down process are examined more fully in the later discussion of optional coverage. But remember, coverage for the medically needy is not optional in a 209(b) state.

ii. Others

In addition to the groups noted earlier, several others also fall within the categorically needy classification. 42 C.F.R. 432.110–432.170. Although a complete listing and explanation of these groups goes far beyond the concerns of the elderly, a sample listing will help reveal the broad scope of the category. For example, states participating in Medicaid must provide coverage to those receiving TANF who would have been eligible for AFDC (Aid to Families with Dependent Children) when AFDC was eliminated in 1996. The state must also provide Medicaid to individuals who receive mandatory state income supplements; to individuals who were eligible for Medicaid in December 1973 as an "essential spouse" of an aged, blind, or disabled, individual who was receiving cash assistance, if certain conditions are met; and to individuals who were eligible for Medicaid in any part of December 1973 as inpatients of medical institutions or residents of intermediate care facilities that were participating in the Medicaid program and who have continuously met the eligibility requirements in effect in December 1973 and remain institutionalized and who continue to need institutional care.

Further, the state must provide Medicaid to those who meet all current requirements for Medicaid eligibility except the criteria for blindness or disability and were eligible in December 1973 as blind or disabled and continue to meet the December 1973 criteria; to individuals entitled to Social Security benefits in August 1972 who were receiving certain other benefits, or were eligible to be in an optional group covered by Medicaid, and who would be eligible for SSI or a state supplement but for the 1972 Social Security cost of living increase; and to certain children and pregnant women. In states that provide Medicaid to aged, blind, and disabled individuals receiving SSI or state supplements, the state must provide Medicaid to individuals receiving Social Security benefits who were eligible for and receiving SSI or state supplements but became ineligible for those payments after April 1977 and would remain eligible but for Social Security cost-of-living increases; such states must also provide Medicaid to certain disabled widows and widowers aged 60 to 64 who would be eligible for SSI except for early receipt of Social Security benefits.

The state must also provide limited Medicaid coverage to Qualified Medicare Beneficiaries (QMBs), who are individuals entitled to Medicare Part A, whose resources do not exceed twice the maximum allowed under SSI, and whose income does not exceed 100 percent of the official poverty line. 42 U.S.C. 1396d(p). For QMBs, Medicaid engages in "Medicare cost-sharing," which includes the payments of Medicare premiums, coinsurance, and deductibles. At the state's option, the cost-sharing may include payment of premiums for enrollment of a QMB with an eligible health maintenance organization or competitive medical plan.

b. Optional Coverage: The Optional Categorically Needy

i. Generally

Section 1396a(10)(A)(ii) permits states to extend Medicaid coverage to a long list of groups known as the "optional categorically needy." The state decides whether to extend Medicaid coverage to such groups. Among these groups, several are of particular importance for the elderly. For example, the state may provide Medicaid coverage to those who are eligible for SSI benefits but not receiving them; those who would be eligible for SSI but for the receipt of state supplementary payments; those who are terminally ill and have chosen hospice care but would be eligible under the state plan if they were in a medical institution; and those who are institutionalized but would be eligible under the state plan, or eligible for SSI or state supplemental payments, if they were not in a medical institution.

Also, under a Medicaid waiver program the state may cover individuals who would be eligible under the state plan if they were in a medical institution and for whom it is determined that, but for the provision of home or community-based services (HCBS), they would require the level of care provided in a hospital, nursing facility, or an intermediate care facility for the mentally retarded. Because most elders would prefer not to be institutionalized, this program is potentially quite important. The waiver may provide medical assistance for case management services, homemaker/home health aide services and personal care services, adult day health services, respite care, and other medical and social services that can contribute to the health and well-being of individuals and their ability to reside in a community-based setting. To obtain the waiver, however, the state must demonstrate to Health and Human Services (HHS) that the program will be as cost-effective or more cost-effective than institutionalization. 42 U.S.C. § 1396n(d).

ii. Institutionalized Individuals in Income Cap States

A state may also extend Medicaid benefits to individuals who are in a medical institution at least 30 consecutive days, who meet resources requirements under the state plan, and whose income does not exceed three times the federal SSI benefit rate for an individual. 42 U.S.C. § 1396a(10)(A)(ii)(V); § 1396b(f)(4)(C). States that use this approach are called "income cap" states. (In contrast, institutionalized individuals in some states are not subject to an income cap approach, but rather to a more liberal medically needy program permitting "spend-down," as discussed later.) Note that the statute imposes a maximum income cap; in fact, states may adopt a cap that is less than three times the federal SSI benefit rate.

In 2009, the SSI benefit rate for an individual was $674. In an income cap state that has adopted the maximum cap, an individual whose monthly income exceeds $2022 (that is, 3 x $674) is thus ineligible for coverage in that year. An individual whose income exceeds the cap cannot spend-down the excess income on incurred medical expenses to create eligibility. Moreover, he cannot disclaim or refuse income to create eligibility.

For example, assume that Ann has countable resources of $25,000 and monthly income of $2021 in 2009. (For a review of the rules concerning resources and income, see the later discussion in this chapter and also the more detailed discussion in Chapter 7 on SSI.) In contrast, assume that Bob has no resources, but he has monthly income of $2022. Both Ann and Bob reside in the same income cap state. Each enters a nursing home that costs $5000 a month. Ann will not be immediately eligible in an income cap state because of her excess resources; however, she may use her excess resources for the monthly cost of the nursing home. After using her resources for five months, she will no longer have excess resources. Because she will then satisfy both the resources and income test, she will be Medicaid-covered.

Bob, however, is less fortunate. Because his income exceeds the cap, he is ineligible for coverage, even though he is totally lacking in resources. The income spend-down process is unavailable in an income cap state, and the state will ignore his attempts to create eligibility by his refusal of pension, Social Security, or other income. Bob may decide to move to a state that uses the more generous "medically needy" approach for institutionalized individuals instead of the income cap approach. Alternatively, he may attempt to remain in the income cap state and create eligibility through the use of a so-called Miller trust, as discussed later in this chapter.

iii. Other

Although of less importance to elders, some other groups included among the optional categorically needy include individuals who would meet the income and resources requirements under AFDC (TANF) if child care costs were paid from earnings; individuals under age 21 who meet the income and resources requirements of AFDC (TANF); and individuals under 19 who would be eligible for Medicaid if they were in a medical institution. A more thorough listing and explanation is provided in the regulations beginning at 42 C.F.R. 435.200.

c. Optional Coverage: The Medically Needy

In light of the stringent requirements associated with the mandatory categorically needy and many optional categorically needy classifications, the Medicaid program permits states to extend coverage under the more generous rules of a medically needy classification.

A person is medically needy if he meets the nonfinancial eligibility requirements for payments under SSI or AFDC (TANF), does not meet the financial requirements to be categorically needy, and yet does not have sufficient income and resources to pay for his medical care. In medically needy states, an individual who has incurred medical expenses and satisfies the resources requirement may spenddown his excess income on those expenses to qualify for Medicaid coverage.

If the state uses a medically needy program, it must provide coverage to certain pregnant women, minors, newborns, and women post-pregnancy. A state may provide coverage to the aged, blind, and disabled. A large majority of states employs the medically needy rules for noninstitutionalized elderly individuals. Most states also extend medically needy rules to institutionalized elders.

By statute, the methodology a state uses for determining income and resources eligibility for the medically needy status of an aged individual can be no more restrictive than the methodology employed under the SSI program in a state employing the SSI program. 42 U.S.C. § 1396a(C)(i).

i. Spend-Down: Institutionalized Individuals

An example of the spend-down process for the medically needy will show how it is more generous than the income cap approach to Medicaid coverage for institutionalized individuals (discussed earlier). Assume that in 2009 Bob has monthly income of $2022 and no resources. He enters a nursing home with a monthly cost of $5000 for private pay patients. As we saw earlier, in an income cap state Bob would not be eligible for Medicaid because his income is $1 greater than three times the SSI benefit rate for 2009. In a medically needy state using the spend-down process, however, Bob qualifies for coverage because he has no excess income once his incurred medical costs are taken into account. (Since he had no resources, he also satisfies the resources test.)

In return for Medicaid coverage, Bob will only retain a small personal needs allowance (which must be at least $30 a month for an individual) from his income. His other income will be used to pay his Medicare and other health insurance premiums, deductibles, or coinsurance charges, and then the balance will be applied toward the monthly nursing home bill. 42 C.F.R. 435.725. Medicaid pays the remaining amount.

Not surprisingly, Medicaid reimbursement of the nursing home is typically less than the amount paid by private patients.

Most states with medically needy programs permit spend-down; those that do not use the income cap approach (discussed previously).

ii. Spend-Down: Noninstitutionalized Individuals

Outside the institutional setting, individuals who meet the resources standard but have excess income may also become medically needy — and thus Medicaid eligible — under a different kind of spend-down process. The income standard is based on family size and may not exceed 133 and 1/3 percent of the state's AFDC payment to a family of similar size. The AFDC payment amount is taken from the program as it existed in 1996 (before AFDC was replaced by TANF) and is adjusted for inflation. 42 C.F.R. 435.800 et seq.

For example, assume that Ann has income of $800. She has incurred medical expenses of $500. Further assume that the applicable state AFDC payment (as adjusted) is $270. Thus, the applicable medically needy income threshold is $360 (that is, 133 and 1/3 percent of $270). To become medically needy, Ann must spend down $440 of her $800 so that she has no more than $360 of income remaining. Once she does so, she is eligible for Medicaid, which will pay the remaining $60 of her medical bills.

E. Income and Resources

As with SSI, Medicaid eligibility hinges upon satisfaction of both an income and a resources test. In fact, in a substantial majority of states, Medicaid programs simply borrow the applicable income and resources tests from SSI. A person who is eligible for SSI in such a state is therefore also eligible for Medicaid. 42 U.S.C. § 1396a(a)(17). States that are not SSI states are called 209(b) states, as discussed earlier.

For married couples, SSI eligibility rules generally consider the income and resources of both spouses under a "deeming" process. This deeming process also occurs in determining Medicaid eligibility of a married person 65 or older in states that base Medicaid eligibility on SSI rules. Section 209(b) states must employ a deeming process at least as stringent as that used in SSI states; however, they may employ a more stringent deeming process. 42 C.F.R. 435.602(b). The Medicaid deeming rules do not include the income and resources of non-spouses.

The following discussion highlights the determination of income and resources under the SSI program. (A more detailed discussion is found in Chapter 7.)

1. Income

Under SSI, income is calculated monthly. Income is anything received during a calendar month that is or can be used to meet one's need for food or shelter. It may be in cash or in kind. In-kind income is not cash, but is food or shelter or something one can use to obtain food or shelter. The regulations also provide a detailed list (with examples) of things that are not income. 20 C.F.R. 416.1103.

Before determining whether the applicant satisfies the income test, however, the monthly income must be further classified as earned or unearned, and exclusions must be applied to arrive at countable income. Ultimately, it is an individual's countable income that determines whether he satisfies the SSI income test.

a. Earned and Unearned Income

Earned income includes wages; net earnings from self-employment (estimated for the year and spread over twelve months); sickness or disability payments received within the first six months of stopping work; and royalties for publications and honoria for services.

Unearned income is any income not earned. This includes food or shelter given to an individual or received by an individual because someone else paid for it; private pension and annuity payments; periodic public benefit payments (including, most importantly, Social Security); civil service annuities; workers' compensation; life insurance proceeds; gifts and inheritances; dividends and interest; and many other things.

In valuing unearned income for in-kind support and maintenance, the SSI program begins with one of two rules: the one-third reduction rule or the presumed maximum value rule. When an individual lives in another's household throughout the month and receives both food and shelter from within the household, the value of the food and shelter is presumed to be one-third of the monthly SSI benefit rate. The presumption is irrebuttable.

In other settings involving in-kind support and maintenance, the presumed maximum value rule applies. For example, the presumed maximum value rule applies if the individual lives with another but buys his own food. The presumed maximum value is twenty dollars more than one-third of the applicable SSI benefit rate. This presumption is rebuttable, however. If the individual shows that the actual value of the shelter (or food, depending upon the circumstances) is less than the presumed amount, then the actual value applies.

b. Countable Income

In determining an individual's countable income, SSI provides certain exclusions. One is a $20 general exclusion. The general exclusion is first applied against the individual's unearned income. If any part of the $20 is not used up, the remainder is applied toward the individual's earned income.

The SSI program also excludes the first $65 of earned income. Once that amount is excluded (subtracted) from earned income, the program then excludes one-half of the remaining earned income. This reduced earned income amount is added to the reduced unearned income to arrive at countable income.

In 2009, the SSI federal benefit rate for an individual was $674. If the individual's countable income was less than $674, he would thus satisfy the income test.

For example, assume that Mark receives a monthly Social Security check for $400. He also earns $465 from part-time employment. To his unearned income of $400, SSI would apply the general exclusion of $20. Thus, $380 will be the total amount of Mark's unearned income that will be considered in determining his countable income. (Because the general exclusion amount ($20) is applied fully against Mark's unearned income, none is left to apply against earned income.) To Mark's earned income, first SSI would apply the $65 exclusion, leaving $400; second, SSI would exclude one-half of this $400. Thus, $200 will be the total amount of Mark's earned income that will be considered in determining his countable income. In sum, Mark's countable income is

$380 (unearned) plus $200 (earned), which equals $580. Mark satisfies the income test in 2009 because his total countable income is less than $674.

2. Resources

Resources include cash and other assets that one can convert to cash to obtain support and maintenance. For almost two decades, the applicable SSI resources limit has been $2000 for an individual and $3000 for a married couple. (For Medicaid purposes, these amounts may be lower in 209(b) states.) Cash resources are counted at face value; other resources are generally counted at their equity value.

a. Countable Resources

While the applicant must disclose all resources, not all resources are included in determining eligibility under the resources test. Rather, the test focuses on the individual's countable resources. 20 C.F.R. 416.1201–.1266.

One important resource excluded from those that are counted is the applicant's ownership interest in the home that is his principal place of residence (including adjacent land and outbuildings). If the individual lives elsewhere (such as in an institution) but intends to return to the home, the exclusion generally applies. As a result of the Deficit Reduction Act of 2005 (DRA), however, states may not pay for Medicaid long-term care services for an individual whose equity value in the home exceeds $500,000 or, at the option of the state, up to $750,000. (These amounts will be indexed for inflation beginning in 2011.) Prior to the DRA, there was no equity cutoff amount that would make an individual ineligible for Medicaid long-term care. Even today, the state can elect not to apply the home-equity cutoff amount in cases of documented hardship. Moreover, if the community spouse or a minor or blind or disabled child lives in the home, the cutoff rule does not apply. 42 U.S.C. § 1396p(f).

Note also that the home-equity cutoff rule is a rule of limited application under Medicaid. The general rule that a home of any value is excluded for the purpose of determining eligibility for Medicaid still applies in other Medicaid contexts. In other words, the cutoff rule applies only in regard to Medicaid payment of long-term care services (and even then has a number of limitations).

Household goods are also excluded in determining countable resources. This exclusion includes furniture, appliances, and electronic equipment such as personal computers and televisions. Personal effects such as items ordinarily worn or carried by the individual are also excluded. Educational and recreational items such as books and musical instruments are also excluded. One automobile is totally excluded regardless of value if it is used for transportation for the individual or a member of the individual's household. The value of property essential to self-support is not counted, within certain limits.

The cash surrender value of life insurance policies is excluded from the countable resources calculation so long as the total face value of all life insurance policies on any person does not exceed $1500. Moreover, the value of burial spaces for the individual, the individual's spouse, or any member of the individual's immediate family, is excluded from countable resources. Up to $1,500 each of funds specifically set aside for the burial expenses of the individual or the individual's spouse are similarly excluded. The burial fund exclusion applies only if the funds are kept separate from all other resources not intended for burial of the individual or his spouse and are clearly designated as set aside for burial purposes.

b. Spend-Down

Before applying for Medicaid, an individual may be able to spend down excess countable resources by converting them into noncountable resources. For example, the individual might use excess countable cash resources to purchase a new car (an excluded resource) or to improve the house (an excluded resource). Note that if the individual purchases a new car but also retains his old one, the equity value of the old car itself becomes a countable resource, since the value of only one car is excluded from countable resources.

F. Spouses and Institutionalization

Relatively few individuals can afford the costs of long-term institutionalization without assistance. Moreover, Medicare does not provide such assistance. When an unmarried person is institutionalized, he typically must use substantially all of his own assets before Medicaid will cover the remaining costs. When a married person is institutionalized and his spouse remains noninstitutionalized, however, requiring him to use substantially all of his assets might impoverish his spouse. This is particularly true if she has few assets of her own or if her assets are deemed available to him during his institutionalization. In the Medicare Catastrophic Coverage Act of 1988, Congress established rules intended to protect the noninstitutionalized spouse (the so-called "community" spouse) from such impoverishment.

An institutionalized spouse is an individual who is in a medical institution or nursing facility, is likely to require institutionalization for at least 30 consecutive days, and is married to a spouse who is not institutionalized. 42 U.S.C. § 1396r-5. Section 1396r-5 provides important rules concerning the treatment of spousal income and resources and also grants the community spouse allowance rights.

1. Income

a. Attribution Rules

As a general rule, no income of the community spouse is deemed available to the institutionalized spouse during any month in which an institutionalized spouse is in an institution.

In determining whether non-trust property income belongs to the community spouse or to the institutionalized spouse, the name of the payee controls. If payment of income is made solely to W, and not to her husband H, then the income belongs to W. If the payment is made to W and H, one-half of the income belongs to each. If the payment is made to W and H and also to a third party, the income is considered available to each spouse in proportion to the spouse's interest; if no interest is specified, then one-half of the total payment to W and H is attributable to each. If property produces income and there is no instrument establishing ownership of the property, then the income is attributed equally to H and to W. These attribution rules, however, are rebuttable to the extent that the institutionalized spouse can establish by a preponderance of the evidence that the ownership interests in income are otherwise than under the attribution rules.

In determining whether trust income belongs to the community spouse or to the institutionalized spouse, the trust provisions control. In the absence of a specific provision in the trust, then the income payment is considered available (1) only to the payee, if the payment is made solely to H or solely to W; (2) equally to both, if the payment is made to both H and W; or (3) in proportion to the interests of H and W, if the payment is made to H and W and a third party.

b. Allowance: MIA

Protecting the community spouse's income is an important step in preventing her impoverishment. But what happens if her income is insufficient for her protection? MCCA rules establish a community spouse monthly income allowance (MIA) payable, under certain conditions, from the institutionalized spouse. The MIA is computed by deducting the community spouse's actual income from a minimum monthly maintenance needs allowance (MMMNA).

By statute, the MMMNA itself consists of two amounts. The first amount is a base allowance generally determined by taking 150 percent of the federal poverty guidelines figure for a family of two and dividing it by twelve. Updated federal poverty guidelines go into effect on July 1 of each year. For the period from July 1, 2008, to June 30, 2009, the annual figure for a family of two was $14,000, and 150 percent of that amount is $21,000. The monthly amount was thus $1,750 (i.e., $21,000 divided by 12.) A state may in fact use a more generous approach, but its formula ultimately cannot render an amount that exceeds an annual MMMNA cap (described further below).

The second amount used in computing MMMNA is an excess shelter allowance (ESA). Calculation of the ESA begins by determining the sum of two numbers: (1) the community spouse's expenses for rent or mortgage payments, taxes and insurance, and the required maintenance charges for her principal residence, and (2) a standard utility allowance (or if the state does not use such an allowance, her actual utility expenses). Ultimately, the ESA is the amount by which this sum exceeds 30 percent of the applicable base allowance (described in the preceding paragraph). Thirty percent of $1,750 (the base allowance in this example as described above) is $525. For example, if Wanda is a community spouse who has housing expenses and a utility allowance totaling $600, then $75 (that is, $600 less $525) will be the ESA that applies towards the MMMNA. The MMMNA in this example would be the sum of base allowance of $1750 plus the ESA of $75. In other words, MMMNA would be $1,825. For a comparison of spousal impoverishment financial standards from 1998–2009, see http://www.cms.hhs.gov/MedicaidEligibility/Downloads/1998-2009SSIFBR110708.pdf.

Once the MMMNA has been computed, the community spouse's MIA can be determined by subtracting her actual monthly income from her MMMNA. Continuing with the example from the preceding paragraph, if Wanda's income consists of a monthly Social Security check of $500 and a pension check of $525, her income would be $1025. Thus, her MIA would be $800 (i.e., the $1,825 MMMNA less her actual income of $1,025). The $800 must come first from her institutionalized husband's income; however, if his income is insufficient to satisfy her MIA, then his resources may be used to produce the needed $800 monthly figure.

As mentioned above, the MMMNA is generally limited in amount by an annual cap. (For example, the cap for 2009 was $2,739.) If either spouse establishes that the community spouse needs income above the level otherwise provided by the MMMNA due to exceptional circumstances resulting in significant financial duress, however, a larger amount may be substituted. Moreover, if a court has entered an order against an institutionalized spouse for monthly income to support the community spouse, the community spouse MIA shall not be less than the amount of the monthly income. Finally, the statute also guarantees either the community or institutionalized spouse with the right to a fair hearing concerning the amount of monthly income available to the community spouse.

The MIA is perhaps the most substantial offset generally taken from the institutionalized spouse's income before the nursing home is paid. Another offset from his income is his personal needs allowance (which may not be less than $30 a month and receives priority over the MIA). Other offsets to be paid after the personal needs allowance and the MIA include a family allowance for certain dependents and an amount for certain incurred medical or remedial care expenses of the institutionalized spouse not subject to payment by third parties. 42 U.S.C. § 1396r-5(d)(1). If the total of these offsets is significant, they may deplete the institutionalized spouse's income and Medicaid may have to foot the entire nursing home bill.

2. Resources

The MCCA also provides the noninstitutionalized spouse with a community spouse resource allowance (CSRA). In essence, the CSRA is the value of a married couple's nonexempt resources that a community spouse may retain without adversely affecting the Medicaid benefits of the institutionalized spouse.

a. The "Snapshot"

To determine the CSRA, most states first take a "snapshot" (an informal term commonly used for the evaluation) of the total value of nonexempt resources to the extent of the ownership interest of either the institutionalized spouse or community spouse. This evaluation reflects the couple's nonexempt resources at the beginning of the first continuous period of institutionalization for the institutionalized spouse. The nonexempt resources of either spouse are generally considered to be available to the institutionalized spouse.

Even if the institutionalized spouse is not applying for Medicaid immediately upon institutionalization, either spouse can and should request the state to undertake this snapshot evaluation when institutionalization occurs, because a retrospective evaluation can be difficult and riddled with errors and uncertainty. (If a spouse requests the evaluation before applying for Medicaid, the state may require a reasonable fee for providing and documenting the resource assessment.)

Once the snapshot is taken, the couple can determine the CSRA and the amount of resources that the institutionalized spouse must spend down.

b. CSRA

From the snapshot of the couple's total nonexempt resources, the community spouse is entitled to retain a portion known as her CSRA. A state may adopt a CSRA within a range that is adjusted annually. In 2009, the minimum amount of nonexempt resources a state may allow a community spouse to retain was $21,912; the maximum was $109,560. For example, if a married couple's total nonexempt resources are less than $21,912 in 2009, then in any state the community spouse would be able to retain them all as her CSRA.

Some states adopt the maximum CSRA amount as the CSRA for all community spouses in the state. If the couple's nonexempt resources exceed $109,560 in 2009, then in such a state the community spouse would keep $109,560. The excess would have to be spent down. If the couple's nonexempt resources were less than $109,560, the community spouse would keep all.

Other states permit the community spouse to retain one-half of the couple's nonexempt resources up to the maximum amount. Under this commonly-used approach, if the couple's nonexempt resources equaled $150,000, the CSRA would be $75,000; the remaining $75,000 would have to be spent down. If the couple's nonexempt resources equaled $250,000 in 2009, then the community spouse would keep the maximum, $109,560, and the excess would have to be spent down.

If the CSRA is greater than the value of assets titled in the name of the community spouse, the institutionalized spouse will need to transfer assets to the community spouse to meet the CSRA. If he is incapacitated, the transfers may be made by his conservator or his agent under a durable power of attorney. 42 U.S.C. § 1395r-5(f)(1).

Resources that the community spouse acquires after the institutionalized spouse is determined to be eligible for Medicaid belong to the community spouse alone. 42 U.S.C. § 1396r-5(c)(4). The statute does not address the proper treatment of resources acquired by the institutionalized spouse after he is determined to be eligible for Medicaid, however. Uncertainty also exists about the treatment of resources acquired by either spouse during the period between institutionalization and the application of the institutionalized spouse for Medicaid.

As with questions about MIA, either spouse is entitled to a fair hearing if dissatisfied with a determination of the CSRA.

G. Asset Transfers and Institutionalization

1. Current Law: The Five-Year Look-Back

Individuals anticipating institutionalization may wish to create Medicaid eligibility while preserving their assets for family members. Thus, individuals sometimes transfer assets to third parties as outright gifts or for far less than fair market value in the period leading up to institutionalization. Individuals also sometimes engage in the creative use of trusts in attempting to create Medicaid eligibility. Medicaid rules seek to minimize such attempts through "look-back" provisions that factor in the individual's transfers of countable assets or the home for less than fair market value. These rules are mandatory as applied to institutionalized individuals. These asset transfer penalty rules applicable to institutionalized individuals also cover those seeking home or community-based services under a waiver program. 42 U.S.C. § 1396p.

The look-back period for transfers made on or after February 8, 2006 is five years. The look-back occurs and the penalty period generally begins when the individual is eligible for medical assistance under the state plan (that is, he meets the income and resources tests) and he would otherwise be receiving institutional level care based on an approved Medicaid application if the penalty period were not considered.

The period of Medicaid ineligibility is determined by dividing the total uncompensated value of the individual's transfers within the look-back period by the average monthly cost to a private patient of nursing facility services in the state or community at the time of application. For example, Jane entered a nursing home on March 1, 2008, and filed a Medicaid application. Her income and assets would make her otherwise eligible for Medicaid; however, she gave $50,000 to her niece in 2007. Because the uncompensated transfer occurred within the look-back period, the value of that transfer must be considered. If the average cost of nursing home care where Jane lives is $6,250 a month, then Jane will be ineligible for eight months ($50,000 divided by $6,250 per month) beginning on March 1, 2008.

The asset transfer penalty rules apply not only to transfers by the institutionalized individual, but also to those of his spouse. If the husband and wife both require institutionalization and would otherwise be eligible for Medicaid but for the transfers, the state must apportion the period of ineligibility between the two.

If the individual has an ownership interest in an asset held in a tenancy in common, joint tenancy, or other form of co-ownership, the asset is considered transferred when the individual or any other person takes action that reduces or eliminates the individual's ownership or control of such asset.

Concerning transfers of assets, the term "assets" also includes funds used to purchase a promissory note, loan, or mortgage, unless the note, loan, or mortgage has a repayment term that is actuarially sound, provides for payments to be made in equal amounts (with no deferral and no balloon payments), and prohibits the cancellation of the balance upon the death of the lender. The statute also treats the purchase of an annuity as the disposal of an asset for less

than fair market value under various circumstances, such as when it is not actuarially sound. Further, the statute provides that, with respect to a transfer of
assets, the term "assets" includes the purchase of a life estate interest in another individual's home unless the purchaser resides in the home for a period
of at least one year after the date of purchase.

2. Exempt Transfers

The asset transfer penalty rules apply to transfers of countable assets and
the home. (This is so even though the home itself is generally a noncountable
resource in determining Medicaid eligibility.)

A transfer of the home is exempt from the transfer penalty rules, however,
if the individual has transferred the home to his spouse; a child who is under
age 21 or blind or disabled; a sibling who has an equity interest in the home
and who was residing in the home for at least one year before the individual
became institutionalized; or a child residing in the home for a period of at
least two years before the individual's institutionalization and who provided care
to such individual that permitted him to remain at home.

Also exempt are assets that were transferred to the individual's spouse or
to another for the sole benefit of the spouse; assets that were transferred
from the individual's spouse to another for the sole benefit of the spouse;
assets transferred to the individual's child under 21 or blind or disabled (or
to a trust solely for the benefit of such a child); and assets transferred to a
trust established solely for the benefit of an individual under 65 years of age
who is disabled.

Section 1396p also exempts uncompensated transfers when the individual
(or his representative) satisfactorily demonstrates that the assets were transferred exclusively for a purpose other than to qualify for Medicaid; that all of
the assets transferred for less than fair market value have been returned to the
individual; or that the individual intended to dispose of the assets either at fair
market value or for other valuable consideration. Further, the statute exempts
uncompensated transfers when the state determines that the denial of eligibility would work an undue hardship.

3. Trusts

a. Generally

The Medicaid statutes include specific rules that substantially limit the use
of the inter vivos trust as a tool for creating Medicaid eligibility. Under the
rules, an individual is considered to have established a trust if his assets are

used to form all or part of the corpus of the trust. Such a trust is also attributed to him if it is established by his spouse, a person (including a court or administrative body) with legal authority to act for him or his spouse, or a person (including a court or administrative body) acting at the direction or upon the request of the individual or his spouse. By statute, the term "trust" includes any legal instrument or device that is similar to a trust.

If the trust corpus consists of assets of the individual and another person, the rules apply to the portion of the trust attributable to the individual's assets. Except for three specific kinds of trusts (discussed in the following section), the rules apply without regard to the trust purposes, trustee discretion, trust restrictions on distributions, or restrictions on the use of trust distributions. 42 U.S.C. § 1396p(d)(2)(C).

For revocable trusts, the corpus is considered an available resource to the individual. Payments from the trust to or for his benefit are considered income. Payments from the trust to others are considered transfers subject to the look-back rules and the asset transfer penalty.

For irrevocable trusts, if there are any circumstances in which payment can be made to or for the benefit of the individual, the portion of the income or corpus from which such payment can be made is considered a resource available to the individual. The payment from that portion of the corpus or income to or for the benefit of the individual is considered income to the individual. Payments from that portion of the corpus or income for any other purpose, however, are considered transfers subject to the look-back rules and the asset transfer penalty. Similarly, portions of an irrevocable trust (corpus or income) from which no payments can be made to the individual are considered transfers subject to the look-back rules and the asset transfer penalty. Thus, if Mike sets up an irrevocable trust and retains no right to any form of distribution, the corpus will not be an available resource and the income will not be income to him. If he establishes the trust within the five-year look-back period, however, the value of the corpus will be considered an uncompensated transfer subjecting him to a period of ineligibility.

The state may waive the trust transfer rules if the individual establishes that their application would work an undue hardship on him.

b. Trusts Exempted from the General Rules

Section 1396p(d)(4) exempts three very specific kinds of trusts from the general transfer rules applicable to trusts. These trusts are sometimes referred to as (d)(4) trusts.

A trust is exempt if it contains the assets of a disabled individual under age 65 and is established for his benefit by a parent, grandparent, legal guardian, or a court, as long as the state will receive all amounts remaining in the trust upon the death of such individual (up to the amount equal to Medicaid benefits paid on his behalf under the state plan).

A trust is also exempt if it is established for an individual and the corpus is composed only of pension, Social Security, and other income to the individual; the state will receive all amounts remaining in the trust upon the death of such individual (up to an amount equal to Medicaid benefits paid on his behalf under the state plan); and the state Medicaid program covers institutionalized individuals under an income cap approach only (and not under a medically needy program). Such a trust is sometimes called a "Miller" trust, based on a court opinion that recognized its validity before the current rules were codified by Congress. Such a trust is an important planning tool in income cap states.

Finally, certain "pooled" trusts are exempt. To be exempt, the trust must contain the assets of an individual who is disabled. The trust must be established and managed by a nonprofit association. The trust must maintain a separate account for each beneficiary of the trust, even though the accounts are pooled for investment and management purposes. The trust accounts must be established solely for the benefit of individuals who are disabled, and they must be established by the parent, grandparent, or legal guardian of such individuals, by such individuals, or by a court. To the extent that amounts remaining in the beneficiary's account upon his death are not retained by the trust, the trust must pay to the state from the balance in his account an amount equal to the total amount of medical assistance paid on behalf of the beneficiary under the state plan.

4. The Counselor Penalty

The concern that many lawyers and others were counseling individuals to create Medicaid eligibility by disposing of their assets in ways that avoided the look-back penalty led Congress to enact 42 U.S.C. § 1320a-7b. The statute makes it a crime for anyone "for a fee knowingly and willfully [to counsel or assist] an individual to dispose of assets (including by any transfer in trust) in order for the individual to become eligible for" Medicaid if "disposing of the assets results in the imposition of a period of ineligibility." Apparently counsel or assistance does not violate the statute if the applicant is successful in his attempt and thus avoids any period of ineligibility. On its face, the statute provides that those who violate its terms are subject to a fine of up to $10,000, imprisonment for up to one year, or both.

Although the provision has not been repealed, it appears unenforceable. In 1998, the New York Bar Association sought a preliminary injunction in federal district court against enforcement of the statute. The bar association asserted that the provision is unconstitutional because it violates free speech, is over-broad, and is vague. During the proceedings, the United States Attorney General notified Congress that the Department of Justice would not enforce the provisions. The court granted the preliminary injunction.

5. Transfers before February 8, 2006

The Deficit Reduction Act (DRA) of 2005 created a uniform five-year look-back period applicable to transfers for less than fair market value. For un-compensated transfers between August 19, 1993, and February 7, 2006, however, Medicaid rules employed two different look-back periods. A three-year rule applied to nontrust transfers, and a five-year rule applied to transfers into trusts. In contrast to the DRA rules, the period of ineligibility under the earlier rules ran from the date of the transfer.

For example, assume that Lon gave $120,000 to his brother on February 1, 2006. On February 1, 2007, Lon entered a nursing home and applied for Medicaid. The average cost of nursing home care in Lon's state or community is $6000 a month. Because the uncompensated transfer occurred within three years, it must be considered. Lon's period of ineligibility is thus 20 months (i.e., $120,000 divided by $6000). Under the pre-DRA rules, however, the period of ineligibility would begin to run on February 1, 2006, the date of the transfer, and not February 1, 2007.

6. Noninstitutionalized Individuals

As mentioned earlier, states must apply the asset transfer penalty rules to institutionalized individuals seeking Medicaid. States may, at their option, extend the rules to noninstitutionalized individuals seeking Medicaid. If states choose to apply the rules to noninstitutionalized individuals, the ineligibility period cannot be greater than that determined under the formula for institutionalized individuals. In other words, it cannot be greater than that resulting when the total uncompensated value of all assets transferred is divided by the average monthly cost to a private patient of nursing facility services in the state or community.

H. Medicaid Liens, Adjustments, and Recoveries

Assets exempt from consideration in Medicaid eligibility determinations are not exempt from a state's effort to obtain reimbursement for Medicaid benefits paid to the individual. Section 1396p(a) provides the rules for the imposition of a lien against an individual who has received Medicaid benefits. Section 1396p(b) provides the rules for adjustments or recoveries against an individual's estate for medical assistance received under the state plan.

1. Inter Vivos Liens

Except in two instances no lien may be placed upon the property of a living individual who has received medical assistance under the state plan. First, a lien may be imposed pursuant to a judgment that the benefits were incorrectly paid on his behalf. Second, a lien may be imposed upon the real property of an institutionalized individual if he is required as a condition for receiving services to spend down all but a minimal amount of his income required for personal needs *and* the state has determined (after notice and opportunity for a hearing) that he cannot reasonably be expected to be discharged from the institution.

This second exception is limited by the following restrictions: no lien may be imposed on the individual's home if his spouse is lawfully residing in the home; if his child who is under 21 or is blind or disabled is lawfully residing in the home; or if his sibling is lawfully residing in the home and has an equity interest in the home and was residing there at least one year immediately before the individual was institutionalized. Moreover, any lien that is properly imposed on an institutionalized patient's real property dissolves upon the individual's discharge from the medical institution and return home. 42 U.S.C. § 1396p(a).

2. Recovery from the Estate

a. Generally

Section 1396p(b) provides that, in several instances, the state shall seek adjustment or recovery for amounts correctly paid under the state plan.

For permanently institutionalized individuals described under the lien provisions, the state must seek recovery or adjustment from his estate or upon sale of the property subject to a lien.

For an individual who was 55 or older when he received medical assistance, the state must seek recovery or adjustment from his estate, but only for medical assistance consisting of nursing facility services, home and community-based services, and related hospital and prescription drug services. The statute, however, provides the state with an option to further seek recovery of any items or services furnished to the individual under the state plan.

The state agency must have procedures under which it can waive the adjustment or recovery rules if they would work an undue hardship.

b. Long-Term Care Insurance

The statute permits states to establish "qualified State long-term care insurance partnership" programs. The term refers to an approved state plan amendment that provides for disregarding assets or resources in an amount equal to the insurance benefit payments that are made to or on behalf of an individual who is a beneficiary under a long-term care insurance policy, if certain requirements are met. (The term also includes certain early partnership plans in existence as of May 14, 1993. The topic of long-term care insurance partnership programs is discussed more fully in Chapter 10.)

Among the requirements placed on partnership policies under the program are the following: the policy must cover an insured who was a resident of the state when coverage first became effective under the policy; the policy must be a qualified long-term care insurance policy issued not earlier than the effective date of the state plan amendment; and the policy must contain inflation protection provisions if sold to an individual who has not attained the age of 76.

For an individual who has long-term care insurance that satisfies the statutory requirements, the estate is protected against recovery or adjustment in an amount equal to the insurance benefits payments that were made to him under the policy. If the estate exceeds that amount, then the state must seek adjustment or recovery from the remaining estate for the medical assistance paid to him for nursing facility and other long-term care services.

c. The Estate

What constitutes the estate against which a recovery or adjustment action may be made? The statute provides states with much leeway in answering this question. The statute defines "estate" to include all real and personal property and other assets included within the individual's estate as defined for purposes of state probate law. In other words, the estate clearly includes the individual's property and assets that would pass under a will or by intestate succession.

The statute further gives states the option to include any other real and personal property and other assets in which the individual had any legal title or interest at the time of death (to the extent of such interest), including assets passing to a survivor, heir, or assign of the deceased individual through joint tenancy, survivorship, life estate, living trust, or other arrangement. Although this is a significant expansion of the traditional definition of estate, it is consistent with a modern trend that allows creditors to reach nonprobate assets.

I. Procedures

1. Application

Federal regulations require the state to publish and make available, in simple and understandable terms, bulletins or pamphlets that explain the rules governing eligibility and appeals. Upon request, the agency must furnish (in writing or orally) information about eligibility requirements, available Medicaid services, and the rights and responsibilities of applicants and recipients.

One can typically file a Medicaid application at a local social services office, human services office, or welfare department. Applications may be available at hospitals, public health departments, and similar places. The written application must be on a form prescribed by the state Medicaid agency and signed under a penalty of perjury. The application may be made by the individual or his authorized representative. If the applicant is incapacitated, someone acting responsibly for the applicant may make the application. The agency must allow individuals chosen by the applicant to accompany, assist, and represent the applicant during the application process or a redetermination of eligibility.

To complete the application, the individual will need to provide his Social Security number (unless he obtains an exception based on established religious objections); proof of age, marital status, residence, and citizenship; and proof of income and resources and governmental benefits. (In most SSI states, the Medicaid agency does not require a separate application for Medicaid from an individual who is receiving SSI.)

2. Determinations of Eligibility

Except in unusual circumstances, the agency must determine an applicant's eligibility within forty-five days (ninety days for applicants applying on the basis of disability). The agency must send each applicant a written notice of the agency's decision on his application. If eligibility is denied, the agency must state the reasons for the action, the specific regulation supporting the action, and an explanation of his right to request a hearing.

If the applicant is deemed eligible, the agency must make eligibility for Medicaid effective no later than the third month before the month of application if the individual (1) received services at any time during that period of a type covered under the plan and (2) would have been eligible for Medicaid at the time he received the services if he had applied.

The agency must have procedures designed to ensure that recipients make timely and accurate reports of any change in circumstances that may affect their eligibility. With regard to circumstances that may change, the agency must redetermine the eligibility of Medicaid recipients at least every twelve months.

The agency must give recipients timely and adequate notice of proposed actions to terminate, discontinue, or suspend their eligibility or to reduce or discontinue services they may receive under Medicaid.

3. Hearings and Appeals

a. Generally

The state plan must provide an opportunity for a fair hearing to any person whose claim for assistance is denied or not acted upon with reasonable promptness. 42 U.S.C. § 1396a(a)(3). The state agency must also grant an opportunity for a hearing to any recipient who requests it because he believes the agency has taken an action erroneously. The agency does not have to grant a hearing, however, if the sole issue is a federal or state law requiring an automatic change adversely affecting some or all recipients.

At the time the individual applies for Medicaid, or at the time of any action affecting his or her claim, the agency must inform the individual in writing of his right to a hearing; of the method by which he may obtain a hearing; and of his right to represent himself or use legal counsel, a relative, a friend, or other spokesman. "Action" means (among other things) a termination, suspension, or reduction of Medicaid eligibility or covered services. A state or local agency generally must mail a notice at least 10 days before the date of an action.

The agency must allow the applicant or recipient a reasonable time, not to exceed 90 days from the date that the notice of action is mailed, to request a hearing. The agency may require that a request for a hearing be in writing. The agency may respond to a series of individual requests for a hearing by conducting a single group hearing. At a group hearing, however, the agency must permit each person to present his own case or be represented by his authorized representative.

If the agency mails the 10-day notice of action and the recipient requests a hearing before the date of action, the agency may not terminate or reduce services until a decision is made after the hearing, unless (1) it is determined at the hearing that the sole issue is one of federal or state law or policy and (2) the agency promptly informs the recipient in writing that services are to be terminated or reduced pending the hearing decision. If the agency's action is sustained by the hearing decision, the agency may institute recovery procedures against the applicant or recipient to recoup the cost of any services furnished the recipient.

The agency may reinstate terminated services if a recipient requests a hearing not more than 10 days after the date of action. The services must continue until a decision is made after the hearing unless, at the hearing, it is determined that the sole issue is one of federal or state law or policy. The agency must reinstate and continue services until a decision is rendered after a hearing if (1) action is taken without the proper advance notice; (2) the recipient requests a hearing within 10 days of the mailing of the notice of action; and (3) the agency determines that the action resulted from other than the application of federal or state law or policy.

b. Hearing Procedures

The state's hearing system must provide for (1) a hearing before the agency or (2) an evidentiary hearing at the local level, with a right of appeal to a state agency hearing. The hearing system must meet the due process standards set forth in Goldberg v. Kelly, 397 U.S. 254 (1970) and other standards as specified in the regulations.

All hearings must be conducted at a reasonable time, date, and place and only after adequate written notice of the hearing. All hearings must be conducted by one or more impartial officials or other individuals who have not been directly involved in the initial determination of the action in question.

At a reasonable time before the date of the hearing and during the hearing itself, the applicant or recipient, or his representative, must be given an opportunity to examine the content of his case file as well as all documents and records to be used by the state or local agency at the hearing. He must have an opportunity to bring witnesses, to establish all pertinent facts and circumstances, to present an argument without undue interference, and to question or refute any testimony or evidence, including an opportunity to confront and cross-examine adverse witnesses.

Ordinarily, the agency must take final administrative action within 90 days from the date the individual filed his request for a hearing. Once a decision is made, the agency must notify in writing the applicant of that decision and his right to request further review either through a state agency hearing or judicial review (if such further review is available to him). Whether judicial review is ultimately available in state or federal court will depend upon the claim.

c. Local Hearings and Appeals

When a local evidentiary hearing is adverse to the applicant or recipient, the agency must (1) inform the applicant or recipient of the decision; (2) inform him that he has the right to appeal the decision to the state agency, in writing, within 15 days of the mailing of the notice of the adverse decision; (3) inform him of his right to request that his appeal be a de novo hearing; and (4) discontinue services after the adverse decision.

Unless the applicant or recipient specifically requests a de novo hearing, the state agency hearing may consist of a review by the agency hearing officer of the record of the local evidentiary hearing to determine whether the decision of the local hearing officer was supported by substantial evidence in the record. A person who participated in the local decision being appealed may not participate in the state agency hearing decision.

Checkpoints

- Concerning the general structure of the Medicaid program, you should understand the role of the federal and state government and the importance of the state medical assistance plan

- Concerning state programs, you should understand the difference between SSI states and 209(b) states and the different rules that apply concerning coverage in each

- Concerning income and resources, you should understand how they are determined and why they are important

- Concerning Medicaid's coverage of long-term institutionalization, you should understand

    - The general rules, including eligibility rules in spend-down and income cap states

    - The treatment of the community spouse

    - The treatment of asset transfers

- Concerning Medicaid recoupment procedures, you should understand Medicaid's rules concerning liens, adjustments, and cost recovery from the estate

- Concerning grievances, you should understand generally Medicaid's rules for appeals

Chapter 10

Long-Term Care

Roadmap

- Many elders need long-term care to assist them with their medical needs or the activities of daily living
- Long-term care may be furnished by
  - Family and friends
  - Community- and home-based services organizations
  - Paid caregivers
  - Board and care homes, assisted living facilities, and continuing care retirement communities
  - Nursing homes
- The costs of long-term care may be financed by
  - Family and friends
  - Personal savings of the individual
  - Proceeds of a reverse mortgage
  - Accelerated death benefits under a life insurance policy
  - Medicaid or other governmental programs
  - Long-term care insurance
    - May provide skilled and custodial care in a nursing facility or at home
    - May include various protections for the insured, including inflation protection and nonforfeiture benefits
    - May be tax-qualified
    - May be a state partnership policy that protects assets
    - Often contains many limiting provisions that a prospective purchaser must carefully consider

A. Introduction

Many elders require the on-going assistance of others in taking care of their medical needs or in satisfying the activities of daily living (ADLs). In other words, they need long-term care. Although no universally-accepted definition of long-term care exists, the term broadly encompasses a large variety of services provided to individuals with a chronic illness, disability, or cognitive or other impairment.

Estimates from the federal government indicate that twelve million Americans will need long-term care by 2020. Of course, an individual may require long-term care at any age; however, the elderly are more likely than others to need such care. A study from the Department of Health and Human Services indicates that a person who reaches age 65 has a forty percent chance of needing nursing home care at some point; about one in ten people who enter a nursing home is likely to stay there for five years or longer. Although the cost of nursing home care varies widely among states, the national average cost of such care in 2001 was $56,000 per year; by 2008, the cost was over $70,000 per year. Experts agree that the costs will continue to rise substantially, and some suggest that the costs could triple within the next fifteen to twenty years.

This chapter examines long-term care and the often difficult choices that individuals must make to ensure that their long-term care needs will be met.

B. Who Furnishes Long-Term Care?

Long-term care includes skilled care and custodial care (also called personal care). In essence, skilled care is care that must be performed by a trained medical professional, such as a licensed nurse or therapist. Long-term skilled care is usually provided in a nursing home, but may be provided elsewhere. In contrast, custodial care is care that helps the individual meet other needs. Most often custodial care helps the individual meet the activities of daily living. The most common of these activities (and the ones most often included in long-term care insurance policies) are bathing, continence, dressing, eating, toileting, and transferring.

Depending upon the elder's needs, long-term care can often be provided by many different persons in many different settings. If the elder has adequate resources and sufficient capacity, she may remain at home and hire her own caregivers. Even if she is unable to afford paid caregivers, she may be able to remain at home if her long-term care needs are not great. For example, community-based services such as meals-on-wheels, personal care, chore services, transportation services, and a range of activities for seniors may be available free or at low cost if she qualifies. In many states, Medicaid will pay for some long-term care services provided at home for certain individuals whose income and resources do not exceed minimal amounts. (In contrast, note that although Medicare provides medically necessary home health care when the Medicare-insured patient meets certain requirements, Medicare does not generally provide long-term care. Medicare is certainly not designed to provide or pay for long-term custodial care.)

The federal government and many state governments have subsidized senior housing programs to assist low-income elders and persons with a disability. At least some of these programs also offer residents assistance with meals, housekeeping, laundry, and shopping.

Family members and friends may furnish long-term care to an elder. In many instances, the elder continues to live in her home with the assistance of such family members and friends, who may or may not live with her. Alternatively, an elder may move into the home of a family member or friend who can assist her. When the elder's long-term care needs are not great and her disposition is good, such a solution can be a happy one that strengthens family or friendship bonds. Some families maintain a separate apartment for an elderly parent or relative whose long-term care needs are primarily custodial. These units typically contain their own living space, kitchen, and bath. They may be part of the family home or a free-standing structure on the same lot.

The demands of caring for a chronically ill or disabled elder, however, are often substantial; very often they are too much for one family member or friend alone, particularly if that caregiver also must work outside the home. Community-based services and other programs may provide some relief for the caregiver. If they do not provide adequate relief, however, and the elder cannot hire additional help, long-term care at home may not be a feasible solution to meet the needs of the elder.

Board and care homes (often called "group" homes) are group living arrangements that provide assistance with ADLs for individuals who do not need nursing home care and yet cannot live on their own. Often the cost to the resident is based on a percentage of the resident's income. Many board and care homes do not receive Medicare or Medicaid payments. Consequently, they are not monitored under the rules of those programs; other monitoring may be minimal. If family members know that they will be unable to visit the elder frequently, this lack of monitoring may be a significant factor weighing against the use of a board and care home. Nonetheless, board and care homes play an important role in providing long-term care, and some of them provide outstanding care.

Depending upon the policy and the group home, long-term care insurance may pay for the insured to live in a board and care home.

Assisted living facilities (ALFs) are an increasingly available option to elders needing long-term care. ALFs are group living arrangements that assist the elderly resident in meeting the activities of daily living. The resident's unit may be a "one bedroom plus bath" arrangement or it may be an apartment. The ALF may have all units under one roof, or various units in different buildings. At most ALFs, residents eat some or all of their meals together. ALFs often provide social and recreational activities for residents. The costs vary substantially across the country and even within a particular locale. Factors typically affecting costs include the size of the unit, the services and help provided, the needs of the resident, and the location of the facility within the community. Residents typically pay a monthly fee for the unit and additional fees for services they receive. The cost of an upscale ALF that provides substantial amenities is often high.

Continuing care retirement communities (CCRCs) are designed to provide various levels of care for their residents. In a CCRC, some elders may live in their own apartment or home; others may live in an assisted living facility to receive help in meeting the activities of daily living; and yet others may reside in a nursing home so that they can receive higher levels of care. As a resident's needs increase, she may transfer from one living arrangement to another within the CCRC. For example, an elder may initially reside in her own apartment, may later move to the CCRC's ALF when she needs more assistance, and then move to the nursing home as her needs further increase. (The CCRC contract typically requires the resident to use its nursing home if the resident needs nursing home care. Thus, the prospective resident should carefully examine the CCRC nursing home and available records concerning it.) CCRCs usually charge a substantial entry fee; the fee may be several hundred thousand dollars at some CCRCs. The resident must also pay a monthly maintenance charge (which may be several thousand dollars). This maintenance charge will generally increase with inflation. CCRCs may offer an all-inclusive "life care" contract, which guarantees that the resident in the CCRC's ALF or nursing home will pay the same fees as a resident who lives in her own apartment or home. CCRCs are generally the most expensive of those entities that provide long-term care. Although the costs vary among CCRCs, those costs are almost always high. Only a very small part of the elderly population can afford to live at a CCRC. (Board and care homes, ALFs, and CCRCs are discussed more fully in Chapter 11.)

Most individuals who can no longer receive care at home or in the community will ultimately reside in a nursing home. Nursing homes provide both custodial and skilled care. (Nursing home regulation is discussed in detail in

Chapter 11.) Nursing homes help residents with the activities of daily living and also help residents with their medical needs. The cost of nursing home care varies substantially across the country and even within a particular state.

C. Paying for Long-Term Care

Even when an elder's long-term needs are for custodial care, not skilled care, the cost of meeting these needs can be substantial. How, then, does the elder pay for long-term care?

As of 2009, the United States still has no national health insurance program that provides universal coverage for the long-term care needs of its citizens. Although Medicare provides health insurance for most of the elderly population, it was not designed to cover long-term care. Medicare supplement policies (so-called "Medigap" policies) are private insurance policies that provide varying amounts of additional health care coverage. Like Medicare, however, Medigap insurance is not designed to cover the costs of long-term care.

1. Family Members and Personal Savings

When the elder's needs are neither too demanding nor costly, family may voluntarily provide the long-term care services. A notable example is the care that one spouse often provides when the other spouse needs long-term custodial care. When the elder needing care is a widow or widower, however, the elder may look to her adult children for assistance. As an alternative to the direct provision of services by the elder's family members, those family members may use their own resources to pay for the costs of such services.

In many instances, the elder's family members can neither provide the care the elder needs nor afford to pay third parties to provide that care. Adult children of the elder often work full-time jobs to meet their financial obligations and the needs of their own spouses and children. Though these adult children may want to assist their parent, they may not have the time and resources to meet her needs. In some instances, the elder has a history of difficult relations with her family. In such cases, the elder's family may not be willing to assist her even if it has the time and means to do so.

Many elders will rely on their personal savings and other assets to pay for long-term care. Should they incur long-term care costs, they will pay those costs from their bank accounts, investments, pensions, income, annuities, or other resources. Many people who use this "self-insurance" approach to long-term care do so by default, because they are unable to afford long-term care insurance or because they have simply failed to consider it as an alternative. Some individuals may have decided that they were unlikely to need long-term care, and thus that they could not justify paying the costs of a long-term care policy. Yet others are content to rely on personal savings and resources because they are wealthy enough to easily absorb even the substantial costs that long-term care can bring. Some people cannot obtain a long-term care policy because of their health conditions.

2. Reverse Mortgage

An individual whose house is her principal (and perhaps only) substantial asset might consider a reverse mortgage as a means of financing her long-term care while remaining at home. Under the Housing and Urban Development (HUD) reverse mortgage program, a homeowner sixty-two or older may borrow against the equity in her home if she owns the home outright or has only a small mortgage balance remaining on the home that can be paid off at the closing. (The eligibility, disclosure, and other requirements imposed under state, local, or private lender programs may differ from those under the HUD program. This discussion focuses on the HUD program.)

The amount she can borrow will depend upon her age, applicable interest rates, and the home's value. The older she is, the more she will be able to borrow as a percentage of the home's value. The maximum she can borrow is generally the lower of the appraised amount of the home or the FHA mortgage limit ($417,000 as of November 2008). Payments (loan advances) to the borrower can be made on a monthly basis, through a line of credit, or through a combined monthly payment/line of credit approach. If the borrower receives periodic payments, they can be structured for a fixed term or, alternatively, for as long as she lives in the home. The mortgage debt does not have to be repaid as long as she continues to live in the home.

Assuming that the elder is able to remain in the home until her death, debt payment (principal plus interest) is not due until she dies. Typically, the home is sold at that time and the sale proceeds are used to repay the lender. Any excess goes to the elder's survivors. (The survivors, however, may choose to pay the debt and retain the home.) If the proceeds are insufficient to satisfy the debt, HUD pays the lender the amount of the shortfall. Because the borrower remains the owner of the home, upkeep and taxes are her responsibility. If the borrower otherwise qualifies for Medicaid and Supplemental Security Income, she must take care to spend her loan proceeds by the end of each month to ensure that they do not become disqualifying excess resources. The loan proceeds are not taxable income to the borrower; however, interest charged on the loan is not deductible until it is paid at the end of the loan. To inform and protect consumers, the prospective borrower is required to receive counseling by a HUD-approved home equity conversion mortgage counselor.

The fundamental risk of a reverse mortgage for the borrower comes in assuming that the borrower will be able to remain in her home long enough to make the mortgage a good bargain. If she dies, sells, or moves away (whether voluntarily or because of necessity) shortly after the mortgage, her bargain may be costly. The bargain also may be costly for her if her home appreciates substantially in value following the mortgage. In some circumstances, the person considering a reverse mortgage might find that selling her home and moving elsewhere is a better option than the mortgage.

3. Life Insurance

In some instances, an individual may use her life insurance to help pay for her long-term care. If the life insurance policy contains an accelerated death benefit (ADB) rider, the insured in essence can obtain cash advances against the policy amount. The individual may apply these monies towards the cost of her long-term care. The details of such riders can vary substantially, and typically the insured can only exercise her rights under the rider when she is expected to die within a short time. As an alternative to the ADB, the insured who is terminally ill or chronically ill may be able to sell her life insurance policy to a third party (a viatical settlement provider) in a viatical settlement. Often the payment from the viatical settlement provider is fifty to eighty percent of the insured's death benefit, depending on the insured's remaining life expectancy. The provider receives the full death benefit at the insured's death.

Federal tax provisions exclude accelerated death benefits and viatical settlement proceeds from income if certain conditions are satisfied. 26 U.S.C. § 101(g); § 7702B. Most importantly, to receive this favorable treatment, the insured must be terminally ill or chronically ill. A terminally ill person is one who has been certified by a physician as having an illness or physical condition that is reasonably expected to result in her death within two years of the certification. A chronically ill person is one who is not terminally ill, but who has been certified within the preceding twelve months by a licensed health care practitioner as (1) being unable to perform (without substantial assistance) at least two activities of daily living (eating, toileting, transferring, bathing, dressing, and continence) for at least ninety days due to loss of functional capacity; (2) having a level of disability similar to that described in the preceding clause; or (3) requiring substantial supervision for protection against threats to her health and safety due to severe cognitive impairment. In the case of chronically ill individuals, a per diem limitation applies in determining the amount that may be excluded from income. The limitation is the greater of a daily set amount (adjusted annually for inflation) or the actual costs incurred for qualified long-term care services.

4. Medicaid and Other Governmental Programs

Because the costs of long-term care are so great, many elderly Americans must rely on governmental programs to help ensure that their long-term care needs are satisfied. Medicaid is by far the most important of such governmental programs. A joint federal/state government program, Medicaid is designed to assist people with little income and few resources. Eligibility requirements and services provided vary substantially among the states. Medicaid pays the costs of nursing home care for those who qualify, and it may pay for some long-term care services for the recipient in the community or at her home. (See Chapter 9.)

A newer program, the Program of All-Inclusive Care for the Elderly (PACE), is designed to provide comprehensive medical, rehabilitative, and social services for the elderly who are frail enough to meet state standards for nursing home care. The services can be provided at various places, including inpatient facilities, adult day health centers, or the individual's home. PACE is only available in states that have chosen to provide it under their Medicaid program. In areas where a PACE program exists, however, the program often allows the individual to receive services at home and thus avoid being institutionalized. The program is financed by both Medicaid and Medicare, and the individual may have to pay a monthly premium.

Other governmental programs, such as those designed for veterans, may also provide some long-term care benefits for those elders who satisfy eligibility requirements. Benefits for veterans may include nursing home care and some at-home care.

5. Specialized Insurance for Long-Term Care

Increasingly, middle-aged and older Americans who can afford to do so are purchasing long-term care insurance. Long-term care policies are private insurance policies. Companies offer a wide variety of policies, and the multitude of choices can be bewildering. Among the important choices are the kind of coverage to be provided, the place where coverage is to be provided, the amount of coverage, the duration of coverage, premium payment options, the age at which to purchase a policy, and whether the policy is tax qualified or is a state partnership policy. Long-term care policies are expensive, and many Americans cannot realistically afford them and should not attempt to buy them. Americans of at least moderate wealth, however, may want to consider the purchase of such a policy. Because of the growing importance of such insurance and the many considerations involved in choosing such a policy, long-term care insurance is discussed in detail in the following section.

D. Long-Term Care Insurance

1. Generally

Until the 1980s, payment for long-term care typically came either from an individual's personal resources or, for those who qualified, from the government. In the 1980s, private insurance companies introduced nursing home insurance, which has evolved into today's more comprehensive long-term care insurance. Although federal laws govern the treatment of certain aspects of long-term care policies, by and large state laws determine the rules governing the issuance and provision of long-term policies within a particular jurisdiction.

The National Association of Insurance Commissioners (NAIC), an organization that includes the chief insurance regulators from all states, the District of Columbia, and four territories of the United States, issues model laws, regulations, and guidelines for state adoption when national uniformity of laws seems appropriate. States choosing to adopt the models may adopt them intact or may make modification to the models. NAIC's models include those regarding long-term care policies. Although numerous differences still exist among state law concerning long-term care policies, many states have relied substantially on NAIC's recommendations.

"A Shopper's Guide to Long-term Care Insurance" is a guide that NAIC prepares to help individuals understand long-term insurance policies and the wide variety of provisions such polices may contain. The guide is written in a simple and straightforward manner and contains worksheets to help the individual assess her needs for a long-term care policy. Most states require an insurance company and its agents to provide the guide to prospective purchasers of long-term care policies. (The guide can also be purchased from NAIC for a nominal amount and is widely available online at the websites of insurance companies, consumer groups for the elderly, and state insurance departments.)

Although the cost of long-term care insurance premiums can vary significantly depending upon the policy provisions, most individuals without significant income or assets will find long-term care policy premiums difficult to pay. In contrast, estate planners now frequently recommend that a client who has at least moderate wealth consider purchasing a long-term care policy to protect her income and assets for herself and her family. Such a client can typically tailor the policy to meet her needs and wishes concerning the kinds of care to be provided, the place where such care will be provided, and so forth.

Before purchasing a long-term care policy, the individual should make sure that she will be able to pay not only the current premiums for the policy, but also the increased premiums that are likely to be charged in future years. An individual for whom current premium payments will be a stretch is generally not a good candidate for a long-term care policy, particularly if her future income stream and the value of her assets are not likely to increase sufficiently to keep up with probable increases in her premium. Individuals who must rely on their Social Security to live, or who receive government assistance such as Supplemental Security Income, typically should not purchase a long-term care policy. The same is true of a person who has already qualified for Medicaid. Medicaid will pay for the costs of some or all of the long-term care needs of poor individuals; commentators (and the NAIC) generally agree that these individuals should not place themselves in further financial need currently by incurring the significant costs of a long-term care policy.

As with any decision concerning the purchase of private insurance, the decision to purchase long-term care insurance involves a balancing of risks. The cost of such insurance is great, and many individuals who purchase it will never need it; however, the cost of long-term care can be enormous, and the individual who does not have long-term care insurance may see her estate depleted or substantially depleted if she is among the large number of elderly individuals who require long-term care.

If the individual decides to purchase such a policy, her choices are many. The more bells and whistles she adds to her coverage, however, the higher her premiums will be. Unfortunately, she often cannot accurately predict whether she will need a particular bell or whistle, and thus she must base her choice on speculation, her willingness to tolerate risk, and her ability to afford additional coverage. The older she is when she obtains the policy, the higher her premiums will be. (The oldest of the old—the group of elders 85 and older—generally cannot obtain long-term care insurance.) Although many observers recommend that an individual consider purchasing a long-term care policy by her mid-fifties, at that age many individuals have difficulty imagining their future need for long-term care. If such an individual still has children to support and educate, her financial obligations to her children may make a long-term care policy seem currently impractical, even if she expects her income stream or assets to increase significantly in future years.

When an individual begins to consider long-term care insurance, she may at first feel overwhelmed by the variety of options facing her. Consumer-friendly publications such as the NAIC's guide and information provided by state insurance departments and advocacy groups provide substantial help in sorting through those options. Nonetheless, to purchase the policy that is right for her, the individual must carefully assess what she wants, what she is likely to need over time, and what she can afford. After she has made this assessment, she must engage in the sometimes daunting task of policy comparison. In sum, a decision to purchase long-term care insurance is not one to be made quickly or lightly.

2. Coverage and Services

In determining what she wants and will probably need from a long-term care policy, the prospective purchaser can benefit from asking herself, "who, what, when, and where?" This list of "w" questions leads the purchaser to inquire about the following: "Who provides the long-term coverage I want at the best rates? What is the coverage I want and what limitations on coverage am I will to accept? When do I want services to begin and end? Where do I want the long-term care to be provided?"

a. Who Provides Long-Term Care Policies?

i. Generally

Most long-term care policies are purchased as individual policies from a private insurance company. These policies may be purchased from an agent or through the mail. Less common is the joint policy that insures more than one person (such as a married couple). A joint policy may provide a pooled benefit that applies for the entire group of insureds. For example, if a husband and wife have a joint policy with a pooled benefit of $300,000 and the husband receives $250,000 of long-term care benefits prior to his death, then the remaining available benefit for his widow is $50,000.

Some individuals purchase long-term care insurance through a group plan affiliated with a large employer or affiliated with organizations like AARP that have a large membership. The federal government and some state governments also offer group policies to their employees and retirees. Like those who purchase private long-term care policies, individuals who purchase long-term care through a group plan typically pay their own premium. (Although some employers may contribute to the purchase of such policies, the federal government does not pay the premiums of its employees, and membership organizations typically do not contribute to the payment of members' premiums.)

Policy offerings under a group plan may provide guaranteed acceptance or may have relaxed standards for accepting new insureds. Thus, an individual whose application for long-term care might be rejected as a private applicant because of her medical condition may still be able to obtain coverage through a group plan. It is not safe to assume, however, that coverage under a group policy is generally superior to that offered under an individual policy. The prospective purchaser who has an option to purchase long-term care under a group plan should carefully consider her private policy options before making a final decision.

Long-term care insurance is regulated on the state level. The office of the state insurance commissioner may provide helpful information to the prospective purchaser about available policies within the state. Nonetheless, the prospective purchaser should also thoroughly and carefully examine her options for herself.

Once an individual has purchased a policy, most states provide the newly insured with a 30-day period in which to cancel the policy and obtain a refund. This consumer protection provision gives the insured a post-purchase opportunity to ensure that the policy provides the coverage she needs at a price she can afford.

ii. Eligibility Requirements

Insurance companies selling long-term care policies typically examine an applicant's current health condition and her health history before accepting her application and issuing her a policy. (As discussed earlier, some group policies provide for guaranteed acceptance from certain applicants.) If an applicant has a pre-existing condition that indicates she is very likely to require long-term care in the near future, the insurance company will probably deny her application. For other pre-existing conditions, the company may (1) issue a policy excluding coverage for services relating to those conditions; (2) impose a longer waiting period (often six months) before coverage relating to those conditions begins; (3) limit the benefits to be paid for services relating to those conditions; or (4) charge a higher premium.

Underwriting procedures vary among insurance companies. Some companies do not engage in detailed questioning, while other companies do. Some companies examine the applicant's medical records and seek a doctor's evaluation of the applicant's current health. Some companies go farther back in time than others in examining an applicant's health history. Although such detailed inquiry may be burdensome, it is generally better for the applicant who is able to obtain a policy. Companies that engage in only a cursory investigation without checking the applicant's medical record before issuing a policy may later attempt to deny coverage based on medical information they discover after the claim is filed. (Such attempts at "post-claim underwriting" are illegal in a number of states.)

An applicant with a pre-existing condition may be tempted to withhold information concerning that condition. If her application contains incorrect or incomplete information and the insurance company issues a policy, however, the insurance company may later be able to rescind that policy. Rescission for innocent misrepresentations is often limited to two years after the policy is issued; however, if the applicant intentionally misrepresents her health history, the company may be able to rescind the policy years after it is issued. If the company does not (or cannot) rescind for misrepresentation, it may nonetheless be able to deny coverage for services related to the unreported condition. The applicant should thus answer all questions truthfully and completely, and she should retain a copy of her application with her other important papers.

b. What Are the Benefits and Costs?
i. Skilled, Intermediate, and Custodial Care

Most long-term care policies cover skilled and intermediate care in a skilled nursing facility. Many elders do not require skilled nursing care or intermediate medical care, however. Rather, their long-term needs stem from the inability to perform the activities of daily living (such as eating, toileting, transferring, bathing, dressing, and continence). The typical purchaser of a long-term care policy will thus want to ensure that the policy also covers custodial care. For example, a policy might provide that custodial care is available when the insured is unable to perform two ADLs without substantial assistance.

ii. Exclusions

Long-term care policies frequently exclude from coverage certain categories of costs. Among these exclusions are costs for long-term care associated with alcohol or drug addiction; with an injury or illness resulting from an act of war; and with injury that was self-inflicted (including attempted suicide). Policies also typically exclude benefits for treatment that the government provides or pays for. Although policies also exclude coverage for costs associated with mental or nervous disorders or diseases, an important exception applies for those who develop Alzheimer's or other dementia. State law typically requires insurance companies to pay for costs associated with Alzheimer's or dementia. (Note that this rule applies to those individuals who develop Alzheimer's or dementia after purchasing the policy. The insurance company does not have to insure a person who has Alzheimer's or dementia at the time she applies for a policy.)

iii. Premiums

(a) Generally

Long-term care policies are expensive. Many factors affect the premium an insured will have to pay, including the various options the insured chooses concerning kinds of benefits, the maximum daily benefit, the length of benefits, and the place(s) where benefits will be provided. The older an applicant is, the more likely she will need long-term care. Thus an older applicant generally will pay a substantially higher premium than a younger applicant. Moreover, premiums for policies offering substantially the same benefits may vary among companies. The cheaper policy does not necessarily provide the better bargain, even if the stated coverage is similar to that of policies offered by other companies. In addition to examining the policy itself, the prospective applicant may want to examine the licensing status, rate increase history, and complaint records of the company issuing the policy. Some or all of this information may be available from the office of the state insurance commissioner. The careful prospective purchaser will also check the financial stability of a company before purchasing a long-term policy. This information may be obtained from insurer rating services such as Moody's or Standard & Poor's.

The prospective purchaser of a long-term care policy should understand that premiums may increase over time. An insurance company cannot set a premium increase on an individual basis (for example, because of the insured's use of the policy to obtain long-term care benefits), but it can set premium increases for entire classes of insured individuals. Substantial premium increases can impose financial hardships on retired persons or others living on a fixed income. For this reason, experts agree that a prospective applicant should carefully consider not only her current ability to pay premiums, but also her probable ability to pay the increased premiums that are likely to come in future years.

Most states require that long-term care policies be "guaranteed renewable." In other words, once the insured obtains a policy, the issuing company must allow her to renew it when the next premium is due. Guaranteed renewability, however, does not protect the insured against premium increases.

(b) Inflation Protection

Assume that a fifty-five year old woman purchases a long-term care policy with a maximum daily nursing home benefit of $200, which reflects the average daily nursing home costs in the area where she lives at the time she purchases the policy. The policy has no inflation protection. The insured faithfully pays her premiums and, twenty-five years later, she needs nursing home care. Because nursing home costs will almost certain have risen substantially over this time frame, her $200 daily benefit cap means that she will have to shoulder a major part of the cost of her care out-of-pocket. (Studies indicate the cost of nursing home care has risen about five percent per year in recent years.)

To minimize this risk, prospective purchasers of long-term care insurance should carefully consider a policy with automatic inflation protection. Under such a policy, maximum daily benefits increase on an annual basis and typically by a fixed percentage (often 5%) either during the life of the policy or for a specified time frame. The inflation adjustment may be simple, thus increasing the benefit cap by the same amount each year. Alternatively — and far better for the insured — the inflation adjustment may be compounded, thus increasing the benefit cap by a larger amount each year. Most state laws now require companies to offer some form of inflation protection. State law may even require companies to offer inflation protection with compound interest. By federal statute, "state partnership" policies must include compound annual inflation protection to purchasers under 61 and must include some level of inflation protection for purchasers aged 61 through 75. Federal statutes also require tax-qualified policies to offer inflation protection. (State partnership policies and tax-qualified polices are discussed later in this chapter.)

Automatic inflation protection can increase the cost of a long-term care policy significantly. This is especially true for younger purchasers, who are the most in need of inflation protection.

Even if a policy does not include automatic inflation protection, the company issuing the policy may allow the insured to increase her benefits from time to time. This is generally a less satisfactory solution to the problems posed by inflation, however, and may be subject to several restrictions.

(c) Payment Options

Depending upon the state and the insurance company, a company may offer the applicant the option of paying premiums under a continuous plan or under a limited-time plan. Most individuals pay premiums for their long-term care policies on a continuous basis (usually monthly, quarterly, semi-annually, or annually). Premiums are usually lower under this option. Under a continuous payment plan, individuals typically pay premiums until the trigger for benefit eligibility is satisfied. As mentioned above, premiums may increase over time for various classes of policies.

The individual who would like to pay up her policy over a fixed-time frame may prefer a limited-time premium payment option. For example, she may be able to pay the entire premium amount at one time. Alternatively (and perhaps more commonly), she may choose to pay over a ten- or twenty-year period. Another limited-time premium payment option allows the insured to pay up to a certain age (usually tied to retirement, such as age 65). By satisfying one of these options, the individual who takes out a policy at an early enough age will not have to worry about premium payments during her retirement years and the potential strain such payments might impose. Once her policy is paid up, she owes no further amounts, and the insurance company cannot cancel the policy. The trade-off, of course, is that premium payments will be larger under a limited-time premium payment plan. Also, if the limited-time payment plan does not guarantee a fixed premium over the applicable time period, the premium is subject to increase during the applicable payment period.

(d) Nonforfeiture Benefit

Insurance companies may offer (or state regulators may require that insurance companies offer) certain policy protections relating to premium payments. The optional protections increase the cost of a policy, however. A nonforfeiture benefit guarantees that the insured will receive some benefit from her long-term care policy even if she allows the policy to lapse, as long as she satisfies certain conditions. One kind of nonforfeiture benefit is a "return of premium" provision. Under this provision, if the insured allows the policy to lapse after a stated time period, the company will return some part of her premium payments to her. The guarantee of premium returns generally adds substantially to the cost of the policy.

A less expensive alternative is the "paid-up policy" nonforfeiture benefit option offered by some companies. If the insured has chosen this option, she will receive a substitute policy when she allows her original long-term care policy to lapse (again, as long as she meets all of the stated conditions for the option to kick in). She pays no further premiums. For example, the paid-up policy may be one under which she has the same benefit period but a reduced daily benefit amount or, conversely, one in which she has the same daily benefit amount but for a reduced benefit period.

Because a nonforfeiture benefit chosen by the applicant will increase the cost of the policy, the applicant may choose to forego the nonforfeiture benefit option. If she does, some states require the insurance company to provide a contingent benefit upon lapse. Under such a provision, the insured receives a benefit when the policy lapses if at the time of the lapse her premiums have increased to a certain percentage above her initial premium. In effect, the contingent benefit upon lapse functions as a default nonforfeiture benefit. The benefit typically is either a paid-up policy with a shorter benefit period or a continuation of the current policy with reduced benefits that allows the premium to remain unchanged.

(e) Waivers, Death Refunds, and Downgrades

A variety of other provisions can affect premium payment. For many applicants, one of the most important of these provisions is a waiver of premium clause. Such a clause provides that the insured no longer must pay premiums once she has begun to receive benefits. Depending upon the policy, the waiver of premiums may be effective immediately upon the receipt of benefits or may become effective only after the insured has received benefits for a certain time period (often two to three months). Although some companies still offer the waiver of premium clause as an option, today most companies include such a provision as a standard part of their long-term policies.

An insured may have the option of choosing a provision for a refund of premiums at death. Although this option can increase the cost of the policy, it may be attractive to an individual who hopes to leave assets for her estate. If the insured has paid premiums for a certain time period, at her death the company will repay to her estate part or all of her premium payments less any benefits the company has paid. The provision may also include other limitations on the refund. For example, it may require that the policy holder die before reaching a certain age, such as 65 or 70.

If an insured lacks the financial ability to pay increased premiums necessary to prevent the lapse of the policy, she may be able to downgrade her policy to one with lesser coverage and a lower premium charge. Although the new policy may not provide all of the protections she wants, reduced coverage may be better than none at all. Moreover, if she allows her current policy to lapse and that policy has no nonforfeiture benefit provision (or she is not eligible to invoke the provision), she may otherwise feel that her prior premium payments were all for naught.

(f) Notice to Third Parties

State law may require an insurance company to allow the insured to name a third party who will receive notice from the company if the policy is about to lapse because of the insured's failure to pay a premium. Some companies may voluntarily offer the insured this opportunity. Such a provision can be very important, particularly for the insured who has become cognitively-impaired. If the insured is incapable of making a decision to renew the policy, or is capable but has forgotten to renew, the notice provision will allow the third party to arrange for the payment of the overdue premium and prevent the policy from lapsing.

3. Policies Providing Special Benefits under Federal Law

Two kinds of long-term care policies that satisfy certain federal laws offer the insured special benefits. One such policy offers limited tax benefits, while the other also helps the insured preserve part of her estate for her successors.

a. Tax-Qualified Policies

The Health Insurance Portability and Accountability Act of 1996 (HIPAA) introduced the Tax-Qualified Long-term Care Insurance Contract. To be qualified, such contracts (also called TQ policies or qualified contracts) must satisfy the requirements of 26 U.S.C. §7702B. If the requirements are met, then amounts received under the policy for long-term care are excluded from the insured's income up to a daily per diem amount as defined in the statute. The statute sets a dollar amount that is adjusted annually for inflation; however, the statute further provides that if the insured's actual costs incurred are greater than the dollar amount, the actual costs are to be used in determining the exclusion.

The statute also provides that the insured may treat part of the amounts she paid (that is, part of her premium payments) for the TQ policy as a medical expense subject to the rules of 26 U.S.C. § 213. Section 213 permits an individual to deduct that part of her medical expenses that exceeds 7.5 percent of her adjusted gross income. Under section 213(d)(10), the amount of medical expense the insured can claim relating to the TQ policy varies with the age of the insured. In 2009, for an individual with an attained age of 40 or less before the end of the taxable year, the limitation was $320; if her age was more than 40 but not more than 50, the limitation was $600; if her age was more than 50 but not more than 60, the limitation was $1,190; if her age was more than 60 but not more than 70, the limitation was $3,180; and if her age was more than 70, the limitation was $3,980. (These amounts are indexed (adjusted) annually.) For example, if the insured were 61 in 2009 and paid a $3,500 premium payment for her TQ policy, she could add $3,180 to her other medical expenses. If her total medical expenses exceeded 7.5 percent of her adjusted gross income, she would have a deduction under section 213 (if she itemizes). In fact, the ability to treat a portion of premium payments as medical expenses often has little or no effect on the income tax owed by most insureds.

To qualify as a TQ policy, the policy must be guaranteed renewable. It cannot impose medical necessity as a trigger for benefits. Coverage must be for qualified long-term care services. Such services are defined under 26 U.S.C. § 7702B(c) to include services for a chronically ill individual that are provided pursuant to a plan of care prescribed by a licensed health care practitioner. Such an individual must be unable to perform at least two activities of daily living for at least 90 days due to loss of functional capacity; or must have a similar level of disability; or must require substantial supervision to protect the individual from threats to health and safety because of her severe cognitive impairment.

The policy must also meet several consumer protection requirements. 26 U.S.C. § 7720B(g). The policy must offer a nonforfeiture benefit provision. An individual tax qualified policy must also offer inflation protection. The policy must also meet certain disclosure requirements under 26 U.S.C. § 4980C that are taken from the NAIC model act and model regulation. The policy must also meet other requirements taken from the act and regulation. Among these other requirements, the policy must have provisions protecting the insured from unintentional lapse, prohibiting post-claims underwriting, and prohibiting prior hospitalization as a prerequisite to benefit eligibility.

b. State Partnership Policies

Many commentators have observed that the demands on state Medicaid long-term programs would decrease if more people would purchase long-term care insurance to finance their long-term care needs. The Deficit Reduction Act of 2005 (DRA 2005) allows states to provide individuals with an incentive to purchase long-term care insurance. Under the Act, states may create a qualified state long-term care insurance partnership through an amendment to their state Medicaid plan. 42 U.S.C. § 1396p(b)(1)(C). Many states have already done so. The general structure of the partnership program is described below. Not everyone agrees that it will ultimately result in substantial savings to the Medicaid budget.

States adopting the partnership program have an "asset disregard" provision that applies to an individual who has received long-term care insurance benefits under a qualified policy. When such an individual exhausts her insurance benefits and applies for Medicaid long-term care, Medicaid will exclude from consideration the value of the long-term care insurance policy benefits paid to or on behalf of that individual. For example, assume that Betty is an elderly widow with assets exceeding the Medicaid long-term care eligibility limits. Normally she would not be eligible for Medicaid long-term care until she spent down those assets and brought herself within the standard long-term care Medicaid eligibility limits for the state. Betty lives in a state with a long-term care insurance partnership program, however, and she purchases a qualified long-term care partnership insurance policy with benefits of up to $100,000. When Betty subsequently needs long-term care, her policy pays until she exhausts her benefits. Once her benefits are exhausted, Betty may shield up to $100,000 of assets (the value of benefits paid by the policy) and yet be able to qualify for Medicaid long-term care if her long-term care need continues and she otherwise meets all Medicaid eligibility criteria. Note that if Betty still has *other* excess assets when her policy stops paying, she will not be eligible for Medicaid currently. She will have to spend down the other assets. Thus, exhausting the long-term care policy benefits is no guarantee that Medicaid eligibility will immediately follow. When the insured applies for Medicaid, however, she will be able to shelter from consideration the amount of the policy benefits paid. (A few states — California, Connecticut, Indiana, and New York — had plans that were approved in the early 1990s as part of a model demonstration program. The details of those plans can be even more generous to the purchaser of a long-term care policy.)

The DRA 2005 statutory requirements on such policies include the following: the policy must cover an insured who was a resident of the state when coverage became effective; the policy must be a tax-qualified long-term care policy (as defined in 26 U.S.C. § 7702B(b)) issued not earlier than the effective date of the state Medicaid plan amendment; and the policy must meet a variety of provisions from the NAIC model act and model regulation. The NAIC requirements include provisions guaranteeing renewability, protecting against unintentional lapse, mandating disclosure, reporting, filing, and so forth. If the NAIC changes its model act or model regulation, within one year the Secretary of Health and Human Services must decide whether to incorporate the changes. 42 U.S.C. § 1396p(b)(5)(C). The DRA also requires the Secretary to develop reciprocity rules that entitle an insured to have her policy recognized in other states that have partnership programs.

A state partnership plan policy must provide for compound annual inflation protection for an individual who has not attained age 61 as of the date of purchase. If the individual is 61 but not yet 76 when the policy is purchased, the policy must provide some level of inflation protection. If the purchaser has attained age 76 at the date of purchase, the policy may (but is not required to) provide some level of inflation protection.

4. When Are Benefits Provided?

Long-term care policies contain various limitations on the provision of benefits. These limitations commonly include (1) a total maximum benefit that the policy provides and a maximum daily, weekly, or monthly benefit that the policy provides; (2) trigger mechanisms for coverage to begin; and (3) an elimination or waiting period before coverage begins. Most policies also contain certain exclusions from coverage. The prospective purchaser should carefully note gatekeeping provisions in the policy. These provisions are those that determine when the insured is entitled to the receipt of benefits. When long-term care policies were relatively new, policies often provided that an insured was not eligible for benefits unless she had had a hospital stay of three days. (This is similar to the Medicare prerequisite for skilled nursing facility care coverage.) This limitation is not found in most policies issued today, and in fact is prohibited by law in most states.

a. Maximum Benefit Limits

The prospective applicant should note carefully two monetary limitations found in most policies. One limitation is the total maximum benefit that the company will pay on the policy. This may be stated as a dollar amount (a maximum benefit amount), or it may be stated in years of coverage (a maximum benefit period). The minimum benefit period is typically one year. It is possible to obtain a benefit period tied to the lifetime of the insured. Only a few policies, however, do not limit the total benefit they will pay. The greater the total maximum benefit, the greater the cost of the policy.

The second limitation is a daily, weekly, or monthly cap on benefits paid by the policy. Again, many policies allow the insured to choose this amount, but the insured will pay more for a larger benefit cap. Typically, the applicant chooses a policy amount based on her projections of probable nursing home costs for her long-term care. Before purchasing the policy, it is important for the applicant to investigate nursing home costs where she believes she will be receiving long-term care and to factor in probable increases in those costs over time. The daily, weekly, or monthly benefit cap is usually expressed in dollars, but occasionally may be expressed as a percentage of nursing home cost. If the policy covers care at home, the daily, weekly, or monthly benefit cap may also be expressed as a percentage of the nursing home amount.

b. Trigger Mechanisms

A key component of any long-term policy is the description of benefit triggers—i.e., the criteria by which the company determines that the insured is entitled to benefits. Triggers may vary from policy to policy, although state law sometimes mandates certain triggers and precludes others. Federal laws pertaining to tax-qualified policies also mandate certain triggers and preclude the use of certain triggers. For example, some long-term care policies require a doctor's certification that the insured requires long-term care, but this benefit trigger cannot be used in a tax-qualified policy.

Under most policies, an insured is entitled to benefits if she is unable to do certain activities of daily living (ADLs) without substantial assistance. The most common activities described in policies are eating, toileting, transferring, bathing, dressing, and continence. For example, the policy might provide that the insured is entitled to benefits when she can no longer perform two of these six ADLs. By statute, federal tax-qualified policies must consider at least five of these six ADLS and require that the insured is unable to perform at least two of them for a period of ninety days. 26 U.S.C. §7702B(c). The prospective purchaser of a long-term policy should clearly understand the policy's definition of inability to perform an ADL, because some definitions are more restrictive than others.

Some individuals need long-term care because of their cognitive impairment. Thus, many long-term care policies provide that an insured is eligible for coverage if she cannot pass certain cognitive tests. The prospective purchaser should note the policy's definition of cognitive impairment and the tests for benefit eligibility. In the early stages of Alzheimer's, an individual may still be able to perform most or all of the ADLs. Thus, the typical prospective purchaser will want to make sure that the cognitive impairment criteria for eligibility are an alternative to the ADLs criteria.

c. Elimination Period

Many policies contain an elimination period (also known as a waiting period or deductible period). The elimination period is the time that must pass after the insured requires long-term care before policy benefits begin to be paid. The elimination period is typically stated in days. The shorter the elimination period, the smaller the out-of-pocket expenses for the insured, but the greater the cost of the policy. The insured usually may choose from a range of elimination periods. A zero-day deductible period (available with some policies) means that policy benefits are payable immediately when the insured requires long-term care. Such a policy is substantially more expensive than a policy with a ninety-day deductible period, which imposes the full costs of care on the insured for three months. If the policy provides for different kinds of benefits (for example, nursing home care and home care), the policy may contain different elimination periods for the different kinds of benefits.

Elimination period provisions can be tricky, and the prospective purchaser should examine them closely. For example, assume that the insured requires nursing home care and has a thirty-day deductible period. Once she has been in the nursing home thirty days, her long-term care benefits begin to be paid. She later improves, no longer requires long-term care, and returns homes. Two years later, she again requires long-term care. Will she have to meet the elimination-period requirement a second time? Some policies only require the insured to satisfy the elimination period once; others impose the elimination period for each episode of care. Some policies taking this latter approach, however, may view a subsequent need for long-term care as a continuation of the original episode of care if the two occur within a certain time frame.

Another important concern is the way in which the elimination period must be satisfied. If the insured has a ninety-day elimination period and requires long-term care for the months of January, March, and April, has she satisfied the elimination period for benefits to begin? If the policy requires the elimination period to be satisfied by a long-term care need over consecutive days, the answer is no. If the policy permits her to satisfy the elimination period by tallying all days of long-term care need, however, the answer is yes. Even if the policy permits tallying all days of long-term care need, yet another question of counting may arise: what constitutes a day of long-term care need? For example, if the insured has a thirty-day elimination period and requires long-term care four days a week throughout one month, has she satisfied her elimination period requirements? Under some policies, the answer is yes, because the entire week is counted. Other policies, however, only count the actual days in which she receives care. Under this latter approach, the insured will have accumulated substantially less than the total of thirty days that the policy requires.

d. Restoration of Benefits

If a policy provides for a maximum dollar benefit of $100,000 and the company pays $25,000 in long-term care fees for the insured, the insured's remaining dollar benefit is $75,000. This is true even if following the company's payment of the $25,000 the insured does not require further long-term care for several years. A restoration of benefits clause, however, restores the total amount of benefits payable under a policy to its original maximum if the insured does not use or require long-term care for a stated period of time (often six months) after receiving prior benefits. Thus, in the preceding example, if the policy had contained a clause restoring full benefits after six months, the insured's maximum dollar benefit would return to $100,000 if six months passed before she required further long-term care.

5. Where Are Benefits Provided?

a. Facilities Covered

Even if a person has a long-term care policy and is receiving long-term care at a facility, her policy may not pay for care at that particular facility. Once again, policy coverage varies. The long-term care policy may cover care in any state-licensed care facility or may exclude certain state-licensed facilities. The policy may require that the facility have a certain government certification, or provide for a certain number of patients, or provide certain kinds of care. Often long-term care policies exclude unlicensed facilities such as "rest" homes or "old age" homes. When purchasing the policy, the prospective insured should examine carefully the places at which the policy will pay for her long-term care. She may also want to ensure that the policy will cover long-term care in new kinds of facilities that arise in the future and that provide superior care.

b. Alternatives to Nursing Home Care

Although long-term care policies originated as nursing home insurance, today's options often allow the insured to receive benefits in many other settings. Once again, many of these options come at a price. Options include home health care, personal care in the insured's home, respite care, hospice care, care in assisted living facilities, and services provided by adult day care and community facilities.

Because almost everyone wants to avoid living in a nursing home, the prospective purchaser of long-term care often desires a policy that pays for in-home long-term care. Policy options vary substantially. The individual may obtain a policy that pays for home health care from a licensed professional who is an employee of a licensed agency, or it may extend payment to include home health care from a licensed professional who is not affiliated with a licensed agency. Some policies provide options that pay for homemaker services, including meal preparation, light housekeeping, and errands run for the insured. (At least some policies will pay family members to perform these services under certain conditions.)

Unsurprisingly, such in-home long-term care coverage may increase the cost of the policy or may include substantial restrictions on the benefits. For example, the company may require that a company employee or other case manager visit the insured and assess her needs and the propriety of in-home care. A policy may impose a lower daily policy limit when the care is provided at the insured's home under the generally accurate premise that much long-term care can be provided more cheaply outside a nursing home.

Respite care typically refers to care provided for short periods of time by someone other than the regular caregiver. Respite care generally benefits the patient and the regular caregiver, for it allows the regular caregiver an occasional break from the substantial stress and demands that may come with the care giving role. Hospice care is care provided for a terminally ill person with a life expectancy of no more than six months. Hospice care may be provided in the home or in a hospice facility.

Checkpoints

- Concerning long-term care, you should understand that long-term care includes not only the provision of medical care, but also custodial care and assistance with the activities of daily living (i.e., bathing, continence, dressing, eating, toileting, and transferring)
- Concerning long-term care, you should be able to describe various ways in which an individual may satisfy her long-term care needs through the assistance of
  - Family and friends
  - Community- and home-based services organizations
  - Paid caregivers
  - Board and care homes, assisted living facilities, and continuing care retirement communities
  - Nursing homes
- Concerning the costs of long-term care, you should be able to describe various ways in which an individual may pay for such care, including the use of
  - Personal savings and the resources of family and friends
  - Proceeds of a reverse mortgage
  - Accelerated death benefits under a life insurance policy
  - Medicaid or other governmental programs
  - Long-term care insurance
- Concerning long-term care insurance, you should understand the way in which long-term care insurance policies work and are regulated, including
  - Eligibility requirements
  - Premium provisions and payment options
  - Inflation protection
  - Nonforfeiture benefits
  - Waivers, death refunds, and downgrades
  - Tax-qualified policies
  - State partnership polices

Checkpoints *continued*

- Benefit limits
- Trigger mechanisms
- Elimination periods
- Restoration of benefits

Chapter 11

The Home

A. Introduction

Most people hope to remain in their home as they grow older. This desire to "age in place" is understandable: the home, however humble, is often filled with special memories of family, friends, and significant events. It contains furnishings and accessories acquired over a lifetime. The home is a place of profound meaning for most individuals, but it may have particular meaning for the elderly person who stringently seeks to maintain autonomy.

Many individuals are fortunate enough to remain at home, living independently until death. Some individuals, however, will require assistance to remain in their homes. Many other individuals will have physical, mental, or financial needs that require them to leave their homes and reside elsewhere.

This chapter presents an overview of several housing options available to elderly individuals.

B. Private Dwellings

1. Home Ownership

The home is important to the typical elderly person not only because of the memories and memorabilia it contains, but also because the home represents stability in her life. The elderly person may feel that as long as she remains at home, she is still in control of her life. (These feelings of stability and control provide one reason why a person may want to remain in her home even when reasonable observers would conclude that the home itself is uninhabitable.) A person who has lived in her home for a number of years often becomes rooted to the place. The longer she has been there, the deeper her roots. If a new residence will take her away not only from her current home but also from the community where she has long resided, her difficulties of adjusting to the new residence may be compounded. A distant move may permanently separate her from longtime friends and from social and religious groups that have played an integral role in her life.

The following discussion examines some ways in which an elderly person may be able to remain in her longtime residence even though she is physically, mentally, or financially vulnerable. The discussion also briefly examines financial and other consequences when a person sells or gives away her home.

a. Monitoring and Home Modification

Many elderly individuals are able to remain in their homes, living independently until death. Some elders may choose to wear a pendant or watch (such as those offered by various companies for a fee) that will allow them to have emergency personnel dispatched to their homes at the push of a button.

Some elderly individuals can remain in their home without any structural modifications to the home. Other individuals will need to alter the physical structure of their home to accommodate their physical needs. Because an elder's ability to bathe is often the first of the activities of daily living that is impaired, one common home modification is the installation of grab bars in showers and around tubs. The individual may also require an elevated toilet or grab bars around the toilet. If the elder becomes wheelchair bound, she may need to install ramps and doorway modifications to assist her in moving about her home. If her home is on two or more floors and she is wheelchair bound or cannot climb stairs, she may need to install a small elevator or a stairway lift chair.

b. Family, Friends, and Community Programs

Family and friends may provide the assistance the elder needs to remain in her home. In many instances, family and friends provide such assistance without charge. For example, family members may share the responsibilities for ensuring that the elder is eating properly, taking her medications, and is otherwise well-cared for. Although such responsibilities seem to fall disproportionately upon adult daughters (and daughters-in-law), other family members sometimes play a major role in ensuring the elder's well-being at her home.

An elder who has family members who can see to her needs on a part-time basis may also be able to remain at home with the assistance of an adult day care program. For example, if Hazel's principal caregiver is her adult daughter Paula, who also has a full-time job, perhaps an adult day care program can provide the necessary supplemental care for Hazel while Paula is at work during the day.

A state that satisfies certain criteria may obtain a Medicaid waiver to provide home- and community-based services to individuals who would otherwise require institutionalization. 42 U.S.C. § 1396n(c), (d). The elder may also receive some assistance through various programs available in her community. Programs such as meals on wheels can help to provide needed services to homebound, frail, or at risk elders.

c. Paid Caregivers in the Home

Although Medicare will provide some home health care if the individual meets stringent requirements, Medicare was not designed to, and generally does not, provide long-term care (at home or elsewhere). Some private Medicare supplement insurance policies (known as Medigap policies) may also pay for certain expenses associated with at-home recovery, but they too do not cover the cost of long-term care.

An individual in need of long-term care who wishes to remain at home may contract with a caregiver to provide such care. The individual may use a private agency, advertisements, word of mouth, or other formal or informal means to find someone who she believes will be a reliable caregiver. If the individual needs round-the-clock care, it may be to her advantage to hire caregivers who work in shifts. When a single caregiver provides services around the clock, stress and tension upon the caregiver can be overwhelming. Many cases of abuse in the home occur when the elder is cared for by one caregiver who is the primary (and perhaps only) person who has regular contact with the elder.

In fact, most instances of elder abuse appear to arise when the caregiver is a member of the elder's own family. Often the elder and an adult child will enter into an informal agreement in which the elder provides the child with room and board in return for the care the child is to provide to the elder. If the child is without monetary resources of her own, the child's financial dependence upon the elder can lead to resentment. If the child also has a substance abuse problem, the probability that elder abuse will occur increases substantially. Financial dependence and substance abuse do not necessarily mean that a caregiver will engage in elder abuse; however, these factors should be considered in selecting a caregiver for an elder.

Sometimes an elder will orally promise "to give" or "to leave" her house to a child or other relative or friend if that person will move into the elder's house and care for her. If, despite the care that is given, the elder then fails to deliver a deed to the house or fails to include a will provision devising the house to the caregiver, the caregiver may be out of luck. The oral promise alone is insufficient to satisfy the statute of frauds or statute of wills. Moreover, a court may presume that a close relative has performed her care giving role gratuitously. On rare occasion, however, principles of equitable estoppel or part performance may suffice to permit the caregiver to enforce the promise. Alternatively, the court may provide the caregiver with an award in quantum meruit in some circumstances.

In an attempt to avoid future disputes about the caregiver's duties and her right to payment, an elder and her caregiver sometimes now use a written life care agreement that details the terms of the contract between them. The drafting of such agreements is probably best left to experienced professionals, for the elder and the proposed caregiver who draft their own document may easily fail to consider the many various contingencies that can arise.

The costs of long-term care, even when provided at home, can be substantial. Long-term care insurance that includes home care coverage is one way to help defray those costs while allowing the individual to remain in her home. Perhaps because of the strong desire of the typical person to remain in her home, most long-term care insurance policies sold today include coverage for home care. In fact, recently over 40 percent of total long-term care benefit payments were made to provide home care for policy holders. (About one-third of total benefits were paid for assisted living expenses, and the remaining benefits were paid for nursing home care.) Thus individuals who can afford to pay the premiums — which are often substantial — are increasingly purchasing long-term care policies with provisions for home care. The insured must meet certain criteria (or "triggers") for coverage to begin. These triggers will vary from policy to policy. Some policies even pay family members who provide the care, although such provisions may contain particularly stringent gate-keeping rules to protect the insurance company against spurious claims.

Following the Deficit Reduction Act of 2005, states are permitted to establish programs that link long-term care insurance and Medicaid rules. Many states have responded by adopting such programs. If the individual purchases a qualified policy and subsequently requires long-term care and exhausts the policy benefits, she may qualify for Medicaid and yet shelter assets equal to the value of the policy benefits paid. For example, Mary purchases a long-term care policy with benefits of $200,000. Mary subsequently requires long-term care, which pursuant to policy terms is provided at her home. If she exhausts her benefits and applies for Medicaid long-term care, the state will ignore the first $200,000 of her assets. Such state partnership programs linking long-term care benefits and Medicaid eligibility provide an added incentive for the individual to purchase a long-term care policy. (For more on long-term care, see Chapter 10.)

d. Reverse Mortgages

In some instances, the principal factor in determining whether an elderly individual can remain in her home is not her mental or physical condition, but rather her financial one. The elderly individual who enjoys good health and owns her home outright may not be able to remain there if she cannot pay property taxes and maintenance, repair, insurance, and utility fees, or if the payment of such expenses leaves her without adequate means of meeting her other needs.

An individual whose house is her principal (and perhaps only) substantial asset might consider a reverse mortgage to obtain the money she needs to remain at home. Unlike the traditional mortgage under which the homeowner makes regular payments to satisfy her mortgage debt, the reverse mortgage allows the homeowner to receive payments from the lender without any obligation to repay the debt until she dies or moves out of the home (whichever comes first). Moreover, the individual can never owe more than the value of her home.

Under the Housing and Urban Development (HUD) reverse mortgage program, a homeowner sixty-two or older may borrow against the equity in her home if she owns the home outright or has substantially paid off her mortgage debt. (The eligibility and disclosure requirements imposed under state, local, or private lender programs may differ.) All but a few reverse mortgages issued in recent years are "home equity conversion mortgages" (HECMs) insured by the federal government. The applicant's income, health, and credit history are irrelevant in determining her eligibility for an HECM.

The federal statute governing such loans requires that the mortgagor receive counseling from a HUD-qualified, independent third party who is to discuss with the mortgagor other options available to her and the financial implications of the HECM. The disclosure must indicate that the HECM may have tax consequences, may affect the mortgagor's eligibility for federal and state assistance programs (such as Medicaid and SSI), and may have an impact on the mortgagor's estate and her heirs. The mortgagor is also to receive full disclosure of all costs that will be charged to her. 12 U.S.C. § 1715z-20. Most homes owned in fee simple and used as a family dwelling are eligible. Also eligible is a leasehold (1) under a lease for not less than 99 years which is renewable or (2) under a lease having a remaining period of not less than 50 years beyond the date of the 100th birthday of the youngest mortgagor. 24 C.F.R. 206.45. A condominium designed as a one-family dwelling is also included. Special rules apply to certain kinds of homes. For example, mobile homes are eligible if the home was built after June 15, 1976, is on a permanent foundation on land owned by the applicant, and meets HUD certification requirements.

The amount an individual can borrow will depend upon her age, applicable interest rates, and the home's value. The older she is, the more she will be able to borrow as a percentage of the home's value. (When spouses who co-own a home apply for an HECM, the HECM is based on the age of the youngest homeowner. At least one of the spouses must be sixty-two, however.) The maximum value of the home considered under the HECM program is the lower of its appraised value or the FHA mortgage limit. If the FHA limit will not generate a loan sufficient to meet an applicant's needs, she may instead pursue a proprietary or "jumbo" reverse mortgage. Compared to an HECM, however, a proprietary reverse mortgage will probably have a higher interest rate and will limit the loan amount to a lower percentage of the home's value. For most people, the protections and rates offered by an HECM make it the better choice.

Payments (loan advances) to the borrower can be made on a monthly basis, through a line of credit, or through a combined monthly payment/line of credit approach. If the borrower receives periodic payments, they can be structured for a fixed term or, alternatively, for as long as the borrower lives in the home. By statute, the HECM debt does not have to be repaid as long as she continues to live in the home. If the HECM loan is to co-owners, the mortgage debt does not have to be repaid until the last surviving homeowner moves from the home. Although the typical borrower will not prepay the mortgage debt, an HECM must provide that the borrower can prepay the debt in whole or in part without penalty if she chooses to do so. Assuming that an owner is able to remain in the home until her death, debt payment (principal plus interest) is due upon her death. Typically, the home is sold and the sale proceeds are used to repay the lender. Any excess goes to the borrower's survivors. (The survivors, however, may choose to pay the debt and retain the home.) If the home is sold and the proceeds are insufficient to satisfy the borrower's debt, HUD pays the lender the amount of the shortfall.

Because the borrower remains the owner of the home following the reverse mortgage, upkeep and taxes continue to be her responsibility. If the borrower otherwise qualifies for Medicaid and Supplemental Security Income, she must take care to spend her loan proceeds by the end of each month to ensure that they do not become disqualifying excess resources. The loan proceeds are not taxable income to the borrower, and interest charged on the loan is not deductible until it is paid at the end of the loan.

Some individuals and couples want or need a smaller home as they grow older. They may want to move from a multiple-story home to a home all on one level. Their needs may include a home with wide doorways and wheelchair accessibility. The Housing and Economic Recovery Act of 2008 added a new provision to the HECM statute that, beginning in 2009, allows the purchaser/mortgagor to purchase a new principal residence and obtain an HECM on the home at the same time. Using this simultaneous procedure, the elder avoids the need for a second closing for the reverse mortgage and its attendant costs. For example, John, an elderly widower, has decided to downsize. He sells his longtime home for $250,000 and purchases a smaller, more elder-friendly home or condominium. The cost of the new home is $125,000, and John hopes to remain in that home until he dies. In purchasing the new home, he could pay cash and still have $125,000 left from the sale of his former home. Alternatively, he could pay part of the purchase price of the new home and finance the remaining part with a reverse mortgage. By taking the latter approach, he will increase his cash flow and he will have no monthly mortgage note to pay on the new home.

The 2008 amendments also provide new limitations on origination fees that are chargeable to the mortgagor under an HECM. The maximum origination fee is $6000. The amendments provide that the $6,000 cap is to be adjusted in future years in increments of $500 based on the increase in the Consumer Price Index, but only when the percentage increase in the index as applied to the maximum origination fee produces dollar increases that exceed $500. 12 U.S.C. § 1715z-20(r)(6).

The fundamental risk of a reverse mortgage for the borrower comes in assuming that the borrower will be able to remain in her home long enough to make the mortgage a good bargain. If she dies, sells, or moves away (whether voluntarily or because of necessity) shortly after the mortgage, her bargain may be costly. The bargain also may be costly for her if her home appreciates substantially in value following the mortgage.

e. Selling the Home (Tax Consequences)

i. General Rule of Gain Exclusion

If the older person decides to sell her home, an important consideration is the tax treatment of the proceeds. The tax code provides that, as a general rule, an individual may exclude up to $250,000 of gain from the sale of property if within the five years ending with the date of sale she has owned and used the property as her principal residence for periods aggregating at least two years. 26 U.S.C. § 121(a). Although the statute does not define "principal residence," IRS regulations and rulings indicate that eligible properties include not only traditional homes, but also properties such as house trailers, houseboats, and a house or apartment that a tenant is entitled to occupy as a stockholder in a cooperative housing corporation. 26 C.F.R. 1.121-1(b). The exclusion is generally unavailable if during the two-year period preceding the date of sale the taxpayer made any other sale to which the exclusion applied.

For example, Jane purchased her home in 2004 for $150,000. Thus, $150,000 is her "basis" in her home. She made no permanent improvements to the home that would cause an upward adjustment to her basis. She did not use the home for business or rental purposes that might have allowed her to claim depreciation that would have reduced her basis. (If Jane had purchased her home prior to May 7, 1997, under certain conditions her basis would have be adjusted downwards for any untaxed gain from the sale of a prior residence.) Jane lived in the home until 2009. In 2009, Jane sold the home for $350,000 without incurring any realtor or other fees (which would have reduced her amount realized). Thus, Jane has a gain of $200,000. Because the home was her permanent place of residence in which she resided for at least two of the five years preceding the sale, she is eligible for the exclusion. In this example, none of the gain is included in Jane's gross income.

In the case of married couples filing a joint return, the maximum exclusion is increased to $500,000. This larger exclusion is available if (1) within the five years ending with the date of sale, either or both spouses have owned and used the property as a principal residence for periods aggregating at least two years; and (2) neither is ineligible for the exclusion because, during the two-year period preceding the instant sale, he or she made another sale to which the exclusion applied. (Under a special rule enacted in 2007, beginning in 2008 a spouse also may exclude up to $500,000 if the sale occurs not more than two years after the date of death of the deceased spouse and the preceding requirements are otherwise satisfied at the time of the deceased spouse's death.)

For example, Jane and her husband Ken purchased their home in 2004 for $150,000 and sold it in 2009 for $640,000. They lived in the home the entire period and had no adjustments to their basis. In the sale, they incurred legal and realtor fees of $40,000 (thus reducing the ultimate amount they realized). If Jane and Ken file jointly, they can exclude their entire $450,000 of gain ($640,000 less 40,000 of fees less the $150,000 basis). This is true whether they own the home together or whether the home is titled solely in the name of one spouse.

In contrast, assume that Jane and her longtime committed partner, Karen, purchased the home in 2004 as joint tenants for $150,000 and sold it in 2009 for $640,000. They lived in the home the entire period and had no adjustments to their basis. In the sale, they incurred legal and realtor fees of $40,000 (thus reducing the ultimate amount they realized). Jane and Karen cannot file jointly, because their relationship is not recognized under federal law. Nonetheless, each co-owner can take advantage of the $250,000 exclusion. Karen and Jane each will realize gain of $225,000 (i.e., for each, $320,000 sales price less $20,000 fees less $75,000 basis). Thus, in this instance the entire gain will be excluded. If the home belonged solely to Jane, however, the entire gain of $450,000 would be attributable to Jane, and thus she would have $200,000 of taxable gain after applying the $250,000 exclusion.

The taxpayer who meets the applicable requirements may elect to apply the general rule of exclusion upon the sale of a remainder interest in a principal residence. 26 U.S.C. § 121(d)(8). An important exception, however, precludes the election if the sale is to certain parties bearing a relationship to the taxpayer as described in various code sections. Among others, these parties include the taxpayer's spouse, ancestors, lineal descendants, and siblings.

The Housing Assistance Tax Act of 2008 added a new restriction on the exclusion of gain. Under section 121(b)(4)(C)(ii)(I), the exclusion does not apply to so much of the gain from the sale or exchange as is allocated to periods of nonqualified use after December 31, 2008. A period of nonqualified use is a period in which the property has not yet become the principal residence of the taxpayer or the taxpayer's spouse or former spouse. Thus, if the taxpayer purchases a home on January 1, 2009, rents the home to others for three years, then lives in the home for two years before selling it, sixty percent (i.e., 3 years of nonqualified use divided by 5 years) of his gain is attributed to the nonqualified use (rental) and will not be excluded. (Some confusion exists in the numbering of the provision. Congress enacted two (b)(4) paragraphs. The nonqualified use provision was located in the second of them. It seems probable that Congress intended the nonqualified use provision to be numbered (b)(5).)

ii. Special Rule: Out-of-Residence Care

A special rule under 26 U.S.C. § 121(d)(7) counts the time certain taxpayers reside in a licensed facility (including a nursing home) in determining the aggregate period of use and ownership of the principal residence. The rule applies to a taxpayer who (1) becomes physically or mentally incapable of self-care and (2) owns and uses the property as her principal residence for periods aggregating at least one year of the five-year period preceding the sale. If she meets these requirements, then she is treated as using the home as her principal residence during any time in the applicable five-year period in which she resides in a facility that is licensed to care for an individual in her condition.

For example, Margaret purchases a home in 2009. Eighteen months later, she is incapable of self-care, and she enters a nursing home that is licensed to care for an individual in her condition. She sells her home after she has been in the nursing home for six months. Because Margaret met all of the requirements for the special rule to apply, her period of nursing home residence is added to her actual residence in her home. Thus, her period of use and ownership at the time of the sale is two years.

iii. Reduced Maximum Exclusion: Sale for Health Conditions

In some instances, a taxpayer is entitled to a reduced maximum exclusion when she does not satisfy all of the requirements to claim the full maximum exclusion. One instance in which a reduced maximum exclusion is available is when the sale is by reason of a change in health. 26 U.S.C. § 121(c)(2). A sale is considered to be by reason of a change in health if the primary reason for the sale "is to obtain, provide, or facilitate the diagnosis, cure, mitigation, or treatment of disease, illness, or injury" of a qualified individual "or to obtain or provide medical or personal care for a qualified individual suffering from a disease, illness, or injury." 26 C.F.R. 121-3(d)(1). A sale that merely permits the individual to enjoy enhanced general health or well-being does not qualify, however. As a safe harbor, the regulations provide that a sale based on a physician-recommended change of residence for health reasons does qualify.

To arrive at the reduced exclusion, the statute first examines two time priods: (1) the aggregate period during the five years preceding the sale in which the property was owned and used as the taxpayer's principal residence; and (2) the period after the date of the most recent prior sale by the taxpayer to which the general exclusion applied. The shorter of those time periods is then divided by two, producing the applicable factor for determining the amount of the reduced maximum exclusion.

For example, John purchased a home in 2009. Shortly thereafter, John's health began to deteriorate rapidly and significantly. One year after the purchase, John sold the home and moved across the country to live with his daughter. His doctor recommended the change of residence. Within the past two years, John did not have any gain on the sale of a prior home that he excluded. Because John did not use the home as his principal place of residence for two of the five years preceding the sale, but because he did move by reason of a change in health, he is permitted a reduced maximum exclusion. He lived in the home for one year of the two that were needed to claim the full $250,000 exclusion. Thus, he may exclude gain of up to $125,000 (i.e., 1 year/2 years x $250,000).

The statute also permits certain individuals to take advantage of the reduced maximum exclusion when they sell their homes to provide medical or personal care to the person suffering from the health condition. For example, Mary purchases a home in 2009. Her elderly father, who lives in another state, develops a chronic illness and requires substantial care. Mary sells her home one year later to move across the country to provide necessary care for her elderly father at his home. Mary may exclude gain of up to $125,000 (i.e., 1 year/2 years x $250,000).

f. Donating the Home

For various reasons, the elder may decide to give her home to a child, grandchild, or other person. Before making such a decision, however, the elder should carefully consider the pros and cons of such a choice. If she makes the gift in an effort to qualify for long-term care under Medicaid, her effort often will be thwarted by the Medicaid look-back rules. If she plans to make the gift simply as an act of love towards the donee, she should be well aware that an outright inter vivos gift, once made, is irrevocable in most circumstances. In making an outright gift of her home, she will be giving up legal dominion and control of the home (even if the donee allows her to live there). Moreover, the donee's creditors will be able to reach the home and force a sale. (Note that if she transfers the home in exchange for the transferee's agreement to care for her, the transfer is based, at least in part, on contract, not gift.)

For the individual of average wealth with a home of average value, the gift of the home will not typically produce significant tax consequences for her estate. If her home has appreciated significantly in value following the time she purchased it, however, in some settings her prospective transferee might be better served by obtaining the property at her death rather than through a lifetime gift. In the typical setting, a donee succeeds to the donor's adjusted basis in the donated property. (The basis is increased by the portion of any gift tax paid resulting from the appreciation in value of the gift compared to the amount of the gift. The basis may not exceed fair market value (FMV) of the property at the time of the gift). A devisee or heir, however, receives a basis that is equal to FMV of the property at the decedent's death. 26 U.S.C. §§ 1014, 1015. For example, assume that Alice purchased her home for $50,000. Because the neighborhood has become increasingly desirable, however, the home is now worth $400,000. If Alice gives the home to her son, he will succeed to Alice's basis of $50,000. In contrast, if Alice devises the home to her son (or if he receives it as her heir), his basis will be the FMV of the property at Alice's death. If market prices in the neighborhood remain constant, the latter result means that his basis will be $400,000. Thus, if the son ultimately sells the home, he will have a larger taxable gain as a donee than as a devisee or heir. Should he sell the house for $450,000, his gain will be $400,000 if he is a donee, but only $50,000 if he is a devisee or heir.

If the elder's property has declined in value, different considerations are likely to come into play. For example, once again assume that Alice purchased her home for $50,000. If the FMV of Alice's home is $40,000 at her death, her son as devisee or heir will receive a $40,000 basis in the home. (This is a so-called "stepped-down" basis, in contrast to the "stepped-up" basis that applies when the property has increased in value.) If Alice gives her son the home when it is worth $40,000, then his basis for determining gain will be Alice's basis ($50,000), but his basis for determining loss will be the FMV of the property ($40,000) when he received it. If the son as donee subsequently sells the home for $30,000, he will thus have a $10,000 loss. If he sells the home the home for an amount of at least $40,000 but not more than $50,000, he will be considered to have no gain or loss. If he sells the home for $60,000, he will have a $10,000 gain. 26 C.F.R. 1.1015-1(a)(1), (2).

For decedents who die during 2010, the basis of property acquired from a decedent will be the lesser of the decedent's adjusted basis or the FMV of the property at the decedent's death. 26 U.S.C. § 1022(a). This provision however, is among the estate and gift tax provisions that expire on January 1, 2011.

2. Rental Units

Even if she can afford to remain in her home and is physically and mentally able to do so, an elder may conclude at some point that she would prefer to rent. By moving to an apartment or other rental unit, the elder may reduce the costs and responsibilities associated with maintenance, insurance, and taxes. If the new residence is a traditional apartment or rental unit, however, the elder may later find that she will again have to move because the residence is not designed to allow an elder to age in place. Thus, in downsizing, the individual should not only consider a residence that currently meets her needs, but also consider her probable future needs if she wants to age in place at the new residence.

a. Government Assistance Programs

For the elderly poor, rental or other housing assistance may be available through subsidies from programs funded by the United States Department of Housing and Urban Development (HUD). Public housing is the most important federal housing assistance program for low-income elders. Public housing is not limited to mass apartment developments, but may include single family houses. There are thousands of public housing authorities (PHAs) in the United States to which HUD administers federal aid. The applicant for residency may experience a long waiting period at many PHAs, and a PHA may even decline to add new names to a long waiting list when the demand far exceeds available housing. Some public housing units or developments are built specifically for low-income elders. Many of those built in the 1960s and 1970s, however, are simply traditional apartments that are not designed to meet the needs of the elder who wishes to age in place. In recent years, some innovative PHAs have developed units that are designed with those needs in mind. Some of these developments also partner with others who provide supportive services for elderly residents.

The Section 202 Housing for the Elderly program provides funds to nonprofit organizations that construct and develop housing for seniors. The only federally funded program designed specifically to address the problem of housing for elders, the program has resulted in the construction of approximately a quarter of a million residential units for elders since 1959. The typical unit is a one-bedroom apartment with kitchen and bath that has features designed especially for the older resident. The vast majority of residents in such apartments are elderly females. Residents must be at least 62 and their incomes must not exceed 50 percent of the area's median income. Because of high demand and occupancy rates, often an individual seeking housing in a Section 202 facility faces a lengthy waiting period. Budget appropriations for the program are a constant concern, and grow more so as the population ages.

The Housing Choice Voucher program (part of the Section 8 program) is also important to many elders. The program permits an individual to apply the voucher towards the housing of her choice. The voucher amount is based on the fair market rental value as established by HUD for the locality.

b. Age Discrimination and Accommodations in Housing

The federal Fair Housing Act prevents housing discrimination in many contexts. The Act, however, generally excludes from coverage the sale or rental of a single family dwelling by an owner who does not own more than three such dwellings at one time, is not in the housing business, and does not use the services of a real estate broker or similar persons. The Act also generally excludes the rental of a unit by an owner in an owner-occupied dwelling intended for no more than four families. Even though such properties are generally excluded, the owner cannot engage in discriminatory advertisements under the Act.

Whether renting or purchasing, many elders would like to live in a housing community for elders. The Fair Housing Act, however, generally prohibits discrimination based on familial status in the sales or rentals of properties to which it applies. 42 U.S.C. § 3604. Congress added the familial status classification to prevent or at least deter discrimination against families with children. Nonetheless, the Act contains certain exemptions to the familial status provision that permit the existence of elderly housing communities. For example, the familial status provision does not apply to housing provided under a state or federal program that HUD determines to be designed and operated for the assistance of the elderly. 24 C.F.R. 100.302.

Housing is also exempt from the general strictures of the FHA's familial status rules if it is "62 or over" housing. Such housing is intended for and solely occupied by persons 62 or older. Housing will meet this requirement even if (1) there were persons residing there on September 13, 1988, who were under 62, as long as all subsequently-accepted occupants are at least 62; (2) there are unoccupied units, as long as the units are reserved for persons 62 or over; or (3) there are units occupied by housing employees (and their families residing in the same unit) who are under 62, as long as the employees perform substantial duties that relate to the management or maintenance of the housing. 24 C.F.R. 100.303. For example, John is sixty-seven and his wife Mary is sixty-one. They are both retired and seek to move into an elderly housing community that has a "62 or over" housing exemption. The housing community cannot rent to the couple if it seeks to retain its "62 or over" housing exemption, because Mary is only 61.

Housing is also exempt from the FHA familial status provision if it satisfies the "55 or over"/"80 percent" rule. Under the rule, at least eighty percent of occupied units must be occupied by at least one person 55 years of age or older. The regulations also contain detailed rules for interpreting the availability of the exemption. The housing will satisfy the "55 or over"/"80 percent" rule even if (1) on September 13, 1988, under eighty percent of the occupied units were occupied by at least one person 55 years old, provided that at least 80 percent of the units occupied by new occupants after that date are occupied by at least one person 55 years old; (2) there are unoccupied units, as long as at least eighty percent of the occupied units are occupied by at least one person fifty-five years of age or older; (3) there are units occupied by housing employees (and their families residing in the same unit) who are under 55, as long as the employees perform substantial duties that relate to the management or maintenance of the housing; or (4) there are units occupied by persons under 55 who are necessary to provide a reasonable accommodation to disabled residents. For new construction, the requirements do not have to be met until at least twenty-five percent of the units are occupied. To qualify as housing designed for those who are 55 or older, the housing facility or community must also publish and adhere to policies and procedures that show its intent to operate as housing for persons 55 and over. The housing facility or community must also be able to produce a verification of compliance through reliable surveys and affidavits. 24 C.F.R. 100.305.

The Fair Housing Act also contains provisions designed to prevent discrimination against individuals with a handicap. These protections are potentially important to many elders, who are increasingly likely to suffer a handicap or disability as they age. A handicap is a "physical or mental impairment which substantially limits one or more major life activities; a record of such an impairment; or being regarded as having such an impairment." 24 C.F.R. 100.201. Major life activities include caring for one's self, performing manual tasks, speaking, hearing, walking, seeing, breathing, learning, and working.

The person with a handicap must be permitted to make reasonable modifications of the existing dwelling if such modifications may be necessary to afford her the full enjoyment of the premises. With rental properties, the landlord may, when reasonable, condition his permission to the modification on the agreement of the renter to later restore the interior of the premises to its premodification condition, excepting reasonable wear and tear. For example, if a tenant with a handicap needs grab bars in the bathroom, a landlord cannot refuse to allow her to install them at her own expense. The landlord may require her to remove the grab bars at the end of her tenancy and restore the wall's exterior to its original condition. (The tenant would not have to remove any interior reinforcement of the wall that was necessitated by the installation of the grab bar, however, since the reinforcement would not be visible when the wall's exterior is repaired, and the reinforcement would not interfere with the landlord's or a subsequent tenant's use and enjoyment of the property.) Similarly, if a tenant uses a wheelchair, a landlord cannot refuse to allow her to widen doorways at her own expense so that her wheelchair can pass through. The federal regulations, however, indicate that the landlord generally could not condition his permission on restoration of the premises at the end of the lease under these circumstances, because the wider doorway will not interfere with future use and enjoyment of the premises. 24 C.F.R. 100.203.

The Act also makes it unlawful for any person to refuse to make reasonable accommodations in rules, policies, practices, or services, when the accommodations may be necessary to afford the person with a handicap equal opportunity to use and enjoy a dwelling unit. This provision extends not only to the dwelling unit itself, but also to the public and common use areas. For example, assume that an apartment building has a no-pets policy, but a blind applicant requires the use of a seeing eye dog. In this circumstance, the owner or manager must permit the dog to live in the apartment with the applicant. In another example provided by the regulations, an individual applies for an apartment in a large complex with a large parking lot. Parking is on a first-come, first-served basis. The applicant, however, is mobility impaired and cannot walk more than a short distance. He requests that a parking space be reserved for him near the unit where his apartment will be. The regulations indicate that the apartment owner or manager cannot refuse to make this accommodation. 24 C.F.R. 100.204.

Finally, the Act also imposes design and construction requirements that apply to covered multifamily dwellings constructed for first occupancy after March 13, 1991. Such buildings must have at least one entrance on an accessible route unless it is impractical to do so because of the terrain or unusual characteristics of the site. Such buildings must also be designed and constructed so that (1) public and common use areas are readily accessible to and usable by persons with a handicap; and (2) all the doors for passage into and within the premises are wide enough to permit passage by persons in wheelchairs. Moreover, all premises must contain (1) an accessible route into and through the covered dwelling unit; (2) light switches, electrical outlets, thermostats, and other environmental controls in accessible locations; (3) reinforcements in bathroom walls to allow later installation of grab bars around the toilet, tub, shower, stall, and shower seat, where such facilities are provided; and (4) usable kitchens and bathrooms so that an individual in a wheelchair can maneuver about the space. 24 C.F.R. 100.205.

C. Congregate Living

1. ALFs and CCRCs

An increasing number of elderly Americans are choosing congregate living in facilities, complexes, or settings that provide various services and amenities. These include assisted living facilities (ALFs) and continuing care retirement communities (CCRCs). Such facilities are governed primarily by state law and regulation, although the nursing home component of a CCRC is also subject to federal law and regulation. In an increasing number of states, a Medicaid home- and community-based services waiver permits the state to offer Medicaid coverage for certain services in an assisted living facility.

There is no universally-accepted definition or description of an ALF. Most often, however, an ALF provides each of its residents a separate, private occupancy unit as well as certain amenities and services such as medication reminders, laundry service, shared dining facilities, and assistance with the activities of daily living (particularly bathing and dressing) and other personal care. The facility may provide some health services. The facility may also provide recreational and social activities and transportation to medical appointments or local activities. State licensure requirements vary. Each year the National Center for Assisted Living publishes a state-by-state overview of assisted living facility regulations. It is available at www.ncal.org/about/state review.cfm.

The cost of residing at an ALF depends upon many various factors, including its location, the amenities and services it provides, the quality and training and number of staff, and its general desirability. The resident typically must pay an entrance fee plus a monthly service fee. Those who can afford assisted living may find that it is a good option that will allow them to age in place once they have established their home there.

A newer, more expensive and more comprehensive alternative is a continuing care retirement community (CCRC). CCRCs provide a full range of housing options in one location, thus helping to ensure that the resident can spend the rest of her life in one place. The CCRC provides facilities or units designed for those who are still able to live independently, for those who need assistance, and for those who require nursing home care. For example, Ann, an elder who is still able to live independently, enters into a contract to reside at a CCRC. She will live in a CCRC cottage, apartment, or other dwelling until she requires assistance. When she requires such assistance, she may be able to remain in place or, depending upon the terms of her contract, she may move to another unit designed specifically as an assisted living facility. If at some point she requires nursing home care, the CCRC contract will probably require that she move to the facility's nursing home. The CCRC resident must pay both an entrance fee and a monthly service fee.

CCRC entrance contracts are generally classified as one of three kinds: (1) the extensive or "life care" agreement, which is characterized by a substantial entry fee that will entitle the resident to lifetime health care without a substantial increase in her monthly service fee; (2) the modified agreement, which imposes a smaller entry fee and provides the resident with only a certain number of days of care each year, requiring the resident to pay for further care when it is needed and thus increasing her monthly service fee; and (3) the fee-for-service agreement, which typically imposes the smallest entry fee, but requires the resident to pay all costs of health care out-of-pocket.

The terms of a CCRC contract can vary significantly from one CCRC to the next. For example, a CCRC may make some part of the entry fee refundable on a sliding scale over a stated time period, after which no refund is available. A CCRC may also require residents to have long-term care insurance. A prospective resident should particularly note the contract terms relating to the monthly payment for services and health care. What services and health care are covered, and how are increases in monthly fees determined? A CCRC may provide a guarantee that the resident will be able to age in place on its campus, but the prospective resident should make sure that the CCRC is a place where she will want to spend the rest of her life and that she can afford the potentially high costs of living there.

A majority of states now have laws regulating CCRC business operations. The independent living and assisted living components of CCRCs are generally not governed by federal law or regulation. A CCRC nursing home, however, must comply with federal laws and regulations.

2. Board and Care Homes

Like assisted living facilities, board and care homes may allow the elder to have her needs met in a "homelike" setting. The differences and distinctions between board and care homes and ALFS are sometimes difficult to make. Some commentators consider board and care homes to be a form of assisted living, and indeed a state may subject board and care homes to the same rules and regulations it applies to an ALF. States may employ various names for board and care homes.

Board and care homes existed long before the advent of the formal ALF. Compared to an entity formally designated as an ALF, board and care homes are usually much less expensive. Residents at a board and care home tend to be less wealthy than residents of a facility designated as an ALF.

Depending upon the board and care home and the training of its staff, the board and care home may provide many of the same services available at an ALF. Residents of a board and care home frequently require assistance with the activities of daily living. Staff at the board and care home may also ensure that residents take their prescribed medications at the proper time and in the proper amounts. A board and care home usually does not provide skilled nursing care (and is not licensed to provide such care), and thus costs of the home are seldom covered by Medicare or Medicaid.

Along with the many thousands of licensed board and care homes in the United States are many thousands of unlicensed, "mom and pop" operations. While the size of licensed board and care homes may vary considerably, unlicensed board and care homes typically have no more than four to six residents at one time.

Some observers have expressed concern that board and care homes whose residents are the elderly poor (such as those living on Supplemental Security Income) often provide a questionable quality of care to those residents. Generalizations are dangerous, however. Board and care homes that cater to wealthier residents are likely to charge more and may have a higher-paid staff; even so, the income of residents is no guarantee of the quality of care at a board and care home. Certainly, the substantial differences in the quality of care across the spectrum of board and care homes should cause some wariness among would-be residents. One considering residence at such a home should proceed with caution. Elders with no family or friends in the community to visit, assist, or protect them once they move in may be at increased risk for neglect or abuse.

A person considering a board and care home for herself or her loved one should check its history with the agency (if any) that issues a license for the home, carefully inspect the home, make unannounced visits on several occasions at different times, and ask current and former residents and their families about the home.

3. Nursing Homes

a. Generally

The typical elder values her autonomy. She does not want to spend her final days, months, or years in a nursing home. As a nursing home resident, she may have to sacrifice privacy and freedom under rules that require her to share a room with a stranger, to eat meals on a schedule from a menu not of her choosing, and to restrict her behavior and lifestyle to meet nursing home policy. Yet many individuals ultimately have no choice but to become nursing home residents. This final section of the chapter focuses on nursing home regulation and the long-term nursing home resident, for whom the facility becomes home.

Some nursing home residents are private pay residents, while others rely on Medicaid to pay for their long-term nursing home stay. Federal Medicaid requirements have had a profound effect on the operations of most nursing homes throughout the country, and many of these requirements are discussed in the following pages. (In contrast, Medicare is not examined in detail in the following discussion. Although Medicare requirements apply to most nursing homes, the Medicare program is generally not designed to cover long-term nursing home care. Instead, Medicare most frequently covers a patient's relatively short stay in a nursing home during which she receives rehabilitative or skilled nursing care and then returns home. See Chapter 8.)

The more complex the patient's long-term condition, the more likely it is that she will require a nursing home stay. Long-term nursing home care is a practical necessity for some individuals. Assisted living facilities and board and care homes do not provide the comprehensive medical, rehabilitative, and round-the-clock services that nursing homes provide. Undoubtedly, efficiency is often a factor in determining a patient's need for nursing home care. If a patient's condition requires that she be seen by doctors, nurses, therapists, and other professionals on a regular basis, often she will be unable to bring them to her home or unable to visit them at their individual offices. Even long-term care insurance policies with provisions for home care will often be insufficient to meet all of a patient's needs at her home if those needs are substantial and continuous. As a nursing home resident, however, she will have easy access in one location to a variety of health care and elder care professionals who are employed by or affiliated with the nursing home.

Most nursing homes exist independently. Some exist as part of a continuing care retirement community, however, and hospitals may also have nursing home facilities within their premises. At the end of the twentieth century, the average stay of then-current nursing home residents was about 2.4 years; the average stay for a discharged patient was about eight months. According to the National Clearinghouse for Long-Term Care Information, twenty-seven percent of residents stay in a nursing home less than three months. Twenty percent stay three months to one year. Thirty-four percent stay one year to five years, and nineteen percent stay more than five years. See http://www.longtermcare.gov/LTC/Main_Site/ Understanding_Long_Term_Care/Services/Services.aspx.

b. Nursing Home Costs and Comparisons

For an individual with extensive needs, the cost of providing nursing home care can be less than the cost of providing comparable care at home. Nonetheless, nursing home rates are not cheap. The cost of a particular nursing home will depend in large part upon its location, staff, facilities, whether it participates in Medicare and Medicaid, and the services it provides. Various estimates of average annual nursing home costs indicated that the cost of a semi-private room in 2008 was around $70,000. A private room cost around $80,000 annually. By contrast, the average annual cost in 2008 for a resident in an assisted living facility was around $39,000. A 2008 report indicated that rates for private room nursing home patients in Alaska and in New York City run substantially more than $150,000 annually; Louisiana was the only state with a private room annual cost of less than $50,000. (The report is available at http://www.prudential. com/media/managed/LTCCostStudy.pdf.)

Those interested in locating and comparing nursing homes may find the federal government's "Nursing Home Compare" tool helpful. The tool is located at the Medicare website, www.medicare.gov. The tool provides an overall rating for each nursing home, as well as information concerning health inspections, nursing home staffing, quality measures, whether the home participates in Medicare and Medicaid, the number of certified beds, and the type of ownership. The vast majority of nursing homes participate in Medicare or Medicaid, or both, by obtaining the proper certification.

Despite the helpfulness of online information concerning nursing homes, no one should select a nursing home without first visiting it and making her own investigation.

c. Federal Laws and Regulations

The Nursing Home Reform Act (NHRA) was enacted as part of the Omnibus Budget Reconciliation Act of 1987 (OBRA 87). Principal goals of the NHRA were to improve and ensure the quality of nursing home care and to recognize and protect the rights of a nursing home resident. The applicable statutes and their requirements are found at 42 U.S.C. § 1395i-3 (Medicare) and 42 U.S.C. § 1396r (Medicaid). Regulations begin at 42 C.F.R. 483.1. The Medicare statute applies to skilled nursing facilities (SNFs), which are those primarily designed to provide skilled nursing care and related services or rehabilitation services. The Medicaid statute applies to nursing facilities (NFs), which include those primarily engaged in providing (1) skilled nursing care and related services, (2) rehabilitation services, or, (3) "on a regular basis, health-related care and services to individuals who ... require care and services (above the level of room and board) which can be made available to them only through institutional facilities." The quoted clause from the statute refers to general nursing home care, which is so important to many elderly residents. By statute, the SNF or NF is not one primarily engaged in the care and treatment of mental diseases.

If a facility is Medicare- or Medicaid-certified, the statutory and regulatory requirements generally apply to benefit all patients or residents. Thus, if Jane is a resident at a certified nursing home whose long-term care costs are paid by Medicaid and Karl is a resident there whose long-term care costs are paid from his own assets or from his long-term care insurance, Karl will generally receive the same protections and benefits that Jane receives. Because Medicaid is the principal governmental program providing long-term nursing home care, the following discussion analyzes the statutory requirements of 42 U.S.C. § 1396r.

i. Requirements for the Provision of Services

(a) Quality of Life

The statutory requirements relating to the provision of services begin with this mandate: "A nursing home must care for its residents in such a manner and in such an environment as will promote maintenance or enhancement of the quality of life of each resident." 42 U.S.C. § 1396r(b)(1)(A).

Each nursing facility must maintain a quality assessment and assurance committee. Committee members include the director of nursing services, a physician designated by the facility, and at least three other members of the facility's staff. The committee must meet at least quarterly to identify quality assessment and assurance issues and to develop and implement plans of action to correct quality deficiencies.

(b) Scope of Services and Activities under Plan of Care

The statute further requires that a nursing facility provide services and activities to attain or maintain the highest practicable physical, mental, and psychosocial well-being of each resident in accordance with a written plan of care. The plan of care must describe the medical, nursing, and psychosocial needs of the resident and how such needs will be met. The plan is initially prepared by a team that includes the resident's attending physician and a registered professional nurse with responsibility for the resident. To the extent practicable, the resident, her family, or her legal representative is also to participate. The plan of care must be periodically reviewed and revised by the team after each assessment (described in the next section) mandated by the statute.

(c) Resident Assessment

The nursing facility must conduct a comprehensive, accurate, standardized, reproducible assessment of each resident's functional capacity. The assessment describes the resident's capability to perform daily life functions, denotes significant impairments in her functional capacity, and includes the identification of medical problems. The assessment is based on a uniform minimum data set established on the federal level and uses an instrument that is specified by the state. The assessment is conducted or coordinated by a registered professional nurse who must sign and certify the completion of the assessment. Monetary penalties may be imposed upon anyone who willfully and knowingly certifies a material and false statement in such an assessment, or who willfully and knowingly causes another to make such a certification. Also, the state may require independent assessors to assess the residents if it determines that there has been a knowing and willful certification of false assessments.

The facility must conduct the initial assessment no later than fourteen days after the date of the resident's admission to the facility. (To avoid duplicative testing and effort, the facility is to coordinate the assessment with any state-required preadmission screening program.) The facility must conduct an additional assessment at least once every twelve months. Also, the facility must conduct an assessment promptly if there is a significant change in the resident's physical or mental condition. Finally, the facility must examine the resident no less than once every three months and, if appropriate, revise the resident's assessment to assure its continuing accuracy.

(d) Provision of Services and Activities

To fulfill the residents' plans of care, the nursing facility must provide (or arrange for the provision of) (1) nursing and related services and specialized rehabilitative services to attain or maintain the highest practicable physical, mental, and psychosocial well-being of each resident; (2) medically-related social services to attain or maintain the highest practicable physical, mental, and psychosocial well-being of each resident; (3) pharmaceutical services (including procedures that assure the accurate acquiring, receiving, dispensing, and administering of all drugs and biologicals) to meet the needs of each resident; (4) dietary services that assure that the meals meet the daily nutritional and special dietary needs of each resident; (5) an on-going program, directed by a qualified professional, of activities designed to meet the interests and the physical, mental, and psychosocial well-being of each resident; (6) routine dental services (to the extent covered under the state plan) and emergency dental services to meet the needs of each resident; and (7) treatment and services required by mentally ill and mentally retarded residents not otherwise provided or arranged for (or required to be provided or arranged for) by the state. The services provided or arranged by the facility must meet professional standards of quality. 42 U.S.C. § 1396r(b)(4)(A).

A nursing facility must provide licensed nursing services that are sufficient to meet the nursing needs of its residents. The facility must provide such services twenty-four hours a day. Further, the facility must use the services of a registered professional nurse for at least eight consecutive hours a day, seven days a week. A waiver from these general requirements is available in limited circumstances. For the nursing facility to obtain such a waiver, the facility must demonstrate its efforts to comply with the general requirements. Also, the state must determine that, among other things, a waiver will not endanger the health or safety of individuals staying in the facility.

(e) Required Training of Nurse Aides

Nurse aides perform a great amount of the day-to-day work at nursing homes. A nurse aide is any individual providing nursing or nursing-related services to residents in a nursing facility but who is not a volunteer, a registered dietician, or licensed health professional. (A licensed health professional is a physician, physician assistant, nurse practitioner, physical, speech, or occupational therapist, physical or occupational therapy assistant, registered professional nurse, licensed practical nurse, or licensed or certified social worker.) The statute generally provides that a nursing facility must not use a nurse aide on a full-time basis for more than four months unless the aide (1) has completed a training and competency evaluation program, or a competency evaluation program, approved by the state and (2) is competent to provide nursing or nursing-related services. 42 U.S.C. § 1396r(b)(5)(A).

The facility must not permit an individual to serve as a nurse aide or provide services for which the individual has not demonstrated competency. Also, the facility must not use such an individual as a nurse aide unless the facility has inquired of any state nurse aide registry that the facility believes will include information concerning the individual. Such a registry generally contains information indicating that the aide has successfully completed a nurse aide training and competency evaluation program or a competency evaluation program approved by the state. The registry also includes documented findings of neglect or abuse or misappropriation of resident property involving an individual listed in the registry.

If a nurse aide who has completed a training and competency evaluation program goes for two years without performing nursing or nursing-related services for monetary compensation, the aide must complete a new training and competency evaluation program or a new competency evaluation program.

The nursing facility must provide regular performance review and regular in-service education to assure that individuals used as nurse aides are competent to perform services as nurse aides. The facility's responsibility includes training for individuals providing nursing and nursing-related services to residents with cognitive impairments.

(f) Physician Supervision and Clinical Records

By statute, the nursing facility must generally require that the health care of every resident be provided under the supervision of a physician. Alternatively, at the option of a state, the nursing facility must require that each resident's health care be provided under the supervision of a nurse practitioner, clinical nurse specialist, or physician assistant who is not an employee of the facility but who is working in collaboration with a physician. Each facility must ensure that a physician is available to furnish necessary medical care in case of emergency.

Each facility must also maintain clinical records on all residents. These records include a resident's plan of care and a resident's assessment, as well as the results of any pre-admission screening.

(g) Required Social Services

If the nursing facility has more than 120 beds, it must have at least one social worker (with at least a bachelor's degree in social work or similar professional qualifications) employed full-time to provide or assure the provision of social services.

(h) Information on Nurse Staffing

A nursing facility must post daily (for each shift) the current number of licensed and unlicensed nursing staff directly responsible for resident care in the facility. The facility must display the information in a uniform manner and in a clearly visible place. A nursing facility must, upon request, make this information available to the public.

ii. Requirements Relating to Residents' Rights

The statute provides residents with a detailed "bill of rights." These include general rights, transfer and discharge rights, access and visitation rights, the right to equal access to quality care, rights relating to admissions policies, rights protecting resident funds, and charge limitations for Medicaid-eligible individuals. 42 U.S.C. § 1396r(c). The rights are elaborated upon in the regulations, beginning at 42 C.F.R. 483.10.

(a) General Rights

(1) Specified Rights

The statute requires a nursing facility to protect and promote the rights of each resident, including several that are specified in the statute.

The resident has the right to choose a personal attending physician, to be fully informed in advance about care and treatment, to be fully informed in advance of any changes in care or treatment that may affect the resident's well-being, and (except with respect to a resident adjudged incompetent) to participate in planning care and treatment or changes in care and treatment.

The resident also has the right to be free from physical or mental abuse, corporal punishment, involuntary seclusion, and any physical or chemical restraints imposed for purposes of discipline or convenience and not required to treat the resident's medical symptoms. The facility may impose restraints to ensure the physical safety of the resident or other residents, but only upon the written order of a physician that specifies the duration and circumstances under which the restraints are to be used. An exception allows the facility to impose restraints in emergency settings until it can obtain such an order.

The resident has a right to privacy with regard to accommodations, medical treatment, written and telephonic communications, visits, and meetings of family and of resident groups. The statute specifically notes, however, that the right to privacy does not require the facility to provide the resident with a private room. The resident has a right to confidentiality of personal and clinical records. The resident (or her legal representative) also has a right of access to her current clinical records within twenty-four hours after making a request. The twenty-four hour period excludes hours that occur during a weekend or holiday.

The resident has the right to receive services with reasonable accommodation of individual needs and preferences, except where the health or safety of the individual or other residents would be endangered. This right includes the right to receive notice before the room or roommate of the resident in the facility is changed. The resident also has the right to voice grievances with respect to treatment or care that is (or fails to be) furnished, without discrimination or reprisal for voicing the grievances. Moreover, the resident has the right to prompt efforts by the facility to resolve grievances the resident may have, including those with respect to the behavior of other residents.

The resident has the right to organize and participate in resident groups in the facility. (Also, the resident's family has the right to meet in the facility with the families of other residents in the facility.) The resident has the right to participate in social, religious, and community activities, as long as they do not interfere with the rights of other residents in the facility. The resident also has the right to examine, upon reasonable request, the results of the most recent survey of the facility conducted by the federal government or by the state with respect to the facility and any plan of correction in effect with respect to the facility.

The resident has the right to refuse a transfer to another room within the institution if the purpose of the transfer is (1) to relocate the resident of a skilled nursing facility (SNF) from the distinct part of the institution that is an SNF to a part of the institution that is not an SNF, or (2) to relocate the resident of a nursing facility (NF) from the distinct part of the institution that is an NF to a distinct part of the institution that is an SNF. The resident's exercise of his right to refuse a transfer under these provisions does not affect his eligibility or entitlement to Medicare or Medicaid benefits. 42 C.F.R. 483.10(o).

The list of specified rights also provides that the resident will have any other rights established by the Secretary of Health and Human Services.

(2) Notice of Rights

To ensure that the resident is aware of her rights, a nursing facility must inform each resident, orally and in writing at the time of admission to the facility, of her legal rights during the stay at the facility. The written description of legal rights must include a statement regarding the protection of residents' personal funds. It must also indicate that a resident may file a complaint with a state survey and certification agency concerning resident abuse and neglect and misappropriation of resident property in the facility.

The facility must inform the resident of the requirements and procedures for establishing eligibility for Medicaid. For each resident who is entitled to Medicaid, the facility must inform the resident of the items and services that are included in nursing facility services for which the resident may not be charged. It must also inform her of those items and services that the facility offers and for which the resident may be charged and inform her of the amount of the charges for such items and services. The facility must provide this information at the time the Medicaid-eligible individual is admitted to the facility or when a current resident becomes Medicaid eligible.

The regulations provide a detailed list of services included in Medicare or Medicaid payment for which a facility may not charge a resident. Among those services are required nursing and dietary services, required activities programs, and room/bed maintenance services. The facility also may not charge for routine personal hygiene items and services that are required to meet the needs of residents, including, but not limited to, the following: hair hygiene supplies, comb, brush, bath soap, disinfecting soaps or specialized cleansing agents when indicated to treat special skin problems or to fight infection, razor, shaving cream, toothbrush, toothpaste, denture adhesive, denture cleaner, dental floss, moisturizing lotion, tissues, cotton balls, cotton swabs, deodorant, incontinence care and supplies, sanitary napkins and related supplies, towels, washcloths, hospital gowns, over the counter drugs, hair and nail hygiene services, bathing, and basic personal laundry. The facility also may not charge for medically-related social services the resident requires.

The facility may charge the resident for many items, however, as long as the items are requested by the resident, the facility informs the resident that there will be a charge, and no payment is made by Medicare or Medicaid. Among such items are the following: a telephone, a television/radio for personal use, and personal comfort items (including smoking materials, notions and novelties, and confections). The facility may also charge for cosmetic and grooming items and services in excess of those for which Medicaid or Medicare will pay, personal clothing, personal reading matter, gifts purchased on behalf of a resident, flowers and plants, social events and entertainment offered outside the scope of the activities program, and noncovered special care services such as privately hired nurses or aides. The facility may also charge for a private room, except when it is therapeutically required (e.g., when isolation is necessary for infection control at the facility). Charges may also apply for specially prepared or alternative food requested by the resident in substitution for the food generally prepared by the facility.

The facility cannot charge a resident for an item or service that the resident does not request. Moreover, the facility cannot require a resident to request any item or service as a condition of admission or continued stay. If the resident (or the resident's representative) requests an item or service for which a charge will be made, the facility must inform the resident (or the representative) that there will be a charge for the item or service and must indicate what the charge will be.

(3) Rights of Incompetent Patients

If a resident has been adjudicated incompetent under state law, her rights generally devolve upon her representative as appointed or designated under state law to act on her behalf.

(4) Use of Psychopharmacologic Drugs

The statute limits the use of psychopharmacologic drugs. The facility can administer such drugs (1) only on the orders of a physician; (2) only as part of a plan designed to eliminate or modify the symptoms for which the drugs are prescribed; and (3) only if, at least annually, an independent, external consultant reviews the appropriateness of the drug plan of each resident receiving such drugs.

(b) Transfer and Discharge Rights

In general, a facility may not transfer or discharge the resident from the facility except in one of the following six circumstances: (1) the transfer or discharge is necessary to meet the resident's welfare and the resident's welfare cannot be met in the facility; (2) the transfer or discharge is appropriate because the resident's health has improved sufficiently so that the resident no longer needs the services provided by the facility; (3) the safety of individuals in the facility is endangered; (4) the health of individuals in the facility would otherwise be endangered; (5) the resident has failed, after reasonable and appropriate notice, to pay (or to have paid on the resident's behalf) for a stay at the facility; or (6) the facility ceases to operate.

Before transferring or discharging a resident, the nursing facility must notify the resident (and, if known, an immediate family member of the resident or her legal representative) of the transfer or discharge and the reasons underlying it. The facility must also record the reasons in the resident's clinical record. Generally, the facility must give the notice at least thirty days in advance of the resident's transfer or discharge. An exception applies if one of the circumstances listed in (1) through (4) of the preceding paragraph applies, or when the resident has not resided in the facility for thirty days. In the case of an exception, the facility must provide notice as many days before the date of the transfer or discharge as is practicable.

Each notice must indicate the resident's right to appeal the transfer or discharge under state law. It must also include the name, mailing address, and telephone number of the state long-term care ombudsman. If the resident has a developmental disability, the notice must include the mailing address and telephone number of the agency responsible for the protection and advocacy system for developmentally disabled individuals. In the case of mentally ill residents, the notice must include the mailing address and telephone number of the agency responsible for the protection and advocacy system for mentally ill individuals.

The facility must provide sufficient preparation and orientation to residents to ensure safe and orderly transfer or discharge from the facility. Before a resident is transferred for hospitalization or therapeutic leave, the facility must provide written information to the resident and an immediate family member or legal representative concerning provisions under the state plan regarding the period (if any) during which the resident will be permitted to return and resume residence in the facility, and the policies of the facility regarding such a period. At the time of the transfer of a resident to a hospital or for therapeutic leave, the facility must provide written notice to the resident and an immediate family member or legal representative of the duration of any such period. The facility must also establish and follow a written policy for readmission, if needed, on a first-available bed basis for (1) Medicaid-eligible residents (2) who are transferred from the facility for hospitalization or therapeutic leave and (3) whose leave exceeds a period paid for under the state plan for the hold-ing of a bed for the resident at the facility.

If a facility voluntarily withdraws from Medicaid participation but contin-ues to provide services of the type provided by nursing facilities, the with-drawal is not an acceptable basis for the transfer or discharge of residents of the facility who were residing in the facility on the day before the effective date of the withdrawal (including those residents who were not entitled to medical as-sistance as of such day). Instead, the provisions of 42 U.S.C. § 1396r continue to apply to such residents. The facility must provide new residents with oral and written notice that the facility is no longer participating in Medicaid and obtain an acknowledgment of their receipt of such information.

(c) Advance Directives

At the time a resident is admitted, the nursing home must provide written in-formation to the resident concerning her right under state law to make decisions concerning medical care, including the right to accept or refuse medical or sur-gical treatment and the right to formulate advance directives. The facility must also provide the resident with its written policies respecting the implementation of such rights and must document in the resident's record whether or not she has executed an advance directive. A facility may not condition the provision of care on an individual's decision to execute or refrain from executing an advance directive. A facility also may not otherwise discriminate against an individual be-cause of her decision to execute or refrain from executing an advance directive.

(d) Access and Visitation Rights

A nursing facility must permit immediate access to any resident by any rep-resentative of the Secretary of Health and Human Services, by any represen-tative of the state, by an ombudsman (or by certain agencies in the case of a resident who is mentally ill or has developmental disabilities), or by the resi-dent's individual physician. The facility must generally permit immediate ac-cess to a resident by immediate family or other relatives of the resident; however, the access is subject to the resident's right to deny or withdraw consent at any time. Subject to reasonable restrictions and the resident's right to deny or with-draw consent at any time, the facility must permit immediate access to a res-ident by others who are visiting with the consent of the resident. The facility also must permit reasonable access to a resident by any entity or individual that provides health, social, legal, or other services to the resident, subject to the resident's right to deny or withdraw consent at any time. Finally, the facility must permit representatives of the state ombudsman, with the permission of the resident (or the resident's legal representative) and consistent with state law, to examine a resident's clinical records.

(e) Equal Access to Quality Care

A nursing facility must establish and maintain identical policies and practices regarding transfer, discharge, and the provision of services required under the state plan for all individuals regardless of source of payment.

(f) Admissions Policy

In its admissions practices, a nursing facility cannot require individuals applying to reside or residing in the facility to waive their rights to benefits under Medicaid or Medicare. The facility cannot require the individual to provide oral or written assurance that she is not eligible for, or will not apply for, benefits under Medicaid or Medicare. (An exception applies to this last prohibition if the facility is part of a state licensed, registered, certified, or equivalent continuing care retirement community.)

The facility must prominently display written information and must provide oral and written information on how to apply for and use Medicaid and Medicare benefits. It must also provide information on how to receive refunds for previous payments covered by such benefits. The facility may not require a third party guarantee of payment to the facility as a condition of admission (or expedited admission) to, or continued stay in, the facility. This prohibition, however, does not prevent a facility from requiring an individual with legal access to a resident's income or resources to sign a contract (without incurring personal financial liability) to provide payment from the resident's income or resources for such care.

For an individual who is entitled to Medicaid for nursing facility services, the facility may not charge, solicit, accept, or receive any gift, money, donation, or other consideration as a precondition of admitting (or expediting the admission of) the individual to the facility or as a requirement for the individual's continued stay in the facility other than the amount required to be paid under the state plan. This prohibition, however, does not prevent a nursing facility from soliciting, accepting, or receiving a charitable, religious, or philanthropic contribution from an organization or from a person unrelated to the resident (or potential resident), as long as the contribution is not a condition of admission, expediting admission, or continued stay in the facility. Also, the prohibition does not prevent a facility from charging a Medicaid-eligible resident for items or services the resident has requested and received that are not specified in the state plan as included in the term "nursing facility services."

The federal statute does not preempt stricter state or local laws concerning admissions practices of nursing facilities that are designed to prohibit discrimination against individuals who are entitled to Medicaid under the state plan.

(g) Protection of Resident Funds

Upon the written authorization of the resident, a nursing facility must hold, safeguard, and account for the resident's personal funds under a system established and maintained by the facility. The facility, however, may not require residents to deposit their personal funds with the facility.

Upon written authorization of a resident, the facility must manage and account for the personal funds of the resident deposited with the facility. The facility must deposit any amount of a resident's personal funds in excess of $50 in an interest bearing account (or accounts) separate from any of the facility's operating accounts. The facility must credit all interest earned on the separate account to that account. The facility must maintain any other personal funds in a non-interest bearing account or petty cash fund. The facility must also assure a full and complete separate accounting of each resident's personal funds, maintain a written record of all financial transactions involving those personal funds deposited with the facility, and afford the resident (or a legal representative of the resident) reasonable access to that record.

The facility must notify each resident receiving Medicaid under the state plan when the amount in the resident's account reaches $200 less than the applicable Medicaid resource limit. The facility must also inform the resident that if the amount in the account (in addition to the value of the resident's other nonexempt resources) reaches that amount, the resident may lose eligibility for Medicaid or for Supplemental Security Income. When a resident dies, the facility must convey promptly the resident's personal funds (along with a final accounting of such funds) to the individual administering the resident's estate.

The facility must purchase a surety bond or otherwise provide satisfactory assurance to cover the security of all personal funds of residents deposited with the facility. The facility may not impose a charge against the personal funds of a resident for any item or service for which payment is made under Medicaid or Medicare.

(h) Limitation on Charges for Medicaid-Eligible Individuals

For certain Medicaid-eligible individuals, a nursing facility may not impose charges for nursing facility services covered under the state plan that exceed the payment amounts established by the state for such services. The term "certain Medicaid-eligible individual" means an individual who is entitled to Medicaid for nursing facility services in the facility but for whom such benefits are not being paid because, in determining the amount of the individual's income to be applied monthly to payment for the costs of such services, the amount of such income exceeds the payment amounts established by the state for such services. 42 U.S.C. § 1396r(c)(7).

(i) Posting of Survey Results

A nursing facility must post the results of the most recent survey of the facility conducted pursuant to 42 U.S.C. § 1396r(g). The posting must be in a place readily accessible to residents and family members and legal representatives of residents.

iii. Requirements Relating to Administration and Other Matters

The statute generally requires that a nursing facility be administered in a manner that enables it to use its resources effectively and efficiently to attain or maintain the highest practicable physical, mental, and psychosocial well-being of each resident. The facility must provide notice to the appropriate state licensing agency if a change occurs in (1) the persons with an ownership or control interest; (2) the persons who are officers, directors, agents, or managing employees; (3) the corporation, association, or other company responsible for the management of the facility; or (4) the individual who is the administrator or director of nursing of the facility.

A nursing facility must be licensed under applicable state and local law, and the administrator of a nursing facility must meet federal standards. A facility generally must meet provisions of the Life Safety Code of the National Fire Protection Association applicable to nursing homes unless the facility obtains a waiver or unless there is a fire and safety code imposed by state law that adequately protects residents of and personnel in nursing facilities.

A nursing facility must establish and maintain an infection control program designed to provide a safe, sanitary, and comfortable environment in which residents reside and to help prevent the development and transmission of disease and infection. The facility must be designed, constructed, equipped, and maintained in a manner to protect the health and safety of residents, personnel, and the general public.

The facility must operate and provide services in compliance with all applicable federal, state, and local laws and regulations and with accepted pro-

fessional standards and principles that apply to professionals providing services in such a facility.

iv. State Responsibilities Relating to Nursing Facility Requirements

As a condition of approval for its Medicaid plan, a state must provide for specification and review of nurse aide training and competency evaluation programs
and of nurse aide competency evaluation programs. The state also must establish
and maintain a registry of all individuals who have satisfactorily completed the nurse
aide training and competency evaluation program. The registry must provide for
the inclusion of specific documented findings by the state of resident neglect or
abuse or misappropriation of resident property involving an individual listed in
the registry, as well as any brief statement of the individual disputing the findings.
The state must make information in the registry available to the public.

For transfers and discharges from nursing facilities, the state must provide
for a fair mechanism for hearing appeals. For nursing facility administrators,
the state must implement and enforce nursing facility administrator standards.
The state also must specify the resident assessment instrument to be used by
nursing facilities. As a condition of approval for its Medicaid plan, each state
must develop (and periodically update) a written notice of the rights and obligations of residents of nursing facilities (and spouses of such residents).

A state must have in effect a preadmission screening program for making determinations for mentally ill and mentally retarded individuals. The state also
must have special "resident review" requirements for mentally ill or mentally
retarded residents.

Each state is required to maintain procedures and adequate staff (1) to investigate complaints of violations of requirements by nursing facilities and (2)
to monitor, on-site, on a regular, as needed basis, a nursing facility when there
has been a failure to comply with the statute or when compliance is in question.

v. Federal Responsibilities Relating to Nursing Facility Requirements

By statute, the Secretary of HHS must ensure that requirements governing
the provision of care in nursing facilities under approved state plans are adequate to protect the health, safety, welfare, and rights of residents and to promote the effective and efficient use of public moneys. The Secretary also
establishes requirements for the approval of nurse aide training and competency
evaluation programs, including requirements relating to (1) the areas to be
covered in such a program (including at least basic nursing skills, personal care

skills, recognition of mental health and social service needs, care of cognitively impaired residents, basic restorative services, and residents' rights) and the content of the curriculum; (2) minimum hours of initial and ongoing training and retraining (including not less than 75 hours in the case of initial training); (3) qualifications of instructors; and (4) procedures for determination of competency. The Secretary also establishes requirements concerning the minimum frequency and methodology to be used by a state in reviewing its program compliance.

The Secretary establishes guidelines for minimum standards that state appeals processes must meet to provide a fair mechanism for hearing appeals on transfers and discharges of residents from nursing facilities. The Secretary also develops standards to be applied in assuring the qualifications of administrators of nursing facilities. The Secretary specifies a minimum data set of core elements and common definitions for use by nursing facilities in conducting resident assessments, and establishes guidelines for the utilization of the data set.

The Secretary promulgates the regulations that define those costs that may be charged to the personal funds of residents in nursing facilities who are individuals receiving Medicaid with respect to nursing facility services and those costs that are to be included in the payment amount for nursing facility services.

vi. Survey and Certification Process

The state plan must provide that the state is responsible for certifying the compliance of nursing facilities (other than facilities of the state) with the requirements of section 1396r relating to the provision of services, resident rights, and administration. The state is to conduct periodic educational programs for the staff and residents (and their representatives) of nursing facilities in order to present current regulations, procedures, and policies.

(a) Investigation of Neglect, Abuse, and Misappropriation

The state must provide a process for the receipt and timely review and investigation of allegations of neglect and abuse and misappropriation of resident property by a nurse aide or by another individual used by the facility in providing services to a resident. After notice to the individual involved and a reasonable opportunity for a hearing for the individual to rebut allegations, the state must make a finding as to the accuracy of the allegations. If the state finds that a nurse aide has neglected or abused a resident or misappropriated resident property in a facility, the state must notify the nurse aide and the registry of such finding. If the state finds that any other individual used by the facility has neglected or abused a resident or misappropriated resident property in a facility, the state must notify the appropriate licensure authority. A state may not make a finding that an individual has neglected a resident if the individual demonstrates that such neglect was caused by factors beyond the control of the individual.

For findings of neglect, the state must have a procedure to permit a nurse aide to petition the state to have his or her name removed from the registry upon a determination by the state that (1) the employment and personal history of the nurse aide does not reflect a pattern of abusive behavior or neglect and (2) the neglect involved in the original finding was a singular occurrence. The federal statute provides that in no case shall a determination on such a petition be made prior to the expiration of the one-year period beginning on the date on which the name of the petitioner was added to the registry.

(b) Surveys

Each facility is subject to a standard survey, to be conducted without any prior notice to the facility. An individual who notifies (or causes to be notified) a nursing facility of the time or date on which such a survey is scheduled to be conducted is subject to a civil money penalty not to exceed $2,000. The Secretary must annually review each state's procedures for scheduling and conducting standard surveys to ensure that the state has taken all reasonable steps to avoid giving notice of such a survey through the scheduling procedures and the conduct of the surveys themselves. 42 C.F.R. § 488.307.

The regulations provide that for each facility, the state survey agency must conduct standard surveys that include all of the following: (1) a case-mix stratified sample of residents; (2) a survey of the quality of care furnished, as measured by indicators of medical, nursing, and rehabilitative care, dietary and nutrition services, activities and social participation, and sanitation, infection control, and the physical environment; (3) an audit of written plans of care and residents' assessments to determine the accuracy of such assessments and the adequacy of such plans of care; and (4) a review of compliance with residents' rights requirements.

Each nursing facility is subject to the standard survey not later than fifteen months after the date of the previous standard survey. The statewide average interval between standard surveys of a nursing facility cannot exceed twelve months. A standard survey (or an abbreviated standard survey) may also be conducted within two months of any change of ownership, administration, management of a nursing facility, or director of nursing in order to determine whether the change has resulted in any decline in the quality of care furnished in the facility.

If a standard survey indicates that a nursing facility has provided a substandard quality of care, the facility is subject to an extended survey. Other facilities, at the Secretary's or state's discretion, are also subject to an extended survey (or a partial extended survey). The extended survey must be conducted immediately after the standard survey (or, if not practicable, not later than two weeks after the date of completion of the standard survey). In the extended survey, the survey team reviews and identifies the policies and procedures which produced the substandard quality of care and determines whether the facility has complied with all of the applicable statutory requirements. An extended survey review must include an expansion of the size of the sample of residents' assessments reviewed and a review of the staffing, of in-service training, and, if appropriate, of contracts with consultants. The statute provides that an extended or partial extended survey is not a prerequisite to the imposition of a sanction against a facility on the basis of findings in the standard survey.

Standard and extended surveys are to be conducted based upon a protocol developed, tested and validated by the Secretary and by a team of individuals who meet the minimum qualifications the Secretary establishes. Each state is responsible for implementing programs to measure and reduce inconsistency in the application of survey results among surveyors. The survey team is a multidisciplinary team of professionals (which is to include a registered professional nurse). An individual who is serving (or has served within the previous two years) as a member of the staff of, or as a consultant to, the facility surveyed respecting compliance with the statutory requirements cannot be a member of the survey team. Similarly, an individual who has a personal or familial financial interest in the facility being surveyed cannot be a member of the survey team. No individual shall serve as a member of a survey team unless the individual has successfully completed a training and testing program in survey and certification techniques.

The statute also provides for validation surveys, by which the Secretary conducts onsite surveys of a representative sample of nursing facilities in each state in a sufficient number to allow inferences about the adequacies of each state's surveys. The Secretary is to conduct such surveys each year with respect to at least five percent of the number of nursing facilities surveyed by the state in the year, but in no case in less than five nursing facilities in the state.

(c) Disclosure of Results of Inspections and Activities; Ombudsman's Role

All survey and certification information (including statements of deficiencies) concerning nursing facilities must be made public within fourteen calendar days after such information is made available to those facilities. If a state finds that a nursing facility has provided a substandard quality of care, the state must notify (1) the attending physician of each resident with respect to which such finding is made and (2) any state board responsible for the licensing of the nursing facility administrator of the facility. Each state also must provide its state Medicaid fraud and abuse control unit (established under 42 U.S.C. § 1396b(q)) with access to all information of the state agency that is responsible for surveys and certifications.

The state must also notify the state long-term care ombudsman of its findings of noncompliance by a facility with any of the requirements concerning the provision of services, residents' rights, or administration of the facility. The state long-term care ombudsmen program is provided for at 42 U.S.C. § 3058g. To receive federal appropriations for the protection of vulnerable elders, a state must have a state long-term care ombudsman office and a state long-term care ombudsman program. The office is headed by an individual, known as the state long-term care ombudsman, who has expertise and experience in the fields of long-term care and advocacy. The ombudsman serves on a full-time basis and must, personally or through representatives of the office, identify, investigate, and resolve complaints (1) that are made by, or on behalf of, residents and (2) that relate to action, inaction, or decisions that may adversely affect the health, safety, welfare, or rights of the residents of providers of long-term care services.

The ombudsman may also investigate public agencies and health and social service agencies regarding these matters. By statute, the ombudsman must provide services to assist residents in protecting their health, safety, and welfare, and other rights. The ombudsman is charged with informing residents about means of obtaining various services, ensuring that residents have regular and timely access to the services provided through the office, and ensuring that residents and complainants receive timely responses from representatives of the office to their complaints. The statute authorizes the ombudsman to represent the interests of the residents before governmental agencies and to seek administrative, legal, and other remedies to protect the health, safety, welfare, and rights of the residents. The ombudsman also plays an important role in analyzing, commenting on, and monitoring the development and implementation of federal, state, and local laws, regulations, and other governmental policies and actions that pertain to the health, safety, welfare, and rights of the residents concerning the adequacy of long-term care facilities and services in the state. The ombudsman is to facilitate public comment on such laws, regulations, policies, and actions; promote the development of citizen organizations to participate in the program; and provide technical support for the development of resident and family councils to protect the well-being and rights of residents.

In carrying out the duties of the office, the ombudsman may designate an entity as a local ombudsman entity and may designate an employee or volunteer to represent the entity. To be designated as a local ombudsman entity, the entity must be free of conflicts of interest and not stand to gain financially through an action or potential action brought on behalf of individuals the ombudsman serves.

The state must ensure that representatives of the ombudsman's office have access to long-term care facilities and residents. The representative must also have appropriate access to review a resident's medical and social records with the consent of the resident, her legal representative, or when the resident is unable to consent and has no legal representative. The ombudsman's representative must also have access to a resident's records as necessary to investigate a complaint when a resident's legal guardian refuses to give the permission, as long as the representative has reasonable cause to believe that the guardian is not acting in the resident's best interests and the representative has obtained the approval of the ombudsman. The representative also must have access to the long-term care facility's administrative records, policies, and documents that are available to the resident or the general public. Finally, the representative must have access to (and, on request, copies of) all licensing and certification records maintained by the state with respect to long-term care facilities.

vii. Enforcement

The statute provides states with substantial enforcement powers when a facility fails to meet the requirements of the statute concerning the provision of services, residents' rights, or administration of the facility. The state may terminate the facility's participation under the state plan. The statute also provides other specified remedies, including the following: (1) denial of Medicaid payment under the state plan; (2) a civil money penalty, with interest, for each day of noncompliance; (3) appointment of temporary management to oversee the operation of the facility; and (4) closure of the facility or transfer of residents, or both, in the case of emergency. The statute mandates certain remedies in particular circumstances. The statute also permits states to establish alternative remedies if the alternatives are as effective in deterring noncompliance and correcting deficiencies as those specified in the statute.

The statute imposes mandatory enforcement rules on facilities that fail to comply within three months after the noncompliance is found. Mandatory enforcement rules also apply to facilities that have been found to have provided substandard quality of care on three consecutive standard surveys.

As an incentive for facilities to provide high quality care, a state may establish a program to reward nursing facilities that provide the highest quality care to residents who are entitled to Medicaid. These rewards may take the form of public recognition, incentive payments, or both. The costs of such a program are considered to be expenses necessary for the proper and efficient administration of the state plan.

Regarding enforcement and the imposition of remedies for state nursing facilities, the Secretary of Health and Human Services has the authority and duties of a state. The Secretary may also impose remedies upon other nursing facilities in a state if they fail to comply with the requirements concerning provision of services, residents' rights, administration of the facility, or the federal requirements imposed on states relating to nursing facilities.

Importantly, the statute provides that its remedies are in addition to those otherwise available under state or federal law and shall not be construed as limiting such other remedies, including any remedy available to an individual at common law.

d. Private Actions against Nursing Homes

Private actions by residents and their families against nursing homes have increased substantially in recent years. Successful plaintiffs have received large damages awards in many cases. Most claims against nursing homes are based on negligence, although some are based on intentional tort, breach of contract, civil rights violations, or other theories.

Today, many claims against nursing homes are brought under state elder abuse provisions. Increasingly, elder abuse provisions explicitly permit the victim or her survivors to sue for damages that include the victim's pain and suffering. This ability of the victim's survivors to receive damages for the victim's pain and suffering is important, because often pain and suffering are the most substantial part of the victim's damages. Using statutes or case law predating the advent of modern elder abuse and neglect provisions, a nursing home may argue that a plaintiff cannot recover for pain and suffering when the victim is dead. If accepted, this argument often would provide a substantial disincentive for an elder abuse lawsuit by the family of a deceased victim and would provide a substantial incentive for nursing homes to delay litigation until the victim died. In Matter of Guardianship/Conservatorship of Denton, 945 P.2d 1283 (Ariz. 1997), the court rejected such an argument based on the language of the state elder abuse provision. The family could thus recover for the deceased victim's pain and suffering.

Nursing homes generally provide both medical and custodial care, and it is often important to distinguish which form of care caused the injury in question. The structure and content of modern elder abuse statutes often encourage the victim or her survivors to fashion the claim as an elder abuse claim when possible. Some elder abuse statutes, however, exclude medical providers from their reach; others may exclude medical providers from suit unless the conduct in question was not willful or wanton or reckless. If an elder abuse claim against a medical provider is precluded, the victim (or her survivors) must bring the action under another theory, such as medical malpractice. Unfortunately for the plaintiff, medical malpractice claims generally have a shorter statute of limitations. Increasingly, such claims are also subject to financial caps on damages. Moreover, plaintiffs in malpractice actions often must jump through substantial evidentiary and procedural hurdles that are not part of a plaintiff's elder abuse action.

In some jurisdictions, a state nursing home residents' bill of rights gives the nursing home resident or her successors a private cause of action for a violation of those rights. In states where the state nursing home residents' bill of rights does not expressly provide a private cause of action, courts have been reluctant to find an implied cause of action. Commentators have suggested that when the state bill of rights does not provide a private cause of action, the state attorney general may nonetheless use the bill of rights to enforce a resident's rights in some instances.

Plaintiffs bringing tort claims against nursing homes often face a host of practical problems. One common problem is a lack of competent witnesses, including the victim in many cases. In some such cases, the injury itself or the circumstances surrounding the injury may help to prove the plaintiff's claim. Survey and inspection evidence collected by the state, when admissible, may also strengthen the claim. In proper circumstances, courts have imposed liability upon the parent corporation of an offending nursing home under various theories for piercing the corporate veil. Moreover, owners of a nursing home generally cannot insulate themselves from liability simply by hiring an independent contractor to run the day-to-day operations of the home.

In instances involving intentional tort, a nursing home employee—quite often a nurse aide—inflicts the injury upon the resident. In these cases, an important issue is whether the nursing home can be held vicariously liable for the acts of the employee. Some opinions focus on whether the acts were within the scope of the employee's employment and permit vicarious liability only when the acts are within that scope. Determining which acts are within the scope of employment is not always easy, however, and some courts do not use the test. In some jurisdictions, nursing homes have been held vicariously liable when they are found to have been complicitous actors or partners authorizing, ratifying, or otherwise approving the employee's actions. Other factors that may be important in finding that a nursing home is vicariously liable include the following: failure to adequately train staff; failure to maintain a proper record of staff training; failure to adequately discipline employees who violate procedures or policies; failure to maintain a proper record concerning discipline; and failure to perform adequate background checks of employees, including but not limited to those checks mandated by law.

Checkpoints

- Concerning the elderly individual who needs physical, emotional, or financial assistance but wishes to remain at home, you should be able to explain various options, including
  - Home modifications
  - The use of volunteer or paid caregivers
  - Long-term care insurance
  - The use of a reverse mortgage
- Concerning the elderly individual who chooses to sell or give away her home, you should be able to explain the consequences of such a decision
- Concerning the elderly individual who chooses to rent or to purchase a home in a community for older residents, you should be able to explain
  - The options available under the Fair Housing Act
  - The protections available under the Fair Housing Act to accommodate her needs
- Concerning the elderly individual who chooses to or who must live in a congregate living facility, you should be able to explain
  - Board and care homes, ALFs, and CCRCs, and the principal differences among them
  - Nursing home regulation, including generally
    - Requirements concerning the provision of services
    - Requirements relating to residents' rights
    - Requirements relating to administration
    - State and federal responsibilities
    - The survey and certification process

Chapter 12

The Professional Responsibilities of the Lawyer

Roadmap

- Representation of the elderly client is potentially fraught with difficult questions of professional responsibility
- Among the most common concerns are
  - The treatment of confidences
    - When the client is a fiduciary
    - When engaging in joint representation of clients
  - The treatment of conflicts of interest and
    - Concerns about informed consent
    - Identifying the client
    - Whether a drafting lawyer may accept a fiduciary position under the document the lawyer drafted for the client
    - Whether a lawyer may accept a gift or bequest from a client
  - The treatment of a client with diminished capacity, including
    - How to maintain a normal lawyer-client relationship
    - When to take protective action for the client
    - Emergency scenarios
    - When the lawyer may draft and supervise the execution of legal documents for such a client

---

A. Introduction

The practice of law has become increasingly depersonalized and business-like in many respects. Nonetheless, it remains a noble profession bound by stringent ethical rules. These rules are not designed to burden honest lawyers, but instead are intended to benefit lawyers and their clients and to protect the integrity of the profession. The rules benefit lawyers by reminding them, albeit in varying degrees, of their obligations to, and the permissible range of their actions for, clients and others affected by their conduct. The rules benefit clients by protecting them from lawyer misconduct. The rules also may protect third-party non-clients, such as when a lawyer for a fiduciary owes some duties to the persons represented by the fiduciary.

This chapter focuses on some of the rules of professional responsibility that elder law attorneys most often encounter. Because most states have adopted the Model Rules of Professional Conduct promulgated by the American Bar Association (ABA), this chapter relies principally on the Model Rules (2002) in discussing the lawyer's ethical obligations. The lawyer must always consult the particular rules and their interpretation in the applicable jurisdiction, for even states that have adopted the Model Rules often alter them in various ways. Moreover, ethics opinions from different states may interpret the same rule in different ways.

The drafters of the Model Rules and Comments are becoming increasingly attuned to the ethical problems of lawyers whose work is primarily in estates and trusts and elder law. Even so, the Model Rules do not always provide neat and precise answers to questions such lawyers face. The American College of Trust and Estate Counsel (ACTEC) has compiled an excellent secondary source of guidance for these lawyers in its *Commentaries on the Model Rules of Professional Conduct* (4th edition 2006). Because the ACTEC Commentaries are designed to fill in some of the gaps where the Model Rules and Comments do not provide sufficiently detailed guidance for lawyers engaged in trust and estate work, this chapter also discusses selected guidance from the Commentaries.

The ABA provides the Model Rules to the public on its website at http://www.abanet.org/cpr/mrpc/mrpc_toc.html. The ACTEC Commentaries are available from the ACTEC website at http://www.actec.org/public/CommentariesPublic.asp.

Several broad questions frequently recur in the practice of elder law. Among these questions are the following: (1) Who is the lawyer's client? (2) May the lawyer represent joint or multiple clients? (3) How does the lawyer address the need to reveal client confidences? (4) How does the lawyer represent a client who is at substantial risk of harm and can no longer act for herself? These and other questions are addressed in this chapter.

B. Lawyer Competence

Model Rule 1.1 states that "A lawyer shall provide competent representation to a client." The importance of the rule cannot be overstated. The lawyer for the elderly client often holds that client's future in hand.

The complexity of representation undertaken by lawyers for the elderly runs the gamut. Comment 4 to Rule 1.1 acknowledges that the lawyer may undertake representation if he can achieve the necessary skill through reasonable preparation. The implied converse of that statement indicates that a lawyer who cannot achieve the requisite skill even with research and study should not undertake the representation. Under Rule 1.2(c), the lawyer may limit the scope of representation to those concerns with which he is competent if the client gives informed consent. Alternatively, the lawyer may consult or associate with another lawyer who is competent on the matters in question, as long as he first obtains the client's informed consent.

In representing the elderly client, the competent lawyer will emphasize to the client the importance of receiving full and accurate information from the client. To help the elderly client establish an estate plan or demonstrate eligibility for various governmental benefits, the lawyer must have a full and accurate picture of the client's wealth. In drafting wills and trusts, the lawyer often must learn the precise nature of the client's family relationships and understand the terms that the client uses. For example, assume that an elderly client states that he wants his entire estate to pass to his "children." The client, however, is not using the term children in its legal sense. Rather, he is using the term to refer to his biological child with his late wife, to his stepson, and also to a foster child the couple reared. Assume further that the client does not intend for the term "children" to include his nonmarital child whom he was legally obligated to support but whom he has never seen. In such a case, the client is clearly unaware of the legal meaning of "children" for inheritance purposes. If the lawyer does not question the client further, but instead merely drafts and supervises the execution of a simple will leaving the client's estate equally to his "children," the client's intentions will go unfulfilled. The estate will probably pass to the client's two biological children, and the stepson and foster child will be excluded. In today's world filled with nontraditional family structures, the competent lawyer will not assume that a client's use of terms such as child, parent, or sibling connotes a legal relationship or that a client has no nonmarital relatives. Similar problems may arise when clients describe property ownership. Is the client using a layperson's interpretation of a property term? While the lawyer is generally entitled to rely on the information the client provides, the lawyer also has an obligation to assist the client in revealing that information in a complete and accurate way.

A lawyer's obligation to be thorough and knowledgeable will often require the lawyer to investigate before acquiescing in a client's request or before accepting representation of a prospective client. For example, in In re Brantley, 920 P.2d 433 (Kan. 1996), the Kansas Supreme Court noted that the lawyer in question had failed to investigate his client's bank records and obtain an accurate report of the circumstances of certain bank transfers before alarming the client (who was in a nursing home) with a false statement about the source of the transfers. Further, the lawyer proposed a voluntary conservatorship for the client without interviewing her face-to-face, instead relying in part on a brief phone conversation with her and on the statements of her stepson. The lawyer subsequently obtained an ex parte order based on "inaccurate, incomplete, and unsupported representations." In filing later for an involuntary conservatorship for the client, the lawyer stated that the petition included a letter from a certain doctor indicating that the client was "completely disoriented as to person, place, and time." In fact, the petition contained no such letter and the lawyer subsequently admitted that he made up the existence of the letter and the language it supposedly contained.

Questions of the lawyer's competency may arise when the lawyer fails to properly supervise the execution of estate planning documents. Although a few states have forgiveness doctrines that permit courts to recognize defectively-executed probate documents if clear and convincing evidence supports recognition, many states still require strict compliance with the formalities of execution. A competent lawyer knows the execution requirements of the jurisdiction and ensures that they are followed. Some lawyers occasionally permit or request an administrative assistant or paralegal to supervise the execution of a will or other estate planning document. In some jurisdictions, this practice may be an improper delegation of the practice of law; even if the supervision of will execution or other estate planning documents does not constitute the unauthorized practice of law, the delegation of the task is questionable. Should anything go wrong, the lawyer will probably be held responsible for the problem.

C. Scope of Representation and Allocation of Authority

Rule 1.2(a) generally requires the lawyer to abide by the client's decisions concerning the objectives of the representation. The lawyer is permitted to take action that is impliedly authorized to carry out the representation. Paragraph

(c) of the rule permits the lawyer to limit the scope of the representation if the limitation is reasonable and the client gives informed consent. Paragraph (d) provides that the "lawyer shall not counsel a client to engage, or assist a client, in conduct that the lawyer knows is criminal or fraudulent." Comment 11 to the rule notes that the lawyer may have special obligations when the client is a fiduciary. This comment is important in the lawyer's representation of guardians, conservators, agents, executors, administrators, and trustees in their fiduciary role. Because the fiduciary has obligations to third parties, the lawyer may also have certain obligations to them, even though they are not the lawyer's clients.

The ACTEC Commentaries on Rule 1.2 suggest that in some instances a prudent course of action is for the lawyer to meet with the fiduciary and those to whom the fiduciary owes a duty. For example, if the lawyer is representing a trustee, the lawyer may explain that the lawyer is representing the trustee (the fiduciary) and not the beneficiaries, that the lawyer may provide occasional information to the beneficiaries, and that the beneficiaries may wish to retain their own counsel. Increasingly, ethics rules are permitting lawyers to disclose the client's breach of fiduciary duties when necessary to protect the beneficiaries. Failure to disclose may result in lawyer liability to the beneficiaries for their loss. Section 51 of the Restatement (Third) of the Law Governing Lawyers recognizes a lawyer's duty of care to those to whom the client owes a fiduciary duty when the lawyer represents the client in the client's role as fiduciary.

The decision to disclose a client's fiduciary breaches, where permitted, is a difficult one for the lawyer, who must be vigilant to protect client confidences and avoid conflicts of interest. The lawyer must carefully examine the rules of professional responsibility in the jurisdiction where the lawyer practices to determine under what circumstances, if any, disclosure is permitted or required. To reduce the lawyer's concern over the client's potential fiduciary breaches, the lawyer may specifically condition representation upon the fiduciary's agreement to permit the lawyer to disclose breaches of fiduciary duty to the beneficiaries or to the court supervising the fiduciary relationship. Some states do not permit disclosure by the lawyer in the absence of a representation agreement that permits disclosure. In any event, the lawyer cannot assist the fiduciary in criminal or fraudulent conduct.

D. Diligence, Communication, and Fees

Model Rule 1.3 directs the lawyer to act "with reasonable diligence and promptness." Comment 3 notes as follows: "Perhaps no professional shortcoming is more widely resented than procrastination." The lawyer representing elderly clients should take special care to remember the rule and the comment. Many an elderly client will need the lawyer to fulfill her request quickly. For example, the dying client who requests her lawyer to draft her will may die intestate if the lawyer does not act promptly. In People v. James, 502 P.2d 1189 (Colo. 1972), the lawyer failed to prepare a will for at least eight months after he was employed to do so by a seventy-five year-old client. The Colorado Supreme Court agreed with the disciplinary committee that the lawyer's failure "was grossly negligent and showed a total lack of responsibility," particularly since the client was an aged person. The lawyer was disbarred.

An elderly client seeking state or federal government benefits will also often need her lawyer to act diligently in representing her interests. In cases involving requests for benefits, the client may suffer from the inherent delay associated with benefit programs and bureaucracy; her suffering should not be compounded by the dilatory practices of her lawyer.

When possible, a prudent practice in the early phase of representation is for the lawyer, with the client's agreement, to establish a schedule for the completion of various tasks. This course of action is suggested by the ACTEC Commentaries on Rule 1.3. The practice is particularly appropriate when the lawyer is solely responsible for completion of the tasks, as is typically the case in will drafting and much estate planning. If subsequent events require the lawyer to deviate from the schedule or timetable, the lawyer should promptly discuss the matter with the client to establish a revised timetable.

Model Rule 1.4 requires the lawyer to maintain reasonable communication with the client and to inform the client promptly when the client's informed consent is required. The rule also requires the lawyer to explain matters as reasonably necessary to allow the client to make informed decisions. Comment 6 to the rule notes that the lawyer should typically provide information appropriate for a "comprehending and responsible" adult. It notes further, however, that the lawyer may be unable to provide full information to a client of diminished capacity. In such instances, Model Rule 1.14 requires the lawyer to maintain, as far as reasonably possible, a normal lawyer-client relationship with the client of diminished capacity.

The ACTEC Commentaries suggest that the lawyer should meet with the client personally, when possible, at the beginning of the representation. The lawyer should then confirm the elements of the representation in an engagement letter to the client. Personal meetings with a client or prospective client typically provide the best opportunity for direct and complete communication. If it appears likely that others will later contest the client's capacity to engage the lawyer or to execute legal documents, a personal meeting is particularly important, for it provides the lawyer with the opportunity to assess the capacity of the client and the reliability of the client's expressed wishes.

The Commentaries also warn that "a lawyer should not provide estate planning documents to persons who may execute them without receiving legal advice" and "should be hesitant to provide samples of estate planning documents that might be executed by lay persons without legal advice." For example, these warnings are implicated when a lawyer receives a client's request for "a blank power of attorney for my mother" or similar requests.

In many instances, the lawyer-client relationship becomes dormant once the lawyer has completed the client's requested tasks. When representation is in a dormant phase, does the lawyer have a continuing duty to inform the client of changes in the law that might affect the client regarding those tasks that the lawyer has previously undertaken? The Commentaries indicate that, when the representation is dormant, the lawyer may periodically communicate with the client concerning the propriety of renewed review (such as with an estate plan) or concerning changes in the law that would affect the client regarding those tasks previously undertaken. The lawyer is not obligated to do these things, however, in the absence of an agreement to do so.

Model Rule 1.5 provides that "[a] lawyer shall not make an agreement for, charge, or collect an unreasonable fee or an unreasonable amount for expenses." The rule also provides a nonexclusive list of factors to be considered in determining reasonableness. When a new lawyer-client relationship begins, Comment 2 to the rule requires the lawyer to establish promptly an understanding with the client concerning fees and expenses. The comment further suggests that the lawyer provide the client with a copy of the lawyer's customary fee arrangements, the nature of services the lawyer will provide, the lawyer's fees or the basis for determining the lawyer's fees, and the client's responsibilities for costs, expenses, and disbursements.

The ACTEC Commentaries note that most states permit a lawyer to serve in the dual roles of fiduciary and lawyer to the fiduciary and to receive compensation for services rendered in both roles. For example, the lawyer may serve as executor of an estate and also as lawyer to the executor. The Commentaries note, however, that "it is inappropriate for the lawyer to receive double compensation for the same work." ACTEC Commentaries on Model Rule 1.5.

"Who is the client?" is a question that often arises in the practice of elder law. For example, an adult daughter may bring her elderly mother to the lawyer's office and offer to pay the lawyer to draft and supervise the execution of her mother's will. In accordance with other authorities, the ACTEC Commentaries provide that the client is the person for whom the lawyer is performing the services in question, regardless of who is paying the lawyer's fees. Determining the identity of the client is crucial, for it is the client to whom the lawyer owes most duties. Model Rule 1.8(f) also comes into play here, for it prohibits the lawyer from receiving compensation from one other than the client unless (1) the client provides informed consent; (2) there is no interference with the lawyer-client relationship or with lawyer's independent, professional judgment; and (3) the client's confidences are protected as required under Model Rule 1.6.

E. Confidences and Conflicts of Interest

1. Confidences

Model Rule 1.6(a) provides that a lawyer may not reveal information relating to the representation of a client without the client's informed consent unless the disclosure is impliedly authorized to carry out the representation or unless the disclosure is otherwise permitted under certain exceptions listed in paragraph (b) of the rule.

Among the exceptions to the general rule, a lawyer is permitted to reveal such information to the extent the lawyer reasonably believes necessary (1) "to prevent reasonably certain death or substantial bodily harm"; (2) to prevent a criminal act or fraud by the client that is "reasonably certain" to cause "substantial injury" to another's property or financial interests "and in furtherance of which the client has used or is using the lawyer's services"; or (3) to prevent, rectify, or mitigate a substantial injury that is reasonably certain to occur or has already occurred to another's property or financial interests from the criminal act or fraud of the client "in furtherance of which the client has used the lawyer's services." Other exceptions exist, and one of these is particularly worth noting: Model Rule 1.6(b)(6) also permits the lawyer to reveal information relating to the representation of a client to the extent the lawyer reasonably believes necessary "to comply with other law or a court order."

As Comment 2 to the Rule indicates, a duty to preserve client confidences is needed in part to ensure full and frank communication by the client to the lawyer. This duty extends not only to matters the client specifically states to the lawyer, but also to "all information relating to the representation, whatever its source." Comment 3. The exceptions to the duty of confidentiality acknowledge that, in some instances, other individuals and society have superior interests that will permit a lawyer to make certain revelations to the extent necessary to protect those interests.

Under Model Rule 1.6(b)(1), which permits revelation to prevent reasonably certain death or substantial bodily harm, a lawyer might reveal the gross elder neglect or abuse committed by his client who is a caretaker for a parent. Before making such a revelation under (b)(1), the lawyer would have to conclude that reasonably certain death or substantial bodily injury is likely to occur from the client's conduct. In making the revelation, the lawyer must reveal only what he reasonably believes necessary to prevent the harm.

As part of the estate planning process, the elder client will frequently execute a durable power of attorney for financial matters. Often the agent's authority springs into effect when the principal becomes incapacitated. If the principal/client later becomes incapacitated and the agent is authorized to carry out the principal's legal affairs, the lawyer may open the client's files to the agent as necessary for the agent to fulfill his legitimate role. Providing such files to the agent would not be a violation of Rule 1.6 once the agent is authorized to act for the principal. In contrast, if the agent named under a springing durable power of attorney requests such information before he has authority to act, the lawyer could not reveal the information without the client's informed consent.

a. Fiduciary Representation

A lawyer may be called upon to represent a conservator, guardian, trustee, executor, administrator, agent, or other fiduciary. Fiduciary representation is a common part of elder law practice, but it can present particularly difficult problems for the lawyer when the lawyer learns that the client/fiduciary is violating fiduciary duties. For example, a lawyer who advises a conservator may learn that the client/conservator has twisted or ignored the lawyer's advice and instead formed a criminal plan to use the estate for the client's own purposes. In such instances, Model Rule 1.6(b)(2) permits the lawyer to divulge information to the extent necessary to prevent substantial injury to the protected person's financial interests. If the lawyer does not learn about the client/conservator's crime until after it has been committed, (b)(3) permits such a revelation if such revelation would mitigate or rectify the client's action or help prevent further injury. Comment 14 to the Rule suggests that, when practicable, the lawyer should encourage the client to take appropriate remedial measures before the lawyer makes a revelation under Rule 1.6(b).

The exceptions to the general rule of nondisclosure permit but do not require revelation from the lawyer. Comment 15 indicates that the lawyer's decision not to disclose is not a violation of the rule. Nonetheless, other laws (and certain parts of other Model Rules) may *require* disclosure. For example, laws in some states specifically name lawyers as mandated reporters of suspected fiduciary elder abuse. Laws in other states impose upon all citizens a duty to report elder abuse; such statutes make no exclusions for lawyers. Discerning when another law supersedes Rule 1.6's duty of confidentiality can be difficult. Comment 12 implicitly acknowledges this, stating that the matter "is a question of law beyond the scope of these Rules." If, however, the other law does require disclosure, then the lawyer may do so without violating Rule 1.6. Rule 1.6(b) specifically permits lawyers to make revelations to the extent the lawyer reasonably believes them to be necessary to comply with such laws. Moreover, as Comment 15 also notes, in some instances the lawyer must disclose even if such disclosure is not apparently permitted by Rule 1.6. For example, the lawyer's duty of candor under Rule 3.3 may require a lawyer to disclose a client's misconduct to a court.

Although the preceding discussion focused on Model Rule 1.6, the rules concerning client confidences vary among the states. Some states clearly prohibit the revelation of client confidences that are permitted under Model Rule 1.6. If rules prohibit the lawyer from revealing the misconduct of a client/fiduciary and the client is unwilling or cannot rectify his or her misconduct, in some instances the lawyer will have no choice other than to withdraw from representation.

At the outset of representation, the lawyer may condition representation upon the client's agreement to permit the lawyer to reveal fiduciary misconduct to the appropriate court or beneficiaries. The fiduciary's informed consent can often significantly reduce the lawyer's uncertainty about the propriety of such revelations.

b. Joint Representation

Sometimes clients with similar, but not identical, interests will ask a lawyer to represent them together. This is often the case, for example, with a married couple seeking to engage in estate planning. Joint representation in such settings can be more economical for the couple than separate representation. When all of the relevant family information is provided to the lawyer as a unified whole, joint representation can also lead to a better coordinated estate plan. Most often, estate planning will be nonadversarial in nature. Yet before agreeing to represent clients jointly, the lawyer must carefully consider whether he can represent them in light of his professional obligations under Rule 1.6 (confidences) and Rule 1.7 (conflicts of interest). When the prospective clients' interests are largely aligned, as is typically the case for example with Medicaid planning for an elderly married couple, the lawyer usually will be able to undertake joint representation.

Prospective clients who first visit the lawyer together may not reveal possible conflicts in front of each other. The ACTEC Commentaries suggest that a lawyer may want to interview each of the prospective clients separately before agreeing to undertake joint representation. The lawyer may be more likely to learn of potential conflicts through separate interviews. For example, a husband and wife who seek estate planning assistance will often appear allied in their wishes during the joint interview; however, a separate interview with each may in fact reveal substantial differences in their wishes, particularly if either has children outside the relationship.

When meeting potential joint clients, such as a husband and wife, the lawyer should thoroughly explain his professional obligations and discuss the conditions of representation with them. The lawyer should discuss the extent to which matters revealed by one joint client will be shared with the other joint clients. The ACTEC Commentaries on Rule 1.7 (conflicts) note that "representation of a husband and wife as joint clients does not ordinarily require the informed consent of either or both of them." Some estate planners, however, undertake to represent related clients as separate clients on related matters, protecting the confidences of each client in the absence of an informed consent confirmed in writing. The ACTEC Commentaries admonish that separate representation in such cases should be taken "with great care."

In the absence of a contrary agreement, when potential multiple clients consult the lawyer together on related legal matters, a presumption arises that the lawyer will represent them jointly, "with resulting full sharing of information between the clients." ACTEC Commentaries on Rule 1.6. Even so, the prudent course of action is for the lawyer, at the outset of representation, to enter into a formal, written agreement with the clients memorializing their instructions concerning the treatment of confidences. The lawyer should provide the clients with copies of the agreement.

Even with a written agreement that contemplates full sharing between or among the joint clients, in some instances the lawyer may be obliged to withdraw when a conflict arises. This may occur, for example, if one joint client reveals information potentially adverse to the other joint client and the revealing client refuses to allow the lawyer to share the information with that other joint client. Typically, the lawyer should first encourage the revealing client himself to share the information with the other joint client. If the revealing client refuses to do so, the lawyer may remind the revealing client of the joint representation agreement. The ACTEC Commentaries note that the lawyer may also inform the revealing client that the lawyer may face a malpractice action or disciplinary action if the information is not provided to the other client. If lawyer withdrawal is ultimately necessary, the withdrawal itself may waive red flags in front of the nonrevealing client.

2. Conflicts

a. Generally

Model Rule 1.7(a) provides generally that "a lawyer shall not represent a client if the representation involves a concurrent conflict of interest." A concurrent conflict is one in which (1) the lawyer's representation of one client is directly adverse to another client or (2) a significant risk exists that the lawyer's responsibilities to a present or former client or a third party will materially limit his representation of another client. Such a conflict also exists when the significant risk arises from the personal interests of the lawyer.

The general prohibition of Rule 1.7(a) contains an exception in paragraph (b). Despite a concurrent conflict, the lawyer may represent a client if (1) the lawyer "reasonably believes" he can give diligent and competent representation to all affected clients; (2) his representation is not otherwise forbidden by law; (3) the representation does not include claims by one client against another client in the same litigation or before a tribunal; *and* (4) "each affected client gives informed consent, confirmed in writing."

Multiple representation often raises serious questions of conflicts and consent. As Comment 14 to Model Rule 1.7 notes, there simply can be no informed consent by a client to some conflicts. Comment 15 points out that, in other instances, the conflict is such that a lawyer cannot reasonably believe that he can provide competent and diligent representation to each affected client. In either case, the exception of paragraph (b) is not applicable and the conflict precludes the representation.

b. Consent

Assuming that a conflict is waivable (or "consentable"), the lawyer must obtain each client's informed consent in writing. While the writing itself may impress the seriousness of the matter upon those clients, it typically does not eliminate the need for the lawyer to discuss risks and benefits, as well as alternatives, with the clients. Model Rule 1.7, Comment 20. In this respect the writing is similar to a medical informed consent document. Like a doctor, a lawyer should not view informed consent as the document itself, but rather as a process. That process should provide the clients with the opportunity to ask questions and to reflect upon their choices.

Comment 22 indicates that clients may be currently able to waive prospective conflicts of interest—i.e., conflicts that develop after the representation begins—but only if the requirements of paragraph (b) are satisfied. Whether a client's consent to waive future conflicts satisfies the requirements for an informed consent will depend upon several factors, including the lawyer's discussion of such potential later-arising conflicts and the client's experience and understanding of legal matters (including material risks). Comment 22 states that a consent that "is general and open-ended ... ordinarily will be ineffective, because it is not reasonably likely that the client will have understood the material risks involved." The ACTEC Commentaries contain warnings about Comment 22 to Model Rule 1.7. They note that a particular jurisdiction or state disciplinary authority employing the rule may emphasize that the text of the rule itself refers only to *concurrent* conflicts of interest, not *prospective* conflicts of interests. Thus, the views expressed in Comment 22 may not apply in a particular state. The Commentaries also warn that an attempt to have a client waive a prospective conflict of interest may possibly implicate Rule 1.8(h)(1), which provides that a lawyer shall not "make an agreement prospectively limiting the lawyer's liability to a client for malpractice unless the client is independently represented in making the agreement."

Even if a client has validly given her informed consent in writing, she may later revoke it. Model Rule 1.7, Comment 21. In the case of common representation by the lawyer, revocation of consent by one client will often require the lawyer to withdraw from all representation. Comment 31 notes that when one client requests the lawyer not to inform another client of information materially affecting common representation, common representation "will almost certainly be inadequate." Such a request should immediately remind the lawyer of his duty of loyalty to each client, of each client's right to be informed of information affecting the representation, and of each client's "right to expect that the lawyer will use that information for that client's benefit." Not surprisingly, Comment 31 suggests that the lawyer, at the outset of representation, "advise each client that information will be shared and that the lawyer will have to withdraw if one client decides that some matter material to the representation should be kept from the other."

c. "Who's the Client?"

In a number of cases, an existing client has requested that the lawyer draft estate planning documents for an elderly relative. Sometimes, the existing client informs the lawyer concerning the proposed substantive provisions of the document, brings the relative to the lawyer's office, is present at the execution of the document, and pays for the lawyer's services. Often the existing client is the sole or principal beneficiary of the document, which reduces or eliminates the possibility of provisions for the elder's other relatives. Such scenarios are inherently problematic. A careful lawyer can and should avoid them. Among the ethical questions that arise are the following: "Who is the client?";

"Is the elder a person of diminished capacity?"; "Is there a significant risk that representation of the elder will be materially limited by the lawyer's responsibilities to the existing client?"; and "Can the lawyer accept payment from the existing client if the elder is the client in this matter?"

In fact, the client in this setting is the elder if the elder has the capacity to seek the lawyer's assistance with regard to the proposed matter. (If the elder lacks that capacity, then the lawyer may not draft a will or trust and provide it to the existing client for execution by the elder.) If the elder is the client, then Rule 1.8(f) precludes the lawyer from accepting payment from the existing client unless (1) the elder gives informed consent; (2) there is no interference with the lawyer's independent professional judgment or with the lawyer-client relationship between the lawyer and the elder; and (3) the elder's confidences are protected as required under Model Rule 1.6. In the setting described in the preceding paragraph, the lawyer should meet with the elder separately—i.e., outside the presence of the existing client—to preserve the elder's confidences and to help ensure that the elder's proposed estate plan is indeed her own, not one founded upon the undue influence of the existing client. On the matter of undue influence, the lawyer should also inform the existing client and the new elder client that a presumption of undue influence could very well arise if the existing client insists on participating in the preparation and execution of the will or trust.

If representation of the existing client is such that the lawyer cannot reasonably believe that he will be able to provide competent, diligent representation to the elder, then the lawyer cannot undertake the representation, even if the elder purports to give informed consent in writing. Such might be the case, for example, when the elder's relative is an existing, long-term client and the lawyer's relationship with that existing client would impair his duties of loyalty and independent judgment in representing the elder.

d. The Drafting Lawyer as Fiduciary or Attorney for the Fiduciary

A client who employs a lawyer to draft a will almost always designates an executor to supervise the administration of the estate. A client who employs a lawyer to draft a trust will designate one or more trustees to manage the trust. The client may ask the lawyer to serve in one or both of those fiduciary roles. The lawyer who serves in such a fiduciary capacity will often find that his compensation for fiduciary representation substantially exceeds his compensation for drafting the will or trust document. As critics have aptly noted, the lawyer who is asked to serve as fiduciary under the document he is drafting for his client is hardly financially disinterested.

The Model Rules do not explicitly cover this scenario. The ACTEC Commentaries state, "As a general proposition, lawyers should be permitted to assist adequately informed clients who wish to appoint their lawyers as fiduciaries." In most states, a lawyer may serve as lawyer and as fiduciary upon the client's request as long as the lawyer (1) has properly informed the client of all relevant information, (2) has not improperly solicited the role of fiduciary, (3) has not unduly influenced the client to make the appointment, and (4) has not otherwise violated Model Rule 1.7 in accepting the appointment. The lawyer should engage in a careful discussion with the client before the lawyer accepts the fiduciary appointment. For example, the lawyer should advise the client concerning other possible choices regarding the fiduciary role. Thus, the lawyer should discuss the ability of a layperson to undertake the fiduciary role with lawyer assistance. The lawyer should also advise the client about the relative costs associated with the choice of a fiduciary. On this matter, the lawyer should discuss his personal financial interest in serving as fiduciary. The lawyer may also suggest to the client that she consider consulting independent counsel before making the appointment.

The ACTEC Commentaries note that Rule 1.7 is implicated when a significant risk exists that "the lawyer's interests in obtaining the appointment will materially limit the lawyer's independent professional judgment in advising the client concerning the choice of an executor or other fiduciary." Because of public fear of lawyer overreaching, some states have adopted or considered additional restrictions to limit the circumstances in which a client may appoint the lawyer/scrivener as fiduciary in the document in question. These restrictions may also impose limits upon "dual" compensation—i.e., compensation to the lawyer as lawyer and compensation to the lawyer as fiduciary. In a few areas of the country, local rules of court impose additional requirements upon a lawyer drafting a document that names him as fiduciary.

e. Client Gifts, Bequests, and Business Transactions

Each year, state courts issue a disheartening number of opinions concerning lawyers who have taken advantage of their positions to acquire a client's assets by gift, bequest, or business transaction.

Model Rule 1.8(a) generally prohibits lawyers from entering into business transactions with a client and from knowingly acquiring "an ownership, possessory, security or other pecuniary interest adverse to the client." An exception exists if (1) the transaction and its terms are fully disclosed to the client, are fair and reasonable, and are transmitted in a writing that the client can reasonably understand; (2) the lawyer apprises the client of the advisability of seeking independent legal counsel and the client is given a reasonably opportunity to do so; and (3) the lawyer obtains the client's informed, written consent to the essential terms of the transaction (including whether the lawyer is representing the client in the transaction).

Model Rule 1.8(c) provides, "A lawyer shall not solicit any substantial gift from a client, including a testamentary gift, or prepare on behalf of a client an instrument giving the lawyer or a person related to the lawyer any substantial gift unless the lawyer or other recipient of the gift is related to the client." (The rule defines "related persons" to include "a spouse, child, grandchild, parent, grandparent or other relative or individual with whom the lawyer or the client maintains a close, familial relationship.") Comment 6 notes that the rule does not preclude simple gifts to the lawyer that meet "general standards of fairness." Even a substantial gift may be valid if the client made the gift freely and knowingly, with no improper solicitation on the part of the lawyer. Because the lawyer is deemed to be the dominant party in his relationship with the client, however, a presumption of undue influence may arise any time that the client makes a substantial gift to the lawyer. If such a presumption arises, to retain the gift the lawyer will have to show that the client was not susceptible to undue influence or had the advice of independent, meaningful counsel before making the gift.

Unless the lawyer is related to the client, he may not draft a will or other instrument that gives him a substantial gift. He also may not draft the instrument in a way that provides for his relatives. For example, a lawyer may not draft the client's will to provide for the lawyer's daughter, if the lawyer and his daughter are not related to or do not have a close familial relationship with the client. Note, however, that this prohibition does not prevent the lawyer from drafting an instrument naming him (or his partner or associate) as an executor or to another fiduciary position upon the client's request. Model Rule 1.8, Comment 8. The lawyer as executor or fiduciary may be entitled to substantial compensation; however, compensation for services is not the same as a substantial gift from the client. The naming of the lawyer as a fiduciary is also not considered a "business transaction" between the lawyer and the client. The comment observes, however, that when the client seeks to have the lawyer serve as fiduciary, the general conflict provisions of Model Rule 1.7 apply.

The ACTEC Commentaries observe that the rule extends "to all methods by which gratuitous transfers might be made by a client." Substantial gifts could thus be in the form of nonprobate transfers such as trust interests, payable-on-death or transfer-on-death accounts, life insurance, and survivorship properties.

F. The Client with Diminished Capacity

1. Generally

One of the most serious ethical questions that an attorney in the field of elder law can face is how to maintain a proper lawyer-client relationship with a client who has diminished capacity. Model Rule 1.14(a) states that "the lawyer shall, as far as reasonably possible, maintain a normal client-lawyer relationship" when a client has diminished capacity.

Capacity, of course, exists along a broad spectrum. When the capacity of the client is only slightly diminished, the lawyer may be able to maintain an ordinary client-lawyer relationship with that client in all respects. Even a client with significantly diminished capacity may be able to understand the general purpose of the legal representation, to reliably express her wishes concerning the progress and direction of that representation, and to make legally binding decisions. At the far end of the spectrum, even individuals who are unable to make certain legally binding decisions may have strong opinions concerning the decisions that are made for them by others. Thus, wards and protected persons may be able to rationally and reliably express their wishes concerning guardianship or conservatorship matters or concerning their legal representation in proceedings concerning guardianship or conservatorship matters. Comment 1 to Model Rule 1.14 sums up the scenario as follows: "[A] client with diminished capacity often has the ability to understand, deliberate upon, and reach conclusions about matters affecting the client's own well-being." Model Rule 1.14 mandates that the lawyer treat each client with attention and respect, regardless of the client's disability.

Comment 2 to Model Rule 1.14 indicates that when a lawyer represents the legal representative of a person with a disability, the lawyer should, to the extent possible, accord the represented person the status of client. The comment further indicates that this treatment is particularly important in regard to maintaining communication. Nonetheless, when a legal representative (such as a guardian or conservator) seeks the lawyer's services, in most cases the lawyer must ultimately look to the decisions made by the legal representative for the person with diminished capacity. This does not mean, however, that the lawyer owes no duties to the person with diminished capacity. Even if the lawyer had no preexisting client-lawyer relationship with the person with diminished capacity, the lawyer may have obligations to that person when representing that person's legal representative. Model Rule 1.2(d) prohibits the lawyer from counseling the legal representative to engage in conduct that is criminal or fraudulent. In recent years, statutes and judicial opinions have increasingly required lawyers representing a guardian or conservator to take action to prevent or rectify guardian or conservator misconduct. The lawyer representing the fiduciary may thus, as part of the engagement agreement, want to seek the fiduciary's permission for the lawyer to reveal fiduciary misconduct to the court, to the ward or protected person, or to third parties interested in the ward or protected person.

The ACTEC Commentaries suggest that a lawyer who represented a client before the client suffered diminished capacity may in proper instances be considered to continue to represent that client after the fiduciary appointment. Thus, the lawyer may continue to meet with and counsel the client, even though the client may lack the ability to enter into contracts or other legal obligations. The ACTEC Commentaries also note that a lawyer may in appropriate cases represent the fiduciary who is appointed for a client or a former client. If, however, there is a conflict of interest between the fiduciary and the ward or protected person, the ward or protected person may be unable to waive the conflict as a result of the ward's or protected person's lack of capacity and corresponding inability to give informed consent. Moreover, because the lawyer must reasonably believe that he will be able to provide competent and diligent representation to each client, the lawyer may not engage in joint representation of the fiduciary and the ward or protected person if the representation of one client will materially limit representation of the other client.

2. Protective Action

Paragraph (b) of Model Rule 1.14 permits (but does not require) the lawyer, in certain settings, to act to protect the client with diminished capacity. Before taking protective action, the lawyer must reasonably believe that "the client has diminished capacity, is at risk of substantial physical, financial or other harm unless action is taken and cannot adequately act in the client's own interest." In this setting, the lawyer may take reasonably necessary protective action. The rule indicates that the protective action may include consultation with those who themselves can act to protect the client. The rule further states that the protective action in appropriate cases may include seeking to have a guardian ad litem, conservator, or guardian appointed for the client.

When the lawyer can no longer maintain a normal lawyer-client relationship with the client and the lawyer believes the client to be at risk of substantial harm and unable to protect herself, the lawyer who decides to take protective action will often have a variety of options to consider. In some instances, the lawyer can protect the client without significant intrusion into the client's life. For example, if the lawyer can successfully counsel the client to wait before making an important decision, no further "protective action" may be necessary.

Such might be the case, for example, where the client's diminished capacity is temporary due to the use of certain medications. Alternatively, if the client retains the capacity to execute a durable power of attorney, the lawyer might explain how the use of an agent could help the client. If the client has already executed a durable power of attorney, the lawyer might consult with the client's designated agent and might suggest to the client that she allow the agent to make decisions that will protect her from substantial harm.

In other settings, more intrusive protective action may be appropriate. The lawyer may consult with family members of the client if the lawyer reasonably believes they will be able to take the necessary protective action. If the client is at risk of substantial harm resulting from abuse, neglect, or exploitation, lawyer consultation with state social services or Adult Protective Services may be appropriate. (As mentioned earlier, some states may require the lawyer to report suspected incidents of abuse.) To make decisions about the proper protective action to take, the lawyer may need assistance in assessing the client's capacity. Comment 6 to Model Rule 1.14 notes that, in appropriate circumstances, the lawyer may obtain guidance from a proper diagnostician.

Consistent with the law's increasing respect for the autonomy of the individual, the lawyer taking protective action should do so in the least instrusive manner that will result in the necessary protection of the client. Moreover, the lawyer should consider the client's wishes and values as well as the client's best interest. Although the rule permits a lawyer to petition for the appointment of a guardian ad litem, conservator, or guardian for the client, petitioning for a judicially-appointed legal representative will typically be a measure of last resort. As Comment 7 notes, "In many circumstances ... appointment of a legal representative may be more expensive or traumatic for the client than circumstances in fact require." Nonetheless, if the client is at risk of substantial harm and other courses of action appear unlikely to protect the client adequately, seeking a legal representative may be appropriate. Comment 7 further notes, "Evaluation of such circumstances is a matter entrusted to the professional judgment of the lawyer."

3. Client Confidences

Model Rule 1.14(c) recognizes that Rule 1.6 protects information relating to the representation of clients, including those clients with diminished capacity. Nonetheless, paragraph (c) provides that when the lawyer takes protective action under Model Rule 1.14(b), "the lawyer is impliedly authorized under Rule 1.6(a) to reveal information about the client, but only to the extent reasonably necessary to protect the client's interests." Comment 8 to Model Rule

1.14 indicates that when the lawyer makes such a disclosure in taking protective action, the disclosure is impliedly authorized even in the face of client opposition. Yet because the lawyer's consultation with third parties may itself impose substantial risks for the client, Model Rule 1.14 carefully limits the lawyer's disclosures to those reasonably necessary. The comment notes that the lawyer's position in these circumstances is "unavoidably difficult." The comment states, "At the very least, the lawyer should determine whether it is likely that the person or entity consulted with will act adversely to the client's interest before discussing matters related to the client." For example, the lawyer should be wary of revealing information to a client's relative who may be reasonably expected to use that information to upset the client's long-established estate plan.

4. Emergencies

Comments 9 and 10 to Model Rule 1.14 address persons who are unable to establish a lawyer-client relationship but who are facing emergencies. Comment 9 to Model Rule 1.14 states that in emergency scenarios involving a threat of imminent and irreparable harm to the person, the lawyer may be able to take protective action even if the person is unable to establish a lawyer-client relationship, if the person or someone else acting in good faith on the person's behalf consults the lawyer. Before taking such protective action, however, the lawyer should have a reasonable belief that the person has no other lawyer, agent, or legal representative to act for the person. The comment indicates that the lawyer should take only that action reasonably necessary to preserve the status quo or prevent imminent and irreparable harm to the person.

Comment 10 admonishes the lawyer to "regularize" the relationship with the person or "implement other protective solutions" as quickly as possible. The comment ends by observing that the lawyer normally will not seek compensation for emergency actions.

5. Advance Directives and Other Legal Documents

Today, the process of estate planning increasingly involves the client's use of advance directives that provide guidance in the event of the client's incapacity. The capable client's careful use of durable powers of attorney, revocable trusts, health care proxies, living wills, and other formal written directions can substantially reduce or eliminate concerns about the propriety of legal decision making for the person with diminished capacity. The ACTEC Commentaries on Model Rule 1.14 note that lawyers representing competent adults in estate planning matters should routinely advise the client of the availability of these legal tools that can protect the client's interest in the event of the client's incapacity.

Inevitably, some individuals will postpone the execution of advance directives until their mental capacities have begun to ebb substantially. When these individuals then approach their lawyer to supervise the drafting and execution of advance directives or other estate planning documents, the lawyer may question whether the client retains the capacity necessary to execute those documents. Comment 6 to Model Rule 1.14 provides that the lawyer should consider and weigh various factors in evaluating the degree of the client's diminished capacity. These factors include the consistency of the client's decision with her long-held goals and wishes, the propriety of the decision from a standpoint of fairness, the variability of the client's state of mind, and the client's ability to explain her reasoning process and to understand the consequences of her request.

Different capacities are required to execute different legal documents. At the lowest end of the spectrum is perhaps testamentary capacity. Even for will execution, however, black letter law requires the testator to know the objects of her bounty, to understand generally what she owns, and to be able to make and understand her plan of disposition. The ACTEC Commentaries warn that the lawyer should be particularly cautious in helping a client modify her estate plan when her testamentary capacity is uncertain. The lawyer should not draft and supervise the execution of estate planning documents when the lawyer reasonably believes the client lacks the required level of capacity. As some cases have noted, however, the lawyer is not the guarantor of the client's capacity. Consistent with this observation, the ACTEC Commentaries note that, in light of the importance of testamentary freedom, "the lawyer may properly assist clients whose testamentary capacity appears to be borderline." The commentary further warns, however, that in such cases the lawyer should take care to document evidence regarding the capacity of the client.

Checkpoints

- Concerning the representation of elderly clients, you should understand
  - The duty and challenge of providing competent representation, particularly when the practice of elder law runs the gamut from simple, common tasks regularly engaged in by general practitioners to highly specialized work involving estate and tax planning and many various kinds of state and federal benefits
  - The importance of defining clearly the scope of representation and the fees to be charged, acting diligently for the client, and maintaining communication with the client throughout the representation
  - The duty to maintain client confidences and the exceptions to that duty, and the particular concerns that may arise when
    - Representing a client who is acting as a fiduciary for an elder
    - Representing a client with diminished capacity who is at substantial risk of harm and who cannot act in her own interest
    - Representing clients jointly
  - The general prohibition on representing a client when a conflict of interest exists, including
    - A conflict that exists because of the lawyer's own interest
    - A conflict between a current and prospective client
    - A conflict between or among joint clients
    - The circumstances under which a conflict may be waived
  - The duty of maintaining a normal lawyer-client relationship with a client of diminished capacity as far as reasonably possible, but noting that in certain instances when the client is at risk of substantial harm and cannot act for herself, the lawyer may take protective action as reasonably necessary,
    - Taking the least intrusive action necessary to protect the client
    - In appropriate cases, consulting with others who can act to protect the client, including family members, designated fiduciaries, or diagnosticians, but revealing information only as reasonably necessary
    - Perhaps even petitioning to have a guardianship or conservatorship established for the client when no other less intrusive alternative is available

Mastering Elder Law
Master Checklist

The following reflects the topics covered in each chapter. A good understanding of the material requires a detailed knowledge of each of these topics.

Chapter One • Elder Abuse

❏ Concerning elder abuse generally, you should
  • Understand various theories about why abusers engage in abusive conduct
  • Understand that elder abuse is a widespread social problem that has only begun to be recognized in recent decades
  • Be able to recognize warning signs of elder abuse

❏ Concerning kinds of elder abuse, you should be able to define and distinguish
  • Physical abuse
  • Sexual abuse
  • Exploitation
  • Emotional abuse
  • Neglect
  • Abandonment
  • Self-neglect

❏ Concerning statutory provisions addressing elder abuse, you should understand
  • The role of Adult Protective Services agencies
  • The way in which reporting statutes work
  • The way in which an abuse investigation is conducted
  • Services available to the abused elder
  • Criminal and civil remedies for the abuse

❑ Concerning miscellaneous matters relating to elder abuse, you should understand
- The nature of new statutory developments that limit an abuser's ability to benefit financially from his abuse
- The potential statutory hurdles against bringing an elder abuse claim against a medical provider
- Various evidentiary and criminal matters such as the possibility of sentencing enhancement
- The importance of abuse registries
- The general nature of nursing home litigation

Chapter Two • Guardianships and Conservatorships

❑ Concerning guardianships and conservatorships generally, you should understand that
- Proceedings are governed by state law, and terminology varies among the states
- Under the UPC, guardians are appointed to make personal decisions for a ward, and conservators are appointed to manage the estate of a protected person

❑ Concerning guardianship and conservatorship proceedings, you should understand
- The appointment process, under which a guardian or conservator should be appointed only when a respondent is incapacitated and requires guardian or conservator assistance
- The least restrictive alternative doctrine, which requires that courts impose the least restrictive alternative consistent with the respondent's abilities
- The due process protections that the law affords to the respondent to the proceeding
- The role of guardians ad litem and visitors
- The typical burden and standard of proof
- The role of a priority list among candidates for appointment as guardian or conservator
- The nature and value of modern guardianship and conservatorship reform

❑ Concerning guardians and conservators, you should understand
- The role of substituted judgment and best interest determinations
- Fiduciary compensation
- Duties and powers of the fiduciary, including

- Powers by default
- Actions requiring court approval
- How the fiduciary role is terminated
- The role of temporary, emergency, and successor guardians and conservators

Chapter Three • Wealth Management and Property Transfers

❏ Concerning wealth management and property transfers, you should understand that
- Many elders wish to avoid having a guardianship or conservatorship imposed
- Many elders use various agency and property tools, including durable powers of attorney as well as more traditional nonprobate and probate devices

❏ Concerning the durable power of attorney, you should understand
- A durable power of attorney is a document executed by a principal that will allow her agent to act for her even though she is incapacitated
- The distinction between a durable power of attorney immediately effective and a durable power of attorney with a springing power
- The potential advantages and disadvantages of using a durable power of attorney
- The principal distinctions between the Uniform Durable Power of Attorney 1979 and the Uniform Power of Attorney Act 2006
- The general nature of agent powers and duties

❏ Concerning nonprobate properties, you should understand
- Nonprobate properties, which are properties that pass to beneficiaries outside probate
- General principles of survivorship properties, including
  - Joint tenancies and tenancies by the entirety
  - Joint bank accounts and their difference from convenience accounts
- General principles regarding other nonprobate assets, including
  - POD and TOD accounts
  - Totten trusts
  - Revocable trusts
  - Insurance
  - Gifts inter vivos and causa mortis

❏ Concerning probate properties, you should understand
- Probate properties, which are properties that pass through the probate process at the owner's death

- General principles of intestate succession, including
  - Methods of representation
  - The treatment of individuals in nontraditional families
- General principles regarding family protection provisions
- General principles regarding wills, including
  - Rules of execution
  - Methods of revocation
  - Revival and dependent relative revocation
  - Common rules of construction regarding
    - Integration, incorporation by reference, and republication
    - Events of independent significance, lists of tangible personal property, and additions to trusts
    - Antilapse, abatement, and ademption
  - The treatment of disinherited relatives, including
    - Spouses
      - In separate-property states
      - In community-property states
    - Issue
  - Bases for will contests and the treatment of penalty clauses

Chapter Four • Health-Care Decision Making

❏ Concerning health-care decision making generally, you should understand principles of informed consent, the right to refuse life-prolonging treatment, advance directives, and assistance in dying

❏ Concerning informed consent, you should understand
- What the physician must disclose
- The standards of disclosure
- Physician defenses
- The requirement of causation

❏ Concerning the right to refuse life-prolonging treatment, you should understand
- The bases for a right to refuse treatment
- The state interests that are implicated when one refuses life-prolonging treatment
- The results when a provider ignores the patient's decision to refuse treatment
- The problems that may arise when a third-party seeks to refuse or withdraw life-prolonging treatment from an incompetent patient, including
  - Who should be the third-party decision maker

- Constitutionally-permissible standards of proof that a state may impose upon the party seeking to refuse or withdraw such treatment for the patient
- The distinctions between substituted judgment and best interest decisions

❏ Concerning advance directives, you should understand
- Living wills
  - Their applicability and limitations
  - General requirements under most state laws
- Powers of attorney for health care
  - Their applicability
  - General requirements under most state laws
- The Uniform Health-care Decisions Act
  - Its applicability and principal concepts
  - Its inclusion not only of provisions for living will instructions and the designation of an agent, but also provisions for a surrogate decision maker when there is no agent or guardian

❏ Concerning assistance in dying, you should understand
- State assisted suicide bans
- The United States Supreme Court rulings that uphold state assisted suicide bans against attack from those seeking physician assisted suicide
- The general way in which "Death with Dignity" statutes apply in Oregon and Washington to permit physician assisted suicide in very limited circumstances
- That no constitutional right to euthanasia exists in the United States, and that no state has attempted to legalize euthanasia

Chapter Five • Age Discrimination in Employment

❏ Concerning the federal Age Discrimination in Employment Act (ADEA), you should understand
- The ADEA protects covered individuals forty and over from age discrimination by covered employers
- The ADEA covers hiring and firing decisions; conditions, terms, and privileges of employment; and retaliation claims

❏ Concerning covered employment, you should understand the definitions of employer and employee, including
- How to determine employer status
  - Must have twenty employees in twenty weeks in current or preceding calendar year

- Nonprofit and charitable organizations are not excluded as employers
- Religious organizations may be included in some circumstances
- Under the eleventh amendment, nonconsenting states are immune to ADEA suits by private citizens seeking damages
- How to determine employee status
  - Test is derived from common law, not statute
  - An individual's title is not necessarily determinative of his employee status

❏ Concerning employer defenses, you should understand generally the
- Bona fide occupational qualification defense
- Reasonable factor other than age defense
- Bona fide seniority system defense
- Bona fide employee benefit plan defense
- Good cause defense
- Law enforcement officer and firefighter exception
- Bona fide executive or high policymaker exception

❏ Concerning forms of ADEA lawsuits, you should understand
- The disparate treatment claim
- The disparate impact claim
- The retaliation claim

❏ Concerning procedural issues under ADEA, you should understand
- The rules for timely filing of a charge
- The rules for filing private suit in federal district court
- The role of the EEOC
- The difference between deferral and nondeferral states and the effect on procedure
- The rules concerning waiver of ADEA rights
- The employer's obligation to provide notices and maintain records

❏ Concerning remedies, you should understand the availability of injunctive relief, back pay, reinstatement or front pay, costs, attorney fees, and liquidated damages

Chapter Six • Social Security, Retirement, and Pension Programs

❏ Concerning Social Security, you should understand
- The FICA tax and the financing of the program
- The importance of the earnings record
- How one establishes insured status
- How retirement benefits are determined, including

- The way in which primary insurance amount (PIA) is calculated
- The effect of receiving early retirement benefits and the application of the retirement earnings test
- The effect of deferred receipt past full retirement age
- The windfall elimination provision and the government pension offset
- Who is entitled to auxiliary benefits and how those benefits are calculated
- The general nature of the Social Security disability program
- The role of the representative payee
- The anti-assignment provision of the Social Security Act
- The administrative and judicial review process

❏ Concerning public retirement or pension programs, you should understand generally
- The railroad retirement system
- The federal CSRS and FERS systems
- The typical aspects of state and local plans
- The military retirement system
- Veterans' benefits

❏ Concerning private-sector pension plans, you should understand
- The distinctions between defined benefit plans and defined contribution plans
- The role of ERISA
- The general treatment of spouses and ex-spouses of plan participants
- The general rules concerning distributions, taxation, and rollovers

Chapter Seven • Supplemental Security Income

❏ Concerning Supplemental Security Income (SSI) generally, you should understand that it is a program for persons of limited means who are blind, disabled, or sixty-five or over

❏ Concerning SSI eligibility rules, you should understand
- The examination and treatment of income and resources
- The effects of institutionalization
- The effect of marriage
- The deeming process

❏ Concerning income, you should understand that
- In-kind income is income not in the form of cash or a negotiable instrument
- The recipient's countable income must be less than the SSI federal benefit rate

- Countable income consists of earned income and unearned income
  - Earned income includes wages, net earnings from self-employment, royalties, honoria, and certain other payments to the applicant
  - Unearned income is any income that is not earned, including Social Security and various other benefit payments, dividends and interest, pensions and annuities
- Special valuation rules apply to in-kind support and maintenance
- Important exclusions from earned income and unearned income exist in calculating countable income

❏ Concerning resources, you should understand that
  - The recipient's countable resources must not exceed the monthly countable resources limit under SSI
  - Countable resources are typically considered on their face value
    - Various important resources are excluded from the determination of countable resources
    - Among the exclusions from countable resources are the home, household goods and personal effects, and one vehicle

Chapter Eight • Medicare

❏ Concerning Medicare Part A, you should understand
  - How Part A is financed
  - The differences in coverage for hospital insurance, SNF care, home health services, and hospice
  - The payment structure (deductibles, copayments, and coinsurance) for the different kinds of coverage under Part A

❏ Concerning Medicare Part B, you should understand
  - How Part B is financed
  - The general kinds of coverage offered
  - The payment structure (deductibles, premiums, copayments, and coinsurance)

❏ Concerning the Medicare Advantage program (Part C), you should understand
  - How it differs from Original Medicare (Parts A and B)
  - The various advantages and disadvantages of the program

❏ Concerning Medicare Part D, you should understand
  - How prescription drug plans work in general
  - The payment structure (deductibles, premiums, copayments, coinsurance, and the "donut hole")

❏ Concerning all parts of Medicare, you should understand generally the tiers of the appeals process

❏ Concerning all parts of Medicare, you should understand generally the rules of enrollment and the penalties that accompany untimely enrollment

❏ Concerning Medigap insurance policies, you should understand
- Policies are not part of the Medicare program, but instead are obtained privately and are completely optional
- Policies are intended to supplement coverage under Original Medicare
- Congress has attempted to simplify the selection process and protect consumers by standardizing policies

Chapter Nine • Medicaid

❏ Concerning the general structure of the Medicaid program, you should understand the role of the federal and state government and the importance of the state medical assistance plan

❏ Concerning state programs, you should understand the difference between SSI states and 209(b) states and the different rules that apply concerning coverage in each

❏ Concerning income and resources, you should understand how they are determined and why they are important

❏ Concerning Medicaid's coverage of long-term institutionalization, you should understand
- The general rules, including eligibility rules in spend-down and income cap states
- The treatment of the community spouse
- The treatment of asset transfers

❏ Concerning Medicaid recoupment procedures, you should understand Medicaid's rules concerning liens, adjustments, and cost recovery from the estate

❏ Concerning grievances, you should understand generally Medicaid's rules for appeals

Chapter Ten • Long-Term Care

❏ Concerning long-term care, you should understand that long-term care includes not only the provision of medical care, but also custodial care and assistance with the activities of daily living (i.e., bathing, continence, dressing, eating, toileting, and transferring)

❏ Concerning long-term care, you should be able to describe various ways in which an individual may satisfy her long-term care needs through the assistance of
- Family and friends
- Community- and home-based services organizations
- Paid caregivers
- Board and care homes, assisted living facilities, and continuing care retirement communities
- Nursing homes

❏ Concerning the costs of long-term care, you should be able to describe various ways in which an individual may pay for such care, including the use of
- Personal savings and the resources of family and friends
- Proceeds of a reverse mortgage
- Accelerated death benefits under a life insurance policy
- Medicaid or other governmental programs
- Long-term care insurance

❏ Concerning long-term care insurance, you should understand the way in which long-term care insurance policies work and are regulated, including
- Eligibility requirements
- Premium provisions and payment options
- Inflation protection
- Nonforfeiture benefits
- Waivers, death refunds, and downgrades
- Tax-qualified policies
- State partnership polices
- Benefit limits
- Trigger mechanisms
- Elimination periods
- Restoration of benefits

Chapter Eleven • Home

❏ Concerning the elderly individual who needs physical, emotional, or financial assistance but wishes to remain at home, you should be able to explain various options, including
- Home modifications
- The use of volunteer or paid caregivers
- Long-term care insurance
- The use of a reverse mortgage

❏ Concerning the elderly individual who chooses to sell or give away her home, you should be able to explain the consequences of such a decision

❏ Concerning the elderly individual who chooses to rent or to purchase a home in a community for older residents, you should be able to explain
  • The options available under the Fair Housing Act
  • The protections available under the Fair Housing Act to accommodate her needs

❏ Concerning the elderly individual who chooses to or who must live in a congregate living facility, you should be able to explain
  • Board and care homes, ALFs, and CCRCs, and the principal differences among them
  • Nursing home regulation, including generally
    • Requirements concerning the provision of services
    • Requirements relating to residents' rights
    • Requirements relating to administration
    • State and federal responsibilities
    • The survey and certification process

Chapter Twelve • The Professional Responsibilities of the Lawyer

❏ Concerning the representation of elderly clients, you should understand
  • The duty and challenge of providing competent representation, particularly when the practice of elder law runs the gamut from simple, common tasks regularly engaged in by general practitioners to highly specialized work involving estate and tax planning and many various kinds of state and federal benefits
  • The importance of defining clearly the scope of representation and the fees to be charged, acting diligently for the client, and maintaining communication with the client throughout the representation
  • The duty to maintain client confidences and the exceptions to that duty, and the particular concerns that may arise when
    • Representing a client who is acting as a fiduciary for an elder
    • Representing a client with diminished capacity who is at substantial risk of harm and who cannot act in her own interest
    • Representing clients jointly
  • The general prohibition on representing a client when a conflict of interest exists, including
    • A conflict that exists because of the lawyer's own interest
    • A conflict between a current and prospective client
    • A conflict between or among joint clients

- The circumstances under which a conflict may be waived
- The duty of maintaining a normal lawyer-client relationship with a client of diminished capacity as far as reasonably possible, but noting that in certain instances when the client is at risk of substantial harm and cannot act for herself, the lawyer may take protective action as reasonably necessary,
  - Taking the least intrusive action necessary to protect the client
  - In appropriate cases, consulting with others who can act to protect the client, including family members, designated fiduciaries, or diagnosticians, but revealing information only as reasonably necessary
  - Perhaps even petitioning to have a guardianship or conservatorship established for the client when no other less intrusive alternative is available

Index